Couldn't Have a Wedding without the Fiddler

"Ken Perlman's comprehensive study of fiddling
on Prince Edward Island makes a beautiful beginning
for the Charles K. Wolfe Music Series. With rich commentary
from the fiddlers on learning, style, and social occasions,
with Perlman's historical research, sensitive observation,
and deft analysis, *Couldn't Have a Wedding without the Fiddler* is among
the very best musical ethnographies ever published."

—HENRY GLASSIE

Professor Emeritus at Indiana University and author
of *The Stars of Balleymenone*

"It is amazing to see Ken in action. Before long fiddlers are sitting
down in the kitchen playing their familiar tunes and talking freely
about fiddling, completely oblivious to the recording apparati.
He is extremely keen in perceiving, identifying, and describing
the peculiar nuances found in the fiddlers from different Island
communities. These qualities carry over to assessing us Islanders;
he has the ability to highlight and accentuate the little eccentricities
we all possess, the knowledge of which helps us to know
and better communicate with each other."

—FR. J. CHARLES "FATHER CHARLIE" CHEVERIE

Priest of the Diocese of Charlottetown
and former director of the Prince Edward Island Fiddlers' Society,
Queens County Chapter

KEN PERLMAN

Couldn't Have a Wedding without the Fiddler
The Story of Traditional Fiddling on Prince Edward Island

CHARLES K. WOLFE MUSIC SERIES
Ted Olson, Series Editor

The University of Tennessee Press / Knoxville

The Charles K. Wolfe Music Series was launched in honor of the late Charles K. Wolfe (1943–2006), whose pioneering work in the study of American vernacular music brought a deepened understanding of a wide range of American music to a worldwide audience. In recognition of Dr. Wolfe's approach to music scholarship, the series will include books that investigate genres of folk and popular music as broadly as possible.

Copyright © 2015 by The University of Tennessee Press / Knoxville.
All Rights Reserved.
First Edition.

Library of Congress Cataloging-in-Publication Data

Perlman, Ken.
 Couldn't have a wedding without the fiddler: the story of traditional fiddling on Prince Edward Island / Ken Perlman. — First edition.
     pages cm. — (Charles K. Wolfe American music series)
 Includes bibliographical references and index.
 ISBN 978-1-62190-097-9 (paperback)
 1. Fiddling—Prince Edward Island—History.
 2. Music—Social aspects—Prince Edward Island—History.
 3. Prince Edward Island—Social life and customs. I. Title.

ML863.7.P7P47 2014
787.2'162110717—dc23   2014023337

That was the three most important people in the town: the minister was first, the schoolteacher was next, and the fiddler was next. Couldn't have a wedding without the fiddler!

ARCHIE STEWART
(Milltown Cross, Prince Edward Island)

CONTENTS

Foreword	
Ted Olson, Series Editor	xi
Acknowledgments	xv
Introduction	xvii
1. Cradled on the Waves	1
2. The Third Most Important Person in the District	19
3. "Music Was the Next Thing to Eatin'"	47
4. The "Gift" and Other Attitudes about Fiddling	65
5. "That's the Way We Had to Learn"	83
6. "I Could Bring What Was in My Mind Out on the Fiddle"	103
7. "Knights of the Bow"	129
8. "I'd Have to Say It Was a Bad Instrument"	151
9. "Everybody Got a Different Style to Play"	175
10. "It's Always Better with Accompaniment"	199
11. "The Devil Was in These Fiddle Contests"	213
12. The Dances	235
13. The Role of Radio and Recordings	263
14. The Repertoire	295
15. "It's Amazing How Quick It Did Go Down"	317
16. "If Everybody Does a Little Bit, Great Things Can Happen"	339
17. "There's Been a Big Revival of Music on the Island"	377

Appendix A. Musical Examples	393
Appendix B. Lists of Interview Sessions	403
Appendix C. Lists of Collected Tunes	413
Appendix D. Pronunciation Guide	419
Appendix E. Discography and Suggested Listening	421
Glossary	425
Bibliography	429
Index	441

ILLUSTRATIONS

Photographs

I.1.	Dancing at Rollo Bay Festival Tuning Shed, July 1992	xviii
I.2.	Ken Perlman with an Earthwatch team, August 1992	xxi
I.3.	North Shore of PEI Near Monticello, Kings County, July 1991	xxx
1.1.	Fishing boats and shacks, northeastern Prince County, August 1992	11
2.1.	Archie Stewart, Chester MacSwain, and Ken Perlman, August 1991	21
2.2.	Step dancers at Atlantic Jamboree, Abram-Village	28
2.3.	Stanley Bruce, Margaret Ross MacKinnon, and Attwood O'Connor, August 1996	33
3.1.	Largus MacInnis, July 1992	51
3.2.	Jackie Webster, Carl Webster, and Donnie MacDonald, August 1992	55
4.1.	Stephen Toole, August 1992	70
4.2.	Sidney Baglole, August 1992	75
4.3.	Francis MacDonald, July 1991	82
5.1.	Dennis Pitre, August 1996	88
5.2.	Robert Arsenault, October 2006	93
6.1.	Eddy Arsenault, August 1991	111
6.2.	Edward P. Arsenault, August 1992	115
7.1.	Johnny Joe Chaisson and his brother Phonsey, July 1992	130
7.2.	Zélie-Anne Arsenault Poirier, August 1992	145
7.3.	Ervan Sonier (Fiddle) and Anne-Marie Gallant Arsenault, August 1991	150
8.1.	Leonard and Claire McDonald, July 1992	156
8.2.	Joe MacDonald at St. Andrews, August 1992	165
8.3.	Andrew Jones, August 1991	174
9.1.	"Young Peter" Chaisson, July 1991	177
9.2.	Alan Jabbour demonstrating classical playing posture	186
9.3.	Gus Longaphie illustrating typical playing posture on PEI	187

9.4.	Alvin Bernard and Edwin Simmons, July 1992	198
10.1.	Kevin Chaisson and Paul MacDonald, August 1991	200
10.2.	Peter Doiron (Right) and grandson Adam Driscoll, August 1996	212
11.1.	Elmer Robinson, Eddy Arsenault, and Eldon MacArthur, July 1992	220
11.2.	Step-Dancer at Atlantic Jamboree, August 1991	234
12.1.	"Ladies in the center," Goose River Dance, November 2006	242
12.2.	"Swing your partner," Monticello Ceilidh, July 1992	247
12.3.	Allan MacDonald, George MacPhee, and Ken Perlman, with Marlene Gallant, July 1991	255
13.1.	Don Messer and His Islanders, probably late 1940s	272
15.1.	Louise Arsenault with her mother, Marie, and sister, Zelma, November 2006	320
15.2.	Ward and Allan MacDonald, October 2006	327
16.1.	Fr. Charles Cheverie leads Queens County and Eastern Kings County Fiddlers, July 1992	347
16.2.	Finale at Festival Acadien, September 1992	355
16.3.	Richard Wood, August 1992	365
16.4.	Jenny McQuaid and Teresa Wilson, July 1992	367
17.1.	Victor Doucette, November 2006	385
17.2.	Angus McPhee and Cynthia Jay Crane, July 1991	387

Maps

1.1.	Prince Edward Island	2
1.2.	Prince Edward Island and its environs	4

Tables

14.1.	Most widely played tunes	296
14.2.	Tune genres, 1991–92	301
14.3.	Sources of the Island repertoire	308
B.1.	List of interviews, 1991–92	403
B.2.	List of interviews, 1999	408
B.3.	List of interviews, 2006	409
C.1.	Additional tunes collected on Prince Edward Island, 1991–92	413
C.2.	Tunes encountered for the first time in 2006	416

FOREWORD

Most Americans, when they think of Prince Edward Island, think of Lucy Maud Montgomery's 1908 novel *Anne of Green Gables* and its seven sequels. Widely read for the past century and often recast in film and television adaptations, these novels have been among the most internationally popular exports of Canadian culture. Fascination with Montgomery's fictional representation of a late Victorian-era Prince Edward Island community has generated a particularly fervent strain of cultural tourism. But as Ken Perlman demonstrates herein, fiddling is the province's most exciting cultural attribute, and this book makes the case that this living tradition is fully as compelling and as worthy of attention as the romanticized aura generated by Montgomery's enchanting fictional world.

Couldn't Have a Wedding without the Fiddler: The Story of Traditional Fiddling on Prince Edward Island perfectly complements Perlman's previous efforts to document that province's fiddle music. Long a leader in the interpretation of Prince Edward Island's music heritage, Perlman in this new study presents a contextualized portrayal of that Province's fiddle scene by combining ethnographic data with solid musicological analysis. The inclusion of compelling oral histories throughout this book adds a measure of immediacy and vibrancy to the study. *Couldn't Have a Wedding without the Fiddler* illustrates that not all that long ago fiddling on Prince Edward Island was integral to everyday life, and, in the era prior to modernization, was associated with a host of social activities, from weddings and dances to housewarmings and harvests. All told, Perlman's decade-long documentation of the Island's fiddling scene has resulted in a book that is clearly among the more significant studies of a local North American music tradition to be published in recent years.

Perlman has built a reputation as a diversely talented music interpreter. He was perhaps first known as the author of several acclaimed music instruction books; a few of these books, from the late 1970s and early 1980s, popularized the melodic clawhammer banjo style by challenging old-time banjoists to perform fiddle tunes on their instruments in intricate drop-thumb arrangements.

A virtuoso performer on the clawhammer banjo and a skilled practitioner of the fingerstyle guitar, Perlman has several commercial recordings to his credit. On his earliest recordings, he focused on arrangements of old-time banjo and guitar of fiddle tunes from Scotland, Ireland, England, and New England. Throughout the 1990s Perlman's major focus shifted to adapting the tunes he collected on Prince Edward Island to banjo and guitar. This interest has continued, but since the early 2000s he has also been exploring Appalachian fiddle tunes; nowadays he often performs with acclaimed Appalachian-style fiddler and folklorist Alan Jabbour, with whom Perlman recorded a CD of fiddle and banjo duets called *Southern Summits*.

In 1989, while visiting Prince Edward Island for the first time, Perlman attended a town fair in the northeastern part of the Island and was deeply intrigued by the fiddling he encountered. As he traveled around the province, he concluded that Prince Edward Island "was simply teeming with fiddle players." Encountering widespread fiddling excellence across that province, Perlman learned that Prince Edward Island's heritage of instrumental music had been largely overlooked both by the media and by earlier folk music collectors. Perlman decided to document the lives and music of many Prince Edward Island fiddlers, and a grant from a Massachusetts organization permitted him to begin this project in 1991.

What Perlman found on Prince Edward Island were vivid recollections of a remarkably fertile fiddling tradition in which fiddlers were central fixtures in everyday social life. During his visits, Perlman identified approximately two hundred fiddlers with strong instrumental abilities, and in 1991–92 he recorded the fiddle repertoires of and conducted oral histories with over one hundred of them. The initial fruits of these documentation efforts included an instruction book entitled *The Fiddle Music of Prince Edward Island: Celtic and Acadian Tunes in Living Tradition* (Mel Bay Publications, 1996) and a 2-CD compilation of fiddle music field recordings entitled *The Prince Edward Island Style of Fiddling* (Rounder Records, 1997). A review in *Fiddler Magazine* declared that the instruction book was "the most important published contribution to the study of a Canadian Maritime fiddle tradition," while the Prince Edward Island Heritage Foundation gave heritage awards to both Perlman's instruction book and his Rounder compilation CDs.

After his original funding ran out in 1992, Perlman maintained his interest in the fiddlers he had worked with and continued to visit the Island frequently. He has returned twice for additional collecting work—a short self-funded trip in 1999 and a much larger project in 2006 that was funded by a grant from a Canadian museum. In 2006, Perlman conducted follow-up sessions with about twenty fiddlers from the original project, and he recorded and collected oral histories from about forty additional fiddlers. This later documentation combined with his earlier collections form the core of *Couldn't Have a Wedding without the Fiddler*.

When Scot Danforth, director of the University of Tennessee Press, and I first announced the Charles K. Wolfe Music Series, our initial intent was to focus upon the specific music genres (country, bluegrass, old-time, gospel, blues, and folk) and regional music cultures that had long fascinated Dr. Wolfe (1943–2006) during his pioneering career as a historian of Southern vernacular music. But Dr. Wolfe's scholarly interests extended to music genres associated with places far beyond his adopted home state of Tennessee. Hence, Perlman's Prince Edward Island study is a perfect book to launch this new series. Not only does Perlman explore an overlooked music culture located far from the exhaustively studied South, but, like earlier books by the namesake of this series, Perlman's study is both groundbreaking in its research and passionate toward its subject. We hope that future offerings in the Charles K. Wolfe Music Series will, like *Couldn't Have a Wedding without the Fiddler* and in the spirit of Dr. Wolfe, invoke a profound love of and a deep respect for music wherever it is made.

TED OLSON
Charles K. Wolfe Music Series

ACKNOWLEDGMENTS

Thanks to Dan Gillis of Bayfield (PEI) and Philadelphia, and to his Iona Foundation, for the initial invitation to Prince Edward Island and for general support thereafter.

Thanks to the following organizations for material support:
- The Arlington (MA) Arts Council
- The Canadian Museum of Civilization of Gatineau, QC (since renamed the Canadian Museum of History)
- The Earthwatch Organization of Watertown, MA
- The Institute of Island Studies of Charlottetown, PEI
- The John and Clara Higgins Foundation of Washington, DC
- The Kittredge Fund of Cambridge, MA
- The Prince Edward Island Fiddlers' Association

Thanks to these Earthwatch volunteers who worked on the 1991–92 project:
June Alexis, bj Altschull, M. E. Anderson, Jane Bloom, Fran Browne, Helen Callbeck, Ann Carter, Wilbur Dehart, Phyllis Dickson, Joan DiLeonardi, Ed Dixon, Katie Dilkes, Lucy Duschene, Joyce and Don Fast, Bev Gallagher, Anne Gefell, Gay Gilbert, Marghie Goff, Sue Gundlach, Edwina Haddad, Gail Hardman, Sylvia Harris, Mike Hird, Steve Jones, Tania Juzak, Lionel King, Esther Koblenz, Annabelle and Hank Kressman, Alice Kujala, Diana Leonard, Thane Mathews, Vicki McLeod, Jan Migaki, Allan Miller, Elaine Miller, Beryl Muspratt, Sandy Myers, Barbara Peacock, Judith Perry, Gavine Pitner, Elnor Ragan, Ben Roberson, Cary Rona, Kay Scott, Jim and B. J. Seitzer, Tzerl Seltzer, Jackie Settlage, Sharon Smith, Holly Spangenburg, Sallie Sprague, Joanie Streets, Randy Sulkin, Jan Tappan, Pam Vasquez, Holly Williams, Elizabeth Wulfsburg, and Gail Zaks

The following individuals provided additional help transcribing interviews:
Paul Harty, Vicki McLeod, Elizabeth Wulfsberg Muzzey, and Deborah O'Hanlon

Thanks for assistance in proofreading and editing:
Susanne Even and Fran Waksler

Thanks for help with the introduction:
Andrea Kronman

Thanks for help in obtaining research materials:
Barbara McOwen and Jan Tappan

Thanks to the following Prince Edward Islanders for guidance, general encouragement, and material assistance:
Eddy and Rita Arsenault; Peter Arsenault; Kevin, Kenny, and "Young Peter" Chaisson and their families; Fr. Charles Cheverie; Philippe Leblanc; Richard Lepage; Allan and Ward MacDonald; Margaret Ross MacKinnon; George MacPhee and his sisters Emmalina MacPhee Crossman, Mary MacPhee Warren, and Teresa MacPhee Wilson; Gail Mullen; Denise Reiser; the Sisters at St. Michael's Parish House (Corran Ban); and Alan Stanley

Portions of the following articles by Ken Perlman appear in this work and are reproduced here by permission:

- "That Old-Time Music: Fiddlin' and Dancin' on Prince Edward Island," *The World and I* (March 1993): 240–51.
- "And It Was Good Pastime: Old Time Fiddling on Prince Edward Island," *Island Magazine* 35 (Spring/Summer 1994): 23–30.
- "A Lovely Sweet Music: Old Time Fiddling on Prince Edward Island," *Sing Out!* 39, no. 2 (November 1994): 32–44.
- "Couldn't Have a Wedding without the Fiddler: Old Time Fiddling on Prince Edward Island," *Fiddler's Magazine* (Spring 1995): 4–11.
- "Tune-Recall among Traditional Fiddlers on Prince Edward Island," *Canadian Folk Music Bulletin* (September–December 1997): 8–12.
- "Me Head Was Full of Music: Learning Fiddle Tunes on Prince Edward Island," *Old Time Herald* (Winter 1997–98): 22–27.
- "The Devil's Instrument Revisited: Prince Edward Island as a Case Study," in *Crossing Over: Fiddle and Dance Studies from Around the North Atlantic*, vol. 3, ed. Ian Russell and Anna Kearney Guigné, 228–38 (Aberdeen: Elphinstone Institute, 2012).

INTRODUCTION

Prince Edward Island in eastern Canada is home to one of the oldest, strongest, and most vibrant fiddling traditions in North America. Fiddling was first established there by Scottish immigrants in the late eighteenth century, was influenced by Irish immigrants arriving a generation or two later, and was seasoned by the unique rhythmic sensibilities of the original European inhabitants of the Island: the Acadian French.

Couldn't Have a Wedding without the Fiddler is drawn from the oral histories of roughly 150 fiddlers and other "Islanders." Although much attention in this book is devoted to both the music and the milieu, the main focus is on the fiddlers—their central role at dances and celebrations, how they learned their skills and their music, their values and attitudes, and how they related to each other, their communities, and their environment.

I encountered Island fiddling for the first time in July 1989 at a town fair in northeastern Prince Edward Island known as the Monticello Tea Party.[1] It was one of those crystalline summer days when the sun is hot but there is a bit of chill in the air from a moderate breeze coming in from the not-too-distant shore. The tar road was lined with red soil, and beyond that as far as the eye could see were brilliant green fields and clusters of wildflowers. A local talent show was in progress, with an audience composed of perhaps a couple of hundred people from the surrounding area, ranging in age from babies to octogenarians.

About halfway through the program, three people got on stage. One had a guitar and one carried a fiddle and bow, while the third, a stately woman in her early thirties whose knee-length skirt revealed remarkably well-developed calves, stood at center stage and waited expectantly. The fiddler—a cherubic-faced man in his late forties wearing a baseball cap—tucked the body of his instrument right into his collarbone with its face aligned almost vertically; he held his bow with the natural, easy grip of a man who has been playing nearly as long as he can remember.

He began to play, his right foot beating out a strong tattoo on the stage floor, and the tone of his fiddle—crisp, clean, and lively—rang out across the grounds. He struck up a moderate-tempo tune called a strathspey, and the

PHOTO I.1. DANCING AFTER HOURS AT THE ROLLO BAY FESTIVAL TUNING SHED, JULY 1992 (PHOTO BY EARTHWATCH TEAM).

woman began to step-dance, holding her arms almost motionless while her legs and feet carried out intricate combinations of steps in close time with the subtle rhythms of the tune. And when the fiddler segued into a much faster reel, her feet shifted into overdrive, matching the tune's faster rhythms precisely with ever-new combinations of steps. The fiddler's expression had been serious and full of concentration, but as the intensity of his playing increased, his countenance grew serene. Meanwhile, the dancer was wearing a broad grin as she redoubled her efforts. The effect was riveting, and I thought to myself, "This is how I've always wanted to hear the fiddle played; this is how I've always wanted to see it danced to!"

Over the next several days at a series of family get-togethers and musical evenings, I got to hear perhaps a couple of dozen more local fiddlers of similar caliber. And on my way back to Boston, I wondered why no one had ever recorded this compelling style of fiddling, and why it was virtually unknown to outsiders.

Roughly a year later I was back on Prince Edward Island, this time to lay the groundwork for a project to collect tunes and oral histories from Island fiddlers. My first step was attending PEI's largest fiddling event: the Rollo Bay

Scottish Fiddle Festival.[2] Held outdoors on the site of a former potato field near the town of Souris in northeastern Prince Edward Island, the event drew several thousand people, or roughly 5 percent of the entire Island population. Throughout its two-day span, dozens of local fiddlers and step dancers took their turns performing to an audience of aficionados, many of whom viewed the proceedings while seated in parked vehicles and expressed their appreciation via the honking of car horns. One special attraction at Rollo Bay was the Prince Edward Island Fiddlers' Society, whose performances featured dozens of fiddlers playing reels, jigs, and other kinds of fiddle tunes in unison.

After the conclusion of the official program, diehards congregated in a small, corrugated metal outbuilding known as the Tuning Shed. There, one fiddler after another played to the point of exhaustion, as onlookers got up to step-dance singly or in groups as the spirit moved them—like witnessing at a Quaker meeting. Meanwhile, on the nearby dance stage, a fiddler and accompanists played marathon medleys of fiddle tunes, while Islanders of all ages step-danced or formed up to dance square sets (the Island name for square dancing).

Not long afterward, I attended an old-time square dance in St. Peters. Residents had converted an old railroad station into a dance hall, which on that particular evening was filled to capacity. Local fiddlers took turns providing the music, and at any one time perhaps half the crowd was up on the floor making their way through the figures of a Souris Set (the most popular square set of northeastern Prince Edward Island). To those accustomed to Southern, New England, or Western-style square dancing, the version danced at St. Peters might seem a little peculiar since dancers formed one or two big circles instead of many small squares. And when it was time to "swing your partner," couples stutter-stepped as they turned, dipping together on the offbeats so that the overall effect resembled a ring of pistons.

As I grew to know the Island, I became increasingly impressed by the sheer number of local events that prominently featured fiddle playing. Not only were there several annual fiddle festivals, but nearly every town and cluster of rural districts sponsored annual town days (fairs), benefit concerts, step-dancing recitals, and weekly community talent shows known as *ceilidhs*. Programs fully devoted to old-time square dancing were less common, but nearly every Island dance featured at least a couple of square sets on the program, and nearly every Island dance band had a fiddler on the roster.

I also came to understand that Prince Edward Island was teeming with fiddle players. Just going about my daily rounds, sometimes it seemed that nearly everyone I encountered either was a fiddle player, was related to a fiddle player, or (at the very least) knew where one could easily be located. During the course of my initial investigation, I identified 150–200 fiddlers whose playing was of sufficient merit to warrant recording, and I strongly suspect that there were as many more whom I failed to locate. This estimate does not take into account the hundreds of Islanders who could play sufficiently well in a pinch to scratch out a couple of tunes on the instrument. Nor does it factor in the scores of youngsters or older Islanders who had recently taken up the instrument through some local instructional program or under the auspices of the Prince Edward Island Fiddlers' Society.

When the project was officially launched in the summer of 1991, my focus was almost exclusively on the music and only tangentially on the (mostly) old folks who made it. As a banjoist and guitarist who had spent most of his adult life immersed in both the Appalachian and the Celtic music scene, I had often heard about and come to admire the accomplishments of the great music collectors of the twentieth century: men such as Cecil Sharp, John and Alan Lomax, Frank Warner, Samuel Bayard, and Alan Jabbour.[3] Surely this was my opportunity to follow in their footsteps.[4]

As I spoke to fiddler after fiddler, however, I found myself increasingly fascinated by their colorful stories of the not-so-distant past, when fiddling was an essential aspect of community life. Nearly every Island district organized its own dances and had its own stock of skilled fiddlers, whose playing was so lively it literally impelled dancers to "get up on the floor." And as implied by the title of this book, during this era, holding any important event in the community without having a fiddler on hand to provide the music was almost unthinkable. These stories, drawn from what I like to think of as the Golden Age of Island fiddling—generally referred to more prosaically in this narrative as "the traditional period"—are the foundation upon which much of this book is based.

The process of modernization came very late to Prince Edward Island. Many advances that urban North Americans take for granted—such as electricity, paved roads, and automobile travel—were not part of rural Island life until well into the 1950s. People rarely traveled more than a few miles (the distance of a comfortable wagon or sleigh ride), and for the most part rural communities fended for themselves and organized their own entertainments. Winter nights were long, and without a dance to look forward to, life might have been dull indeed!

Essentially, the district fiddle dance was the centerpiece around which the life of many communities revolved. Local families took turns making their homes available, and a fiddler or two would be summoned from the surrounding area to provide the music. "Them times," just about any excuse was considered sufficient justification for organizing a dance—whether it was raising money for local institutions such as school and church, rewarding neighbors for helping out with important tasks such as house-building or plowing, celebrating a wedding, marking a holiday, greeting visitors from "away," or merely giving vent to high spirits.

Most of the fiddlers interviewed for this project were old enough to have grown up during this era. They learned their skills, developed their attitudes about playing, and forged their playing styles at a time when community life was nearly the same as in the days of their great-grandfathers. For the most part, these "old-time" fiddlers carried these skills, attitudes, and styles nearly intact into the modern era. And because they learned through emulating older players within the isolation of their districts and musical individualism was an important Island attitude, most of them developed highly distinctive styles and approaches to repertoire.

PHOTO I.2. KEN PERLMAN (*CENTER*) WITH ONE OF HIS EARTHWATCH TEAMS AT SHORE NEAR MONTICELLO HEADQUARTERS, AUGUST 1992 (PHOTO BY EARTHWATCH TEAM).

Even when radio broadcasts and recordings became widespread on Prince Edward Island in the 1930s and '40s, they had considerably less impact there than on many other twentieth-century fiddling cultures.[5] For the most part, Island fiddlers eagerly adopted new repertoire from radio and recordings, but these media had surprisingly little influence on their playing styles. After 1939, the airwaves of Atlantic Canada came to be dominated by fiddlers from the neighboring provinces of New Brunswick and Nova Scotia, and—as one result—PEI fiddling was almost unknown to much of the outside world until well into the 1990s.

When twentieth-century technology and social organization did become firmly established on Prince Edward Island in the 1950s and '60s, they almost put an end to Island fiddling. As the lure of new forms of entertainment such as television and films became irresistible, Islanders ceased gathering for dances with their neighbors. A new generation coming of age found its own music, and fiddling was increasingly looked at as something that appealed only to the old folks. This decline was stemmed to some degree by a revival (that is, an organized rekindling of interest) that got under way in the mid-1970s, and fiddling slowly made its way back to prominence, adapting in the process to a new set of social conditions.

Coming full circle, the fiddling and dance scene that I first encountered on Prince Edward Island turned out to be a complex mixture of old and new elements. Nearly all the venues and organized elements—fiddle festivals, town days, regularly scheduled ceilidhs and old-time dances, fiddle instruction programs, and the Prince Edward Island Fiddlers' Society—were products of the fiddling revival and had been in place for fifteen years or less. What survived from the past were the spirit and infectious rhythms of the music and the fiddlers' sweet, powerful, and highly individualistic playing styles.

About This Project

Through informants' recollections, I was able to piece together a coherent picture of the Island's musical life from about the turn of the twentieth century to the present. Because these recollections often included stories heard during youth from older relatives and neighbors, I could frequently push the narrative back to the time of "the old people" (that is, the generation in their prime during the final decades of the nineteenth century). To extend the story back still further, and to flesh out areas where oral accounts were inconclusive or contradictory, I relied on archival records or secondary sources. In terms of the latter, I am particularly indebted to James Hornby's excellent master's thesis, "The Fiddle on the Island."

Oral histories were collected during three periods. The first and most extensive period of collecting, sponsored by a Massachusetts organization called Earthwatch, took place over a period of several months in 1991 and 1992. I subsequently conducted two follow-up projects—a relatively brief series of interviews in 1999 and a much larger set in 2006 funded by the Canadian Museum of Civilization of Gatineau, Québec, since renamed the Canadian Museum of History.

Earthwatch sent along eight teams of six to eight volunteers, each of which took up a two-week residency.[6] They performed such tasks as running audio and video recording equipment during interviews, taking photographs, and transcribing speech. More important, their presence helped turn each interview session into a festive occasion, thereby encouraging even the most taciturn informants to speak freely.

With the help of fiddler George MacPhee, we set up our headquarters in the district of Monticello, about ten miles northwest of the town of Souris. The house MacPhee found for us to rent had been his childhood home; its general reputation as an important former venue for fiddling and house dances gave us a stamp of legitimacy right from the start. Our position in the region was greatly enhanced by the fact that until then, the eastern sector of Prince Edward Island had never been much of a tourist attraction. Consequently, we outsiders came to be viewed both as novelties and as the objects of considerable local interest.

Fiddlers were located largely through word of mouth. To this end, informants were asked to recommend other players, and casually encountered Islanders were routinely quizzed about any fiddlers they happened to know. Eventually this process became a bit of a game, and many a fiddler we had previously interviewed would approach us at a musical event and ask—with a hand shielding the corner of the mouth in a mock effort to avoid being overheard—"And did you get Archie?" or "Did you get Joe?" In fact, we later learned that at least some of the fiddlers we interviewed relished comparing notes with each other about their experiences with us.

As things turned out, our project had several points in its favor. For one thing, playing the fiddle for neighbors or other visitors upon request proved to be an old Island tradition. More important, the time was ripe for conducting a project of this nature. There was a definite awareness that the days of those with clear memories of "them times" were numbered, and many fiddlers seemed more than eager to tell their stories for the benefit of future generations.

The interviewing and music-recording process did not always go smoothly. The first few sessions conducted in the carpeted living room at our Monticello headquarters, for example, were halting and uncomfortable affairs that yielded little in the way of useful information. We were still trying to sort out what the problem was when the time came to conduct our first session off-site, about fifteen miles southwest of our headquarters in Poplar Point at the home of fiddler Jimmy Banks. We were heading for the living room to set up our equipment when Banks said, "Let's do this in the kitchen; we always play in the kitchen. When there's a carpet down, you can't hear your own foot tapping." Taking the hint, we held almost all subsequent interviews in kitchens, and the general atmosphere improved considerably!

Since most fiddlers brought along one or more accompanists to interview sessions, we encouraged the latter to add their reminiscences whenever they felt comfortable doing so. This policy almost always yielded useful information, and at some interviews the accompanist proved to be the one who was the most articulate and informative individual on hand.

Not all the Islanders interviewed were accomplished fiddle players. Among those whose insights and perspectives I sought during all three periods of interviewing were music instructors, dancers and dance instructors, community leaders, event organizers, fiddle makers and repairers, radio executives and personalities, traditional singers, and academic folklorists. I was also able to gain insight into the Island fiddling scene by observing and videotaping a variety of local musical events, such as fiddle festivals, town days, old-time dances, fiddle-club meetings, community talent shows, and private music parties.

Stylistic Notes

By and large, transcripts of fiddlers' comments are verbatim, and every effort was made to preserve their idiosyncratic syntax, rhythm of speech, and imagery. I did make certain changes in the interests of clarity and conservation of space, however, such as the insertion of some proper nouns and other key words without marking them with brackets; deletion of repetitions, digressions, and nongermane sentence fragments without using ellipses; and occasionally moving sentences around within a quotation so that a point strongly made verbally carried equal weight when rendered in print.

Although the selection and placement of punctuation when transcribing speech is necessarily somewhat arbitrary, I have tried to use it to the best of my ability to make the meaning of quoted passages as clear as possible. There is only one specialized symbol in the quotations, namely, the em-dash (—),which is used to separate sentence fragments from complete sentences or to separate two consecutive fragments.

I have adopted the convention of using the present tense to refer to the time of the original Earthwatch project (that is, 1991–92), and I tend to use the present tense when introducing fiddlers' comments (for example, "As so and so says, notes, observes. . ."), even when the informant has since passed away. A more recent present is evoked by means of such expressions as "at the time of the 2006 follow-up" and "at the time of this writing."

For the sake of streamlining, quotations or paraphrased speech from the 1991–92 interviews are not footnoted. Instead, only informants' names are noted in the text. The first time a particular informant is quoted in a given chapter, however, mention is also made—depending on which is more relevant—of his or her place of birth, childhood residence, or current residence (a complete listing of interviews from all three projects appears in appendix B). When a quotation, paraphrase, or other piece of information derives from the 1999 or 2006 interviews or from a conversation or exchange of letters or e-mails between author and informant outside the interviewing context, this is indicated via a conventional note.

All the original audio recordings, video recordings, and photographs collected during the 1991–92 and 2006 projects are archived as Accession #AV2007-33 at the Canadian Museum of History in Gatineau, Québec. All quotations and photographs derived from the 2006 project are copyrighted by the Canadian Museum of History.

Understanding Community Nicknames, or "Handles"

Until fairly recently, most Island communities were populated by only a few family groups, often resulting in a paucity of surnames. To assist with identification, Islanders employed a system of nicknames, or "handles," to identify individuals. Most handles consist of a person's first name followed by his or her father's first name. For example, Kings County fiddler George MacPhee is known in and around his native Monticello as "George Mel" (George, the son of Mel), and his oldest son Mel is known as "Mel George." Similarly, Prince County fiddler Edward Arsenault is known as "Edward à Polycarp" (Edward, son of Polycarp), or sometimes simply "Edward P Arsenault."

Two-name handles are sometimes not sufficient to identify an individual, in which case a grandfather's or (if the person is an outsider) even a spouse's name can brought into play. Kings County fiddler Kenny Chaisson, for example, is known around his native Bear River as "Kenny Joe Pete" (Kenny, son of Joe, grandson of Pete). Alternatively, the legendary Prince County fiddler Joe Arsenault of St. Nicholas was known as "Joe à Bibienne" (Joe, husband of Bibienne). Sometimes, descriptive nicknames are also used. One particularly tall and thin fiddler, for example, was known to his community as "Joe the Post." These various naming systems are sometimes combined. Archie Stewart of Milltown Cross, Kings County, for example, tells us that a man known locally as "Black Sandy" had a son whose nickname was "Big Alec"; the latter's full handle was then "Big Alec Black Sandy."[7]

Putting This Work into Perspective

While researching background material for this book, I had occasion to read many area studies that focused in whole or part on other traditional fiddling cultures. It quickly became clear that fiddling on Prince Edward Island shared many attitudes and practices with counterparts in Britain, Ireland, and diverse parts of North America stretching from Newfoundland to Arizona. Each of these regions had what amounted to its own Golden Age, when people danced in local kitchens or barns to the music of accomplished local fiddlers and fiddling was pressed into service to help harness community labor and resources.[8]

This kind of musical life had its roots in pre-emigration Scotland and Ireland and was carried by immigrants across the Atlantic in the late eighteenth and early nineteenth centuries. Wherever conditions were ripe, these Scottish and Irish immigrants established communities in the New World with customs relating to fiddling and music making that paralleled in many respects those they had left behind in the Old. And while these far-flung communities evolved quite different ways of life in response to the circumstances of their respective environments, they retained a common bond insofar as elements of this old-world musical life were preserved. What's more, because repertoire and other musical ideas diffused around North America via travel, commerce, and the print media, this original bond was maintained, if not strengthened, throughout much of the nineteenth century.

Under pressure from social forces unleashed through technological change and the growth of mass culture, traditional (or "old-time") fiddling and the way of life that fostered it were in sharp decline throughout much of North America by the first decades of the twentieth century. In the 1920s, several well-publicized campaigns—the best known of which was led by industrialist Henry Ford—were organized to stem fiddling's decline. In their wake came fiddle contests, folk festivals, and other events aimed at both maintaining the interest of existing players and bringing attention to the art. Although such efforts succeeded in producing a great deal of short-lived hoopla, they were ultimately unsuccessful. By the time of the Second World War, what had once been a nearly universal music culture had shrunk to a relatively few pockets.

One special characteristic of the PEI experience is how late in the twentieth century its Golden Age persisted. In many portions of Prince Edward Island, both old-time fiddling and the community life that supported it were in full flower well into the 1960s and later—perhaps a full generation longer than just about anywhere else in North America. Although this way of life was largely gone by the time I arrived on the scene, its spirit survived in the music and recollections of nearly every Island fiddler who was then over thirty-five. And as their stories in these pages bring PEI's musical practices, customs, and attitudes to life, they provide a window into our collective musical heritage as North Americans and an insight into the kind of preurban community life that many of our forebears experienced.

I have mentioned that one of my initial ambitions was to emulate the great twentieth-century music collectors. There is a romantic corollary to the great-collector story that still circulates in the music scenes I frequent: that the source musicians they visited were essentially rustic artist-philosophers who amassed their musical treasure troves in isolation and strictly for the love of the music. Although old-time Island fiddlers were clearly products of a vanishing kind of community life—not "rustic philosophers" at all—at the end of the day there are aspects of this fundamental truth that seem even more compelling than the original story: that the music and the fiddle sound they loved (and to which I felt so strongly drawn) were once the life blood of their communities, that nothing of importance happened without them, and that you "couldn't have a wedding without the fiddler."

NOTES

1. On Prince Edward Island the term *tea party* harks back to large-scale nineteenth-century church picnics. There is no connection whatsoever with either the Boston Tea Party that preceded the American Revolution or the American antitax Tea Party movement of the early twenty-first century. For more on Island tea parties, see chapters 1 and 2.
2. "Scottish" in this context indicates a connection not with Scotland but with the fiddling of neighboring Cape Breton Island; see chapters 13 and 16.
3. Cecil Sharp (1859–1924) was a pioneer in collecting English folk dances and Appalachian folk songs; John Lomax (1867–1948) and Alan Lomax (1915–2002) were giants in the field of American folk song collection, associated in particular with perfecting the practice of documenting folk music via field recordings; Frank Warner (1903–78) collected folk songs in the American South and the Adirondacks; Samuel Bayard (1908–97) is best known for his work among Pennsylvania fiddlers; and the collecting work of Alan Jabbour (1942–) among fiddlers in North Carolina, Virginia, and West Virginia helped launch the Appalachian fiddle-music revival.
4. I did, in fact, devote myself systematically to collecting tunes as part of the project; see Perlman, *Fiddle Music of* PEI. As of this writing, a website devoted to traditional PEI fiddling is under construction that features a large sampling of the music recordings made during both the 1991-92 and 2006 projects; it will be jointly sponsored by the Canadian Museum of History and the Robertson Library at the University of Prince Edward Island. The tentative name for the site is "Bowing Down Home: Traditional Fiddling on Prince Edward Island." Several versions of the URL have been reserved, with the most likely version being www.bowingdownhome.ca; readers are encouraged to check Internet search engines for availability or contact the author through his website, www.kenperlman.com.
5. During that era, neither radios nor phonographs required an electrical-power grid to operate. As discussed in chapter 13, early phonographs were spring-powered, and radios could be powered by storage batteries.
6. Earthwatch recruited volunteers for hundreds of different projects each year through a printed catalog. Volunteers each paid a sum to participate in the project of their choice. Funds collected by Earthwatch were split roughly fifty-fifty, with half financing a given project and the rest going toward the organization's administrative expenses.
7. These customs have roots in Scotland; see, for example, MacPhail, *Master's Wife*, 87; and Dunn, *Highland Settler*, 136–37.
8. Some of the many parallels between Island musical customs and those from other fiddling traditions are noted throughout the book but discussed in detail toward the end of chapter 2.

Couldn't Have a Wedding without the Fiddler

PHOTO I.3. NORTH SHORE OF PEI NEAR MONTICELLO, KINGS COUNTY, JULY 1991 (PHOTO BY KEN PERLMAN).

CHAPTER ONE
Cradled on the Waves

As with any social phenomenon, fiddling on Prince Edward Island is deeply interwoven within a fabric of time and place. And while a full analysis of the Island's geography, climate, history, political economy, and sociology lies far beyond the scope of this book, nevertheless there are certain factors—ordinarily the purview of these fields—that must be addressed before we can devote ourselves fully to fiddling's story.

Prince Edward Island is Canada's smallest province in terms of both land area and population. The Island is only about 140 miles long by 40 miles at its widest. It is divided into three counties, which (going from east to west) are named Kings, Queens, and Prince (see map 1.1). The population in the early 1990s was about 130,000. Of these, approximately 30,000 lived in the Island's two urban areas: the provincial capital, Charlottetown, in central Queens County and the city of Summerside in eastern Prince County. The rest lived either in small towns—Souris, Montague, Rustico, Borden, Kensington, Miscouche, O'Leary, Alberton, and Tignish—or scattered among the hundreds of rural districts that dot the landscape.

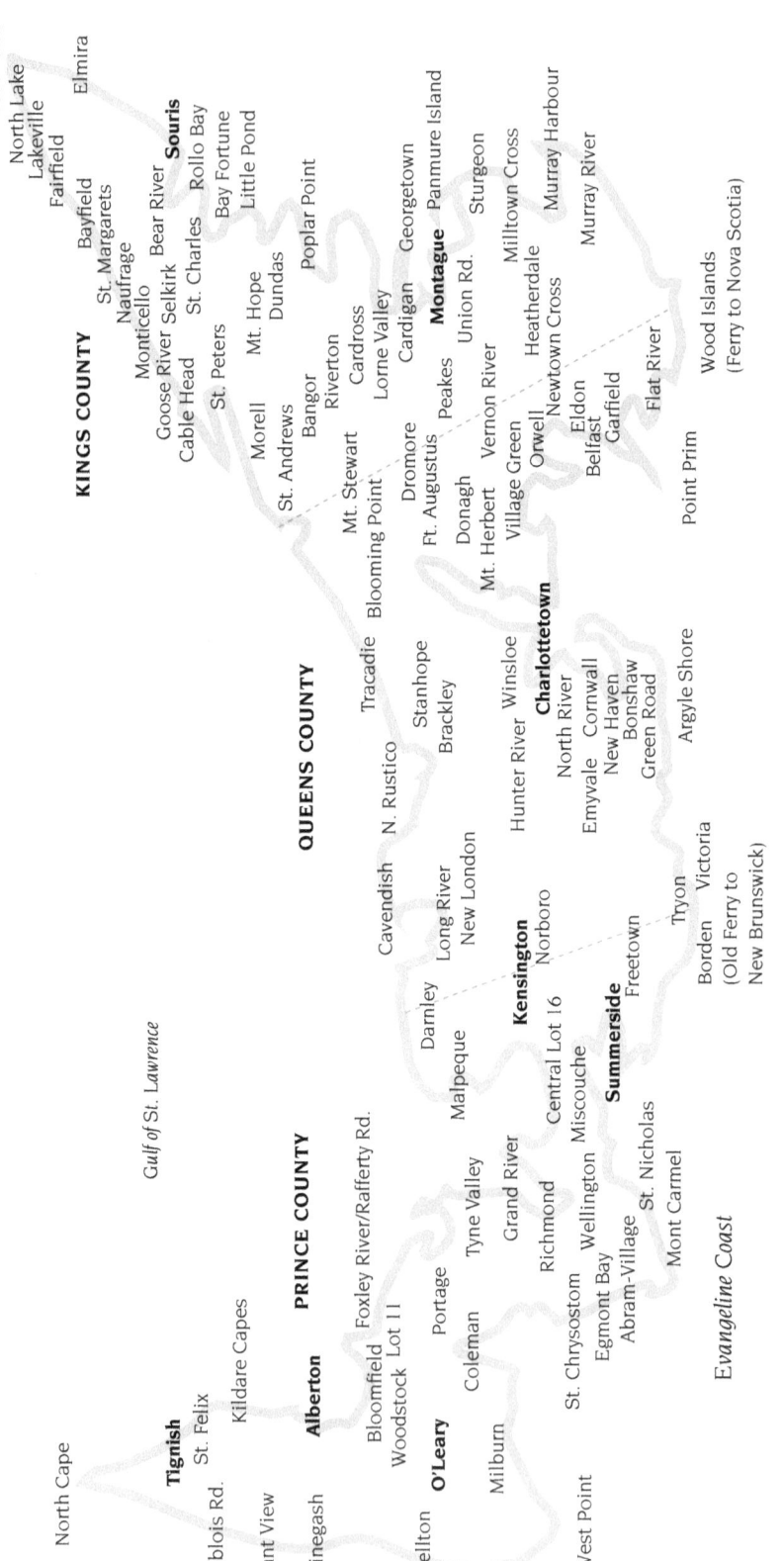

MAP 1.1. PRINCE EDWARD ISLAND, SHOWING COUNTY LINES, MAJOR TOWNS, AND MOST DISTRICTS MENTIONED IN THE TEXT.

Prince Edward Island rests in the Gulf of St. Lawrence in a crook formed by the neighboring provinces of Nova Scotia and New Brunswick (these three are known collectively as the Canadian Maritime Provinces, or simply as the Maritimes). Geologically speaking, it consists of a single red sandstone plateau, and the terrain is flat to rolling with but a single site (currently the home of the Island's sole ski lift) that rises to an altitude as high as five hundred feet. Much of the Island is lined by tall bluffs that fall away abruptly to a rocky shoreline. Because Island sandstone is quite soft, these bluffs erode at a fairly rapid pace. In fact, Teresa MacPhee Wilson (b. Monticello) reports that residents along the north side of Kings County have seen a succession of shore roads washed into the sea, and they have moved their homes and churches inland several times over the years to keep them from sharing the same fate.

The Gulf Stream flows not far off the north shore of Prince Edward Island—giving it the relatively warm ocean waters that make it eastern Canada's prime beach resort. Summers are short, cool, rainy, and intensely green; winters are long, cold, and harsh. Most Islanders seem relatively unperturbed by climate, but they are much more likely to complain of summer humidity than of winter cold.

Prince Edward Island is populated for the most part by the descendants of three major ethnic groups: the Acadian French, the Highland Scots, and the Irish. The Highland Scots predominate in eastern Kings County, as do the Acadians in southern and western Prince County. The Irish are scattered throughout the Island, but several areas might be regarded as enclaves. Among these are Charlottetown and its environs, western Prince County, and the northeastern Queens County region surrounding Fort Augustus. Other ethnic groups of significance on the Island include the Mi'kmaqs,[1] Lowland Scots, English, Welsh, and Lebanese.

Most Islanders belong either to the Catholic Church or to one of several Protestant denominations, notably the United Church of Canada. Because the Catholic Church numbers among its adherents most Islanders of Acadian, Irish, and Highland Scots descent,[2] its adherents form the largest bloc. Worship tends to be decentralized, and the Island is dotted with charming churches—many of which imitate on a small scale and in wood the architecture and ornamentation of stone counterparts in Britain, Ireland, and France.[3]

As has been the case since the earliest days of settlement, the most common occupation is farming. Although almost the entire Island was once under cultivation, many farms have been abandoned over the past few generations,

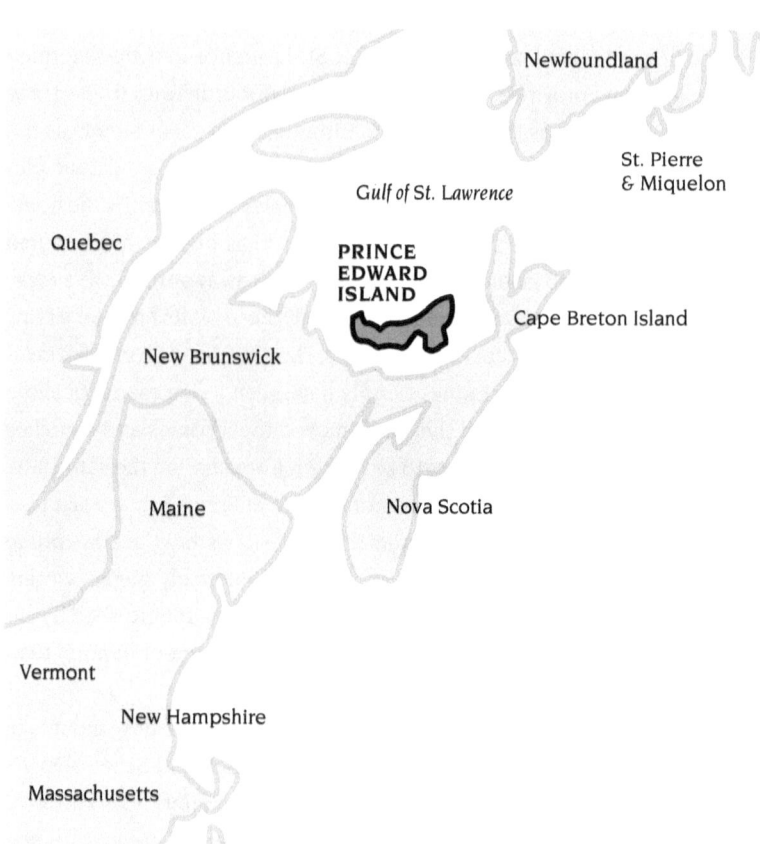

MAP 1.2. PRINCE EDWARD ISLAND AND ITS ENVIRONS.

and the land has been allowed to go back to thickly grown young spruce forest. Until quite recently—when it was overtaken by occupations related to tourism—fishing was the second most common form of work on Prince Edward Island. Nowadays, only the lobster fishery is viable. As far as the pursuit of ground-fish (cod, hake, and flounder) is concerned, the relatively recent closing of the Atlantic fishery was merely a last straw for what had already become a moribund pursuit.

With poet's insight, the Mi'kmaqs called the Island Abegweit (pronounced "AH-beg-way"), which means "cradled on the waves." Jacques Cartier claimed the Island for France in 1534 and named it Île Saint Jean; the British annexed it in 1758 and changed its name twice—first to Isle of Saint John and then in 1799 to its modern appellation.

When the British took control of the territory after the Seven Years' War, or French and Indian War (1756–63), they moved almost immediately to deport its approximately four thousand Acadian inhabitants back to France.[4] This *grand dérangement* led to much hardship, with substantial numbers perishing of disease or shipwreck en route. Some Acadians who made it back to France later emigrated once again to the New World and made new homes for themselves in French-owned Louisiana, where their descendants have subsequently become known as Cajuns.[5]

Despite British efforts, some Acadian families escaped deportation by concealing themselves from the military authorities. Still others were eventually permitted to return to the Island when the ban on Acadian settlement was relaxed. By 1798, these remaining Acadians had formed three communities: Bay Fortune in northeastern Kings County, Rustico in northwestern Queens County, and Malpeque in northeastern Prince County. A census taken that year in these communities listed only thirty family names, and to this day nearly all Island Acadians bear one of these original thirty.[6]

With the Acadians for the most part out of the picture, Britain sought to resettle the land with its own peoples. To this end, the Island was divided into sixty-seven *lots* of about twenty-thousand acres each. These lots were sold or presented by the British government to wealthy or politically connected individuals who were then charged with populating and developing their holdings.

The Highland Scots were the first British group to settle en masse on the Island. The decline of the clan system following the Jacobite Rebellion of 1745, and the subsequent Clearances (a movement aimed at ridding the Scottish countryside of its tenant farmers, or crofters), created a large pool of castoffs from whom immigrants could be recruited by PEI's newly appointed landlords.[7] These landlords generally arranged for Highlanders to cross the Atlantic on specially chartered ships in the company of their fellow clanspeople. When they reached the Island, these clan members often settled on adjoining lands, and they were thus able to retain many of their original family and social ties.

One of the first groups of Highland Scots to arrive on Prince Edward Island consisted of about 250 members of the MacDonald clan—most of them Catholics from the West Highlands and from such Western Isles as South Uist and Barra. They were recruited by the Island landlord John MacDonald, who was also Laird of Glenaladale in Scotland. These MacDonalds sailed on board the *Alexander*, landed at Tracadie Bay in northeastern Queens County in 1772, and settled on two nearby lots.[8] This expedition essentially set the pattern for Highlander immigration over the next few decades.

Probably the largest such venture was organized by Thomas Douglas, Fifth Earl of Selkirk. In 1803, Lord Selkirk arranged for the transportation of some eight hundred Presbyterian Scots—mostly from the Isle of Skye—to his lands near Orwell Bay in what is now southeastern Queens County. There they founded the district known as Belfast.[9]

Large-scale Irish immigration to Prince Edward Island did not get under way until roughly 1810, when a declining economy and increased population pressure encouraged many Irish to try their luck abroad. Unlike the Highlanders, the Irish came mostly as individuals or small families rather than as part of clan or extended-family groups. At first immigrants from southeastern Ireland predominated, but by the 1830s the center for Irish emigration had moved northward, with the largest contingent by far having its origin in County Monaghan. By the 1840s, Irish immigration to Prince Edward Island had pretty much ceased, and the waves of immigrants heading for North America in the wake of the infamous potato famine bypassed the Island almost entirely.[10]

By the time the Irish appeared on the Island, most desirable land was already occupied. Consequently, they were generally forced to settle on poorer-quality lands that were relatively inaccessible to roads or water transportation. Nevertheless, as the only one of the Island's three major population groups to be native English speakers at the time of their arrival, the Irish may have had an easier time adjusting to Island life than did their Acadian or Highlander counterparts.[11] And when compulsory English-language education was instituted throughout Prince Edward Island in the mid-nineteenth century, Islanders of Irish background were the ones most often recruited as teachers. This has left a legacy of Irish expressions, turns of phrase, and even a slight hint of "brogue" among nearly all "anglophone" Islanders.

As for the Acadian French and Highland Scots, they spoke their native languages almost exclusively until fairly late in the nineteenth century, when compulsory English-language education plus an urge toward assimilation among the young gradually set the Island on the path toward becoming the anglophone culture it is today. Nowadays, almost all Island Acadians speak fluent English, with French remaining the predominant native tongue only within certain distinctly Acadian areas.[12] Most Acadians who live outside these enclaves have grown up with English as their mother tongue; for the most part, they are culturally indistinguishable from their Scots- and Irish-descended neighbors.

Most youngsters of Highland Scots ancestry spoke fluent English by 1900, but older generations continued to converse in Scots Gaelic well into the twentieth century.[13] Although all the Islanders from Scots background who form part of this study are Anglophones, many recall parents and grandparents for whom Gaelic was the native tongue. This account, for example, is from Largus MacInnis of Lakeville, Kings County:

> There was an old lady, used to live in Munn's Road. She'd call in. My two grandmothers was livin' with us. Grandma Campbell smoked a clay pipe and the other old lady, they called her Big Daisy, she smoked a pipe. And what they smoked was dried Twist.[14] Whoa! The smell of the smoke would pretty near knock a young feller down. But they'd get those two old clay pipes packed with tobacco and get them going. There'd be just a blue fog of smoke going and they'd be talking away in Gaelic.

Political Economy

The lot system that was put into practice when the British first occupied Prince Edward Island had some unfortunate consequences. For one thing, few landlords ever visited their North American holdings, and they were for the most part unconcerned with such matters as land development, improving agricultural methods, or seeing to the general prosperity of their tenants. Moreover, because tenants who improved their land were often assessed higher rents, they had little incentive to increase efficiency or productive capacity.[15]

After considerable struggle, the lot system was finally done away with in 1875, but it left in its wake a long-term legacy of agricultural inefficiency and rural poverty. The system also left one more bequest; the shape of the old lots is still reflected in the locations of secondary roads and property lines all over the Island. Also left behind were place-names: the area surrounding Emyvale, Queens County, for example, is still often referred to as Lot 65; and Prince County still has a few communities that bear such names as Lot 11 and Southwest Lot 16.

Although the Island experienced some good times in the mid-nineteenth century—fueled mainly by tariff-free trade with American ports and by growth in the local shipbuilding industry—this period of prosperity gradually faded away under the new Canadian Federation.[16] From the time of its inception in 1867 until well into the twentieth century, the Canadian federal government followed transportation and tariff policies that consistently favored the growth of manufacturing and agriculture in central and western Canada over shipping and agriculture in the Maritimes. As one manifestation of this policy, stiff tariff barriers were instituted to inhibit the lucrative American trade, which had the effect of depressing prices for Island produce, while forcing Islanders to buy relatively expensive manufactured goods made in central Canada.[17] Consequently, the Island's economy was relatively stagnant from the 1880s until the 1950s. In fact, as recently as 1950 the per capita income on Prince Edward Island was only half the Canadian national average.[18]

One major consequence of a poor local economy in the years following confederation was a continuous stream of emigration to other North American regions—notably Boston and other parts of New England, Ontario, and western Canada. Despite large average family size, the Island population actually declined between 1891 and the 1940s. Another important consequence of these hard times was that for several generations Prince Edward Island remained an economic and cultural backwater. In many fields—such as transportation, education, agriculture, energy, and communications—the ways of doing things throughout much of the Island remained practically unchanged from the 1880s until after the Second World War. During this period, most rural Islanders went about their daily activities only minimally affected by the many radical changes experienced during this period elsewhere in North America.

"The Farming Was the Same All the Way down the Road"

By the turn of the twentieth century, most Islanders made their living through an occupation called "mixed farming." They owned their land, and for the most part they subsisted, but they were rarely out of debt. Hard work was often the only thing that kept disaster at bay. Merlin Quinn of Cardross, Kings County, describes what a typical mixed farm in his area was like.

> The farming back in them days around here was the same all the way down the road. There was a farm about every five chains from here to the school, so each farm was five chains wide.[19] Each farmer would have two to three acres of potatoes, half an acre of corn, and an acre of turnips; each farmer would keep one brood sow, and she'd have a couple of litters of pigs per year. A pretty good farmer would have four nice milk cows. And the grain was the same, a pretty good farmer would have twenty acres of grain or so in. When digging time would come, we'd have three acres of potatoes, our neighbor would have three, and so on. We all had to use a horse if we went to the store or went to church: horse and wagon. A good farmer was considered he'd have two horses. There was an odd farmer was only able to afford to have one horse; he was referred to sometimes as a "one horse

farmer." That brought that down in history; if a person wasn't doin' that great, he was called a one horse farmer. I remember going to school in my bare feet. In fact, I remember in the summertime, the only girl in the school that would have shoes on would be the teacher. We didn't think anything about it 'cause that's the way it was. Everybody had the same deal.

According to Art O'Shea of Iona, Queens County, the following chores had to be done every day: feed the hens, gather the eggs, clean the pigpen, water the horses and feed them oats, hand-carry water, feed and milk the cows, separate the milk and cream via a hand separator, slice turnips (winters only), pick wild berries (summers only), throw down hay and straw and clean the stables, check on the animals after nightfall, manage the woodpile, fill the wood box, saw and split the wood, and go for groceries (often with eggs for barter).[20] Then there was the really hard work: planting, cultivating, and harvesting.

For the most part this was not a cash economy; farmers grew and made much of what they consumed and bartered for the rest. In the Hungry Thirties (as the Great Depression is locally known), this self-sufficiency was to come in handy. To many Island farmers, as Stewart MacIntyre (b. Fairfield, Kings County) tells us, this period seemed only a slight intensification of the usual level of travail.

> There was good times in the Hungry Thirties because practically everything that you used, your food and your clothing, for instance, grew on the farm. People on salaries lost their jobs, they suffered. But a farmer he could put on a good meal. I was in charge of the East Point Coast Guard station at that time, and I was on salary. One day, I was around collecting for the Red Cross, and I went to this farmhouse. They had a tale of woe, no money, and it was quite a big family. But it was just noontime, the dinner table was set and there were two nice fowl on it, and all the fittings. So when I went back home, I started figuring up what it would cost me to put that dinner on the table. When I was done, I had nothing left over for breakfast or supper!

In many parts of the Island, until the onset of the Second World War, many merchants refused to offer cash in return for most farm produce. Instead, farmers would generally receive just a notation in the merchant's ledger that entitled them to a certain amount of store credit. Stewart MacIntyre describes the process.

> Any excess that wouldn't be used by the family, they could sell it in town. You'd haul it in, and in those days you drove your team down along the shore and through the runs into Souris; that was eight miles. You would leave home about three o'clock in the morning, and you wouldn't get back until nine o'clock that night. For oats,

you would get half cash, because they used to ship it to England for their horses and it was in strong demand. So you would get half cash for oats. But for potatoes you would get nothing, for poultry you would get nothing, or anything like that. It would just go onto your account, which would run for the year, see. And the rest of the year, you bought on that account. There was no money in farming whatsoever.

Such exploitative practices were later ameliorated in some parts of the Island through the growth of agricultural cooperatives, in which producers banded together to achieve a better position relative to the market. Some such cooperatives included farmer's institutes, grain banks, egg circles, dairy cooperatives, shipping clubs, and a potato growers' association.[21]

Fishing and the "Lumber Woods"

As noted above, fishing was until quite recently the second most common occupation on the Island. Until the growth of fisherman's cooperatives in the late 1920s, few fishermen had any independence. Most owned no boat or gear of their own. Instead they worked a company boat and fished "half-line" (that is, they paid the company half the catch in rent). Most were unemployed all winter and lived off credit from the fishery, so they were always paying off what they owed. Like most of their agricultural counterparts, few ever saw cash.[22]

In the Tignish area, as described by Joseph Doucette of Deblois Road, Prince County, many men employed in the fishing or fish-processing trade had to live away from home in company housing during the fishing season. Consequently, the countryside was virtually depopulated during that period each year.

> The poor class of people went to the shore, workin' in the factories and fishin'. They boarded there, they stayed there, they slept there and had their meals there. So there was not that many people in the country then; in the spring of the year there wasn't too many. In the summertime, coming into the fall and into wintertime, people was home, but they didn't have that much to do.

In winter, many young men—even those with growing families—were often forced by the need for ready cash to take jobs off-Island. Most of them sought work cutting and hauling timber in the "lumber woods" of Maine, New Brunswick, Nova Scotia, and Québec. Attwood O'Connor of Milltown Cross, Kings County, for example, spent seven winters in the lumber woods because "there was nothing else to do around here; you just jumped on the train, went over and got a job in the woods."

PHOTO 1.1. FISHING BOATS AND SHACKS, NORTHEASTERN PRINCE COUNTY, AUGUST 1992 (PHOTO BY KEN PERLMAN).

This practice was commonplace as early as the 1860s when Larry Gorman—a Prince County man who later became a renowned regional songwriter—worked in the lumber woods of New Brunswick's Miramichi Valley.[23] It was still going strong in the late 1940s when then-teenaged Danny MacLean (b. Garfield, Queens County) elected to seek his fortune in the lumber camps of Québec. As can be surmised from MacLean's account, there had been little change in lumbering technology in the intervening years:

> I worked there all one winter. It was all bucksaws then; there was no power saws. The wood was all piled up on the mountains. Then you hauled it off the mountains and piled it on the frozen lakes, then the river would drive it down to the mills in the spring. I hauled a team there, too, hauled wood down off the mountain [in] bobsleds.

"You Helped Your Neighbor and They Helped You"

Rural Islanders developed a system in which the warmth of community relationships compensated to some degree for the physical hardship and material privations of daily life. As Stewart MacIntyre remembers, "That was the tone of the times. You helped your neighbor and they helped you, and I don't think people would have been able to get along otherwise."

For one thing, neighbors generally pitched in when any local family was faced with such labor-intensive jobs as cultivating and harvesting. MacIntyre, for example, recalls that as a child he was often "lent" by his parents to help out the neighbors.

> My father was in charge of the Coast Guard station; we had no land of our own. But we children had to go and help out the farmers around, and you couldn't very well refuse. They planted potatoes and that was all done by hand, all horse-drawn machinery. I remember the first time we went; the chap who farmed next door, he was supposed to be a little tight with money. My sister and I, she'd be about six years old and I wouldn't be more than eight, and he got us to plant potatoes for him. So we planted potatoes all day and in the evening. And we were warned before we left, "Don't take any money, he's a neighbor and you can't charge." We protested, but he pushed the money in our pocket. It was twenty-five cents apiece, I think. So, I suppose when we got home we looked guilty, and it turned out that we had the money. Well, they didn't know what to do. They were going to send it back at first, then they decided that the old chap might think that he hadn't given us enough. So they confiscated the money and give us a lecture and that ended it. But that was the tone of the times.

Another major locus for cooperation was the one-room community school. The province provided only a portion of its upkeep, and each rural district was required to raise the remainder from among its own inhabitants.[24] In addition to requiring such fund-raising, the local school served as an important community focus in numerous other ways. Jenny McQuaid (b. Naufrage, Kings County) describes it as follows:

> It was their school where they worked together to raise funds, or to get something for it. Parents did care if the school was warm, and they'd see that there'd be wood there. They cared that everybody got home on a stormy day, and the person with the horse and sleigh would see to it that these kids would get home. And if the kids weren't in school today, well, you knew very well why they weren't there; the word was around they were sick or had measles or something. You had all that instant feedback about everybody. And if there was a death in the community, school closed. It was caring for each other and knowing one another, and it just had that sense of family.

Much time, especially in the winter, was spent in visiting neighbors and whiling away the evenings in their company. And as noted by Cosmas Sigsworth (b. Corraville, Kings County), if there was a party or celebration, everyone soon knew about it: "Word got around: neighbor tells neighbor. Somebody'd be goin' in down the road, drop in and tell so and so—So on and so forth. There was a lot of friendliness. Everybody knew everybody, I think. More friendliness then than now." Neighbors also knew they could depend on each other. As Merlin Quinn describes, "People were honest. There was a lot of principle, strong principles that they lived by. A lot of old people, if they'd give you their word, that was just as good as a note in the bank!"

Social division by age group was unknown. Young and old took part in the same tasks and engaged in the same social activities. Therefore, according to Jenny McQuaid, as a youngster at a district social event you would expect to "dance with somebody who'd be twice your height maybe, and three times your age." And when it came to community tasks, any youngster who could pull his or her own weight was accorded adult levels of respect.

Because economic survival was so tenuous, hard work was considered as important a characteristic as neighborliness. Consequently, community values centering on its importance were regarded as self-evident and universal truths.

> Hard work ... was a pre-eminent virtue, and its opposite, laziness, a character flaw which elicited the greatest contempt. From the time of earliest settlement there had been no easy way to make a living on the Island. There was only one safe route to survival, the uphill road of industry and labor. ... To be known as [a hard worker] was the highest compliment bestowed in the rural order.[25]

"You Didn't Get Very Far with a Horse and Sleigh"

Adding to local isolation and the need for self-sufficiency was the state of transportation. Islanders rarely traveled more than a few miles from their homes until the coming of widespread automobile transportation in the 1950s and '60s. Joe MacDonald sums up local transportation during his youth in northern Kings County as follows:

> We had no cars. In the wintertime, the roads weren't plowed and the roads all filled up in the fall of the year. We used horses and sleighs and mind you, you didn't get very far with a horse and sleigh. From here to Mt. Stewart was four miles; that's a big trip! You'd go to Mt. Stewart, that's where we bought our groceries, and back again on a cold day in the wintertime. That was far enough! An odd time, people would take a horse and sleigh to Charlottetown, which is twenty miles, and back is forty miles. They'd make it in a day, but it's pretty rough on the horse."

There had been a railroad on Prince Edward Island since the late nineteenth century, but it never provided residents with a practical alternative to horse-drawn transportation. Its builders—who had been paid according to how many miles of track were laid—responded with a poorly designed serpentine system that was good for little other than moving produce from farm to warehouse.[26] According to one wag, these trains were so slow, "one could step off the moving train, fill his pockets with mushrooms or blueberries, then step in again."[27]

Fiddling Comes to the Island

Fiddling and fiddle music were originally carried across the Atlantic to Prince Edward Island by Scottish and Irish immigrants.[28] Although a detailed account of the development of fiddling and fiddle music in the Old World is beyond the scope of this book, nevertheless a few general observations can be made to serve as background.[29]

When the violin was introduced to Scotland in the late seventeenth century, its superior tone, response, and playability soon led musicians to take it up and abandon other bowed instruments that had previously been in circulation, such as the *fidhel* (pronounced "fi'ull"), rebec, and viol. Violin design was copied by local craftsmen, and before long the instrument—which had also come to be referred to as the *fidhel* or *fiddle*—was well established in both urban and rural areas of the Scottish Lowlands. By the middle of the eighteenth century, just about all classes and regions in Scottish society were evincing a great passion for fiddling and fiddle-accompanied dancing. The two most popular such dances were the indigenous Scotch reel and an import from England known as the country dance. The upper classes and urban bourgeoisie danced in private ballrooms or at events with paid admission known as assemblies, while crofters and other less-prosperous rural folk danced in local cottages or on the village green.

This growing interest in fiddling encouraged the development of a class of fiddle virtuosos and fiddle tune composers, of whom perhaps the best known were Niel and Nathaniel Gow, William Marshall, and Daniel Dow. These men, and dozens of others, published collections of new and traditional fiddle tunes—reels, strathspeys, airs, jigs, and hornpipes—which ultimately served as the foundation of this musical genre (for more on fiddle tunes and fiddle tune collections, see chapter 14).

The first records of the violin's presence in Ireland date to about 1720.[30] Not until the late eighteenth century, however, did the violin became widely popular in Ireland as a dance-accompaniment instrument; it was also around this time when Irish fiddlers begin to seriously apply themselves to playing jigs and reels. Many of the earliest fiddle tunes played in Ireland were probably imported from Scotland, but by 1800 Irish composers were turning out tunes of their own in great abundance. Of special note were the hundreds of jigs composed about this time to accompany an indigenous couples' dance that featured elaborate stepping.

Island oral tradition has it that fiddlers accompanied Highland settlers across the Atlantic. According to Francis MacDonald of Morell, Kings County, for example, his mother's side of the family traces its descent from fiddlers aboard the ship *Alexander* when it first landed at Tracadie Bay in the 1770s. Similarly, Dan McPhee (b. Bayfield, Kings County) notes that his musical forebears settled on the Island not long afterward: "I don't know how many shiploads of MacPhees came from the Hebrides and settled here. The lot extended from this shore here [near Monticello], to the south shore just east of Souris. And there was fiddlers amongst them, a lot of them."

The same ships that brought the first Highland fiddlers to the Island also brought its first bagpipers.[31] Bagpipes had been the dance-accompanying instrument of choice in Scotland and Ireland prior to the ascendancy of the fiddle, and Scots continued dancing to the pipes at outdoor venues throughout the eighteenth century. According to Hughie McPhee of Bayfield, Kings County, a piper named Toganny McPhee came to Prince Edward Island from Scotland late in the eighteenth century and settled on a grant of land in Rock Barra. Similarly, the following account comes from a family whose Scottish ancestors sailed for the Maritimes not long after the Glenaladale party landed in Tracadie Bay.

> When the immigrants landed on shore, they formed up and danced a Scotch Reel in which my grandaunt led off. Bishop Fraser was there and after listening to my uncle Ronald MacDonald the piper he exclaimed with delight, "That man has the best little finger on the chanter I have ever known."[32]

Along these lines, it is known that Scottish pipers Eachan and Con Duiligh Rankin settled in the Belfast area of Prince Edward Island not long after the founding of that settlement. They had learned their art from their father, Neil Rankin, the last of his line to serve as hereditary court piper for the MacLean chieftains on the Isles of Mull and Coll.[33]

Along with their fiddles and pipes, the very first Highland settlers and their Irish counterparts carried with them a powerful musical heritage of both vocal and instrumental music. They also brought along many practices associated with music making—such as holding community dances in or around the home and using music and dance parties as a reward to neighbors for donating their labor. Such customs were well established in Island districts by the 1820s, when a traveler named John MacGregor reported an active musical life characterized by frolics (dances held following communal work: see chapter 2) and other kinds of dance parties: "The amusements of the farmers and other inhabitants settled in different parts of the island are much the same as they have been accustomed to before leaving the countries they came from. Dances on many occasions are common."[34]

MacGregor also tells us that at the time of his visit to Prince Edward Island, a division of labor existed among fiddlers and bagpipers in which the latter handled most outdoor dances and the former all those within doors.[35] This arrangement seems to have persisted until about the last quarter of the nineteenth century, when the use of bagpipes as a dance-accompaniment instrument began to decline. By the end of the nineteenth century, the bagpipes could still be heard on certain ceremonial occasions, but their role as a dance-accompaniment instrument had pretty much come to an end.[36]

By the middle of the nineteenth century, new tunes, dances, and musical ideas imported from Britain and from other parts of North America were becoming a significant factor in shaping both Island fiddling and its milieu. Such importation probably first led Island churches to the strategy of employing fiddle dances to raise funds. Accounts of the resulting church picnics—often called "tea parties" to stress their alcohol-free nature—begin to appear in Island newspapers as early as the 1860s (for more on tea parties and similar events, see chapter 2). Before long, most Island communities were also employing fiddle dances to raise funds for local schools and other activities.

The fiddle-based music and dance scene described in the following chapters was pretty much in place on Prince Edward Island by the 1880s, and it retained its general shape until the gradual collapse of rural district life in the decades following the Second World War. As we shall see, the particular state of technology, infrastructure, and social organization that prevailed during this period made fiddlers and their music essential to the smooth operation of community life.

NOTES

1. The Mi'kmaqs (pronounced "MIK-maks") are the Island's First Nation inhabitants.
2. The Protestant Reformation did not penetrate very far into the Scottish Highlands, whose inhabitants held onto their original faith at least in part as an act of defiance against the British government.

3. Smith, *Historic Churches of* PEI, 11–12.
4. Acadia was the name given to French holdings in what is now New Brunswick and mainland Nova Scotia. Most of its French inhabitants had moved to Prince Edward Island in the 1750s after Acadia was ceded to Britain. All Island French were thereafter known as "Acadians."
5. Arsenault, *Island Acadians*, 33–36.
6. Arsenault, *Island Acadians*, 51–54.
7. In 1745, many Highland clans supported the claims to the British throne of Charles Edward Stewart (known as "Bonnie Prince Charlie") and joined him in an uprising against the British government. Because most Highland crofters were armed retainers of their respective clan chiefs, the British felt more secure with them out of the picture.
8. *Arrival of the First Scottish Catholic Emigrants*, 50–51.
9. Clark, *Three Centuries*, 67–69.
10. MacDonald, *New Ireland*, 5–9.
11. Scots Gaelic was the native language of the Highland Scots at the time of immigration. Use of the Gaelic language in Ireland had been declining for generations because of a long-term British policy of suppression. The areas from which most Irish immigrants to Prince Edward Island originated were already almost entirely English speaking by the late eighteenth century. See MacDonald, *New Ireland*, 13–15, 22.
12. These areas are (going east to west) Rustico, the Evangeline Coast, Cascumpec, and Tignish.
13. The last known native Gaelic-speaking Islander died in the 1980s. See Shaw, *Gaelic in* PEI, 1.
14. Hickey's Twist was a locally manufactured chewing tobacco.
15. Clark, *Three Centuries*, 42–52.
16. Although there was considerable initial opposition on Prince Edward Island to joining the Canadian Federation, it finally agreed to sign the Articles of Confederation in 1873 after being offered several inducements by the new federal government, such as help with railroad construction debt, assistance in abolishing the lot system, and establishment of a regular ferry service.
17. In all fairness, it should be noted that some ill-effects of Canadian federal policies were inadvertent. For example, Maritimers expected to make up for the loss of the American market by access to the British West Indian sugarcane trade. Unfortunately, this trade declined markedly after 1880 as beet-sugar production rose. See Mackintosh, *Economic Background*, 34.
18. Schwartz, "Economic History of PEI," 93–107.
19. A chain is twenty-two yards.
20. O'Shea, *It Happened in Iona*, 105–8.
21. Webster, "Cooperatives and Credit Unions."
22. Webster, "Cooperatives and Credit Unions," 184–87.
23. Ives, *Larry Gorman*, 53.
24. The old school district boundaries were about four to five miles apart. At some point, Islanders began to use the term *district* (that is, school district) in lieu of such terms as *village* or *community*, a practice that continues to this day.

25. Weale, "No Scope," 5.
26. Clark, *Three Centuries*, 138–43.
27. O'Shea, *It Happened in Iona*, 34.
28. There are no records pointing to an Acadian fiddling tradition on PEI that predate British annexation. However, an intriguing diary entry by a Rev. Wm. Drummond dating to 1770 makes note of an Acadian dance party. Unfortunately, Drummond mentions neither whether instruments were played nor what kinds of dancing took place. Quoted in Kennedy, "Is Leis an Tighearna," 155.
29. The history of Scottish fiddling and fiddle music is particularly well documented; see such works as Alburger, *Scottish Fiddlers and Their Music*; Collinson, *Traditional and National Music of Scotland*; Emmerson, *Rantin' Pipe and Tremblin' String* and *Social History of Scottish Dance*; and Johnson, *Scottish Fiddle Music in the Eighteenth Century*. For Irish fiddling history, see Breathnach, *Folk Music and Dances of Ireland*; O hallmhurain, *A Pocket History of Traditional Irish Music*; and Vallely, *The Companion to Irish Traditional Music*.
30. Mac Aoidh, *Between the Jigs*, 24–25.
31. The kind of bagpipes originally brought to the Island was in all likelihood a version of the Scottish war-pipes (see chapter 6). I have found no mention in print, diary, or oral histories of the Irish *uilleann*, or elbow, pipes (also known as the "union pipes") being played on PEI prior to the modern era.
32. MacLeod, "Glenaladale Pioneers," 317.
33. Kennedy, "Is Leis an Tighearna," 316–20 (Kennedy cites a work in Gaelic by Neil Morris Rankin, the title of which translates roughly to "Clan Duiligh: The MacLean Pipers" [*Transactions of the Gaelic Society of Inverness* 37 (1934–36)]). As Scottish noble houses became increasingly British in cultural outlook in the years following the Jacobite rebellion, they gradually divested themselves of their court pipers and other hereditary retainers.
34. MacGregor, *Historical and Descriptive Sketches*, 73.
35. MacGregor, *Historical and Descriptive Sketches*, 2:451, quoted in Hornby, "Fiddle on the Island," 16.
36. The one part of the Island where interest in piping remained highest was in and around Belfast—the very site to which the Rankins had first immigrated. The Island's lone Highland Games, known as the Scotch Gathering, was founded in this area around the middle of the nineteenth century, and since then pipers have provided accompaniment for Highland dancing at this event.

CHAPTER TWO

The Third Most Important Person in the District

Just as they banded together to ensure their survival and educate their young, so too did the inhabitants of each Island district collaborate in organizing their recreation and entertainment. The most popular leisure activity by far in rural Prince Edward Island from the 1880s through the decades immediately following World War II was the fiddle dance. These dances served as a major focus of district social life. They provided an important respite from toil and family responsibilities. They served as a gathering place where locals could bask in the warmth of social relationships. Their energizing, often electric atmosphere was an outlet for pent-up feelings. Most important, these events offered Islanders the opportunity to engage in their two favorite pastimes—listening to fiddle music and dancing square sets.

Fiddle dances in rural Prince Edward Island went year-round. In the colder months, most dancing took place at house parties, which in Acadian communities were known as *soirées musique* or *veillées musiques*.[1] In more clement seasons, fiddle dances were an essential element of larger, often multi-community celebrations such as frolics, weddings and wedding showers, church picnics, and socials. Dances held in the schoolhouses and community halls had no special season and could take place just about anytime.

The fiddlers whose playing made all these dances possible generally resided locally and pursued their livelihoods in much the same manner as everyone else. Whenever there was a dance in the offing, it was considered their duty to make themselves available to play. They generally expected no payment for their time and talents, which at least in principle were contributed as expressions of neighborliness. Fiddler Alvin Bernard of Long River, Queens County, and guitarist Edwin Simmons of Darnley, Queens County, offer this account:

> SIMMONS: Every community had one or two people. If something was going on, they were expected to show up with the violin, and whatever it was.
>
> BERNARD: To make the music.
>
> SIMMONS: There'd generally be a bunch of people; they'd listen to it and dance. And every time there was a wedding, they always had the bridal shower thing. The fiddler was always supposed to show up for that, and there was music there, too. Anything that went on in the community, really; somehow or other music was generally involved before the night was over.
>
> BERNARD: There was generally one fiddler in every district, pretty well. I don't know why, but he'd play all the music.

Because so many local activities would have been impoverished or even impossible without them, fiddlers in "them times" served a crucial role in community life. This role is put into perspective by Archie Stewart of Milltown Cross, Kings County.

> One thing boy, you were always welcome! I heard an old fellow saying one time, the three most important people in the district. The minister was first, the schoolteacher was next, and the fiddler was next. That was the three most important people in the town: the minister or the clergyman, whichever it happened to be, and the schoolteacher, and the fiddler. Couldn't have a wedding without the fiddler!

On a more formal plane, Bishop Faber MacDonald (b. Little Pond, Kings County)[2] puts it this way:

> The violin was integral to the fabric of social life on Prince Edward Island for years and years and years. The people took it here and they developed their gifts here. In small rural communities there were always one, or two, or three, or a number of fiddlers who were raised up, and they were the ones who kept social life going and kept the dances going.

I begin my exploration of the fiddler's role on Prince Edward Island by depicting in detail the most common form of district fiddle dance: the house party.

PHOTO 2.1. *LEFT TO RIGHT:* ARCHIE STEWART, CHESTER MACSWAIN, AND KEN PERLMAN AT MILLTOWN CROSS, AUGUST 1991 (PHOTO BY EARTHWATCH TEAM).

"Probably Once a Week Somebody Would Have a House Party"

House dances, or house parties, were sometimes organized to help celebrate family milestones such as birthdays, anniversaries, homecoming visits, and housewarmings. They could also serve as a means of focusing community labor on a particular task. As Archie Stewart points out, however, just as often no particular excuse was necessary.

> Back then there was no radios, there was no television, and that was the only entertainment we had; in the wintertime probably once a week somebody would have a house party. And everybody would bring a pound of sugar and they'd make fudge and we'd have fudge. Then they'd clear all the stuff out of the kitchen, and I'd get the fiddle out, and away they'd go. And they'd dance till twelve or one o'clock, and that was an evening's entertainment. There was nothing else! And it was good pastime.

Neil MacCannell (b. Lorne Valley, Kings County) offers this description of the house parties held in the communities around his childhood home:

> The house parties were usually during the winter in the slacker times. An announcement would be made that this house party was at such and such a home. And people usually traveled from up to a distance of three or four miles: in horses and sleighs, in snowstorms, usually. The fiddler usually came in a horse and sleigh, too, and his fiddle would be so cold and full of frost, he'd have to warm it up over the old kitchen stove before he could even play it. He'd start playing, and the people would get up and dance: pick their partner. Men would get up and pick their partners. The men would be on the floor first, and when the music started, then the ladies would come up and join their partners. They were all ages, even from teenage up to eighties, some of them.

As Danny MacLean (b. Garfield, Queens County) tells us, someone who was willing to travel to neighboring districts could sometimes take part in several house parties per week.

> There was pretty near always a party somewhere every night in the wintertime. Now take Iona. I used to play for parties up there, here and there and everywhere. They'd have a party just to have a party; there was no special occasion or nothing. They'd get together and they'd have lots of food, and they'd have the liquor. They'd have a house dance in their own house, and then the next time it would be in another house. But the parties were all over the place.

"The Feller with the Fiddle! Nothing Happened Till He Got There"

When a house party was in the offing, invitations were distributed for the most part by word of mouth. On the appointed evening, relations, neighbors, and friends would converge at the hosts' home. Those who lived within a radius of two or three miles generally came on foot, while others from farther away arrived in horse-drawn vehicles.

For those intent on joining the festivities, neither snow nor ice was considered much of an obstacle. Jimmy Halliday of Eldon, Queens County, for example, often walked miles across frozen Orwell Bay to get to a dance, while Johnny Morrissey (b. Newtown Cross, Queens County) offers this recollection:

> I was at dances over at Earnscliffe across the ice with horse and sleigh. If there was good ice and there was a party over there, people would go. Sure, any place there was a dance they'd like to go. If you knew the people pretty well and knew they wouldn't chase you [away], you'd go.

House parties were usually held in the kitchen, since most rural Island kitchens—designed to accommodate the sit-down meals of a dozen or more children plus parents, grandparents, and in-laws—were more than big enough to serve this purpose. If the kitchen was not deemed suitable, some other room in the house with a solid floor became the dancing room. Archie Stewart sums it up as follows:

> Years ago them old houses, the kitchen or the front room [parlor] had a polished hardwood floor. You'd just gather up the chairs and the tables and put them out someplace and away you go: dance all night! Years ago a house was no good if there was no place to dance in it.

According to Emmett Hughes of Dromore, Queens County, in his area it was customary for Islanders to wear their finest clothes to these events: men wore suits if they had them, and women donned their best dresses. Given that at the time it was perfectly acceptable to wear overalls to church, this gives a sense of just how high house parties ranked on the local social scale.[3]

Most house parties got under way about seven or eight o'clock in the evening. Gus Longaphie of Souris, Kings County, tells us that once the kitchen was cleared, the hosts would "put benches round: stack a couple of blocks of wood and lay a plank along it to seat the people when they come in."

If there was no fiddler in residence, the host family would naturally have tried to line one up. According to Jimmy Halliday, for example, many times someone would come to his door and ask, "Can you come tonight and play?" If no local fiddlers were available, however, community members would have to come up with someone else to provide the music. Dennis Pitre of St. Felix, Prince County, for example, recalls having himself gone "with some other guys to get a fiddler. He wouldn't come—Coax and coax and then drive to another place, then keep goin' till you get one." Similarly, Archie Stewart remembers the many times people from a neighboring district sought him out.

> I've had people drive fifteen miles in a horse and sleigh to pick me up, take me to play for a house party. And at three o'clock in the morning they'd drive me back home. They used to go to great lengths to get a fiddler. And if there was no fiddler in their own district, they'd have to go to another district to get a fiddler.

With the kitchen set up, the dancers would wait expectantly for the fiddler's arrival, as Frank O'Connor of Kildare Capes, Prince County, recounts: "If it was in the wintertime, you'd hear a set of sleigh bells jingling. You'd look out through the window and here comes such and such a fellow. Well, he had his fiddle with him and we're in for a night of music!" Looking at it from the fiddler's point of view, Ervan Sonier of Summerside describes the excitement occasioned at a house party when he walked in the door:

> You'd get there, and, my gosh, as soon as you get in the house it's the same as Santa Claus came in with a bunch of toys: the feller with the fiddle! Nothing happened till he got there. And then move the stove, and kick the chairs all to one side or outside or somewheres, and then start the dance. Then of course, make sure you got something for the fiddler: he's got to be fed!

The fiddler would grab a chair, get situated in the corner, and strike up a lively jig, reel, or set tune—his only accompaniment being his own foot keeping strong time on every beat.[4] Generally, people sitting on the benches would have their feet going as well, tapping out the time along with the fiddler. In certain communities, individuals who had "good timing" might add an additional level of rhythm by playing spoons, striking an old pie-plate with a stick or kitchen utensil, or beating on the bass strings of the fiddle with a pair of sticks or knitting needles.[5]

When players of more formal accompaniment instruments were on hand, they would begin to play along as soon as the fiddler touched bow to string. Before the Second World War, the accompaniment instrument of choice at house parties was the pump organ. Later on, use of the pump organ declined as pianos and guitars came into vogue (for more on formal and informal accompaniment instruments, see chapter 10).

It might take a while before the dancing got under way. Neighbors and relatives would chat among themselves or help put the finishing touches on a *lunch* (that is, a snack or late-evening repast). As Jimmy Halliday notes, "You'd probably set around for a while and talk; they'd just socialize for a little while before the dance would start." Similarly, Leonard McDonald from Emyvale, Queens County, adds, "You might have to play probably for a half hour before anybody would get up to dance."

"They Danced to the Old-Time Music"

Eventually, a square set would be organized, and as Archie Stewart puts it, "they danced all night to that music like I played there now; they danced to the old-time music, the older tunes, you know." Each community had its own particular version of a square set that was danced over and over as the night progressed, and dancers were generally able to function without benefit of a caller.[6]

All Island square sets are descended from a nineteenth-century European dance known as the quadrille, and they have retained from their common ancestor the practice of dividing each dance into discrete segments called figures. In most Island communities during this era, the local square set was made up of four figures. Each figure had different steps to it, each was accompanied by a different tune, and there was always a short pause between figures for dancers and musicians to take a breather. At the conclusion of the last figure, there would generally be a still longer pause while dancers regrouped; then the cycle would start over again.

Although no universal standard dictated which kinds of tunes worked best with what figures, most fiddlers had their own notions on the subject. Emmett Hughes, for example, favored using jigs for the first figure and reels for the other three. Jimmy Banks of Poplar Point, Kings County, in contrast, played a hornpipe for the first figure, a jig for the second, a set tune for the third, and a reel for the fourth. Archie Stewart describes his own tune-selection process:

> You played something that suited the time that they were dancing to. There was a certain beat of music for each section of the set.[7] Like when you started, you wanted a fairly slow beat, because it was a slow back and forth. Then, for the second figure you wanted a good lively tune. And then for the third figure you wanted something like a jig, something you could march to. For the last figure, for the grand chain, that was a good fast tune [a reel]. See, a lot of those old fellows, in the grand chain when they got a couple of drinks in them they wanted to step-dance along right in the set, so you'd want to play something good and fast for them.

Until fairly recently, according to Jimmy Banks, fiddlers would never play a medley to accompany set dancing. Instead, they would generally play a single tune throughout a given figure.

> You wouldn't change your tune in the middle of the figure, 'cause if you did, you might be on a different time [tempo] and upset all their time on their dancin'. In my young days, when you'd sit down to play for a bunch of dancers, especially if they were the older fellows that was used to dancin' those breakdowns or reels,[8] you had to play the tune pretty exact. You didn't want to be driftin' off, not playin' every turn as you should, or they'd soon tell you, you weren't playin' right! You had to be careful how you were playin' when you were playin' for some of them fellows, because they knew their music.

By the time the square sets got under way, the house party was pretty much in full swing. As Hélène Arsenault Bergeron (b. St. Chrysostom, Prince County) tells us, these parties were not "sit politely and quiet affairs."

> The better the fiddling is, the livelier the music, the louder the party gets. And the louder the party gets, the livelier the music gets! The kitchen parties that we had at my grandfather's and at our house, everybody was always jumping up to dance because the fiddling, the music, was so lively. I think that style of fiddling was developed to make people dance. So it's not something you just want to sit and listen to, it's something you want to jump up and dance to.

Here is how Robert Arsenault (b. Abram-Village, Prince County) describes the house-party atmosphere:

> It's a very high-energy kind of feeling. It lifts the spirits and it makes you want to tap your feet and get up and dance, because it's a very lighthearted feeling. And once the party gets going it's a very electrifying kind of thing. It's a very high, charismatic kind of feeling. It's a very positive feeling, I think, as well. Many people have called it a devilish feeling: my memories of people who say, "Oh, you got the devil in you," and this kind of thing.

Sometimes these high spirits just came from exhilaration, exertion, and appreciation of the music; sometimes they were helped along by consumption of alcohol. Archie Stewart tells this story, for example, of a dancer who would not be deterred from self-expression by an overcrowded room:

> The old man of the house, he got a few good shots of 'shine into him.[9] They had a range in the kitchen, and I was sittin' back there playin'. This range was settin' over there, and the house was so full you couldn't move in it; they couldn't get room to dance. But the old feller he got feeling pretty good, and he wanted to step-dance. He opened down the oven door, and he step-danced there all night. It must've been a tough oven door; he wasn't a very big man, he only weighed about a hundred 'n' twenty-five pounds soakin' wet, but he step-danced all night on the oven door! There was no room anyplace else.

Along these lines, Joseph Doucette of Deblois Road, Prince County, tells of some dancers who were so carried away by drink and high energy that they failed to notice that as a prank he had turned his bow upside down and that for a while no sound was actually coming out of his instrument: "I seen one night a couple of fellers on the floor, and I was playing the violin, driving her for all it was worth. After a while I turned the back of the bow like this [*he demonstrates*], and they were still dancing! They never stopped."

Spirits tended to get most out of control when a house party took place in one of those rare districts that had no local fiddlers. Dennis Pitre notes, "If you were at a house where there was a house party only once a year and you went there to play music, it might get a little rough before the night was over!" He also tells this story about one fiddler-deprived district:

Andrew Jones was telling me one time he was invited to a house party. They hadn't heard music for a long while, and they were all excited to dance the square dance. He said, "I used to take quite a while to tune the fiddle, and they danced the first figure of the dance when I was still tuning the fiddle!" Just when he was tuning, they were dancing. I guess they must have been pretty excited.

Since the typical Island kitchen was only large enough to accommodate a single set of dancers (that is, four couples lined up at right angles in square-dance formation), house-partygoers would have to take turns dancing, as Cosmas Sigsworth (b. Corraville, Kings County) reports. "When one set would be finishing, there'd be another bunch standing up waiting to get in. And if you didn't get in quick, you were out of it! The fiddler didn't have to sit down and play all night waiting for somebody to get up and dance." To allow still more people the opportunity to get on the floor, some families would clear a second room and make it available. As Bill MacDonald (b. North Lake, Kings County) tells us, "They danced two squares at a time: two different rooms, and the piano and the violin would be in the center."

When there was more than one fiddler present at a house party, they would usually share the task of providing music. If the house was big enough, each fiddler would play all night in a separate room. Largus MacInnis of Lakeville, Kings County, for example, recalls some parties at which "there'd be dancin' in two or three rooms. They'd have a fiddler in the kitchen and one in the dining room." More often, fiddlers would just take turns playing for the dancing. As Cosmas Sigsworth puts it, "You take your turn, play for a set or two, and someone else plays for another set. This is the way it used to go."

Rarely would two or more fiddlers play together at a dance. Because each fiddler had his own *twist* (distinct personal version) for every tune in the repertoire, there was concern that joining forces would only result in a jumbled rendition. In general, only close relatives or friends who had previously ironed out their musical differences regarded playing together as a viable option (for more on tune twists, see chapter 6).

"Would You Play Me a Tune? I Want to Step-Dance"

Over the course of an evening, there might be a few occasions when there was a break in the continual stream of square sets. At these junctures, some other activity—usually a display of individual prowess such as step dancing, singing, or storytelling—might temporarily take center stage.

PHOTO 2.2. STEP DANCERS AT ATLANTIC JAMBOREE, ABRAM-VILLAGE, AUGUST 1992. FIDDLER IS PETER ARSENAULT (PHOTO BY EARTHWATCH TEAM).

In the case of step dancing, this change of pace provided no respite for the fiddler. As noted by Ervan Sonier, "While you were having your rest, that's what you done; you played for a step dance. Once the set was over, somebody would come up and say, 'Would you play me a tune? I want to step-dance!'" Leonard McDonald explains:

> It depended on how big a crowd there was. Maybe there'd be people waiting, and you'd play square dances almost all night. But if there was a lull, if there wasn't too big a crowd and everybody could get on the floor that wanted to, maybe they'd have a break and maybe two or three fellows would step-dance. Somebody would go up to me and say, "Play for such and such a fellow to step-dance." There were some good step dancers then. Both men and women step-danced: excellent dancers and they'd keep perfect time!

Generally each step dancer had a favorite tune whose rhythms best suited the kind of steps he or she liked to do. Through long association, the district fiddler often knew each dancer's favorite tune and would strike it up as soon as the latter came forward. Otherwise, as Archie Stewart notes, the dancer would "ask for his tune when he'd get up to dance." He further cautions that "you didn't change tunes [in the middle] because you might put him off his step."

At some house parties, a number of step dancers would get up to dance at the same time. Peter Doiron (b. North Rustico, Queens County) recalls, "We had a lot of step dancers come to our house parties. I remember the floors in the old house would be just sagging as they were dancing; you could just see them bouncing!" Similarly, Jimmy Banks offers this recollection:

> Sometimes they'd get competin' with one another. One feller would get up and start step-dancin' pretty good, then another feller would decide he was gonna see if he couldn't do a little better than that and he'd get up. There'd be four or five of 'em at it by and by at one time. [*Question*: How did you decide who the best one was?] It wouldn't do to make a decision which was the best, you might start some trouble!

Most districts also boasted at least a couple of residents known for their singing or songwriting abilities, and they would sometimes be called upon between square sets to entertain the company with a couple of selections. Most singing was performed unaccompanied during this era, although Clifford Wedge of Miminegash, Prince County, tells us that by the 1940s he and many other rural Island singers had begun to accompany themselves on keyboard instruments or guitar. Wedge notes that at house parties he generally played backup guitar for fiddlers during the dancing, but once or twice over the course of an evening he was asked to sing to his own accompaniment.

Whether the inhabitants of a district were English or French speaking, the most frequently performed songs were either disaster ballads or locally composed community satires. Some disaster ballads commonly performed at house parties were "Peter Emberly" (fatal lumbering accident), "The *Gracie M. Parker*" (shipwreck), "The Norway Bum" (man driven to drink when a fire destroys his family and home), "Frozen Charlotte" (death from exposure), and "Le Meurtrier de sa Femme" (in English, "The Wife-Murderer").[10]

Alternatively, dancers taking a breather might be regaled with stories and anecdotes from local raconteurs. Among Islanders of Highland Scots extraction, for example, a common theme for stories was the interaction of ancestors or contemporaries with such supernatural beings as the devil, fairies, witches, ghosts, *sluagh* or *swoog* (a shadowy force that carries off the unwary), and *forerunners* (mysterious noises or bright lights that foretell illnesses, deaths, or other disasters in the community).[11]

"Sometimes It Would Be Getting Quite Bright When We Were Getting Home"

As the house party was winding down, a snack or meal known as lunch was generally served, prepared by the women of the district and served by the hostess. This meal generally consisted of baked goods, sandwiches, and tea, but it could involve—as Wilfred Gotell of Georgetown, Kings County, puts it—"a full-course meal with a couple of chickens cooked." Bill MacDonald remembers it this way: "I've seen my mother make lunch for fifty. Because in those days we lived handy the road, you see. And everyone went by and heard the music, they'd come in. No one was ever turned away."

House parties were generally over by about one or two o'clock in the morning, but as Cosmas Sigsworth tells us, sometimes they persisted far into the night: "Those things went on. Sometimes it would be getting quite bright when we were getting home." Leonard McDonald remembers one house party at his place, for example, that was still going strong well into the next day.

> I had a party in the barn here one time. At 4:30 a.m. I was in the house here having a rock in the rocking chair and I said, "I think I'll go out to the barn and play for a square dance." I went outside, and the floor was filled front to back: old folk and young. After that we went to bed, but they were still going at eight o'clock the next morning. That wasn't typical, but I mean that could happen.

Even when the dance was over, it took a while for the exhilaration to subside. Residents dallied as they sorted look-alike galoshes in the mudroom,[12] and they lingered in last-minute conversation: an activity referred to by some as the "standing ceilidh." If the weather was mild, fiddlers and accompanists might find a congenial spot on the way home and play still a few more tunes before going their separate ways, as guitarist Lemmy Chaisson of Rollo Bay, Kings County, reports.

> We'd come home after a dance, and we'd sit out in front of my house down below the hill here by the mailbox until the sun come up in the morning. He'd keep on playing tunes to get me to follow him, and that's how I learned to play behind them. So it was mostly Peter Senior that kept me at it,[13] and we used to go at it every other night of the week.

Although the house party was only one of several district dance events, it can be regarded as the prototype. The other events share many significant details with the house party—how the word went out, methods of travel to and fro, the way in which fiddlers were obtained, how the festivities got under way, the role of fiddlers and accompanists, the kind of dancing performed, the ensuing atmosphere of exhilaration, the kinds of performances that were sometimes held between square sets, the serving of lunch, and the standing ceilidh. The major differences between house parties and these other events involve such issues as function, size and duration, venue, the number of communities involved, and the nature of associated activities.

"They'd Go and Cut His Wood, and That Night They'd Have a Dance"

When house parties were held during the growing season, they were often associated with a frolic, or bee.[14] The idea here is quite simple: a family needing to plow the fields, dig potatoes, or carry out some other labor-intensive activity would invite all able-bodied members of the community in to help. After the work was done, the host family offered up a substantial meal, followed by a night of dancing. Joseph Doucette of Deblois Road, Prince County, explains the process as follows:

> Supposin' that you had a piece of wood to cut, and you were alone. Well, they'd make what they called a bee; others call it a frolic. He'd ask a bunch of men, or they'd offer themselves. They'd go and cut his wood, and that night they'd have a dance at the house. Sometimes it was the women, spinning: a spinning party. And then they'd dance.

As noted in the previous chapter, traveler John MacGregor found frolics well established on the Island as early as the 1820s, and mention of such events appears frequently in published diaries and other firsthand accounts that deal with nineteenth-century Island life. Among the activities mentioned as occasions for frolics are barn raising, land clearing, stump pulling, plowing, harvesting, wool milling or waulking,[15] spinning, and weaving.[16]

According to Archie Stewart, many kinds of frolics were still fairly common when he was a youngster during the 1920s and '30s.

> They'd have a hookin' frolic or a barn raisin' bee. Used to have plowing frolics, too, stumpin' frolics: dig out the stumps, clearin' land. And if somebody's barn burnt, everybody'd come in and they'd call it a barn raisin' bee. Somebody'd make up a jug of beer, the women would bake up a whole lot of stuff, and they'd have a great time: put the barn up in a day. And mostly they'd have a little shakedown in the evening, any excuse to have a dance back then. I remember one year, there was a man on the road, he was sick and couldn't put his crop in. One day, every farmer on

the road went and they worked up his land and sowed all his grain and put in his potatoes, and the whole damn thing all in one day. And then they had a dance.[17]

Although the practice of holding frolics on Prince Edward Island was in decline prior to the Second World War and had pretty much come to a close by the 1950s, the younger generation continued to hear tales of frolics past from older relatives. Margaret Ross MacKinnon (b. Flat River, Queens County), for example, often heard about the rug-hooking frolics once held at her grandmother's home.[18] Similarly, George MacPhee of Monticello, Kings County, learned about plowing frolics from his father, Mel MacPhee.[19]

> There'd be probably half a dozen teams of horses come and plow. There'd be a big keg of beer set, and at night there'd be a big party. The women would all gather in and they'd cook; and they'd make a great big supper for them. All the fiddlers would take their turns. There was a plowin' frolic down in Hollow River that lasted for two days! The first day they done the plowin'. The second day they done the drinkin'!

Archie Stewart points out that as the frolic was declining, it was replaced to a certain extent in Island life by the practice of holding benefit concerts. "When somebody has trouble or somebody's got cancer or somebody loses something, they all get together and go to a benefit concert and everybody chucks in ten or twenty dollars and they have a program."[20] These events, which were still going strong into the 1990s and beyond, are essentially community talent shows featuring singing, recitations, fiddling, and step-dancing demonstrations.

Weddings, Showers, and Shivarees

The old-time Island wedding was essentially a house party writ large: there was more food, more drink, more dancing, and a lot more people. Generally, fiddlers from several neighboring districts would be on hand, and they would be expected to take turns playing. As "Young Peter" Chaisson of Bear River notes, "Them times before somebody got the date of the weddin', they always made sure that there was a fiddler available."

Wedding celebrations generally took place in late spring or summer. They were held at the bride's home and were attended not only by the people of the district but also by friends and acquaintances from miles around. The dancing was often held outdoors on a specially constructed platform called a dancing saloon. The floor of the saloon would be made of good stout boards,

PHOTO 2.3. *LEFT TO RIGHT*: STANLEY BRUCE, MARGARET ROSS MACKINNON, AND ATTWOOD O'CONNOR AT MILLTOWN CROSS, AUGUST 1996 (PHOTO BY KEN PERLMAN).

and a framework would be constructed overhead that could be covered with evergreen boughs or tarpaulins to keep off the sun.

As Attwood O'Connor describes, guests at these festivities could look forward to generous meals, plentiful drink, and an opportunity to engage in virtually continuous square dancing until at least the wee hours of the morning.

> After they'd get married they'd be comin' home and they'd have their big supper; it would be a table spread there for everybody. And my God you'd be eatin' half the night. The table was set all the time: you got hungry, go eat! You'd dance there all night, too: all square dancing. And a big pot full of moonshine and a dipper in it to drink it out of. Everybody'd be into that!

The old-time weddings were notoriously long-lasting. As Emmett Hughes puts it, "A wedding was anywheres from the afternoon to daylight in the morning. They went clean through the night and sometimes the second day along with it." Similarly, Attwood O'Connor tells this story:

> I started one time playing for a wedding on St. Marys Road. I started three o'clock in the afternoon playin' and I never stopped till six o'clock the next morning. That was a long old time! I was never so glad when it ended; I was pretty near going

to break the fiddle! That's the way it was over there; you just had to be playing as long as they were dancin'.

In many districts with a strong Scottish heritage, the bride, groom, and other members of the wedding party opened the wedding celebration by performing a *wedding reel*, a dance whose elaborate footwork required that all participants be adept step dancers. According to George MacPhee, this dance was always performed to a certain group of tunes, which included "Christy Campbell," "Christy Miller," and another tune known only as "The Prince Edward Island Wedding Reel" (see appendix A, example 2.1). He adds that the wedding reel was always followed by another similar dance called "The Friends' Reel" or "The Reel of Honor" (see appendix A, example 2.2).

> They used to go in to dance the wedding reel; that would be pretty near the opening of the wedding, getting it going. The wedding party get up and done their dance: the bridesmaid and the best man and the bride and groom. They always had somebody that could step-dance good, [who] they took in the dance with them. They'd [all] go around and then they'd stop in front of each other, and they'd step-dance.

The custom of dancing a wedding reel immediately following the wedding supper was brought to the Island by Highland immigrants, and it is in fact still danced in the Hebrides.[21] The Hebrides version of the dance—and almost certainly the version first brought to Prince Edward Island—would be a variant of the foursome, or Scotch reel. Essentially, the dance begins with two couples standing at opposite ends of the floor: bride with best man, and bridesmaid with groom. Over the course of the dance, and after much complicated stepping and maneuvering, bride is united with groom, and bridesmaid joins best man.[22]

Various fiddlers recall seeing a much-reduced version of the wedding reel danced sporadically into the 1940s and '50s, but by the 1960s it was almost certainly gone from the Island scene. Interestingly, as the art of step dancing began to decline, the custom of dancing the wedding reel was prolonged by appointing stand-ins, as Jimmy Banks describes: "Them wedding reels, you generally had to get a good step dancer. If the bride and groom wasn't good to dance, they generally stood on the end and got some of the older, good dancers for to dance in their place."

Right after the conclusion of the Second World War, the sheer number of young men returning home all at once led to a sudden spike in the number of weddings. Since it was still customary to celebrate the occasion with nonstop square sets, fiddlers' services were at a premium. Ervin Rafferty (b. Rafferty

Road, Prince County), for example, had his own wedding around this time and reports that he had to line up fiddler Elmer Robinson, then of Mount Pleasant, quite far ahead. Not only this, but on his wedding day Rafferty had to drive his horse and sleigh five miles each way in the dead of winter to carry Robinson to and from the event.[23]

Fiddlers were also asked to play for two events closely related to old-time weddings: the country shower and the shivaree. Most rural districts would hold a *country shower*, or prewedding celebration, for both bride and groom together. Leonard McDonald recalls, for example, that around his home district of Emyvale, Queens County, "they'd have the shower at home, like. All the neighbors turned out to the shower and the house would be packed. Then you'd dance all afternoon and into the evening." Alternatively, Elliott Wight (b. Flat River, Queens County) describes a somewhat different version of the event.

> They'd do it for anybody in the community that's getting married; they used to have a shower and everybody would come and bring a small gift. They'd give them the gifts, and while they were getting the lunch, we'd be playing for a couple of square dances. And that's called a country shower.

The *shivaree* is an old Scottish custom associated with the aftermath of wedding festivities. Essentially, shivarees are a bit like Halloween trick-or-treat. When the bride and groom first come to occupy their home, community members gather outside and make a racket by yelling and beating on an assortment of metal and wooden objects. They then refuse to go away without a snack or other small gift. As Merlin Quinn of Cardross, Kings County, recalls, however, shivarees on Prince Edward Island often served as just another excuse for initiating a house party.[24]

> When Edna and I came home from our honeymoon, we had this house ready to move into. And when we got there, the crowd—first they went around and just made a lot of noise, so we invited them in. They came in and they brought fiddle, guitar, and all that. They played and danced, and we had some lunch and tea. And that was the way that shivaree went over, anyway.

Benefits and Benefit Dances

Prior to the modern era, rural communities on Prince Edward Island were responsible for supporting three local institutions—church, school, and community hall. Each local parish or congregation had a church, a clergyman, and perhaps a church hall to maintain. Many districts had a community hall built and maintained by community labor on donated land. And as Teresa MacPhee Wilson (b. Monticello, Kings County) explains, every district also needed to help support the operations of its local one-room schoolhouse.

> Everything was done by the people in the district. The teacher didn't draw full pay from the government. So the people had to pay into the supplement, and extra money had to be given by the district. If not, the teacher didn't get her full pay. That's how it was done in those days.

In lieu of collecting taxes or tithes, most churches or districts would appoint committees to organize one or more benefit events. According to Merlin Quinn, for example, in central Kings County each community appointed three trustees and a secretary—each with two- or three-year terms—whose responsibility was to raise funds for the local one-room schoolhouse.[25] They would meet periodically to plan events and would then spread the word concerning their decisions to the neighbors.

Another major force in community organizing was the Women's Institute.[26] Ella Chappell of Cornwall, and later of York, Queens County, tells us that members of the Women's Institute would meet monthly not only to plan events but also to gossip and discuss common reading projects. Meanwhile, their husbands would be gathered together in the kitchen drinking tea and swapping anecdotes and yarns.[27]

As a result of all these activities, there would be church or school picnics in summer, indoor socials in winter, and schoolhouse or hall dances year-round. At nearly all such events, the opportunity to dance square sets was offered as a major incentive for attending. Whenever there was a dance, local fiddlers were expected to be on hand and to donate their services free of charge.

A variety of strategies were employed to raise funds at Island benefits, such as collecting a general admissions fee, selling or auctioning off donated foodstuffs, and assessing the gent a few cents every time a couple got on the dance floor. Such revenues could be further augmented by charging locals for participating in lawn bowling, card playing or dice playing, or various carnival games.

Probably the largest Island fund-raisers were the annual church picnics. The following description is from Joe MacDonald:

> There is a Catholic community here at St. Andrews and then there is the Protestant community at Mt. Stewart, and there'd be the Protestant picnic, the Catholic picnic, and everybody intermingled. And they served meals: good meals, too!

They'd have a big dancing saloon, and the music was all voluntary; fiddlers just went and played and took turns. The dancing was free, too; admission was only for the meal. But there was bowling alleys, they'd charge for that. It'd be only a dime or something. Then there was other things to do. People would come there with a hammer and drive the [weight] up to ring the bell, they had wheels of fortune and shooting galleries, and there was admission to all that.

Church picnics, once known as *tea parties*, had their heyday on the Island during the second half of the nineteenth century. One tea party held in the summer of 1865 on a site overlooking St. Peters Bay in northern Kings County was attended, according to a journalist's estimate, by about three thousand people.

> Every part of King's County was fully represented, to say nothing of a very considerable number from Queen's County. The party was given for the purpose of realizing funds to be applied towards the building of a new [Protestant] Chapel. . . . The tables were abundantly supplied with every delicacy which is usually furnished on such occasions and there was certainly no lack of fair hands to dispense the good things to those who wished to partake of them. . . . [All the] while bagpipes and violins were to be heard in several directions, where the merry dancers regardless of the hot weather kept time to the music for the live-long day with untiring feet.[28]

Such major undertakings had long been in decline by the 1930s, when one Islander's lament for the tea parties of yore vividly evokes their atmosphere.

> I may say that tea parties seem to be much tamer than those of the past, especially the ones held in Souris when I was a boy. We missed the old time fiddlers, the bag piper going around the grounds playing his lively air and followed by a group of youngsters—the many flags floating in the breeze—the different booths scattered here and there covered with branches of maples and studded around with young spruce—the different saloons where noisy clerks shouted their wares of candy, pop corn, chewing gum, ice cream, spruce beer and what not. [We missed t]he merry dancers, and the sound of "Swing your partners!" as they went through their quadrilles and reels.[29]

As an aside, one parish picnic made notorious through a song penned by a local satirist took place circa 1897 in the old district of Groshaut, near present-day St. Charles in northeastern Kings County. Apparently, decorum disintegrated and several fights broke out among parishioners because hard cider had been delivered instead of the sweet cider that was originally ordered. On the event's second day, the local priest, Fr. Walker, restored order by diluting the open cider kegs with water and returning the unopened ones.[30]

Many districts also held picnics, usually known as *socials*, to benefit the local schools. Fund-raising at these events leaned heavily on two methods—selling homemade sweets and assessing couples on the dance floor. Archie Stewart describes, for example, the socials of southern Kings County.

> Every district would have an ice cream social: make the ice cream themselves. Everybody would give so much cream. They'd all gather at the schoolhouse in the afternoon. The women would bake cakes. And they'd make up this big batch of homemade ice cream and then that night they'd sell it. I think you got a saucer of ice cream and a piece of cake for ten cents. Ours used to be at the school down here. But they'd have an ice cream social all over the country; each would have them at different times. And when the strawberries would get ripe, they'd have a strawberry festival: ice cream and strawberries. They'd have a dancing saloon built outside, and they'd have a dancin' floor built: so much a set to dance. We used to build a little place off the saloon, just big enough for the guitar player and a fiddler to sit in. You'd set in there and play all night, and battle the mosquitos!

Indoor socials to benefit church or school were held in the cooler seasons. A general admissions charge would be collected, supplemented by an auction of pies or boxed dinners. Wilfred Gotell notes, for example, that at the box socials held to benefit the local church in Georgetown, Kings County, "Every family would bake a box; you could either buy your own box and sit down and eat it, or give it in and buy someone else's. You'd eat, and then there'd be a dance after." Frank O'Connor of Kildare Capes describes the pie socials of western Prince County.

> The women in the district, each one would bake a cake or a pie or whatever: then they'd take it and after the dance was over they'd auction it off. And of course if there were some girls and they had boyfriends, it would be a terrible thing if a girl had a pie up for sale and her boyfriend didn't buy it! He either bought the thing, or else he was in the doghouse. Those were some of the things that happened. [*Question:* Did people bid up the prices?] Oh, absolutely!—Especially somebody that had a little bit of spite in for the other fellow.

Fund-raising in the form of small benefit dances went on in most districts throughout the year. These more modest affairs were held in the schoolhouses, in church halls or community halls, or even in local homes. Proceeds from schoolhouse dances were generally earmarked exclusively for the school budget, whereas moneys gathered at hall dances or house dances could be directed toward any common purpose.

When completely emptied out of furniture, most schoolhouses and community halls were capable of accommodating at least several sets of dancers.[31] According to Leonard McDonald, "Instead of charging admission at the door, they would charge you about five cents to dance. They'd go around with a hat; when they'd get you lined up for the square dance, somebody would go around and collect." Emmett Hughes describes the schoolhouse dances in the Fort Augustus, Queens County, area:

> A big crowd then would be about a hundred. The school was small; it wouldn't hold any more. In the summertime, there was so many you couldn't get in to dance the set; you couldn't get in the place. But I played for them as many as six nights a week at one time, and farmed along with it. You get home at two o'clock and you gotta get up again at six. You didn't have much sleep!

The smallest benefits of all were those held in local homes, at events referred to in some districts as "parlor socials." Teresa Wilson recalls, for example, that her parents and other Monticello families would take turns hosting church benefits in their homes.

> They played old-time music in a couple of rooms in the house, and perhaps in another room if the house was big enough you'd play cards. In our house they danced in the kitchen and down in the front room and played cards in the back room. They played dice, too. They played dice for probably some prize, and probably ten cents a throw. Then they'd clean off the table and served the lunch, and then they went back at the dancing again.

Not all benefits were held to support church, school, or community hall. In the town of St. Peters around 1910, for example, a group of youngsters financed the construction of the Island's first skating rink by organizing a tea party.[32] And during the Second World War, according to Stewart MacIntyre (b. Fairfield, Kings County), dances organized under the auspices of the Carry On Canada campaign were held at the Elmira Hall in northeastern Kings County to support the war effort.

"In the Christmas Concert, the Children Would Always Dance a Square Dance"

When important religious holidays came along, means were generally found to integrate fiddling and fiddle dances into the general festivities. Following the calendar around, here are some examples covering the holidays Twelfth Night (Epiphany), Les Jours Gras (Shrovetide), St. Patrick's Day, and Christmas.

In Acadian communities, January 6, or Twelfth Night, was celebrated with a custom known as "Le Gâteau des Rois" (Kings' Cake). The community would gather to consume a special cake, into which certain tokens had been baked. The first man and woman to discover these tokens in their portions would be declared King and Queen; they then "would call upon individuals to sing a song, tell a joke, play a musical instrument or to perform a step dance. And the people called upon had to obey."[33] Because the holiday was observed in the Catholic Church as a Sunday, square dancing and other forms of social dancing were not permitted. "Step dancing was acceptable, however, and plenty of it was done to the lively reels played by the local fiddler, whose presence was indeed imperative."[34]

Another Acadian custom was the celebrations preceding Lent known as Les Jours Gras, culminating on the well-known February Tuesday known as Mardi Gras. Since no square dancing was allowed during Lent, the general idea was to get in as much as possible in the weeks leading up to it. People in the district took turns hosting house parties during this period, and there would be a dance almost every night. Celebrations grew most intense on the two days before Lent, which begins on Ash Wednesday. A house party would commence on a Monday after supper, and one square dance followed another until dawn. Everyone would go home for a few hours of sleep, then gather again for a final round of dancing beginning early Tuesday afternoon, since all dancing had to cease precisely at midnight.[35]

In mid-March, many Island districts celebrated St. Patrick's Day by staging a St. Patrick's Play at the local community or parish hall. Generally, as Rita Morrison (b. St. Andrews, Kings County) notes, "there'd be three acts to it and the local people would perform." According to Stephen Toole of Green Road, Queens County, "They'd have an intermission in between each act, and they'd probably have step dancin' and fiddlin' [then] for entertainment."

Many communities also held an annual Christmas concert, an event that—because of the solemnity of the occasion—was supposed to focus mainly on singing and poetry recitations. Nevertheless, fiddling and dancing often managed to work their way in. Teresa Wilson, for example, tells the following story concerning one such event:

> In the Christmas concert the children would always dance a square dance. And my father or Neil McCormick or somebody would be Santa Claus. Neil McCormick would probably play the fiddle; and of course Santa played a tune, too, before he'd leave, a dead giveaway who Santa Claus was. My father was Santa Claus one time, the first time I ever remember seeing Santa Claus. I had no idea who this chap was that come in. There was no radios then, you know, or anything; and I was

too little to realize that there was such a thing as Santa Claus. They took me up to the concert at the school and this big man came in, in sort of a mask on for Santa Claus, and a white fur on his hat and all this. My father had his own fur coat on, but it never dawned on me who it was. He came in and picked up the fiddle, and he started to play. Then they lit the candles and got up to dance. But he backed up and brushed against the tree with all those candles lit, and the fire went up the back of his coat: burnt the fur off the back of his coat, just a strip. Anyway, he got away from the tree, and they got the candles out. So on the next day my older brother Gerard said to me, he said, "I think that was Dad," he said, "that was Santa Claus last night. You come and see!" He took out the fur coat and showed me where the burn was on the coat. I put two and two together after that.

Origins and Parallels

House parties, frolics, and other related events almost certainly have roots in Old World musical customs. The Island house party probably blends together elements from two commonplace features of eighteenth- and early nineteenth-century Scottish and Irish rural life: the indoor social dance and the ceilidh. Beginning in the eighteenth century and extending into the time of living memory, fiddle dances were held in farmhouse kitchens of the Scottish Lowlands and around the firesides of Highland crofts, or tenant farms. Similarly, in Ireland around the time of emigration to Prince Edward Island, many rural folk lived in communal settlements called *clacháns*, where after a day's work neighbors and kin would often congregate in village kitchens for an evening of music and dancing.[36]

Other aspects of the house party—particularly its centrality in community social life and its role as a venue for solo performances by talented locals—hark back to the ceilidh, a custom that was widely practiced throughout much of the eighteenth and nineteenth centuries in the Scottish Highlands and in rural parts of Ireland. Following the workday, neighbors would gather together at a designated home in the community. Participants would be called upon in turn by the man of the house to entertain the gathering, each according to his or her own special gift. Many descriptions of ceilidhs focus specifically on oral pursuits such as singing, storytelling, and informal debates, but others also mention solo performances on instruments such as fiddle, bagpipes, and *trump* (jaw harp), along with episodes of solo dancing.[37]

As for the ultimate origin of the frolic, suffice it to say that dancing following harvesting or other work activities in the Scottish and Irish countryside was widely reported. Crofters in the Scottish Highlands, for example, held dances following the completion of various stages in the production of wool cloth.[38] Similarly, on Donegal clacháns, a family with work to be done would hire a fiddler; the neighbors then gathered together to complete the task, and all concerned would meet afterward for a night of dancing.[39]

Beginning in the eighteenth century and continuing in some cases into the 1950s, reports from social observers of very close analogues to both house parties and frolics have emanated from myriad North American communities. In terms of house dances, such descriptions point to the following common features: spreading invitations by word of mouth, clearing the kitchen or parlor via carrying out the furniture; music supplied by a local fiddler playing unaccompanied or with rudimentary accompaniment; social dancing in the form of square sets, reels, or contra dances;[40] episodes of solo dancing, singing, and storytelling; the serving of a repast; and so on. Similarly, accounts of frolic-like events throughout North America—so widespread that many folklorists refer to them merely as "work parties"—point to a task tackled by community members, who are then rewarded for their participation with a meal followed by a house or barn dance.

In New England and New York State, house dances were once accorded such colorful names as *junkets*, *heel burners*, *kitchen hops*, or *kitchen whangs*, and work parties were held in the form of corn huskings, barn raisings, "sugaring-offs" (maple sugar making), sheep shearings, quilting bees, hay gatherings, or harvestings.[41] In Newfoundland, house parties were known as *house* or *kitchen times*, although on that island throughout much of the twentieth century, accordionists were more likely than fiddlers to be supplying the music.[42] On Cape Breton Island, house dances served as the most common fiddling venue through the nineteenth and early twentieth centuries, when "any gathering, particularly a milling frolic or wedding, was considered to be a reasonable excuse for a dance."[43] In New Brunswick, well-known fiddler Don Messer started his career around the time of the First World War by playing at the house dances that followed barn raisings near his home at Tweedside.[44] Finally, from all over the American South and Southwest we are told of husking and quilting bees, log rollings, rail splittings, house and barn raisings, corn shuckings and grindings, peanut shellings, cotton pickings, and harvestings, all of which "frequently wound up with dances, euphoniously called 'frolics'. . . [with] music furnished by backwoods fiddlers."[45] In Kentucky, such events were called *workin's*, where "they'd invite people come and help them do their work . . . and then they'd have a dance that night."[46]

It is reasonable to surmise from the foregoing that both the house dance and the frolic crystallized in North America at a fairly early stage of settlement, then diffused among far-flung communities along with trade and other forms of contact. Certainly, some American observers have maintained the view that such institutions were a necessary aspect of the pioneer and premechanized rural experience and that the fiddlers who made them possible served as an important component in the development of Western civilization in North America.

> [I]n decades past the fiddler and his fiddle were the center of community activities. Nearly every community had at least one fiddler or more. . . . Barn raisings, husking bees, weddings, entertainments, shivarees, wakes and almost every other social function required the presence of the fiddler and his beloved instrument.[47]

Moreover, the ubiquity of such parallels strongly suggests a general connection, perhaps even a kinship, among rural communities throughout North America prior to the jazz age.

The Island Fiddler

The various dances and other events described in this chapter give a rough outline of the Island fiddler's role. He played at house parties, frolics, weddings and wedding showers, church and school picnics, box and pie socials, schoolhouse dances and hall dances, workplace dances, and holiday celebrations. His music not only enriched community social life but also served as a lens to help focus community energies and resources on essential activities, projects, and institutions.

Although these events are no longer part of the Island scene, some of their features survived into the 1990s and beyond. House parties, for example, lived on to a certain extent in the guise of weekly old-time dances. On these occasions, local fiddlers provided the music, local people danced square sets throughout the evening, step dancers and singers sometimes performed in the breaks between square sets, and some of the old air of excitement was rekindled. In addition, a lunch—usually cakes and sandwiches cut into small squares washed down by strong Island tea—was customarily served near the end of the proceedings.

The array of benefit events just discussed gradually faded away in the 1950s and '60s as the provincial and federal governments increasingly took over responsibility for providing education and other social services. Nevertheless, Island communities looking to raise funds for special projects have spawned a new generation of annual and occasional fund-raisers—such as church suppers, town days, and benefit concerts—all of which seek to draw an audience with shows featuring performances by local fiddlers, step dancers, and other local talent.

NOTES

1. *Soirées* and *veillées* are synonyms meaning "evenings." Old songs, diary entries, and newspaper accounts make clear that Island Anglophones once used the term *spree* for this kind of event, but I did not encounter that usage during the course of this project. The Acadian term *parties de cuisine* (kitchen parties) came into vogue during the 1990s, largely through stage presentations conducted by the then-popular band Barachois (for more on Barachois, see chapter 16).
2. As a young clergyman, MacDonald played a major role in the Island's fiddling revival (see chapter 16); he was appointed bishop of Grand Falls, Newfoundland, in 1980.
3. Emmett Hughes, personal interview, Nov. 25, 2006, Prince Edward Island Fiddling Project (hereafter cited as PEIFP), Interview #57.
4. In the interest of smooth prose, the pronouns *he* and *his* will often be used in lieu of *he and she* and *his and her*, respectively, especially when the narrative is for the most part referring to men. For a detailed discussion of Island fiddle tune genres, see chapter 14.
5. In other parts of North America, this last activity was referred to as "beating straws" or using "fiddle sticks."
6. Prior to World War I, many Island communities also danced four-hand or eight-hand reels; for a detailed discussion of Island dancing, see chapter 12.
7. The term *set* is used on the Island not only to refer to the kind of dancing ("square set") but also to denote a full dance cycle; "section of the set," then, is another way of saying "figure." In addition, the term *set* can also be used to indicate a dance formation (as in "set of dancers"). The operative meaning of the term should in general be clear from the context.
8. *Breakdown* was another name for the eight-hand reel; see chapter 12.
9. '*Shine* is the popular term for moonshine, the name common throughout much of North America for privately (and often illegally) distilled spirits.
10. A detailed account of the Island vocal-music tradition is beyond the scope of this book. For the work of two well-known Island anglophone songsmiths, see Ives, *Larry Gorman* and *Lawrence Doyle*. For Acadian disaster ballads (known in French as *complaintes* [laments]), see Arsenault, *Complaintes acadiennes*. Disaster ballads generally focused on the accidental or violent deaths of people in their prime of life. The lyrics were composed by local or regional songsmiths, who often borrowed pre-existing Scottish or Irish ballad melodies.
11. See, for example, Shaw, *Gaelic in* PEI, 7–10. For some Acadian tales and anecdotes, see Arsenault, *Contes, légends et chansons*. As an aside, in July 1992 George MacPhee's sister Gloria told me of one mysterious bright light, reported long before the days of local electrification by her grandfather Roddy Joe MacPhee of Monticello, Kings County.

Apparently this light turned out to be the forerunner—not of any local death but of present-day Monticello's only street lamp, which was unknowingly built on the very site where Roddy Joe encountered his vision.

12. Emmett Hughes interview, Nov. 25, 2006.
13. That is, "Old Peter" Chaisson of Bear River, Kings County. This handle distinguishes him from his nephew "Young Peter" Chaisson, who is his junior by about fifteen years.
14. In the pages that follow, the reader will encounter some confusion among various accounts on whether the term *frolic* applies only to the communal work activity, only to the dance afterward, or to both activities together. In my narrative, I use the term to refer to the dual activity, but otherwise I allow each informant to speak with his or her own voice.
15. Milling or waulking was the process of preparing raw wool for spinning by soaking it in urine, then pounding it until workable. There has been considerable attention paid to the songs and folklore associated with waulking in both Scotland and the New World; see Shaw, *Folksongs and Folklore*, 6, 72–74. For a detailed account of the waulking process on Prince Edward Island, see [Mellick], *Timothy's Boyhood*, 103.
16. See Johnstone, "Letters and Travels," 77, 141; Brehaut, *Pioneers on the Island*, 63, 73–74; Cotton, *Chapters*, 49–50; [Mellick], *Timothy's Boyhood*, 103; and Shaw, *Tell Me the Tales*, 80.
17. Archie Stewart, personal interview, Aug. 8, 1999.
18. Margaret Ross MacKinnon, personal interview, Aug. 10, 1999.
19. George MacPhee's father's full first name was Malachi; his community handle was "Mel Roddy."
20. Archie Stewart interview, Aug. 8, 1999.
21. In Gaelic the dance is known as *Ruidhleadh na Banais*. See Flett and Flett, *Traditional Dancing in Scotland*, 46.
22. "Stephen Rory MacNeil and the Wedding Reel," in MacGillivray and MacGillivray, *Cape Breton Ceilidh*, 133–34.
23. Ervin Rafferty, personal interview, Nov. 22, 2006, PEIFP interview #51. Robinson also played at Rafferty's fortieth and golden wedding anniversaries but did not live long enough to make it to the sixtieth, which was held in 2005.
24. In parts of New York State, housewarmings for the bride and groom (often featuring fiddling and dancing) were known variously as shiveries, mock serenades, hornings, horning bees, skimmertons, or skimiltons. See Bronner, *Old-Time Music Makers*, 6.
25. Merlin Quinn, in Carl and Jackie Webster interview, Oct. 24, 2006, PEIFP, Interview #12.
26. This organization was founded in 1913 to better the cultural lot of farmers and other rural workers, and it is still Canada-wide in scope, with its headquarters in Toronto. See also Arsenault, *Island Acadians*, 177.
27. Ella Thomson Chappell, personal interview, Nov. 17, 2006, PEIFP Interview #42.
28. *Charlottetown Examiner*, July 10, 1865, 2.
29. George Leard, "Tea Parties," ms. dated Sept. 1936, George Leard Files, Robertson Library, University of Prince Edward Island, vol. 10.
30. The song, entitled "The Picnic at Groshaut," and the story surrounding it appear in Ives, *Lawrence Doyle*, 20–26.

31. Island schoolhouses were roughly forty feet long by twenty-five feet wide, while community halls tended to be perhaps half again as large as that.
32. Pratt, *Brief History*, 9.
33. Arsenault, "Le Gâteau des Rois," 25.
34. Arsenault, "Le Gâteau des Rois," 26.
35. Camella Arsenault, "Acadian Celebrations," 30.
36. For Scotland, see Flett and Flett, *Traditional Dancing in Scotland*, 37–38; for Ireland, see O hallmhurain, *Pocket History*, 66–67.
37. For the ceilidh as a primarily oral phenomenon, see Carmichael, *Carmina Gadelica*, xxii; and Breathnach, *Folk Music and Dances*, 47. For accounts of instrumental music at Scottish ceilidhs, see Emmerson, *Social History*, 140–44. The word *ceilidh* (spelled *ceili* in Ireland) has undergone a significant evolution over the past few generations. In contemporary Scotland and on Prince Edward Island, it often denotes a formal musical evening featuring local talent, particularly one at which admission is charged. In Ireland, the term nowadays generally refers to an evening of traditional social dancing.
38. Dunn, *Highland Settler*, 56–57.
39. Lord George Hill, *Facts from Gweedore* (Belfast: Queen's University Institute of Irish Studies, 1971), quoted in Mac Aoidh, *Between the Jigs*, 30.
40. Contra dancing and square sets share both a common ancestry and many similar "steps"; see chapter 12.
41. See Tolman and Page, *Country Dance Book*, 17; Pichierri, *Music in New Hampshire*, 55; Bronner, *Old-Time Music Makers*, 5–6, 48; and Damon, *History of Square Dancing*, 12, 28–29.
42. Wareham, "Ethnography of 'Times,'" 24, 79.
43. Dunn, *Highland Settler*, 105. See also McKinnon, "Fiddling to Fortune," 22.
44. Sellick, *Canada's Don Messer*, 4. For more on Messer's career, see chapter 13.
45. Cash, "Taylor County," 41. For other accounts of frolic-like activities, see, for Alabama, Cauthen, *With Fiddle*, 152–56; for Arizona, Kartchner, *Frontier Fiddler*, xvi; for Georgia, Wiggins, *Fiddlin' Georgia Crazy*, 7; for North Carolina, Nevell, *Time to Dance*, 39; for Texas, Townsend, *San Antonio Rose*, 17; for Virginia, Morgan, *Virginians at Home*, 86; for West Virginia, Milnes, *Play of a Fiddle*, 26, 112.
46. Clyde Davenport, quoted in Perlman, "Traditional Banjo Player," 17.
47. Del Ryke, "So Hell Is Full," 181. Delores Del Ryke was active in the state fiddle association movement in the United States during the 1950s and '60s.

CHAPTER THREE

"Music Was the Next Thing to Eatin'"

> My parents loved music, both of them.
> They always said that music was the next thing to eatin'.
>
> Attwood O'Connor (Milltown Cross, Kings County)

Fiddling, fiddle music, and fiddle dances were deeply woven into the fabric of PEI social life. The house parties, weddings, community dances, and other events described in the previous chapter were only their most obvious manifestations. In addition to these, most Island districts and towns were home to a steady stream of informal and impromptu musical episodes and gatherings.

If no dance was in the offing, most Islanders were nearly as happy to while away their leisure hours just listening to fiddle playing. As Lemmy Chaisson of Rollo Bay, Kings County, notes, "There's not too many people around here wouldn't just sit down and listen to a fiddle, or fiddle music, 'cause it's really enjoyable, you know!" Joe MacDonald of St. Andrews, Kings County, puts it this way:

> It [fiddle music] overrides every emotion in the world. It does away with sadness, it does away with—If you were mad, and you listen to a good piece of fiddle music, the next thing, you're in great humor. I think it overrides fear. That's the way it hits me, anyway. When I listen to some of those good players, you know, I'm just in seventh heaven!

Those who had the most ready access to this favored pastime were members of the Island's many fiddling families: households in which at least one parent and several children played fiddle and accompaniment instruments. Zélie-Anne Arsenault Poirier (b. Abram-Village, Prince County)[1] grew up in the home of Joe à Bibienne Arsenault, one of the most renowned fiddlers of the Evangeline Coast. She describes a typical evening at home.

> We had an old-fashioned organ, we had an old guitar. Always a couple of fiddles in the house—had to be, there was too many playing. And we used to have square dances in the house, there were so many. We had fourteen one winter, fourteen in the house, so lots of nights we had square dances. We were never short of music and that's for sure. Anyone at all that could grab a fiddle played for the dance. We could all play: one would grab the fiddle and played, and the others would dance.

Teresa MacPhee Wilson, who grew up in the fiddling family of Mel Roddy MacPhee of Monticello, Kings County, tells us that her father often had an ulterior motive for getting the children to dance in the evening.

> He played the fiddle for us and he'd get us all dancing: that was usually the roundup. He'd have us all on the floor to dance. He'd play and he'd play, and we'd dance and we'd dance and we'd dance. As soon as ever he'd finished, he'd say, "All right, off to bed now, everybody!" Then he'd get a chance to read the paper.

Louise Gallant Arsenault (b. 1956 in Mont Carmel, Prince County) reports on the family musical evenings that took place in her home as recently as the mid-1960s.[2]

> In the evenings we only had the [kerosene] lamp; we never had the electricity at the time, either. So it was like more or less a real nice family togetherness there, you know. It was an old pump organ there, and my mother would play that when my father played the violin. But whenever I would take the violin out, my dad would get on the organ. And we'd play a lot, just me and him together. Then one of my brothers would join in with the guitar, and then my sisters would dance. I have two sisters, and we used to step-dance, the three of us together. I couldn't be there just doing nothing. I had to grab the guitar, or I would step-dance, or play the spoons. I just couldn't stay still!

As the children of such families grew up and had children of their own, this often created an extended family in which music and dance served as an important part of both celebrations and routine gatherings. Robert Arsenault (b. Abram-Village, Prince County) describes it as follows:

> This music was always part of when relatives came and visited. Parents and uncles played every time there was visitors. Instead of fighting among family members,

play music and play cards—no arguments! It bridged the generation gap and the opinion gaps, too. Sunday afternoons were always traditionally a time where the neighbors came to visit, or relatives, or whatever. And there was always some fiddling happening. Other than that, there was always parties and special occasions, and Christmas: and a lot of music played there. Whenever anybody came to visit as well, there was always get-togethers then. There was always all kinds of different occasions that was an occasion to play.

"Our House Seemed to Be a Place for Them All to Come"

Such fiddling households often served both as community gathering places and as unofficial community centers. Neighbors would gravitate there on evenings, on Sunday afternoons, or at other leisure moments just to see what was going on. Sometimes they would merely sit around and take in the music. On other occasions, as Zélie-Anne Poirier puts it, they "used to come down and sing and dance and God knows what."

Locals in the Belfast, Queens County, area, would often drop in at fiddler Angus Leslie MacLean's home looking for music, dancing, or other excitement. If it was summer, they could dance outside on the little dancing saloon that had been constructed in the yard. In the colder months, they sat around on the floor and took in the goings-on, as recalled by MacLean's son Danny.

> My father played, and my brothers and my sister. Sometimes they'd have about three of them fiddles going at once. People would come round in the wintertime, and, well, our house seemed to be a place for them all to come. Come Sunday, they'd be sitting all around the walls in there, just talking and carrying on, and wrestling and playing, and singing and stuff like that: Indian wrestling and sometimes boxing, too.

In the area surrounding the district of Milltown Cross in south-central Kings County, community members looking for music would descend a couple of times a week on fiddler Philip O'Connor's household, as described by his son Attwood.

> My father's house, that was the gatherin' place of the community. We'd be in there singin', playin', dancin': had the floor half wore out from dancing on it when we were kids. This happened once or twice a week. Maybe there'd be twenty-five or thirty'd be in there. The noise was pitiful! My father used to play fiddle, and I played, and Arnold, my oldest brother, and Elsie, my oldest sister, she played, Melville played, we all played. Every one of us, we'd take turns. Sometimes we had two or three fiddles going, an organ, and a couple of guitars.

On Sunday afternoons in the Bear River, Kings County, area, many locals eager to hear music used to head for fiddler Joe Pete Chaisson's house, as his son Kenny reports.

> We were around it all the time when we were young. My uncles, they were all good violin players, and they used to go out home to my father's place after church. And I mean just automatically, people on the road they'd just go there after church: fifteen, twenty, thirty people. And they'd sit around the livin' room, and my uncles would just play. They'd do that all Sunday afternoon, Sunday night. The people would just come in after church and they'd be just sitting around the veranda, there'd be music going, and it was the thing then, you know. They'd maybe get up and give a few steps [step-dance], and maybe even go into a set.

Along these lines, Chaisson's brother Kevin recalls that as recently as the 1960s when a major snow warning was issued, the cars of those hoping to be *storm-stayed* (marooned) at Joe Pete Chaisson's could be seen lined up all along the Bear River Road.[3]

Alternatively, some households known in the district to be especially hospitable to musicians became popular spots for spontaneous visits from local fiddlers and their accompanists and from neighbors eager to hear them play. As reported by Jenny O'Hanley McQuaid, one such place was the O'Hanley household of Naufrage, Kings County.

> In those times, I remember J. D. MacAdam played the fiddle, Chester played the organ, and Albina step-danced. They used to come to our place quite often, because we had an organ and a fiddle and that; they'd come a lot of different Sunday nights, and they'd play till the cows come home! Then my sister had some boyfriends and a lot of them were fiddlers, and Connie Gallant lived next door, and he's an exceptionally good fiddler. So with the boyfriends and the fiddlers and people comin' in, you'd have a house party almost every time you turned around.

As implied above, just about any household featuring young women of marriageable age would become a popular gathering place, and if the company was large enough the attempt would be made to get up a square set. For example, Largus MacInnis of Lakeville, Kings County, recalls one house in his district that had more or less cornered the local market for eligible young women.

> They used to have parties over here at [the] Roses'. There'd be a bunch come in and they'd dance; somebody could play the mouth organ or the fiddle or bang a dishpan. They had a pump organ; the girls could play and they'd also sing. See, there were a lot of girls over there, and then the boys used to gather of an evening. And if there was a fiddler there they'd have a dance.

PHOTO 3.1. LARGUS MACINNIS AT LAKEVILLE, JULY 1992 (PHOTO BY KEN PERLMAN).

In this setting, as Teresa Wilson puts it, you were considered a "pretty good boyfriend if you were able to play the fiddle: welcome around here especially!"

When a young man who played fiddle and a young woman who played keyboard or guitar felt a mutual attraction, these informal gatherings afforded them the opportunity both to be together and to cooperate on the task of music making.[4] Cosmas Sigsworth (b. Corraville, Kings County), for example, met his wife, Rita, this way.

> When I got to be a little bit better on the fiddle and played a few tunes, my girlfriend she used to play guitar. So, me playing the fiddle and her playing the guitar, I decided that I needed a lot of practice. In fact, we both needed a lot of practice: together! So it gave an excuse. Sometimes we wouldn't take the fiddle out of the case! But it got me to where I was going; finally I got her persuaded to marry me. We only lived two miles apart. At dances we'd play music together. As I said, I figured we needed more practice. "How about Wednesday night, meet for practice?" "OK." All and all, I was working on this: "I wish she was mine, wish I could take her home and keep her." So finally I got her persuaded. We got married, and that was the beginning of a long, happy life. We'll be celebrating forty-nine years of wedlock next month. So we hope to make it to the fifty!

Having a fiddler over for a social visit was another effective way to conjure up a musical occasion. Merlin Quinn of Cardross, Kings County, for example,

"Music Was the Next Thing to Eatin'" 51

remembers that his parents often invited Cosmas and Rita down from nearby Corraville with instruments in tow. "They'd come down on a Sunday night and they'd have the fiddle and the guitar. They'd play and we'd have lunch, and, oh, it'd be twelve o'clock or better before they'd leave. We just loved their music, and we'd sit around and listen to them."

Many households kept instruments around just so that they would be available in the event that musicians happened by. Jim MacDougall of Grand River, Prince County, for example, estimates that when he was growing up, just about "every second house would have a fiddle in it." Similarly, Kenny Chaisson offers the following account:

> If you went up through the north side or up east,[5] any of them places, if you went to a house, like I often went with my father hundreds of times, if you'd have no violin with you, you'd go into this house and they'd pull one out from underneath the bed! It was just an automatical thing which was all over the place at that time.

Along these lines, Vincent Doucette recalls that residents of his home district of Deblois Road, Prince County, virtually held fiddles and other instruments in common.

> Everybody had their musical instruments in their houses. The people that were more well-off had pianos and organs and stuff like that. Like Mrs. Ryan across the road—She had a piano there, so we used to go there and fool around with it. And at my grandfather's they had an organ, so when you'd go there on Sundays you'd get to practice that. And, of course, at our place we had a guitar and a fiddle, so there was always music, and everybody used to play music almost every day. That's why at that time there was a lot of music.

"If Anybody Came That Could Fiddle, It Just Stopped Everything"

Some households valued the opportunity to hear music so highly that a fiddler's visit—even in the middle of a busy workday—could occasion the suspension of all work. According to Attwood O'Connor, "That's the way it was at home. If anybody come in playin', singing, or anything, that was it—Sit down and enjoy it!" Similarly, Merlin Quinn tells this tale:

> My father loved the fiddle. So if anybody ever came in that could play fiddle, it just stopped everything right off. That was the end of the work! We all went in, and stopped there as long as they'd play. Didn't make no difference if it was the middle of the day or what. And we'd stay and listen to the fiddle. I remember this truck driver who could play the fiddle. He'd come up and we'd start to load the potatoes. We'd put the load

on, I guess. But then nothin' would do but he'd come in. Oh, the fiddle would come out first thing. Perhaps the teapot would go down: maybe a cup of tea. But as long as they wanted to play, there was no hurry to get back to work, and that was it. My father was a great worker, worked hard all the time, never stopped. But at the same time, if there was somebody come in with a fiddle, my father stopped everything.

The farm was not the only place where work sometimes took a back seat to fiddling. According to Alvin Bernard of Long River, Queens County, a visit to Jimmy Bearisto's barber shop in eastern Prince County exposed the customer to a quite bit more than just scissors, combs, and razors.

He used to cut hair there in Kensington, and he played the fiddle. And every time you'd go in, there'd be some fiddler in there playin', eh. People used to go in there, sit down and listen to the music. Jimmy would get your hair half cut and think of a tune. "Did you ever hear this tune?" Then he'd leave you and go and play the tune, eh. He'd do that quite often! There used to be lots of music in there at one time. Lots of good fiddlers, they'd go in there and play and get their hair cut.

Ivan Day (b. Norboro, Prince County) adds this recollection of Bearisto and his shop:

I didn't go in very often that Jimmy didn't have a new tune for me: "I had a dream the other night and I thought of an old tune." And he'd want to play it for you. I went in one day, and he was cuttin' this old fellow's hair. So he said, "I'm gonna play it for you." I said, "Not today, Jimmy, I'm in a hurry." "No, no, you just wait a minute." He turned the old fellow in the chair around so he was facing the back of the barber shop with this shawl still around his shoulders. And Jimmy went and got the fiddle, and he played the tune for me. I seen the old feller sittin' in the chair, and he'd turn his head trying to see what was going on behind him. Jimmy didn't think about him at all; he was more interested in playin' that tune for me.[6]

In the district of Coleman Corners in western Prince County, mill operator Warren Leard notes that when a fiddler brought his grain in for grinding, part of the workday was always devoted to music.

There'd be people coming to the mill, like, from all the surrounding areas. It would be probably after we'd do the work for them. We'd take a little time, invite them in for a cup of tea, a few tunes, have a little talk with them, and invite them back. And then they'd come back again sometimes.

In western Prince County near Tignish, politicians often brought in local fiddlers to play at their meetings. Fred Richard from the nearby district of St. Peter and St. Paul, for example, was asked to take on this task when he was a young man. He offers this account:

> If you went to a meeting of politics, I'd play maybe a couple of tunes there and you'd get the old politicians, or maybe the strong liberals or the strong conservatives would be gettin' up and givin' a step, and everybody would be just whoopin'.[7]

PEI's railway was another place where fiddling might be encountered during working hours. Sir Andrew MacPhail records this story, for example, about a fiddler named Pat Bolger whose music was frequently heard in the Orwell, Queens County, area around the turn of the twentieth century:

> He would play the fiddle and anyone who liked might dance in the aisle. In passing the stations of Highland settlements, he would play derisory tunes. It often happened that there was a Highlander on the train who had brought with him his bagpipes . . . and he would remember tunes equally irritating as he passed through an Irish settlement.[8]

According to Joe MacDonald, playing on the trains was still a fairly common occurrence as recently as the 1930s and '40s.

> You'd hear people playing there, all right; you could play the fiddle on the train. There was a blind Indian always playing on the train, and he made a little money at it. He lived here in St. Andrews, and his name was Noel Sapphere.[9] He drove to the station, he'd get on the train, he'd play the fiddle, and people would give him a little money. Then he'd sit in the car till Charlottetown.

"People Would Go to Any Lengths to Get Them to Play"

If all else failed, locals with a yen for fiddle music or dancing would simply go looking for a fiddler. Generally, they would descend upon his home during leisure hours, hoping either to start a small dance on the spot or to lure him away to entertain the company elsewhere. As Emmett Hughes of Dromore, Queens County, notes, "Usually the house that got affected the worst with the house parties was the one that had a fiddler there; they could land there anytime!" Similarly, fiddler Wilfred Gotell of Georgetown, Kings County, tells us,

> They used to call our old place the halfway house—A couple guys together, and have a bottle, then "Let's go up to Wilfred's!" Of course, they'd come in and have a few drinks, and they'd want to hear the music and the fiddle. So it would end up to be a party there that night. And many's the time that happened.

Music seekers would sometimes approach a fiddler during his workday and ask for a few tunes. According to Carl Webster of Cardigan, Kings County, for example, people came to his house at all hours to get his father, Jack Webster, playing.

PHOTO 3.2. *LEFT TO RIGHT:* JACKIE WEBSTER, CARL WEBSTER, AND DONNIE MACDONALD AT MONTICELLO HEADQUARTERS, AUGUST 1992 (PHOTO BY EARTHWATCH TEAM).

> When people would come to the house, Dad would always play the fiddle for them, day and night. If someone come along in the daytime, no matter if he was cultivatin' potatoes with horses, he'd stop, tie the horses up, and go in and play for an hour or two.

Occasionally, Islanders eager to hear music would even rouse a fiddler right out of his bed, as Jimmy O'Connor of Murray Harbour, Kings County, recalls.

> Dave Beck, he was about the best around here when I was younger; he played for a lot of dances around. One night we went up there, a bunch of us, and we got him up in the middle of the night. We got him out in the car playing. Then somebody said for me to play, and he said, "You got just as good a fiddler here with you as I am." Oh, I thought that was something! I couldn't play near as good as he could, but that's what he said. Then he got out and left; he just wanted to get out of the car and go back to bed, I guess.

In this story from Ivan Day, he was on the receiving end of a similar late-night delegation:

> I remember there was a party back in Frank Murphy's one night up in Norboro, and they come to me, got me out of bed at 10 or 10:30: "They want to have a dance back there!" I said, "I can't play for a dance alone; you go get Bill Durant." They got Bill, I went with them, and we played till daylight. So that was often done too. You suddenly took a notion, you went and got the fiddler. And lots of fiddlers, they got them out of bed same as they got me out of bed that night.[10]

Modesty is a deeply ingrained Island virtue, and it was usually the custom for fiddlers to put on at least a token show of reluctance when asked to perform. Sometimes, as in the following account from Largus MacInnis, this reluctance was quite genuine, especially when the fiddler had already put in a hard day's work.

> There was one fiddler over across the road here, Billy MacDonald: "Billy Lauchy" we called him.[11] Well, sometimes he'd come and sometimes he'd balk. The way it was, he used to do the farming home, and after you've chased after a team of horses all day you didn't feel too much like fiddling. But most times he'd go.

When a fiddler offered more than token resistance to playing, strenuous attempts were made to change his mind. As John Cousins of Bloomfield, Prince County, describes, "People would go to any lengths to get them to play: coax and coax. And some of them were shy men. It took a long time, and in a good many cases it took lubrication, you know." He goes on to recount this story:

> That's no job for you if you're shy, to play the fiddle. But this particular fellow, and this is the God's truth, they used to get him to play the fiddle, and he'd sit and face the corner; he couldn't face the people he was playing for. Somebody told me about goin' into the house, and this man was sittin' in the pantry playing the fiddle and they were sittin' listenin' in the next room.

If a fiddler had a reputation for not playing on demand, someone he was known to be especially fond of might be recruited to make the request. Hilda MacPhee MacDonald (b. Selkirk, Kings County) tells this story about just such a stubborn fiddler from nearby Cable Head named Jimmy Simmons:

> He was a great big tall man to white whisker.[12] He wouldn't play for everybody, no sir! They'd be dyin' to hear him play, and he wouldn't play for them. He was pretty funny that way, you know. But he'd play for me when I'd ask him! Ronnie MacKinnon was runnin' the general store, and he would get me to go in to get Jim to play a tune. So after I'd be in talkin' to him for a while: "Jim, will you play a couple of tunes?" He'd pick up the fiddle and they'd be at the window listenin', you know. God, was he great to play!

Regardless of what method of persuasion was employed, the individual who brought the fiddler along—or finally got him to take out his instrument—was often the man (or woman) of the hour, as Vincent Doucette tells us: "If you didn't have anybody musically inclined in the family and you could go someplace and bring a fiddler over for a party, you were all set. If you could get a fiddler over there it would be all the proper thing."

Of course, the ultimate method for having a fiddler around when there was none in the family was to take one in and provide his food and shelter. Ervan Sonier of Summerside recalls that his grandfather used to extend hospitality in such fashion to an itinerant fiddler named Jack Proveau.

> Where was he from? Anybody who'd feed him! He'd stay at your place all year, play the fiddle, if you fed him. I don't know of him having a home; he might have. I know he stayed at my grandfather's winter after winter. Wherever there was a bite to eat. He'd probably leave here and go to Tignish, stay up there a month at one place and a month at another. I never knew his address, wouldn't know where he come from.

"It Was About the Biggest Square Dance I've Ever Played For"

Islanders who worked "away" for extended periods of time brought their love for fiddle music and dancing along with them. During their winters in the lumber woods, for example, Islanders often joined together with like-minded workers from New Brunswick, Nova Scotia, and Québec to hold music-and-dance parties in the camps. And as Danny MacLean reports, anyone known to be a fiddler would probably be coaxed into helping provide the music for these parties.

> One place I worked, all the lumbermen had a bunkhouse, and they used to have parties there on the weekends. Different ones would be playing and dancing. And singers, too, there'd be great singers! But mostly there'd be a step dancer; there wasn't enough room to square-dance.

And when the men returned from the lumber woods in the off-season, there would also be plenty of music making on the train ride home, as Attwood O'Connor describes.

> Coming home, we'd get a bottle and get to fiddling and guitars goin' in the train: play there for hours. We never thought of laying back and having a sleep or a rest. There'd be always somebody on the train playing, singing. Yeah, we'd always be happy with a few dollars in one pocket and a bottle in the other! They'd play there for hours all the time the train was running.

In the mid-1950s, Island fiddlers Omar Cheverie (b. Souris, Kings County) and Harold Dockendorff (b. Mt. Hope, Kings County) were among the hundreds of Maritimers hired to help construct new facilities at the joint US-Canadian Air Force Base in Goose Bay, Labrador. Since both men brought their instruments along, they soon became major sources of entertainment for their workmates. Dockendorff notes, for example, that he and a few fellow musicians would congregate after supper each night to play music in the washroom: "That was our entertainment. And there was two or three step dancers there; they'd get a piece of plywood on the floor and whoop it up."[13]

Even the rigors of war were not necessarily an obstacle for Islanders bent on enjoying the fiddle. During World War II, for example, Eddy Arsenault of St. Chrysostom, Prince County, recalls that while stationed in Halifax he often had the opportunity to swap tunes with other Canadian fiddlers in the service and that on one occasion one of those joining in was Cape Breton fiddle-great Angus Chisholm (for more on Chisholm, see chapter 13). Arsenault spent the latter part of the war driving a supply truck in France, and although he rarely had a chance to play fiddle during this period, fate thrust one in his hands while he was on leave in Glasgow, Scotland, during the height of victory celebrations.

> It so happened that me and a guy from Québec, we were in a pub there right close to the square and it was on V-E Day. We noticed there was quite a thing going on down the square. And there was a guy there, he was just playing around with the fiddle so I just asked him if I could play a couple of tunes. So me and that fellow from Québec, who played guitar, we started to play. And all of a sudden I noticed they were dancing—Well, I couldn't see the end of it! It was about the biggest square dance I've ever played for; they were there by the thousands, not just by the dozen! And after a while I said, "This is too much for us, we'll have to quit or we'll be really in trouble." So we just played for a couple of dances and we took off.

"It's Singing a Fiddle Tune with a 'Deedle-Deedle-Dum'"

When no fiddler was available, many Islanders were able to amuse themselves by singing fiddle tunes, an activity known in anglophone communities as *jigging* or *tuning* and in francophone communities as *musique à bouche* or *turluter*.[14] There is more to this art than just singing the melody of a fiddle tune. Generally, the singer tries in his rendition to imitate the phrasing of the fiddler and the rhythmic pulsation of the fiddler's bow. Instead of just humming the melody, he or she uses nonsense lyrics or abstract vocables to articulate the notes of a tune. To enhance the rhythmic effect of the music, the "tuner" taps his or her feet in the same powerful way that a fiddler would. As Hélène Arsenault Bergeron (b. St. Chrysostom, Prince County) describes, "It's singing a fiddle tune, not with words but just with a 'deedle-deedle-dum,' and tapping your feet at the same time."

This activity was in all likelihood brought to the Island by its original Scottish and Irish settlers. In Scots Gaelic it is known as *puirt-a-beul*, while in Irish Gaelic the terms are *pointaireacht* or *point bhéil*. In Irish-English, the equivalents are *mouth music, lilting*, or—in what seems to be a clear antecedent for Island practice—*jigging*.[15] In the Scottish tradition, some make a clear distinction between *puirt-a-beul*, in which melodies are performed using nonsense lyrics, and *diddling*, in which a tune is articulated using vocables of the "deedle-deedle-dum" variety.[16]

Given this rubric, most Island tuning of the last few generations would certainly be considered "diddling," although one might easily surmise that true *puirt-a-beul* would have been more common when Scots Gaelic was still widely spoken. Along these lines, George MacPhee of Monticello, Kings County, tells this story about an older neighbor who—as a signal to MacPhee's mother that it was time to put on the kettle—always tuned a set of Gaelic lyrics to an old Scottish piping reel:[17]

> Old Jim Carter that used to live here, he used to tune a lot when he got older; he was great to tune and great to sing old songs. He used to come over home when we were kids. He'd always have that tune before he'd get a cup of tea, he'd start tuning that tune, eh, in Gaelic. He'd get sittin' down and get his pipe goin', and he'd get tunin' then. Then he'd get the kids step dancin', and he'd go to judge which would be the best dancer. Of course he always picked the girls, eh!

Some English-language *puirt-a-beul* is still in circulation on Prince Edward Island, mostly in the form of fragments. The following example is from Teresa Wilson, who tells us that this rhyme was once popular among children on the north side of Kings County. It is sung to the well-known reel "Red-Haired Boy."

> I went to the river and I couldn't get across,
> And I paid ten dollars for an old dead horse.
> The horse wouldn't go so I traded for a hoe,
> And the hoe wouldn't dig so I traded for a pig.
> And the pig wouldn't squeal and I traded for a wheel,
> And the wheel wouldn't run; I traded for a gun.
> The gun wouldn't shoot so I traded for a boot,
> The boot wouldn't wear, and I traded for a bear.

> The bear wouldn't climb, and I traded for a dime,
> The dime wouldn't pass, and I threw it in the grass;
> [*Spoken:*] And that was the end![18]

Jigging tunes in the sense of "diddling" was a very popular activity in the Island district. Men and women jigged as they went about their daily chores, and they also jigged for recreation. Here's how Attwood O'Connor remembers it:

> We all used to do it. Well, my soul, it'd be likely to be any time, through the day or night, go around whistlin', tunin', jiggin', what they call it! [*Question:* While you were working?] Sure, the best time: made your work a lot lighter. At least you sounded contented, anyway! My oldest daughter used to get after me about that: "Dad, you're forever whistling a tune or singing something. You don't even know you're doing it."

As Teresa Wilson notes, it was not unusual to step outside your door on a mild summer evening and find the night air filled with the sound of your neighbors' jigging.

> In the evening after her work would be done, Janie MacKinnon would take a chair out on the veranda over there. She would tap her foot, and she'd just tune one tune after the other; she'd take probably an hour, an hour and a half. There were no trees around here then. It was all clear land, and we could hear her tuning from here.

"If They Couldn't Get a Fiddler Years Ago, Someone Would Tune"

Sometimes a person who was "good to jig" might be asked to accompany a square dance. As Archie Stewart of Milltown Cross, Kings County, tells us, "Some of those fellows were noted for being able to tune for the dances; old fellows years ago, they were good at it."

According to most Island fiddlers, it was indeed the "old people"—those generations in their prime of life before 1900—who truly excelled at jigging. When the old people were on the go, Islanders frequently danced square sets to jigging at house parties and community dances. As Cosmas Sigsworth notes, "I remember my mother talking about that; a couple of older ladies could jig tunes like you wouldn't believe, and people would get up and dance to it." Similarly, Jenny McQuaid tells us, "In Mom's day, at dances, sometimes the only music they had was that tuning or jigging."[19]

Skilled jiggers were reportedly able to match the fiddler note for note and accent for accent. At some house parties and community dances, they even helped increase the volume of music by forming an ensemble with the fiddler, as reported by Teresa Wilson.

> I heard my mother sayin' that before her time they had two—They called them "tuners": two women, or a man and a woman. They'd sit on each side of the fiddler, and they tuned the tune with the fiddler.[20] Mom's mother was one of those; she knew every tune really well.

The practice of jigging for square dancing in Island rural districts continued on a limited basis up to the start of the modern era. Ervin Rafferty (b. Rafferty Road, Prince County), for example, reports that a neighbor named Mrs. Lizzie Sullivan "could do that to perfection. She could have a bunch of people up there doing a square dance. She could diddle like that and keep time with her feet; you'd swear it was an instrument of some kind playing the tune."[21] Similarly, guitarist Chester MacSwain of Peters Road, Kings County, remembers tuning for square sets as recently as the early 1960s.

> I done that once. Jackson and I stood up in an old vacant house; it had one good room left in it and the floors still in. They'd have a dance there, and him and I'd stand there, play the guitars, and tune all night. That was their music. Of course, we wouldn't be able to talk for a week after.

One setting where jigging for square sets remained relatively commonplace was the district school. Pupils would be encouraged to dance during lunchtime breaks, and music would be provided by those children who were the best tuners. Jennie McQuaid recalls that at Monticello school, "if it wasn't fit to do something outside, you'd get some form of music going, usually jigging or dancing; quite often it was square dancing." Teresa Wilson, who was a schoolmate of Ms. McQuaid's, remembers it this way:

> I think they did it in nearly all the schools. It was at the dinner hour. The teacher pulled her desk over in the corner, and she went at whatever she was doing. I was one of the ones that was doing the jigging, and we danced square sets in the school for our dinner hour and we learned how to swing [our partners].

As implied above in George MacPhee's story about Old Jim Carter, step dancing to jigged accompaniment was also common practice on the Island. As Archie Stewart notes, there "could be a bunch in the house at night, and someone would be a step dancer in the crowd. If a fella was there that could tune, he'd tune and the other fellow would get up and he'd crank 'er down, boy!"

In the port of Tignish in western Prince County, fisherman coming off their boats at the end of the workweek would often step-dance to the tuning of their mates, as reported by Dennis Pitre of nearby St. Felix and Vincent Doucette.

DOUCETTE: I remember if you were at the harbor Saturday afternoon after everybody was all done fishing, one guy'd be jigging and the other fellow'd be step dancing. They'd keep it up a long while. That's the way they'd practice their steps.[22]

PITRE: There were a lot of good step dancers, those days, really good. But then there'd be someplace where there was no fiddler, so somebody had to jig for them, eh. And the step dancers would be just step dancing on the wharf or anyplace.

DOUCETTE: The guys would be happy probably havin' a few glasses of malt beer on Saturday afternoon. And if they had no fiddle music, that was their entertainment.

When a family had several members that excelled at step dancing but had no fiddlers in residence, this tended to be a great incentive for developing jigging skills, as Teresa Wilson describes.

There was a family of MacKinnons lived down in Goose River, and every one in that family were very, very good step dancers. None of them could play a musical instrument, but they could really tune. Mary Kay and Dolphus MacKinnon, they used to tune and dance at the same time, which is difficult because you get out of breath.

"We Used to Do a Lot of Jigging Just as Kids"

Most Island children learned to jig at a fairly early age, and jigging fiddle tunes was often a common children's play activity. As Clifford Wedge of Miminegash, Prince County, tells us, "When we were younger, we used to do a lot of jigging just as kids, fooling around. Might be walking along the road, a bunch of us; somebody'd start jigging and everybody'd join in."

Teresa Wilson notes that Monticello children would compete with each other to see who could "learn to jig a tune the quickest, and how many tunes we knew." She also recalls that children in her community made a game out of emulating the vocables and tuning styles of local adults.

Another thing we used to do was imitate people tuning. Everybody'd tune different, eh. They said whatever tongue-twister you had. My Father always said, "Da rappa daddle dit / rappa raddle diddle ah." And Mom was, "Dom diddle eye-dle addy / diddle diddle dye-dle ah." It's different, eh? The sounds come out different! We'd be imitating them doing it.[23]

This ability to jig would often progress to another common children's play activity, in which the youngster pretended to be a fiddler, as reported by Ervan Sonier.

Two pieces of stick, and I used to take them and go through the motions of playing. Then I would tune, and I'd be playing the sticks and tapping my feet. They'd be back watching me doing that and they used to get a great kick, I remember. And I couldn't play then at all.

As we shall see in chapters 5 and 6, jigging often played a vital role in passing on the art of fiddling. To begin with, many youngsters would eventually tire of the "pretend" fiddling described above and become motivated to attempt the real thing. Equally important, jigging served as an important intergenerational tune conduit, enabling nonmusicians to become actively involved in shaping the repertoire of the next generation of players.

Another important notion to carry forward: in many Island districts fiddlers and their music often served as the first defense against boredom. Whenever locals felt the need for a little excitement, the strategy most frequently employed was to find a fiddler and try to coax some music out of him. So to the fiddlers' already fairly extensive job description we can also add the following two items: community jukebox and on-demand entertainer.

NOTES

1. Zélie-Anne Arsenault Poirier remarried a few years after this interview and changed her surname to Gaudet.
2. From roughly 1995 to 2005, Louise Arsenault played fiddle in the popular touring ensemble Barachois; see chapter 16.
3. Kevin Chaisson, personal interview, Aug. 1993.
4. It was generally the young man playing the fiddle and the young woman playing an accompaniment instrument, rarely the other way around; see chapter 7.
5. To residents of northern Kings County, "up east" means toward East Point, roughly ten to fifteen miles east of Chaisson's childhood home in Bear River.
6. Ivan Day, in John Gauthier interview, Nov. 16, 2006, PEIFP Interview #40.
7. Fred Richard, personal interview, Nov. 7, 2006, PEIFP Interview #25. In Island parlance, to "give a step" means to step dance at a public gathering.
8. MacPhail, *Master's Wife*, 150.
9. This Mi'kmaq fiddler, known locally as "Blind Newell," was awarded a special medal at the Great Fiddle Contest of 1926; see chapter 11.
10. Ivan Day in John Gauthier interview, Nov. 16, 2006, PEIFP #40.
11. This community handle indicates that this man was the son of Lauchy MacDonald.
12. That is, "with white whiskers," perhaps a borrowing from the French construction, as in "à la barbe blanche."
13. PEIFP personal interviews: Omar Cheverie (Interview #59), Nov. 26, 2006; and Harold Dockendorff (Interview #43), Nov. 18, 2006.
14. *Turluter* (pronounced "toor-loo-TAY") is sometimes rendered as an Anglo-French hybrid: "turlutting."

15. In Scots and Irish Gaelic, the term *port/puirt* means "instrumental air" and *beul/bhéil* means "mouth." Because in Irish Gaelic the word *puirt* denotes both "instrumental air" in general and "jig" in particular, the path by which the term *jigging* became associated with mouth music is obvious. See Breathnach, *Folk Music and Dances*, 63.
16. See Johnson, *Music and Society*, 105; and Collinson, *Traditional and National Music*, 93–95. A systematized version of diddling called *canntaireachd*—in which each scale note and kind of ornament is assigned a specific vocable—was used as a teaching tool at eighteenth-century piping colleges. See Cannon, *Highland Bagpipe*, 67–69.
17. As an aside, the idea of using jigging as a signal features in an Irish folktale: a servant lilts one tune to let her lady know the coast is clear for a suitor's visit and another when the lady's father is lurking about; see Mac Aoidh, *Between the Jigs*, 74–75.
18. Teresa MacPhee Wilson, personal interview, Nov. 14, 2006, PEIFP Interview #37. Notation for "Red-Haired Boy" appears in dozens of tune books, including the classic O'Neill's *Music of Ireland*.
19. This is a not-uncommon phenomenon in North American fiddling cultures. For New Hampshire, see Pichierri, *Music in New Hampshire*, 55; for Québec, see Lederman, "Fiddling," 456; and for Newfoundland, see Wareham, "Ethnography of 'Times,'" 208–9. Similarly, according to Samuel Bayard (*Hill Country Tunes*, xxiii), in Pennsylvania when no fiddler was available to play for a dance, the company sang dance airs to improvised or traditional rhymes.
20. In some parts of Ireland, pairs of female lilters—often an adult with a low voice teamed with a young girl with a higher voice—sometimes provided music for house dances. See Mac Aoidh, *Between the Jigs*, 29.
21. Ervin Rafferty, personal interview, Nov. 22, 2006, PEIFP Interview #51.
22. This scene echoes a vignette from Mark Twain's *Life on the Mississippi*: "Next they [the raftsmen] got out an old fiddle, and one played and another patted juba and the rest turned themselves loose on a regular old-fashioned keelboat breakdown" (14).
23. The tune being jigged here is the opening couple of bars of "Lord MacDonald's Reel" (see appendix A, example 3.1); for the full tune, see Perlman, *Fiddle Music of PEI*, 45.

CHAPTER FOUR

The "Gift" and Other Attitudes about Fiddling

Because fiddling played such an important role in district life, it is not surprising that Islanders would develop a deeply felt set of ideas about it. Many of these attitudes deal with the issue of what makes a "good" fiddler: both in the sense of musical mastery and in terms of personal demeanor and social role. These attitudes in turn became important factors not only in shaping fiddling style but also in defining the terms by which fiddlers and their communities related to one another.

Probably the most widespread notion about fiddling on Prince Edward Island is that the ability to play constitutes an inborn gift. John Cousins of Bloomfield, Prince County, expresses it as follows:

> The term people use for that, to become a good fiddler, the term everyone used ad nauseam was "a gift." You were given this gift. And people used that sincerely. Only a few people were given this gift, but if you became a good fiddler that was a gift you had been given—by who knows whom. But that's the way it was.

The gift of fiddling has two components. First, as Islanders express it, the fiddler must not simply "have music in him" but must in fact be "just full of music." In other words, he or she must not only have a powerful musical memory—one that is capable of absorbing a new tune after just a few hearings—but also be able to translate that tune directly from the imagination to the strings of an instrument. Second, the fiddler must possess a level of natural physical ability sufficient for attaining technical expertise. The gift of fiddling, then, can be summed up as an inborn combination of musical imagination, musical memory, and eye-hand coordination, which is as much discovered by the player as it is developed.

> You got to be full of music, and if you're not full of it, you needn't try; you won't learn. Some people has got a great ear for music, but they don't have the coordination, and that's no good. You've got to have it all, and very few people do. (Joe MacDonald: St. Andrews, Kings County)
>
> I think it's got to get born in you. I think you're gettin' it from birth. You either have music or you don't have it, one thing or the other. (Attwood O'Connor: Milltown Cross, Kings County)
>
> To be a fiddler you have to have the whole thing. You have to have the tunes and the music in you, and you also have to have the rhythm. I suppose it's the same as anything else. There are people who are good carpenters and they are born carpenters, eh. Some can learn the trade but they'll never be as good a carpenter as the one that's born to it; it comes out of him without having to learn or study about it. I don't know what to make of it, but that's my belief anyway. (Teresa MacPhee Wilson: b. Monticello, Kings County)

Where does the gift come from? For many, such as Wilfred Gotell of Georgetown, Kings County, the ability to play fiddle is "a gift from the Heavenly Father." This attitude coincides quite closely with certain teachings of the Catholic Church regarding the divine origin of human talents in general, as frequently expressed in homilies by the local clergy.[1] On a more mundane level, most Islanders also see the gift of fiddling as an inheritable trait, like hair and eye color. This inheritable trait then passes along family lines—a theory that was naturally reinforced by the presence in many communities of large fiddling households, such as the Chaissons of Bear River, the MacLeans of Garfield, and the Joe à Bibienne Arsenaults of Abram-Village. Most would agree with Angus Leslie MacLean's son Danny, who states, "To make a good fiddler, you kind of inherit it, because families that got music in them, it seems to go right down through the centuries." Similarly, Gus Longaphie of Souris, Kings County, tells us, "This type of thing has got to be an inheritance. The little bit of fiddling I got, I suppose I got it inherited from my father. I think it's grading down from one generation to another."[2]

Being an agricultural people versed in the practice of animal husbandry, Islanders have developed several theories that predict where the inheritable gift of fiddling might fall. Cosmas Sigsworth (b. Corraville, Kings County), for example, notes that a family with fiddlers on both sides is most likely to produce a good player.

> It's natural inheritance. Good musician crossed with a good musician, you could get a better musician, right? That's kind of a coarse way of saying it, but that's the way. The natural inheritance from two sides, I'd say, would increase the ability compared to someone that had music just on one side. I think they have a musical inheritance that other people don't have. They got two sources to draw from, the mother and the father's side.

Another popular take on fiddling inheritance has it that great talent skips a generation. Therefore, the player with the most potential gifts is likely to have fiddling grandfathers on both sides. According to Joe MacDonald, there are also two other commonly held theories on the subject: one posits that "fiddling will come out again every third generation," while the other describes a cyclical process that "goes up for three generations, and down for three generations."

Islanders also have a tendency to see fiddling style as inborn and therefore inheritable. There is a fine young fiddler from Bear River, Kings County, for example, named "J.J." Chaisson who has two well-known fiddling grandfathers: Joe Pete Chaisson on the mother's side of the family and Johnny Joe Chaisson from nearby Souris on the father's side. Although as a child J.J. was exposed almost exclusively to the fiddling of Joe Pete's kin, it was once widely assumed that his ultimate style would also draw heavily from the paternal line.[3] Here's how Fr. Charles Cheverie explained it at the time:

> J.J.'s got Joe Pete's blood all right, but it's not exactly the same background. His father would come from Johnny Joe, who would have his own style of playing. Even though J.J. is playing a lot of the same tunes as his cousins [on the maternal side], and probably learned them from his [maternal] uncle Peter, I dare say after a while that his playing will become different.

If fiddling runs in families, it should certainly run in nationalities. Most Islanders feel that ethnic identity is associated with the ability to learn fiddling. Ironically, despite the long association of both Irish and Highland Scots with the instrument, many Islanders feel that the gift of fiddling falls most often, and most powerfully, among the Acadian French. Alvin Bernard of Long River, Queens County (who himself claims English ancestry), expresses it this way:

I suppose it's the Scotch too, but we find the French, eh, it's bred and born in them! They sit down and just do it so easy. I think they get their feet going before they get their bow going. It's gotta be handed down from generation to generation, I guess. That's the way we look at it.

Interestingly, the birth of nonmusical individuals to an intensely musical household is seen merely as an exception that proves the rule. Family and community members expend considerable energy trying to figure out which nonmusical ancestor donated their genes to the deprived. Teresa Wilson, for example, explains the lack of musical talent in two of her thirteen siblings as follows:

They were the only two in the family because Mom's father had absolutely no music in him. So they picked it up traditionally from him. Mom's father loved music, and he just couldn't play. He'd try dancing, but he couldn't dance for nothing! And he loved it probably more than the one that could do it. They didn't pick up any music because they were just like him: just picked up different genes or something.

The other side of the coin is the sense that it was pointless for individuals not possessed of the gift to even attempt the instrument. Ms. Wilson tells this story about one of her elder brothers, for example, which illustrates the futility of trying to learn when the gift was lacking:

There wasn't an ounce of music in him, but he just loved that fiddle. He would come in at dinnertime, and he would get the fiddle down in the front room. He'd start playing, [and] he'd get us to guess what tune he was playing. Oh, golly, that was the worst guessing game I ever got involved in! We didn't want to offend him, so we'd start guessing, and he would say, "Don't you know any tunes at all?" So he never did learn to play. And Aunt Hilda said [one of her sons] was the same.[4] He tried so hard to learn to play that fiddle and he never could. He didn't have any music in him to come out of him, [and] that was it.

This complex of attitudes created an unfortunate consequence. Since it was generally assumed that people without a known fiddling heritage had no gift, musically inclined individuals from nonmusical families often felt discouraged from taking up the instrument. Jenny O'Hanley McQuaid (b. Naufrage, Kings County) describes it as follows: "I think that was the general idea, that you had to have it in your genes and there wasn't much point in anyone else trying. If you didn't have music in your family, you might as well not bother! I think that would be the general impression."

Taking this a step further, youngsters from nonmusical families with an interest in fiddling often had to struggle against the skepticism of their neighbors. Robert Crane (b. Riverton, Kings County), for example, tells of a childhood friend named Lorne MacKay who had gotten hold of a fiddle but did not have his own bow. Crane's father knew that a neighbor named Angus Mahann had a couple of extra bows, and he suggested that MacKay try to borrow one. Here's how the youngster fared:

> He went to up Angus for the bow, and Angus said, "What do you want the bow for?" He said, "There's no damn music in any of the MacKays I ever heard tell of." And he was right, there was none of the other MacKays ever played music. But Lorne, he turned out not too bad [a player]![5]

In this atmosphere, even accomplished fiddlers are prepared to produce a pedigree, as if talent unsupported by heritage might be suspect. For example, Elmer Robinson of Woodstock, Prince County, notes, "My background is not bad. My father played the fiddle, both my grandfathers played the fiddle, and my uncle Will Harvey on my mother's side of the family, he was one of the champion fiddlers of the Island!"[6] Similarly, here's how Stephen Toole of Green Road, Queens County, sums up his family's musical background:

> The fiddling came from my father's side through my grandmother, who was a McCatty. Her brother Michael McCatty was a real bang-up player. I heard the old gentleman playing back in the thirties when he was over eighty years old, and I guess that's who my father took after. That's the side of the house that the music came from.

When confronted with a successful first-generation fiddler, Islanders often feel the need to rack their brains for a suitable forebear, as in this story told by John Gauthier (b. Stanhope, Queens County).

> I was playing at the wedding of a cousin of mine in Rustico[, Queens County,] in 1946 or '47. I took a break, I went in and set down with a plate full of little sandwiches, and sat beside this elderly gentleman. He said, "What's your name?" I told him. "What's your father's name?"—"Grandfather's name?"—"Oh, yes." He said, "You had a great-uncle Charlie who was a fiddler," and he said, "I could have sworn it was him playin' out there." Believe what you like; I didn't even know I had a great-uncle Charlie.[7]

Some first-generation fiddlers seem embarrassed by their lack of a clearly defined musical heritage, which in some cases leads to the creation of makeshift pedigrees. One fiddler from southern Kings County, for example, frequently reminds neighbors that the source of his musical talent is a Newfoundland-born grandmother with "I forget how many brothers, and they all played the fiddle." Another case concerns an outstanding young Queens County fiddler without a single known fiddling ancestor. Since it is assumed that talent on

PHOTO 4.1. STEPHEN TOOLE AT HIS ARGYLE SHORE COTTAGE, AUGUST 1992 (PHOTO BY EARTHWATCH TEAM).

this level could not appear spontaneously, two theories have grown up to offer an acceptable explanation. The first is a variant of the "Great-Uncle Charlie" gambit: it posits fiddling ancestors "way back," of whom there is no living memory. The second theory, favored by the youngster's father, can be summed up as follows: since both sides of the family lived for generations in districts noted for fiddling, at some point a marriage must have brought the gift into the family gene pool, where it lay dormant until the current generation.

"God's Gifts Are Given to Us Not for Ourselves"

Most Islanders agree that possessing the gift of fiddling carried with it an important responsibility. For whenever fiddlers were called upon by friends and neighbors to play, they were expected to share their gift willingly. This notion that those blessed with the gift of music had a distinct duty to the community was central to many an Island sermon, as described by Bishop Faber MacDonald (b. Little Pond, Kings County).

> I used to talk about the social nature of the gift. See, the gifts, God's gifts, are given to us not for ourselves. They're entrusted to us for everybody. And the human person, when he engages himself or herself in the delivering or the giving of himself through his gift, he matures and grows. There's something that happens to the human person when he or she is involved in giving himself to others, you see. And so these gifts are invitations to go out, invitations to give of yourself.

That many fiddlers, Catholics and Protestants alike, intrinsically accepted this view is indicated by the following comments.

> I must've played for hundreds of weddings and never took a cent yet. I had the talent, and I had nothing to do with it. It didn't cost me anything. What I figured is a lot of people didn't have it, and that may sound like bragging. What I mean by that is, it's a God-given gift and you have nothing to do with it. Oh, it was all right; it didn't hurt me a bit. I wish I could do it now! (Joe MacDonald, Catholic)

> It comes from my religion, I guess. I guess we were brought up to do that, share your gifts. I know myself, if somebody asked me to play I mostly said yes. I don't know why, I just helped them out, I guess. So you just go, play what you can play and do the best you can do. I wish I could do better! (Alvin Bernard, United Church of Canada)

In practice, such religious teachings amplified an equally powerful network of community obligations in which playing for dances or local entertainments was seen as an expression of neighborliness, like helping the neighbors harvest potatoes. Together, these religious and secular constraints defined the fiddlers' role in the district. Essentially, it was the fiddler's *duty* to provide the music for house parties, weddings, frolics, benefit dances, concerts, and any other kind of dance or fund-raising event. Not only did fiddlers have to provide the music without demanding recompense,[8] but there was also a strong implication that they had to keep on playing as long as the neighbors wished to go on listening or dancing. As Rita Morrison (b. St. Andrews, Kings County) tells us, "If they came, they'd play all night, and everybody kind of expected that, that they'd play all night; they'd never get tired of playing, they'd just play." Sometimes such expectations were not at all subtle. Harold Dockendorff (b. Mount Hope, Kings County), for example, describes one occasion when the only way he and his accompanist cousin could get away from a schoolhouse dance was by escaping out the window: "We were just driving out of the yard when they realized we were leaving, and some of them gave chase tryin' to catch up the car."[9]

Because the fiddler's participation in community events was seen in terms of duty or obligation, he was often taken for granted by his neighbors. When there was a dance in the offing, the fiddler was sought after and treated well. When his music was no longer needed, however, the fiddler's special talents were more or less forgotten. As soon as the dance was over, he was treated the same—and evaluated by the same standards—as anyone else in the district. Elliott Wight (b. Flat River, Queens County) points out, "I don't think that anyone ever thought it was much of a thing to be able to play the fiddle. You just played and that was it; there was nobody really praised you up too much because you could play. It was just a skill just like doing carpenter work." Similarly, Alvin Bernard and Edwin Simmons put it this way:

> SIMMONS: He was pretty important when they wanted to party, but otherwise they weren't thought of all that highly.
>
> BERNARD: If they wanted music, they thought he was a pretty good guy, I guess. They wanted him to play at the hall for nothing. They expected him to go, eh.
>
> SIMMONS: They would possibly be quite offended if he refused; I guess they would be! But [otherwise] he got treated on an equal basis as anyone else.

It was perhaps only when a district lacked one of their own that the fiddler's worth was fully appreciated, as illustrated in this story from Hélène Bergeron (b. St. Chrysostom, Prince County):

> I was talking to an older dancer a few months ago, and he said, "You were fortunate in St. Chrysostom, you had all the musicians there to play for dances. Us in St. Philippe," he said, "we only had—We had to use a horseshoe." They used a horseshoe and a big spike and just played it like a triangle, and they had a harmonica and spoons and jigging. That's what they had to make their dances with there.

"He Gave Them People the Urge to Get Up and Dance"

A fiddler might have a gift for remembering tunes and excellent musical coordination, but he is not considered successful unless his playing is so lively that people are literally driven to get up and dance. This liveliness is considered to be an inherent aspect of the fiddler: another gift, if you will. This gift is communicated through a fiddler's music directly to listeners, who in turn become so filled with vitality that they cannot help but express it on the dance floor. Archie Stewart of Milltown Cross, Kings County, describes it this way:

> You get some kind of a message from your music through to the people. I've seen at a dance hall where the people would be all sittin' around and nobody'd be up

dancin', and the thing would be pretty quiet and not much goin' on. A certain fiddler would come in and pick up that fiddle and start to play, and in five minutes that dance floor was full. He gave them people the urge to get up and dance. There was something in his music that got through to the people. There was something there that made them want to get up and express their feelings by dancing.

As one might suspect, great fiddlers are said to have the gift of liveliness in abundance. According to Cosmas Sigsworth, for example, renowned fiddler Jack Webster from nearby Cardigan had "great life to his music: if you were listening to him, you would just get filled with life. He was a great lively player!" Similarly, it was said of Angus Leslie MacLean that "when he started to play the fiddle he'd pick your feet right off the floor!"[10]

Youngsters who seem on the road to becoming good fiddlers are also said to possess this inherent quality of liveliness. For example, here's how Kenny Chaisson described the playing of his aforementioned nephew J.J. when the latter was about nine years old:

> He's probably got a flow of music; he seems to be able to make people move. I don't know what it is, it's somethin' you can't see or explain, but he seems to be able to pump the adrenaline up a little bit. It does somethin' to you, and JJ's got that type of rhythm, eh.

There are several aspects to the Island notion of musical liveliness. First, the player must produce a *tempo* (playing speed) that is neither too slow nor too fast. As Stephen Toole notes, the important thing is producing a tempo that is compatible with the Island style of dancing.

> Too slow is no good. Too slow a music is no good for a square dance; you have to be lively. [*Question*: Can a fiddler play too fast?] Well, there's dance time. You take Island music here and Cape Breton music. It's about the same dance time, the same stride and swinging. They swing around in dances, and you can't swing to too fast a tune, just to a medium speed.

The player must also have a steady and unerring rhythmic sense that never allows the beat to waver. As George MacPhee of Monticello, Kings County, observes, "If you don't have good time in your music I suppose it don't sound too good: there's an off beat on it."

Fiddlers must do more than just keep steady timing, however. They must also reflect with their bowing the subtle rhythmic nuances that characterize the movements of Island square and step dancing. This allows dancers to move precisely along with the music instead of fighting it, which in turn produces both an exhilarating sensation of lift and a longing to get up on the floor. This last quality—often referred to as having "good timing on (or 'to' or 'with') the music"—probably more than anything else defines liveliness.[11] Angus Leslie MacLean, for example, is said to have "had terrific time with his music";[12] Reg Banks of Poplar Point, Kings County, tells us that late fiddler Hector MacDonald of nearby Bangor had "great timing on his playing"; and George MacPhee says that the late J.D. MacAdam of Bear River, Kings County, "really had a great touch on his music. He played a lovely great sweet music, and great timin' to his music."

This emphasis on liveliness has shaped the PEI fiddling style for generations. Until the modern era, it was quite rare for fiddlers to perform for a listening audience. True appreciation of the fiddler's music and true understanding of his or her musical gift were only to be found on the dance floor. Similarly, the greatest tribute you could offer a fiddler was to get up and dance to his music.

Islanders are quick to praise lively fiddling and fairly persnickety about tolerating fiddling that is perceived to be insufficiently lively. They also tend to "vote with their feet" at community dances and house parties, and—as Wilfred Gotell observes—they won't get onto the dance floor unless the music moves them to do so. "It takes a snappy tune to get them to move, to get them up on the floor, you know. It's what you got to do, but if you play for fifteen or twenty minutes and no one moves, it's kind of discouraging. You figure you're not doing too good a job."

When Islanders felt stuck at a dance with an insufficiently lively player, the appearance on the scene of a fiddler known to have better "timin' to his music" would evoke not only a general sense of relief but sometimes overt expressions of appreciation such as applause and backslapping. This situation is depicted by a well-known Kings County song called "The Spree at Montague," in which a house party is ruined by a fiddler who was unable to get comfortable with a borrowed instrument (referred to below as "number one"), then rescued by a willing substitute.

> When the shouts that marked his coming had died away and gone,
> He took that very fiddle, condemned by number one.
> Saying, "Boys get to your places. Ask what you want in time,"
> And the walls of the old mansion rang with music sweet and fine.[13]

This love for lively music apparently does not diminish with age. Sidney Baglole (b. Lot 16, Prince County), for example, tells about the time he was asked to play regularly at a senior citizens' home in nearby Summerside after numerous predecessors failed to make the grade. "You have to be lively. You

PHOTO 4.2. SIDNEY BAGLOLE AT FREETOWN, AUGUST 1992 (PHOTO BY EARTHWATCH TEAM).

have to play lively for dancin', you know. Now, they've had poor players in the senior citizens' [home], and they didn't like them. The music was no good, they said. No, they want something that's right lively!"

"He Was a Very Sweet Player"

Most Islanders feel that a good fiddler should have a sweet, smooth sound that soars above the cares of every day. George MacPhee, as already noted, describes the playing of J.D. MacAdam as a "lovely great sweet music," while Wilfred Gotell says of his father, John Charles Gotell (1893–c. 1970), "He was a very sweet player; he wasn't rough, and he was very sweet. And he had fairly big fingers. I'd often watch him and wonder how he could bring such a sound out of a fiddle." Similarly, Pat Doucette (b. Miminegash, Prince County) likens the sound of well-known Tignish-area fiddler Willie Thibodeau to the song of the Sirens:

> You ever hear tell of the mermaid when the ship went through? To me, Willie was somethin' like that. It was sweet just like angels. His music would draw you to the

sound; you couldn't walk away from him, I'm not kidding! [Not] if you had any music in you.[14]

Like musical talent and liveliness, the tone that a fiddler could get out of his instrument was considered an inherent quality. Moreover, as Stephen Toole tells us, unless you had the right kind of inborn sound you would never become a good player.

> The old people used to say that if you couldn't take the right sound out of a fiddle, you'd never be a fiddler. Every fiddler will go over the strings, and everybody has their own sound. But the old people said that you had to be able to take a sound out of it, and a musical sound out of your fiddle, 'fore they could judge whether he was going to make a fiddler or not.

As one might suspect, a conflict can arise between playing sweet and playing lively. Specifically, as one's playing gets more vigorous there is a tendency to ignore the niceties of tone. So while smoothness is widely admired, it is generally acknowledged that there might easily be circumstances, such as a rowdy dance or the second day of an Island wedding celebration, when rough playing is unavoidable. It should also be noted that many Island fiddlers whose music is considered vigorous but hardly smooth are generally accepted as good dance players. Of the latter, Elliott Wight observes, "Some players, although they can play good, they're rough players, like. I see the hairs all hanging off the bow where they're breaking off, that type of thing."

"I'd Try to Play as True as Possible"

No matter how sweet or lively a fiddler's playing might be, he will not get the full respect of his peers or neighbors unless his tunes are relatively *true*. What this means is that the major themes (strains) of each tune—as it is locally known—must be played more or less intact. Otherwise, the tune is said to be *cut up*, *cut short*, or *chopped up* (that is, incomplete). As Leonard McDonald of Emyvale, Queens County, notes, "Well, I tried to play true. I'd try to play as true as possible. I hate people chopping up the tunes. It's probably not always the way they're written, but it's the way I know them."

At least some of this desire for "trueness" stems from a general theme of Island life, which Paul MacDonald of Charlottetown sums up as, "If you don't do it right, you don't do it at all." Another element at work here derives from a general tendency in Scottish culture to revere tune composers while attempting to preserve their compositions as close as possible to published versions. As Joe MacDonald notes, you should "put everything in that the fellow who wrote it, that the composer wrote into it." Kenny Chaisson expresses it as follows:

> There's so many people who play, but they don't play a lot of stuff right. But my father[, Joe Pete,] always liked pretty well sticking to the basic tune; if somebody had made a tune, he figured the least people could do was probably get as close to being right as possible. I think you'd like to hear it original.

Another element, as noted by Stephen Toole, is a sense that for the sake of one's reputation it was best not to stray too far.

> I like to learn them and play them right. There is some people that will learn a tune, but they haven't really got it down right. And you don't like to play a tune that way, 'cause somebody in the audience that can play—That other guy, he would say, "Well, that fellow's not playing that tune right."

In practice, trueness is by no means an absolute value. When fiddlers are forced to make a choice between playing true and playing lively, liveliness wins out almost every time. The dilemma is as follows: when faced with a complex or "crooked"[15] tune, does the fiddler try to play all the notes or jettison a few in the interests of keeping good timing on the music? This issue can be avoided to a certain extent by subtly changing phrases of the tune so that notes fall under the fingers in a more congenial manner, while leaving the original melody relatively unscathed. Apart from this, most fiddlers would probably agree with Archie Stewart, that the fundamental task is to keep the dance rhythm intact even if a few notes have to go.[16]

> When you're playin' for a dance, you set back and play. You don't care whether you got all the notes in. The fellows that are dancin' aren't going to question you. Another thing, too. When you start to get tired—At twelve o'clock at night you start cuttin' corners, and that gets to be a habit after a while. I never played the fiddle for someone to sit down and listen to; I played the fiddle for people to dance. And that makes a difference. You have good timin' and you're makin' good music. What difference if you got all the notes in it or not? Doesn't make any difference to me. They can make fun of me all they like!

It is also worthy of note that in practice the Island concept of trueness embraces a wide variety of approaches to the same tune, each representing a somewhat different take on significant portions of the melody. To understand this apparent contradiction, we need to take a look at both the local style of tune assimilation and the importance ascribed to individual tune versions, which are known as *twists*. These subjects are addressed in detail in chapter 6, but suffice it to say here that tunes are believed to have both essential and inessential elements and that fiddlers are permitted, even encouraged, to vary the inessential ones.

"Suppose You Played for a Hundred Years, You Could Always Learn"

Most players feel that a good fiddler should have a fairly large repertoire. Danny MacLean, for example, recalls that his father, Angus Leslie, "could play all night and never play the same tune twice." Stephen Toole expresses it this way:

> Well, the fiddler has to know a good selection of dance tunes. He has to be able to play a good selection of tunes: jigs, and reels, and waltzes. [*Question:* Just how many tunes would he have to know?] Well, it would be hundreds, anyway. Maybe you could know a hundred jigs; you could know a hundred reels and hornpipes.

No matter how many tunes the fiddler knows, it is never considered sufficient. According to Reg Banks, "Suppose you played for a hundred years, you could always learn something." Similarly, Gus Longaphie observes, "You can never know too many! The same as a mechanic or a carpenter or a machinist of any kind. You can always learn. You can never know too much."

In this atmosphere, it is not surprising that even fiddlers in their eighties are still busy adding to their repertoires. Among the approximately one hundred tunes that eighty-year-old Sidney Baglole played for us over the course of his interview session, for example, were several that he had only recently learned from Cape Breton radio broadcasts. Similarly, eighty-five-year-old Charlie Sheehan of Bear River tells us, "There's always some new ones [tunes] popping upon the radio in the evenings. As the tune comes on that I like, I tape it and then I can pick at it and learn it." (The influence of radio on the Island fiddling repertoire is discussed in chapters 13 and 14.)

Not only must fiddlers continually add to their repertoires, but they are also expected to continue improving in other aspects of their playing. Most important here, as Dennis Pitre of St. Felix, Prince County, tells us, is the notion that each player should continue tinkering until he or she has come up with the best possible version for each tune.

> I think about music there's no end to it, like. Even if you learn a tune, then, gee, there's something more in it that you could learn a little better. You can keep learning and keep learning. I guess that's the beauty of it, because if you got to a stage where that's it, I don't think it'd be any good.

"Not a Proper Thing to Go and Be Up Front, You Know!"

One strong thread that runs through traditional Island culture is the discouragement of self-aggrandizing or self-promoting behavior. It simply is not proper to seem too eager to draw attention to oneself. Consequently, the appropriate stance for fiddlers, dancers, and other talented members of the community is to wait to be coaxed at least once or twice before plying one's craft.[17] Robert Arsenault (b. Abram-Village, Prince County) describes how the process works for step dancers.

> They'd want so-and-so to get up and dance; and they wouldn't want to dance. They would go get 'em, and then they'd dance. They'd have to be encouraged, of course, because it's not a proper thing to do, not a proper thing to go and be up front, you know. You have to be asked!

As recently as the 1990s, youngsters who showed great promise on the fiddle were told in no uncertain terms by their elders to avoid demanding special treatment or putting on airs. They were also given to understand that ignoring this advice could cause them to be ostracized by both peers and community adults.[18]

Given this background, even fiddlers who command long-standing local respect display a strong reluctance to step forward. According to his daughter Hélène Arsenault Bergeron, for example, renowned player Eddy Arsenault of St. Chrysostom, Prince County, much prefers dance playing to concert playing because it allows him to avoid the limelight. Not only are Island fiddlers self-effacing when it comes to public performances, but they also evince considerable humility with regard to the level of their own playing accomplishments. Along these lines, Arsenault's standard response to a musical compliment is, "Oh, I am the *worst* fiddler!" Similarly, Gary Chipman (b. Charlottetown) puts it this way:

> We don't look at ourselves as gifted musicians, I don't think, or at least I never did. Where's the big deal? And I think the rest of the guys, they probably just have a lot of fun with it. Everybody would like to have something that they're recognized for, and in our case, it happens to be playing the fiddle.

A corollary here was the general feeling that music and dance should be conducted without much in the way of fanfare or unnecessary motion. Consequently, Island fiddlers (at least through the 1990s) generally looked askance at some of the extravagant stage antics engaged in by some modern concert fiddlers, such as swaying soulfully from side to side or fiddling and step-dancing simultaneously.

In part, fiddlers' pronouncements of humility are just a public stance, and some of them no doubt do have a healthy sense of their own musical accomplishments. For others, however, such humility is all too real, stemming in part from such factors as the near-absence of Island fiddling from the media and the virtual disappearance of fiddling from everyday life in the years following modernization.

Still another source for fiddlers' self-doubt was the decidedly mixed view that most communities maintained toward the practitioners of this all-too-necessary art form. Although fiddling may have been regarded as a skill and a pastime, it was most definitely not considered to be "work": a term reserved almost entirely for plowing, planting, carpentry, and other activities that directly manipulated the material world. And while spending hours a day engaged in mastering such material skills was the "one sure path to esteem among your peers,"[19] putting in the same kind of time developing fiddling skills or playing at public events was often seen as frivolity at best and laziness at worst. As discussed in chapter 8, this contradiction between the central role of fiddling and the absence of recompense or special status for its practitioners often created economic, social, and psychological hardships for Island fiddlers over the course of their lives.

Attitudes about fiddling such as the gift of music, playing lively, and playing true are firmly ensconced in the Island ethos. They largely determine who feels motivated to take up the instrument; the kinds of rhythms, phrasing, and tone they try to achieve; the zeal with which they pursue new repertoire; and some of the ways in which they interact with their neighbors. Such attitudes were also at the root of the relatively haphazard method by which youngsters learned to play (as we shall see in the next chapter).

It should be noted that as the Island moves deeper into its fiddling revival, some attitudes described here are in the process of changing. Fiddlers from the most recent generation are far more likely to find themselves in front of a concert audience than playing for any kind of dancing (as noted in chapters 16 and 17). Consequently, the old notion of liveliness is growing increasingly less salient, and constraints against showy, self-aggrandizing public behavior are rapidly disappearing.

NOTES

1. According to Fr. Charles Cheverie of Charlottetown, the notion of talents as divine gifts, along with a corollary that states that such gifts must be used for the benefit of the community, goes back to the teachings of the Apostle Paul (personal interview, Oct. 1, 1997).

2. The notion of fiddling as a divinely proffered or inheritable gift is not confined to Prince Edward Island. For Ireland, see Mac Aoidh, *Between the Jigs*, 55; for Newfoundland, see Quigley, *Music from the Heart*, 8; and for Scotland, see Shoupe, "Musical Families," 21.
3. Johnny Joe and Joe Pete Chaisson were very distant cousins. J.J.'s cousins referred to in the following quotation in the text are the offspring of his maternal aunts and uncles, notably "Young Peter," Kenny, and Kevin Chaisson.
4. The "Aunt Hilda" being referred to is Hilda MacPhee MacDonald (b. Selkirk, Kings County).
5. Robert Crane, personal interview, Nov. 29, 2006, PEIFP Interview #65.
6. Will Harvey won second prize in the Great Contest of 1926; see chapter 11.
7. John Gauthier, personal interview, Nov. 16, 2006, PEIFP Interview #40.
8. Some occasions at which fiddlers could earn money from playing are described in chapter 7.
9. Harold Dockendorff, personal interview, Nov. 18, 2006, PEIFP Interview #43.
10. Bobs West, quoted in Hornby, *Belfast People*, 248.
11. In the Scottish tradition, this aspect of playing was known as *dird*, defined as "the accent given to the notes—that extra something that makes the onlookers' feet tap and gives life and lift to the dancers" (Flett and Flett, *Traditional Dancing in Scotland*, 47–48). In Newfoundland, this is referred to as *dart* (Quigley, *Music from the Heart*, 50), and in Shetland as *lilt* (Cooke, *Fiddle Tradition*, 98).
12. Bobs West, quoted in Hornby, *Belfast People*, 248.
13. Patrick Wm. Farrell, "The Spree at Montague," in Ives, *Lawrence Doyle*, 214–15. Farrell (1864–1950) was from St. Georges, Kings County.
14. Pat Doucette, personal interview, Nov. 9, 2006, PEIFP Interview #29.
15. Island fiddlers use the term *crooked* to refer to a tune that is difficult to play or requires unusual or contorted fingering. Within the contemporary Appalachian fiddling revival, however, the term *crooked* has been commonly employed to refer to tunes with irregular meters; in recent years that usage has also been adopted by the participants of several other contemporary fiddling revivals.
16. These sentiments echo almost exactly the advice once given in remote parts of Scotland to novices by veteran fiddlers: "[N]ever lose time by trying to get in a note—the dancers won't notice if you leave it out" (Flett and Flett, *Traditional Dancing in Scotland*, 47).
17. Wareham ("Ethnography of 'Times,'" 438) mentions the "rule of three," which seems apt here. When someone known as a singer was asked to perform for the company, they were expected to decline twice but accept at the third invitation.
18. Kevin Chaisson, personal interview, June 22, 1992.
19. Weale, "No Scope," 5.

PHOTO 4.3. FRANCIS MACDONALD AT MONTICELLO HEADQUARTERS, JULY 1991 (PHOTO BY EARTHWATCH TEAM).

CHAPTER FIVE
"That's the Way We Had to Learn"

As implied by the previous chapter's discussion of musical gifts, there are three components to the fiddling art—absorbing and remembering tunes, translating them to the instrument, and developing the requisite physical skills to properly interpret them. There was no set path to learning to play the fiddle on Prince Edward Island. There were no rules, no formal instruction, no organizations to oversee progress. Somehow those youngsters who felt drawn to the instrument had to find a way to acquire their playing skills and initial repertoire.

Certainly, the general pattern was to get started quite young. Fully one-fourth of the fiddlers interviewed for the 1991–92 project had taken up the instrument by the age of eight, the median age for getting under way was about ten, and roughly four-fifths had begun by age fifteen. The experience of Attwood O'Connor of Milltown Cross, Kings County, was not uncommon: "I started to play about six, seven year old. I know I couldn't put the fiddle under my chin and reach the neck with my left hand. I had to set it up on my shoulder; that's the only way I could reach it." Similarly, Teresa MacPhee

Wilson (b. Monticello, Kings County) recalls the beginnings of her brother George MacPhee's fiddling career.

> We knew George was going to be a fiddler because he could come around [jig] those tunes so well when he was very, very little. And Dad made a little fiddle for him out of a shingle, and he was sittin' on a little bench that he had here and he was [making like] playin'. And that went on until he got big enough to start to play a real fiddle. And George could play the fiddle very good when he wasn't any more than five or six, and he was still sitting on his little bench.

Those youngsters who waited until well into their teen years or later to attempt the instrument were for the most part from nonfiddling households. Consequently, they had more difficulties to overcome in getting under way.

What drew youngsters to the fiddle? Part of the answer stems from the fiddler's high visibility in community life. Just as the fireman's colorful presence in many North American communities leads some youngsters to fantasize about following in his footsteps, so too did the fiddler's salient role as the center of the entertainment have a similar effect on Island youngsters. Merlin Quinn of Cardross, Kings County, puts it this way:

> Oh, the fiddler was the king in my day! If you could only play the fiddle or squeak a tune at all, you were something, you were really something. To play the fiddle, somebody who'd come in that could play the fiddle, they were treated like a king.[1] It just simply seemed to me to be the thing to be able to do. It was so great! I could whistle and I could jig, and I could sing and so could my father, who as I said was a good singer but he couldn't play. And I thought if you could only put one of them tunes on here [*points to the fiddle*], what a great thing it would be! Even if it was a song or two, it would be so great!

Most youngsters who ultimately became successful fiddlers, however, were inexorably drawn to the instrument itself: both to its sound and to the kind of expression possible on it. In essence, this fits in quite neatly with the notion of fiddling as divine gift or calling.

> Ever since I could even remember hearing music, I loved the sound of the violin. Whatever there was about it I don't know, but I remember waking up at night when I was a very small child, and hearing the fiddle music. There'd be probably a fiddler or some musicians come in to my father's place. They'd have a session, and I liked the music. (Francis MacDonald: Morell, Kings County)

> I'd be walking up to me grandfather's and I'd be passing this house, and I'd hear the violin going. I'd stand, I'd listen. I wouldn't go in, but I'd just stand out in the yard and listen to the music. It sounded good to me! So that's how I got to be kind of interested in the violin. (Johnny Morrissey: b. Newtown Cross, Queens County)

> Violin music I was always attracted to; I liked it. When I got a chance to go to a square dance with my cousin, I would go and sit on the corner of the stage and listen to the fiddler all night. I would not move. Scared I'd miss something! (Sterling Baker: Montague, Kings County)

Nearly every male who was drawn to fiddle music in this way took a stab at playing the violin.[2] Playing fiddle tunes on other instruments was done, but it was looked upon as something of a curiosity. Even the language used to describe the two acts is different. You "play the tune" on fiddle, but you merely "play the tune *right out*" on other instruments like piano, guitar, mandolin, or flute. The implication here is that practitioners on keyboard, fretted, or wind instruments can produce a musically correct, recognizable version of a tune, but only when the melody appears on fiddle does it retain its essence and heart. Even today, adept players of fiddle music on other instruments are generally consoled with remarks such as, "You know, *you* could play the fiddle!" And Joe Kearney of Sturgeon, Kings County, had this to say about the efforts of our Earthwatch research team:

> You fellows goin' around lookin' for music can't help but learn to play the fiddle. Because you should! If you got the music in you, and you're pickin' it out, and writin' it down, and tapin' it there, and looking through that [video camcorder]—Let me tell you that there's no reason why you shouldn't learn. No trouble to play the fiddle!

"My Father Used to Chip Fiddles out of a Cedar Shingle"

As implied in chapter 3, for many youngsters the very first stage of playing took the form of pretend-fiddling. In its most basic form, this involved using "two pieces of stick" to simulate fiddle and bow in the manner previously described by Ervan Sonier. Beyond this, some families would provide their offspring with a fiddle-shaped toy to offer a feel for the instrument. The most common such toy was a two-dimensional fiddle-shaped surrogate cut from a wood shingle, supplemented by a toy bow carved from a block of scrap wood. Here's how Wilfred Gotell of Georgetown, Kings County describes them:

> My father worked in a lumber factory there in Georgetown, and he used to bring home little pieces of hardwood. So I'd make my own bow [hair] out of white thread. You can imagine my mother had a hell of a job keepin' white thread on the go, eh. It would be a little bow about that long [*indicates about six inches*], and that'd do the trick. My father used to chip fiddles out of a cedar shingle. And then we'd wrap the white thread around them for strings, fasten it, and get a piece of wood and put it

in for a bridge. My brothers and I'd think we were doing good, playing along with him on our shingles when he'd be playing the tune on fiddle. I'd say I was about five at the time.

Francis MacCormack (b. St. Charles, Kings County) notes that with a bit of ingenuity these fiddle surrogates could be improved to the point that real music could be coaxed out of them. In his family, youngsters used sturdy No. 12 black thread for strings, and for resonance they tied an empty sardine can firmly onto the back of the shingle. For a bow, they sharpened a stick lengthwise and rubbed spruce gum or rosin along the point. According to MacCormack, the result had "quite a ring to it; it was next door to a Strad!"[3]

Other fiddlers mentioned different fiddle toys. Lenie Bolger (b. Lot 11, Prince County), for example, notes that his first violin was made from a cigar box.[4] Jimmy O'Connor of Murray Harbour, Kings County, reports that a neighbor fashioned him a makeshift instrument by putting a violin bridge on a ukulele. And when Fr. Charles Cheverie of Charlottetown was a young boy, he got a tin fiddle that handled pretty much like the real thing.[5]

"I'd Get the Tune into Me Head"

Most fiddlers report that even before they first came to pick up the instrument, they already had a substantial stock of tunes committed to memory. They were exposed to these tunes as a part of growing up in the old Island districts, and—before they were even aware of making an effort—the tunes had stuck. In terms of process, the important point is that the music exists first in the mind of the player. Only afterward does he or she make the attempt to play it on the violin. Joe MacDonald of St. Andrews, Kings County, puts it this way:

> I'd get the tune into me head and then express it on the fiddle. By the time I was old enough to get hold of a fiddle, me head was full of music then. For everything I heard stayed there, and I had no trouble—I had all kinds of music to express on the fiddle out of me head.

The most important source for these budding players' initial stock of tunes was the fiddling or "jigging" they heard in their homes or surrounding community. As Johnny Morrissey describes it, "I had tunes in me head at the time when I was quite young, just from listening to people singin' or jiggin' or whatever." Similarly, Zélie-Anne Arsenault Poirier (b. Abram-Village, Prince County) observes, "I'd heard so many tunes you wouldn't believe: my head was full of them there. You just hear them once, and if it was played long enough you just pick it up." Similarly, Leonard McDonald of Emyvale, Queens County, states,

> My mother and father didn't play. But a lot of these old tunes—The first tune I played there was my mother's favorite tune, it was "The Flowers of Edinburgh."[6] And when we'd be kids sitting on her knee she'd jig these tunes to us, and that's where we learned them. She knew an awful lot of tunes, like. She could jig nearly any tune. And those tunes came right from the old country.

Although youngsters born to musical households had a distinct advantage in acquiring their first tunes, those not so blessed were often able to learn tunes by absorbing the music emanating from the homes of neighbors.

> Now out in Millburn where my mother was born, there was fiddlers lived on either side. There was one house on one side and there was three fiddlers, and on the other side there was four fiddlers. One family's name was Boxton, the other family was Guilfoy. So she heard music from when she was yay high [*holds palm a few feet above the floor*], and it just came natural to her. (Cosmas Sigsworth: b. Corraville, Kings County)

> My [future] brother-in-law was living right next door, and he was a fisherman. He was playing fiddle then, but we were eleven in the family, eh. My mother says, "You don't go in there now, it'll bother the neighbors." He'd get home from fishing and go in the house, and he'd start playing. And I put my ear right against the shingles on the outside of the house and tried to get something out of it. (Dennis Pitre: St. Felix, Prince County)

Because of all this exposure, youngsters would be jigging their first tunes long before they got their hands on a fiddle.[7]

> You were brought up on that. You could jig reels and jigs, and whistle them when you were five or six year old. And when I was real young, me father used to send me to neighbors, they had a gramophone, and I could learn tunes and come home and whistle for him to learn them: even before I went to school. You had the tunes already, you knew the tunes. (Emmett Hughes: Dromore, Queens County)

> I was no more than six or seven. Dad used to [be] down in the evening in the front room and playin' the fiddle. And of course, I'd saunter down with my two sticks and I'd sit down beside of him. He'd play the fiddle, and I got where I used to jig the tunes [with him]. And I learned all the tunes that way. Every tune he could play, I could jig the tune. (Omar Cheverie: Souris, Kings County)[8]

To sum up, then, youngsters such as Omar Cheverie, George MacPhee, Ervan Sonier, and countless others were capable at a very early age of imitating the

PHOTO 5.1. DENNIS PITRE AT ST. FELIX, AUGUST 1996 (PHOTO BY KEN PERLMAN).

motions of playing on their toy instruments, while tapping their feet like a fiddler and simultaneously jigging relatively complex fiddle tunes virtually note for note.

"You Lived Dangerously if You Took the Fiddle"

The next step was to get consistent access to a real instrument. If there was no fiddle already in the home and none could be begged or borrowed from friends or relations, a youngster might have to wait months or years until a sufficient amount was saved to purchase one. Sometimes a bit of ingenuity helped short-circuit the process. For example, at age twelve Dennis Pitre found a fiddle in a catalog priced at about twenty dollars; to get that amount he gathered roughly two thousand empty bottles and turned them in for a bounty of one cent each.[9] And when Herb MacDougall (b. Bangor, Kings County) was about ten, he pieced his first fiddle together from bits he found in a case lying in the attic.[10]

In contrast, the primary challenge for children from fiddling households was to establish that they were sufficiently responsible to be entrusted with the family instrument. After all, as Teresa Wilson points out, fiddles were easy to damage or put out of adjustment, and accessories were costly or inconvenient to replace.

> My father was very, very strict with the fiddle. It was Depression time, and it wasn't easy to buy rosin or it wasn't easy to buy strings, so you had to be very good and very able to handle the situation pretty well before you'd be allowed to have the fiddle. When Mom would be home alone with us, I'd plead with her to let me have a try at it. She'd give it to me, and she'd warn me not to grease the bow. And I never could figure out this "grease the bow" thing till I grew up, 'cause I thought you'd have to rub grease on it.[11] I'd say, "I'm not going to put any grease on the bow." But you lived dangerously if you took the fiddle. You'd make sure you'd rosin that bow before you put it back, because Dad would know right away that you had it.

Since fiddling parents were generally reluctant to allow access to the family fiddle, it often required an act of relatively courageous initiative for youngsters to get started. In one common pattern, the child would grab the instrument on an occasion when the fiddling parent was out of the house, and—after much "squawking"—succeed in getting a tune or two out of it. This accomplishment was then unveiled, the parent would be pleased, and from then on the child was allowed to play.[12] Following are a few fiddlers' stories that more or less fit this vignette.

> My father wouldn't leave me take the fiddle, so I'd sneak it. When I'd see him coming, I put the fiddle away. But one day he caught me. I was playing a tune, not too bad. So he give me a growling first about taking the fiddle: "Your father told you not to take that fiddle!" After a while he said, "Try that again." I tried the tune, so after that I could take it, with his permission, of course. (Andrew Jones: Pleasant View, Prince County)

> One day when my father and mother went to town, I decided it was a good time to try the fiddle. So I took it out and I decided I should try to tuning it. So right off the bat I broke a string. That didn't go very good. When my father come home that evening, he went to play the fiddle and there was a broken string on it. So he asked me, "Did you have this fiddle out today?" and I said, "Yes," and he said, "What were you trying to play?" I said, "I thought I'd try to tune it first." "Yeah," he said, "that's a pretty good way to start." Then he said, "Here put a string on," and he said, "Here, put it in tune." I had quite a battle with it, and he wound up putting it in tune for me. So I started from there. (Reuben Smith: Blooming Point, Queens County)

> [One] morning my father get up, hitched the horse and the sleigh, and once he went over the hill I knew he couldn't come back too quick. And my mother had a

big wash out, and she was taking it out to the clothesline, and I knew by the size of it she was going to be out there for a while. So I pull out my father's fiddle and started playing on it, and by gosh I was gettin' a few little things on it. At dinnertime one of my [older] brothers come in, and I said, "You know I had my father's fiddle out this morning, and I was pickin' a few tunes out on it." He said, "You were? Let's hear it." I got this fiddle out and I started playing it, and he thought it was just great. I had a sister that could play the pump organ some, so she got on the pump organ and we started playin' some of those tunes. So that night when my father come home, [she and I] went in the living room—there was no lights and no electricity, see, and no heat in it—and got the fiddle out, and we started playin'. First thing, the door opened, and my father stuck his head in just grinnin' from ear to ear. (Jim MacDougall: Grand River, Prince County)[13]

In some families, access to the family instrument was forbidden because a parent did not want the youngster to face a fiddler's lifestyle (more on this in chapter 8). As Kevin Chaisson of Bear River, Kings County, recounts, such opposition was not always successful.

Grandpa didn't want any of the boys in that family playing fiddle. And the reason [for] that was because Grandpa used to be around playing for weddings, getting home when the sun would be coming up in the morning. He just out and told 'em, he said, "I don't want you fellows to see as many sunrises as I have." And this is why he didn't want Daddy to play, he didn't want any of the boys to play. But my grandmother, she used to jig all those tunes. She'd jig tunes to my uncle Peter and Daddy.[14] Matter of fact, if I'm not mistaken, my father was playing for a [square] set before my grandfather even knew that he played the fiddle! But when Grandpa seen that there was nothing he could do, my father was playing the fiddle then. And every one of the boys played, except one.

In other cases, parents played favorites, giving some children easy access to the fiddle, while denying others that privilege. Danny MacLean (b. Garfield, Queens County), for example, notes that because of such family dynamics he did not have an opportunity to learn until as a teenager he left home and went to work in the lumber woods of New Brunswick. Another object of parental disfavor was MacLean's brother Clarence. He stayed home and managed to sneak the fiddle sufficiently to learn to play. Because he was always looking over his right shoulder to see if the coast was clear, however, he developed the lifelong habit of playing with his head cocked to the right, and his fiddle braced well to the right of the breastbone.[15]

It should be mentioned here that even after a novice had acquired the right to use the family fiddle, access to it might still be fairly limited. Few households had more than one or two fiddles on hand, and family members would have to take turns practicing. Sometimes this was a fairly orderly process, as in this case reported by Stephen Toole of Green Road, Queens County:

> It wasn't very much a problem. Maybe my father would play for a while after supper, then I would play after a while, probably after I'd finished learnin' my lessons at night. And then my brother would play. We wouldn't be all playing' together.

In other households, however, getting hold of the fiddle was more of a free-for-all. Frank O'Connor of Kildare Capes, Prince County, for example, tells this story:

> We had a family of ten children, and everybody played. In the hard times in the thirties, we had about one mouth organ, an old pump organ that was pretty wheezy, and one fiddle my dad played. And at first he wouldn't allow any of the rest of us to touch it for fear if we broke it we wouldn't have another one. But it used to be a scramble for the ten of us. [Question: How was it decided who got to play?] Oh, devious methods throughout!—You'd kinda fool somebody into thinking you were goin' outside, but you went down in the front room and grabbed the fiddle and played a tune. That type of thing.

Youngsters from nonfiddling households also had to sort out a few logistical issues before they could actually get down to playing. They were often shy about asking questions of established players, and even when questions were asked, the ensuing responses were often less than completely satisfying. Fred Richard (b. St. Peter and St. Paul, Prince County), for example, reports that when he first tried to draw a bow across the strings nothing happened. He asked around and was told that to make the strings sound he needed rosin. So down he went to the general store and asked for some. What they sold him was a five-pound bag of resin meant for waterproofing boats. It did the trick, but the quantity was so great that in 2006 at age seventy he still had some of that original supply left.[16] Similarly, after Herb MacDougall had succeeded in reassembling the fiddle he found in the attic, he noticed that the bow stick had nothing attached to it.

> I said, "What goes in this?" They said, "It's usually hair from a white stallion." So I was thinkin' to myself, "We have a black stallion, and the color probably wouldn't matter." And, of course, instead of askin' [my parents] to go out and take some hair from his tail, and he had a long tail; it'd be a twelve-hundred-pound horse— He was standing, and his tail was close to the edge of the stall. I reached in and grabbed a bunch of hair from his tail. And of course he kicked and that. It was a dangerous thing when I think back, 'cause I was only nine or ten then. I just ripped

it out of his tail; I had to do it quick! So, anyway, I didn't have enough. It took me about a week or two before that horse would be in that position again. So I did it again. And got enough [hair], at least to partially fill the bow.[17]

"I Learned Just by Watching Somebody Else"

There was very much of a sink-or-swim attitude toward learning music on Prince Edward Island. Johnny Joe Chaisson of Souris, Kings County, for example, recalls that his father demonstrated "how to tune the fiddle. Then he said, 'There, you're on your own!'" Omar Cheverie reports that the advice he got amounted to, "Here's the fiddle, and the bow. Now if you're going to be able to play the fiddle you're going to have to learn it yourself."[18] Similarly, Tony Smith (b. Tracadie Cross, Queens County) reports that well-known fiddler Bill Weatherbie from Charlottetown offered to help his son George out with a few pointers, but only if the latter could first figure out on his own how to work the bow.[19] Three major factors contributed to this state of affairs: the notion that fiddling was a gift, logistics created by large family size, and the lack of any coherent teaching tradition.

As noted earlier, fiddling was considered to be a gift that an individual either possessed or lacked. If a youngster had the gift, he or she would find a way to learn; if he or she did not, there was nothing to be done about it. This attitude applied not only to the art as a whole but also, as Merlin Quinn notes, to the specific skills involved.

> I don't know anybody can teach you how to bow. I guess you can improve, the same as you can improve with your fingers. You're only blessed with so much. If you have fingers that are big and kinda stiff like mine, all you can do is try to train them to do the best you can with what you've got. But you can't compete with somebody that's got better fingers. Same thing with the bow. If you have a stiff bow, you can train it and do the best you can with it, perhaps by making up the difference with real good fingers. You do the best you can with what you've got.

Next was the issue of family size. In a typical Island household with a dozen or more children in residence, it was difficult for any one child to command sufficient parental focus to become the object of concentrated teaching. Robert Arsenault (b. Abram-Village, Prince County) sums it up as follows:

> Whoever had a talent to pick things up picked it up. You just fended for your own self and developed your own skills, you know. Just picture this: there was fourteen kids there, right? I don't know how much individual attention you figure parents

PHOTO 5.2. ROBERT ARSENAULT AT MEADOWBROOK, OCTOBER 2006 (PHOTO BY KEN PERLMAN).

can give to anybody. This is survival of the fittest! So I guess at a very young age people fend for themselves. They're out there harvesting and planting, and fishing, and doing whatever has to be done.

Along these lines, youngsters' learning often went on under the radar, and it was entirely possible to become a fairly adept player without one's family being aware of it. Francis MacCormack, for example, tells this story:

They came home from the army once, my three oldest brothers, and of course a little bit of moonshine was flowin' around. My older brother says, "It's funny Francis don't play the fiddle," and I'm just on pins and needles, just dying for the fiddle, eh. "Oh, no," my dad says, "I never heard him." He didn't, either. And I piped up; I said, "I can play." My dad looked at me and said, "You can?" And I said, "Yep!" And my brother says, "Give him the fiddle." I took the fiddle like a piece of bread, boy, molasses and all, and I let 'er go. My Dad's eyes opened up. "Holy cow," my brother says, "boy, can he ever play!" I had a great time, then.[20]

Finally, there's the issue of instruction. In short, fiddlers had no idea how to go about teaching a youngster to play. For the most part, they played by instinct with little concern for the fine points of technique. The important thing for them was what came out of the instrument—the power, rhythm, and tone of the music—not what went into it. After all, it was liveliness that made people want to get up and dance, not technically superior styles of bowing or noting.

Much of the instruction that was available on the instrument centered on teaching the notes to particular tunes. As Attwood O'Connor and Stanley Bruce tell us, although getting a fiddler to repeat a tune for you was easy, getting them to demonstrate how they went about playing it was quite another story.

> BRUCE: That was the basic problem. The fiddlers didn't know how to show, they didn't know how to teach. If you asked them to play any kind of a tune, they'd play it for you and let you watch them, play it over and over half the night for you if you wanted them to. But they couldn't—They didn't know how to teach you.
>
> O'CONNOR: They didn't know how to go about teaching. I wouldn't myself. I wouldn't have a clue how to go about teaching anybody to play the fiddle, not a clue.

Most Island youngsters, therefore, learned their fiddling skills by watching, observing, and emulating accomplished fiddlers in the family or community.[21]

> I learned just by watching somebody else. You sat just as close as you could to who was playing the fiddle and watch what he was doing, and try and learn. That's the way we had to learn. (Jimmy Banks: Poplar Point, Kings County)

> I used to watch the other fiddlers. Like when I'd get a chance to go anywheres where anyone was playing, and I'd be a-watchin' them and listenin'. I really was terribly interested in it! (George MacPhee)

Along these lines, when Wilfred Gotell wanted to learn how to note, he would "try to watch [his] father's fingers, where they went on the strings." Similarly, when "Old Peter" Chaisson of Bear River, Kings County, wanted to learn to hold the bow, he watched his "father and the other old fiddlers"; he said, "I just figured that was the way it should be held and that was it!"

The process of acquiring fiddling skills was not entirely ad hoc, however. To begin with, as reported by Jimmy Banks, "If you asked the older fiddlers for some information, they'd tell you: the right way to tune the fiddle, and how to handle the bow, and [to] try to loosen up as much as you can." Similarly, in the following account, Dennis Pitre may lament the absence of instruction, but with a little initiative he was able to get the basic assistance he needed to get under way:

> I think I was around twelve years old when I finally got enough money to send for a fiddle. Then I couldn't tune it. So I had a cousin that used to play, and he was fishing. Him and his father, they'd come down in a horse and wagon. And I'd wait till about two o'clock in the afternoon. They'd be goin' home, so I'd run to the gate to the road with the fiddle. And the old feller would stop the horse, and I'd give it to his son. He'd tune the fiddle in the wagon there. Back in the house and try! But nobody ever showed me anything. You just had to pick it up on your own by yourself.

Some fiddling parents would make the effort try to pass on a few pointers to their offspring. In one oft-reported pattern, a parent would hold the fiddle and produce appropriate noting changes on the fingerboard, while the youngster operated the bow. In this way the child was able to get the experience of bowing a tune without having to worry about pitch or fingering. Since this process required very close contact and coordination between parent and child, these lessons were often remembered by the latter with great fondness.

> First off, I'd sit on my father's knee, and he held the fiddle. And he worked the fingers while I worked the bow. So I could get an idea about it. That's what was the start of it. (Roland Jay: Mount Stewart, Queens County)

> My father used to take the fiddle, and he'd play the tune with the fingers, and I'd take the bow, eh. I used to stand in front of him and take the bow, and work it up and down. He'd play the left hand, and I'd play the bow. (George MacPhee)

Another area where parents might offer assistance was rudimentary noting.[22] Hilda MacPhee MacDonald (b. Selkirk, Kings County) recalls that her father assisted her progress by "showing [her] where to put [her] fingers to play the tune." Alternatively, as cited by Louise Arsenault of Mont Carmel, Prince County, tunes would be jigged or played slowly to the youngster on a phrase-by-phrase basis, while he or she tried to reproduce them by hunting for notes on the instrument.

> My father, he's the one that taught me a lot of tunes that I know today. I had a good ear, but he would have to tune me the tunes. He would tell me every note, because when I was smaller it was harder for me to learn. But as long as he would make the music to my ear I would pick up the music really quick.

Finally, youngsters might encounter parental instruction in the form of maxims designed to hasten his or her progress.

> My father told me, "Your biggest problem will be to coordinate your fingers and the bow." And it was. I'd get my fingers going, the bow would stop; I'd get the bow going and my fingers would stop. It took a while, but I finally mastered it. He also

> told me, "Just hold the bow with the thumb and [fore]finger, let your [other] fingers rest on the bow. Don't squeeze it, hold it light." (Attwood O'Connor)

> What my father did tell me was that most of the music wasn't the fingers. It was the bow, the way you handled the bow for the tunes, see. Some fiddlers have a better bow, a better arm, than others. A real good violin player, you watch his hand on the bow and the tune, the rhythm, there's where it's from. It's not the fingers. The bowing arm has to be loose, you see. (Joseph Doucette: Deblois Road, Prince County)

Youngsters from nonfiddling households often tried to find a local player to oversee their first steps. In some cases, as Merlin Quinn tells us, this involved assistance with specific skills.

> I got help from a neighbor who was living across the fields here named Art MacEachern. I had the tune in my head and I could hum it, but I couldn't figure out how to get it on the fiddle. I used to walk over to his place, and he helped me out with it. He just simply showed me the fingering.

Alternatively, such oversight from an adult fiddler might focus on repeating a tune sufficiently for the youngster to commit it to memory, as Alvin Bernard of Long River, Queens County, reports:

> My father couldn't play or my mother and grandmothers. My grandfathers on either sides couldn't play. I just liked old-time music, and I liked the fiddle. A fellow down the road there named Andrew Johnson could play, so when I was about twelve years old I bought a fiddle, and I asked him if he could teach me how to play. So I started taking a few lessons from him. It was just by ear. He'd play a tune and I'd try to follow him. The lessons were free, and I went for a couple of years, just more or less in the wintertime.

There was more to this kind of teaching relationship than tune repetition, however. While the older fiddler was playing, an enterprising youngster also had the opportunity to closely observe playing mechanics. If the novice had good visual memory, he would be able to bring these mechanics to mind later on and incorporate them into his own playing.

Some families were more proactive about their youngsters' musical progress. David Gaudet (b. Peter Road, Prince County), for example, tells us that an older brother would sometimes send him upstairs to learn a particular tune and not let him back down till he had mastered it.[23] According to Teresa Wilson, her parents tried to motivate her brother George MacPhee by raising the specter that without sufficient practice he might be overtaken in terms of progress by Marie MacIntyre, the young daughter of a family friend.[24] Finally, "Young Peter" Chaisson of Bear River, Kings County, reports that his father, Joe Pete, was quite insistent about enforcing a practice regimen for his sons.

> We used to have a back rink in the old house, and I'd be looking out the window watching them playing hockey and trying to concentrate on practicing the tune. And you didn't leave the house and play hockey until you practiced that tune and knew it. I resented it at the time when I was a kid, but [now] I enjoy the music, really love it!

"My Fingers Would Get Desperate Sore"

Once they were effectively launched, the next step for novices was trying on their own to find melodies on the fiddle. As Johnny Joe Chaisson observes, "I could jig the tunes all right, but it was to get them on the fiddle that was the hard part." Joseph Doucette describes the process.

> How'd I go about it? Go hide somewheres, so I wouldn't give my mother a headache. It's the same as learning a song. You have to get the air of it. Once you have the air of it, then try to place the fingers where they should go. And remember where the place was, see. That's why it takes a long while. Then once you have the hang of it, it's no problem then.

At this stage, the inevitable screeching cacophony that a new fiddler can produce sometimes tried family patience, as Archie Stewart of Milltown Cross, Kings County, reports.

> You drove everybody crazy tryin' to learn to play, and everybody persuaded you that you were making an awful racket. You didn't want to play in front of anybody. My mother used to ban me down in the livin' room. I'd run all the way home from school so I'd get a little spell to play the fiddle before I had to go out to do the chores around the farm. I'd grab the old fiddle and run down and shut the door, and get in there and saw away till supper was ready. You know there wasn't a rat or a cat or a dog left within a half mile; they all left!

But family members would rarely complain too vigorously. After all, as pointed out by Jimmy Banks, having another fiddler around meant there would be more house parties, benefit dances, and other community celebrations in the offing: "Oh, yeah, they always encouraged you to play, no matter how much noise you were making or how bad it was. They'd never tell you to put it away or anythin' like that, you know, because that'd only discourage you!"

Those who were ultimately successful at fiddling spent many long hours struggling with the process of learning to play. Many practiced as often as they could get their hands on a fiddle, their technique growing naturally as they mastered successively more difficult tunes.[25] As Dave Thomson (b. West Royalty, Queens County), reports, along with the drudgery came a feeling of excitement as each new hurdle was overcome, each new tune committed to memory: "I used to practice so much that my fingers would get desperate sore, so I'd just borrow mom's silk gloves and that would help. I'd be up at 5 o'clock in the morning playin' the fiddle. I just loved it!"

Most fiddlers report that once they got under way, their progress was quite rapid. Some were playing for dances within a few months of taking up the instrument. As Charlie Sheehan of Bear River, Kings County, observes, "I was about six months learning before I started to play at dances. It may not have been all that good, but they were dancing to it!" Many others were playing for dances within a couple of years. When there was a substantially longer incubation period, it was often more an issue of a fiddler's age than it was of his proficiency. In other words, the youngster might have become good enough to play for dances, but he was not yet allowed out at night. As Jimmy Banks points out, "At nine years old we didn't get around them days like young people do now. And if there was a dance anywheres, you were lucky enough just to get to go to it."

Quite often, a youngster's first experience playing for dances came in the form of being thrown into the breach as an emergency substitute. According to Jackie Webster of Cardigan, Kings County, his father, Jack Webster, was only twelve when he played for his first dance: "The fiddler at a local house party became drunk and couldn't play any more. Our father as young as he was finished out the set."[26] Similarly, George O'Connor of Kildare Capes, Prince County, tells this story:

> I think the funniest thing was the first dance I played for, only eight or nine years old. The fiddler doesn't show up, they tell you to play! All you could play was "Red Wing" or "Cock of the North."[27] Your knees are going like a jackhammer. Pete Ned was supposed to come and play, and he didn't show up and they gave me the fiddle.

As for Jim MacDougall, his first call came at age sixteen when two men appeared on his doorstep late one night after he had already gone to bed.

> There was a dance in the hall in Grand River and there was no fiddler. Somebody knew that I could play three or four tunes, and they thought if my father would let me go, they could get me. So they came up with the horse and sleigh, that's about two and a half miles. And I remember my father comin' up the stairs to my bedroom and askin' me if I wanted to go down and play for a dance at the Grand River Hall. Boy, boy, I was just all aglow! So I get up, get dressed, grabbed the fiddle, and away I went down. Of course, it's just an old gas lantern hangin' in the center and an old wood stove, and no electricity, so you had no amplifiers: just one fellow with a guitar playin' that night. Just the two of us, we just sat back in the corner and played.[28]

"Whatever You're Trying to Play There, You're Not Playing It Right"

Although Islanders' general attitude toward acquiring fiddle technique may have been laissez-faire, the same can definitely not be said of their attitude toward repertoire. In fact, once youngsters had sorted out the initial problem of finding melodies on fiddle, older family and community members continued to coach and correct them on the trueness of the tunes they played. This coaching took two forms. First, as noted by Cosmas Sigsworth, if the youngster's memory was incomplete, an effort would be made to help to fill in the blanks.

> My mother knew all the older tunes. When I could get a little bit of a tune at a dance, all I had to do was bring it home to Momma. And I'd pester her all day until I got it. [Question: How did your mother teach you the rest of a tune?] She just hummed the tune; she was full of music!

Alternatively, as Jimmy Banks observes, if the youngster's memory was faulty, adults would sometimes intervene and make sure the tune was played correctly.

> Campbell's father was a good player, and of course he wouldn't play very much. But he'd be listenin' to us playin'. If we were makin' mistakes he'd stop us. He'd say, "Look, boys, whatever you're trying to play there you're not playing it right! You'd better do it right or else not learn it that way, or it'll be no good!" Oh, yeah, he'd notice we weren't playing the tune right, you know.

Children were not the only recipients of such tune coaching. When Edward P Arsenault of Wellington, Prince County, took up the instrument as an adult, for example, his wife, Marie—who had grown up in a musical family—assumed the responsibility for overseeing his progress.

> EDWARD: I was thirty-two years old when I started, and that's a bad mistake. My wife bought me the first fiddle, eh. What a mistake she made then! Oh, my God. It must have been five years before I learned to play a few tunes right. I'd be in my bedroom all by myself, and I used to start to play a tune. All of a sudden, I'd hear a knock at the door: "That's not the way that tune goes!" Then she'd start to tune it to me.
>
> MARIE: I did that for ten years, sittin' on the foot of the bed.
>
> EDWARD: She was very sharp. She's got a sharp ear. I'd hear a tune and then I tried it, but it wasn't all right. It was a few notes [wrong], you know. She'd hear that, so she'd come over and correct it.
>
> MARIE: I can't stand that. It's gotta be played right or not at all!

As was the case for these Arsenaults, in some families one individual became the resident authority on tune correctness. According to Teresa Wilson, for example, "My mother knew the tunes really well: she could set my father straight on his tunes if he had any mistakes at all." In the home of Stewart MacIntyre (b. Fairfield, Kings County), his father was the musical authority.

> I built the first radio receiver that was in the eastern end of the country in 1922, and that was a sensation of course. One night I was listening to an orchestra in Philadelphia, and they announced that one of the leading violinists in the US was going to play an old Scotch tune. I called my father, and he came and put the headphones on, and he listened. When the feller was done, I said, "Do you know the tune?" "Yes, I do," he said, "but he wasn't playing it right!" And he wasn't, either. He was a classical violinist, and he couldn't play that old-time stuff right. My father knew every Scotch or Irish tune that ever existed. And a lot of the tunes I played in the early days, I learned from him. He used to jig them and I learned them.

In fiddling households with several musicians in residence, learning a new tune sometimes became a cooperative endeavor. As Teresa Wilson recalls, each family member would contribute whatever part of the tune he or she remembered, and a composite version would eventually emerge.

> We'd all be at it together, get it all down pat, and my father would play it. I remember yet the first time my father played the "Princess Reel."[29] A cousin of mine came here, and he played it on the pump organ. Well, I'm telling you! After he left, we all hammered at that tune until we got it. Then my father learned to play it on fiddle, and he made a good job of it, too. [Question: How did this work?] I'd remember one little bit. And they'd go over it and they'd say, "No, I think it's like this." Then we played it on the organ, and we tuned it, and we did everything until finally we had it.

Youngsters drawn to the fiddle had to figure most things out on their own: how to get hold of an instrument, how to manipulate bow and noting fingers, and how to translate music from mind to strings. Given the ad hoc nature of fiddle learning, it's no wonder that Islanders resorted to the catch-all notion of "giftedness" to explain the accomplishments of those who managed to thrive musically under this system. As we shall see in the next chapter, this sink-or-swim training method generally produced fiddlers with independent musical visions and highly honed musical memories.

NOTES

1. As noted in the previous chapter, such privileged treatment for fiddlers generally lasted no longer than the events where they played. By way of analogy, more or less the same thing might have been said of professional baseball players prior to the days of free agency, but this did not stop countless North American youngsters from seeking to emulate them.
2. For females the situation was more complex; see chapter 7.

3. Francis MacCormack, personal interview, Oct. 15, 2006, PEIFP Interview #02. A Strad, short for "Stradivarius," is a violin made by the famous Italian luthier Antonio Stradivari (1644–1737), whose instruments are generally considered to have great richness of tone.
4. Cornelius "Lenie" Bolger, personal interview, August 12, 1999.
5. Fiddling toys have also been reported elsewhere. Using two sticks or bits of kindling for fiddling-play has been noted in Cape Breton (Garrison, "Traditional and Non-traditional Teaching," 146). In Newfoundland, fiddler Emil Benoit started on a wood-shingle fiddle (Quigley, Music from the Heart, 9). Cigar-box fiddles were used in West Virginia and Alabama, while tin fiddles have been noted in Cape Breton, Alabama, and Ireland. See Mac Aoidh, Between the Jigs, 33; Cauthen, With Fiddle, 51, 108; Garrison, "Traditional and Non-traditional Teaching," 146; and Milnes, Play of a Fiddle, 127.
6. "The Flowers of Edinburgh" is a classic Scottish tune, dating to the eighteenth century. For its early publishing history, see Gore, Scottish Fiddle Music Index, 37.
7. Cauthen writes (in With Fiddle, 45–47) that in Alabama the offspring of some fiddling families could "hum or whistle a number of fiddle tunes before they even picked [a fiddle] up."
8. Omar Cheverie, personal interview, Nov. 26, 2006, PEIFP Interview #59.
9. Dennis Pitre, personal interview, Nov. 9, 2006, PEIFP Interview #28. As an aside, in the 1970s when Pitre's arthritis forced him to give up fishing at a relatively early age, he took over the local bottle-redemption business.
10. Herb MacDougall, personal interview, Nov. 20, 2006, PEIFP Interview #47. His father had once played but had given up the instrument years before MacDougall was born.
11. Getting sweat or food residue on bow hair, referred to here as "greasing the bow," would block its ability to absorb rosin, which in turn would make getting sound out of the strings more difficult.
12. Having to "sneak" the fiddle because parental misgivings has been frequently reported in other fiddling cultures. See, for example, Milnes, Play of a Fiddle, 42, 127; and Cauthen, With Fiddle, 48–49, 83.
13. Jim MacDougall, personal interview, Nov. 22, 2006, PEIFP Interview #52.
14. Kevin Chaisson's father is Joe Pete Chaisson; the uncle referred to is "Old Peter" Chaisson.
15. Clarence MacLean, personal interview, Oct. 27, 2006, PEIFP Interview #17. Ordinarily, a right-handed fiddler would brace the fiddle on the left side of the breastbone; see chapter 9.
16. Fred Richard, personal interview, Nov. 7, 2006, PEIFP Interview #25.
17. Herb MacDougall interview, Nov. 20, 2006.
18. Omar Cheverie interview, Nov. 26, 2006.
19. Tony Smith, personal interview, Nov. 24, 2006, PEIFP Interview #56.
20. Francis MacCormack interview, Oct. 15, 2006.
21. This learning style seems to have been typical in British, Irish, and North American fiddling cultures. See, for example, Garrison, "Traditional and Non-traditional Teaching," 183–84; and Maloney, "Irish Music in America," 329.

22. Finding notes on the violin, which has no distinct markings or divisions to serve as guides, is a process that many beginners initially find quite daunting
23. David Gaudet, personal interview, Nov. 8, 2006, PEIFP Interview #26.
24. Teresa MacPhee Wilson, personal interview, Nov. 14, 2006, PEIFP Interview #37.
25. This parallels an observation by Garrison (in "Traditional and Non-traditional Teaching," 190) that for fiddlers technical improvements arose primarily "as byproducts of listening and observing undertaken in pursuit of [an expanded] repertoire."
26. Quoted in Hornby and Weyman, "Memories of Jack Webster," 3.
27. "Red Wing"—composed by Kerry Mills and originally published in 1907—has become a staple of the fiddling repertoire throughout North America. Many Island fiddlers reported that "Cock of the North," a Scottish jig first published in the 1820s, was the first tune they attempted to play.
28. Jim MacDougall interview, Nov. 22, 2006.
29. "Princess Reel" probably originated in New Brunswick in the 1920s; standard notation for the tune appears in Perlman, Fiddle Music of PEI, 46.

CHAPTER SIX
"I Could Bring What Was in My Mind Out on the Fiddle"

The formative musical experiences described in the previous chapter foster a style of learning that allows for the rapid, and seemingly effortless, assimilation of new tunes. This style of learning—far from turning the musical imagination into a passive sponge—is not only highly active but also far from neutral, in that it promotes faithful transmission of certain fundamental features of tunes while encouraging wide variation in detail. This tendency toward variation is then expanded by local attitudes that encourage fiddlers to experiment with and develop truly personal versions of the tunes they play, ultimately resulting in just about as many *twists* (takes) on any given tune as there are active fiddlers. Finally, the tune-recall mechanism not only explains how tunes spread and circulate among local fiddlers but also is fundamentally involved in the process by which new tunes enter the Island repertoire.

Fiddle playing on Prince Edward Island is based on a repertoire of dance melodies—reels, jigs, hornpipes, strathspeys, set tunes, marches, and waltzes—which collectively are known as *fiddle tunes* (for explanations of fiddle tune genres, see chapter 14). While fiddle tunes may not seem complex when compared to, say, orchestral music, nevertheless many of them have intricate melodies that are tricky both to play and to remember. Even so, many Island fiddlers report that at the height of their powers, they were able to absorb a completely new fiddle tune in just a few hearings. Archie Stewart of Milltown Cross, Kings County, observes, for example, "Back when I was younger, I could hear a tune probably twice and I could play it," while his neighbor Attwood O'Connor says, "There was one time I heard a tune twice and I had it: I could sit down and play it." Similarly, "Old Peter" Chaisson of Bear River, Kings County, asserts, "It came pretty simple to me when I think of it: just hear a tune a couple of times, eh, that was it!"

The fact is that most successful Island fiddlers established a personal style and strategy for learning tunes by ear quite early in the game. The initial stages have already been described: tunes heard frequently around the home or community were first absorbed into memory, jigged out loud, located on the instrument, and finally critiqued by input from family and community. From this early training, fiddlers developed the ability to quickly grasp and reliably express previously unfamiliar tunes. As Archie Stewart tells us, "You'd hear a tune that's catchy and it's going through your mind. I could pick up the fiddle and bring that tune out; I could bring what was in my mind out on the fiddle."

Styles of Tune Recall

An analysis of fiddlers' descriptions identified three styles of tune recall, which I term *conscious recall*, *subconscious recall*, and *visualization*. In all likelihood, all three styles are employed to some degree by all players, with the proportion of each varying among individuals.

No matter which recall style is operative, the process always begins with hearing a new tune played at a house party, frolic, benefit dance, or informal gathering or on the radio or gramophone. For assimilation to occur, the fiddler first has to be particularly attracted to the tune. As Bill Koughan of Donagh, Queens County, describes it, "When you hear another fiddler playing it and you like the tune, well, you'll learn it. If you hear something you don't like, you are not going to bother with it."

In conscious recall, the fiddler has the tune in mind immediately after its initial hearing. He or she then goes home and attempts to work out the melody.

> I could be on the floor dancing a set, and then a tune would come along that I took a liking to. I'd learn that tune. I'd have that one when I went home. And when I'd

get home, it would take me a little while to learn to pick it up on the fiddle. But before the night would be out, I'd have the tune and be able to play it. If I didn't like it, I wouldn't make no pass at it. (Charlie Sheehan: Bear River, Kings County)

In subconscious recall, the tune is somehow absorbed by the fiddler's mind. He or she cannot think of it immediately, but sometime later the tune resurfaces.

> The way I picked up tunes, I'd go to a dance, I'd hear a tune that I liked, I'd take particular notice to that tune. Then when I'd go home I'd go to bed, and the tune would be still floating around in me head. So perhaps in a week's time I'd think of the tune, and I'd start whistling it. It'd come to me like that! I don't know how it'd register: there, I guess, in me brain. And then it'd take that long for me to get it out, like. That's the way I found to learn a tune. (Johnny Morrissey: b. Newtown Cross, Queens County)

Along these lines, Jim MacDougall of Grand River, Prince County, reports that absorbed tunes would often spring to mind while practicing. He would be playing a familiar tune, suddenly think of a new one, and start playing it almost automatically: "It's like tellin' stories, eh, one leads to another; I think tunes are about the same way."[1]

For many fiddlers, the retrieval of such "absorbed" tunes was associated with awakening from sleep. This was a widely reported phenomenon. In almost every case, fiddlers report that if they did not make a dash for the instrument and try to play the tune on the spot, it was lost.

> Now some of the old fiddlers—Ward Crane used to say that he'd hear a tune. He'd go to bed and he'd go to sleep. He'd wake up at four o'clock in the morning, and he'd have every bit of that tune. He said he had to get up then and get the fiddle and play it. If he didn't, by the time he got his breakfast over it was gone. Now Otis Jackson, he said the same thing. He'd go to bed and this tune would be in his mind, and he'd wake up at three o'clock in the mornin'. He'd get up, went down to the livin' room, and picked up the fiddle and played that tune. He said if he didn't do it then, by the time he'd get up and got his breakfast, the tune would be gone. It seems that your subconscious mind brings it—It's there, and your subconscious mind brings it out. (Archie Stewart)

> I can hear a tune today and I won't have one turn [section] of it. But I'll go to bed tonight and get up tomorrow morning and take the fiddle and play it, the whole tune right through. That's the way I learn. It just hits me overnight. I've seen myself getting up at half past three and four o'clock in the morning, taking the fiddle, and going over a number. I don't know if I dreamt about it or if it shot through my mind or what. But anyway, in order to get it—If I didn't pick it up then, I'd miss it. (Gus Longaphie: Souris, Kings County)

A new tune could appear in mind just about any time. When this occurred in the middle of a workday, the fiddler was presented with a dilemma. Should he be "responsible" and continue with his tasks (in which case the tune might be forever lost) or drop everything and get out the fiddle?[2] John Cousins of Bloomfield, Prince County, tells how a fiddler from nearby Millburn named Guy Boulter (1895–1972) is said to have handled this situation.

> Guy would go to cut grain. Now, in order to cut grain you had to haul a binder. To haul a binder you needed three horses. A binder was the heaviest piece of machinery that was on the farm for horses to haul. It was quite a complicated maneuver to hitch a three-horse team. Anyway, they said Guy Boulter would, if he was out on the binder, he'd be out cuttin' grain, and a tune would be goin' through his head. He'd be thinking of this tune. It'd get to him so bad that he'd get off the binder, he would drive to the barn, he would unhitch the horses, and he would put them in the barn. And he would sit down and play that tune on the fiddle. He couldn't stop himself.[3]

Visualization is the process by which players of an instrument associate certain sounds with particular movements of the hands or fingers. For fiddlers, this involves the ability to associate a particular note with the position of a given finger on a particular string.[4] When a musician is able to visualize in this way, it helps him or her identify the notes of the tune as they go by. As Paul MacDonald of Charlottetown describes, "You know the sounds of certain fingers, what the tone is that the fiddle projects when[, for example], your third finger's playing on the E string instead of your second finger."

The reason that visualization is such an effective tool is that it so well anticipates the process by which tunes enter muscle-memory. As a tune is perfected, the sequence of sounds (or "notes," if you will) is translated into specific muscle movements. For some musicians, these specific movements are translated into a series of images that unfold as the tune progresses, each a split second before the corresponding maneuver is actually performed. For such musicians, these images are retained in mind as much as is the melody.

By watching and retaining the image of another's fingers operating during a performance, then, a fiddler can substantially streamline the process of memorization. In other words, he or she begins the process of translating the tune into muscle-memory before it is physically attempted. Archie Stewart describes the process as follows:

> If I was learnin' a tune there now, I'll learn the high part of that tune right quick. On the high turn of the tune, which I can hear real good on the sharp [high-pitched]

music, I can almost visualize where every one of his fingers was goin' when he was playin' that tune. But when he gets down on the low strings I can't do that, because my [poor] hearin' comes against me there. The sound tends to run together. I couldn't figure out where he was puttin' his fingers on the low strings. But if I sat down and watched him playin' then I'd get it, 'cause I'd watch where he put his fingers.

"Putting Your Own Twist on a Tune"

For most fiddlers, the initial tune-recall experience is often only the beginning of the process. To understand more fully how fiddlers proceed from these beginnings, the reader needs to understand a bit more about the structure of fiddle music. Most fiddle tunes have two sections, each four or eight measures long, which Islanders call the *low turn* and the *high turn*. The low turn generally centers on the lower strings of the fiddle, while the high turn moves up to the instrument's higher strings.[5] The highlight of each turn consists of one or more distinctive phrases, or *themes*. These themes are joined together by less distinctive bits of melody, which can be referred to as *secondary* and *connecting phrases*. Finally, each turn generally ends with a relatively generic bit of melody, known as a *cadential phrase*.[6]

When I discussed the recall process with fiddlers and compared transcriptions of their respective tune versions, it became clear that in general certain parts of fiddle tunes are remembered and reproduced more consistently than others. Specifically, those bits that are most salient or "catchy" tend to be transmitted relatively intact among players. Those bits of tunes that are less catchy or more generic, in contrast, are less consistently transmitted and tend to vary markedly from fiddler to fiddler. As noted above, variations among the tune versions of different fiddlers are known on Prince Edward Island as *twists*, and developing one's personal tune version is called *putting your own twist on a tune*. Here's how the process works.

The first stage of recall might bring only one "turn" to mind or even just one theme from a single turn. In this case, as George MacPhee of Monticello, Kings County, tells us, fiddlers hope that additional exposure will allow them to fill in the missing pieces.

> Sometimes you'd get the whole thing, and more times you'd get part of a tune. You'd be trying to get it, and you'd have to get ahold of somebody that could play the fiddle. And you'd find out from them, and see what way it went and try to get the rest of it.

Such filling in often required seizing the moment when a potential tune source came within range. Reg Banks of Poplar Point, Kings County, for example, tells this story:

> I learned the high turn of "Lord McDonald's Reel" from Jack Webster. He used to drive the mail through here: sixteen miles from here to Cardigan, with horse and sleigh in the winter, and horse and wagon in the summertime. Sometimes I'd take the violin out to the mailbox and meet Jack, and he'd play "Lord McDonald's Reel" for me; he'd take about five minutes of his time and play the tune. He must have had a pretty good nature to put up with it!

At the next stage, the fiddler has assimilated all the tune's major themes but still must fill in around them. In other words, musical phrases must be inserted between the themes to stitch them together, and a suitable ending must be found for each turn. There are three ways in which such phrases can be filled in. First, the fiddler directly emulates the secondary, connecting, or cadential phrases used by another musician. Second, the fiddler composes entirely new phrases (or reuses ones that he or she has previously composed for use in other tunes). Third, and this seems to be the most common pattern, the fiddler draws standard phrases, appropriate in terms of tune genre, key, and *mode*,[7] from a personal stock or "storehouse." In other words, over the course of a lifetime each fiddler acquires in memory a stock of "internal" phrases and endings, drawn from those in circulation among other fiddlers in the region. When assembling an initial version of a tune, he or she then selects the ones that first come to mind or seem to fit best.[8]

The end product of this kind of tune recall is often a pastiche of recently remembered and previously assimilated elements, all actively stitched together in the fiddler's musical imagination. Because the previously assimilated elements (that is, the connecting and cadential phrases) are either uniquely composed or selected from a large pool, each fiddler's tune version is well on its way toward becoming a unique twist right from the start.[9]

There is an interesting parallel here to styles of composition and recall that have been noted among tale-tellers and ballad singers in Europe and elsewhere in North America. The fiddler who uses a preexisting cadential phrase to finish off a turn, for example, finds an analogue in the bard who employs a stock verbal phrase—such as "her lily white hands" or "her raven black hair"—to finish off a line of poetry or round out a ballad stanza.[10]

Transcriptions of fiddlers' tune versions do show some variation in terms of themes, but most of these involve what might be termed "equivalencies"—

phrases that may differ from each other slightly in terms of notes or note sequence but for all intents and purposes create the same musical effect. For example, a note or two might be inserted or left out, a couple of adjacent notes might be interposed, a run of notes might proceed a little differently between the same origin and destination, an arpeggio might have notes in a slightly different order, and so on.[11]

Some musical examples that illustrate the phenomenon of twists in Island fiddling can be found in appendix A, examples 6.1–6.4.

- Example 6.1 shows twists on the high turn cadential phrase of "Lord MacDonald's Reel," as played by ten different Island fiddlers. For added perspective, the very last entry is from the well-known late nineteenth-century Scottish tune compendium, the *Skye Collection* (1887). A version of the entire turn appears as example 6.1a.
- Example 6.2 shows twists on the cadential phrase from the low turn of "Princess Reel," as played by ten different Island fiddlers. A version of the entire turn appears as example 6.2a.
- Example 6.3 depicts twists on a secondary/connecting phrase from the high turn of "Pigeon on the Gatepost," as played by ten different Island fiddlers. For added perspective, the very last entry shows the version of this passage from *O'Neill's Music of Ireland* (1903). A version of the entire turn appears as example 6.3a.
- Example 6.4 contains versions by ten different Island fiddlers of the main theme for the low turn of "Paddy on the Turnpike." For added perspective, the very last entry is from the classic work *Ryan's Mammoth Collection* (1883). A version of the entire turn appears as example 6.4a.

Understanding how tunes are assimilated allows us to more precisely define the Island concept of "true" playing (as discussed in chapter 4). The catchy themes of tunes can vary along certain lines, but only insofar as that variation does not fundamentally alter their character. Secondary, connecting, and cadential phrases, however, are essentially left to the discretion of the individual player.

Tune recall is far from foolproof. Even assuming that a tune's main themes have been faithfully assimilated, there is still much that can go awry, often resulting in "corrupt," or at least curious, tune variants. Here are some examples.

- The fiddler joins together low and high turns that were originally part of two separate tunes, resulting in a *hybrid variant*. Because both turns are intact, hybrids sometimes circulate in their own right—especially if the two original tunes were not widely known by local players.[12]
- The fiddler "recalls" a turn that joins together themes from what were originally two or more different tunes, resulting in what might be termed a *hybrid turn*. Twists with hybrid turns tend not to circulate on the Island and—when performed in public—often lead to declarations that a fiddler is "chopping up his tunes."[13]
- An episode that is perceived as tune "recall" actually leads the fiddler to unwittingly compose an entirely new theme or turn (more on this phenomenon later in the chapter). This can lead to a hybrid *turn* that is a composite of remembered and composed themes or to a hybrid *tune* in which one turn is remembered and the other is a product of the fiddler's musical imagination.
- The stitching-together process results in connecting or cadential phrases with too few or too many beats. Because the unusual number of beats makes them impractical to use for dance accompaniment, such variants tend not to circulate on Prince Edward Island.[14]

"After the Rough Work Is Done, You Gotta Put on the Trimming"

Adding to the growth of distinctive twists is the fact that many fiddlers continually tinker with their tunes, either to make them more playable or in hopes of improving their overall sound. Above all, as Eddy Arsenault of St. Chrysostom, Prince County, describes, artistic considerations are the main driving force behind the tinkering impulse.

> The more you play the tune, the more you can add on to it. The more you play it, the more you can add a few note here and there, a few strokes of the bow. It's like buildin' a house. After the rough work is done, you gotta put on the trimming, you got to do the finishing inside. But the fiddler's about the same thing, you see. You could play the piece with just the basic note, but you could also add some note on it to make it a little bit fancier. After a while, you put the extra note in there in

PHOTO 6.1. EDDY ARSENAULT AT ST. CHRYSOSTOM, AUGUST 1991 (PHOTO BY EARTHWATCH TEAM).

order to put the finishing touch on it. After a while when you got more practice, you add more note and more color to it.

One way in which fiddlers put "trim" on their tunes is by adding double-stops, grace notes, or other forms of *ornamentation* (see chapter 9). Another is by continually coming up with new twists on the various phrases of the tune. According to Jackie Biggar (b. Tyne Valley, Prince County), "It just comes to you as you're playing. You hear a note should be there, or maybe shouldn't be there. When you're home you'll think of it, then you try it and, 'God, that don't sound too bad!'"[15]

Fiddlers are continually borrowing twists from each other. When one player likes another's twist on a given phrase, he'll probably try to incorporate it into his own playing. According to Dennis Pitre of St. Felix, Prince County, sometimes the motivation stems from a feeling that the other fellow's twist may be "truer" than one's own: "I play the tune and I think I have it, and I get excited. I play it that way for quite a while. Then all of a sudden I hear the tune again from somebody. And I realize, 'Something in there's missing, something else is in the tune!' So I try and learn it." Alternatively, as Eddy Arsenault tells us, a fiddler may decide to adopt another's twist simply because it seems more interesting or esthetically pleasing than his own.

> Sometime a feller will put a certain twist onto a tune; I'll have a try at it 'cause it seems to sound a lot better. There's a tune here we call the "Princess Reel." I used to play it a little differently a while back, but now I change it a little bit. I heard a fellow play it another way and I liked it. So I twisted it around.

Looked at from the other side, when another player borrows your twist, that is seen as a form of personal validation, as Jackie Biggar observes:

> You know you're doing a good job when people start playing your tune the way you play it, 'cause that tells you that people want to listen to your playing. If you play a tune and you put your twist on it and nobody [else] does it, then you know you're not doing too good of a job. If you put your twist—If you put your own signature twist on a tune and, first thing you hear, somebody else is playing it, and next thing you hear, some other feller's got it, you know you've done your job.[16]

As the fiddler continues to play a given tune over time, he tends to accumulate multiple twists on one or more of its phrases. These various twists on the same phrase will then be used alternately on different repetitions of the tune, according to the whim of the musician. For example, Eddy Arsenault may have adopted that other fiddler's twist for a phrase of "Princess Reel," but the original twist still shows up every so often in his playing (both twists on "Princess Reel" are illustrated in appendix A, example 6.5).

The upshot here is that Island fiddlers rarely play a given tune exactly the same way twice. There are almost always little details that vary from repetition to repetition. Alvin Bernard of Long River, Queens County, tells us, "I don't think I play a tune every time the same way; I shift it every time I play it." Eddy Arsenault (with tongue firmly planted in cheek) describes the process as follows: "Well, sometime I add something on, something a little bit different here and there. It all depend how a feller feel. If a feller had two drink of rum, probably he'd put a little less thing in than if he have four drink of rum!"

"I Would Stick to the Way That I Played It"

Island fiddlers are far from apologetic when it comes to the issue of their own twists. To begin with, twists are seen in terms of personal satisfaction. In the words of Buddy Longaphie (b. Souris, Kings County), "You dress the tune up a little bit to suit yourself." Second, twists are looked at as a kind of musical brand that makes a particular version of a tune one's own. Finally, there is an implication in Island lore that twists flow inexorably from some aspect of the personality. As Allan MacDonald of Bangor, Kings County, puts it, "Your own twist is what comes out of the brain, you don't do it intentionally."[17] As a matter of personal integrity, then, Island fiddlers feel that there is no point in slavishly copying their colleagues' tune versions, despite being capable of doing so.

> Well, you're not just going to do it exactly as the other fiddler. [*Question*: Could you do so if you wanted to?] Well, yes. But every fiddler's got their own version of playing, and you're not just going to play it the same way as he does. You can pick it up in your own mind, and you're going to play it in your own mind, like. (Stephen Toole: Green Road, Queens County)

> Every fiddler is different, that's for sure! There's not one fiddler that plays the same as you. I would listen to Eddy Arsenault play, and I would learn one of his tunes, but I would play it a different way. Then later I would listen to him again and I'd think, "Oh, no, I learned it the wrong way!" But I wouldn't change; I would stick to the way that I played it. I just have my own way of playing tunes. And I imagine another fiddler would listen to my playing, and they wouldn't probably play that tune in the same way as I do, because they have their own style of playing. (Louise Gallant Arsenault: Mont Carmel, Prince County)

Equally at work here is the widespread notion that a musical world without fiddlers' twists would be dull indeed. As Alvin Bernard observes, "Every fiddler plays different, eh. Puts a few notes in or takes a few out. It's a good job they do, eh. If we all played the same there'd be no variety."

Along these lines, the relatively recent rise on the Island of fiddling societies whose members perform published, standardized versions of tunes has made some fiddlers more self-conscious about their twists than had previously been the case. Although most fiddlers are still proud of them, some nonetheless have begun to feel the need to justify their take on the music.

> I was talkin' to one old-time fiddler one day. I said, "I don't have a lot o' the tunes right." He said, "Who's right or who's wrong?" He said, "When you pick up the fiddle and play a tune," he said, "that's your rendition of that tune. That's the way you think that tune sounds the best. I pick up the fiddle, I play the same tune, I got a few little different twists." And he said, "That's my version of that tune." He said, "Every fiddler has his own version of each tune. This here 'playin' them exactly right,'" he said, "that's for the birds!" (Archie Stewart)

> My idea is whoever makes the tune sound the best—Hell with the [written] note, play it that way! All those people that put the music on paper, they're only human beings same as the rest of us. So if you can put a few little frills in a tune and it sounds better, sure, why not play it. So someone might say to you, "Well, that's not the way it's written down, eh." The heck with the way it's written down! I like it this way, and I'm goin' to play it this way. You got to stick your neck out a little bit sometimes. (Hugh Gotell: b. Georgetown, Kings County)

Such attitudes are probably not unique to Prince Edward Island and indeed may be endemic to many or even most oral-based fiddling cultures. As early as 1802, for example, the introduction to a well-known Scottish fiddle tune collection laments, "[W]e cannot avoid mentioning that in every part of Scotland where we have occasionally been, and from every observation we were able to make [we] have not once met with two Professional Musicians who play the Same notes of any Tune."[18]

"A New Tune Would Come into My Head"

The art of composing (the local term is *making*) new tunes has probably been widespread on the Island since its first days of fiddling, and many fiddlers we spoke to had made at least a tune or two over the course of their playing careers. In 1991–92, there were perhaps just a few fiddlers who could be described as serious tunesmiths. Bill MacDonald (b. North Lake, Kings County) had made a sufficient number of tunes to fill at least a couple of notebooks, while Emmett Hughes of Dromore, Queens County, was just about to publish *A Composition of Fiddle Tunes*, featuring nearly seventy original tunes.[19] Only two local composers—Edward P Arsenault (of Wellington, Prince County) and Kenny Chaisson (b. Bear River, Kings County)—had made tunes that were circulating to any extent among other players. By the mid-1990s, Kenny's brother Kevin Chaisson had begun to seriously apply himself to composing, and many of his tunes have since become quite popular. By 2006, there were at least a few dozen Islanders who were actively composing fiddle tunes, including a substantial contingent of younger players coming up through the fiddling revival (for more on local composing, see chapters 13, 14, and 17).

As some Island fiddlers describe tune making, its similarity to the process of subconscious tune recall is striking. In short, the new tune spontaneously springs to mind more or less in its entirety. As Bill MacDonald recounts, the fiddler then has to make a grab for his instrument, or the tune may disappear forever.

I've gotten up in the night. I would wake and couldn't get back to sleep, and a new tune would come into my head. And the only way that you can capture it is—I get up, close the door, get the violin, and put just a few bars of it on the tape recorder I have out there. Now, if you only get half, if you only get one turn, as we say, then the other half will come later. You can hear it coming, you know. Tuesday I went out to my daughter's cottage, twenty-five miles out. I was coming back in, and there was a beautiful tune going through my head. It's gone now; it may never come again. I whistled it all the way in, but when I got here I didn't have it![20]

Not all fiddle composing occurs in this manner, and in fact some students of the process mention other, more systematic approaches, such as allowing one's fingers to wander over the fingerboard in scale-like patterns until a pleasing basis for an opening theme is hit upon.[21] Regardless of the initial compositional method employed, coming up with a completed tune tends to involve the same process of assembly described above for recalled tunes. In other words, newly composed themes are generally stitched together with preexisting secondary, connecting, and cadential phrases.[22]

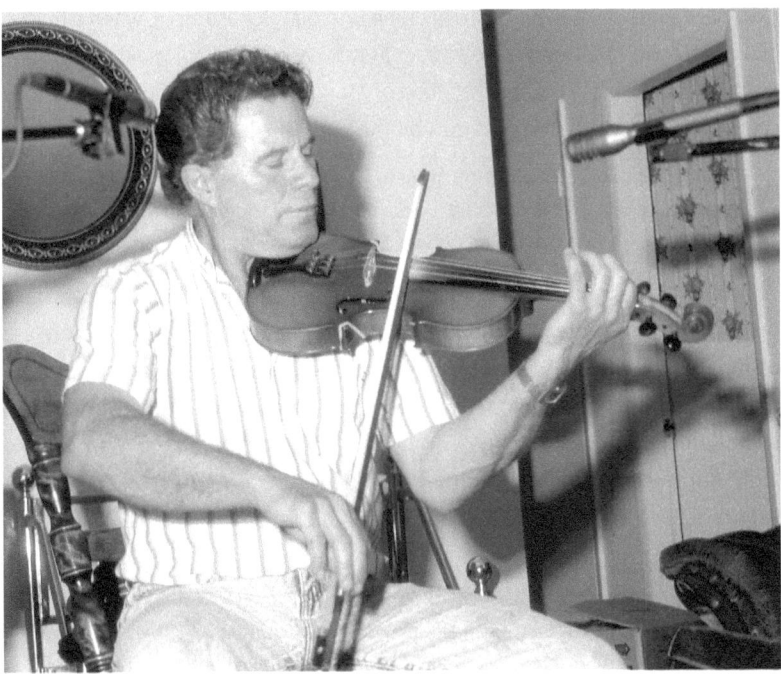

PHOTO 6.2. EDWARD P ARSENAULT AT WELLINGTON, AUGUST 1992 (PHOTO BY EARTHWATCH TEAM).

The psychological similarity between making and recalling also leads to the following dilemma. Does the tunesmith have a totally new tune in mind, or is he merely recalling one that has long lain dormant in the subconscious mind? Consequently, when a tune maker believes that he has come up with a new tune, virtually his first act is to ask friends and relations whether they have heard it before. For example, here's how Edward P Arsenault's wife, Marie, describes the moments immediately following the composition of his best-known tune:

> You came out and you asked me, "Is this a new tune?" And that's what you played, "The Acadian Reel." I really liked it, and I said, "Yes it is, and it is lively!" And you said, "But what are we going to call it?" I said, "That sounds right like Acadian music, so why don't you call it 'The Acadian Reel.'"[23] And that's how the name stuck.

This confusion between composition and recall can also be taken in another direction, especially when the moment of creation immediately follows sleep or some other not fully conscious episode. Specifically, the following question arises: was the new tune produced spontaneously by the awakener's imagination, or was it merely recalled after having been placed there by some external agent? Such a query might come into play, for example, when a fiddler claims to have "dreamed" a new tune. In this case, credit for making the tune might not be taken. George MacPhee of Monticello, Kings County, describes one such incident, which occurred on the night his father passed away.

> I dreamt that tune one night. After my father died, I dreamt he was playing it, and it was kind of going over in my mind. I woke up, I took the fiddle, and the tune stuck with me. I don't know what kind of tune it is, or where it came from.[24]

There is a subtext to MacPhee's story, suggesting that the tune may have been sent by his father's spirit at the moment of passing. Similarly, there are other accounts of Islanders who came upon new tunes with assistance from the supernatural. One such story surrounds the origin of a tune from northeastern Kings County known variously as "Toganny's Tune" or "Fairy at the Well" (for the notation of this tune, see appendix A, example 6.6). The following account is from Hughie McPhee of Bayfield.

> When they first came to the Island [in the late 1700s], Toganny and Pitt McPhee got grants of land close together in Rock Barra. They had to live on it for two months a year to hold onto it, and Toganny was puttin' in his two months. He went to get water from a spring, and it was nice and warm there, so he stretched out and had a nap and fell asleep. And there was a fairy come up from the spring with a set of

pipes or flute and played the tune. When he woke up, Toganny went back to his shanty, got his pipes, and played it.[25]

Whether Toganny McPhee got his tune from a water sprite or from somewhere deep in his own mind, the mysteriousness of the subconscious recall process—whereby a beautiful or lively melody that greatly affects the hearts of one's neighbors pops up inexplicably, out of seeming nothingness—has clearly created on the Island and in many other music cultures an association between the acquisition of music and contact with the spirit world. Scottish tradition, for example, recognizes a distinct musical category known as *fairy songs*, made up exclusively of songs said to have originated among the "little folk."[26] Similarly, Irish lore features numerous tales concerning musically inclined individuals who acquire repertoire via fairies' gifts.[27]

In a sense, such stories are a variant of the "music as God's gift" notion described in chapter 4, a point further emphasized when we learn that fairies' gifts can also include musical talent. According to McPhee family lore, for example, Toganny received not only the tune that bears his name but also a special gift for retaining music that could be transmitted to future generations. One early recipient of Toganny's gift was a nephew, the firstborn child of his niece Annabelle and Hughie McPhee's paternal great-grandfather Angus. This child showed signs of extraordinary musical talent at a very young age: "Her brother would be jiggin' for the child in the cradle at one or two [years old], and the child would jig the tune right back to him."[28]

There was one more class of supernatural beings that was often credited by European and North American folklore with having the ability to transmit music and musical talent to humans: namely, the devil and his minions. That discussion can be found in chapter 8.

"And the Rest of the Fiddlers Picked It Up from Him"

It is now easy to imagine how tunes circulated around the Island, passing from fiddler to fiddler like batons in a relay race. Weddings, frolics, benefit dances, and other such events enabled fiddlers from many communities to hear and ultimately learn from each other. Tunes were also carried about the Island by itinerant fiddlers such as the aforementioned Jack Proveau and Blind Newell, by musically inclined travelers such as the organ-playing cousin who first brought "Princess Reel" to Teresa Wilson's childhood home, or by seasonal workers. In terms of the latter, Jenny O'Hanley McQuaid makes special note of the Acadians from Prince County who worked at the fishing harbor near her home in Naufrage, Kings County.

> A lot of the French people came from Summerside and up west,[29] and they were quite talented musically, and for dancing and singing! So the harbor was a great place for a gathering of people for music and stories. When they were working in the factory or they come to the cookhouse, they'd jig every tune, everything going. It'd be more musical than a fiddler could do it!

Fiddlers' recall was also the route by which new tunes were introduced into the Island repertoire from the outside. The process was as follows. First, some Island fiddler had to encounter the new tune. Once it was encountered, the fiddler had to "take particular notice" of the tune, absorb it, and then find an effective way of bringing it out on his or her instrument. If the result was sufficiently compelling to attract the interest of other fiddlers, the tune would spread.

Prior to the rise of mass media, there were essentially two ways whereby fiddlers could encounter a new tune from outside: they could find it in published or written form or take it directly from another musician via aural transmission. Although both methods are more or less self-explanatory, the ways in which they apply specifically to the Island require further elucidation.

Most rural districts may have been cut off from the mainstream, but the Island as a whole was never particularly isolated. Over the course of the past two centuries, an almost continuous stream of comings and goings has afforded musically inclined Islanders the opportunity to encounter and pick up new tunes. These thousands of separate encounters can be discussed in terms of the following categories: "random" transmission, immigration, and pursuit of trade or employment opportunities.

Community fiddling of the kind described in these pages was practiced throughout the entire eastern half of North America from the late eighteenth through the first decades of the twentieth century. Consequently, tunes could easily pass around the continent from fiddler to fiddler via the same pass-the-baton process that operated on the Island. Once tunes had made it as far as New Brunswick or Nova Scotia, they would be carried across the Northumberland Strait by musically gifted merchants or fishermen.

Immigration on a large scale from Scotland and Ireland may have ceased by the mid-nineteenth century, but it continued on a limited basis for decades more. Similarly, over the generations there has been a small but steady influx of individuals from other parts of North America to Prince Edward Island. Whenever migrants happened to be musical, tunes were brought along. One example is the case of Joe à Bibienne Arsenault, who moved from his home province of Québec to Abram-Village, Prince County, when he married a local woman. As his daughter Zélie-Anne Arsenault Poirier recalls, he played "mostly old crooked tunes from Québec." Some of these—such as the tune subsequently dubbed "Reel à Joe Bibienne"[30]—have since become staples of the western PEI repertoire.

Charlottetown was a thriving international port until fairly late in the nineteenth century, and maritime trade has continued there on a reduced basis through to the modern era. Other active Island ports include Souris, Georgetown, and Montague in Kings County and Summerside in Prince County. While conducting business at or merely passing through such places, an enterprising fiddler could seize the opportunity to pick up a new tune just about any time, as illustrated by the following story from Archie Stewart.

> One time down here at Cahouns' wharf, they were loading potatoes on a ship to go to Newfoundland.[31] There was a dockhand, and he was whistling' a tune. Otis Jackson was one of our old-time fiddlers around here, and he was waiting his turn to take his load off. And he was listening to this fellow whistling. So this tune was going through his mind, and the next morning, a day later, he was down there again waiting for to get on. And the fellow was still whistling the tune. Otis went home, and he said he woke up at three or four o'clock in the morning and he had the tune. The tune was there in his mind. He jumped out of bed, down to the living room, and he picked up the fiddle and he played the tune. He went down the next morning, and the fellow was still whistling the tune. And Otis went aboard, and he said, "Do you know the name of that tune you're whistling?" "Yes," he said, "it's 'The Green Fields of America.'"[32] And Otis, I guess, was the first man that played that tune around this area.

As noted earlier, many Islanders were forced by a poor local economy to work "away" for portions of the year or even for years at a time. Some lived for extended periods in major North American cities such as Boston, New York, Montreal, or Toronto. Such situations naturally created numerous opportunities for encountering new tunes and subsequently carrying them home. One off-Island occupational setting that proved to be a particularly fruitful medium for musical interchange was the lumber woods of New Brunswick, Nova Scotia, Maine, and Québec. Men from all over northeastern North America worked at lumbering, and nearly every camp had a few fiddle players in residence. As Danny MacLean (b. Garfield, Queens County) recalls, "I did learn tunes in the lumber woods; that's mostly where I did learn them." Similarly, Archie Stewart and his long-time accompanist Chester MacSwain describe how the latter's father came back from a stint in the lumber woods with a new tune in tow.

> STEWART: His father was workin' in Nova Scotia. Your father didn't play the fiddle, did he? But he had music in him! He could whistle and pick up a tune. He learned that tune over there, and he come back here.
>
> MACSWAIN: The guy he worked for in the woods played the fiddle, and he always played this tune. And when my father come back, he was whistling this tune all the time. A fiddler down home heard it named Harper Leeco, and he started playing the tune.
>
> STEWART: And the rest of the fiddlers picked it up from him. It still goes as "MacSwain's Reel" here.[33]

A written tradition for fiddle music has coexisted with the oral since the second quarter of the eighteenth century (more on this in chapter 14). While the ability to read music has never been widespread among Island fiddlers, published music nevertheless has often played a major role in the introduction of new tunes. For this resource to come into play, all that was required was a single musically literate individual somewhere on the Island. Such an individual would be capable of translating published tunes to an instrument, thereby making it possible for others to assimilate these tunes by ear and then put them into further circulation.

Every generation within living memory has boasted at least a few Island fiddlers who had the ability to read music. Teresa Wilson (b. Monticello, Kings County), for example, recalls that her father's cousin Ronnie Archie MacPhee was one such person. Another, as Hughie McPhee reports, was his father, John Joe: "My father had a lot of music books and he used to pick up tunes. If he heard a tune from somebody playin' and he found out the name of it, he'd look it up and then he could play it."

According to Fr. Charles Cheverie of Charlottetown, quite often the process of translation from written note to oral tradition required a nonfiddler to serve as intermediary: "Some of the [pump] organists could read music. All you'd have to do was to get an organist who could get the tunes on the keyboard, and the fiddlers will just play them. The fiddlers pick up the tunes in a hurry."

In some cases, fiddlers who played entirely by ear might spend extended periods of time at the home of a musician who had the ability to read. The latter would then play tunes from a book until the former had them committed to memory. Bill MacDonald, for example, recalls hearing about one such musician from the previous generation named Steven Campbell: "He was a schoolteacher and he also studied music. People used to go on trips with horses, and horse and sleigh in winter, spend a weekend with him and learn two or three tunes. This is how they got their music."

Similarly, Fr. Cheverie tells us that both Joe Pete and "Old Peter" Chaisson of Bear River, Kings County, often added to their repertoires through extended visits with Bill Weatherbie, a musically literate Charlottetown fiddler. According to "Old Peter" Chaisson, Weatherbie would sit up late into the night playing tunes from printed collections: "He'd be still sitting there playing, going over tunes, and I'd be picking them up."

Prior to the media age, then, the circulation of printed music and the movements of musically inclined individuals formed a matrix by which tunes spread readily to Prince Edward Island from across the Atlantic and the North American mainland. Tunes could jump almost anywhere via publication, immigration, or pursuit of trade, then spread gradually from any given landing point via random contact among musicians. As detailed in chapter 13, the introduction of audio mass media simply added another element to this matrix, in effect making it even easier for tunes to jump from place to place.

The Island's Bagpipers

Over the past two centuries, the Island's resident bagpipers functioned as an effective conduit for introducing tunes from abroad into the local fiddle repertoire. Although by 1900 the pipes had largely fallen out of favor on Prince Edward Island as a dance-accompaniment instrument, pipers remained very much a part of the Island scene. They performed routinely at local benefit concerts, town days, funerals, and other, less formal occasions. At the Scotch Gathering—an annual Highland Games held since the mid-nineteenth century in Vernon River, Queens County—they generally accompanied the Highland dance competitions. And for many years Charlottetown boasted its own pipe band, known as the PEI Highlanders.[34]

A piping school was established in Summerside in 1990,[35] but prior to that, most Island pipers were either self-taught or trained to their craft in the British or Canadian Army.[36] Since the early nineteenth century, Highland pipers in general—and military pipers in particular—have come to rely on published and handwritten sheet music as the method of choice for transmitting repertoire. With published notation forming such an important tool of the trade, recent generations of military pipers have been routinely well schooled in note-reading skills.[37]

Once they completed their service, many Islanders who received formal training on bagpipes in the military simply returned home. These retired military pipers were in an excellent position to carry new tunes across the Atlantic. To begin with, their musical activities offered local fiddlers plenty of opportunities to hear Scottish piping tunes. Second, these pipers would generally have been aware of musical trends abroad and could direct fiddlers' attention to popular new tunes. Finally, because these pipers were musically literate, they could make tunes from both bagpipe and fiddle tune collections accessible to non–musically literate fiddlers. This last factor would, of course, have been of greatest significance in those cases in which a particular piper also played fiddle.

One noted local fiddler-bagpiper of recent memory was John Dan MacPherson (1920–90) of Caledonia, Kings County. According to Margaret Ross MacKinnon (b. Flat River, Queens County), MacPherson served during World War II as a piper and bagpipes instructor in a Canadian regiment known as the Nova Scotia Highlanders. After returning to the Island, he translated much of his piping repertoire to fiddle.[38] During the 1991–92 project, many fiddlers cited MacPherson as having been both a remarkable player and a major influence.

"Names Escape Me"

One important offshoot of the local tune-recall method is that tunes are filed in memory by melody rather than title. Although nearly every Island fiddler knows the names for perhaps a couple of dozen widely played tunes, otherwise scant attention is paid to tune nomenclature. As Johnny Joe Chaisson of Souris, Kings County, puts it, "When we learn a piece we don't think much of passing their names—just to get the piece down." In fact, to underline the widespread neglect of tune titles on Prince Edward Island, fiddler Kenny Chaisson named one of his original tunes "Names Escape Me."[39]

There are two major factors that contribute to this neglect of titles. First, as Dan McPhee (b. Bayfield, Kings County) tells us, for many older tunes "the names were in Gaelic and they died because the language died." Second, and more important, names for instrumental tunes are generally associated more with a written than with an oral tradition. A piece of music printed on a page needs a title for easy reference, whereas a melody filed directly in memory needs no such verbal handle. In the words of Hugh Gotell, "When you don't play it by note, you don't know the names of them, really." Conversely, Sterling Baker of Montague, Kings County, observes that he became more aware of tune titles in recent years when his weekly job playing for tourists in Orwell Corners, Queens County, had him "mixing with more people who read music. They become interested in a tune you play and they say, 'What's the name of that?'"

It should also be noted that in general the worldwide state of fiddle tune nomenclature is a hopeless muddle. For the past 250 years, compilers of major collections have deliberately published the same tunes under different names— either in an effort to deflect copyright suits or to inflate the size of a given project.[40] Adding to the confusion is the fact that many tunes have acquired numerous national or regional names. On Prince Edward Island, for example, one popular tune in the key of A is known variously as "Twin Sisters," "Speed the Plow," "The Queen's Marriage," "Pride of the Ball," and "Roddy Joe's Reel."

Interestingly, when Island fiddlers began picking up tunes from broadcast and recorded sources, their general level of attention to nomenclature actually declined. For one thing, there was often a substantial time lag between broadcast and recall, thus offering little or no opportunity to associate a name with a particular tune. Moreover, in recent years it has become commonplace to pass around "party tapes"[41] and informally duplicated versions of professional fiddle recordings sans original labeling and liner notes. From the fiddlers' viewpoint, tunes learned from such sources never had any titles to begin with.

Instead of using titles, Island musicians often communicate tune identity by jigging or whistling the opening phrases of a tune or by quickly scratching it out on the fiddle. Kevin Chaisson of Bear River, Kings County, expresses it as follows:

> If I was after [my brother Peter] to play a tune, I'd just kind of jigged a little bit of it to him. But it would be much simpler and much easier if you could put the names up there [points to head] and keep them there. But it was never stressed to us, I guess, when we were learnin' tunes. We just spent more time playing than learning names.

An Island joke that reflects this method of tune communication is recounted by Fr. Charles Cheverie:

> There's a story about a fiddler having a few drinks under his belt and going along pretty well. Well, the local priest came over to say a word to him about his state of insobriety. He says, "Joe, you know all these other tunes, but do you know the Our

Father?" And the fiddler says, "Father, you just whistle the first couple of bars and I'll have it for you in a minute!"[42]

"I Can't See It That There's Ever Any Life in It"

Despite their predominantly aural method of tune learning, reverence for the printed note is quite widespread among Island fiddlers. Certainly, the Island preoccupation with "trueness" carries with it the connotation that a tune's major themes should be fundamentally consistent with what appears in a tune book. Many Island ear-players see the ability to read music as a mysterious and virtually inaccessible process. Essentially, they feel that if they were suddenly blessed with this skill it would not only make them better players but also, as Kevin Chaisson observes, it would open up a world of previously inaccessible material.

> The thing I feel bad about is I wish I could read music, because then you'd have the best of both worlds. You have the music, and you know what? Instead of me sitting down and listening to a tune or getting my brother to play it for me, I could look at the sheet and play it. And then all it's got then to do is go in here [points to head], and then that's it!

Having the knowledge that published tune versions exist creates a general insecurity among Island fiddlers concerning their powers of musical recall. As Reuben Smith of Blooming Point, Queens County, asserts, "We are only grasping out of the air." Joe MacDonald of St. Andrews, Kings County, puts it this way:

> If the music [reading] had been available when I and people my age were young, we would have made better fiddlers because we'd have learned properly. We didn't learn proper; we just learned by ear. Sometimes the tunes would be right, and sometimes they'd be wrong. We just played them anyway.

This said, respect among Island fiddlers for the written note only goes so far. As previously noted, for example, most fiddlers show no particular inclination to relinquish their individual twists. And in practice, those musicians who do learn to play *by note* (that is, via note reading) and acquire their repertoires primarily via sheet music are generally regarded by ear-players with some degree of contempt. The general sense is that learning tunes solely from sheet music promotes playing that is rigid, mechanical, and lifeless. Conversely, those subtle aspects of music that make a tune unique, interesting, and lively can only be absorbed by ear.

> To play by note, I can't see it that there's ever any life in it. It's not lively. You give them the notes and they could play the fiddle. Take the notes away from them and they wouldn't even know how to tune it. So there's no music in you; it's all on paper. (Danny MacLean)

> You can listen to somebody that plays by ear, and you can always hear those little notes and stuff that you don't get from sheet music. They've got them in there. If you listen long enough, you'll hear them, you'll get them. Mostly you get people that learn to play the fiddle by ear: they play snappy music, and it's good and lively. (Reuben Smith)

Although many fiddlers were happy to pick up new tunes from the musically literate, being known as musically literate did not necessarily improve your local standing. Jimmy Halliday of Eldon, Queens County, reports, for example, that he learned to read music during his youth but felt compelled to conceal that fact from other local players: "Those times you did it on the sly. They made fun of you for playing by note then, that it was sissy or something, that it was too mechanical. But it was a good way to pick up tunes!"

The style of recall and tune processing discussed in this chapter deeply affected the way in which fiddlers thought about themselves and conducted their art. First, the focus placed on achieving individual twists effectively turned what might have been regarded as a defect (that is, the nonexact reproduction of tunes) into a highly prized virtue. In addition to promoting unique tune versions, this had the further consequence of spawning a constellation of highly individualistic playing styles (more on this in chapter 9). Second, dedicated fiddlers spent a good deal of their adult lives actively searching both for new tunes and for new twists on old ones; they were therefore highly motivated to put themselves in situations where the various stages of the recall process could come into play. One result of this state of affairs is discussed in chapter 7; fiddlers generally organized their own musical gatherings so that participants played one at a time, thus exposing all new tunes and twists to an eager audience of highly honed ears. Finally, because new tunes had to be caught on the fly, many fiddlers developed the habit of dropping whatever work was at hand and making a beeline for the instrument whenever a new tune came to mind. As we shall see in chapter 8, nonmusician neighbors who witnessed such practices never quite understood the motivation behind them and often interpreted what was clearly a form of artistic dedication as clear evidence of fiddlers' poor work ethic.

NOTES

1. Jim MacDougall, personal interview, Nov. 22, 2006, PEIFP Interview #52.
2. Tune recall upon awakening from sleep, or at inconvenient moments during the workday, has been widely reported elsewhere. See, for Cape Breton, Garrison, "Traditional and Non-traditional Teaching," 143; for Alabama, Cauthen, *With Fiddle*, 61; for Ireland, Maloney, "Irish Music in America," 342; and for Shetland, Cooke, *Fiddle Tradition*, 17.
3. In 2006 I heard a very similar story told about renowned fiddler Jack Webster of Cardigan, Kings County.
4. This association of pitch with finger position is reflected in the speech of Island fiddlers, who sometimes use the term *finger* to mean "note" or "pitch."
5. In most Celtic and North American fiddle cultures nowadays, the low and high sections of fiddle tunes are generally referred to respectively as the A *part* and the B *part*. In Ireland prior to the modern era, the corresponding terminology was *tune* and *turn* (Breathnach, *Folk Music and Dances*, 57). In some regions of the United States, the two parts were once known as *turn* and *chorus* (Bayard, *Hill Country Tunes*, xxi), while in others the terminology was *coarse part* and *fine part*.
6. *Theme*, *secondary phrase*, *connecting phrase*, and *cadential phrase* are terms borrowed from formal music study, not words that Island fiddlers would use.
7. "Mode" is a concept that takes into account both gamut (scale) and patterns of note usage; for more on modes in Island fiddle music, see chapter 9.
8. Bayard (in *Dance to the Fiddle*, 10) describes a similar process taking place among Pennsylvania fiddlers.
9. Bayard (in *Dance to the Fiddle*, 10) uses the term *re-creativity* to describe what amounts to the same phenomenon. This style of recall is related to a widespread compositional method known as centonization, defined as the process of stitching together preexisting elements to make new tunes (*New Harvard Dictionary of Music*, 144).
10. The classic work in this area, dealing with the epic songs of Yugoslavia, is Lord, *Singer of Tales*, esp. 30–67.
11. The engine behind this kind of variation may be related to a method known as *transformations*, used by composers to manipulate melodies while leaving them fundamentally intact. Some common transformation techniques include interversion (order of notes interchanged), reversion (notes in reverse order), contrary motion (same intervals, inverse direction), and inversion (inverse intervals and direction). See Retí, *Thematic Process in Music*, 68–85.
12. One hybrid variant circulating on Prince Edward Island is "Paddy Carrey's Ship" (see Perlman, *Fiddle Music of* PEI, 146), made up of the low turn from the Irish jig "Paddy Carrey's Fortune" and the high turn from the Scottish jig "New Rigg'd Ship."
13. Some other fiddling cultures seem to have no problem with hybrid turns. In Québec, for example, numerous widely circulating pieces contain turns that combine themes from two or more Irish or Scottish tunes.
14. In the Appalachian fiddle music revival, variants of this kind—known as crooked tunes—are highly prized as performance or jam session pieces. As stated in an earlier

note, in recent years several other contemporary fiddling revivals have also borrowed this terminology and perspective.
15. Jackie Biggar, personal interview, Nov. 23, 2006, PEIFP Interview #54.
16. Jackie Biggar interview, Nov. 23, 2006.
17. Allan MacDonald, personal interview, Oct. 24, 2006, PEIFP Interview #14.
18. Niel Gow and Sons, *Part Second of the Complete Repository* . . . (Edinburgh, 1802), quoted in Alburger, *Scottish Fiddlers*, 135. For more in this vein, see Cauthen, *With Fiddle*, 64; and Cooke, *Fiddle Tradition*, 40.
19. Hughes later put out a second volume, entitled *More Fiddle Tunes: Book 2*.
20. Quigley (in *Music from the Heart*, 55) describes a similar incident involving Newfoundland fiddler Emil Benoit.
21. Quigley (in *Music from the Heart*, 67–74) mentions that Emil Benoit frequently used this method. According to Mick Maloney (in "Irish Music in America," 378), composer Ed Reavy embarked upon "a variety of loosely structured improvisations . . . until he hit upon 'a good measure' that 'appealed to him.'"
22. As composer Ed Reavy describes it, one "build[s] up the tune using 'suitable parts'" (quoted in Maloney, "Irish Music in America," 378). Again, the term in musicology for this process is *centonization* (see note 9 in this chapter).
23. For the notation to "The Acadian Reel," see Perlman, *Fiddle Music of* PEI, 84.
24. For the notation to this tune, to which I assigned the title "George Mel's Dream," see Perlman, *Fiddle Music of* PEI, 209.
25. Hughie MacPhee, personal interview, Aug. 10, 1999.
26. Collinson, *Traditional and National Music*, 101–10.
27. In one such tale, a woman who offers shelter on a stormy night to two fairies disguised as fiddlers is told that whenever she sat at a certain spot they would "appear to only her and give her any tune she liked" (Mac Aoidh, *Between the Jigs*, 65).
28. Hughie McPhee interview, Aug. 10, 1999.
29. In Island parlance, *up west* means the western part of Prince Edward Island; *out west* refers to western Canada.
30. For the notation to "Reel à Joe Bibienne," see Perlman, *Fiddle Music of* PEI, 120.
31. It apparently was common practice for Newfoundlanders to sail to Prince Edward Island, load up with potatoes, then sell them for a profit at their home harbors. See Wareham, "Ethnography of 'Times,'" 207.
32. For the notation to this southern Kings County version of "The Green Fields of America," see Perlman, *Fiddle Music of* PEI, 70. The tune Jackson learned is an entirely different piece of music from the well-known Irish tune of the same name.
33. For the notation to "MacSwain's Reel," see Perlman, *Fiddle Music of* PEI, 80.
34. According to Cannon (in *Highland Bagpipe*, 153), the first civilian pipe bands arose in Scotland in the 1880s.
35. The PEI College of Piping was founded by an Ontario native named Scott MacAuley; its role in the Island's fiddling revival is mentioned in chapter 16.
36. Although the bagpipes have played a role in the British Army for centuries, the practice of assigning a complement of pipers led by a "pipe-major" to all Highland

regiments and the Scotch Guards dates to the period of the Crimean War (1854–56). See Cannon, *Highland Bagpipe*, 119–24, 151–52.
37. Cannon, *Highland Bagpipe*, 48–49. The Highland piping tradition has its own tune books, which employ a specialized notation to indicate recommended ornamentation.
38. Margaret Ross MacKinnon, personal interview, Aug. 10, 1999.
39. For the notation to "Names Escape Me," see Perlman, *Fiddle Music of* PEI, 51.
40. In terms of the latter, one flagrant case involves *Ryan's Mammoth Collection* (better known as *One Thousand Fiddle Tunes*), in which many tunes appear several times—each time under a different title.
41. "Party tapes" are recordings of professional fiddlers, usually from Cape Breton, made while they were playing informally at music parties.
42. More or less the same joke is told in Ireland (see Breathnach, *Folk Music and Dances*, 57).

CHAPTER SEVEN
"Knights of the Bow"

It is tempting to view traditional fiddlers as robust, colorful and charismatic merry makers—perennial grasshoppers in an ants' world. Such a perspective, for example, is clearly at the heart of the following nostalgic paean that appeared in the *Charlottetown Guardian* during the 1920s.

> "|They| were like the itinerant bards of Scotland, privileged characters for whom every door was open, who received plaudits and honors everywhere as by divine right, and who created at their coming mirth and merriment galore. These were none other than the sturdy knights of the bow, the old-time Fiddlers."[1]

What was it actually like to be a traditional fiddler on Prince Edward Island? In this chapter, I trace some of the material parameters of the fiddlers' life, such as conditions of music-work, fiddlers' pay, instruments and accessories, relations with fellow musicians, and issues related to illness and aging. I also look at the special challenges faced by female fiddlers in the days prior to modernization.

PHOTO 7.1. JOHNNY JOE CHAISSON (*LEFT*) AND HIS BROTHER PHONSEY AT SOURIS, JULY 1992 (PHOTO BY EARTHWATCH TEAM).

As they approached maturity, fiddlers often found themselves constantly on the go playing for dances and other events in both their own and neighboring communities. Jackie Webster of Cardigan, Kings County, recalls, for example, "My father, Jack Webster, done a lot of fiddling. He played six nights a week some summers at dances, five and six nights every summer." Similarly, Johnny Joe Chaisson of Souris, Kings County, puts it this way:

> Oh, dear God almighty! I played at a whack o' [dances]: from Saint Peters to the East Point. I played down in Forest Hill, Saint Margarets, North Lake, Cardigan, Saint Marys Hall, all over the place. And I played at Clifford Peter's Barn Dance for near about twelve years.[2] That was five nights a week in the fifties and sixties.

Fiddling at Island dances in the days before electronic amplification was often quite strenuous. Merely making oneself heard provided a major challenge, and as a matter of course practitioners were expected to play almost continuously throughout the duration of an event. In addition, fiddlers routinely had to deal with issues of crowd control, to the extent that planning an escape route in the event of violence was a frequently mentioned survival tactic (more on this in chapters 8 and 15). Because a house party, frolic, or wedding could easily extend well into the night, many a fiddler recalls watching the day break on the way home, knowing that a full day's work on the farm or fishing boat lay ahead.

> I'd be playing at dances and you would have to walk for bloody miles, and I would get home in time to go to work, eat breakfast, and be gone: change my clothes and leave. There was a fellow, he used to come around all the time, Lot Jenkins. Many's the time we come home after the sun got up in the morning in the summer: tired, weary, you'd eat your breakfast and go to work all day. Maybe the next night you'd get three or four hours sleep; what could you do? (Attwood O'Connor: Milltown Cross, Kings County)

> Some mornings they'd be getting home and they'd just go right to the cows. I've come home and went right to work without goin' to bed. Not often, mind you, but I have done it, just enough that I can tell about it. Don't think I'd want to tackle that now! (Cosmas Sigsworth: b. Corraville, Kings County)

As long as fiddlers were still young and their energy levels were high, this kind of life was no hardship. As Gus Longaphie of Souris, Kings County, observes, "I used to love to play for the dances back when I was eighteen, twenty, twenty-five. I'd play all night, get up in the morning: a good piece of rum, a couple of eggs, a slice of toast, go to work!" As is discussed at length in the next chapter, however, as fiddlers aged this pattern became increasingly burdensome.

"I Never Made Any Fortune with the Fiddle"

Although stories abound concerning Island fiddlers who displayed remarkable expertise on their instruments, there are precious few describing Islanders who made a paying career from fiddle playing, either at home or "away." Professional fiddling scenes and fiddle-recording industries may have developed by the 1920s and '30s in the American South, Cape Breton, and elsewhere in North America, but practically nothing of this nature appeared on Prince Edward Island prior to the modern era.[3] Opportunities for earning even pocket money through fiddling were extremely limited.

Fiddlers were typically not paid at all for playing at house parties, frolics, weddings, or other dances that took place within the home district, nor were they paid for playing at benefit dances. As Joe MacDonald of St. Andrews, Kings County, notes, "For playing around here you never thought of charging anything; I must've played for hundreds of weddings and never took a cent yet." As Johnny Morrissey (b. Newtown Cross, Queens County) recalls, offering the fiddler good hospitality was usually considered sufficient.

> You wouldn't get paid for house parties. You'd be lucky if you got a bite or two. They'd still want a fiddler; they wouldn't pay him, though—Might give him a few drinks, make him feel good. That is about the way things were goin' in them times.

This said, occasions did sometimes arise at which Island fiddlers could earn money for playing. If a fiddler was invited to play for a house party or dance outside his community, for example, he might expect some recompense. In many cases, this arrangement took the form of collecting contributions. Sidney Baglole (b. Lot 16, Prince County), for example, tells us, "They used to pass the hat around to pay me; sometimes I'd get fifty cents." Ervan Sonier of Summerside, Prince County, sums it up as follows:

> It was hard work playing the fiddle for a dance. And then of course, you got well-paid; you got two dollars! Of course, two dollars then bought you something. You could get a teddy of 'shine for a dollar and a quarter.[4] And you could go down and have your lunch at the Chinese restaurant.[5] Hot chicken was thirty-five cents, so you'd come home with fifteen cents after a belly-full of moonshine and a belly-full of food. So it was quite rewarding! I don't know if there's anybody ever made any money playing the fiddle: probably Don Messer or somebody like that, but around here nobody made money. And then at house rackets [house parties] sometimes they'd start chuckin' silver on the floor, eh—Not always, it depended where you were: a "silver collection," they called it.

As commercial dance venues began to proliferate in the 1940s and '50s, fees for fiddling went somewhat higher. Not even the best-known players, however, were able to command very much. Renowned south Kings County fiddler Jack Webster, for example, according to his son Carl, "would get paid five dollars a night, then he went to six and seven; later years he got ten and twelve dollars." Johnny Joe Chaisson puts it this way: "When I first started, I got a dollar. That wouldn't buy the strings. Then I got up to a dollar and a half. The most I got at the barn dances when I started was ten dollars. Then in the sixties at the last of it, I was getting twenty." When they had no cash to offer, dance organizers would sometimes seek to pay fiddlers in kind. Most such payments were in the form of alcoholic beverages (more on this in chapter 8), but among the items sometimes received were household goods, foodstuffs, and even livestock, as in this story told by Wilfred Gotell of Georgetown, Kings County:

> Once I played down in Murray Harbour. There was five of us, and we had to hire a car and driver to get there. After the thing was over, we went to get paid. And what I got was two 'scovy ducks in a crate.[6] That's what we got paid for that night. I don't think there was a one of us had a cent in our pocket. There we were, two ducks and we couldn't pay the driver! No, I never made any fortune with the fiddle, that's for sure.

The financial aspect of fiddling was not absolutely bleak, however. As has been noted, cash in general was in short supply, and having any on hand was helpful. Moreover, as Emmett Hughes of Dromore, Queens County, observes, one could sometimes make more from a night's fiddling than from a full day's work on the farm.

> I started playing for dances in '45, around there. It was five dollars for three of us: for fiddle, guitar, and mandolin. Of course, then you'd work for twelve dollars or fifteen dollars a month on the farm. At that time, there was no other work anyplace, even in Charlottetown. You could make more money playing.

Instruments and Accessories

With money scarce to begin with and little to be earned from musical pursuits, Island fiddlers rarely had the wherewithal to obtain well-crafted fiddles or bows. As fiddle maker and repairer Neil MacCannell (b. Lorne Valley, Kings County) points out, most instruments in circulation on Prince Edward Island were mass-produced to haphazard specifications around the turn of the twentieth century and were marketed on the Island through mail-order catalogs such as those distributed by Eaton's of Toronto.[7] MacCannell notes, "My mother had an Eaton catalog dated 1899, and you could purchase a violin made in Germany for one dollar, or a deluxe one for five dollars, and a bow for fifty cents!" He has had many such fiddles apart in the course of his business and has come to the following conclusion.

> Most of the instruments don't follow any kind of plan. They don't adhere to any kind of dimensions that any reputable maker would ever use. The back of [a violin] is supposed to be thick in the center, and it becomes thinner towards the edges. But you get instruments apart here, and they'll be thick where they should be thin, and thin where they should be thick. The top [of a violin] is supposed to be even; but [on most local instruments] you'll find it may be half as thick as it should be in some places, and three or four times as thick as it should be in others.

MacCannell also notes that the general quality of violin bows on the Island is similarly dismal. Most are too light, do not balance well, and have lost most of their camber.

Despite the generally poor quality of instruments and bows, Island fiddlers usually do manage to find a way to make them work well enough to suit their purposes. According to MacCannell, this makes the lively, powerful, singing tone they are able to achieve all the more remarkable.

> I have nothing but admiration for anybody who can play with something like that. But somehow they manage to get around it. These fiddlers have all kinds of ability, but the instruments—I thought it's a real shame that they don't have something under the chin that's giving them something for their effort.

Most experienced fiddlers pride themselves on their ability to function no matter what instrument or bow is put in their hands, regardless of its state of craftsmanship, setup, or repair. This was quite a feat, considering that instruments have vastly different tones, string heights, and string spacings and that bows have different lengths, weights, and handling characteristics.[8] As Hilda MacPhee MacDonald (b. Selkirk, Kings County) recalls, "Didn't make any difference. You'd pick up a fiddle and you'd play it, and that's it!" Similarly, "Old Peter" Chaisson of Bear River, Kings County observes,

> I can pretty near pick up—take—any fiddle. If it's a good one or a bad one, you can still try to get a sound out of 'em. I think it's the way you're brought up on it. Like I'd go anywheres when I started out playing, somebody would have a fiddle and get you to come in and play a few tunes. It just came simple to me.

Many fiddlers were painfully aware that the instruments at their disposal were not of the best quality. A good violin plays easily and has sweet, well-balanced tone and good projection, but most Island players would consider themselves lucky to have an instrument that possessed even one of these qualities. From the local viewpoint, as Archie Stewart of Milltown Cross, Kings County, explains, probably the most crucial feature to select for was projection.

> Back in the old days there was no such a thing as a sound system. You had to send your music to the back end of a fifty-foot hall. A fiddle that wouldn't carry out, they couldn't hear it probably twenty feet from the stage. It might be a sweet fiddle to listen to, but she'd be no good to play for a dance with. That's where this fiddle used to come in; this fiddle has tremendous volume [*holds up instrument*]. And she carries out. I'll bet if you were standing out in the road, you could hear this fiddle just as plain as if you were in this kitchen. She carries! And she was great for playing at dances.

Because purchasing a better violin was usually out of the question for most fiddlers, many notions grew up on how to improve the ones they had. One common idea had it that the tone of an instrument would be improved if it were played all the time. Conversely, it was felt that a fiddle needed to be played constantly or its sound would deteriorate. "Old Peter" Chaisson puts it this way:

> Any fiddle, I guess, is the same; it's gotta be played on and kept in shape, I'd say. You can't just leave them for two or three weeks and then pick them up. They gotta be practiced a bit all the time to keep them in shape. Same with yourself, eh. You gotta keep at it all the time: keeps you in the mood and the shape.

While there may be some truth to such notions,[9] MacCannell tells us that many other ideas in circulation are counterproductive or little more than superstition. In terms of the former, it is generally believed that tone can be improved by leaving rosin dust undisturbed on the face of the instrument.[10] This dust actually bonds with the finish of the instrument over time and restricts the range of motion in the wood, thereby causing its tonal response to decline. As for superstition, MacCannell cites the widespread notion that "if you find a snake skin and shove it in through the sound hole, that's gonna somehow improve the sound."[11] He has also been advised that the violins he builds would improve markedly if he used wood from trees that had themselves been regularly exposed to music: "One person told me I'd never make a satisfactory fiddle unless I got wood that grew near a church. Church bells chiming would fill the wood full of music, and that was the only type of wood to use."

Quite a few fiddlers over the years have also taken a crack at making their own instruments. Joe MacDonald, for example, mentions that his Mi'kmaq neighbors near St. Andrews, Kings County, often made their own fiddles; he recalls one in particular built by Peter Scully: "He made a great job—the workmanship was marvelous on it!" Hilda MacDonald notes that her brother Hughie made the two fiddles that were available in her household. Similarly, Charlie Sheehan of Bear River, Kings County, mentions that his father, James, built two fiddles.

> He didn't have a fiddle, so he got working on one. He was a good carpenter, and he made a danged nice job. I can just remember the fiddle when I was growing up. He built a case and everythin' for it, and he hung the case up on the wall pretty high up so us kids couldn't get to it. But one day the case opened and she come down and struck on the floor. It split that fiddle all up! So he built another one.

Some homemade violins were made of unconventional materials. John Cousins of Bloomfield, Prince County, for example, tells of a local player who built an instrument of scrap metal.[12]

> In Campbellton where I grew up there was a man who made a fiddle out of a cream can, one of these big cream cans which were used to store cream in. They called him Ben Bruno,[13] and they said he soldered it all. This fiddle was played by a number of very good fiddlers, and they said it was a wonderful instrument. There's a whole cycle of stories about Ben Bruno and his fiddle. I know there's one song out there about a young fellow who goes to Maine and wants to come home. The only two lines I remember are, "I'll swing the winsome maidens there that's so neat around the middle / To the music of the organ and Ben Bruno playin' the fiddle."

Once an instrument appeared on the Island, it tended to pass from hand to hand through the generations. Many fiddlers I spoke with still played their father's or grandfather's instruments. In a few families, these instruments came along with colorful lore concerning their origins. Stewart MacIntyre (b. Fairfield, Kings County), for example, tells of a grand-uncle named James MacIntyre who brought both a Doctor of Divinity degree and a fine fiddle back from Rome in the 1840s: "Oh, they say it was a beauty; I heard my father saying when [somebody] drew a bow across that violin, you would hear it a mile away!" Similarly, here's how MacIntyre's own instrument came into the family:

> The violin I learned to play on, they called it the MacKenzie violin. It was taken to Fairfield around 1850 by Captain Alec MacKenzie. Captain Alec was dead before my time, but I remember his son playing on it. My father bought the violin from him in 1906 when I was about six years old, and it was a fine, fine instrument.

Along these lines, Hughie McPhee of Bayfield, Kings County, describes how he acquired an instrument from abroad while serving in Holland with the Canadian Army during the Second World War.

> I went up around the town in Rotterdam, and this fiddle was sitting in the window. I went in and I bought it. I didn't pay much for it; it was a hundred and ten guilders, the fiddle and the bow. And I sold three packages of tobacco for a hundred and twenty guilders! I said, "If that's the price of it, okay!"

With cash always in short supply, obtaining the accessories required to keep an instrument operational was also problematic. With a little resourcefulness, however, many fiddlers were able to keep themselves supplied even in hard times. As implied in chapter 5, for example, spruce gum gathered in the woods could be substituted for store-bought rosin, and a bow could be rehaired via clippings from the tail of the family horse. There was no home-grown substitute for strings, however, and—as Sidney Baglole reports—breaking one could mean considerable inconvenience.

> I used to break strings, too. Then I'd be in trouble. Summerside was the only place where you could get strings. It would spoil a day to go to Summerside and back, about twelve or fifteen miles. You'd have to feed the horse, and you'd have to have your dinner, and by the time you'd get home the day would be gone.

The quality of fiddles and bows in circulation on Prince Edward Island has been gradually improving since the early 1990s. This is due primarily to the activities of several enterprising individuals who periodically purchase quantities of relatively decent used instruments and bows at wholesale prices in Boston or Toronto and then informally offer them for sale on the Island. In addition, several professional luthiers (violin makers) have recently set up shop on Prince Edward Island and elsewhere in the Maritimes, and many Island fiddlers are now playing their instruments.[14]

"That's the Big Thing When You Get Together with Other Fiddlers"

Whenever practitioners of the same art or craft gather together, smooth social interaction requires dealing effectively with the issue of competitiveness. Otherwise, such universal emotions as envy, jealousy, pride, and insecurity come into play and—despite the best of intentions—make orderly human relations difficult. Among Island fiddlers, two widespread attitude-clusters take on the role of dealing with this issue. First, there is the notion that playing for dances or for other gathered company is a social duty. When a fiddler gets up to play, he is doing his part, not expressing his ego. A corollary here is that another fiddler attending the same event becomes not a rival for social attention but a colleague who needs to be given the opportunity to fulfill his own social duty. Second, the notion that every fiddler has his or her own unique, or even inborn, style carries with it the implication that there is a certain level at which musicians cannot be compared and where, in fact, all such comparisons are in the "apples-to-oranges" domain. Even a fiddler of very modest accomplishment, then, can reason, "That other fellow might be able to play certain tunes better than I do, but he could never duplicate my sound." Naturally, the same implication tends to keep arrogance among even the most adept players in check.

When there was more than one fiddler on hand at a community dance, they usually shared the task of playing. The fiddler who got things rolling would play for a few square sets or until he needed a breather; he would then hand his instrument on to another player, and so on. As Joe MacDonald puts it, "It was a matter of passing the fiddles from one to the other." More or less the same rule applies at fiddlers' gatherings, when musicians from the same general area come together for a few hours of shared music and good fellowship. These events are essentially jam sessions—like those attended by musicians throughout the Western world—with one important exception. Musicians at jam sessions in Britain, Ireland, and most of North America tend to play together. On Prince Edward Island, however, fiddlers generally take turns playing solo. In other words, the first fiddler plays until he grows fatigued or has performed through an informally allotted time period, then the next fiddler has his turn, and so on.[15] Here's how Fr. Charles Cheverie of Charlottetown describes the procedure:

> It's like musical chairs. Everybody sits around; one guy will play the fiddle, and the piano or guitar player will play with him. Then somebody else plays. "OK, your turn for the hot seat now!" Regardless of the quality of the player, young or old or beginner, seasoned, whatever.

While one fiddler plays, the others generally listen intently, and this is not merely from politeness. After all, as George MacPhee of Monticello, Kings County, points out, since everyone has his or her own sound and collection of twists, there is always something to enjoy about the playing of another: "There's a lot of good fiddlers around, and it doesn't matter if they're a real good player or not. I can sit down and listen to anybody playing, really! I like anybody, their style of playing, anybody that's going to give it a try." More important, each listener is hoping to hear something new: perhaps a new twist on an old tune, or even an entirely new tune. As Alvin Bernard of Long River, Queens County, and Edwin Simmons of nearby Darnley report, listeners then have the opportunity to commit the new twist or tune to memory and use it in their own playing.

> SIMMONS: Everybody's got a tune to try. Everybody always wants to learn a tune from somebody. See, that's the big thing when you get together with other fiddlers, regardless of how good you are.
>
> BERNARD: Learn a new tune if you can, that's the big thing, eh! Keep learnin' tunes, keep addin' tunes. "Did you ever hear this tune?" Fellows would be

> waitin' to pick up a tune or learn them. One fellow might start playin' a tune and play a few bars, and the other fellows would say, "Where'd you get it?" or, "That's a new tune, I want to learn to play that." Then the first fellow will play it over a few times, and the other fellows try to learn it by ear.

Because each player has his own twists, it is never considered problematic to repeat a tune that another has previously played. It is not looked upon as "poaching," nor is it regarded as indicating a limited imagination or repertoire. What's more, since all fiddlers know they will have an opportunity to be clearly heard playing their favorite tunes, no one has the need to dominate the proceedings. In turn, this creates the feeling, "I've had (or will have) my chance, so now I can relax and listen to the others."

It has already been mentioned that Island fiddlers generally avoid ensemble playing at dances and other public events. Essentially, there is concern that playing two or more different twists on the same tune simultaneously would result in a general muddiness of sound.[16] Despite this general reluctance, it is not uncommon for fiddlers at one of their own gatherings to take a crack at playing together. In such instances, they rely on a few conventions to make sure that they "make a good job of it." First, as Archie Stewart tells us, it is agreed upon that each turn of every tune is to be played twice through, as would generally be the case at a dance: "If fiddlers are playing together that's a rule. Because then one fellow knows when the other fellow is going to shift to the other turn of the tune. You play two turns of the low, and two turns of the high, and that's a rule." Next, if the ensemble is to perform a *group* (medley) of tunes, the convention is that each tune is played twice through before going on to the next. As reported by Allan MacDonald of Bangor, Kings County, one fiddler generally takes charge of the medley. Because the others know that the leader is certain to switch following a tune's second run-through, they know exactly when to keep an ear peeled to determine which new tune is coming up.[17]

Many of the attitudes and customs that governed fiddlers' interactions on the Island prior to the modern era operated by virtually removing competitiveness from the playing field. This worked quite well in promoting cooperation among fiddlers at music events and in encouraging acceptance of the state of one's own musical accomplishments. On the down side, most Island fiddlers went through life without having ever learned to deal effectively either with musically competitive situations or with their own competitive feelings. Consequently, when fiddle contests began to proliferate on Prince Edward Island after the Second World War, many fiddlers were unable to deal successfully with the psychological and social pressures they engendered. As described in chapter 11, this ultimately resulted in widespread feelings of insecurity and resentment, long-term grudges, and even periodic outbreaks of violence.

Musical Friendships

When fiddlers gather together, they do more than just play music. They banter with each other; they also share the general details of their lives. They talk about new tunes that they have learned or wish to learn. As Archie Stewart describes, they also discuss the tools of the trade.

> We talk about fiddles, you know. "Did you ever play on this fellow's fiddle or that fellow's fiddle?" "What'd you think of it?" "Do you think it's a good fiddle?" We know pretty near every fiddle that's in the country: that we have played on them. We'd swap ideas about who's got the best fiddle, all this stuff.

Another popular topic for conversation according to Stewart concerns "different fiddlers": who are the best players now and who were the best within living memory. In terms of the latter, stories about exceptional or eccentric players often circulate for years after their passing. This book already includes quite a few tales about such legendary artists as Jack Webster of Cardigan, Jimmy Simmons of Selkirk, Guy Boulter of Milburn, Joe à Bibienne Arsenault of Abram-Village, and Jimmy Bearisto, the fiddling barber of Kensington. Finally, Mr. Stewart mentions that fiddlers also enjoy talking about the dances they have played for over the years.

> When you get in touch with an old fiddler, you get reminiscing about the old days when we used to play for all the dances and stuff like that. When you meet up with another old-time fiddler around your own age, you have a pretty good conversation for a while.

A shared interest in fiddling frequently forms the basis for strong friendships among players. Pairs of fiddling friends might cooperate in learning skills and working on new tunes, and they might even feel comfortable playing together at dances or other public events. Dave Thomson (b. West Royalty, Queens County), for example, recalls that in his younger days he had such a relationship with another young Charlottetown-area fiddler named Gary Chipman.

> We'd play at concerts together over the years. But they used to have to [push our chairs apart] 'cause he was playin' right-handed and I was playin' left-. I remember one time we were pretty near goin' to poke one another's eyes out with the bow.

Similarly, Ervan Sonier and Toussaint Arsenault of Summerside had been close friends since the 1940s, when Sonier returned to the Island after serving in the Second World War. According to the latter, for the next forty years they met weekly at Arsenault's house to play tunes together, accompanied on organ or piano by Arsenault's wife, Anne-Marie. In the late 1980s, Arsenault suffered a stroke that left him generally unable to remember his tunes. When his friend Ervan came by for their weekly session, however, these memories would return. Whenever Sonier began to play, Arsenault would once again be able to join in.

Close friendships also grew up with some frequency between fiddlers and their regular accompanists. Although most Island fiddlers were capable of playing with just about any accompanist, many grew accustomed to the sound and general approach of a single backup player. A certain accompanist's approach to rhythm, for example, might particularly suit the fiddler's style of playing. Or an accompanist might be quick on the uptake and capable of finding chords for tunes even in the most difficult keys. Alternatively, an accompanist might simply share the fiddler's joy in playing, becoming a willing participant in whatever musical adventures or mishaps might come along (for more on accompaniment, see chapter 10).

Once such a relationship was firmly established, this relationship offered additional advantages to the fiddler. A long-term accompanist, for example, would generally know a fiddler's repertoire well enough to cover up errors or even put him back on track in the event of a memory lapse. Moreover, a regular accompanist would also be aware of a fiddler's idiosyncrasies, thus permitting the latter to ignore certain musical conventions with impunity. Archie Stewart, for example, notes that whenever his favorite guitarist, Chester MacSwain, was on hand, he could neglect to repeat the turns of a tune: "I just shift [turns] wherever I feel like it, and he knows what I'm thinking; we've played together for about thirty years, him and I."

Archie Stewart and Chester MacSwain were only one pair of such long-term musical associates. Some other fiddler-accompanist pairings encountered in the course of this project were fiddler Alvin Bernard and guitarist Edwin Simmons in northwestern Queens County; fiddler Elliot Wight and pianist Judy Lowe in the Charlottetown area; and fiddler Dennis Pitre and guitarist Vincent Doucette in western Prince County.

In some cases, fiddler-accompanist pairings have persisted through the generations. Guitarist Lemmy Chaisson of Rollo Bay, Kings County, for example, notes that his father, William, used to frequently accompany "Old Peter" Chaisson. In the 1960s, Lemmy himself took over the task. Nowadays, he routinely accompanies not only Old Peter's nephews Kenny and "Young Peter" Chaisson but also several of Old Peter's grandnephews and grandnieces.

Upon occasion, a fiddler-accompanist pairing has served as a basis for courtship and marriage. We have already noted the case of Cosmas and Rita Sigsworth from the Corraville, Kings County, area. Some other couples forged when a fiddling husband married his primary accompanist are Toussaint and Anne-Marie Arsenault of Summerside, Prince County; Warren and Bernice Leard of Coleman Corners, Prince County; and Leonard and Claire McDonald of Emyvale, Queens County. Then there is the case of piano player Marie Gallant of Wellington, Prince County. Several years after she married Edward P Arsenault, she decided that there should be a fiddler in the family. She bought her husband an instrument, and after several years of practice he became an accomplished player. They then performed together for years afterward.[18]

Ladies of the Bow

Female fiddlers on the Island faced special challenges that are worthy of separate consideration here. As has been noted, fiddling was considered by and large to be a man's calling. As Eddy Arsenault of St. Chrysostom, Prince County, puts it, "Fifty years ago if you had seen a woman play the fiddle it would've been [considered] an awful thing." Part of this was an extension of the division-of-labor attitudes that had men running plows, mowers, and binders, while women devoted themselves to spinning, weaving, and cooking. But there was also a general feeling—because of the rough and rowdy atmosphere at some Island dances—that fiddling was not only too physically taxing for a woman but also no "proper" activity for her. Fr. Charles Cheverie puts it this way:

> In terms of the energy that was required to play volume-wise for dances when there wasn't any P.A. system—You really had to work at it, which might have been difficult for women. But apart from that aspect, there was the stigma that was attached to the fiddle in terms of the boozing component. And in those days it was probably not the place for a woman to be.[19]

Young girls who were drawn to the fiddle were rarely discouraged outright. It just seemed that in many households they received less encouragement and fainter praise for their attempts at fiddling than did their male counterparts.

It was rarely the female child of a household who got the pointers in tuning, bowing, and noting or was the recipient of helpful advice. Rita MacDonald Morrison (b. St. Andrew's, Kings County)—a piano player in her seventies who took up the fiddle in middle age—describes the situation this way:

> But they [females] weren't encouraged as much, maybe, were they? Years ago I wouldn't even think of picking up the fiddle to learn, but now I don't seem to mind. I can pick up the fiddle and try to learn a piece. It wasn't the thing to do then, and there were very few women played, very few. And there was no talk of fiddles for girls in my family either, you know. But for my brothers there was no question of whether they should do it. They just took the violin and played.

Similarly, Teresa Wilson (b. Monticello, Kings County) offers these memories:

> I guess a lot of things was considered to be men-only at that time, and I think playing the fiddle was one of them. When I was about six, one Sunday afternoon we were all at home and I asked my father if he'd let me play, and I played him part of a tune. He was quite surprised, but he didn't give me encouragement to play again, and he never encouraged me into it at all, as a matter of fact. But I was really anxious to play, and when Mom was home alone, sometimes I'd play.

Wilson reports that she "sneaked" the fiddle from time to time and persisted in her efforts to learn, until she was confronted with social pressures of a far less subtle nature.

> I played at a little birthday party, and Josie MacIntyre was there. He said, "I heard you've been playing the fiddle; you'll be like Maggie Butler now." As soon as he said that, that was the end of me life; I didn't want to be like Maggie Butler. And I had no idea what she looked like! Just right there I stopped playin' the fiddle. I didn't play because he discouraged me right there. [*Question*: What about Maggie Butler?] She was an old lady that lived alone, and she was a good fiddler. They just made fun of her because she was playin' the fiddle.[20]

According to Rita Morrison, the situation was quite different with regard to accompaniment instruments. A girl's explorations on keyboard instruments such as organ and piano or on fretted instruments such as guitar and mandolin would generally elicit much in the way of encouragement and helpful hints. "Everybody would always be glad to have you to play with them, you know; and accompaniment's always good help to a fiddler." In keeping with this pattern, when Teresa Wilson shifted her attention to mandolin and guitar with the aim of accompanying her fiddling brothers, she received all the encouragement she could have wished.

> I bought a mandolin over in Moncton[, New Brunswick,] when I was about fifteen, and I brought it home. And I used to play at the dances with my brother Roddy, play the mandolin with him at the dances around. Then [my younger brother] George started playing fiddle, and I was playing the guitar for George, or the piano, or the organ. And we played a lot of weddings and a lot of things like that. But I didn't play the fiddle, I played the guitar or the mandolin, or the piano.

Because most such pressures were relatively subtle, many males were unaware of their existence. They simply accepted the absence of women fiddlers as a fact of life. As Reg Banks of Poplar Point, Kings County, recalls, "The piano was what the ladies always played mostly; it just didn't appeal to them, to play the violin." Similarly, Eddy Arsenault puts it this way: "I don't know why no women ever took to play the fiddle. I don't know why, but probably they didn't want to try or they didn't want to learn. Not that somebody stopped them from playing. It always was men that were supposed to play the fiddle."

Despite this state of affairs, some Island women did try to learn the instrument. Most of those who succeeded grew up in large fiddling families such as the MacLeans of Belfast and the O'Connors of Milltown Cross. Apparently, the drive to make music in these households was so strong that holding any children back from expressing it proved difficult. But even most of these female fiddlers carried on their art in the privacy of their homes. When it came to house parties and dances, as Hilda MacDonald recalls, usually only the men played.

> I never played fiddle very much at the dances. It was always mostly on the organ that I played with the violin players; I'd be killed on the organ all night. The men would take their turns playing. When one man would get done, there was always another to take his place. So I didn't play [fiddle] at many dances, 'cause there'd be men players for that.

Some women were sufficiently bold to ignore this cultural atmosphere and make the effort to play in public. As Johnny Morrissey tells us, one example was Elsie MacLean of Garfield, Queens County.

> I guess all the MacLean boys played,[21] and the girls too: a musical family, full of music! I heard them playing one night in Eldon. Angus Leslie's daughter Elsie, she come into the hall and she was only about fifteen. Well, she come in there and she went up to the stage, and she picked the fiddle up, and she got playin' with her father. God, boys, talk about music—She was good to play the fiddle! She probably knew all the tunes he knew!

The Island family most noted for producing female fiddlers who played outside the home was that of Joe à Bibienne Arsenault of Abram-Village,

PHOTO 7.2. ZÉLIE-ANNE ARSENAULT POIRIER AT ATLANTIC JAMBOREE, ABRAM-VILLAGE, AUGUST 1992 (PHOTO BY KEN PERLMAN).

Prince County. Several of his daughters—Zélie-Anne, Louise, Kate, Rita, and Mary—did not merely become accomplished fiddlers, but for decades they were called upon to provide a significant proportion of the local dance music. Joe à Bibienne's grandson Jacques Arsenault (b. Abram-Village) offers this explanation for his grandfather's ability to break with tradition: "Maybe because Joe Bibienne was a fairly strong-willed character. He traveled 'round a bit for work and stuff, and he was an outsider.[22] He also had different music. And all the girls, they were also pretty rough and tough!"

By the time Louise Gallant Arsenault was playing her first notes on fiddle in the environs of Abram-Village a generation later, community attitudes toward fiddling by females had changed markedly. By then, people had gotten used to seeing Zélie-Anne Arsenault and her sisters playing the instrument, so when Louise came along, she experienced none of the subtle discouragement that had been the lot of so many other young Island girls.

> I would go and play certain places, and they'd say, "My goodness, it's not too often you see a woman fiddler." And it would make me feel good. "My goodness, a little girl that can play the violin, listen to that." And they would pass the hat, and

"Knights of the Bow"

at the end of the evening I would go home very happy. I had my father behind me all the way. He was really encouraging me to keep on going. My whole family was behind me, as far as entering contests and stuff. They would always encourage me to give it a try. It was very exciting!

The Abram-Village area was an exception, however, and prior to the modern era females made up only a relatively small percentage of the Island fiddling population. Although few of them fiddled, women were still very much a part of the music and dance scenes in their districts. They danced; they jigged and whistled; they played accompaniment on piano, organ, and guitar; and in some families they served as resident critics, correcting young and old alike on the quality of their playing and on the accuracy of their tune versions.

As the Island's fiddling revival gathered steam through the 1980s, it had the effect of extending the right to fiddle to Rita Morrison, Teresa Wilson, and other female Islanders of their generation. Hundreds of them took advantage of this new freedom and began practicing at home or learned the rudiments of playing through one of the Island's newly established instructional programs. In the mid-1990s, a substantial number of young girls began taking up the instrument, and by the first decade of the twenty-first century, young females far outnumbered their male contemporaries at almost every fiddle instruction program on the Island (for more on this, see chapters 16 and 17).

Illness and Aging

Most of the fiddlers encountered during the course of this project have maintained an active interest in playing throughout their lives, even through the bleak years when Island fiddle dances had all but disappeared and not so much as a hint of the current fiddling revival was in the air. Because in their day playing the fiddle was a route to neither significant financial reward nor enhanced social esteem, it is probably safe to say that what kept them at it was pretty much what drew them to the instrument in the first place: their great passion for both the sound of the fiddle and the music that is played on it.

Some fiddlers also cite the pleasure they derive from working out new tunes. As Leonard McDonald notes, "The most satisfaction I ever got playing the fiddle is learning: when you think you have mastered a tune, it gives you a great feeling." Similarly, Gus Longaphie observes, "Everybody goes away sometimes: wife and girls goes out drivin', I'd be alone home. I'd think of a tune, I'd go and take the fiddle, I get a pleasure out of it: pick up a new tune, play it for meself!" Still other fiddlers cite the enjoyment that ensues on those occasions when they can still play for dances. In particular, they like partaking of the camaraderie—and watching the pleasure of others as they move to the music. Elliott Wight (b. Flat River, Queens County) puts it this way:

> When you're playing for a dance and you see everybody having a good time, that's probably ninety percent of the battle right there. When you get up to play, and the people get up to dance the minute you start to play, and you know that they like it, it makes you feel good!"

For some, a love for music keeps them playing despite the effects of potentially crippling illnesses or injuries. Johnny Joe Chaisson, for example, lost a joint on his left index finger in a wood-splitter accident, and George MacPhee partially severed the tendons in his left hand with an axe while chopping wood, yet both managed to keep playing. Similarly, Dennis Pitre continues to play despite a painful arthritis condition.

> Sometimes before you start playing, your fingers are pretty painful, eh. But once you get them moving, it's better. Some nights there when we used to play for dances, it was terrible! The pain was so bad I couldn't bend them, and I kind of chewed my fingers just to get more pain, so I could surpass that [original] one: just to get the finger bent. Once you have it bent there, you could play for an hour or more. But then the next morning you would be still all twisted up.

It seems unfortunate that older fiddlers with heart conditions have sometimes been warned off their favorite pastime by local doctors, on the grounds that the vigorous movements involved in bowing adversely affect the chest cavity.[23] Attwood O'Connor recalls how such medical advice ended the playing career of Joe Kearney's brother William, of Sturgeon, Kings County.

> William Kearney was a beautiful fiddler. But he had a heart condition, and the doctor told him to definitely leave the fiddle. "Don't play it," he said. [So] he had to stop. He told me it affected his chest. Whatever's the reason, I don't know. I suppose it's holding your arms up.

Despite such obstacles, many fiddlers have been able to carry their devotion to playing and love for the instrument into old age. When Danny MacLean's father, Angus Leslie, had to move into the local senior citizens' manor, for example, "he wanted to have a fiddle; he was ninety-something and he could still play." Similarly, Teresa Wilson recalls that her father, Mel MacPhee, was literally playing the instrument until the end.

> The last thing my father did was play the fiddle. Mom went in to lie down, and she could hear him pickin' at it; she said when she fell asleep, that's what he was doin'. And when she got up in the morning he was dead. That was the last thing he did, so I guess that's what he always wanted to do. He loved the fiddle!

NOTES

1. "Ye Old-Time Fiddlers Contest," *Charlottetown Guardian*, Mar. 4, 1926, 1. This excerpt is from the front-page editorial that first announced the Great Contest of 1926; see chapter 11.
2. This "barn dance" was a commercial venture, one of many such venues that arose on the Island beginning around the time of the Second World War; see chapter 15.
3. A professional fiddling scene finally emerged on the Island beginning in the mid-1990s; see chapters 16–17. Prior to this modern scene, the only fiddlers with ties to the Island who had any kind of long-term commercial success were Don Messer and members of his band, the Islanders; see chapter 13.
4. A teddy is a small container with a capacity of roughly eight ounces (240 milliliters).
5. During this era, a Chinese restaurant in a small Canadian city such as Summerside would have served standard Island fare alongside (or in lieu of) a distinctly ethnic cuisine.
6. Muscovy ducks are a large, crested breed of domestic fowl.
7. In the United States, many country fiddlers obtained instruments of similar quality through Eaton's American counterpart, Sears, Roebuck and Co. See Blaustein, "Traditional Music," 28.
8. One major point implied by the song "The Spree at Montague" is that the cranky fiddler should have been able to function no matter what quality of instrument was thrust into his hands.
9. Frequent playing will indeed improve the tone of well-built violins made of fine woods, but it probably would not have much effect on the general run of Island instruments.
10. Particles of rosin, the translucent amber-colored cake derived from oil of turpentine that fiddlers rub on their bows for traction, tend to fly off as the bow passes over the strings, especially if the bow has been overrosined.
11. This is probably a variant of the widespread North American practice of placing a rattlesnake rattle inside the fiddle to improve tone. See Sanders, "Honor the Fiddler," 82; and Wolfe, *Tennessee Strings*, 19.
12. Mac Aoidh (in *Between the Jigs*, 33) notes that Donegal tinsmiths often built tin fiddles, whose poor sound production allowed fiddlers to practice at home without disturbing their families.
13. This community "handle," or nickname, identifies him as "Ben, son of Bruno."
14. In 2006, one of the most active luthiers was Richard Lepage, who had moved to Prince Edward Island several years earlier and set up shop in Flat River, Queens County, on a property he named the Fiddle Farm; at the time of this writing he is still in operation.
15. In the gatherings I attended, there seemed to be an unspoken agreement that no fiddler would play for more than about twenty minutes. This "take turns" style of jam session is also practiced on Cape Breton.
16. This attitude has been changing of late because of the rise of fiddlers' societies; see chapter 16.
17. Playing tune medleys is probably a relatively recent development that emulates contemporary Cape Breton custom. Two other medley conventions are shared with

Cape Bretoners: (1) ad hoc changes in mode are permissible, but (2) the leader avoids changing the key center without advance warning.
18. Marie Gallant Arsenault passed away in the mid-1990s.
19. A thorough analysis of Island sex roles is beyond the scope of this book. One might inquire, however, why a dance might be too rough for a woman playing fiddle but not too rough for her on the dance floor or playing accompaniment on pump organ or guitar.
20. Teresa MacPhee Wilson, personal interview, Nov. 14, 2006, PEIFP Interview #37.
21. As noted in chapter 5, some boys in this family learned to play despite discouragement from their father.
22. As noted in chapter 6, Joe à Bibienne Arsenault originally hailed from Québec.
23. According to Dr. Michael D. Rosengarten, editor in chief of *Online Journal of Cardiology*, www.hrt.org (e-mail communication, Nov. 15, 1998), there seems to be no basis for this recommendation in current medical thinking.

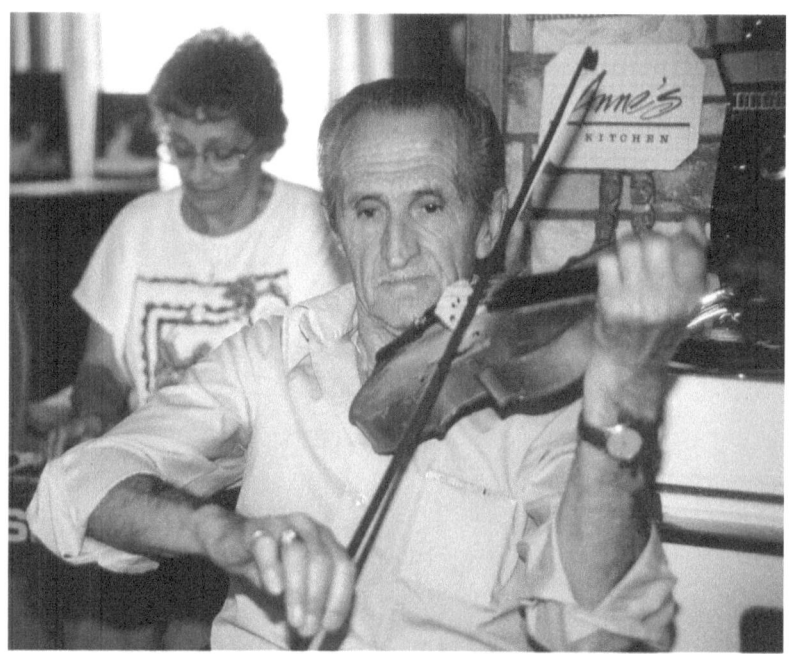

PHOTO 7.3. ERVAN SONIER (FIDDLE) AND ANNE-MARIE GALLANT ARSENAULT AT SUMMERSIDE, AUGUST 1991 (PHOTO BY EARTHWATCH TEAM).

CHAPTER EIGHT

"I'd Have to Say It Was a Bad Instrument"

Although it would be reasonable to assume from their importance in community life that fiddlers as a class would generally have basked in the high esteem of their neighbors, paradoxically, this was often far from the case. In fact, the same individuals whose talents were quickly sought out when a house party was in the offing might otherwise be regarded as persons of dubious character, who were prone to neglect such "real" community duties as farm chores and child rearing in favor of an activity regarded by most as merely an amusement.

> There was a belief here that if a man ever became a fiddler—In order to be a good fiddler, you couldn't be any good for anything else. First of all, it implied an addiction to the instrument. And young fellows, once they started playing it they'd spend all their time playing the fiddle, and do nothing else. You were done for. You would never be a success in life; that was it! That was a strongly held belief. (John Cousins: Bloomfield, Prince County)

> Years ago [a fiddler] wasn't much good for anything else! He was quite often a shiftless sort of a fellow. All they were any good for was a drink of rum and play

the fiddle. That's the way it was. In the old days they were handy to have around for a house party, but they didn't have a very high position at all. (Jimmy Halliday: Eldon, Queens County)

Stories abound, which Islanders take much glee in recounting, that focus on the lack of responsibility to home and hearth shown by fiddlers intent on playing their instruments. Ervan Sonier of Summerside, Prince County, for example, tells the following tale:

> This was a true story, I think. I remember Guy Boulter, a terrific fiddler from up west. And they were going to get Guy. So this afternoon somebody's there with some 'shine. "Come on, Guy, we're goin' to have a party." So he takes off. Now the woman's at the door, and she yells, "Guy," she said, "You're leaving with the fiddle again?" "Yes." And she said, "You know there's not a stick of wood cut about the place?" "Christ, woman," he said, "I'm taking the fiddle, not the axe!" So it was a bad instrument! I'd have to say it was a bad instrument.

Another story told of Boulter—how he unhitched a three-horse team in the middle of a workday and grabbed his fiddle when a tune came to mind—is employed in chapter 6 to illustrate the process of subconscious tune recall. The point of the story as told by Islanders, however, is that this man was so addicted to the fiddle that he would sacrifice both precious energy and potential work time to play it. To his neighbors, then, the main thing about Boulter was not his fiddling prowess but, as John Cousins points out, that "he never made any success of farming at all, because he always neglected his farming." Cousins also tells another story in this vein that goes so far as to blame the decline and disappearance of an entire Kings County community on fiddling:

> Somebody told me that down at Rock Barra, which is near East Point—whether this is a myth or not—Anyway, Rock Barra is now a deserted community. There's nobody there. You drive along, and I don't know if there's a farm there or not. But someone attributed the demise of this community to the fact that there was too many good fiddlers. They just never did anything else but play the fiddle, and they were useless.

Added to this image of the fiddler as shiftless ne'er-do-well was that of the fiddler as perennial alcoholic. As Jimmy Halliday tells us above, the general opinion was "all they were any good for was a drink of rum and play the fiddle." Similarly, Glenna Bowness of Kensington, Prince County, recalls, "Even the good fiddlers years back were considered scum, you know. They fiddled all night and drank, and then they couldn't work the next day, so they were counted as no-gooders."

Finally, fiddlers were also held accountable for the general climate of alcohol abuse and violence that all too often surrounded Island dances. Fr. Charles Cheverie of Charlottetown describes it as follows:

> And then there's the question of high-spirited young people, and maybe middle-aged people, too, who at every dance got into a bit of fisticuffs. It was not uncommon for people in a given region to fight among themselves, but what happened more frequently was people comin' from other communities would get in, and then you'd have fights occurring. I suppose a lot of the priests at that time thought, "If you're not going to behave yourselves, then no more parties." And of course, if you want to get at the source of it: get rid of the fiddler!

Although these stereotypes were supported by a considerable amount of superficial evidence, they effectively concealed an unfortunate set of social arrangements whereby fiddlers were scapegoated by their own neighbors. Powerful pressures and demands placed on fiddlers by both church and community contributed to work neglect and alcoholism. The fiddler's reputation as an alcoholic was considerably amplified by certain attitudes and customs that grew up in response to the Island's long-standing but often ignored Prohibition laws. And as far as violent behavior at dances was concerned, fiddlers were far more often innocent bystanders than active participants.[1]

One of the major foundations upon which these stereotypes rested was a general sense that fiddling and dancing were morally suspect activities. For the source of this notion, one needs look no further than a whole complex of negative attitudes involving both social dancing and dance musicians that have been periodically promulgated throughout much of the Western world by the Christian church. A full understanding of fiddling's place on the Island, therefore, requires that we also take into account the nature and extent of some of these old doctrines.

"That's the Shadow Side of the Story"

The first major component of Island fiddling's negative image is the notion that an obsession with playing drains a person's energies and distracts him from real work. If a fiddler's energies were often drained, however, the real culprit was not so much an obsession with fiddling as it was the virtually continual demands for fiddling services placed on him by church and community. These demands, in turn, were supported by a tightly knit web of beliefs and attitudes.

As previously noted, many Island churches taught that the "divine gift" of fiddling ought to be shared freely with the community and thereby harnessed to its service. All too often, however, this notion of sharing was taken one step further, to the point where this gift was to be shared without hesitation or any hope of recompense and with little regard for the fiddler's own needs or desires. This position was sometimes put forward in no uncertain terms by local clergymen, as in this instance described by Angus McPhee of Mt. Stewart, Queens County:

> They were having dances in the church hall, and of course some of us balked and didn't want to play. Well, an awful cardin' [scolding] the next Sunday after the altar boys. It was a gift from God, and we were supposed to use it: no matter for who it was. So we played after that. [*Question*: Who was it that told you?] The priest—He was tellin' them they all [should have] played. That was his excuse. He said it was a gift from God and you were supposed to use it. Everybody didn't have it, so it wasn't a very good idea not to do it if you could do it. We were doing it for nothing, of course.

Added to church-generated pressures was the network of community obligations. If one farmer had to harvest potatoes, the neighbors dropped everything and helped out. If someone took sick, the neighbors helped with the chores; if someone wanted to put up a new barn, the neighbors pitched in, and so on. In the same vein, local fiddlers were relied upon to provide music whenever it was required.

Fiddlers played for house parties, frolics, showers, weddings, and other community dances. They appeared at fund-raisers that financed church, school, and other local projects. They were also continually on call whenever neighbors simply had the whim to hear music. Fiddlers had to fulfill these musical responsibilities day in and day out, often in disregard of their own needs, interests, state of mind, and general health. In other words, the role of district fiddler on Prince Edward Island had many aspects in common with what is generally regarded as an occupation in Western culture.

As far as Island church and community were concerned, however, fiddling was not a job but merely an amusement, deserving of neither special recognition nor financial return. The fiddler's activities may have been essential to the smooth operation of district social life, but he generally went unpaid unless the neighbors out of the kindness of their hearts tossed him a few coins following a dance. The upshot here was that most fiddlers were essentially working two jobs but getting economic returns for only one.

Even more problematic in this regard was that the aforementioned network of sharing and community obligations went only one way. In other words, the fiddler had numerous obligations to church and community, but they acknowledged none toward him that stemmed from his music making. The neighbors did not see it as their duty to help a fiddler with chores on the day following a late-night house party, nor did local clergymen send along representatives to lighten a fiddler's burden on the days following a benefit dance. As far as the neighbors were concerned, if the fiddler's work was done poorly or not at all, it was his laziness or poor moral character that was at fault, not the system. Bishop Faber MacDonald (b. Little Pond, Kings County) sums up the basic problem as follows:

> That brings up another consideration in terms of the gift [of music], you see. Like [with] everything else, a certain perversion can set in and did set in. In a lot of instances, the community began to think they owned the fiddler. So just as the individual fiddler himself can lose sight of the fact that his gift is not exclusively for himself, the community can have the same kind of possessiveness. Maybe the church and community would use the fiddler to promote their cause, whatever the cause might be. He was key to an event that was going to raise money to build something, a church building or some social building. And maybe the church and maybe society could certainly bear some responsibility for a lack of awareness, of not cultivating an awareness of who this guy was for us.

Indeed, many fiddlers found themselves chafing under the pressures generated by their neighbors' unrelenting stream of demands.

> If you played the first four nights of the week, and a good friend come along and said, "Look, I'm having a house party Friday night, will you come and play?" Now what are you gonna say? You can't just say, "No, I won't do it for you." And that was another thing. If you played for one fellow, then the other fellow'd say, "Well, you played for him, why aren't you playin' for me?" You kind o' get trapped into the thing, you know. It got pretty tiresome at times. (Archie Stewart: Milltown Cross, Kings County)

> If you went to one, how could you say no to the next fellow? That's the sort of thing you got into. You felt obliged, you know. Like you went to play for this fellow over here. Then this fellow down there, his daughter is getting married next week and he's gonna have a shower and a wedding: "You played at his house, how come you won't play at mine?" I mean, that don't work! You know them all; they're all your neighbors. (Leonard McDonald: Emyvale, Queens County)

PHOTO 8.1. LEONARD AND CLAIRE MCDONALD AT THE "PIGPEN," KELLYS CROSS, JULY 1992 (PHOTO BY KEN PERLMAN).

And every once in a while, a fiddler would be driven to the breaking point. In the following instance cited by Andrew Jones of Pleasant View, Prince County, one hard-pressed musician chose an unusually effective method for letting his neighbors know that he'd had enough.

> One fellow I remember named Blanchard, he was the only fiddler around then. He played all night and was played out. At the last of it he refused to play, so they coaxed him and coaxed him. They had an old-fashioned stove, them with the round oven on it. And they asked him to play anyway, so he opened the door and put the fiddle in there, with a big fire on! So after a while they started smellin' the glue. The dance was over then! That's how he got rid of playing.

If under these conditions fiddlers began to systematically neglect their farming or fishing, who could blame them? Bishop MacDonald describes the dynamic as follows:

> He's worn out! It took a lot of stamina. Some of them had to travel long distances to play at a place, you know: the horse and sleigh in the winter, the horse and wagon in the summer. In the summertimes they'd have to travel eight or ten miles to play,

play all night, drive back, and then to have to do their work next day. So there was quite a price to pay from their part. People expected a lot from this man, you know. And any individual who feels used and exploited will feel a lot of pain after a while, and degraded, no matter who he is. And then eventually he has to get some way to still that pain, or he has to find ways to continue to be able to produce when he doesn't even feel like producing anymore. And so then you get into the "more rum for the fiddler" syndrome, see? That was the expression, "more rum for the fiddler," and many of them got trapped in that. That's the shadow side of the story.

In their image of him as "lazy no-gooder," then, many Islanders failed to understand that the fiddler was actually very busy indeed helping to entertain his neighbors. And if these same neighbors truly believed that providing music was indeed pastime and not work, they conveniently ignored their own complicity in both creating music events and demanding that fiddlers play for them.

It may well be asked how Island fiddlers' lopsided social role—characterized by high demands from neighbors with little offered in return—could evolve in a society whose prime principle was reciprocity. Just why was fiddling not considered "work," and why did the act of fiddling not serve as a unit of currency in the exchange of obligations?[2] The answer may well lie in church teachings that have at times placed fiddling and social dancing beyond the pale. Certain doctrines—preached throughout the Western world at different times and with varying degrees of intensity by nearly every Christian denomination, Catholic and Protestant alike—branded the fiddle as the devil's instrument and declared many of its practitioners to be in active league with Old Nick himself.

The Devil's Instrument

There are two major currents of thought behind church opposition to dance playing in general and fiddling in particular.[3] The first is an offshoot of the belief that musical talent, music memory, and even music composition can derive in whole or in part from denizens of the spirit world, such as sprites and fairies; all too often, such relatively benign pagan relics were literally demonized by the church in an effort to enforce religious hegemony. The second principle, stated in secular terms, is as follows: by transporting participants to an emotional plane that transcends ordinary social and psychological restrictions, activities such as fiddling and dancing place themselves in league with the dark forces of human nature, personified in the figure of the devil.[4] In turn, both these notions fed off a variant of the secular stereotype described above, that both dancing and playing dance music are not only distracting and addicting but also inherently subversive to the social fabric.

Ultimately, stories associating fiddling and the devil became a popular theme in European and North American folklore. Such tales follow three major motifs. First, pieces of music or musical talent are acquired through chance encounters with the Evil One. In a story from Donegal, Ireland, for example, a fiddler named Mooney runs away from a nagging wife and encounters by the roadside a dark stranger (the devil), who borrows Mooney's instrument and plays a wonderful jig. Upon discerning the stranger's identity, Mooney delightedly extends his hand and declares, "Shake hands with your relations, my friend. I'm married to your sister!" He later recalls the tune and plays it locally, where thereafter it becomes known as "The Devil and His Sister."[5] In the nineteenth century, rumors suggesting an infernal gift of this kind had a profound effect on the reputation of famed violin virtuoso Niccolò Paganini (1782–1840). During Paganini's lifetime it was often asserted that he owed "his extraordinary technical feats . . . to some Faustian pact with the Devil."[6] Because of such rumors, for years after the maestro's death the Catholic Church denied his heirs the right to bury his remains in consecrated ground.[7]

Second, the devil engages an already accomplished player in competition. One recent manifestation of this motif is a well-known country-music song called "The Devil Went Down to Georgia," in which Lucifer wagers a golden fiddle against the musician's soul.[8] The devil is defeated in this instance, but there are other tales of this ilk in which he emerges victorious.[9] Finally, the devil or one of his minions appears suddenly at a dance with instrument in hand. A tale circulates in Newfoundland, for example, in which the new fiddler at a party in Barbados turns out to be the Lord of Flies, and all those present are compelled by his music to dance until their feet are literally worn away.[10]

Although church opposition to dancing and dance musicians in Britain, Ireland, and North America was more or less ongoing, the strength with which this message was promoted ebbed and flowed. In the latter half of the seventeenth century, for example, many regions were dominated by austere Protestant sects whose clergy spoke out consistently against "promiscuous"[11] dancing and—the violin not yet being in significant circulation—also against pipers, flutists, and violists.[12] By contrast, a few generations later, the first Scottish and Irish immigrants to Prince Edward Island grew up in an atmosphere of musical tolerance, although clerical fulminations against music and dance would certainly have been within living memory. PEI's first generations of immigrants would also have been familiar with some of the eighteenth- and early nineteenth-century Scottish fiddle tune titles that in effect "send up" the relationship between dance music and Old Nick posited by seventeenth-century clergy. Some examples of this phenomenon include "Deil among the Tailors," "The Devil and the Dirk," "Devil's Dream," "Devil's Hop," "Devil in the Kitchen," and "Deil Stick the Minister."[13]

In the mid-nineteenth century, a powerful current of religious revivalism coursed through Great Britain, Ireland, and North America, bringing with it a climate of repression directed toward both dance musicians and social dancing. Because the fiddle had by this time become the dominant dance-accompaniment instrument in these regions, most antimusic proscriptions were aimed squarely at fiddlers and their instruments. In Scotland, for example, "there are many horrifying stories from this period of ministers ordering public bonfires of fiddles, excommunicating farmers for holding barn-dances on their premises, and so reducing the demand for fiddles that the instruments had to be sold off at auctions at nominal prices."[14] In Ireland, many parishes banned dancing of all kinds, thereby sending many local fiddlers and pipers to the workhouse, while some priests "scoured the countryside hunting for courting couples and purging fiddlers from crossroads dances."[15] On Cape Breton Island, numerous Catholic and Protestant clergymen "held to the puritanical view that pipes and fiddles were instruments of the devil." The most notorious of these was Fr. Kenneth MacDonald, priest of the Mabou–West Lake Ainslie Parish from 1865 to 1894, who at one point "had all the pipes and fiddles [in the area] gathered up and burned."[16] Stories in a similar vein also emanate from many regions of the American South.[17]

Prince Edward Island experienced its own Christian revival during the mid- to late nineteenth century, and there too zealots among the clergy spread the message connecting fiddling, dancing, and the infernal. That these teachings bore at least some fruit is evidenced by one Kings County man, who notes in his memoirs that he "got the impression that a fiddle was a wicked instrument, that it had as many devils as the man of Gadara."[18] Similarly, a Queens County woman was so sure of the connection between fiddling and the devil that during a house party several pranksters convinced her that an infernal visitation was in progress by merely stopping the flue and directing smoke into the kitchen. According to one account, an exorcism had to be performed before she would once again consent to enter that dwelling.[19]

Dancing of any kind was forbidden in certain communities, although such strictures were much more common in Protestant than in Catholic districts. Along these lines, the following account describes a late nineteenth-century gathering in which the strict Presbyterian principles of one Kings County family were put to the test by their new neighbors:

> One of the neighbor boys came in with a suspicious looking parcel and soon we heard the thrum, thrum, thrum of the fiddle in one of the rooms. This was followed up by a lively little tune. This was just to start cautiously to see how it would be received.... There being no protest another tune was given, and soon some of the light footed ones tripped about on the nice smooth floor. Before we realized it, a real housewarming was in full glow.[20]

As was the case in many other regions, the destruction of a musical instrument could serve as a rite of passage for those who wished to declare a newfound piety. The following two accounts of this phenomenon originate from heavily Protestant southeastern Queens County. The Mr. Macdonald cited below is Rev. Donald McDonald (1783–1867), the Scottish-born founder of the McDonaldites congregations and probably the most prominent exponent of the Christian revival on Prince Edward Island.

> When Angus Joiner (McLeod) . . . became a convert of Mr. Macdonald, he was admonished by him to put aside the violin he loved to play "as belonging to the flesh." Angus took it out and destroyed it with an axe.[21]

> Musical instruments were not held in favor. One young man who performed very well on the bagpipes abandoned the practice at the time of his conversion; and to prove his sincerity destroyed the instrument which he had made with his own hands.[22]

Although this crusade against musicians and musical instruments had for the most part subsided on the Island by the end of the nineteenth century, remnants persisted for generations. Eddy Arsenault of St. Chrysostom, Prince County, for example, recalls that when he was a boy in the 1920s, local priests often spoke out against music and dance; and when at age fifteen he took up the instrument, on some level he felt himself "the worst sinner."[23] Similarly, Archie Stewart reports that during the same period "there'd [still] be a certain amount of old ladies in the district who didn't believe in dancin' and drinkin', and they'd be kickin' up a row."[24]

As the years passed, the grip of the church on Island music and dance continued to slacken. In some Acadian districts in Prince County, for example, square dancing would still be forbidden on Sundays, but even that stricture could sometimes be relaxed with permission from the curé.[25] And Margaret Ross MacKinnon (b. Flat River, Queens County) reports that although secular music playing was still banned on Sundays in southeastern Queens County until well into the 1960s, Angus Leslie MacLean "used to go down to the [music] room and devise schemes to play his tunes [so] that nobody would hear."[26]

In some areas where strictures against music playing had generally relaxed, those aimed at dancing remained in force for the devout until relatively recently. Danny MacLean (b. Garfield, Queens County) notes, for example, that his grandfather Lauchy MacLean was a good fiddler, but "he wouldn't play at no [dance] parties; he just didn't believe in parties because we were kind o' religious people." By the 1970s a Baptist church based in northeastern Kings County may have been the last holdout in this regard, as reported by Kenny Chaisson (b. Bear River) and his distant cousin Lemmy Chaisson of nearby Rollo Bay.

> LEMMY CHAISSON: If you go east of Souris, it'd be the worst place you could ever play. They were great listeners but they wouldn't dance, mostly because the most populated area up there was Baptist, and they weren't allowed to do that at the time. They wouldn't go to dances for anything. Even young people my own age, they weren't allowed to dance.
>
> KENNY CHAISSON: You could almost see the change coming over the years, how the number of people who started dancing [increased]. And they loved listening to the music, eh, but it was just sort of against their—
>
> LEMMY CHAISSON: Their upbringing was not to [dance], and I guess they just didn't do it. But now, most of those people that wouldn't dance are all up on the floor dancing; even the seniors there. It's fantastic the way it has changed.

Interestingly, just as churches in many contemporary North American communities might express disapproval for gambling in general but employ the game of chance known as bingo to help raise money, so too did Island churches begin to sponsor fiddle dances as fund-raising events. As a result, even in the mid-nineteenth century during the heart of PEI's Christian revival, players of the devil's instrument were continually being called upon to use their God-given gifts to help raise money for religious causes. Ultimately, as we have seen, fiddle dances became a major revenue source for Island churches of nearly all denominations.

By the 1920s, the prevailing attitude of the Catholic Church and most mainstream Protestant denominations toward fiddling began to shift markedly.

Ironically, by that time these churches had begun to view fiddle music and dance as potential buffers against the spread of new and far more dangerous musical threats, such as jazz, blues, and the sexually provocative styles of dancing that came in their wake.[27] And by the 1970s, clergymen throughout the Maritimes were actively engaged in leading revival movements dedicated to the preservation of fiddling.

Although the complex of attitudes painting fiddling as evil had lost much of their virulence on the Island by the lifetimes of the fiddlers interviewed for this project, vestiges were undoubtedly lurking in the background, ready to amplify any negative impressions about the art and its practitioners that the public might otherwise entertain. In this atmosphere, the "sharing" of musical gifts was probably regarded as an opportunity by which fiddlers might partially redeem themselves from the sin of playing. Such an opportunity would then be seen as its own reward, making further recognition or recompense unnecessary.

"More Rum for the Fiddler"

The second aspect of the Island fiddler's negative image paints him as an inveterate alcoholic. Although many Island fiddlers did indeed turn to alcohol as a refuge from the many conflicting pressures they experienced, this is only part of the story. Again, it was the fiddler's neighbors—in pursuing their own amusements—who promoted his drinking on the one hand, then blamed the victim for moral weakness on the other.

At many district dances, fiddlers were continually plied with alcohol. As far as his neighbors were concerned, having a "happy" (that is, inebriated) fiddler on hand was ideal, since he would then be likely to continue playing throughout an entire occasion without protest. As Fr. Charles Cheverie recalls, "It was quite customary to have the fiddler treated with these drinks. The old saying 'more rum for the fiddler' was very common, and in some cases the more rum, the better fiddling. So you paid accordingly." The following two stories indicate just how far some house-party denizens would go to see that fiddlers were kept well-oiled:

> I was playin' for a weddin' down Panmure Island. And as the weddin' got goin' in the evenin', there was all kinds of stuff to drink there. A fellow come in, and he had a teddy of moonshine. He wanted me to have a drink out of it. I said no, I haven't got time. You know, there was one set right after another. So he went to the cupboard and he got a spoon, and he pulled a chair up in front of me and he sat down. He

opened the bottle, and I was playing away. And he'd fill the spoon with the moonshine. He'd put it in my mouth. And I'd drink it! He fed me the whole bottle. At one o'clock, the fiddle went over my shoulder and down behind me and hit on the floor. I was scared to turn around. So that ended the dancin' that night. That was a common occurrence, you know; the fiddler would get drunk and that'd end the dance. It was this fiddle here: there's the chip I knocked out of her! (Archie Stewart)

Right across the road here was a fellow who made the best beer, in large quantities. I was playing for a house party down there one night, and I didn't drink very much at the time, but he made sure I was well enough looked after. I was playing by this old kitchen stove, and on the tank of the stove he set a glass and a great big pitcher of beer. And I was to fill my own glass. And every time the pitcher would get down about that much [indicates a few inches], he'd fill it up. Never the glass: he'd fill the pitcher! I thought, "Now you've got quite a system here! I like it!" But that was typical. That's why I think so many fiddlers turned out to be alcoholics, because the fiddler was always well looked after. (Leonard McDonald)

Along these lines, the gift of a quantity of rum or 'shine was often considered fair payment for a night of playing outside the community. Robert Crane (b. Riverton, Kings County), for example, tells this story involving his father, the well-known fiddler Ward Crane:

This "Big Joe" Kennedy from St. Teresa's drove in, wanted us to go play for this weddin'. "I don't think we can go, Joe." Of course, he kept coaxin' and coaxin'. "No, I don't think we can go." And after a while Joe reached inside of his shirt and pulled out a big full quart: "Try a taste of that, Ward." So then my father turned around to me and said, "What do you think Bob, will we go? All right, we'll go." It was before dark we landed down there in Cardigan. And we played till about four o'clock in the mornin' and drank rum all night. And you know what pay we got? We got home at the gate, there in the driveway; and he handed [my father] a quart of rum, about three-quarter full.[28]

Another aspect of the fiddler's reputation as an alcoholic derives from a custom that calls for rural Islanders at public events to do their drinking in private; drinking in public was simply not socially acceptable. So while most Islanders could consume alcohol with impunity at dances by merely moving outside the spotlight of public attention, fiddlers had no such luxury. Being virtually chained to their chairs playing for square sets and step dancing, fiddlers had to imbibe in plain view, thereby labeling themselves at best as louts and at worst as drunks with no self-control.

As Fr. Charles Cheverie tells us, this habit of drinking in private developed as a method of evading detection by Revenuers, Mounties, and other government enforcers during the seventy-odd years that Islanders were subject to Prohibition laws. "On the Island in Prohibition days in particular, a lot of the drinking was done—it picked up a peculiar social style and custom. You brought your pint in your back pocket or your coat pocket, and you went outside behind the barn to consume it."

Laws aimed against the consumption or manufacture of alcoholic beverages on Prince Edward Island go back to the 1870s, and in 1906 the Legislative Assembly put the entire Island under a permanent Prohibition Act.[29] As authorities in the United States were to subsequently discover, Prohibition never stemmed the flow of liquor or succeeded in curtailing its use. Instead, the process of distributing and drinking alcohol was merely driven underground. As one observer commented, "It is noteworthy that those periods in which all-out attempts were made to make the province 'dry,' were the very ones in which rum runners discharged thousands of gallons of liquor upon its shores . . . , and in which 'moonshiners' had stills in almost every bush."[30]

The predominant method for making moonshine during the Island's Prohibition days relied on the fermentation of molasses, which was plentiful and cheap because of long-standing trade links with the British West Indies. A mixture of molasses, water, and yeast was prepared and allowed to ferment for about ten days. The result was then poured into a metal cream can, which was capped with a makeshift wooden stopper wrapped with a flour-encrusted rag to serve as a sealant; the stopper was then wired firmly in place. Coiled copper tubing ran from inside the can through a hole in the stopper and then was directed through a tub of cold water. When the mixture was heated, the distillate would condense as it went through the water. The distiller threw out the poisonous first cup and bottled the rest: roughly a gallon of 'shine. *Molasses beer*—fermented molasses in its nondistilled form, often flavored with such additives as juice or raisins—was often consumed by Islanders in lieu of conventional beer, which is traditionally made from barley or other grains.[31]

Rum-running in particular became quite a profitable business. As Bill MacDonald (b. North Lake, Kings County) points out, cargoes of West Indian rum were picked up from St. Pierre and Miquelon, two islands under French jurisdiction located just off the coast of Newfoundland. He goes on to describe the operation:

> The vessels used to take the rum, and they'd lay off the three-mile limit, then come in handy at night. The fishermen would come in and get boatloads: all kinds of rum,

PHOTO 8.2. JOE MACDONALD AT ST. ANDREWS, AUGUST 1992 (PHOTO BY EARTHWATCH TEAM).

whiskey, hand-brand alcohol, cigarettes, nylons, all kinds of make-up for ladies, and silk scarves—all contraband, eh. I remember seeing sixty kegs, some would be five gallon and some would be ten gallon, all piled up on the shore when I was a kid.

Once the rum had made it safely to shore, middlemen would purchase the liquor at twenty-five dollars per keg; it was then retailed by local bootleggers at about one dollar per *teddy*, which was eight ounces. One of the prime locations for these bootleggers to hawk their wares was outside local dance venues, where teddies of rum or 'shine could quickly disappear into customers' pockets.

Needless to say, rumrunners were often regarded as something approaching folk heroes by many rural Islanders. Joe MacDonald of St. Andrews, Kings County, for example, proudly recounted to us an exploit involving the most famous rumrunner of them all, Captain Edward Dicks (1879–1943). In 1927, Dicks's ship, the *Nelly* J. *Banks*, was seized by the Canadian Coast Guard while it was steaming, loaded with rum, through waters that he later claimed were outside the three-mile limit of Canadian federal jurisdiction. MacDonald's version of the story is as follows:

They sailed into Charlottetown, they unloaded the kegs of rum, and they put 'em in a building at the end of the wharf. [Dicks] put up his crew in the most expensive place in Charlottetown. When it came to trial the next spring, they didn't have a thing! He had his chart, and he showed it to the judge, and the judge just threw [the case] out because the officers had nothing to prove that Dicks was where they said he was. So they had to put the rum back on his ship again. [Dicks] got to the warehouse, and all the kegs in the bottom were all empty. The lads were all goin' down and borin' under the buildin' catchin' the rum, and there was rum all winter in Charlottetown. The [government] had to send a ship to St. Pierre then to replace it. It was quite an embarrassment![32]

In one somewhat bizarre twist to the Prohibition saga, a provision was added to the law in 1919 that allowed an Islander to obtain alcohol legally from the newly created Liquor Commission if he could "secure a permit from his physician certifying that the liquor was for medicinal purposes only."[33] This ultimately set up the following once-commonplace sham. First, an individual went to the doctor and declared, "Doc, I'm awful dry!" The doctor then wrote a permit for the appropriate cure (say, a fifth of rum). Finally, the "patient" presented this prescription at the nearest Liquor Commission outlet and got his rum.[34]

Although the alcohol trade was more or less regularized by the 1950s, the custom of drinking in private persisted among rural Islanders for decades afterward and was still the prevailing norm well into the 1990s. Long after the end of Prohibition, therefore, the fiddler's well-abetted public drinking made him a convenient target for those who found fault with the widespread overindulgence in alcohol that was common practice at Island dances.

"The Evening Wasn't a Success Unless There Was a Fight"

The third and final aspect of the fiddlers' stereotype on Prince Edward Island depicts them fomenters of violence. All too often, house parties, weddings, and other Island dances were associated with fisticuffs, brawling, and other forms of mayhem. For many Islanders, observing or participating in such activities served as the high point of an evening's entertainment. In fact, the question "Can you remember any one house party that stands out in your memory?" almost always led to a description of some kind of battle royal. As Archie Stewart notes with only some facetiousness, "I remember a lot of house parties: a lot of good fights, too! The evening wasn't a success unless there was a fight." Similarly, three western Prince County musicians—Elmer Robinson and Dorothy Rogers of Woodstock, and George O'Connor of Kildare Capes—offer the following assessment:

ROBINSON: That used to be quite a tradition around here!

O'CONNOR: Everybody'd have a white shirt and tie. And the first thing, bang, crash, and nothing but the collar left when they got through with it!

INTERVIEWER: What did people fight about?

O'CONNOR: No trouble at all to find a reason!

ROGERS: They used to speak for a place for the next dance.[35] And some fellow would come along and say, "Can I have your place next time?" He didn't want the girl, he just wanted that place. When the dance would be over, someone else would come and take it, and then the war would be on.

ROBINSON: I don't think we'll fight now over a place to dance. That's all over with!

Although fiddlers sometimes participated in these fracases, neither their music nor their influence lay at the root of the problem. A full explanation of dance-related violence on the Island is beyond the scope of this book, but at least the main dynamics can be pinpointed without too much difficulty. From a distance, some aspects of PEI's once closely knit community life may seem idyllic, but in general this was no utopia. The daily routine was often characterized by hard, physical toil for small economic returns, creating for many a reservoir of pent-up feelings that in the normal course of events was afforded few socially acceptable outlets. Personal privacy was virtually unknown, and behavior was generally kept within narrow bounds by powerful social pressures.

> In the end, the very character of the community was imbued with the qualities of conservation and control. Emotional extravagance became as rare as economic improvidence, and even words were measured out carefully, like coins in a purse.[36]

Even if one assumes that most Islanders got along well with their neighbors, inevitably there were exceptions. And once a grudge had grown up, community life afforded plenty of time and opportunity for it to fester, expand, and even be passed among generations. In fact, given the Island's original settlement patterns, some old scores were probably traceable to events in the old country prior to the days of immigration.[37]

When dances brought Islanders from different districts together, still other factors came into play. For one thing, as Archie Stewart tells us, some men simply had reputations for toughness to uphold.

> Each district had their strong man or their hard man. Each district had somebody they thought could fight better than somebody else, and those two guys would meet, and they'd fight just to see who's the best man. And I seen hard fights: two

fellas fightin' just to see who was the best at it, who was the strongest, who was the best fighter, and that's the only reason they were fightin'. They both had a hard name, and they'd meet and square off, boy, and go at it: the best man win!

More importantly, just below the surface were remnants of long-standing ethnic and religious animosities. Catholics and Protestants, for example, did not mix freely on the Island until the past few generations.[38] As Joe MacDonald recalls, "When I was young, you could feel the bigotry then: all good friends and everything, but [Protestants] didn't muckle around with the Catholic religion, and the Catholics didn't muckle around with the Protestant religion." Similarly, there were hard feelings between Islanders of Scottish descent and their Irish counterparts going back to the days of the old lot system.[39] Finally, Acadians had been treated as second-class citizens by Islanders of British and Irish extraction until well into the twentieth century, thereby creating a legacy of mutual hostility and mistrust.[40]

Add to these various ingredients a high-energy atmosphere and free-flowing alcoholic beverages to lighten inhibition, and no help from fiddling would be required to explode this volatile mixture. And while there was always some precipitating incident—an insult, the competition for dance space, or just an offhand remark that brought unsettled old scores to mind—participants, as Attwood O'Connor of Milltown Cross, Kings County, tells us, were sometimes at a loss afterward to explain just how these free-for-alls had gotten started: "Actually, I don't think that a lot of them knew themselves what was fought about. Somebody'd say something to somebody else in fun, and he'd get cross and hit him, and that started the whole thing."

As the Island slowly modernized after the Second World War, and most dancing moved out of the homes and into regional dance halls, another factor came into play that sharply increased the incidence and scope of such violence. By bringing people together at a considerable distance from their native districts, these halls effectively neutralized even the relatively meager restraints on violent behavior that had once been provided by the presence of family and neighbors (for more on violence in the dance halls, see chapter 15).

"They Made Sure That Nobody Got Hurt around the Fiddler"

As a general rule, the fiddler was actually far less likely than most of his contemporaries to become a direct participant in these melees. For one thing, combatants were usually careful to avoid involving him. After all, if either musician or instrument were put out of service, there would be no more dancing that night! In fact, as Attwood O'Connor recalls, sometimes the fiddler was actually warned that a fight was in the offing, so that he could place himself and his precious instrument out of harm's way.

> As long as you had the fiddle you were all right. They made sure that nobody got hurt around the fiddler. If they got the fiddle broke or the fiddler left, that was it. They've come up and warned me not to go outside the door, that they were going to go out and fight. Phonsey McCarran said, "Somebody would hit you by mistake; we can't get along without the fiddler!"

Fiddlers could not always count on such warnings, however, and as Archie Stewart recalls, it was a good idea when playing for some dances to have an escape route or at least a safe haven for one's instrument, planned well ahead of time.

> I used to play at a dance, and the dance hall was awful bad for fights. I was always scared I'd get my fiddle broke. So I had put a string on the fiddle here [*points to the pegbox*], and I drove a nail up on the wall behind where I used to sit. The minute the fight started, I'd run around—Hung the fiddle up on the nail and waited until the fight was over. Then I took her down and played again. There wasn't much law and order then: survival of the fittest!

At some dance halls, fiddlers actually helped keep trouble to a minimum. Like the saloon pianists depicted in old Hollywood westerns, for example, Dave Thomson (b. West Royalty, Queens County), learned that he could keep the fighting from getting out of control merely by refusing to abandon his post.

> Down here at North River [, Queens County,] we had dances at the Old Fire Hall. There was hardly a night that there wasn't a fight break out. And one of the things you done was you never stopped playing, because that just gets more of them into it. Oh yeah, they'd all gather round the fight then. There was some good ones! They'd just start in the middle of the floor, but you don't pay much attention of it, and keep going. And then it's all over!

When fiddlers did resort to violence at Island dances, it was generally when they had to confront a direct personal threat, as described in the following accounts:

> There was a wedding here, not too far from the church. I got there around nine o'clock, and I was right in the middle of the room with my fiddle between two legs to tune, you know. Somebody grabbed me behind the back of the neck, and they

were really choking me. So I grabbed the fiddle and—Bang! The only thing that stayed in my hand was this [*shows the neck of the fiddle*]. I broke it right off at the side. He was drunk. But he had quite a bruise on the side of his head, I'm tellin' you! (Eddy Arsenault)

I was about eleven years old. My father was very muscular, and he'd played fiddle all night. He had a reputation for being very strong; his trade was blacksmithing. I remember one smart aleck coming to him and saying, "Could I get a demonstration of your ability?"—meaning physical ability, I guess. I think he must have had a couple of drinks. But my father just grabbed this fellow by the shoulders somehow, and I remember him just tossing him up against the wall! That was all there was to it. (Peter Doiron: b. North Rustico, Queens County)

This being said, it is nevertheless true that in 1912 one of the largest brawls ever to take place on Prince Edward Island was fought between two fiddling families from western Prince County, the Daltons and the Doyles. This fracas, since immortalized in Island lore as "the Chew at Campbellton Corner," is colorfully described by John Cousins.

One side had it that when the Doyles got up on the floor to dance, that the Daltons just sawed on the fiddle and made a bad job of it. The other allegation has it that one of Daltons was playing and one of the Doyles kicked the chair out from under him and broke the fiddle. But [in either event,] the challenge was sent out. The priest got wind of it, this being a Catholic community, and for the only time in the history of this area, he intervened from the altar the previous Sunday. He told the people not to have anything to do with this, and he told the protagonists to ease up: didn't do one bit of good! They met at Campbellton Corner. My father said there'd be five hundred people there [including spectators], and I believe him. A number of things happened. Number one, it was the one and only time in the history of West Prince [County] that I'm aware of, where a magistrate read what was called the Riot Act. He came out and stood on the corner, and he read the Riot Act, which empowered him to swear in special constables. And there was a song about it: "Peter Keefe and Underhill, Big Alec and his son / Were sworn in as constables before the fight begun." Now, Big Alec was Big Alec MacDonald, whose sons were fighting on one side. So there was a bit of partisanship. And these men were all big husky devils. Peter Keefe was a boxer, a big, big man, and Underhill Coughlin was a big, big man as well. My father was just a little boy and told me after the fight started he saw very little of it because there were so many people there. But he did see the main bout. The story I heard from several sources is that the Daltons, man for man, probably got the best of it. Art Dalton went toe to toe with Arch Doyle: Arch Doyle was a huge, huge man. And Arch Doyle couldn't touch him. Dalton was a fierce fighter and apparently a good fiddler too! There was other fighting that went on, too. But that was all over a fiddle, or all over fiddling!

Legacy of a Stereotype

These tales of all-too-universal human foibles may bring a knowing smile to the lips today, but it is nevertheless true that many fiddlers suffered mightily because of their generally disreputable image. If in the long run a fiddler faltered in his economic tasks, the neighbors—oblivious to their own role in the matter—merely nodded sagely and pointed to yet another example of the pitfalls attached to fiddle addiction. Even when a fiddler's fortunes were clearly declining, the neighbors would continue to ply him with liquor at house parties while ridiculing his drunkenness, keep him up late providing music while deriding his irresponsibility, and get to brawling over trifles while assuming that he was somehow to blame for this, as well.

Ultimately, fiddling's negative stereotypes led to a general devaluation on the Island of the art itself. After all, how could the local brand of fiddling be of much account if it was produced by a bunch of lazy, drunken reprobates? As noted in chapter 13, during the early years of radio and recordings, this attitude may well have discouraged local promoters from attempting to market the local playing style with any degree of seriousness. Conversely, it seems that most Island fiddlers bought into their neighbors' negative evaluations, and few of them ever made an attempt to professionalize or put themselves forward as participants in the new media age.

As the Island modernized and communities discovered alternative forms of entertainment and fund-raising, most locals were all too ready to cast the fiddler off like an old shoe and to brand him, among his other faults, as being completely irrelevant to the new era. Once fiddlers' music was no longer needed, all that remained in the average Island consciousness was the popular stereotype depicting them as shiftless, drunken, and violent.

NOTES

1. Stereotypes describing fiddlers as drunken, lazy, and violent also grew up in many other Celtic and North American fiddling cultures. Although the focus here is on Prince Edward Island, my sense from examining the secondary literature is that the dynamic described here may well have also been at work in these other regions.
2. There have been many primarily agricultural or barter-based societies in which offering musicians substantial rewards for performing was customary. For an overview, see Merriam, *Anthropology of Music*, 123–44.
3. Clerical proscriptions against dancing among the common folk go back at least as far as the early Middle Ages, although the message gained new strength following the

Reformation (1517–c. 1590). Calvinist sects in particular—such as Presbyterianism and its offshoots—stressed avoiding aspects of life that might serve to stimulate the senses and thereby distract the individual from establishing a personal relationship with God.

4. For a thorough discussion of both principles, see Quigley, *Music from the Heart*, 46–58. Explaining the coexistence in church doctrine of "fiddling as God's gift" with "fiddling as the devil's gift" is beyond the scope of this book. I can, however, suggest as an analogy the weather house barometer, where depending on atmospheric conditions either an ugly hag or a lovely maiden appears on the veranda. Instead of atmospheric pressure, however, the main factor determining which inhabitant appears on the veranda in a given era would be the church's social agenda.
5. Mac Aoidh, *Between the Jigs*, 63–64.
6. Plantinga, *Romantic Music*, 176.
7. Sugden, *Niccolo Paganini*, 136–39.
8. The song first appeared on an LP by the Charlie Daniels Band called *Million Mile Reflections* (1979). The basic melody was adapted from "Lonesome Fiddle Blues" by bluegrass fiddler Vassar Clements (1928–2005); the lyrics were composed by the Charlie Daniels Band.
9. Stories with this motif go back at least as far as the ancient Greeks. The most common pattern is that a mortal challenges Apollo, one of the Muses, or some other deity to a musical competition, is declared the loser, and then is punished severely for having had the effrontery to challenge the divinity.
10. Quigley, *Music from the Heart*, 46.
11. Literally, "mixed" dancing, the term then used to describe men and women dancing together.
12. Attempts at repression in seventeenth-century Scotland may not have been as consistent or far-reaching as some have claimed. See Emmerson, *Rantin' Pipe*, 28; and Emmerson, *Social History*, 69–81.
13. These tunes are listed in Charles Gore, *The Scottish Fiddle Music Index*, part 1: 27–28, and part 2: 10. A similar impulse in the American South inspired by a subsequent period of musical puritanism elicited such titles as "Devil in the Woodpile," "Hell among the Yearlings," and "Hell Broke Loose in Georgia"; see Wolfe, *Devil's Box*, xv.
14. Johnson, *Scottish Fiddle Music*, 213.
15. O hallmhurain, *Pocket History*, 78. See also Carolan, *Harvest Saved*, 24–25.
16. McKinnon, *Fiddling to Fortune*, 24–25. See also Dunn, *Highland Settler*, 54. According to some scholars, the current flowering of Cape Breton fiddling began just after Fr. MacDonald departed this mortal vale.
17. For example, see A. W. Putnam, *History of Middle Tennessee*, 465–66, quoted in "The First Tennessee State Champion Fiddler," *Devil's Box*, Dec. 2, 1968, 7; Milnes, *Play of a Fiddle*, 69–72; Cauthen, *With Fiddle*, 204, 210; and Nevell, *Time to Dance*, 73.
18. [Mellick], *Timothy's Boyhood*, 90.
19. Casey, "PEI Hallowe'en Story."
20. [Mellick], *Timothy's Boyhood*, 92–93.

21. MacQueen, *Skye Pioneers*, 84. This account may overstate McDonald's stance. He played the violin himself in youth, there is nothing specifically antifiddling in his writings, and his biographer M. LaMont (in *Reverend Donald McDonald*, 12) details McDonald's love for music. For an overview of McDonald's career, see Weale, "Time Is Come!" 35–39.
22. MacPhail, *Master's Wife*, 149.
23. Eddy Arsenault, personal interview, Aug. 5, 1999.
24. Archie Stewart, personal interview, Aug. 8, 1999.
25. Georges Arsenault, personal interview, Aug. 13, 1999.
26. Margaret Ross MacKinnon, personal interview, Aug. 10, 1999.
27. See, for example, O hallmhurain, *Pocket History*, 111–13. There is an interesting parallel here. In the mid-nineteenth century, the Catholic Church of Québec grew concerned about the spread of waltzes and other couples' dances among the rural population and began to actively encourage the very same quadrilles and other group dances that for generations they had bitterly opposed; see Voyer, *La danse traditionnelle*, 38–39.
28. Robert Crane, personal interview, Nov. 29, 2006, PEIFP Interview #65.
29. The Legislative Assembly is PEI's provincial legislature.
30. Lewis, "History of PEI Liquor Laws," Dec. 1957, 23.
31. The two fiddlers who offered this information in 2006 requested that I not cite them by name; both expressed reluctance to publicly admit their firsthand knowledge of such matters.
32. Geoff and Dorothy Robinson (in *Duty-Free*, 15–19) tell a more prosaic story based on contemporary newspaper accounts. The Canadian federal government caved in before trial and agreed to restore Dicks's property plus damages and legal fees after the latter went public with a series of "vitriolic" verbal attacks. Dicks sold the boat in 1928. In 1938, the boat was again captured by government cutters, as later described in "The *Nelly J. Banks*," a song by Lennie Gallant (MacKinnon and Belsher, *Prince Edward Island Music Series*, 16). The boat was destroyed in 1953.
33. Lewis, "History of PEI Liquor Laws," Nov. 1957, 40.
34. Archie Stewart, personal interview, Aug. 1993.
35. In Island parlance, "to speak for a place" meant reserving a place for the couple to dance in a square set.
36. Weale, "No Scope," 6.
37. Similarly, Dunn (in *Highland Settler*, 102–3) reports that on neighboring Cape Breton Island some brawls at dances could be traced to clan animosities that had originated in Scotland.
38. Catholic settlement on Prince Edward Island was forbidden by law in the early days of British control, and Catholics throughout the British empire were denied the vote until the 1830s; see, for example, Smith, *Historic Churches of PEI*, 13–14.
39. Generally, the earlier-arriving Scots held most of the best land, while the Irish had to be content with the dregs. Islanders of Scots and Irish background came into deadly conflict with each other over the distribution of land during the Belfast Riots of 1847; see MacDonald, *New Ireland*, 17.
40. Arsenault, *Island Acadians*, 101–36.

PHOTO 8.3. ANDREW JONES AT PLEASANT VIEW, PRINCE COUNTY, AUGUST 1991 (PHOTO BY EARTHWATCH TEAM).

CHAPTER NINE

"Everybody Got a Different Style to Play"

This chapter explores the playing styles of traditional PEI fiddlers as manifested in the early 1990s.[1] A musical style can be defined as that aspect of a musician's sound that immediately identifies him or her to the experienced ear as a member of a distinct musical group or subgroup. In terms of group style, similarities of sound are the result of many factors, such as shared playing techniques, shared attitudes, and a common set of life experiences. On the individual level, stylistic differences flow not only from such dimensions as talent, skill level, and taste but also from relatively small variations among players along a wide range of technical parameters. Because the characteristics of a musical style are often quite difficult to communicate via language, readers are highly encouraged to supplement the following discussion by listening to recordings of Island fiddling, such as those listed in the discography.[2] And while the following presentation is aimed as much as possible at the general reader, some discussion of music on a technical level is unavoidable.

Island fiddlers tend to be very much aware of the issue of playing style on both the group and the individual level, and most can clearly describe their own place within the stylistic universe of eastern Canadian fiddling. Essentially, each has his or her own personal style, which is a subset of a regional style, which is in turn is placed in relation to other styles played on the Island or in neighboring provinces. Eddy Arsenault of St. Chrysostom, Prince County, puts it this way:

> It don't make any difference where you go. You can go up west to Tignish, you can go east to Souris, you can go Summerside, and everybody got a different style to play.[3] You notice that? Now, in New Brunswick they got a different style, in Nova Scotia they have a different style, in Québec, and in Cape Breton. Now, in Cape Breton they don't play the same at all as they do at all in mainland Nova Scotia: all different! Jesus, it's a funny thing! It don't make any difference where you go; it's all different, it's all different styles.

On the individual level, each player is seen as having his or her own unique style or sound, as described by Johnny Joe Chaisson of Souris, Kings County: "I don't think there's two fiddlers that plays alike that I know of. It's hard to explain, but I got my own time,[4] my own style of playing, and somebody else hasn't got perhaps the same time." Similarly, Merlin Quinn of Cardross, Kings County, offers this assessment:

> Most fiddlers around here are playing their own style. Everybody to my way of thinking has a style. It's Joe playing, that's his style. Then the next night the other guy might play the same tune; it's the same notes and everything, but it's another style of playing.

The following interchange between the brothers Kevin and "Young Peter" Chaisson of Bear River, Kings County, both echoes these viewpoints and suggests a few other Island attitudes about playing style:

> KEVIN: Well, the thing I see about it, we're all individuals. It's just like, all the music, all the players—All I have to do is sit down and listen to a player, and I know who is playing; it's because that style is coming out.
>
> PETER: And where he's from.
>
> INTERVIEWER: How do you know that?
>
> PETER: By his sound, by his style.
>
> KEVIN: That's where the difference comes in as far as I'm concerned. I don't think it's got anything to do with ability; the sound that comes, it's coming from within. That's what I'm trying to get at.

As is the case for the gift of music and the quality of liveliness, then, an individual's sound or style is thought of as an inherent—and perhaps inborn—expression of the personality, to be as much discovered as it is developed.

PHOTO 9.1. "YOUNG PETER" CHAISSON AT MONTICELLO HEADQUARTERS, JULY 1991 (PHOTO BY EARTHWATCH TEAM).

Because one's own style comes from within, efforts to consciously imitate the styles of other players are strongly discouraged. Attwood O'Connor of Milltown Cross, Kings County, for example, declares, "I never believe in trying to imitate somebody; I just play in my own way, sometimes good, sometimes bad!" Similarly, Danny MacLean (b. Garfield, Queens County) remarks,

> A good fiddler should play his own way. He should never try to copy somebody else's. You'll hear this tune and you try and play it like this other fellow, and it's ninety-nine times out of a hundred the other fella is just playing it his own way, too. Everybody plays different!

Such attempts at imitation are seen as not only undesirable but also futile. There is no point in trying to exactly reproduce another player's sound since when all is said and done you wind up just sounding like yourself. As Merlin Quinn puts it, "Even if you're trying to imitate some great fiddler, you generally still come up with your own style of fiddling." Looked at another way, the wide variety of fiddling styles found on Prince Edward Island simply makes the world a more interesting place. In the words of Leonard MacDonald of Emyvale, Queens County, "If we all played exactly alike it wouldn't matter who played, would it."

As Kevin Chaisson also implies above, most Island fiddlers are so familiar with the individual styles of the colleagues who live in their area that they can generally identify them at musical events sight unseen. Fr. Charles Cheverie of Charlottetown also reports, "I'm sure if I hear somebody playing in the next room not knowing who it was, I could probably identify who's playing." How does this process of style recognition work? Jimmy O'Connor of Murray Harbour, Kings County, explains that each fiddler essentially has his or her own "voice" on the instrument. Recognizing it, then, is no different from identifying an artist on a popular recording.

> When you hear somebody singing a song on the radio, even if you [haven't] heard their name, you know who it is just by their voice. And the same with a fiddler, you can hear the difference. You can tell them all when they're playing because they're all different. They never play the same; they've [each] got a little different turn. You can tell pretty well once you know the fiddler, just by the sound.

Regional Styles

As implied above by "Young Peter" Chaisson, most Island fiddlers are also capable of pinning down within a few miles the home districts of complete strangers on the basis of their playing sound. To carry the vocal analogy just cited a little further, this process would be akin to identifying an anglophone singer's regional accent as American-Southern, Canadian-Maritimes, British, Irish, and so on.

One of the most fundamental regional distinctions that Islanders recognize separates the fiddlers of eastern Prince Edward Island, or Kings County, with its strong Scottish heritage, from those of western Prince Edward Island, or Prince County, with its strong Acadian heritage. Fiddlers from Kings County tend to favor moderate tempos, a smooth and controlled style of bowing, and a relatively ornate approach to embellishment, or *ornamentation*; they also play a repertoire that contains a high proportion of tunes considered by Islanders to have a Scottish origin.[5] Fiddlers from Prince County, in contrast, favor faster tempos and manifest a more vigorous and far less controlled approach to bowing. In fact, some players extend bow strokes so far afield that the implement seems in danger of flying out of their hands. They tend to decorate their tunes with rhythmic accents, or *syncopations*, and to play more of a "French"[6] and general North American repertoire. Here's how two fiddlers from the eastern side express some of these differences:

> If you get the traditional style of music from the west end of the Island, it's French. They play faster, and they play a little different from the way we play. And they got different tunes. (Archie Stewart: Milltown Cross, Kings County)

> It's mostly a Scottish accent to it in this part of the country. And when you get up to the western part of PEI, it's still reels that are played, only with a different flavor. When you go up west you'll find it's a French accent to the music. (Sterling Baker: Montague, Kings County)

This French "accent" (Fr. Charles Cheverie calls it a "French twang") is characterized by Hélène Arsenault Bergeron (b. St. Chrysostom, Prince County) as a unique rhythmic sensibility coming from Acadian culture that finds expression in both local dancing and fiddling styles.

> The style right here in the French area, I find that it has a drive that's different from other areas of the Island. The dancers from this area have something a little unique, and I guess it's the French roots. Just like the French fiddling style: there's a little shuffle thing that comes out in the music; I don't know if it's the dancing that inspires it or the music inspires the dancing, but one sort of mirrors the other.

The various differences between east and west become most extreme as one approaches the two outer edges of the Island, represented in the public mind by the two towns cited earlier in this chapter by Eddy Arsenault, namely, Tignish in western Prince County and Souris in northeastern Kings County. This stylistic continuum extends through to the neighboring provinces. Fiddling from Cape Breton (located to the east of Prince Edward Island across the Gulf of St. Lawrence) is seen as still more "Scotch"[7] than that of northeastern Kings County, while fiddling from New Brunswick (to the west of Prince Edward Island across the Northumberland Strait) is regarded as still more "French" than that of western Prince County.

Although this east-west divide has been in place throughout living memory, it has been sharpened over the past couple of generations as fiddlers from northeastern Kings County have increasingly borrowed repertoire and stylistic elements from the highly professionalized Cape Breton fiddling scene (more on this in chapter 13). As detailed in chapter 16, much of the impetus behind this trend has come from a single extended fiddling family: the Chaissons of Bear River. The family's place in the stylistic continuum is defined as follows by "Young Peter" Chaisson:

> We were born listening to my father's [Cape Breton fiddling] records and listening to him followin' a certain style on the fiddle, and it just come natural, I guess. They say there's an Island sound, and they say there's Cape Breton sound; well,

we're somewhere in between. Because you go to Cape Breton and they can tell an Island player, eh. But my grandfather's music and my father's music was a lot different. Like my grandfather was more of the Island-flavor type music, and Daddy adopted the Cape Breton Scottish sound.

Fiddlers from the center of the Island (roughly coinciding with the area occupied by Queens County) tend to play a style that blends the characteristics of east and west. As Cody Myers of New Haven, Queens County, describes it, these *central-Island* fiddlers incorporate some Scottish elements into their playing, but their music also tends to have a bit of the "French twang" to it.

> I grew up in the center part of the Island, and that's again a distinct kind of fiddling from Prince County and Kings. Prince County's mainly Acadian, and there's a lot of French. They might be playing Scotch tunes, but they have the French and Acadian touch. And certainly down east's fairly Scotch in its content. The center's kind of a half of each and a lot of neither.

As Myers implies, there is no one central-Island style. Instead, there is a stylistic continuum, in which fiddlers from eastern Queens County play with more of a Kings County flavor, and those from western Queens County play with more of a Prince County flavor. Also in the mix for some center-Island fiddlers are elements borrowed from the up-tempo, "no-frills" playing style of Don Messer, who dominated fiddle broadcasting on Island radio from 1939 through 1957 (more on Messer below and in chapter 13).

Although many regional fiddling traits are associated in the public mind with ethnicity, they generally hold regardless of the ethnic background of the player. Western Prince fiddlers Sidney Baglole, Elmer Robinson, and Andrew Jones, for example, have playing styles that are not unlike those of their Acadian French neighbors.[8] Similarly, the Chaissons are not the only fiddlers with Acadian surnames who play the "Scotch" northeastern Kings style; some other Acadian surnames found in the ranks of fiddlers who play that style are Cheverie, Longaphie, and Gallant.

With all this emphasis on Scottish versus Acadian elements, there is a tendency for Islanders to ignore the Irish influence. Because the pattern of Irish settlement was scattered, no one Island style that can be identified as distinctly Irish survived into the modern era. Instead, Irish elements have been subtly incorporated into what is generally regarded as "Scotch" in the east and "French" in the west. We know that there are many tunes of Irish origin in circulation. We can also assert with some confidence that the Irish brand of step dancing, as carried to Prince Edward Island by its first generations of Hibernian immigrants, was probably a major determinant of Island dance rhythms (for more on this, see chapter 12). Beyond this, Irish fiddling practices and tastes have certainly helped shape the general stylistic pool. As far as Island fiddling in general is concerned, then, my guess is that Emmett Hughes of Dromore, Queens County, is correct in asserting, "There's as much of it is Irish, as it is Scotch."[9]

In addition to the Kings, Prince, and central-Island styles, several subregional stylistic pockets can be identified. Just south of Montague in southern Kings County, for example, fiddlers such as Archie Stewart, Attwood O'Connor, and Joe Kearney play a smooth, lilting style that differs noticeably in terms of tempo, bow articulation, and manner of ornamentation from styles that predominate elsewhere in Kings County. Nearby in southeastern Queens County around the districts of Belfast and Flat River, fiddlers from that area such as Danny MacLean, Johnny Morrissey, and Elliott Wight share many stylistic elements with South Kings players but have a somewhat more syncopated approach to bowing. Another enclave is the Evangeline Coast of Prince County, where one of the major factors holding fiddlers together stylistically is the influence of Eddy Arsenault's powerful, soaring sound. Still one more probable pocket is south-central Queens County, where similar approaches to bowing and musical phrasing among such players as Stephen Toole of Green Road and Leonard McDonald of Emyvale suggest the presence of what was once a stylistic community.

Various fiddlers' accounts strongly suggest that at one time nearly every cluster of districts was the seat of its own distinct regional substyle. With the onset of improved roads and widespread automobile travel in the 1950s and '60s, however, plus the development in the '70s of fiddling association and festivals, players from different areas were brought into contact who might otherwise never have had the opportunity to meet. One unavoidable consequence of these changes has been a homogenization among substyles. When Emmett Hughes was asked, for example, to define the difference between his own eastern Queens County style and the one played across the line in Kings County, he observed, "There's not that much difference now. This last thirty years you see one another a lot more; I guess they copied some good parts from here, and we copied some good parts from there."

Before proceeding further, I should address two seeming contradictions. The first involves the conflict between the notion of unique inborn sound and the presence on the Island of several distinctive regional styles and substyles. The resolution here can be found through an analogy to the phenomenon of tune twists. Just as fiddlers pride themselves on performing true tune versions while reveling in their own twists, so too can they see themselves as Kings, Prince, or center-Island players while feeling completely at home with their own stylistic idiosyncrasies. In other words, certain features of a shared sound are considered essential, whereas others are left to the discretion of the individual. Second, one may well ask how a general stance rejecting direct emulation can persist in the face of so much evidence that suggests widespread stylistic borrowing. Again, there is an instructive analogy to tune twists. Fiddlers in general resist changing their tune versions, but they gladly borrow bits and pieces of each other's twists if they so desire. Similarly, most fiddlers avoid wholesale copying of another's style, but they will eagerly latch onto those particular features that catch their fancy.

"Traditional Prince Edward Island Music; It's a Mixture of Scotch, Irish, and French"

The realization among Island fiddlers that there might be a general sound underlying their individual and regional sounds probably had to await the consistent contact with alternative styles brought along by the first decades of radio broadcasts. Although these broadcasts brought sporadic exposure to Québecois and Appalachian fiddling, the two genres that had by far the most pervasive media presence on Prince Edward Island were Don Messer style and Cape Breton style. Ultimately, both these last two styles became standards against which the local sound could be measured. Archie Stewart puts it this way:

> We had our own music before Don Messer ever came to Prince Edward Island, we had our own style of playing. I think maybe this area here plays traditional Prince Edward Island music; it's a mixture of Scotch, Irish, and French. A lot of fiddlers on the Island changed to Cape Breton–style playing when it became popular, but there's quite a few fiddlers that didn't. There's Attwood [O'Connor] over here, there's me, there's Joe Kearney; and a bunch of us fiddlers from southern Kings here, we don't play Cape Breton–style music. We play the way we learned to play when we were young; we still play the traditional way that the old fiddlers around here like Billy Murphy and Ward Crane and Otis Jackson, the style that they played. We still play that same style of music.

Whereas most Island fiddlers saw Cape Breton fiddling as an elaborate, polished cousin, they generally regarded Don Messer's playing as fundamentally alien both in principle and in execution. As further discussed in chapter 13, for Messer the violin served as a cog in an elaborately orchestrated ensemble; it was not expected to function outside the band context as a solo dance-accompaniment instrument. In his system, other instruments took over many of the roles that had traditionally been the fiddler's purview. Rhythmic accents were provided by a rhythm section, ornamentation was handled by the winds section, layered sound was provided by the interplay of several instruments, and so on. Because most locals evaluated Messer's playing as if he were a local dance fiddler, some of the following criticisms leveled at it are of course unfair. Nevertheless, such statements provide an excellent starting point for identifying some salient characteristics of the general Island sound.

> His playing just didn't have the guts. I found it really didn't have that much feel in it, that it was too, no timin' on the notes; it was just one straight line. I like the dips and the cuts and the grace notes. (Kenny Chaisson: b. Bear River, Kings County)

> He played with a short, quick bow, and we didn't figure there was enough swing to that. (Archie Stewart)

> He was too diddly. He really never took the sound out of the fiddle. The way he played just like that little short bow hand, he's kinda jiggling out the tune. [*Question*: Do you think the fiddler should dig in?] Well, yes, you take the sound out of it. (Danny MacLean)

Turning these critiques around, we can say that Island sound has the following characteristics: strong rhythmic accents (that is, "timin' on the notes"), a bow stroke that swings with the rhythm of the music and bites into the strings (that is, "takes the sound out"), plus at least some fleshing out and decoration of the melodies ("cuts" and "grace notes").

As noted in chapter 4, "timin' on the notes" is an important aspect of *liveliness*, the crucial musical characteristic that makes community members, tired as they are after a hard day's work, want to get up and dance. Again, for a performance to be considered lively, the tune must be played so that its rhythms exactly reflect the tempo and rhythmic nuances of Island dance. Ultimately, such dance rhythms become inseparable from the melody and thereby serve as a universal and indelible aspect of the Island fiddling sound.

The need to "take sound" out of the fiddle results in part from the kind of playing conditions under which most Island fiddlers operated. They learned their craft in the days before sound amplification, and they had to play with sufficient sound volume so that their music projected above the din of a house party, wedding, or benefit dance. "Taking sound" also has two other functions. First, it is the method of choice for marking rhythmic accents, which in turn help contribute to perceived liveliness. Second, this extra bow pressure is an important way for the fiddler to communicate emotion to dancers.

These playing conditions also contributed to the development of other stylistic features— such as sawstroke bowing, elaborate foot-tapping styles, and use of double-stringing—which are described in detail below. Also described below is the elaborate system of ornamentation that Island fiddlers employ for decorating melodies.

Some other general traits of Island style are more difficult to put into words. Certainly, this writer has the strong impression that deep within the fabric of the music are reflected certain characteristic aspects of past and present Island life: the gentle rolling of the landscape; the crash of the sea on the Island's red bluffs; the graceful shape of its wooden churches and farmhouses; the creaking rhythms of the old horse-drawn buggies, sleighs, and plows; the crackling of kitchen fires barely keeping at bay the snow-laced winds of winter; and the puffy clouds that careen over painfully green flower-strewn meadows in summer. One might also perceive in the music's powerful, singing tones a current of poignancy, a trait that Robert Arsenault (b. Abram-Village, Prince County) traces to the travails of musicians' ancestors.[10]

> The music is a reflection of what a people's entire experience has been up to the day they were playing the thing. It has to do with whatever historical things they went through: like the Scottish Highlanders got kicked off their land and they ended up here. The Acadians got kicked off of their lands and ended up here. The Irish fled because—You know, it's all this misery that brings people together. We all inherit it, what our ancestors had before, and here we are and this is what it is: feelings that are being transmitted in music. I think that the Scottish and Irish and Acadian fiddlers when they play are a witness to the nature of things and to the nature of that person's own entire cultural inheritance.

Alongside such intangibles, Island playing styles and sub-styles can also be described in terms of several technical parameters. Among these are foot-tapping style; the manner of holding the fiddle, noting hand, and bow; bowing mechanics; double-stringing; the use of grace notes and other embellishments; and the tonal and modal systems. By looking at which elements are shared among fiddlers and analyzing how they vary, I can more precisely describe differences among individuals and define regional styles. For a clearer image, the reader should bear in mind throughout the following descriptions that Island fiddlers generally perform while seated.

"The Only Accompaniment Was His Feet"

One universal characteristic of Island fiddling is that the act of playing involves the entire body. While the fiddler's upper half is engaged in manipulating the instrument, the lower half is busy beating out the time. Jimmy Halliday of Eldon, Queens County, for example, has this to say about one of the most accomplished local fiddlers of an earlier generation:

> Joe Griffin, he'd play all night long for dancing, and the only accompaniment was his feet. He didn't need a piano or an organ; his feet would be going anyway, so I suppose there was accompaniment there. He must have had terrific energy; he'd pick his feet way up off the floor all night long.

Essentially, this foot tapping amounts to a sedentary dance whereby time is kept by alternately striking the floor with heel and toe. There are one-footed and two-footed tapping styles. In the one-footed style that predominates among eastern PEI fiddlers, the heel is levered forward with supporting action from the hip to stomp out the down beat, then the toe is levered back with support from the knee to mark the offbeat. When playing *reels* (fast-tempo dance tunes with eight notes per measure; see chapter 14), either heel or toe hits the floor four times per measure (that is, every second note). In the two-footed tapping style that is popular primarily among western PEI fiddlers, the player appears to be virtually step dancing on the floor. In practice, each foot has a separate role. One performs the levered, leg-supported movement described above, while the other stomps more or less in place—landing in such a way that it rocks from heel to toe. These various movements are timed so that heels and toes strictly alternate, ensuring that for a reel either a heel or a toe hits the floor eight times per measure (assuming 2/2 time, that means once for every eighth note).

This style of keeping time not only marks the basic beat for dancers but also allows for other levels of communication. First, tapping clearly marks the subtle offbeat accents, or syncopations, of Island dancing, thereby enhancing the dancers' experience of liveliness. What's more, as Robert Arsenault observes, fiddlers can communicate through their tapping both the air of excitement at the heart of the dance and their own exhilaration at being able to play the music they love at full throttle.

> A fiddler carries his own level of feeling with him when he plays. A fiddler is a dancer, and his whole entire body plays. Do you notice the action of his arms and the whole physical thing? It's all tied into one! It is this feeling that is being communicated to people who dance.

This style of keeping time arose because until the 1930s instrumental accompaniment at Island dances was rare and fiddlers had to provide their own rhythmic support. Even after instrumental accompaniment became commonplace, however, Island fiddlers continued strongly tapping out the beat. In part, this practice persisted merely through inertia. More important, this tapping style served as a form of insurance: even when faced with slipshod instrumental accompaniment or an especially rowdy crowd, fiddlers with strong tapping styles could always be confident of maintaining a rock-solid rhythm.

Playing Posture

When the violin is held in the manner recommended by formal violin teachers, the instrument is tucked under the chin, with the belly positioned roughly parallel to the collarbone, and tilted only slightly downward from the player's left to right (photo 9.2). From the Island fiddler's viewpoint, this position has two

PHOTO 9.2. FIDDLER-FOLKLORIST ALAN JABBOUR DEMONSTRATES THE CLASSICAL METHOD FOR HOLDING FIDDLE AND BOW; MR. JABBOUR PLAYED IN BOTH THE JACKSONVILLE AND MIAMI, FLORIDA, SYMPHONY ORCHESTRAS EARLY IN HIS CAREER (PHOTO BY KAREN SINGER JABBOUR).

PHOTO 9.3. THIS PHOTO OF GUS LONGAPHIE OF SOURIS, KINGS COUNTY IS A GOOD ILLUSTRATION OF THE PLAYING POSTURE GENERALLY FAVORED BY ISLAND FIDDLERS (TAKEN AT MONTICELLO HEADQUARTERS, AUGUST 1991, PHOTO BY EARTHWATCH TEAM).

major drawbacks relative to bow handling. First, to merely reach the strings, both elbow and forearm must in general operate from a fairly elevated position. Second, the curvature of the bridge requires that the elbow be raised still higher to give the bow access to the fourth string of the fiddle (that is, the string lowest in pitch).[11] The problem here is that an elevated bowing arm is under considerably more stress than it would be if its general locus were brought lower down.

To allow for less stressful bowing mechanics, many Island players hold the fiddle tilted at an extreme angle, so that the belly of the instrument is almost perpendicular to the collarbone (see photo 9.3). This allows the fiddler to maintain arm and elbow at a much lower position, thereby permitting him or her to reach the fourth string without significantly elevating the arm from this initial position.[12] Some Prince County fiddlers solve the fourth-string problem in a different way. They hold the fiddle closer to the horizontal and at opportune moments rotate the bass side of the instrument up to bring the fourth string into the path of the bow.

Ultimately, there are probably as many strategies for holding the instrument on Prince Edward Island as there are fiddlers. Some brace their instruments against the chest or upper abdomen. And as noted in chapter 5, Clarence MacLean of Garfield, Queens County, developed the habit of planting his fiddle on the opposite side of the breastbone from the norm.

As for the noting hand, many if not most Island players brace the heel of that hand on the underside of the instrument, wedged firmly against the heel of the neck. The wrist is then collapsed backwards, and the fingers are positioned so they are hovering directly over the strings (also shown in photo 9.3). This noting hand position serves two functions. First, it helps stabilize the instrument in the absence of a chin rest or shoulder support. Second, it allows the fingers to be set more or less exactly to play within the range of notes employed by most fiddle tunes.[13] Because Island fiddlers rarely need to shift the noting hand up and down the fingerboard, they have no need for the poised noting-hand position (with slightly arched wrist) favored by trained violin players (and illustrated in photo 9.2).

Bowing

To obtain the level of sound volume they need, most Island players use the *sawstroke* as their essential bowing motion. In a sawstroke, only one melody note is obtained per bow stroke, giving the appearance of a sawing action. Because much attention is devoted to developing upstrokes that are as strong as downstrokes, this sawing approach allows the same high level of attack to be brought to bear on each note.

Slurring (obtaining more than one note from a single bow stroke via action of the noting fingers on the bowed string) can certainly be found in Island fiddling, but the technique is generally used either for ornamentation (see below) or to set up a particular direction for the next bow stroke. In the latter case, fiddlers use slurs most commonly to ensure that the notes falling on a tune's strong beats, or *downbeats*, are played by downstrokes. Every so often, however, a sophisticated player will seek a particular phrasing by going against the grain and employing slurs to specifically set up an up-bow on a downbeat.

Sawstroke bowing has the advantage of offering maximum control and sound volume, but it can yield a fairly wooden sound unless the player develops a high level of fluidity in terms of arm and wrist movement. Consequently, achieving such fluidity is of prime concern to most Island fiddlers. As Attwood O'Connor notes, "If you're gonna play, you can't hold a stiff arm, what I call a crowbar arm; you have to let your arm go limber."

Because the favored method for holding the instrument allows the bowing hand to be held relatively low relative to the position of the strings, the wrist is able to serve as the major driving force of the bowing motion. As Dave Thomson (b. West Royalty, Queens County), points out, "You really should play with more of it in your wrist. It makes it easier, rather than the whole arm goin'." This wrist-driven sawstroke ultimately becomes so natural for experienced fiddlers that they can virtually do it in their sleep.

The wrist not only drives the movement of the bow but is also a major determinant of bow pressure. Such bow pressure requires a delicate level of balance, since the favored sound requires enough to produce some bite but not so much that the tone becomes harsh and scratchy. In turn, this wrist-generated bite both communicates intensity and allows—through the intermittent application of additional force—for the rhythmic accents of Island dance to be positioned precisely within the continual stream of notes.

It is instructive in this regard that tunes new to the Island often undergo a subtle transformation that allows for the insertion of appropriate dance accents. One case in point is "St. Anne's Reel," which first entered the repertoire via Québec radio in the 1930s. The following account is from Andrew Jones of Pleasant View, Prince County:

> We used to play "St. Anne's Reel" the old way. That didn't go very good with step dancing. Somebody'd get up and dance, and they'd get kind of mixed up because there was slow action into it. So amongst our friends we changed it to suit the step dancer. We'd get them to dance, we'd follow the step dancer with the bow, and we'd jig it up according to his steps. That's the way we got it; we jigged it up a little bit to suit the step dancer.[14]

Island fiddlers also use several additional strategies to reduce wear and tear on the bow arm. Unlike the method recommended by formal violin pedagogy, for example, they generally "choke up" on the bow and hold it some distance away from the frog. They also tend to use fewer than four fingers (plus thumb) to grip the bow.[15] As for bow handling, Island fiddlers tend to use a relatively small portion of the bow for each stroke, and many play with the locus of string contact near the tip of the bow, where balance is easiest. This being said, those fiddlers who play with a multifinger grip closer to the frog, with slightly longer strokes, and with a locus closer to the center of the bow, generally muster a more powerful, singing sound.

One additional dimension that should be considered is range of motion. The bow is propelled via intricately coordinating the levered movements of hand, wrist, forearm, upper arm, and shoulder. Managing the process so that it is accomplished with minimal movement in each sector yields the most efficiency and the smoothest, most controlled sound. Although a wider than optimum range of motion in any sector yields a rougher, less-controlled sound, some fiddlers prefer such a sound on aesthetic grounds and actively cultivate a wider range of motion than is absolutely necessary.

"They Used the Double-String Effect to Take the Place of the Bagpipes"

As an additional strategy to increase sound volume and resonance, Island fiddlers often bow two strings at once. There are several strategies for using double strings in Island fiddling: open neighbor strings, anticipated stopped strings, priming, and fingering forms.

- *open neighbor strings*: When bowing a melody note, the fiddler takes the higher or lower open neighbor along for the ride.
- *anticipated stopped strings*: When logistics permit, the bow stroke carries the melody note plus the string on which the following note is located. Sometimes the neighbor string is stopped early just so it can be played together with the melody string.
- *priming*: The player in effect doubles the sound of an open string by finding the same pitch on the lower neighbor string.
- *two-string fingering forms*. These are fingering patterns that yield a series of double strings for a given key. (Examples for the keys G, D, and A are shown in appendix A, example 9.1). Formally trained violinists refer to two-string fingering patterns as *double-stops*; some Island fiddlers call them *chords*, probably by analogy to guitar chord fingering configurations.

To make double-stringing easier, fiddlers often recarve standard violin bridges to flatten out some of their pronounced convex curvature. As Attwood O'Connor explains, "You can hit two strings a lot easier; you don't have to keep tripping your arm up and down all the time, and it's a lot easier to get across the strings." Another strategy to make double-stringing more effective for the keys A and D involves placing the violin in one of two alternative tunings, known locally as *high bass* (ADAE) and *high counter* (AEAE).[16] According to Archie Stewart, use of high counter tuning had fallen out of favor by the time his generation had reached maturity. Instead, many Island fiddlers sought to achieve roughly the same effect by "bridging" the third and fourth strings with the first (index) finger at A and E, respectively. They then would note on top of these bridged strings with their remaining fingers.

Double-stringing may have originally been adopted as a device for increasing sound volume, but it has become prized in its own right as an important method for elaborating and otherwise dressing up tune versions. For one thing, as Francis MacDonald of Morell, Kings County, observes, double-stringing offers the opportunity to create a musical drone (continually sounding tone) that emulates the sound of the bagpipes.

> I think we use double strings as much as we can to give us more volume, a different tone, anyway. I think it was originated from the bagpipe tunes, the old Scottish bagpipe marches. The fiddlers used the double-string effect to take the place of the drone in the bagpipes. I think that's how most of that came about.

Second, many fingering forms yield *intervals* (tone combinations) known as *thirds* or *sixths*. Because these tone combinations are the building blocks of major, minor, and seventh chords,[17] the use of fingering forms gives the music a very full sound, even when performed unaccompanied. Leonard McDonald explains:

> I'll tell you I play a lot of chords [fingering forms] on the fiddle because I had nobody to accompany me. You'd play alone, you'd get all the notes in that you could, and double notes if you could. Do you notice when I'm playing, I'm hitting a lot of times two strings? There's chords on the fiddle, same as on anything else. But the more sound I could get out of the fiddle the better I liked it. Some people might like the clear notes and leave it clear,[18] but not me.

Because the nonmelody string in any double-string pair can be above or below the melody, the overall effect is of a second musical line that corkscrews around the melody. This spiraling second line is yet another distinctive feature of Island style.

Ornamentation

Various kinds of quick notes and rhythmic figures can be employed as decorative devices. Such *ornaments* can be added via either the bow or the fingers of the noting hand. Bowing ornaments are shown in appendix A, examples

9.2a–e, while noting ornaments (sometimes known as *graces* or *grace notes*) are shown in appendix A, examples 9.3a–f.[19]

Bowing ornaments used on Prince Edward Island include *snaps*, *cuts*, and a technique I have dubbed the *suppressed stroke*. The snap, or *Scotch snap*, is a rhythmic device performed by a quick pair of alternate-direction bow strokes, always beginning on a downstroke. It is usually written as a sixteenth note followed by a dotted eighth note (appendix A, example 9.2a), implying that the second note sounds three times as long as the first. Snaps are played more or less as written in contemporary Scottish fiddling, but on Prince Edward Island and Cape Breton they are played so that the second note is only twice as long as the first, yielding what amounts to a tied-note triplet (example 9.2b). Although snaps appear primarily in such quintessentially Scottish tune genres as pipe marches and strathspeys, many Island fiddlers integrate them into their renditions of reels and jigs as a form of syncopation, particularly in "Scotch"-leaning Kings County. When played in *jig time* (that is, 6/8 time), a snap is expressed in notation as an eighth note followed by a quarter note, as shown in example 9.2c.

Cuts (appendix A, example 9.2d), or *birls* as they are known in Scotland, were probably adapted to fiddle from the bagpipes.[20] Paul MacDonald of Charlottetown recalls how this technique was first explained to him by "Old Peter" Chaisson of Bear River, Kings County.

> He just basically said there's two short notes and one long one; in musical terms what it is are two sixteenth notes and an eighth note at the end. Then he said whenever you have a long note, which meant a quarter note, you can substitute in "cutting." So it's just those three notes, and he told me that it was always down-up-down with the bowing.

Use of the cutting technique was once commonplace among Island fiddlers, particularly among those from Kings County. When Neil Cheverie of Elmira, Kings County, was declared winner of PEI's first major fiddling competition in 1926, for example, he was lauded for his ability to "bring in the cuts, slurs and grace notes which are characteristic of old-time fiddle."[21] Although cutting had fallen into disuse among most Island players born in the first half of the twentieth century, interest in the technique has revived over the past few decades because of the influence of Cape Breton fiddling.

The suppressed stroke is a method for creating strong syncopations; it is employed most by Prince County fiddlers but is used to a certain extent by nearly all Island players. The technique, which Louise Arsenault of Mont Carmel, Prince County, calls *shuffles*, is accomplished as follows. When the fiddler wants to specially accent a weak-beat note (generally an upstroke), he or she lightens pressure on the following downstroke (the strong beat), so that only the slightest "scratching" tone is heard instead of a pure note. This makes for an audible break in the stream of notes, thereby creating the impression that the strong-beat note has been omitted altogether. This break then offers the sense that the preceding weak-beat upstroke has been accented. The suppressed stroke can be indicated with an x-shaped note head (plus a tie), as shown in appendix A, example 9.2e.

Most noting-hand ornaments are produced by slurring. Perhaps the most common ornament is the *slow grace*, or *delayed note* (appendix A, example 9.3a).[22] For this technique, the player bows a note just below an important melody note and then slurs into the melody. Although a slow grace is not considered an integral part of the melody, in some instances (assuming 2/2 or 4/4 time) it can sound as long as an eighth note. Two other ornaments—the *quick grace*, which generally comes from above (example 9.3b), and the *double grace* (example 9.3c)—are usually performed by quickly touching an open or stopped sounding string with a free left-hand finger. There are two other noting-hand ornaments commonly used on Prince Edward Island. One is related rhythmically to the double grace, but in this instance the player ascends or descends to the melody note via two quick scale steps (examples 9.3d–e). Finally, there is what I call a *reverse double-grace* (example 9.3f). For the reverse double-grace, the player starts with an already stopped, sounding string. Then, without actually lifting the finger off the string, he or she releases and quickly reapplies pressure. Taking all these components together, this maneuver suggests the sound of a conventional double grace.

Tonal and Modal Systems

Comparing a major scale (do-re-mi-fa-so-la-ti-do) played on fiddle by traditional Island players with the same scale played on piano reveals at least three major differences. Generally, the third scale step (mi) and the seventh step (ti) of the Island fiddle scale are often somewhat flatter, while the fourth step (fa) is often somewhat sharper. This means that for a major scale in the key of A, the fiddler plays the notes C# and G# somewhat flat and the note D somewhat sharp, relative to the piano. Conversely, for a natural-minor scale in the key of A, Island fiddlers play both C-natural and G-natural a little sharper than what would be the case on piano.

To complicate matters further, there are some tunes in which the fiddler intentionally plays the third note of the scale at a pitch that is about halfway between its major-scale and minor-scale values, yielding what is known as a neutral third. For such a tune in the key of A, for example, a fiddler might play a note lying between C# and C-natural, yielding the pitch known as C-*neutral*.[23]

The tonal system described above is not unique to Prince Edward Island. It is shared with traditional players from other Celtic-based fiddling traditions, and to some degree it probably shares a common origin with the Highland bagpipes scale.[24] Although those brought up on the piano's *equal-tempered scale* may react to certain pitch values in traditional Celtic-based fiddling by assuming that the latter are "out of tune," this is not the case: the prevailing concept of pitch among traditional fiddlers simply differs from the one that is currently dominant in mainstream Western culture.

Many Island tunes also employ modes that may sound unusual to the mainstream ear. The term *mode* refers not only to an ordering of notes in a scale but also to the rules concerning how the notes in that scale are used. In addition to the several inversions of the diatonic scale referred to as *Church Modes* (Dorian, Mixolydian, Ionian, and so on), a few inversions of the pentatonic scale,[25] and several *hexatonic* (six-tone) scales, there are also several *enriched modes* in circulation. Enriched modes are of particular interest, since they often call for different inflections (that is, sharp, flat, neutral, or natural values) of the same pitch in different contexts. For example, a melody in A might feature C# in ascending passages and C-natural in descending passages, or it might feature C# on the high strings of the instrument and C-natural on the low strings.[26]

Individual and Regional Styles, Revisited

Now that we have looked at the various playing dimensions that Island fiddlers have in common—and described some parameters by which they tend to differ—we are in a much better position to see how individual and regional styles relate. Just as each Island fiddler has his own *twist* for each of the tunes in his repertoire, so too does he have his own approach along a wide variety of parameters. He has his particular style of tapping out the beat. He holds the fiddle at a particular angle relative to the collarbone and braces it at a particular spot under the chin or lower down. He chokes up on the bow a given distance, applies a certain portion of its length to the strings, and tends to use a certain length of bow on each stroke. He has a particular level of arm and wrist flexibility that reflects his own notions about what level of "bite" or sweetness is desirable in terms of tone. He would also have his own manner of applying ornamentation, his own style of using double strings, his own way of applying slurs and accented up-bows, and so on.

On the regional level, the Island's east-west fiddling dichotomy can be now defined with greater precision. Fiddlers from Kings County usually employ the one-footed tapping style; they often hold the belly of the fiddle perpendicular to the collarbone; and they tend to develop bowing styles with a relatively concise range of motion. They often use snaps as a syncopation strategy and prefer using drones, grace notes, and cuts for ornamentation. In contrast, fiddlers from Prince County tend to use the two-footed tapping style. Many of them hold the fiddle at a less extreme angle than that of their Kings County counterparts and tilt the fourth string into the path of the bow. They generally develop bowing styles with a wide range of motion. Bowed accents, such as those produced by the suppressed stroke, are a major feature of their music. They are somewhat less likely to use drones, graces, and cuts than are Kings County players.

The wide variety of individual and regional fiddling styles observed on Prince Edward Island in the 1990s was highly unusual for this late date. For many other fiddling genres that survived into the late twentieth century—Irish, Scottish, Cape Breton, Appalachian, and so on—the playing of a single dominant fiddler or a small coterie of players with significant media exposure or music-contest success was so widely emulated that most individual idiosyncrasies and regional differences rapidly passed from the scene (more on this in chapters 11 and 13). For reasons described later, no such dominant style, or *superstyle*, had developed on Prince Edward Island by 1990 despite over half a century of exposure via media and live appearances to several powerful external templates.

NOTES

1. Many of the observations made here may no longer apply to the most recent generation of players coming up through PEI's fiddling revival; see chapters 16–17.
2. A website devoted to traditional Prince Edward Island fiddling based on the author's field recordings is now under development. For more information, see note 4 in the introduction.

3. Tignish and Souris are at opposite ends of the Island; Summerside is about fifteen miles east of Arsenault's native St. Chrysostom.
4. By "my own time," Chaisson is referring what PEI fiddlers call "timing on the notes"; see chapter 4.
5. The term *Scottish* (or more commonly, *Scotch*) is used by Islanders to refer to the eastern style and its repertoire and also to refer to fiddling from Cape Breton. This term should not be taken to imply a direct connection between styles played in Kings County and any contemporary Scottish fiddling style.
6. On the Island, the term *French* refers specifically to the Acadian French from Prince Edward Island and its provincial neighbors New Brunswick and Nova Scotia. Occasionally, the term also encompasses the Québecois, but it almost never refers to the inhabitants of France.
7. By the late 1990s, Islanders—presumably because they had become attuned to trends in World Music marketing—had begun using the term *Celtic* instead of *Scotch* to describe Cape Breton fiddling.
8. Baglole and Robinson are English surnames (the former is specifically Cornish), while Jones (at least in origin) is a Welsh surname.
9. Note that use of the term *Irish* here does not imply an association with contemporary Irish fiddling, whose sound changed markedly after about 1930; for more on this, see chapter 13.
10. As a parallel, in his cross-cultural study "Folk Song Style," Alan Lomax suggests a strong association between cultural experience and vocal performance styles.
11. The fiddle's four strings are generally referred to nowadays by number. Under this system, the string with the highest pitch (that is, the thinnest string) is called the *first string*, and so on. In recent years, the first string has been made of plain steel, while strings two through four have been wound with aluminum over a soft central core made of gut, nylon, or composite fiber. See "Violin" in the *New Harvard Dictionary of Music*, 921–92.
12. Around the time of most Scottish immigration to Prince Edward Island, the formally taught manner for holding the violin was actually fairly close to this "perpendicular-to-collarbone" style. See Babitz, *Differences between Eighteenth Century*, 3.
13. Referred to in formal violin pedagogy as *first position*, this range extends over two octaves from G below middle C to the second B above middle C.
14. See, for example, the version of "St. Anne's Reel" (as played by Elmer Robinson of Woodstock, Prince County) that appears in Perlman, *Fiddle Music of* PEI, 73.
15. The standard grip has thumb and all four fingers grasping the bow stick at the frog. See "Bow" and "Bowing" (104 and 105–6, respectively) in the *New Harvard Dictionary of Music*.
16. These names derive from an archaic system of nomenclature in which the strings of the violin were known (lowest pitch to highest) as *bass, counter, tenor,* and *treble*. The fiddle is normally tuned (low to high) GDAE. Using *scordatura* (alternative tunings) in fiddling goes back at the very least to eighteenth-century Scotland; see, for example, Johnson, *Scottish Fiddle Music*, 120.

17. There are two kinds of thirds relevant here: major thirds (two whole steps in length), and minor thirds (one and a half steps in length). Simple chords, or triads, consist of two adjacent thirds sharing a common note. In a major triad, the major third comes first; in a minor triad, the minor third comes first; seventh chords are made up of three adjacent thirds.
18. By "leaving it clear," McDonald means playing the melody line just on a single string.
19. Special thanks to Paul MacDonald of Charlottetown for helping to elucidate Island bowing and noting ornamentation.
20. According to David Johnson (in *Scottish Fiddle Music*, 120), whether eighteenth-century fiddlers borrowed the birl from pipers or vice versa is not entirely clear. He feels that it is instructive, however, that before circa 1750 birls show up in fiddle-music notation only when the tunes are derived from bagpipes. Assuming that the birl did originate on bagpipes, however, its three-note manifestation on fiddle appears to be but a convenient substitute for a whole class of far more elaborate bagpipe ornaments.
21. "Cheverie Won Third Place in Contest," *Charlottetown Guardian*, Apr. 8, 1926, 1ff. For more on this contest, see chapter 11.
22. In formal music, this is referred to as an *appoggiatura*.
23. Fiddler Iain Fraser of Jedburgh, Scotland (personal interview, June 15, 2004), refers in jest to this pitch as "C super-natural."
24. Roderick D. Cannon (in *Highland Bagpipe*, 28–29) points out that the average values of C# and G-natural (the third and seventh tones of the bagpipe scale) coincide very closely with those produced via an old universal tuning system known as *just intonation*. He also points out that bagpipe makers perform final pitch adjustments by tuning each note to make a consonant (sweet-sounding) interval with the drone. Such a system would inevitably cause certain pitches to be tuned differently from the equal-temperament rubric, in which pitch values have been "averaged out" to enable fixed-pitch instruments to play in tune for all twelve keys.
25. All diatonic scales have seven tones; they coincide in terms of pitch relationships with the white keys of the piano. Pentatonic scales have five tones; the most common pentatonic scale (which contains no semitones) coincides in terms of pitch relationships with the black keys of the piano. In a "scale inversion," the first note is moved to the end, and what was previously the second note now becomes the new key-note, or tonic.
26. It is beyond the scope of this book to engage in a lengthy discussion of the modality of Island tunes; for a more detailed discussion, see Perlman, *Fiddle Music of* PEI, 28–30.

PHOTO 9.4. ALVIN BERNARD (FIDDLE) AND EDWIN SIMMONS (GUITAR) AT LONG RIVER, QUEENS COUNTY, JULY 1992 (PHOTO BY KEN PERLMAN).

CHAPTER TEN
"It's Always Better with Accompaniment"

At many an Island house party, wedding, benefit dance, or other musical gathering, the accompanists were often the unsung heroes. It was not uncommon for fiddlers to take turns playing, or for the primary fiddler at such an occasion to be spelled for a dance or two by a substitute. Accompanists, on the other hand, were often at their stations throughout, valiantly maintaining a steady beat despite all the rollicking distractions around them. As Kevin Chaisson of Bear River, Kings County, reports, "When we were young fellows—Jesus Christ, many's the night I sat at the piano for eight or nine hours straight, never even got off. 'Cause there was all kinds of fiddlers around and just one piano player."

By sifting through somewhat contradictory accounts, I have pieced together the following approximate chronology for fiddle-music accompaniment from the earliest period covered by living memory through the early 1990s. Prior to about the mid-1930s, instrumental accompaniment for fiddling was relatively rare on Prince Edward Island. In fact, as Joe MacDonald of St. Andrews, Kings County, tells us, at most rural house parties and other small dances "there was

PHOTO 10.1. KEVIN CHAISSON (PIANO) AND PAUL MACDONALD AT CHAISSON FAMILY CONCERT, ROLLO BAY FESTIVAL GROUNDS, AUGUST 1991 (PHOTO BY EARTHWATCH TEAM).

nothing—only the fiddles, just the fiddles." Nevertheless, accompaniment on keyboard instruments was occasionally available even then at certain larger events, such as church benefits or weddings, and at dances held in the environs of the Island's two major cities, Charlottetown and Summerside.[1] And as Archie Stewart of Milltown Cross, Kings County, points out, accompaniment was available even at smaller dances when there happened to be a keyboard instrument on hand.

> And if you were in a house where there was an organ, there was an awful lot of women who were good to chord on the old pump organ; you'd play the fiddle and the organ. Or the piano: pianos were pretty scarce, people couldn't afford to have pianos, but in the odd place there was a piano. There was one at Alec MacLeod's; we called him Alec Thrasher, and both girls played.

As instrumental accompaniment became more popular through the 1930s and '40s, pump organs increased in number and remained the instrument of choice for that purpose. Then, in the 1940s and '50s, pianos began to supplant pump organs, and guitars—which had previously been rare—rapidly became an important factor.

It is not clear what the state of accompaniment might have been on Prince Edward Island before pump organs appeared on the scene.[2] There are diary and newspaper accounts of dances in eighteenth-century Scotland around the time of emigration to Prince Edward Island that make note of accompaniment by "bass-violin" (that is, cello) or second violin.[3] In addition, most early fiddle tune collections included accompaniment parts for harpsichord or piano along with *continuo* (continuous bass line) indications for viola da gamba or cello. As far as I was able to determine, however, either this early accompaniment tradition was never carried to the Island, or it failed to survive there into the time of living memory.

Although instrumental accompaniment was once uncommon at smaller dances, there were plenty of other ways for community members to help fiddlers keep time. To begin with, those not on the floor dancing would generally echo the fiddler's foot-tapping with their own feet, employing for this purpose the same kind of sedentary dance steps that fiddlers use for timekeeping. "That's why they tapped their feet at the dances," notes piano player Anne-Marie Gallant Arsenault of Summerside, Prince County: "That was an accompaniment for the fiddlers." Community members might also help keep time by making impromptu rhythm instruments out of such common household items as pairs of spoons, pots and pans, buckets, and horseshoes. As Joseph Doucette of Deblois Road, Prince County, recalls, "The feet and the banging of a pan or a set of spoons, that's about it; that was about the height of the orchestra at that time!"

As previously noted, beating on the fiddle strings with sticks or knitting needles was another popular form of accompaniment. The "percussionist" generally stood in front of a playing fiddler and—selecting a spot somewhere on the upper fingerboard away from the path of the bow—beat out a rhythm on the lower (or *back*) strings of the instrument. According to Cosmas Sigsworth (b. Corraville, Kings County), "That beatin' on the back strings, it used to give pretty good time, you know."

Dancing-men were also sometimes used as rhythm instruments. These flat, loose-jointed wooden dolls were manipulated via a stick attached to the doll's back. As the operator moved the stick up and down and brought the doll into contact with a hard surface, its legs and feet could be made to mimic the rhythms and movements of step dancing.[4]

When no fiddlers were available, rhythm players could provide quite serviceable dance music by joining forces with those proficient at *jigging* or *tuning* (that is, singing fiddle tunes; see chapter 3). John Cousins of Bloomfield, Prince County, for example, tells this story:

> A lady I knew quite well was one of the last wooden spoon players; it's a dying art. People would tune, and she used to play the spoons.[5] Between [banging] the spoons and the tuning, it used to hurt her knee, so she put a hockey players' shin guard under her skirt to protect her leg. Which was very good use, a much better use than the hockey players put it to!

Instrumental Accompaniment

As noted above, the pump organ was initially the Island's most popular fiddle-music accompaniment instrument. It can be described as combining aspects of the piano, the accordion, and the player-piano. The instrument is shaped like an upright piano and has a piano-like keyboard. As in the accordion, sound is produced by forcing a stream of air over metal reeds in the instrument's interior. This stream of air is pumped into the instrument by a pair of player-piano-like treadles operated by the player's feet.

Pump organs were at first far more common than pianos because under prevailing conditions they were far more practical: they were relatively light, they required little servicing, and their metal reeds rarely needed tuning. Pianos were more temperamental. Their big wooden soundboards and hundreds of strings were subject to continual stress from the Island's cold, wet climate. In addition, pianos could rarely be moved even a short distance without being put out of whack in some fashion. A family would think twice before letting its prized piano be dragged down to the community hall for a dance.

Pump organ players gradually developed a style that was well suited to accompanying Island fiddling. It involved a fairly static *attack* (approach to striking the keys), with relatively few chord changes. Because pump organ keyboards do not allow for changes in *dynamics* (loudness and softness), musical accents were provided by sustaining certain notes longer: either by hand or via "swell-bars" operated by the player's knees. As Charlie Sheehan of Bear River, Kings County, reports, the overall effect was a gentle wall of sound behind the fiddler.

> At them times [the 1930s into the 1950s] there was usually an organ. Practically everyone would have an organ. There was no pianos much then or guitars. Get a fiddle

and an organ together, it was really nice music! I'd rather an organ with a violin anytime than a piano. You get a nice drone from the organ, you know, a steady sound on it, just keep a drone going all the time. But the piano's just dancing the keys.

Sheehan also points out that accompanists could vary the organ's drone to echo the pitch range being produced on the violin: "When you'd come on the back strings of the fiddle, you'd go back on the back keys on an organ. And if you're on the high strings of the fiddle, then you'd go on the high keys of an organ. It makes a nice sound. It makes a lovely drone to it!"

Beginning around the end of the Second World War, the number of pianos found in rural homes on Prince Edward Island started to increase sharply. There were three major factors involved. Many rural Islanders had installed central heating in their homes, making instruments less prone to climate-based problems. There was more money in circulation, so that more families could afford tuning, repairs, and other routine maintenance. Still another element at work was the example set by the recorded and broadcast fiddle music of the period, which often featured piano accompaniment (see chapter 13).

As pianos became increasingly popular through the 1950s and beyond, pump organs gradually passed from the scene. Most organists were able to make the transition to the piano without too much difficulty. In effect, they took the accompaniment style they had developed on organ and—as much as they were able—transferred it to the new instrument. This created the gentle, rumbling piano-accompaniment style that for several decades graced many an Island dance and benefit concert. Interestingly, some former Island organists also brought along to the piano the habit of pumping their feet as they played, a practice that only seemed truly incongruous when carried out beneath the pedal-less electronic keyboards that became popular beginning in the late 1980s (more on this below).

There were hardly any guitars on Prince Edward Island prior to the 1940s. The first wave of interest in the instrument was sparked by its high profile in country music and western swing recordings. Because there were few guitars to be had locally, youngsters drawn to the instrument had to have them brought in from off-Island. Teresa MacPhee Wilson (b. Monticello, Kings County), for example, describes how she obtained her instrument.

> My first guitar was like a dream come true. I used to be looking in the catalog to see the pictures of guitars, thinking, "Gosh, would I ever love to have one of those!" My brother drove into the yard one day. He was working over in Nova Scotia, and he said, "Go out and look in the back seat of the car; I got something out there

for you." And it was one of those Palm Beach guitars.[6] Boy, was I ever made up! I never thought to say hello to him or anything. I just took off with the guitar. I'll never forget my fingers, how sore they were.

At first, most Island guitar playing was confined to vocal accompaniment. Guitarists quickly discovered, however, that the same kinds of chord configurations and strumming patterns used to back up songs would also suit quite well when played behind a fiddler.

Although the guitar's balanced sound and easy portability presented many advantages, the instrument did not gain general acceptance until the mid- to late 1950s, as Fr. Charles Cheverie of Charlottetown recalls:

Guitar in those days was a real second-rate instrument. You were "cowboyish," and you were not considered to be too elite. But I enjoyed it, and I had a lot of fun at it. And when I come back from the seminary by this time Elvis Presley was coming along, and guitar was a great thing.

By the 1960s, the guitar had become firmly established at Island dances. In many parts of the Island, it was beginning to displace both pump organ and piano as the primary accompaniment instrument, especially at smaller events where hauling in a relatively massive keyboard instrument might not seem worth the effort.

In the early 1990s, the dominant style of guitar accompaniment on Prince Edward Island involved using a *pick*, or plectrum. Generally, players used standard "open-position" chord shapes in the left hand. The predominant plucking techniques could be described as either *flail-strumming* or *pick-strumming* (in flail-strumming, the guitarist creates a wall of sound by rapidly brushing down and up on all strings; in "pick-strumming," he or she plucks individual bass notes on downbeats and other main beats, and then strums on secondary beats).

A few other instruments have played a role in fiddle accompaniment on the Island. For example, there is occasional mention in this regard of banjos (both five-string and four-string varieties) and mandolins. In addition, there are also accounts of harmonica players who were able to provide support for a fiddler by *doubling* (simultaneously playing) the melody.

Not all fiddlers initially welcomed the proliferation of instrumental accompaniment. Most of them eventually came to understand, however, that having a good keyboard or guitar player behind them made their own playing sound more accomplished and lively. Having solid musical support not only made establishing and keeping the beat much easier, but it made playing a lot more pleasurable. As Joe MacDonald reports, "I used to think that the other stuff spoiled the fiddle, but it's not the case; it's always better with accompaniment." Here's how Danny MacLean (b. Garfield, Queens County) describes it:

> I'll tell you, if you have somebody good to accompany you when you're playing, that makes an awful difference. And if you get used to playing with him, that makes an awful difference. Like they've got the same rhythm, you know. If you're going to play fiddle for a dance, say you had a guitar and a piano, too, that makes for good lively old-time music.

Before long, finding an accompanist or two for a house party or other district event was nearly as important as locating a fiddler, and (as noted above) accomplished accompanists became the backbone of just about every Island dance.

"I Got Stuck on the Piano"

Although fiddlers may have been irresistibly drawn to their instruments, many accompanists were firmly guided to theirs by family and community. As already noted, for example, musically inclined females were discouraged from fiddling but received considerable encouragement for developing keyboard skills. Similarly, some males were also specifically groomed as accompanists by a fiddling parent, as in this instance described by Bill MacDonald (b. North Lake, Kings County):

> I didn't learn to play the violin, because I got stuck on the piano [playing for] my dad. That's why I learned all those tunes; I learned them to accompany him. I didn't care for playing the piano, but there was no one else to play. My sisters and brothers all quit and then I was stuck with it.

We have already seen how many women grew to resent being channeled in this manner. For their male counterparts, such feelings of resentment would be compounded by a sense that they had been denied an important birthright. Even when such men learned to play fiddle in later life, they often evinced a regret for time lost and a feeling that they might have "made a better job" on the instrument had they not been deflected from it in childhood.

Not all male accompanists were conscripted to the task. For example, many took up accompaniment when their attempts at fiddling met with little success. For these disappointed fiddlers, learning a keyboard or fretted instrument provided an alternative route for participating in community music making.

Alternatively, some successful male fiddlers learned accompaniment skills to increase their level of musical participation at dances and other district events. Even when it was another's turn to play fiddle, they could continue taking part in music making by contributing on pump organ, piano, or guitar.

Kevin Chaisson of Bear River, Kings County, describes still another path. In his case, at least, learning piano accompaniment served as an effective means for deflecting a much-loved but extremely demanding parent bent on producing a brood of top-notch fiddlers. As a teenager, Chaisson struck a deal with his father, Joe Pete: the youngster would devote himself seriously to piano accompaniment in exchange for avoiding any further family pressure to pursue fiddling.[7]

Chording

Although most *keyboard* (organ or piano) accompanists learned their basic skills by emulating local musicians, a substantial minority were able to take advantage of at least some formal training. There had long been a certain number of trained keyboard teachers scattered throughout the Island to whom promising youngsters could be sent for instruction.[8] Not surprisingly, the most likely recipients of such formal training were the keyboard teacher's own children. Rita Morrison (b. St. Andrews, Kings County), for example, offers this recollection:

> My grandmother was a music teacher. She taught my mother to play the organ, and that's why she played very well. My mother played in the church, and she would play anything on the organ. I never heard her chording with the fiddlers, but she could play any piece [from] notes.

As Rita Morrison's recollection of her mother implies, the formal keyboard training that a rural Islander was likely to receive centered on a "classical" or religious repertoire. Rarely did it address even the basics of *chording* (fiddle accompaniment). As far as chording was concerned, then, trained keyboard players were pretty much in the same boat as the self-taught. In other words, they might hope for a few pointers and some general encouragement from accomplished chorders in the family or community, but for the most part they had to pick up the art on their own.

While it is beyond the scope of this book to cover accompaniment skills in the same depth as fiddling techniques, a few points can be made. Essentially, there are two aspects of chording that accompanists must master. First, there is *timing*—keeping a rock-solid beat on which the fiddler can rely. As Kevin Chaisson observes, "The thing about playing the piano, especially when you are backup to a fiddler, the most crucial thing is timing. If the timing gets off a little bit, then it throws [off] everything!" Second, accompanists have to come up with an appropriate harmony for each segment of the tune. This in turn has two elements: knowing when to *shift* (that is, when the chord must be changed) and knowing which chord to play. According to Kevin Gotell of Georgetown, Kings County, the sense of when "shifting" is appropriate is just another inborn trait involved in the process of recalling and making music. "It's basically by ear: my ear just tellin' me. I know in the music when the fiddlers are going to shift. And I know if I'm playing a chord and it's not the right chord that the fiddler's in, I know it in my own ear. It's a gift, I guess."

Although the accompanist needs a special talent to hear when a shift is required, he or she can easily learn by rote the specific sequence of chords required for any given tune. As Gotell observes, this is one area in which a novice can count on the most assistance from experienced musicians.

> I know when to shift, but sometimes I have trouble [knowing] which chord to shift to. A few friends can play violin, and as they're playing they shout the chords out. Fred McCullough was one:[9] he could sit and play fiddle with his eyes closed, feet going, and shout the chord out just before the shift.

After mastering the basics, accompanists progress by developing more-sophisticated chording skills. One effective tactic is to seamlessly stitch chords together at their transition points via techniques that are known formally as *bass runs* or voice leading. Kevin Chaisson describes this approach as follows:

> The thing that I like to do—I don't even know what you call it, it's leading in from one chord into the other. I don't know where it came from, it's just something I developed on my own. It's just like different runs [series of notes] and stuff that you would put in. I enjoy doin' it; it makes it somethin' different.

Alternatively, accompanists might offer extra support for the fiddler by doubling the melody, an art known on Prince Edward Island as *playing the tune right out*. For piano players or organists, this means playing dance tunes at full throttle with the right hand while maintaining a chording rhythm with the left. This kind of melody playing is no mean feat on keyboard—particularly for those without sufficient formal training to make use of thumb or finger pivots to shift hand location[10]—and those who did it well were often locally renowned. Teresa Wilson, for example, recalls that her mother was an expert at this kind of playing: "There was hardly a tune that she couldn't play. She played the reels really nice and really swift and kept good timing on the organ. She played the tune right out, so in order to go along with her you'd have to know your tune real well."

"Make Sure the Piano Player Knows What You're Going to Do"

There are many ways that fiddlers and accompanists work together to bring about an effective performance. As Kevin Gotell implies above, for example, they often cooperate on selecting appropriate chords. Such collaborations were not always smooth, however, particularly when the musicians involved were friends or relations. Kevin Chaisson, for example, offers this account:

> Oh, my God! My brothers and I, we used to get into some awful squabbles over the music. I remember lots of times we'd get into it, trying to figure out what chords to use [and] what way to put them. I'd be sitting down and my brother Kenny would say, "There's another chord missing, there's something missing, eh?" So we'd work on it, and I'll try to get it in there if I can at all.

Some of the same conventions that help groups of fiddlers play together are also employed by fiddlers and accompanists; for example, each *turn* of the tune is almost always repeated, and each tune in a medley is generally played twice through. Fiddlers and accompanists also share several other conventions. For example, when an accompanist wishes to request a tune from a fiddler, he generally jigs or whistles its first few bars. When a fiddler wishes to indicate a particular key, he often runs his bow back and forth a few times on a telltale double stop. Archie Stewart explains,

> If I was going to play a tune now and he's sittin' there I do this [*plays the double-stop G–B on strings 3 and 2*], and he knows I'm goin' to play in G. If I do this [*plays the double-stop D–F# on strings 2 and 1*], he knows I'm going to play in D. If I do this [*plays A's in unison on strings 3 and 2*], he knows I'm going to play on A. If I do this [*plays the double-stop C–E on strings 4 and 3*], he knows I'm going to play on C.

Alternatively, many fiddlers use the verbal cues "A and G" or "G and F" to indicate "modal" (nonmajor) tunes in the keys of A and G, respectively.[11]

Accompanists also expect that a fiddler will stay within the same key when moving among tunes in a medley.[12] Should the fiddler wish to shift keys, he is supposed to either warn the accompanist in advance or shout his intent just prior to the change. As Allan MacDonald of Bangor, Kings County, notes, "If you shift from one chord [key] to another, you make sure the piano player knows what you're going to do." When this obligation is neglected, it tends to create a degree of annoyance. As Emmett Hughes of Dromore, Queens County, recalls, repeated transgressions of this kind could ultimately cause a fiddler to be ostracized.

> This one fiddler, he was goin' wild playin', and jumpin' from one key to the other. And at the last, nobody wants to play with him. He'd start in G, and then B-flat, and then into A, he'd jump from one key to the other. It doesn't give the accompanist much of a chance when you don't know where they're gonna go to.

Effect on the Tonal System

One striking feature of Island accompaniment prior to the early 1990s was the virtual absence of minor chords, coupled with the use in their place of major chords with the same root.[13] One probable consequence has been the exacerbation of certain tonal tendencies already present in Island fiddle music (see chapter 9). Specifically, some scale notes that were traditionally played somewhat sharp relative to "standard" values may have been driven sharper still by accompaniment practices. The clearest instance involves the fourth note of the major scale in the class of tunes typified by the well-known A major reel "Mason's Apron." The opening theme of the high turn opens with an arpeggio on the tonic chord, A. This is then followed by the same arpeggio pattern played one step higher, which would be expected to outline the chord B minor, or B–D–F# (appendix A, example 10.1a). The tendency among Island accompanists, however, was to eschew the minor and play the chord as B major, or B–D#–F#. Island fiddlers had already tended to play the fourth note of the major scale (that is, D in the key of A) somewhat sharp, and it may be that the use of the B major chord for accompaniment in that passage pushed fiddlers' pitch-sense even further upward. In any event, many Island fiddlers now play those D notes so sharp that they almost sound as D#'s (example 10.1b).

Interestingly, the early 1990s proved to be something of a watershed with respect to the use of minor chords on the Island. Just around that time, many accompanists began to use minor chords consistently in their playing, with pianist Kevin Chaisson serving both as pioneer and as primary role model. By the time of this writing, the use of such chords behind the fiddle has become relatively commonplace, especially among younger accompanists. This change in accompaniment practices may explain at least in part why the latest generation of fiddlers has not developed the sharp fourth scale-degree to the exaggerated extent exhibited by those of the previous generation.

Ensembles

The spread of accompaniment on Prince Edward Island throughout the 1930s and beyond led in due course to the development of fiddle-centered ensembles, which performed primarily at local dances and benefit concerts. Interestingly, the notion of the orchestrated ensemble did not take root,[14] despite numerous examples provided during that era on radio—not only by Don Messer's band, the Islanders, but also by American bands such as the Skillet Lickers and Bob Wills's Texas Playboys. Instead, the typical Island band merely increased the number of accompanists without materially changing the fiddle's role or affecting the texture of the music. In other words, such ensembles generally featured a single fiddle playing melody while all other instruments simultaneously chorded along. If there was more than one fiddler among the crew, they generally took turns playing the lead instrument.

Sometimes, a vocalist who also played guitar or keyboard would join forces with one of these ensembles. During vocal numbers, the fiddler would softly double the melody behind the singer while the rest of the band chorded. For dance tunes, the fiddler would take the lead while the vocalist chorded along with the rest of the band. By the 1970s, this kind of ensemble had become the most common kind of Island dance band; they were still widespread in the early '90s (for more on this, see chapter 15).

Probably the most important recent development in Island accompaniment has been the spread of electronic keyboards, which got seriously under way in the late 1980s. Because these instruments offer both the tonal range of the piano and the portability of the guitar, they have nearly replaced both instruments at many Island music events. Piano accompaniment styles are also rapidly changing, as many younger players have begun to emulate modern Cape Breton piano accompaniment, with its highly syncopated, percussive attack and wide dynamic range. Once again, the pioneer and major role model for this stylistic shift has been Kevin Chaisson.

Two other major developments in Island accompaniment did not come into play until the mid- to late 1990s. First, there has been a dramatic increase in the level of accompaniment skills now available on such fretted instruments as guitar, banjo, and mandolin. Second, orchestrated ensembles—as exemplified by such groups as Barachois and Vishten—have now become a major feature of the Island scene. What's more, the success of such ensembles on the world music and North American festival circuits has played a major role in actively projecting Island fiddle music beyond its local confines (both modern trends are discussed in chapters 16 and 17).

NOTES

1. A few local ensembles featuring keyboard accompaniment also played regularly during the 1930s on Summerside and Charlottetown radio stations; see chapter 13.
2. The pump organ, or harmonium, was first patented in 1848 in Paris, France, by Alexander-Francois Debain; see Gellerman, *American Reed Organ*.
3. See, for example, Emmerson, *Rantin' Pipe*, 108.
4. Similar dolls, now known as *limber-jacks*, are often offered for sale at North American folk festivals.
5. To use spoons as a rhythm instrument, one hand holds two spoons by their handles with their business ends positioned back to back and hovering over a knee. The free hand then strikes the spoons so that they collide with both the knee and each other.
6. Palm Beach guitars were decorated with stenciled palm trees and other tropical designs.
7. As noted in chapter 5, during the traditional period overt pressures of this kind to succeed at music were quite rare.
8. Formal keyboard training for young women was available at some Island convents. In addition, musically gifted Island youngsters were sometimes sent for keyboard training to such cities as Halifax, St. John, and Boston.
9. Fred McCullough was a highly regarded fiddler from the Georgetown, Kings County, area; he was frequently mentioned during the 1991–92 interview sessions as having been an outstanding player and major influence. He passed away shortly before our project got under way.
10. In formal keyboard training, students are taught to play a right-hand ascending scale by pivoting on the third finger, then reaching the thumb underneath to obtain the next note in sequence. Descending, they are taught to pivot on the thumb and reach the third finger over it to obtain the next note in sequence.
11. The most common "alternative" modes found in Island fiddle-music are characterized by a penultimate scale degree that is a full step lower than the tonic. One common strategy for harmonizing tunes based on such modes is to use the major chord whose root is the penultimate scale degree as the dominant chord. Consequently, for an "A modal" tune the tonic chord is A major and the dominant is G major; for a "G modal" tune the corresponding chords are G major and F major, respectively.
12. More precisely, the fiddler is expected to select among tunes that have the same keynote. He may shift at will among different modes with the same keynote.
13. The reference here is specifically to cases in which a minor triad is outlined or strongly implied by the melody but is instead accompanied by the corresponding major triad (that is, A major in place of A minor).
14. An orchestrated ensemble has each instrument playing a previously worked-out part; all parts are designed to mesh together during performance.

PHOTO 10.2. PETER DOIRON (RIGHT) AND GRANDSON ADAM DRISCOLL AT SUMMERSIDE, PRINCE COUNTY, AUGUST 1996 (PHOTO BY KEN PERLMAN).

CHAPTER ELEVEN
"The Devil Was in These Fiddle Contests"

Fiddle contests first got under way on Prince Edward Island in the 1920s and were a common aspect of Island life for about half a century. Unlike what prevailed in many other regions of the Anglo-Celtic world (see below), these Island contests served no grand scheme; nor—apart from an occasional play-off among local winners—were they ever integrated into an organized network. Instead, they served primarily as local entertainments, attractions, or fund-raisers. This chapter discusses the nature, extent, and effects of fiddle contests on Prince Edward Island.

Although traditional-music competitions were conducted in many other locales without causing undue hardship, on Prince Edward Island such contests had a decidedly negative impact on many fiddlers' lives. This impact was so pronounced that when fiddlers began to organize in the 1970s, one of their first collective acts was to remove virtually all such contests from the local milieu.

Given the foregoing, it is worthy of note that the Island's first major fiddle competition—often referred to locally as the "Great Contest of 1926"—was, if anything, a unifying and validating experience for both fiddlers in particular and Islanders in general. It was the largest and most widely publicized musical event of the traditional period and represents perhaps the first time that trends in mainstream North American popular culture impinged directly on Island fiddling.

In early 1926, the newly formed Prince Edward Island Tourist and Publicity Association received a notice from the Intercolonial Club of Boston announcing the latter's intention to hold an "international" fiddling competition in its home city on April 6 of that year.[1] Seizing an opportunity to glean "valuable publicity for the Province,"[2] the association decided to sponsor an Island-wide contest, with the first-place winner to be awarded an expense-paid trip to compete at the Intercolonial competition. On March 4, 1926, the competition was announced on the front page of the Island's largest newspaper, the *Charlottetown Guardian*:[3]

> Let all you young fellows of fifty or so who have twanged fiddle-strings at weddings, tea parties, house-warmings, bean-suppers, barn dances, stumping bees and corn frolics throughout our fair province all these years with such little recognition heretofore! Come with your fiddles and your bows to Charlottetown to the Strand Theatre on March 30th and be assured (whether you win or lose) of a hearty welcome.[4]

Contest rules did in fact dictate that entrants had to be at least fifty years of age.[5] The repertoire was also restricted; contestants could "play quadrilles, schottisches, polkas, jigs, reels, hornpipes or what they please—but it must be genuine old stuff—none of these new fangled fox trots or bear gallops will be tolerated."[6] The announcement further stated that a step-dancing contest would be held in conjunction with the fiddling match.

The Island contest soon spawned considerable excitement, so much so that the *Guardian* ran most articles dealing with it as front-page news. In one column, it was described as "the talk of the Island. . . . [N]othing in recent memory has stirred such enthusiastic interest."[7] Another column proclaimed, "[N]ow in every city, town, and hamlet on the Island the big question is, 'who shall represent P.E. Island at the contest in Boston on April 6th.'"[8]

Ultimately, forty-one fiddlers signed up to participate. To give all of them a chance to be heard, the length of the competition was expanded from one to two days, and its starting time was moved back one day to Friday, March 29.

The timing of the Intercolonial's invitation and the alacrity with which Island officials and news outlets took up the cause all point to a wider context for this story. Before continuing this description, therefore, I will make a small digression and take note of numerous similar events taking place around that time on the North American mainland.

Fiddle Contests and the First North American Fiddling Revival

The mid-1920s represented the peak of a continent-wide effort to revive fiddling and square dancing. Both arts had been in rapid decline in much of North America through the late nineteenth and early twentieth centuries and were in the process of being replaced by the newer music and dance styles associated with the ragtime and jazz ages. Because fiddling was rapidly losing its customary association with social dancing, diehards saw large-scale contests as an alternative means both to maintain the focus of existing practitioners and to attract a new generation to the art. They also hoped that the publicity generated by major contests would revive flagging public interest in fiddling and thereby help stem its decline.[9]

Formal and well-promoted fiddle competitions began to appear in certain parts of the United States in the last third of the nineteenth century.[10] Such efforts gathered steam after the turn of the twentieth century, as increasingly larger and better-publicized contests took place: notably in such areas as West Texas, Dallas, and Atlanta.[11] The visibility of such events increased markedly in the early 1920s when several contest champions also became pioneers in the fields of country music broadcasting and recording. For example, Eck Robertson—a product of the West Texas contest scene—was the first Southern fiddler to record for a major label. Fiddlin' John Carson, who made his early reputation on the Atlanta contest scene, was probably the first Southern fiddler to play on radio; he was also the first country music artist to produce a commercially successful recording. Three other fiddlers whose professional music careers were launched by the Atlanta contests were Gid Tanner, Clayton McMichen, and Lowe Stokes. They later joined forces to form the Skillet Lickers, one of the best-known 1920s "hillbilly" string bands.

Fiddle contests received still another major boost in terms of public attention and media exposure during this era when famed industrialist Henry Ford initiated his own campaign to revive fiddling and square dancing in the United States. One major driving force behind the Ford campaign was a nostalgic or even reactionary social and political agenda. Fiddling and square dancing were associated in the public mind with pioneer values and the Jeffersonian ideal of the yeoman farmer: aspects of culture that were being threatened at the time by cultural, technological, and demographic trends. By promoting the survival of what was already being referred to as "old-time" music and dance, Ford hoped to keep at bay not only modernity but also those contemporary influences he regarded as non-Nordic, or otherwise non-American.[12]

Ford's activities got under way in 1923, when he began holding old-time dances at an inn he purchased in Sudbury, Massachusetts. In 1925, he sponsored a contest in Detroit at which eighty-year-old Jasper "Jep" Bisbee of Michigan was crowned King of Old-Time Fiddlers. Late that same year, a fiddler of similar vintage named Allanson Mellen "Mellie" Dunham of Norway, Maine, was lionized in the American press when he was personally invited by Ford to spend several days at the latter's estate in Dearborn, Michigan.[13]

By 1926, the efforts of Ford and other organizers had pushed interest in fiddle contests to an all-time high throughout North America, and literally hundreds of them took place. One of the biggest was the three-day All New England Contest held in Providence, Rhode Island, in January of that year.[14] Another competition that attracted considerable attention—in part because Scottish fiddle-great James Scott Skinner had agreed to participate—was the four-day World Champion Old-Time Fiddlers' Contest, scheduled that April for Lewiston, Maine.[15] Major contests also took place during the first three months of that year in Detroit, Nashville, Louisville, Chicago, and San Antonio.[16] The largest contest of all was America-wide in scope. Some 1,865 fiddlers competed in local and regional play-offs organized through Ford dealerships. In a final play-off held in Detroit, Uncle Bunt Stephens from Moore County in middle Tennessee was declared national champion.[17]

It is against this background of continent-wide media attention and public frenzy that the Intercolonial Club sent its invitation and that the Island's own Fiddle Contest of '26 was subsequently organized and promoted.

As it drew near, many Islanders must have regarded the impending competition not only as a source of pride but also as a great curiosity. Here a commonplace, virtually taken-for-granted art—hitherto practiced primarily in district kitchens—was suddenly elevated to center stage by the Island's political and economic elite and touted in its major newspaper.[18] What's more, from that same elite came another message—that fiddling was on its way out, doomed by the same forces that afflicted it elsewhere in North America, and if one were to miss this display of expertise, one might never see the like again. Certainly, the *Guardian*'s initial announcement underlined such a perspective:

[T]here is one old time art, not yet altogether lost to us, which—however—through lack of proper appreciation we have allowed to decline sadly from its former prominence. It flourishes now only in out of the way corners in town and country. It is something that we all loved fondly when we were young, but now we think have outgrown with the advent of radio and gasoline. It is intimately connected with the past history of the Island. It was a feature of all the social gatherings of our forefathers. It stirred alike the blood of the Irish, French and Scotch, for it appealed to sentiments that were universal.[19]

Although such laments for fiddling's impending demise turned out to be decades premature, it is easy to see how at the time such a message would have thrust home. In the mid-1920s, Prince Edward Island did indeed appear to be on the brink of what we now refer to as modernization. This was a time of relative prosperity buoyed by the rise of two new agricultural businesses: fox-pelt farming and seed-potato growing. There were also numerous other signs pointing to oncoming modernity: electricity had been available in Charlottetown for decades, regular ferry service with the mainland had just been established, and work was under way on a new system of roads suitable for motor traffic. There was no way to foresee that the onset of the Hungry Thirties would cripple the Island's new agricultural businesses, that poor planning and engineering would undermine much of the hoped-for improvements in road transportation, and that electrification for much of the Island outside its major cities would be delayed for up to forty years.[20]

"It's About the Great Contest in Old Charlottetown"

On the morning of Friday, March 29, 1926, two special trains set off—one from Souris in eastern Kings County and the other from Tignish in western Prince County—each with the task of bringing contestants from these most distant parts of the Island into Charlottetown. According to local lore, only some of the Islanders who boarded these trains with fiddles in tow were actually contestants, while the remainder were just ringers hoping for a free ride to the competition.[21] As luck would have it, a major storm struck the Island that day, and both trains ended up snowbound. Although the train from Prince County made it to Charlottetown by the second day, conditions were so bad in the east that yet a third day had to be added to the contest to give fiddlers from Kings County an opportunity to compete.[22]

The contest, sans most of the Prince and Kings County competitors, got under way as scheduled at Charlottetown's 1,200-seat Strand Theatre, which was "taxed to capacity . . . with a cheering and enthusiastic audience." To expedite matters, contestants were divided into teams, each consisting of a fiddler plus a step dancer. Each team was then scheduled "to perform for a period of eight minutes—step dancing for four minutes, with the remaining four allotted to the fiddler." According to the *Guardian* correspondent reporting the next day, "Many and varied were the different styles of step dancing and tunes played, [with] the audience showing its approval at intervals with dynamic cheering and handclapping."[23]

On the following day, the demand for tickets proved to be so high that an additional venue was established at the nearby Prince Edward Theatre. In the interests of fairness, all contestants were then required to perform for both audiences. Even with two theatres in operation, however, hundreds of would-be spectators had to be turned away. Reported the *Guardian*, "[W]ords fail to describe the enthusiasm and pleasure with which the second night's performance was received—received two-fold it may be said [since] both theatres . . . were crowded to capacity."[24]

Then-fledgling Island radio station CFCY achieved its first major regional notice by broadcasting the entire contest. Since this turned out to be the first radio broadcast on the Island to garner a sizable local audience, it did much to establish CFCY as a viable business (for more on the founding of CFCY, see chapter 13).

Several elimination rounds were required to determine the outcome, but at last the three winners were announced on the evening of April 1. First prize went to one of the late-arriving Kings County contestants: a fifty-year-old farmer and lobster fisherman from the district of Elmira named Neil Cheverie. Second prize went to William Harvey of Ellerslie, Prince County, while third prize went to Robert Weeks of Winsloe, Queens County, who also won the step-dancing championship.[25] In addition, earlier in the proceedings a seventy-four-year-old Mi'kmaq fiddler named Noel Sapphere of St. Andrews, Kings County, had been granted a special medal for "his splendid work on the fiddle."[26] The following verses were penned shortly after the contest and published in the *Guardian*:

> Come all ye young fiddlers, give ear to my song
> Give me your attention, I won't keep you long
> It's about the great contest in old Charlottetown
> Where were gathered the fiddlers of fame and renown
> . . . .

> Then play up your fiddles and play them up strong
> And give them your best as you fiddle along
> You'll need it I'm sure for it's plain for to see
> You'll have to go some to beat Neil Cheverie.[27]

On April 6, Cheverie went on to compete at the Boston contest. He won third prize there, with first prize being awarded to Dan MacDonald, a Boston resident originally from Antigonish, Nova Scotia.[28] A few days later, in what amounted to a rematch of the original contest, Cheverie took second place, behind a Mr. McEachern from Boston.[29]

There was some hope on the Island that the Intercolonial Club competition would be broadcast on Boston station WNAC.[30] Apparently, however, what was big news on the Island was small news indeed in Beantown. Not only was there no broadcast, but the Boston press seems to have ignored the event entirely, deciding instead to focus their attention on the aforementioned World Champion Fiddle Contest in Lewiston, Maine, which took place about the same time.[31]

The Fiddle Contest of '26 was still talked about on Prince Edward Island in the early 1990s. Some merely mentioned it as having been an important event of their youth. Others proudly proclaimed their descent from the prize-winners. Several families touted their ownership of winners' instruments, and in some cases there were more of these claims than there were such instruments to begin with. Fiddle repairer Neil MacCannell (b. Lorne Valley, Kings County), for example, points out that "three different people think they have Neil Cheverie's fiddle."

As recently as the 1990s, some Islanders were still debating whether the judges made the right decision. As one might expect, those from Cheverie's native northeastern Kings County generally felt that justice was done, while some from other parts of the Island felt that their man might have been short-changed. As for the descendants of the participants, some "still [had] hard feelings about the results fifty-five years later."[32]

"That Way You'd Know Who Played the Best"

No fiddle contest as elaborate in its preparation or as powerful in its ability to focus public attention was ever again held on the Island. Nevertheless, the events of '26 firmly established the idea of holding fiddle competitions in the public mind, and for the next half century small- and moderate-scale

PHOTO 11.1. *LEFT TO RIGHT:* ELMER ROBINSON, EDDY ARSENAULT, AND ELDON MACARTHUR AT WOODSTOCK, JULY 1992 (PHOTO BY EARTHWATCH TEAM).

fiddle contests were commonplace. Some such contests were sponsored as commercial ventures by local promoters, businesses, or radio stations; more often they served communities as yet another way to use fiddling as a means to raise funds for local causes (contests were quite effective in this regard: the audience paid an admission price, but only a small proportion of the proceeds ever went out in prize money).[33]

Some of these later competitions still managed to spark the local imagination. Jackie Biggar (b. Tyne Valley, Prince County), for example, recounts a story he heard from older fiddlers about a Charlottetown contest held in the 1940s. Apparently, the judges just could not decide who deserved first prize and kept making the last two competitors—William Harvey and his nephew Elmer Robinson of Woodstock, Prince County—play off against each other.

> Them contests sixty, seventy years ago, everybody played the same tune. That way you'd know who played the best. And I don't know if they were just abusin' the sys-

tem or whether they just enjoyed the music and kept them up there playing, but I think Elmer Robinson and Bill Harvey had to play "St. Anne's Reel" seven or eight times each before they could pick out who was the best. Seven or eight times! They couldn't pick the winner and said, "OK, go at 'er again, boys!" And they'd go back up there, and Elmer, you know how Elmer would step up there just like a peacock, boy! Bill Harvey was gone before my time, but I wish I would have heard him.[34]

Tony Smith (b. Tracadie Cross, Queens County) describes another Charlottetown contest, at which renowned Cape Breton fiddler Winston "Scotty" Fitzgerald was one of the judges. It was held at the Forum, a hockey rink that in the off-season often served as a venue for major public events.

> The contest was almost over when this fellow sauntered in; he was about three sheets to the wind. He said, "I'm gonna play in the contest." So somebody said, "You can't play in the contest. It's almost over." "I'm playing anyway," he said. He had the fiddle in a flour bag, one of them old flour bags they had years ago. So Fitzgerald, he come backstage and said, "Let him play. If he wants to play, let him play." Jeez, when he started to play, I never heard the like for fiddlin'. Oh, a beautiful player. He just stood up there, boy, he let 'er go and as cool as could be. And I never heard of him since. It was the first and last time I ever heard him.[35]

As an aside, Smith identified this mysterious contestant as Lorne MacKay (b. Riverton, Kings County). This is the same Lorne MacKay who, according to a story cited in chapter 4, had trouble gaining credibility for his early fiddling efforts because he came from a nonmusical family.

According to Harold Dockendorff (b. Mount Hope, Kings County), in the late 1940s, radio station CFCY ran a series of contests over the airwaves. Over a period of days or weeks, fiddlers would be brought into their Charlottetown studio to play live, and listeners would call in their votes. Dockendorff notes that Jack Webster of Cardigan, Kings County, won first prize at least a few times in these on-air championships.[36]

Ultimately, three levels of competition developed on the Island. On the lowest level were dozens of district contests, most of which took place in local halls. "Old Peter" Chaisson of Bear River, Kings County, for example, tells us that by the 1940s and '50s nearly every district hall across the seventy-five-mile expanse from Charlottetown to East Point had a contest at some point during the year and that he "was in on them all."

In an effort to limit the number of contestants at these smaller events, judges would sometimes make youngsters qualify before allowing them to compete. Teresa MacPhee Wilson (b. Monticello, Kings County) describes how the process often worked.

> You had to be able to play "Lord MacDonald's Reel" before you were allowed to get into the contest. And I mean that wasn't something that was written down, but that was something that generally was true of every fiddler's contest. It was a difficult tune to play, too. If you could play "Lord MacDonald's Reel," they felt you could play nearly any tune.

On the second tier were annual competitions held in the cities Charlottetown and Summerside and in such major towns as Souris, Montague, Alberton, and Tignish. Jimmy Banks of Poplar Point, for example, describes the procedure at the Montague, Kings County, contest.

> They advertised and you had to send in your entry if you wanted to play. They used to have three nights of it: two nights of competition, and then they'd have a play-off night when the first and second prize [winners] from the first two nights would play off. You were supposed to play a waltz and a jig and a reel: three tunes. And you had a certain length of time to play them in. Then the next fellow come up and took his turn.

Finally, Island-wide competitions were sometimes held, often set up as play-offs involving the winners of the various city and town contests. Archie Stewart of Milltown Cross, for example, was Kings County Champion in 1948 but placed third in a subsequent play-off. Similarly, in 1967 the winners of nineteen local competitions met for a play-off held at Birchwood High School in Charlottetown; Wilfred Gotell of Georgetown, Kings County, was ultimately declared Island champion.

Local promoters sometimes tried to amplify a contest's appeal by inviting fiddlers from neighboring provinces to compete against top Island players. Emmett Hughes of Dromore, Queens County, tells us, for example, that in the late '60s he took part in an event billed as the Maritimes Fiddling Contest, which was held at the Forum in Charlottetown and featured Winston Fitzgerald as one of the judges. Among other Island players participating were Hector MacDonald of Bangor, Joe Pete and "Old Peter" Chaisson of Bear River, and George Weatherbie of Charlottetown. Among those brought in from away were New Brunswick recording artist Earl Mitton and Cape Breton fiddler Angus MacIsaac, the father of present-day recording star Ashley MacIsaac. Hughes was awarded first prize in the competition, which he attributes to the fact that on that occasion he was able to "borrow" Fitzgerald's highly accomplished accompanist.[37]

Winning even a major Island contest was not especially remunerative. On the local level, prizes rarely amounted to more than five or ten dollars in cash, or the equivalent in merchandise.[38] Awards were substantially higher at city and town contests, but as noted by frequent winner Andrew Jones of Pleasant View, Prince County, such awards rarely amounted to more than fifty dollars in the 1950s or—keeping pace with inflation—one hundred or two hundred dollars in the late 1960s and early '70s.

Some of the fiddlers we spoke to competed in countless contests. If the rewards were uncertain and not especially grand, why did they bother? Essentially, participating in contests was one of the very few paths by which Island fiddlers could earn money or attract special recognition from their art. There was little money and precious little positive social attention to be gained playing for dances, there was no paying concert circuit, and after about 1940 there were few opportunities even for the best-known and most accomplished players to appear on local radio (see chapter 13). A contest victory, in contrast, brought in its wake not only prize money but also the special notice of peers and community. "Old Peter" Chaisson expresses it as follows:

> I got into them; you either win or lose, but I was always pretty lucky, got in the second or third or first, or whatever. If you won, boy, that was it, you know! The next fellow'd try to win the next time, and I don't know whether it was the proper way to run it or not. [But] it was quite the thing, I'll tell you!

Frequent winners, then, had a very understandable reason for taking part in the competitions. Some other fiddlers who competed infrequently or without much expectation of winning were also drawn to contests because they simply enjoyed the proceedings. As such players describe it, these events served the role of unofficial conventions; they offered an opportunity to catch up with colleagues, become familiar with the state of the field, learn new tunes, and investigate new ideas and developments.[39]

> I never missed them; I didn't win that many, but I really enjoyed going! It was nice to hear other fiddlers, players that you'd never heard before, didn't know they existed; and they'd be there! I just enjoyed meeting the group and hearing different fiddlers. (Wilfred Gotell)

> I just listened to every note: comparin' with the next fellow. And see the different styles of each—Everybody's got different styles. And pick out who you think is the best; you might not always be right. Oh, I loved it! (Cosmas Sigsworth: b. Corraville, Kings County)

"Some Fiddlers Were Very Deeply Scarred and Wounded by Things That Happened"

Although Island fiddling competitions may have had some beneficial aspects, in general their impact on Island fiddlers seems to have been problematic. The main factors involved can be summed up as follows: most fiddlers were ill-prepared by the cultural milieu for dealing with explicitly competitive situations involving music, the judging was often haphazard and unpredictable, and underhanded tactics among competitors became rampant. This state of affairs led to resentments and grudges that often persisted for decades.

Essentially, the main premise underlying fiddle contests runs contrary to the fundamentally noncompetitive principles upon which relations among Island fiddlers were built. By entering a contest, the individual fiddler is clearly putting himself forward for recognition rather than doing his part in a community project. What's more, the very nature of such contests implies that individual styles are not fundamentally unique, that it is possible to grade them so that one person's playing can be declared superior to all others. As is plain from the following comments, some fiddlers were clearly uncomfortable with such notions:

> I don't think there should be any competition, anyway. Everybody is as good as anybody else, you know. They each have their own style of playing. There's nobody perfect in it. And there's nobody to compare anyone to, 'cause everybody's so different. (Jimmy O'Connor: Murray Harbour, Kings County)

> A contest doesn't prove nothing; to me it proves nothing. The greatest fiddler of the night probably can't play something I can play, and vice versa. So who's the best fiddler? Some fellas can play a beautiful waltz, some can't. (Ervan Sonier: Summerside, Prince County)

Other fiddlers who had no objections to contests in principle still questioned the quality and impartiality of the judging. Although upon occasion prominent fiddlers from out-of-province such as Winston Fitzgerald were engaged to adjudicate competitions, the vast majority of judges at Island contests were local people who may have been great fans but lacked the level of musical understanding required to fairly evaluate competitors' skills. Hughie McPhee of Bayfield, Kings County, for example, describes a contest he witnessed in Souris. He overheard the judge declare that he would award first prize to a fiddler who could play successfully "on the flats" (that is, in the flat keys). The award went to someone who played "High-Level Hornpipe,"[40] a tune usually played in the key of $B\flat$. But what the judge didn't know (and presumably should have known) is that this particular fiddler had transposed the tune to the key of C—which has no sharps or flats—and was therefore no more entitled to win than the next fellow.[41]

Second, most judges tended to be fairly conservative in their tastes, favoring fiddlers who played common tunes over those whose tune choices were more esoteric. As "Young Peter" Chaisson of Bear River, Kings County, points out, "If you could play some of those tunes that were played for years and years, you apparently won the first prize, like if you could make a good job of 'Lord McDonald's Reel.' But if you played something different to the judge's ear, you wouldn't win."

Finally, many judges brought to the job quite a bit of what we now call "baggage": family ties, friendships, or grudges that predisposed them for or against the fortunes of particular players. Folklorist James Hornby (b. Belfast, Queens County) outlines the basic dynamic.

> It's a small community, and anybody's going to be a judge; they're going to get some farmer who had some interest in the music, and he's always going to be related more on one side to X than Y. He's going to work with somebody and not work with someone else, and there's going to be all these other factors that you get in a small society at play.

There was also quite a bit of local favoritism. If a contest took place in Summerside, for example, there was a strong presumption that fiddlers from Summerside would walk off with the prizes. And as for the northeastern Kings County town of Souris, "the word was at that time, there's no use in anybody going to [compete in] Souris; if you're not belonging to Souris, you'll not win anything anyway."[42]

Compounding these inherent biases was the fact that many judges could in effect be "bought." According to Emmett Hughes, for example, it was common practice for fiddlers to curry favor with judges by plying them with alcohol or promising to do so in return for a favorable outcome: "I seen that for meself, they'd treat the judges, which shouldn't have been allowed. They'd go outside and give them a few drinks. Then they'd expect to get first, and they would mostly!"[43]

The upshot here is that serious competitors were almost always suspicious of the results and concerned in particular about whether their performances were being fairly evaluated. As Emmett Hughes describes, this made it particularly difficult for them when they played well but failed to win.

> If you're workin' all day, and you have to hurry home, and hurry to get supper, to try to get there in time, and you knew you were better than the whole lot that got prizes, [and] you got nothin', it didn't go down very good for all with you. Everybody knows damn well when they play—You have a pretty good idea that you sounded as good as anybody up there, and you know when you make a mess of it, too.[44]

There was another factor at work here. Because one's level of musical talent was considered a gift from God and one's liveliness, sound, and style were considered inherent aspects of the personality, for most fiddlers musical style and personal identity were inextricably linked. Consequently, many of them found it difficult or even unbearable to have their playing publicly declared inferior to another's: even on just a single occasion. Some such players might avoid competition entirely, but others—especially in the face of a highly haphazard adjudicating environment—might do nearly anything to win, including undermining a rival's performance. And once a previously innocent player was victimized, he would be likely to either respond in kind or attempt to similarly victimize a third party. As a result, tampering with instruments and equipment, mean-spirited pranks, and other forms of skulduggery became endemic at Island contests.

George MacPhee of Monticello, Kings County, notes, for example, that if you were competing against the friend or relative of an accompanist, he might well sabotage your performance with poor play.[45] Jackie Biggar tells of a contest that took place in Summerside in the late 1960s when he was perhaps sixteen years old. When he got up to play, a far older and better-established fiddler turned down the volume on Biggar's microphone so that his playing could not be heard where it counted.[46] Similarly, Tony Smith points out that if you were a skilled player with a known drinking problem, your rivals would be all too eager enable your addiction. He tells the following story, for example, involving another contest at the Forum in Charlottetown and a well-known fiddler from the Tracadie area named Larry Smith:

> Larry would have got first prize that night. But [some other competitors] got wind of this. They had a couple of hookers [liquor-filled containers] with them, and they got feedin' him behind the stage, they got feedin' him booze, and Larry got pretty full. And "Scotty" Fitzgerald was a judge that night. And he was lookin' at Larry and lookin' at him, and he said, "By Jesus, if he hadn't dropped the bow on the floor, eh." 'Cause that's what happened to him. He said, "If you hadn't dropped that friggin' bow," he said, "you would have got first prize." He said he never saw a fellow who could finger the fiddle that good, eh.[47]

Some other commonly employed stratagems included buttering a rival's bow, asking to try a rival's fiddle and returning it ever so slightly out of tune, and insisting that the rival try your fiddle in hopes that differences in string height and spacing might throw off his sense of finger placement once he had returned to his own instrument.[48]

Not surprisingly, the conditions under which Island fiddle contests were conducted often created resentment and hard feelings among players. At the very least, angry looks or negative comments might be directed toward the victors. As Peter Doiron (b. North Rustico, Queens County) recalls, "In fiddling contests here on the Island there's a certain amount of little darts that are flying back and forth if you happen to play something better than somebody else." At their extreme, such hard feelings could easily erupt into violence, as in the following account from Eddy Arsenault of St. Chrysostom, Prince County:

> One time I went to a fiddlers' contest in Charlottetown, and we were all in back of the stage. And the guy, whoever it was that won the first prize, the other fiddlers didn't like it at all. So everybody started to break their bow and their fiddle. You should have seen the mess in the back of the hall, four or five fiddles all broken up, and bows all over the place. And the fight—oh, God, that's when the fight started!

Even more destructive were the long-standing grudges and high levels of distrust that often built up as a result of these contests. Fr. Charles Cheverie of Charlottetown sums it up as follows:

> When we were kids and we were playing cards at times, inevitably it would end in a fight. Mom would always say, "The devil's in those cards, the devil's in those cards." Well, to paraphrase that, I think the devil was in these fiddle contests. Because an awful lot of hardship really come out of it. There are fiddlers who will not speak to each other on PEI, because going back to their childhood when they had these competitions, there was always the question as to whether they had fair judges.

As the years went by, Island fiddlers became increasingly disillusioned with competitions. At long last, they took matters into their own hands. When the Prince Edward Island Fiddlers' Society was formed in 1975, a proposal came up almost immediately to forbid members from participating in contests. It carried overwhelmingly, and since that time there have been precious few events of this kind held on the Island. Bishop Faber MacDonald (b. Little Pond, Kings County), who was head of the organization during its early years, recalls the dynamics behind the decision.

> You could get the sense that there were some very, very deep feelings about what had happened among fiddlers over the years as a result of them being engaged in competitions. I picked up that some very, very good fiddlers were very deeply scarred and wounded by things that happened. So that was one of the very first meetings that it got out on the floor: "O.K., if we're going to form this society, anybody who's a member will not enter contests." They were adamant on that: "Never again will a member of this society get involved in fiddling contests." Later on, there was still

an attempt on the part of certain organizations to set up the contests, but these guys stayed away from them.

Once local fiddlers stopped supporting them in the late 1970s, fiddle contests pretty much faded from the Island scene. One major exception was the annual PEI Fiddling and Step Dancing Competition in Tyne Valley, Prince County, which had been founded in the 1950s and was generally held during the summer in conjunction with a town day known as the Oyster Festival. Among its most frequent winners were Elmer Robinson (who won so many times that in his later years he was appointed a judge) and Jackie Biggar. Generally, a renowned fiddler from the Canadian mainland—such as Ivan Hicks and Graham Townsend—was brought in both to entertain the crowd and to serve on the judging panel. The event was finally discontinued after the 2005 season because of declining attendance.[49]

In retrospect, it is curious that neither judges nor sponsors tried to systematize award criteria, control foul play among contestants, or otherwise correct the chaotic state of affairs that once prevailed at Island fiddling contests. Perhaps this was still another outgrowth of the negative stereotypes about fiddling discussed in chapter 8. In other words, many Islanders may have viewed all the contest-related fracases, grudges, and personal distress not as an inevitable consequence of a flawed system but as yet another manifestation of fiddlers' poor moral characters. And as long as various communities and organizations benefitted from contest proceeds, there was little incentive to look into the matter more deeply.

Impact and Legacy

The role that fiddle contests played—or failed to play—on Prince Edward Island is probably best understood when placed in a broader historical context. Since the late eighteenth century, most musical preservation movements in the Anglo-Celtic world have relied on contests as their primary strategy for ensuring the genre's survival. In Scotland, such efforts go back to the 1780s, when competitions in Highland bagpiping were organized in London and Edinburgh in hopes of preserving that art. By the 1830s and '40s, this tactic had been extended to dancing, fiddling, and other traditional arts and crafts, with the ultimate effect being the evolution of the Scottish Highland Games movement.[50] In Ireland, preservation activities got under way as early as 1792, when a competition known as the Belfast Harpers's Festival was organized in hopes of preserving the art of Celtic harping in that country.[51] Two subsequent, and ultimately much more successful, Irish cultural-preservation movements also focused on music competitions to achieve their goals. These include the Feis Ceoil Association founded by the Gaelic League in the 1890s and the still-extant Comhaltas Ceoltoiri Eireann, which was founded in 1951.[52] As for North America, the contest-centered American fiddling revival of the late nineteenth and early twentieth centuries ultimately failed: by the late 1920s, popular interest in what had become a media-driven fad began to ebb, and what little interest was left quickly evaporated with the onset of the Great Depression.[53] However, a second and ultimately much more effective round of fiddling-preservation activities that also featured contests as a primary focus would arise roughly a generation later in the form of independent state and provincial fiddling associations.[54] Nowadays, contests sponsored by such organizations—such as the National Oldtime Fiddlers Contest in Weiser, Idaho, and the Canadian Open Old Time Fiddle Championship in Shelburne, Ontario—are a prominent feature of rural North American life.

Whenever such well-developed competition scenes have been established, they have generally exerted a profound influence on playing styles. For one thing, when contests rival or replace playing for dances as a major focus, there is a natural tendency for fiddlers to de-emphasize strong dance rhythms in favor of the kind of smooth, showy virtuosity that impresses judges. This was certainly one of the factors that in the mid- to late 1920s led to the dominance at many Southern contests of the "long-bow" approach, which has since become the prevailing style in bluegrass and swing fiddling.[55] Another common theme is that contests can quickly push up the general level of expertise while also promoting homogenization among players. The process is as follows: because those eager to succeed soon adopt the general approaches of the first few contest winners, these approaches eventually become templates, or *superstyles*, for future generations. Over time, both individual idiosyncrasies and variation among regional styles tend to disappear.[56]

On Prince Edward Island, none of these trends came to pass, and contests had little effect on style or repertoire. I can venture a few theories to explain why this was so. First, apart from the Great Contest of '26, these competitions had no underlying musical aim or organizational focus (and even the stated aims of the '26 contest appear to have been defined primarily by an external cultural movement). Probably in consequence, the judging was for the most part capricious and parochial; there never was sufficient consistency to offer contestants a trend to follow, much less a template. Furthermore, with most judges favoring conservative approaches to technique and repertoire over innovation, these contests if anything served more as a deterrent to change than as a spur to exploring new musical paths. Most important, until the tail end of the contest period, many district dance scenes remained vibrant, and (as discussed in chapter 15) regional dance halls were still thriving. Consequently, most fiddlers remained focused on providing effective dance rhythms and had little motivation to consider modifying their personal playing styles.

All considered, it would seem that the Island experience with fiddle contests has been the opposite of the pattern that has prevailed throughout much of the Anglo-Celtic world. In most other regions, competitions were adopted as a method for promoting musical revival. On Prince Edward Island, contests were virtually eliminated from the local scene at the founding of the Prince Edward Island Fiddlers' Society, which essentially marked the dawn of the Island's own revival. With this most fundamental of tactics cast aside, Islanders had to come up with alternative strategies to promote the survival of fiddling. As discussed in chapters 16 and 17, the strategies they employed in lieu of competitions made it difficult both to kick-start the fiddling revival and to control its course once it was fully under way.

NOTES

1. The Prince Edward Island Tourist and Publicity Association was formed in 1923 to oversee the growth of tourism, which had just been identified as a potential new industry (see MacDonald, *If You're Stronghearted*, 119). The Intercolonial Club, located in the Roxbury section of Boston, was made up primarily of Canadian-born Boston area residents; its successor, the Canadian-American Club, now has its headquarters in Watertown, Massachusetts.
2. "Old Timers Fiddling Contest at the Strand," *Charlottetown Guardian*, Mar. 30, 1926, 1.
3. The *Guardian* describes it as the very first fiddle contest on the Island of any kind, but according to Hornby ("Fiddle on the Island," 67 and "Great Fiddling Contests of 1926," 26), some of his informants recalled local contests that predated this one.
4. "Ye Old-Time Fiddlers' Contest," *Charlottetown Guardian*, Mar. 4, 1926, 1.
5. My best guess on the reason for choosing fifty as age-floor is that in the absence of qualifying rounds, the sponsors may have been seeking to keep the number of contestants down to a manageable size; they may also have been attempting to add gravitas to the proceedings.
6. "Ye Old-Time Fiddlers' Contest," 1.

7. "The Fiddlers Charge," *Charlottetown Guardian*, Mar. 8, 1926, 4, quoted in Hornby, "Fiddle on the Island," 70.
8. "Entrants for the Fiddling Contest," *Charlottetown Guardian*, Mar. 24, 1926, 3.
9. American contest-organizer Wm. Van Jacoway, for example, hoped "to show the present generation . . . that there was sweeter and more inspiring music emanating from the fiddle and the bow than will ever be found in the present day jazz" (*De Kalb [Alabama] Republican* Aug. 14, 1924, quoted in Cauthen, *With Fiddle*, 186).
10. What well may have been the earliest North American violin competitions took place in Williamsburg, Virginia, in 1736–37; see Hulan, "First Annual Country Fiddlers' Contest."
11. For Georgia contests, see Wiggins, *Fiddlin' Georgia Crazy*, 15, 46–61; for West Texas, see Townsend, *San Antonio Rose*, 29–30; for Dallas, see Wolfe, *Devil's Box*, 32.
12. See, for example, Blaustein, "Traditional Music," 35–42.
13. See Blaustein, "Traditional Music," 42–50; see also "Fiddling to Henry Ford."
14. See Greene, *Uncle Joe Shippee*.
15. Skinner (1843–1927) had been the first Scottish fiddler to record commercially (see chapter 13). Quite a bit of reporting on the Lewiston contest appeared in the Boston papers April 7–11, 1926. Two examples are Herbert Baldwin, "Wins Place in Fiddlers' Final Test," *Boston Post*, Apr. 8, 1926, 1ff.; and Arthur Bartlett, "Maine Fiddler Wins Third Night," *Boston Herald*, Apr. 8, 1926, 25.
16. Greene, *Uncle Joe Shippee*, 1.
17. Blaustein, "Traditional Music," 50.
18. The Island's elite class has not figured much in this narrative since discussion of the Land Question and de facto sharecropping in chapter 1. By the 1920s, it consisted primarily of large farmers, merchants, politicians, educators, and intellectuals, most of whom lived in or near Charlottetown or Summerside. Until the modern era, the ethnic and religious makeup of this elite class was overwhelmingly English and Protestant, respectively.
19. "Ye Old-Time Fiddlers Contest," 1.
20. See MacDonald, *If You're Stronghearted*, 112–54, 155–84.
21. Hornby, "Fiddle on the Island," 70.
22. "Old Timers Fiddling Contest Again Meets with Popular Favor," *Charlottetown Guardian*, Mar. 31, 1926, 1.
23. All quotations in this paragraph are from "Old Timers Fiddling Contest at the Strand," 1.
24. "Old Timers Fiddling Contest Again Meets with Popular Favor," 1.
25. "Neil Cheverie Will Represent the Island in Fiddle Contest," *Charlottetown Guardian*, Apr. 1, 1926, 1ff. As an aside, in the course of this project I have interviewed relatives of each of the winners: Omar Cheverie (Neil Cheverie's grandnephew), Elmer Robinson (Harvey's nephew), and Judy Lowe (Weeks's granddaughter).
26. "Old Timers Fiddling Contest at the Strand," 1.
27. Quoted in Hornby, "Great Fiddle Contests," 27. According to Hornby, these lyrics have been attributed to Wm. Joseph Cheverie of Souris.
28. "Cheverie Won Third Place in Contest," *Charlottetown Guardian*, Apr. 8, 1926, 1.

29. "Cheverie 2nd Weeks First in Contests," *Charlottetown Guardian*, Apr. 12, 1926, 1. The winner of the fiddle contest was probably "Big Dan" MacEachern, a cousin of well-known Cape Breton fiddler and composer Dan Hughie MacEachern. Margaret Dunn (in the introduction to *MacEachern's Collection*, vol. 2 [1993]) mentions that "Big Dan" won a major fiddle contest at the Intercolonial Club in 1926 (quoted in Graham, *Cape Breton Fiddle*, 93). Robert Weeks, who had won first place in step dancing on Prince Edward Island, had been sent along with Cheverie to Boston and took first place honors at the step-dancing contest held alongside the second Boston fiddle contest.
30. "Cheverie Won Third Place in Contest," 1.
31. Newspapers consulted include the *Boston Globe*, *Advertiser*, *American*, *Herald*, *Post*, *Telegram*, *Transcript*, and *Traveler*.
32. Hornby, "Fiddle on the Island," 71.
33. Hornby, "Fiddle on the Island," 67.
34. Jackie Biggar, personal interview, Nov. 23, 2006, PEIFP Interview #54.
35. Tony Smith, personal interview, Nov. 24, 2006, PEIFP Interview #56.
36. Harold Dockendorff, personal interview, Nov. 18, 2006, PEIFP Interview #43.
37. Emmett Hughes, personal interview, Nov. 25, 2006, PEIFP Interview #57.
38. Hornby, "Fiddle on the Island," 67.
39. There is some analogy here to the fiddlers' conventions held during the nineteenth century in parts of the United States, often on the courthouse lawns of towns and villages in conjunction with the arrival of the local circuit court. These "conventions" were primarily occasions for conviviality and tune swapping but were sometimes accompanied by concerts and contests. See Combs, "Highlander's Music," 116; and Cauthen, *With Fiddle*, 164–65.
40. For the notation to "High-Level Hornpipe," see Perlman, *Fiddle Music of PEI*, 114.
41. Hughie McPhee, personal interview, Oct. 20, 2006, PEIFP Interview #08. It is generally presumed that playing in the flat keys is difficult on fiddle. Many Island fiddlers, however, have developed fingering strategies and shortcuts that make playing in the keys of F and B♭ relatively accessible.
42. Emmett Hughes interview, Nov. 25, 2006.
43. Emmett Hughes interview, Nov. 25, 2006.
44. Emmett Hughes interview, Nov. 25, 2006.
45. George MacPhee, personal interview, Nov. 25, 2006.
46. Jackie Biggar interview, Nov. 23, 2006.
47. Tony Smith interview, Nov. 24, 2006.
48. Ward MacDonald, personal interview, July 30, 2008.
49. Peter Robinson, personal interview, Nov. 11, 2006, PEIFP Interview #32.
50. See, for example, Emmerson, *Social History*, 242–47.
51. See, for example, Conran, *National Music of Ireland*, 259–65. Unfortunately, in this case such hopes proved forlorn. The task of preserving the harpers' music went to an organist named Edward Bunting, whose *General Collection of the Ancient Irish Music* (1796) serves as the only record we have of this once-great art.

52. For Feis Ceoil (pronounced "Fesh Kool"; in English, "Music Festival"), see McCarthy, "Transmission of Music," 146–49. For Comhaltas Ceoltoiri Eireann (pronounced "KOL-tis kol-TOR-ree E-rin"; in English, "Musicians' Association of Ireland"), see Maloney, "Irish Music in America," 479–81.
53. Blaustein, "Traditional Music," 51–55.
54. See, for example, Blaustein, "Traditional Music," 63–97.
55. In the "long-bow" style, the player slurs many notes off a single bow stroke; this would give quite a different sound than the "sawstroke" described in detail in chapter 9. Wolfe (in *Devil's Box*, 32, 83–85, and 113–14) attributes the contest success and successful playing careers of several noted Southern roots fiddlers, such as Uncle Jimmy Thompson, Lowe Stokes, Clayton McMichen, and Fiddlin' Arthur Smith, to acquiring this bowing style.
56. See, for example, Maloney, "Irish Music in America," 482; and Blaustein, "Traditional Music," 113–19.

PHOTO 11.2. STEP-DANCER AT ATLANTIC JAMBOREE ABRAM-VILLAGE, AUGUST 1991 (PHOTO BY KEN PERLMAN).

CHAPTER TWELVE
The Dances

No book on PEI fiddling would be complete without a detailed look at the kinds of social and solo dances that Island fiddlers have accompanied over the years. Putting these dances in rough chronological order, the list includes the Scotch reel, eight-hand reel, square set, solo step dancing, waltz, and fox-trot.[1] The time frame covered extends from the time of early Scottish immigration in the late eighteenth century through the end of the traditional period.

The *square set*, or *quadrille*, has been the dominant form of old-time social dancing on Prince Edward Island throughout most of the period covered by living memory. Although Islanders adapted the quadrille to a "big-circle" format toward the end of the traditional period (more on this later), this dance is ordinarily performed with four couples facing each other in square formation, as illustrated and described in sidebar 12.1.

The quadrille is a species of *figure-dancing*—so called because each dance is composed by combining and recombining a relatively small number of routines, or "figures." Figure dances were initially collected and codified in the

SIDEBAR 12.1. QUADRILLE MANEUVERS AND DEFINITIONS

```
                    1ST COUPLE
                      O   X

   3RD COUPLE   X                    O   4TH COUPLE
                O                    X

                      X   O
                    2ND COUPLE
```

(x = *gentleman*, o = *lady*.)

The Square: Four couples stand at right angles, and gentlemen each have their ladies at their right hands. The lady at the gentleman's left hand is known as the *corner lady*. *The couple with their backs to the head of the hall are known as the first, or head, couple; the couple opposite them is the second couple; the couple on the first couple's right is the third couple; and the couple on the first couple's left is the fourth couple.** *First and second couples are known as head couples; third and fourth couples are called side couples.*

Source: Hillgrove, *Hillgrove's Call-Book and Dancing Master*, 63–64.

* This numbering system varies among different square dancing traditions. In contemporary American square dancing, for example, the couple to the right of the head couple is generally considered the second couple, and enumeration proceeds on a counterclockwise basis.

---

seventeenth century by a London dancing master named John Playford. In 1651, Playford published dancing directions for over a hundred such dances, with tunes corresponding to each, in a book called *The English Dancing Master*. The book was subsequently republished in several increasingly expanded editions (the eighteenth and last edition, published by Playford's son Henry in 1728, had over nine hundred tunes).

Playford's dances (which became known as *country dances*) were run from three basic formations. Sometimes the dancers formed a circle, other times a square, but most often dancers lined up *longways* (that is, in two facing lines). In the decades that followed, *progressive* longways country dancing became the dominant social dance for all levels of society in England, and it was also widespread in Scotland.[2] The French also adopted country dancing (which they called *contredanse*),[3] and by the early eighteenth century it had become one of the most popular dances of France.[4]

Around this same time, the French began to develop and elaborate their own version of square-formation figure-dancing, which also became widely popular. This specifically French style of square-formation dances became known as *contredanse française* (French country dance), while the longways version of figure-dancing was then referred to as *contredanse anglaise* (English country dance).[5] An alternative name for contredanse française was *cotillon* (rendered in English as *cotillion*).[6]

As danced in the eighteenth century, cotillions were characterized by a *rondo*, or verse-chorus structure (in French, the terms are *couplets* and *refrain*). In the most common pattern, nine different routines—known as *entrées* or *figures generales* in French and *changes* in English—would alternate in succession with a recurring routine, which eventually became known in French as *la figure complète* and in English simply as the *figure*. As the dance evolved, the "changes" became standardized, but each of the many cotillions in circulation had its own unique figure routine.[7]

Both English and French styles of country dancing were widespread in Britain, Ireland, and colonial North America during the second half of the eighteenth century. Interest in longways dancing declined throughout much of the United States in the early nineteenth century, however, perhaps because of feelings of hostility stirred up toward things British by the War of 1812.[8] In any event, square-formation dances ultimately became the dominant style of figure-dancing in much of the United States. The main exception to this trend was the New England region, where interest in longways dancing, or *contra dancing*, remained strong.[9] One longways dance that continued in currency throughout North America was "Sir Roger de Coverley," also known as the "Virginia Reel."

The quadrille originated in France toward the end of the eighteenth century as an offshoot of the *contredanse française*. There were three stages to its development. At first, it became fashionable to dance cotillions grouped together into suites or medleys, known at the time as *pot-pourris de contredanses*. In this earliest stage, each separate contredanse—including all changes and figures—was performed in its entirety. In the next stage, the standardized changes were jettisoned and only the distinctive figures (that is, *les figures complètes*) from each cotillion were danced. By the beginning of the nineteenth century, the most popular such medleys had become standardized, and it was these medleys that became known as "quadrilles."[10] The constituent contredanse figures in essence became integral components of the quadrille, and from then on they were simply referred to as "figures" of the quadrille.[11]

Each quadrille, then, was made up of several distinct segments, known as figures.[12] Each figure had its own steps and music, and each was danced in succession with pauses in between. At first, most quadrilles were made up of five figures. Reflecting both their basic formation and their origin as a medley of once-independent dances, in English-speaking countries quadrilles also became known as "square sets."[13]

The quadrille was formally introduced in Great Britain at the close of the Napoleonic Wars in 1815; the venue was Almack's Assembly Room, an exclusive London dance hall frequented by members of the British nobility. Only four figures were danced upon that occasion—La Pantalon, L'Été, La Poule, and La Trenis—but soon afterward a fifth figure, known as La Finale, was added. A square set consisting specifically of these five figures ultimately became known as the First Set of Quadrilles, or simply the Quadrille.[14]

Scores of different square sets were in circulation during the nineteenth century, each characterized by a unique group of figures.[15] Probably the best-known alternative to the First Set was the Lancers Quadrille (usually referred to merely as the Lancers), whose earliest known mention in print was an advertisement in an 1817 Dublin newspaper. The ad specified an inventor for the dance (one Duval of Dublin) and also named the Lancers' five figures as La Dorset, La Lodoiska, La Native, Les Grâces, and Les Lanciers. At first, the Lancers was merely a relatively obscure rival to the First Set, but by the mid-nineteenth century it had eclipsed its predecessor to become the most popular kind of figure dance in the British Empire.[16]

Some other popular square sets were the Caledonians (or Caledonian Quadrille), the Prince Imperial, the Continentals, the Union Quadrille, the Empire Quadrille, and the Saratoga Lancers.[17] To avoid confusion, in this chapter I use the lowercase form (*quadrille*) to refer collectively to the whole genre but the uppercase form (*Quadrille*) to refer specifically to the First Set of Quadrilles. Some popular quadrille steps are described in sidebar 12.2.

After being introduced in Britain, the quadrille quickly spread throughout Europe and much of North America. Its first documented appearance in the ballrooms of Charlottetown was about 1840: roughly a generation after its London debut. By 1860, it had become the most popular form of social dancing in the colonial capital.[18]

Once established in Charlottetown, the quadrille gradually spread through the Island hinterland, where it gradually replaced two other dances: the Scotch reel and the eight-hand reel (both discussed later). The last holdout was eastern Kings County, where this shift did not take place until roughly the time of the First World War. Just why the changeover in Kings County happened

SIDEBAR 12.2. QUADRILLE STEPS

Allemande Right: Couples join right hands, turn once around each other, and return to place. (Also, *Allemande Left:* Couples join left hands . . .)

Dos à Dos: Couples circle around each other, passing back to back (the French command literally means "back to back"). In English, this maneuver is often written "do-si-do" and pronounced "doe-see-DOE."

Grand Chain: "Each gentleman faces his partner, taking her right hand and passing her . . . presents the left hand to the next lady . . . giving the right hand to the next lady, the left hand to the next" (Hillgrove, 80). Generally, dancers make two circuits of the square and end by facing the original partner.

The Basket, or Ladies in the Center: "Four ladies forward to the centre . . . and join hands. The four gentlemen join hands. . . . [T]he gentlemen raise their hands . . . and the ladies, keeping hold of their hands, stoop, pass backwards, and rise on the outside of the gentlemen's arms, [thus] forming a basket or wreath" (Hillgrove, 81).

Ladies' Chain: "Ladies cross to the opposite's place, giving right hands as they pass each other, and their left hands to the opposite gent who turns them once" (Tolman and Page, 39). They then use the same procedure to return to their partners.

Promenade: Partners each walk hand in hand about the square in time to the music, generally ending up in their original place.

Sources: Hillgrove, *Hillgrove's Call-Book*, 65–97; Tolman and Page, *Country Dance Book*, 33–41.

precisely then is unclear, but some fiddlers attribute it to a general decline of interest in learning complicated stepping patterns (more on this later).[19] The following assessment, for example, from Jimmy Banks (b. 1907) of Poplar Point, Kings County, is typical:

> Then in our day, there was more of that old type of dancing began to go out. An odd one you'd have to play for, but more of the newer Quadrilles and Lancers. Well, they were slower movement to dancing. They didn't have so much step dancing in them.

From Ballroom Quadrilles to Island Square Sets

The ballroom quadrille was a fairly stately affair. Formal dress was called for, along with refined, moderate tempos and slow, deliberate movements. While more-elaborate footwork was current in the early days of the quadrille, after 1840 dancers generally just walked through its steps and figures: even the swinging of a partner (or *turning*, as it was then called) was accomplished without much generation of centrifugal force.[20]

The average nineteenth-century ball-goer would either have taken lessons from a local dancing master or have learned to dance from someone who themselves had experienced this kind of training. Through this process, he or she would have learned all the steps and figures for at least a few different varieties of quadrille. Consequently, there was little need for callers, or *prompters*, until the end of the nineteenth century, when the sheer number of quadrilles in circulation made them a necessary expedient.[21]

Generally, a different piece of music was used to accompany each of a given ballroom quadrille's five figures. The music used for accompanying quadrilles generally reflected the tastes of refined classes of society and was often drawn from marches, operas, operettas, and popular songs of the day. Sometimes, music was specially composed to serve as the accompaniment for the figures of a specific quadrille.

Accompaniment was usually provided by a band or small orchestra. In *Hillgrove's Call Book*, for example, the ideal ballroom ensemble is described as consisting of first and second violins, viola, bass, flute, clarinet, first and second cornets, and trombone.[22] Music and dance were structurally linked in the ballroom quadrille, in the sense that each maneuver was precisely timed to occupy a specific length of music (that is, a certain number of measures, or *bars*). In the first figure of the Quadrille as described by Hillgrove, for example, each maneuver—right and left, balance, ladies' chain, and so on—occupies exactly eight bars of music. This sequence is executed twice to complete one entire figure, for a grand total of sixty-four bars.[23]

Islanders took these formal quadrilles and created new versions of them that suited their own tastes and predilections. The pace of dancing increased, and demeanor became less restrained. Steps were altered or recombined in ways that seemed more convenient or pleasing. The centrifugal swing and "buzz-step"—which is said to have developed in New England in the 1870s—was imported and used in lieu of the more sedate two-handed turn.[24]

There was also a decrease in the number of figures that made up a given square set. Specifically, nearly all the fiddlers we interviewed report that the number of figures danced in their districts during the traditional period was four, instead of the five figures that were standard for ballroom versions. As Jimmy Banks tells us, "Whatever movements was in figure number one, they'd finish that out and then you'd stop. And then there'd be different movements for the next, the number two figure. And there was four in every Quadrille and Lancers; there was four different figures."

Other important changes involved both the music played and the manner of accompaniment. The typical Island set was generally accompanied by a lone fiddler (or a fiddler with ad hoc accompaniment), not by bands or small orchestras. The music employed for dance accompaniment on PEI consisted for the most part of jigs, reels, and other kinds of fiddle tunes, instead of semiclassical and popular material from nineteenth-century ballrooms. And individual fiddlers on PEI decided which particular tunes to use as accompaniment for the various figures, whereas in the ballroom such matters were generally dictated by convention.

Because the dancing in Island square sets was linked to the beat of the music rather than to its structure, fiddlers were not required to sort out a precise relationship between the tunes they played and the steps of a particular figure. Generally, the fiddler would start playing and dancers would begin their routine at just about any convenient point in the tune; they would then continue dancing to the beat until the entire figure was completed.

As the years went by, still more changes occurred on the local level, as each Island district pretty much created its own version of the square set. In fact, just as each fiddler put his own twist on the tunes in his repertoire, it could be said that each district had its own twist on the quadrille. As Jenny McQuaid (b. Naufrage, Kings County) describes it, "Each area had its flavor of dances."

For the most part, each district had only a single version of quadrille in circulation. This local version would then be danced over and over throughout the duration of a given occasion. The focus was not on achieving variety or in effecting a series of complex maneuvers. Instead, the idea was to have a comfortable routine that left enough of one's attention free to allow for relating both to one's neighbors and to the music.

A basis for comparing the routines of Island square sets with those of ballroom quadrilles is provided by those districts that used specific names drawn from the ballroom lexicon—Quadrille, Lancers, Caledonians, and so on—to refer to their own square-set versions. Largus MacInnis of Lakeville, Kings County, recalls, for example, that people in his community danced the Quadrille but that in some surrounding districts they danced the Saratoga Lancers. Similarly, Stephen Toole notes that in central Queens County the local square set was known as the Queen Lancers, while Archie Stewart of

PHOTO 12.1. "LADIES IN THE CENTER" AT GOOSE RIVER DANCE, NOVEMBER 2006. THE FIDDLER IS "YOUNG PETER" CHAISSON (PHOTO BY KEN PERLMAN).

Milltown Cross, Kings County, reports that his neighbors danced the Caledonian Lancers.[25]

By comparing accounts of quadrille steps and figures from such communities with those appearing in nineteenth-century dance manuals, one gets the impression that Island square sets with a local ballroom name each tended to have one or two figures that roughly corresponded to published versions. The other figures in the dance, however, often departed quite markedly from them.[26] This comparison also reveals a considerable amount of borrowing among districts. Communities were not especially fastidious about maintaining the purity of ballroom prototypes, and quadrille steps regarded as particularly appealing tended to circulate freely. This process is strongly indicated, for example, by the presence in nearly all Island square sets of a figure that included the maneuver known as ladies in the center.

Sidebars 12.3 and 12.4 offer relatively full accounts of the square sets danced in two different parts of Kings County during the traditional period.

SIDEBAR 12.3. A QUADRILLE AS DANCED IN THE LAKEVILLE, KINGS COUNTY, AREA

First Figure:
- You started in by salutin' your partner, and then you go eight hands 'round.
- Then the two head couples would go right and left, and the ladies would change [chain] across to opposite gents. Then they'd change back to partners and promenade forward.
- The side couples done the same, and after that was all over, they'd either promenade eight, or they'd go right hand to your partner, grand right and left till they met their partner. Then they'd swing, and then the first figure was over.

Second Figure:
- The first lady [head lady] gave right hand across to opposite gent and back with the left. Then right hand to partner and they'd go half right and left.
- The ladies would change across to their opposite partner [gent], and they'd swing and change back. Then the first lady on the side [side ladies] would do the same.
- The ladies would change across to their opposite and swing, and change back; and you done that twice—the head couples and the side couples. Then, when the last couple got through, they either promenaded around the room or they went right hand to your partner. Once they got back to their partner, that was another figure.

Third Figure:
- They all joined hands and went around. Then they broke away to the left and two couples went four hands around.
- Then they went right and left and changed partners and they changed in line; instead of changing back they kept on going till they got back to their partner.
- And when that was over they doubled up the opposite way and went right and left. And the two ladies changed to their opposite partner and then they changed back.
- Then the four couples promenaded all around the room. And that ended the third figure.

Fourth Figure:
- They started out by grand changing [chaining] and when they got to their partner they done what they called balance your partner. You were supposed to step-dance, and then you'd swing your partner.
- After they promenaded round the room they'd balance their corner lady, and they'd turn around to swing their partner. And then they'd promenade with the lady they balanced till they got back to their partner.
- [Ladies in the center] And then they joined hands and the ladies got in the center and the gents went out, caught hands and went outside and then they put their hands all over the women's heads and went around again.
- And they grand changed to their opposite—to the lady across the room. And—after they swung the lady across the room they turned the lady on their left and then the ladies grand changed and went to their partner—they promenaded back to their places. So that was the end.

Source: Described by Largus MacInnis.

**SIDEBAR 12.4. A "CALEDONIAN LANCERS"
AS DANCED IN THE MONTAGUE, KINGS COUNTY, AREA**

First Figure:
The first part of the set was the two couples here went back and met one another and back again, and then you swang your lady in the corner. Then the other two done the same thing and then that was over.

Second Figure:
Everybody caught hands and went back and forth and then they swang, and they promenaded right around.

Third Figure:
The next part of the set was what we called ladies in the center. The ladies joined hands in the center and the men joined hands, and they went in a complete circle, and then back again, and then they promenaded all around, and then all the way back. They done this twice.

Fourth Figure:
The last part of the set was grand chain. You give your hand to the lady next to you, and you went right around the circle; and when you met your partner you swang. Then the first couple at the head led up, and the lady went right and the gent went left and the rest all fell in and they come back and met, and promenaded up the center, and then they broke and back and forth and then they swang. Till every couple did that, then the set was over.

Source: Described by Archie Stewart.

"We Had to Learn How to Do It"

A nineteenth-century ball-goer may have viewed Island quadrilles as rather rough-and-ready affairs, but in fact rural Islanders had fairly well-defined standards concerning what made good and bad dancing. Although the main emphases may have been on enjoying the music and the company of one's neighbors, dancers still had to know what they were about. For just as fiddlers feared the social repercussions of a playing error, an inexperienced or inept dancer whose awkwardness interfered with the smooth workings of a set might also be taken to task by the neighbors. This state of affairs applied to youngsters in particular. As Teresa MacPhee Wilson (b. Monticello, Kings County) recalls, "It used to be you had to be able to dance the square dance real well, or you just wouldn't be allowed in the set."

There were no formal dancing masters in rural Prince Edward Island. Nevertheless, according to Merlin Quinn of Cardross, Kings County, "We had to learn how to do it; you couldn't just get up on the floor, you know."

As was the case for budding fiddlers, most youngsters learned to dance square sets through observation and emulation of local adults. This being said, some help was available to novice dancers. We have already seen, for example, how dancing square sets was virtually an authorized activity during lunch hour at some district schools. Alternatively, as illustrated by the following story from Merlin Quinn, in some families youngsters were taken aside and taught how to function on the dance floor:

> I wouldn't want to go to a dance and go up and ask a nice girl to dance and not be able to dance. That would be a terrible thing to do. And if it wasn't for my sisters I never would have learned it! I had four sisters, and they used to get after me to take them to the dance in the horse and wagon. And I didn't want to go because I couldn't dance very good, or I couldn't dance at all! So to get me primed, they got teachin' me to dance. We got down in the front room on Sunday evenings and we'd jig [sing the tunes], and they'd show me how to go through the sets. So I finally caught on.

The lack of formal dancing masters on the Island certainly created a need for prompters to cry out the steps. And indeed, Stewart MacIntyre (b. Fairfield, Kings County) recalls that once the use of such prompters "was a general thing. Everything was carried out according to the calls, and it seemed to put a lot of pep in the dancing." As communities became more and more familiar with their own square-set versions, however, the need for prompting declined. By the 1930s, as MacIntyre notes, the practice had for the most part been abandoned.

> It was just a sort of a custom they started, that callers fell out of favor, you know. On that style it went out, and they were left to do what they like. As far as I know, when we did it during the Second War in the Elmira Hall [in northeastern Kings County], that was about the end of it.

One community where dance prompting persisted nearly up to the modern era was Lakeville in northeastern Kings County. According to Largus MacInnis, it was the custom there for one of the male dancers in a set to call out the steps.

> Anytime I called a set I was always dancing. Like if there was a bunch dancing in the parlor, the man from one of the couples that was dancing would call the set. And if there was more dancin' in the kitchen, the man from one of the couples that was dancing [there] would call that set.

The Development of Circular Sets

As the modern era approached, there was a general shift in Island quadrilles from the traditional four-couple squares to "big-circle" formations that could accommodate up to several dozen couples. There were two major factors that led to this development: chaotic conditions at the commercial dance halls that grew up in the years following the Second World War, and the great popularity of a new figure known as swing-all-'round.

The spread of automobile travel allowed Islanders to congregate for dancing at large regional halls, where brawling and other forms of violent behavior were endemic (for more on this, see chapter 15). One major source of friction at these events was competition for room on the dance floor. Because four-couple squares tend to be relatively space intensive, Islanders began tinkering with the formation to accommodate a larger number of dancers. At first, additional couples were added to the sets. Ivan Day (b. Norboro, Prince County), for example, recalls that at one point quadrilles were danced with two or three couples on each side of the square.[27] These enlarged squares proved unwieldy, however, and ultimately Islanders gave up on them altogether. Instead, all those couples who were inclined to dance a quadrille would simply form one or more large circles. Some quadrille routines were adapted to work from these "big circle" formations, and the rest were abandoned.

One quadrille figure that was particularly well-suited to the big-circle format was swing-all-'round,[28] which seems to have first appeared on Prince Edward Island during the 1930s and spread rapidly thereafter. Merlin Quinn explains both its procedure and the main source of its appeal.

> The best figure of all was swing-all-'round 'cause you get to swing all the girls. You'd swing the lady on your left and then you'd promenade with the lady on your left around and then you'd pass her to the guy on your right and you'd turn, swing the next lady on your left and keep goin'. Then you'd swing and promenade each girl till you reached back to meet your partner.

By the 1950s and '60s, several new "regional" versions of the quadrille had evolved at Island dance halls: all featuring big-circle formations and the swing-all-'round figure. These big-circle quadrilles—such as the *Souris Set* in northern Kings County, the *Grand River* in western Queens and eastern Prince Counties, and the *Quadrille and Flux* in western Prince County—became extremely popular on Prince Edward Island and were the only form of quadrille to survive there into the modern era.

PHOTO 12.2. "SWING YOUR PARTNER" AT MONTICELLO CEILIDH, JULY 1992 (PHOTO BY EARTHWATCH TEAM).

Along with the change in formation came a general reduction in the number and complexity of figures. The Souris Set danced in the 1990s, for example, had only three figures, two of which were extremely simple in concept. The second figure consisted entirely of swing-all-'round, while the third figure was composed primarily of just two maneuvers: ladies in the center and grand chain. Only the first figure was relatively complex (see sidebar 12.5).

This general reduction in complexity had at its root two main factors: differences among local versions were never adequately reconciled, and logistical problems created by converting from square to circular formations were never systematically addressed. Although such issues might have easily been overcome by a corps of competent prompters, the practice of using prompters at Island dances—which had fallen out of favor in the 1930s—was never readopted.

SIDEBAR 12.5. FIRST FIGURE OF THE SOURIS SET, CIRCA 1993

- Join hands, circle left
- At own place, swing partner
- Promenade all around
- Head couple with right couple, four-hands round
- Ladies' chain
- Men's chain
- Ladies exchange places, swing opposite
- [Swing partner*]
- Promenade [with partner] all around
- Head couples with left couple, four-hands round
- Ladies' chain
- Men's chain
- Ladies exchange places, swing opposite
- Grand right and left

Source: Described by J. D. MacIntyre of Goose River, Kings County.
* Author has added this detail after observing videos of several dances.

Here is an example of the kinds of problems that can develop when routines developed for conventional quadrilles are adapted to circular sets. As noted in sidebar 12.5, the first figure of the Souris Set as danced in the 1990s calls for head couples to go four hands 'round with side couples on the right and, later, with side couples on the left. Given a circular formation, however, how is it determined which are the head couples? In the absence of prompters to make such calls, this dilemma tends to generate confusion each time the first figure is danced. Adding to the potential difficulties is the issue that without prompters, it is difficult to avoid circular formations containing an odd number of couples, thereby leaving one couple without a counterpart for four hands 'round.

Scotch Reels and Eight-Hand Reels

Prior to the rise of the quadrille, the dances of choice in rural Prince Edward Island were the *Scotch reel* and the *eight-hand reel*. The Scotch reel had been the predominant dance of eighteenth-century Scotland. There were several variants in circulation at the time of immigration to Prince Edward Island, most notably the *circular reel*, the *threesome reel*, and the *foursome* (or *four-hand*) *reel*.[29] In terms of basic procedure, the various kinds of Scotch reel have the following aspects in common:

- The typical set for a Scotch reel is made up of either three or four dancers. In both the circular and foursome reels, it comprises two couples. In the threesome reel, a set is made up of a man and two women, or a woman and two men.[30]
- The dance consists of an alternation of two kinds of footwork, which are known respectively as *setting steps* and *traveling steps*. Traveling steps are employed to negotiate a *traveling figure*, during which dancers describe the outline of a circle, figure eight, or other geometric shape, the way a figure skater might outline such a shape on ice. Setting steps, in contrast, are used to mark time between embarking upon traveling figures. Each kind of Scotch reel has its own distinct traveling figure: a circle for the circular reel, a figure eight for the three-hand reel, and "a figure eight with an extra loop added" for the foursome reel.[31]
- There is almost always a change in tempo and musical accompaniment in the course of the dance. Specifically, the musician plays one or more moderate-tempo strathspeys for the early stages of the dance and then segues into one or more fast tunes, or reels.[32]

As noted in chapter 1, oral tradition has it that virtually the first act of the Glenaladale pioneers upon landing in the New World in the 1770s was to dance a reel on the shore to the skirl of the bagpipes.[33] The earliest published account of Scotch reels danced on Prince Edward Island comes from the 1820s diary of a British traveler named John MacGregor, who declares, "Their dancing is at the very antipodes of our fashionable quadrilling; with them every muscle and limb is actively and rapidly engaged."[34] Another early account dates from 1839, when a forty-three-year-old minister from the district of Belfast in southeastern Queens County was "unfortunately prevailed on to join in a Scotch reel" and ruptured an Achilles tendon at the governor's New Year's party in Charlottetown.[35]

It is virtually impossible to say what specific brands of Scotch reel footwork initially made it across the Atlantic to Prince Edward Island at the time of Scottish immigration. For one thing, there were probably hundreds of different styles of setting and traveling steps in circulation. In the towns and cities of Scotland, each prominent dancing master taught his own version of footwork, while in less-settled areas without dancing masters, each village developed its own variant. Adding to the profusion, different kinds of footwork were employed in different settings. For town greens and other outdoor venues, dancers were up on the balls of their feet and popular steps called for a considerable amount of leaping, hopping, and kicking. For the ballroom, dancers used what might be described as a "refined" version of outdoor footwork. Finally, for informal indoor venues such as parlors and croft kitchens, the emphasis seems to have been more on tapping out rhythms with the feet on hard surfaces.[36]

Although we do not know what styles of Scotch reel footwork were originally brought to Prince Edward Island, we do know the style that has been used for dancing the Scotch reel and its relatives within the time of living memory. To a person, older Islanders who have witnessed such dances describe the footwork employed as "step dancing."

During the mid-nineteenth century, still another version of reel dancing began to spread through the English-speaking world, known as the eight-hand or *eightsome reel*. This new dance was performed by four couples in square formation who employed setting and traveling steps borrowed from Scotch reels to negotiate quadrille-like routines.[37] The eight-hand reel appeared not long afterward on Prince Edward Island, where for a couple of generations it coexisted with its four-hand cousin, as implied by this newspaper account dating to 1862 of a Souris, Kings County, tea party:

> [I]t done us good to witness big plethoric bodies moving with surprising elasticity and frolic through the various nimble "reels" and four or eight hand encounters, and giving . . . the whole force of their minds, and their extremities also, to the business.[38]

The eight-hand reel reached its high point in terms of popularity in rural Prince Edward Island toward the end of the nineteenth century, after which it rapidly lost ground to the quadrille. By the 1920s and '30s (the time frame of the following recollections), reel dancing in general had grown sufficiently rare to be considered a curiosity by the younger generation. In the following descriptions, note that the footwork style is referred to as *step dancing* and that—at least in some parts of the Island—eight-hand reels were also known as *breakdowns*.[39]

> An odd time the old folk would get up and they'd dance what they call a breakdown. It was all step dancing. It was generally four couples got up and they'd face

their partner and dance, and then two couples would dance across the room and back. Then the two end couples would do the same, and they'd keep on dancing. (Largus MacInnis: b. 1918)

There was another dance—I seen it done in our house, my father and uncle and Uncle Henry and my father and all those guys. They had what they called a breakdown. It consisted of step dancin' all the time, right through the set. The girls all lined up on one side and men on the other and they'd step right down to the tune, you know. And then they'd join hands and go through another figure, and they'd step all the way around and square off again. It was just continual step dancin' all through the set. It was beautiful! (Merlin Quinn: b. 1929)

In the early days of the quadrille on Prince Edward Island, carrying footwork directly from the eight-hand reel into the dancing of square sets must have seemed a natural thing.[40] At the next stage, such footwork was confined to certain figures, or to interludes between figures, as noted in the following descriptions:

There would be a grand chain, and when they would stop, they would step-dance. I remember they stood in a circle, the ladies in middle, and the men would catch hands and swing around, and they'd stop and the caller would say, "Make a beer barrel and kick the bottom out of it." That was to start the step-dancing part. (Stewart MacIntyre)

When the figure was done, the four couples would step-dance in between: the whole bunch of them. It was something to see, I'm telling you! Every clown couldn't get up on the floor then, you know. But it was mostly the older people that could do that; the younger generation didn't pick it up at all. (Jimmy Halliday: Eldon, Queens County)

As the proportion of Islanders adept at the art of step dancing declined, so did the custom of incorporating fancy-stepping into Island square sets. Eventually, it all but disappeared from Island social dancing, although as Archie Stewart reports, an individual might still occasionally break into a flurry of steps as a form of self-expression: "Sometimes there'd be two or three fellows clipping it off going around the grand chain, because they'd get feelin' pretty good and they wanted to show off their talents. Some of them didn't have too much, but they made a noise anyway!" As its role in social dancing declined, step dancing increasingly became an art that was practiced and performed on an individual basis. Throughout most of the period of living memory, step dancing was in fact most to be encountered as solo demonstrations between square sets at house parties and community dances.

It makes sense now to take another look at the wedding reel (described in chapter 2), which had once inaugurated rural Island wedding celebrations. As originally danced on Prince Edward Island, the *wedding reel* featured a four-person set akin to a circular or foursome reel.[41] As dance styles changed, however, these same trends were reflected in wedding reel routines. When the eight-hand reel replaced the Scotch reel, the wedding reel was adapted to a square formation. When the eight-hand reel itself declined and fancy footwork was relegated to the confines of an occasional quadrille figure, the wedding reel was also confined to a single quadrille figure (generally the last figure of the dance).

Despite the decline and ultimate disappearance of Scotch and eight-hand reels, many important elements from these older dance styles live on in PEI music and dance. When square sets came along, Islanders transferred the instrumentation and music with which they were already familiar (that is, fiddles and fiddle music) into a new context. They also carried along characteristic rhythms and rhythmic accents from the Scotch and eight-hand reels to quadrille accompaniment. In turn, these rhythms strongly influenced the way in which Island square sets were danced.

Another feature that survived from the Scotch reel was the mid-dance tempo shift. The most obvious modern manifestation of this phenomenon is in Cape Breton step dancing, in which it is still customary to open with a strathspey or group of strathspeys and then segue into one or more reels (Cape Breton fiddlers now also use this format for medleys intended as performance pieces). Following the Cape Breton model, over the past couple of generations this practice has also been adopted by many PEI fiddlers and step dancers.

Origins of Step Dancing

Although determining exactly how step dancing originated on Prince Edward Island is beyond the scope of this book, I can venture a reasonable scenario based both on oral histories and on the secondary literature. In the ensuing discussion, it is important to bear in mind that the style of step dancing practiced on Prince Edward Island almost certainly grew up as a larger regional phenomenon, since very similar approaches to the art can be found in Cape Breton, mainland Nova Scotia, New Brunswick, and Québec.

In Scotland, a modified, codified version of outdoor reel-footwork later served as the basis for modern *Highland dancing*.[42] The informal or kitchen version, in contrast, fell into disuse and did not survive long enough to ever be systematically notated or filmed. However, descriptions written by eighteenth- and early nineteenth-century observers suggest at least a kinship between the kitchen version and what ultimately became eastern Canadian step dancing.[43]

On Prince Edward Island and elsewhere in the Canadian Maritimes, the situation was reversed: the outdoor version of reel stepping soon fell into disuse, while the kitchen version flourished. Opinions diverge as to how matters progressed after that point. Some writers have put forward the theory that the indoor brand of Scotch reel stepping was the sole ancestor of step dancing.[44] Others point to Irish step dancing, English hornpipe dancing, or other imported styles of fancy-stepping as more or equally likely progenitors.

Several kinds of step dancing were popular in Ireland around the time of major immigration to Prince Edward Island, but the most widespread of all was a couples' step dance known as the *double jig*. In this dance, several different steps—the grinding step, the shuffle, the drumming step, the skipping step, the doubled battering step, and so on—were combined to intricately mirror the rhythms of specific tunes.[45] Interestingly, stepping of this kind to jigs did survive into the time of living memory on Prince Edward Island, where—according to Leonard McDonald of Emyvale, Queens County—it was known as *double-dancing*. Similarly, Attwood O'Connor of Milltown Cross, Kings County, notes that he used to dance the "Irish jig," about which his accompanist Stanley Bruce of Heatherdale reports, "It's not that much different than the step dancin', but it's double time."[46]

English hornpipe dancing originated as a localized, rural pastime in the third quarter of the eighteenth century. It was soon refined and elaborated for presentation on the stage; as such, it was carried across the Atlantic to North America, where it became a major attraction in some early traveling circuses.[47] As an intriguing aside, in 1797 the Ricketts' Circus of Philadelphia—featuring renowned hornpipe dancers Samuel Ricketts and John Durang—embarked on an extended tour of Lower Canada (now the province of Québec), including the cities of Québec, Montreal, and Trois Rivieres.[48] Such a tour could have easily sparked or amplified an interest in fancy-stepping in Lower Canada and spread from there to the Maritimes.

Given the above considerations, I will venture the following theory on step-dance origins: during the first two-thirds of the nineteenth century, the Scotch reel served as a crucible wherein Maritimes step dancing gradually took shape. Into this crucible also went elements drawn from Irish step dancing, from English hornpipe dancing, and from other late eighteenth- and early nineteenth-century fancy-stepping disciplines, such as Scottish *treepling* and various regional English *clogging* styles.[49] By the last third of the nineteenth century, Maritimes step dancing had emerged as an all-purpose style that could be applied to any solo or group dance requiring fancy footwork.

"When the Dancer and the Fiddler Are Bang On, I Tell You That's Magic!"

The kind of step dancing performed within living memory on Prince Edward Island is an informal dance.[50] Instead of following a prescribed routine, each dancer assembles a combination of steps that mirrors the unique rhythms of a given piece of fiddle music. In this way, dancer and fiddler have the opportunity to forge a powerful connection. When all is in sync and the dancer precisely mirrors the rhythms of the music, this interaction is considered a thing of great beauty. Here's how Libby Hubley of Kensington, Prince County, describes it:

> You could almost see the music when you watched them dance. Like the high turn would come, and they would perhaps have a little higher step or a little something comical in it. It just brings the music to life. And when it clicks, when the dancer and the fiddler are bang on, I tell you that's magic!

Just as each district once had its complement of fiddlers, each also had its stock of expert solo step dancers. Good step dancers were highly prized, and some of them became local celebrities remembered long after their passing, as implied by this story from Bill MacDonald (b. North Lake, Kings County):

> Jim Cheverie, he's dead now, but he was a champion step dancer. He had over seventy different steps, oh my dear! He could dance all day. He was the only person I saw that could dance all the way up the stairs and all the way down: step-dance on every step all the way up!

Similarly, Vincent Doucette of Deblois Road, Prince County tells this story involving a renowned local dancer named Gill Proveau:

> When they'd have a party at my grandfather's place, they'd go to the barn, and they'd take him a circular saw three feet in diameter, and they'd put that in the middle of the floor. That was his step-dancing platform. He could make cartwheels or flips as he was step-dancing and land in the same place, and not miss a step as he was dancing. He was one of the best around.[51]

Youngsters in rural Prince Edward Island during the house-party era learned their step-dancing skills for the most part through observation and emula-

PHOTO 12.3 *LEFT TO RIGHT:* ALLAN MACDONALD (GUITAR), GEORGE MACPHEE (FIDDLE), KEN PERLMAN (BANJO), AND MARLENE GALLANT (DANCER) AT MONTICELLO TEA PARTY, JULY 1991 (PHOTO BY EARTHWATCH TEAM).

tion of older family and community members. As Joe Conway (b. New Zealand, Kings County) tells us, "I learned mostly from watching people dance. I never took lessons: just watching somebody dance, and watching the way they moved their feet. Then you kind of practice it out yourself."

What makes a good step dancer? As was the case for fiddling, having what it takes begins with inborn gifts: not only the gift of dancing but also a good sense of timing and, as Dan McPhee informs us, the gift of music: "In order to be a good dancer, you have to know the tune; you have to know it perfectly. I imagine that a good dancer probably could play the fiddle if he really put his mind to it, because he knew the tunes so well." McPhee's point here is that the dancer must know the music intimately to prepare in advance a viable routine of steps. This means that he or she should be capable of calling tunes to mind—complete with rhythmic nuances—in the absence of a fiddle or any other instrument. As Donna Chaisson of Bear River, Kings County, describes, "I could just stand there and dance with a tune going on inside of my head; I wouldn't need any music." Along these lines, George MacPhee of Monticello, Kings County, tells this story about a dancer who was able to function just fine without musical accompaniment:

> This one old guy at St. Charles, he was a great step dancer. And he would dance anywheres to anything. So once he came to "Big Peter" MacKinnon's home, and Peter had no fiddle, couldn't play the fiddle. So what [Peter] done, he jacked up the wagon. Then he turned the wheel, held a stick against the spokes, and the old fellow used that [sound] for the dancin'.

Other considerations mentioned by Islanders involve what might be termed dancing technique. For example, as Jimmy Banks recounts, during the house-party era it was considered extremely important for virtually all step-dancing activity to be confined to the legs and feet: "Some fellows had a nicer style of dancin' than others: not too much body action. A lot of good dancers would stand there almost straight; their legs would just work from the hips down." As Wilfred Gotell of Georgetown, Kings County, describes, the older generations also felt strongly that the dancer's feet should barely seem to leave the floor.

> Some of the older step dancers I played for years ago, they were so close to the floor you could hardly get a cigarette paper under the soles of their shoes. That's true, and they were really pretty to watch. None of this "galloping," as I call it now, where they're lifting their legs clean to the knees and pretty near hitting their chins. We used to call it "close to the floor," and that's the way they used to be judged: closer to the floor and get the steps in!

Just as a good fiddler needs to have a large repertoire of tunes, a good dancer needs a large repertoire of *steps* (stepping patterns). An average dancer would know perhaps a few standard steps, a good dancer might know a couple of dozen steps, while a "champion" dancer—such as the aforementioned Jim Cheverie—might know three times that number. As Hélène Bergeron (b. St. Chrysostom, Prince County) describes, "The more steps you learn, then the more combinations are possible. So it's not a matter of ever running out of steps at any point. The step-well will never run dry!"

As noted in chapter 2, in the old days most step dancers would work out a routine of steps to fit a particular tune, and many would not have been comfortable trying to extemporize a sequence of steps to fit another one. There was a relatively small number of tunes (all of them reels) that were popular among step dancers in general. These tunes became part of nearly every fiddler's repertoire, and most have remained current in these repertoires for generations. Probably the most requested step-dancing tune was "Lord MacDonald's Reel," but just about all the most widely played Island reels are current or former step-dancing favorites (a list of the most widely played Island tunes appears in chapter 14).

Just as there are clear stylistic differences on Prince Edward Island between eastern and western fiddling styles, the flavor of solo step dancing also varies significantly along the same geographic continuum. In short, solo step dancing from Acadian-dominated western Prince Edward Island is faster, more syncopated, and more loosely constructed than its counterpart from the predominantly Scottish east.

Waltzes, Fox-Trots, and Dancing Games

The *waltz* developed in central Europe during the second half of the eighteenth century. In the 1780s, Prague and Vienna became the first cities to take up the dance in earnest; in Vienna, it was initially known as *Deutscher Tanz* (German dance) or simply *Deutscher*. In 1812, the waltz made its English debut at Almack's Assembly Room, the same venue where the Quadrille would subsequently be introduced.[52] It initially experienced some resistance in the British Empire from social conservatives, but by the 1830s the waltz was firmly established there. The first records of its having been danced in Charlottetown date to the 1840s.[53]

Although the waltz was hugely popular in most of North America throughout much of the nineteenth century and beyond, it was nearly absent from rural Prince Edward Island until right around the time of the Second World War—roughly a century after its Charlottetown debut.[54] Teresa Wilson (b. 1928), for example, notes that she "never saw waltzing or anything like that until [she] went away to work in Boston." Similarly, Emmett Hughes (b. 1922) of Dromore, Queens County, recalls that at the house parties and dances of his youth it was "all just square sets and step dancing; there'd be no waltzes and all this stuff."

Once the dance finally became established, it served as a break from an evening of otherwise continuous square sets. Before long, as Merlin Quinn recalls, many youngsters were learning to waltz as a matter of course.

> But then there was the old-fashioned waltz, and that wasn't easy to learn. My sister was teachin' school up in one of those districts and wanted me to take her to the dances and go up there on Friday nights and all. That was back in the '50s. And the only way to get me to go was to teach me how to waltz. So one of my sisters put me through that, and that's the only way I learned.

During the 1990s, I often heard the waltz referred to on Prince Edward Island as *round dancing*, presumably because couples generally form a circle and—to make a cosmological analogy—each couple rotates on its own axis as it orbits the midpoint of the room.

A dance game known as the "Paul Jones" was once popular on Prince Edward Island that featured waltzing or waltz tunes as prominent components. There were at least two variants in circulation. In one variant described by Ralph Hardy (b. Alberton, Prince County), the fiddler strikes up a reel and the company proceeds through a grand chain maneuver. Then, at a time of his own choosing, the fiddler starts playing a waltz tune, and each dancer begins to waltz with whomever he or she has by the hand.[55] Tony Smith (b. Tracadie Cross, Queens County) mentions a second version: the fiddler plays a waltz tune while the company conducts a grand chain maneuver. When the fiddler shifts into a jig, each dancer starts to swing with whomever he or she has by the hand.[56]

On Prince Edward Island, the term *fox-trot* is employed as a generic label for just about any up-tempo twentieth-century couples' dance step in duple meter (that is, 2/2, 2/4, or 4/4). Fox-trots began making their appearance in Island dance halls in the 1940s, and the genre served as an important conduit by which twentieth-century pop tunes and dance steps would reach and circulate about the Island. Just about any up-tempo duple-meter pop tune made for effective accompaniment, and just about any couples' step that kept appropriate time—from the two-step and Charleston through the Lindy hop and twist—also seemed to be acceptable.

Since the late eighteenth century, rural Prince Edward Island has experienced almost continual change in terms of its predominant styles of fiddle-accompanied social dancing. The Scotch reel was carried across the Atlantic by the first waves of Scottish settlers; it was joined in the mid-nineteenth century by the eight-hand reel and the quadrille. By the time of the First World War, the quadrille had supplanted both forms of reel dancing and had become the major social dance of rural Prince Edward Island. Couples' dancing in terms of waltzes and fox-trots became popular in the 1940s, a period during which the basic quadrille formation changed from the traditional four-couple square to a big circle. Not surprisingly, significant changes in fiddle-accompanied dancing styles have continued to take place since the coming of the modern era. The quadrille has gone into sharp decline, while both step dancing and couples' dancing have increased in prominence. What's more, step dancing has undergone a major stylistic shift due to the development of organized competitions and instructional programs. (Further developments in Island social and solo dancing are discussed in chapters 15–17.)

NOTES

1. As an aid to the reader, in this chapter each dance or dance genre is italicized when first introduced or discussed.
2. Progressive dances are designed so that any given couple "progresses" a slot or two up or down the line following each repetition of the prescribed routine.
3. Dance scholars generally see the French term *contre*, as used in this context, as a corruption of the English word *country*.
4. This general history is described in several books; an example is Damon, *History of Square Dancing*, 6–8.
5. Although it is natural to assume that the contredanse française was a direct outgrowth of the English country dance, a compelling case has been made that it was actually a hybrid: the result of applying ideas and principles drawn from English figure-dancing to steps and formations drawn from older French dances, notably the *branle*, which was popular from medieval times through much of the seventeenth century; see Guilcher, *La Contredanse*, 70–78. Similarly, Semmens ("Branles, Gavottes and Contredanses," 48) points out that at the turn of the eighteenth century, branles and some popular versions of contredanse française shared a common "step vocabulary."
6. The cotillon was a waist-petticoat worn by the peasant women of rural France. The French pronunciation is "ko-tee-YON"; the English pronunciation is "ko-TILL-yon" (rhymes with "million"). In the early eighteenth century, the terms *contredance française* and *cotillon* referred to two different square-formation dances, but by the mid-eighteenth century they had become interchangeable; see Guilcher, *La Contredanse*, 79–80.
7. Guilcher, *La Contredanse*, 127–31, 152–53.
8. See, for example, Damon, *History of Square Dancing*, 24–25.
9. "Contra dance" seems to be a re-Anglicization of the French term *contredanse*.
10. According to Richardson (*Social Dances*, 57–59), the term *quadrille* was originally used interchangeably with *contredanse française* and only gradually became exclusively associated with the medleys just described. The word originally referred to a small company of cavalry and was derived as a diminutive (*quadriglia*) of the Italian word *squadra* (a company of soldiers in square formation); later it was applied to performances by groups of dancers. Alternatively, *The Harvard Dictionary of Music* (674) credits the Spanish *cuadrilla* (a group of horsemen).
11. Guilcher, *La Contredanse*, 135–36, 151–57. Less technically detailed versions of the same story appear in Damon, *History of Square Dancing*, 27; and Richardson, *Social Dances*, 58–61. Semmens ("Branles, Gavottes and Contredanses," 35–37) notes that in the seventeenth century, branles had also been danced in a similar medley, or multi-segmented, style.
12. In this chapter, the reader will need to get used to multiple meanings for the word *figure*: the term can refer to (1) a routine, or "step"; (2) the "chorus" of a cotillion; (3) one complete segment of a quadrille; or (4) a geometric shape. The meaning intended in any given case should be clear from the context.

13. The term *set* is often used to describe a collection (of dishes, playing cards, and so forth), but particularly in British English its meaning also shades over to encompass a collection of musical pieces performed in succession (that is, a suite or medley), as in "set of jigs," "set of reels," or the "Scottish set" described in chapter 13.
14. Richardson, *Social Dances*, 58–59. In later years, a figure called La Pastorelle was usually substituted for La Trenis (Guilcher [in *La Contredanse*] spells it "La Trenize"). For routines published at the time for each figure, see Rogers, *Quadrille*, 79–86.
15. Presumably, once the quadrille was fully launched as a genre, new figures were composed specifically for the quadrille that had never formed part of any particular cotillion.
16. Richardson, *Social Dances*, 70–73, 91–93, 141–43. Duval had a rival claimant; a source dating to circa 1820 named Joseph Hart as inventor of the Lancers. For specific routines of both Duval's and Hart's versions, see Rogers, *Quadrille*, 87–94.
17. The routines for these various quadrilles appear in Hillgrove, *Hillgrove's Call-Book*.
18. Hornby, "Fiddle on the Island," 31–32.
19. There is an alternative explanation for how quadrilles became established on Prince Edward Island and elsewhere in the vicinity. Dan McPhee (b. Bayfield, Kings County), for example, who is roughly two decades younger than Banks, suggests that square sets were introduced to northeastern Kings County in the 1920s by people of Irish background coming to the area from Boston. This view is echoed by Michael Kennedy (*Gaelic Nova Scotia*, 221–22), who credits local émigrés returning home from Boston circa 1900 with having introduced the quadrille to neighboring Cape Breton Island (interestingly, Kennedy's source for parallel developments on Prince Edward Island is Hughie McPhee of Bayfield, who happens to be Dan McPhee's younger brother). Although these accounts do not mesh well with the version of events put forward by other Island informants, this is certainly an intriguing perspective that is worthy of further study.
20. Hillgrove, *Hillgrove's Call-Book*, 63.
21. Patri Pugliese (independent dance scholar), personal interview, Nov. 1996. In Britain, the use of prompters was commonplace during the first few decades after the quadrille was introduced, but the practice declined after that; see Rogers, *Quadrille*, 41.
22. Hillgrove, *Hillgrove's Call-Book*, 235–36.
23. Hillgrove, *Hillgrove's Call-Book*, 65–69.
24. Similar changes were made in the quadrille by rural folk throughout much of North America; see, for example, Damon, *History of Square Dancing*, 30–38.
25. There might be some confusion here in nomenclature: at least in the ballroom lexicon, Lancers and Caledonians were two different kinds of quadrille.
26. I am indebted for this analysis to Patri Pugliese (personal interview, Mar. 1997), who cautions that the large number of figures (and versions thereof) in circulation in the late nineteenth century make it impossible to determine in any given case precisely which dance prescriptions were originally borrowed. Manuals used for comparison were Hillgrove's *Call-Book and Dancing Master* (1863), Edward Scott's *Dancing as an Art and Pastime* (1892), and Dick's *Quadrille Call Book* (1878).

27. Ivan Day, in John Gauthier interview, Nov. 16, 2006, PEIFP Interview #40.
28. A "swing-all-'round" figure appears in a quadrille known as the Caledonians, but only within the confines of a single set of dancers. Some big-circle dances from the southern United States such as the "Tennessee Mixer" also have a swing-all-'round feature (see Nevell, *Time to Dance*, 195).
29. Flett and Flett, *Traditional Dancing in Scotland*, 1–2, 156–57. Although some authorities feel that the term *Scotch reel* should apply only to the foursome reel, I have elected to use this term as a convenient generic.
30. Flett and Flett, *Traditional Dancing in Scotland*, 130–56.
31. Flett and Flett, *Traditional Dancing in Scotland*, 1, 133, 140–42, 144, 156.
32. Flett and Flett, *Traditional Dancing in Scotland*, 1, 142–43, 157.
33. MacLeod, "Glenaladale Pioneers," 317.
34. MacGregor, *Historical and Descriptive Sketches*, 2:186, quoted in Hornby, "Fiddle on the Island," 31.
35. From the surgical reports of a Dr. Mackieson, described in Lea, *History of the Practice*, 70–71.
36. For outdoor Scotch reel footwork, see Flett and Flett, *Traditional Dancing in Scotland*, 75–86. For indoor reels, see Rhodes, "Dancing in Cape Breton Island," 272.
37. See, for example, Rhodes, "Dancing in Cape Breton Island," 270, 279–80; and Emmerson, *Social History*, 179.
38. "Souris Tea Party," *Charlottetown Examiner*, Aug. 4, 1862.
39. The term *breakdown* was once used in some other North American regions to refer to the last figure of a quadrille, when fancy stepping to fast tunes was encouraged. For example, see Voyer, *La danse traditionnelle*, 79.
40. On neighboring Cape Breton Island, the practice of using setting and traveling steps to negotiate quadrille figures survives to this day.
41. See, for example, Rhodes, "Dancing in Cape Breton Island," 270.
42. See, for example, Emmerson, *Social History*, 242–47.
43. See, for example, Rhodes, "Dancing in Cape Breton Island," 272; and Collinson, *Traditional and National Music*, 158.
44. See, for example, Rhodes, "Dancing in Cape Breton Island," 272–74. This is echoed in Fraser, "Traditional Stepdancing," 24.
45. Breathnach, *Folk Music and Dances*, 44. The graceful high-kicks of modern Irish step dancing did not become an integral part of the Irish milieu until the mid-twentieth century.
46. There is a formal Highland dance also called the Irish jig, but this involves a leaping style of movement similar to what is employed for most other Highland dances.
47. Emmerson, *Social History*, 157.
48. Downer, *Memoir of John Durang*, 47–94. Durang commissioned a Mr. Hoffmaster of New York City to compose the hornpipe that bears his name; Ricketts also had a hornpipe named for him. Both tunes are still widely played in North America.
49. For treepling, see Flett and Flett, *Traditional Dancing in Scotland*, 260–67. Nearly every region in England boasts a clogging tradition; see, for example, Flett and Flett, *Traditional Step-Dancing in Lakeland*.

50. I encountered no living memory of formal dances involving "stepping" footwork on Prince Edward Island, but many accounts from Cape Breton describe stepping as having once served as the basic footwork for such formal dances as the "Fling," "Seann Truibhas," and "Jacky Tar." See Rhodes, "Dancing in Cape Breton Island," 272; see also "Margaret Gillis," in MacGillivray and MacGillivray, *Cape Breton Ceilidh*, 60–61.
51. Vincent Doucette, in Dennis Pitre interview, Nov. 9, 2006, PEIFP Interview #28.
52. Richardson, *Social Dances*, 43–45, 63. A form of waltz sans "close hold" had previously been danced in Britain but in a form that was integrated into longways dancing or cotillions.
53. Hornby, "Fiddle on the Island," 31–32.
54. As was certainly the case in Québec (Voyer, *La danse traditionnelle*, 38–39), church opposition to having men and women consort publicly in close proximity may have been a factor inhibiting the spread of the dance.
55. Ralph Hardy, personal interview, Nov. 23, 2006, PEIFP Interview #53.
56. Tony Smith, personal interview, Nov. 24, 2006, PEIFP Interview #56.

CHAPTER THIRTEEN
The Role of Radio and Recordings

F iddling virtually ushered in the media age on Prince Edward Island. In 1924, Lem Jay (1882–1960), a fox rancher from the district of Fanningbrook near Mt. Stewart, Queens County, was asked by radio pioneer Keith Rogers to play fiddle on a series of test broadcasts for the Island's first radio station, which would soon be granted the call letters CFCY. The station opened for business the following year, and not long afterward, a broadcast featuring Jay's fiddling—conducted from a makeshift studio in Rogers's home on Bayfield Street in Charlottetown—inaugurated the Island's first regularly scheduled live-entertainment radio show. Then in early 1926, CFCY's live broadcasts of the Great Fiddle Contest from the Strand and Prince Edward Theatres in Charlottetown first established the station as a regional presence.[1]

To put this into broader chronological perspective, Jay's first formal weekly broadcast took place roughly five years after the airing of North America's first scheduled radio show, on station KDKA in Pittsburgh, Pennsylvania, and about three years after the first US country-fiddling broadcast, which featured "Fiddlin'" John Carson on WSB in Atlanta, Georgia. At about the same time that

Jay got under way on CFCY, similar shows featuring local or regional fiddling talent were being established in numerous markets around the continent. Two of the most famous—and longest lasting—of such shows were the *National Barn Dance* on WLS in Chicago and the *Grand Ole Opry* on WSM in Nashville, Tennessee.[2]

The music recording industry was also well under way by this time. The phonograph had first appeared in the 1870s, and by 1900 the American retailer Sears, Roebuck and Co. was selling a "Home Gramophone" for five dollars that played wax Edison cylinders. The first phonographs that played disks were introduced in 1909. By the early 1920s, companies such as Edison, RCA Victor, Okeh, and Columbia were collectively producing an average of two million phonographs and one hundred million recordings per year.[3]

One of the first fiddlers to be featured on commercial recordings was noted Scottish virtuoso and composer James Scott Skinner, who cut numerous Edison cylinders and 78 rpm disks for Berliner, Columbia, and several other labels between 1899 and 1922. Recordings of Irish and Québecois fiddlers first began appearing in the late 1910s and proliferated throughout the 1920s and '30s. The first commercial US country-fiddling recording, made in New York City by Eck Robertson for the RCA Victor Company, was released in 1922; over the next twenty years, the music of about three hundred different US country fiddlers would be issued by various labels.[4]

The history of fiddling on local media divides neatly into two phases: the early days (1923–39) and the Don Messer era (1939–58). In terms of off-shore media, recordings and broadcasts emanating from PEI's island-neighbor Cape Breton proved by far to be the most significant, but British, Irish, and other North American sources must also be taken into consideration.

The Early Days: Island Fiddlers on Radio

Lem Jay hosted a weekly ninety-minute fiddling show on CFCY from mid-1925 until 1931. Although he generally performed unaccompanied, piano backup was provided on some shows by his son, Roland,[5] or by his daughter, Edith. According to the latter, her father's presence on radio produced quite a sensation among the neighbors.

> It was a great event to hear my father and I playing over the radio. [T]hey drove from all around the country and came in to Clark's Store to hear us play [over the air].[6] And I remember when we went home after we had been playing, they would

all gather around that night at Mount Stewart, and they began asking me questions about how we did it and what it was like and what the microphone was like and what the studio was like and they fired the questions at us from all directions.[7]

Despite his show's substantial popularity, Jay himself ultimately elected to discontinue it: in part because the Hungry Thirties had adversely affected his farming income and the station refused to reimburse his travel costs. From that time until 1958, he appeared on radio just once a year, offering a special half-hour live broadcast on CFCY's weekly *Outports* show during the week between Christmas and New Year's Day.[8] According to the many fiddlers in this study who recall having heard these annual shows, Jay always included two signature numbers in his program: "Bonaparte Crossing the Alps" and "Jay's Reel."

Several other Island fiddlers appeared on Charlottetown-based radio in the 1920s, both on CFCY and over another station called CHCK, which for a few years during that era shared the former's assigned frequency.[9] Among these fiddlers were two from Kings County (Hector MacDonald of Bangor and Otis Jackson of Peters Road) and two from the Charlottetown area (Robert Weeks and Percy Groom).[10]

There was also fiddle-music broadcasting during this period emanating from the Prince County city of Summerside on station CHGS, which had been founded in 1926 by Holman's Department Store. Perhaps the most prominent act to broadcast on that station was Gaudet's Old Timers, an amateur ensemble organized by local restaurateur "Joe Bun" Gaudet. An old news photo reprinted in a 1973 edition of the *Summerside Journal-Pioneer* identifies band members as Cornelius "Lenie" Bolger and Medius Arsenault on fiddle, Wilfred "Moonie" Gallant on piano, Ernest "Lippy" Gaudet and Ernest Gallant on harmonica, Anthony Arsenault on jaw harp (trump), and Harold Huestis on banjo.[11]

For several years beginning in 1933, the most popular show on Prince Edward Island that featured live fiddling was CFCY's weekly *Kelly and McInnis Program*. The mainstay of this show was a band called the Merry Makers, who performed not only fiddle tunes but also a variety of vocal numbers drawn primarily from American country music and Irish popular music. Although band personnel varied considerably, the best-remembered team included fiddlers Al Dowling of Charlottetown and Hélaire Gallant of Rustico, Queens County.[12]

The most prominent Island broadcast-fiddler of the 1930s was a Charlottetown resident named George Chappelle, whose first appearances on radio were with the Merry Makers. In 1935 at the request of CFCY, he organized a touring band called George Chappelle and the Merry Islanders, which—at least in one configuration—also included Garfield Chappelle on fiddle, Jackie Doyle on piano, Bill Leblanc on drums, Tex Cochran on guitar, and Lawrence Toombs on banjo.[13] In 1937, this group was tapped by the Canadian Broadcasting Company (CBC) to put together a series of fifteen-minute programs for distribution throughout Canada. Over the next couple of years, the band flourished both on air and in live performance, but a falling-out with CFCY management in 1939 led to Chappelle's replacement by a young bandleader from New Brunswick named Don Messer.[14] Messer then in effect became CFCY's flagship fiddler, and he would dominate fiddle broadcasting on the Island for nearly twenty years. Once the Messer era got under way, interest on the part of the local media in promoting other fiddlers all but disappeared.

Island fiddling was featured on radio after 1939 but primarily on an ad hoc or amateur basis. The old Merry Makers band featuring fiddlers Al Dowling and Hélaire Gallant returned to the air in the early 1940s, for example, under the leadership of vocalist Raymond Sellick of Brackley, Queens County.[15] In 1946, the MacCormack Family of the Cardigan, Kings County, area—which featured Dan MacCormack on fiddle with his sisters Mary on piano and Therese on guitar—had a series of weekly shows on CFCY (Dan MacCormack reenlisted in the armed forces later that year and for a while was replaced in the band by fiddler John Gauthier of Stanhope, Queens County).[16] Similarly, for a few years beginning in the late 1940s, fiddler Peter Doiron of North Rustico, Queens County (whose style was heavily influenced by Messer) had an early morning show on CFCY on which he was joined by accompanists Loman MacCauley, Ches Cooper, and Keith Robinson.[17]

Local fiddle-music broadcasting came to an end on CFCY and other Charlottetown stations in the late 1950s when Messer departed for Halifax (more on this later), but it continued informally on the Summerside station, by then renamed CJRW. On weekday mornings from the mid-1950s through the mid-1980s, CJRW aired the *West Prince Party Line*, a fifteen-minute amateur talent show hosted by Lowell Huestis of Summerside.[18] Most of the fiddling broadcast on the show was pretaped under controlled conditions at the CJRW studio, then played periodically to fill airtime.[19] According to Huestis, the fiddler whose playing was featured most on the show was Russell Warren of Miminegash, Prince County (1920–74); some other Prince County fiddlers whose music also appeared regularly were Eddy Arsenault of St. Chrysostom, Toussaint Arsenault and Ervan Sonier of Summerside, Sidney Baglole (b. Lot 16), Howie Getson of Coleman, Lini Bolger (b. Lot 11), Andrew Jones of Pleasant View, and Elmer Robinson of Woodstock. Although no surveys were ever conducted to determine the size of his radio audience, Huestis reckons from informal feedback that it must have been fairly substantial.

> We'd hear stories; whenever 11:30 in the morning came along, people in stores would stop: "We gotta stop, *West Prince Party Line*'s on." And we heard this many times, where people stopped what they were doin', in a garage or somewhere where there were people workin', they would stop and turn up the radio for *West Prince Party Line*.[20]

Several factors would converge to limit the influence of PEI's first generation of homegrown radio performers. Among these factors were the state of the local economy, the infrastructure and technological base, the state of local fiddling attitudes and performance practice, and the aims of local entrepreneurs and opinion leaders.

Although commercial broadcasting may have been well launched elsewhere in North America by the mid-1920s, in general the Island was slow to embrace the new technology. In 1927, there were only 249 radio sets registered in the entire province, and as late as 1936 there were still only 2,159 sets registered.[21] Most rural families had to wait until deep into the 1930s before radios were a realistic option. Teresa MacPhee Wilson (b. Monticello, Kings County), for example, reports that her family did not obtain its first radio until 1938, while Fr. Art O'Shea of Iona, Queens County, recalls that his family's first radio appeared in 1939.[22]

Because most rural Island districts did not receive electric power until the late 1950s or early 1960s, radio sets prior to that time had to be powered by storage batteries akin in size, method of operation, and general unwieldiness to those found in modern automobiles. These batteries had a relatively short active life before needing to be recharged for a fee at the local general store, and their ability to retain a charge declined over time.[23] Consequently, most rural families rationed their listening time fairly strictly. As Elliot Wight (b. Flat River, Queens County) reports, even as recently as the late 1940s, total daily listening time for a typical rural family with a radio in the home probably averaged less than an hour: "At that time we had no electricity in our house, and we used to have a battery radio. And we could only turn it on to hear the news and to hear Don Messer. That was the only two things you could turn it on for."

Some Islanders came up with ingenious methods for dealing with this issue. Francis MacCormack (b. St. Charles, Kings County), for example, recalls that when the family batteries ran low, his older brother used to hook up the radio to an old car battery so that their mother would not miss her favorite shows.[24] Alternatively, John Gauthier notes that a few people around Stanhope powered their radios via a makeshift generator consisting of a wind-driven propeller and electrical coil.[25]

Similarly, phonographs were not especially plentiful in rural Island districts until the 1950s. Because most of these machines—often referred to on Prince Edward Island as "gramophones," in keeping with the old brand name—were spring-driven, this state of affairs cannot be ascribed to the absence of electric power. Instead, the primary issue here was the high cost, relative to local incomes, of both machines and recordings.

This shortage of available radios and gramophones was offset to some degree by the sharing of such devices among neighbors and by the tendency for locals to congregate at general stores or other commercial establishments where these devices were present. It has already been noted, for example, how Lem Jay's neighbors gathered to take in his broadcasts at Clark's General Store in Mt. Stewart. Alternatively, many rural families who owned radios often invited the neighbors in to hear fiddling broadcasts. Largus MacInnis of Lakeville, Kings County, for example, describes how such an invitation sometimes provided the basis for a house party: "When radio started coming in, probably there'd be a place that had a radio, and there'd be old-time music on sometimes. And there'd be a crowd gathered in to listen to the radio, and they'd probably dance."

With its small audience and tiny transmitters, Island radio in its first decade could do little more than serve as "one great big Island hall [where] people felt free to drop in off the street and entertain a little."[26] It was not capable of promoting local talent or creating the kind of broadcast fiddling "industry" that grew up elsewhere in North America during this era. Similarly, the lack of a significant local market for gramophones and recordings at least partially explains why a recording industry devoted to Island fiddling never sprang up, either during that period or in the decades that followed.[27] By way of contrast, it has been documented that for at least three other major fiddling traditions—those of Ireland, Cape Breton, and the American South—phonograph or record dealers hoping to stimulate sales were instrumental in getting a viable recording industry under way.[28]

At the time that radio and recordings first appeared on Prince Edward Island, the state of local fiddling was such that its practitioners were unprepared for active participation in the new media. For performance on radio or recordings to be effective, musicians must be schooled to a more exacting standard of performance practice than they would need to succeed at a district dance. Some of the considerations involved include concern about fine points of technique, tone, and finesse; hitting one's stride immediately and maintaining a solid, consistent attack; achieving mistake-free renditions; and establishing for each number a precise, clean beginning and a strong ending. This kind of performance practice tends to evolve through competition among players when a region has an active contest, concert, or paying dance-playing circuit. Some of the first major fiddlers to record from the Southern tradition, for example, were either established stage performers or had styles well adapted to competing in major regional contests.[29] Similarly, the first Cape Breton recording artists were active participants in a highly competitive, semiprofessional music scene (more on this later).

Another aspect of media-friendly performance practice is adapting to the demands of ensemble playing. Perhaps the most important consideration involved here is the ability to take on a specific musical role without interfering with those adopted by other band members. Such a role might involve playing harmonies and countermelodies; playing introductions, leads, and breaks; or playing complementary rhythmic figures behind a lead instrument or vocalist. For example, one of the major reasons for Don Messer's success was his ability to mesh his own playing within the context of a tight ensemble sound.

On Prince Edward Island, however, fiddling throughout much of this period was still carried out on the district level by unpaid amateurs. As long as a musician had the kind of bowing rhythm that made people want to get up and dance and a pleasing, tuneful sound, that was considered sufficient. Even when contests developed, as we have seen, the judging offered no clear trend to push up the level of professionalism. And although commercial dance halls had begun to appear in rural sections of the Island during this era, disorderly conditions at these establishments were often so pronounced that they tended to suppress rather than enhance the technical level of playing (for more on this, see chapter 15).

Nor was there much incentive to develop ensemble-oriented skills. Fiddling was still for the most part performed unaccompanied, and even when accompaniment was present it was strictly the case of a keyboard or guitar player providing background for the fiddler (fiddlers themselves never had to adapt). Similarly, vocal music was generally performed unaccompanied, and—apart from the jigging of fiddle tunes—there was little precedent for intermingling the vocal and instrumental traditions. Even the fiddlers who appeared with ensembles such as the Old Timers, Merry Makers, and Merry Islanders did little but play melody over a wall of sound provided by multiple accompanists.

The Island's first generation of radio fiddlers might have overcome their initial lack of preparation by adapting their styles to the demands of the new medium. But aside from a few minor concessions—Lem Jay, for example, decreased the vigor of his foot-stomping considerably when on the air to avoid having its sound dominate his broadcasts[30]—there was very little progress during this period toward developing either professional levels of performance practice or a true ensemble approach. After all, doing things in one's own way and maintaining personal twists and idiosyncrasies were cornerstones of Island fiddling. Because playing on local radio offered little in the way of financial recompense or even prestige, there was little incentive for change.

One more point needs to be made here. Most twentieth-century fiddling traditions with substantial media histories can trace their early successes in the field to the activities of one or more important promoters or visionaries who made a personal mission of bringing the local fiddling sound to the outside world. No such individuals ever materialized on Prince Edward Island. The Island's elite and ambitious, who had proved themselves quite capable of mobilizing resources and generating excitement in the days leading up to the Great Contest of '26, were virtually inactive when it came to promoting local fiddling on media.

Ultimately, the styles and repertoires of the Island's early radio players left little mark on future generations. Apart from the two signature tunes that Lem Jay played regularly on his annual show, for example, few fiddlers reported having picked up tunes from Island radio during this era.[31] As for stylistic influence, these early radio fiddlers probably lacked the stature to override two other strongly felt Island attitudes about music: that style was largely inborn and that self-conscious emulation of style was not something to be encouraged.

When compared to the major upheavals in style and repertoire that some other fiddling traditions experienced in the 1920s and '30s because of exposure to fiddling on media, this lack of influence among early PEI broadcast artists is highly unusual. In the Irish fiddling tradition, for example, most new players since the 1930s have tried to emulate the repertoire, ornamentation style, and general approach to the instrument first popularized by the recordings of just three men from County Sligo: Michael Coleman, Paddy Killoran, and James Morrison.[32] In Southern fiddling, the "long-bow" styles of a few 1920s and '30s recording artists—notably, Clayton McMichen, Lowe Stokes, Clark Kessinger, and Arthur Smith—have since become standard practice.[33] And as discussed later in the chapter, the styles and repertoires of the first few Cape Breton fiddlers to record also left a profound mark on later generations.

As previously noted, when a single style dominates the playing choices of the next generations to such an extent that preexisting local styles, local repertoires, and individual twists fade away, that stylistic template is referred to as a *superstyle*. Generally, the first group of media performers or prizewinning contest players from a given musical tradition generate superstyles. What is perhaps most remarkable about the early days of Island fiddling on radio, then, is that it never gave rise to anything approaching a superstyle for Island playing.

Don Messer and His Islanders

As long as CFCY was little more than "one great big Island hall" with informal standards and little at financial stake, it was happy to feature amateur Island fiddling on its broadcasts. By the mid-30s, however, the station was effectively launched as a business, and the amount of money involved had grown considerably. In 1936, it acquired a new 500-watt transmitter and two secondhand steel broadcasting towers. This, plus a strategic location at the edge of the Atlantic Coast, made CFCY potentially one of the most prominent stations in eastern Canada.

To bring this potential to fruition, Keith Rogers hired a Souris, Kings County, native with some Boston radio experience named L. A. "Art" MacDonald to be general manager. It was MacDonald who coined the station's soon-to-be-famous slogan, "The Friendly Voice of the Maritimes."[34] He was also the man who, after a disappointing experience with George Chappelle, decided in 1939 to bring in Don Messer to "fill the dual roles of Musical Director and Orchestra Leader" for a new band, to be dubbed the Islanders.[35]

The general lack of professional-level performance practice among Island fiddlers was almost certainly a major factor in MacDonald's decision to bring in an outsider with a proven track record to headline CFCY's premier fiddle-broadcasting program. Certainly, others who were aware of his thinking at the time stress this viewpoint. Keith Rogers's daughter Betty Rogers Large tells us, for example, "Art figured that it was time to search for talent that would

PHOTO 13.1. DON MESSER AND HIS ISLANDERS, PROBABLY LATE 1940S: (LEFT TO RIGHT) DUKE NIELSEN (BASS), MESSER, WARREN MACRAE (DRUMS), RAE SIMMONS (SOPRANO SAX), CHARLIE CHAMERLAIN (GUITAR), AND JACKIE DOYLE (PIANO). COURTESY PRINCE EDWARD ISLAND PUBLIC ARCHIVES AND RECORDS OFFICE (ACCESSION NO. 4268).

have national as well as regional appeal. He found it in Don Messer. Don was a perfectionist, a true professional and an original."[36] Similarly, Raymond Sellick notes that although there were lots of good fiddlers on the Island in the late 1930s, "they were maybe not up to that category. They wouldn't have fit in, particularly at that time; they were just not professional enough. To have a band that goes all over Canada you can't make any mistakes. Art MacDonald was very fussy; it had to be right or not at all."[37]

There is a widely held opinion among Island fiddlers that the local media lost interest in promoting the local product after Messer arrived and that in general it subscribed to the not-uncommon Island theory that nothing homegrown can possibly be of much worth. Archie Stewart of Milltown Cross, Kings County, sums up this notion.

> What the problem was, we had fiddlers here on the Island that Don Messer couldn't carry rosin to. He came in from another province, and the radio station took hold of him, and they pushed him, and they made records of him, and they put him on television. We had fiddlers on Prince Edward Island that could play rings around Don Messer. And we couldn't—If we had five thousand dollars, we couldn't buy fifteen minutes on the radio station on Prince Edward Island. There was no way; they just wouldn't talk to you. They didn't push their local talent.

This viewpoint may ascribe to the Island media a greater single-mindedness of purpose and policy than was probably the case. Nevertheless, it does indeed appear that once Messer was established, station officials ceased looking in any serious way for local players whose careers might also be worthy of promotion.

Because Don Messer was such an important figure in the history of both Island and Canadian national broadcasting, and because his music left an indelible mark on North American fiddling, it is important here to sketch out the course of his career. He was born in 1909 near the towns of Harvey Station and Tweedside in southwestern New Brunswick. His background and early musical influences were similar to that of most Island fiddlers. His parents were Scottish (the family name is German, but his father's forebears had lived in Scotland for some generations before immigrating to Canada). He grew up on a mixed farm among a family of eleven children, and he attended a one-room schoolhouse. His mother jigged tunes around the house. Messer took up the fiddle at the age of five and learned his first tunes from local fiddlers. While still a youngster, he often played at local house parties and barn raisings with his uncle Jim Messer, accompanied by his sister Emma on keyboard.[38]

Messer's approach to music began to evolve when he traveled to Boston at the age of sixteen to live with an aunt. There he was exposed to note reading, music theory, and some formal music training. He played briefly with a string ensemble and developed an interest in playing in band situations. He also became interested in fiddle tunes from other areas—such as Ireland and the American South—which he had ample opportunity to hear on Boston radio.[39] Interestingly, the time frame of his Boston sojourn, roughly 1925–27, would have put him in a position to attend some of the major fiddle contests that took place in the region during that era (see chapter 11). He would also have been able to witness the emergence of the Southern "hillbilly" sound as a viable commercial genre on American radio and recordings and to witness the commercial success of the Skillet Lickers and other fiddle-centered ensembles.

Not long after Messer's return to Tweedside in the early 1930s, he was hired for a series of regular radio programs on CFBO in the nearby city of St. John. By 1934, he was playing on the radio with a band that eventually became known as Don Messer's Lumberjacks. In 1936, he and the Lumberjacks signed with the local CBC affiliate, CHSJ, to do a show called *Backwoods Breakdown*. This show developed a fairly wide audience, creating sufficient notoriety for the band to tour as far afield as Boston and New York.[40]

When Messer moved his show to CFCY-Charlottetown in 1939, his band became formally known as Don Messer and His Islanders. He brought with him three members of the Lumberjacks: Charlie Chamberlain on vocals, Duke Nielson on bass, and Ned Landry on fiddle. He also recruited Rae Simmons on clarinet and sax (Simmons was a Nova Scotia native who had been employed for years as an announcer on CFCY), along with three musicians who had played with Chappelle's Merry Islanders: pianist Jackie Doyle, vocalist Babe Doyle, and drummer Bill Leblanc.[41] Over the years, Messer would also bring several other musicians into the band, such as trumpet player Harold Macrae, drummer Warren MacRae, vocalist Marg Osborne, and fiddler/guitarist Cec MacEachern.

Messer's show was an immediate success. Within a month it was picked up by the CBC National Radio Network, where it was to continue for almost twenty years. By the mid-1940s the band was becoming known across Canada, and after CBC's International Service began, their broadcasts were also accessible to many parts of the northern United States.[42] One globe-trotting Charlottetown couple even wrote in to attest that the show had been picked up on shortwave broadcast as their vessel was crossing the Indian Ocean.[43]

Messer and the Islanders were also highly active in terms of live appearances and recordings. Right from the start, the band was much in demand for concerts and dances both on the Island and throughout the Maritimes. From the late 1940s through the early '70s, they toured Canada more than twenty times; their high point was the Canadian Centennial (1967), when they made seventy-two concert appearances.[44] In 1942, they began to record on the Apex label, a division of Compo Records of Lachine, Québec (Messer and the Lumberjacks had previously recorded a few sides for Compo in 1937). These records sold quite well throughout Canada, and over the next twenty-five years they were to record approximately three hundred selections for Compo and other labels in both 78 and 45 rpm formats.[45] Many of these recordings have since been reissued on LPs or CDs.

In 1958, when Messer moved to Halifax to establish the television show that eventually became known as *Don Messer's Jubilee*, this was essentially the end of formal fiddle broadcasting on Prince Edward Island. Certainly no Island player was considered to have sufficient stature to replace him. Even if such a player could have been found, the general feeling in the industry at the time was that the era of live fiddle-music broadcasting was probably coming to a close.[46]

As for Messer's TV show, it got under way in 1959 and ran with considerable success on the CBC national network for roughly a decade. The show was still going strong in terms of ratings when it was canceled by CBC management, which, according to Messer's biographer, was impelled to this decision more by political than by financial considerations. When news got out regarding the show's impending demise, radio stations and newspapers across Canada were besieged by heated protests.[47]

Messer's Repertoire and Musical Style

The repertoire performed by Don Messer and His Islanders was sufficiently varied so that it appealed to a large cross section of the Canadian public. Only a small proportion of the fiddle tunes they performed, for example, was derived from either Prince Edward Island or Messer's native New Brunswick. Instead, Messer gleaned most of his fiddle repertoire from his substantial collection of tune books, manuscripts, and recordings. As a result, among the tunes he performed, recorded, and published were selections from a variety of fiddling traditions, including those of Ireland, Scotland, Cape Breton, Québec, the southern United States, and New England. Also in the mix were a substantial number of fiddle tunes composed by him or by other members of his band, most notably, Cec MacEachern and Ned Landry. In addition, a substantial proportion of Messer's radio shows was devoted to material other than fiddle tunes, which represented "everything that was [then] popular—including Dixieland, swing, novelties, hymns, ballads and Irish numbers."[48]

The music of Don Messer and the Islanders was sometimes referred to as "eastern swing" to underscore a certain resemblance of its sound to that associated with Bob Wills, the Texan band leader credited with developing the style known as western swing.[49] Messer tended to bridle at the suggestion that the Islanders played "western or cowboy music,"[50] but certainly it could be said that in terms of style the band was moving along the same path as that of several US fiddle-centered ensembles of that era, such as Wills's Texas Playboys (whose instrumentation was virtually identical to that of the Islanders), Clayton McMichen's Georgia Wildcats, and Fiddlin' Arthur Smith's Dixieliners.[51]

As noted in chapter 9, Messer created a fiddle style to operate within the context of the band he put together. This meant assigning the fiddle a specific role; as he put it, "I play the melody and let the accompaniment fill in the details."[52] To this end, he generally played a relatively straight, unadorned melody line with great precision and assurance but with little in the way of ornamentation, rhythmic nuance, or expressiveness. The task of providing such musical subtleties then became the role of the ensemble. Gary Chipman of Charlottetown sums up the band sound as follows:

> The music was arranged so that the piano player was playing certain runs, and the bass was playing counter runs, and the guitar player was plugging in the holes, and the banjo player was doing something else, and the drummer was doing what he was supposed to do, and the fiddle player was doing the leads, and the clarinet player complemented the fiddle player. It was really a distinct sound; you can listen to ten fiddle players on the radio with bands, and you can tell Messer's band every time.

Although Messer's band was considered entertaining by most PE Islanders, his own playing style had very limited local influence. It did attract some disciples—primarily a few young players then living in the Charlottetown area—but most Island fiddlers were not taken with his approach to the instrument. As has already been noted, Messer's ensemble-oriented style lacked many of the important qualities that PE Islanders valued in their fiddlers, especially when it was evaluated as a solo style apart from the band context. Teresa MacPhee Wilson sums up the general impression.

> When Don Messer and His Islanders first started, the men around the Island who played the fiddle didn't think too much of Don Messer's music. They thought he was—I really don't know what *groich* means in Gaelic, but it's something you kind of make a bad job of, if you're a groich.[53] So my father used to call him "a groich of a fiddler." I heard a fellow from up west [Prince County] was interviewed on the radio. They were talking about fiddling, and this fellow, he said, "I wouldn't go across the road to listen to Don Messer play the fiddle."

Messer's major impact by far on Island fiddling was in terms of repertoire. Most Island players report that his radio shows and live appearances frequently served as sources for new tunes (more on this in chapter 14). When Island fiddlers absorbed tunes from Messer's broadcasts and recordings, however, they generally played them not in Messer's style but in a style thoroughly adapted to the standards of their own districts. Archie Stewart sums it up as follows:

> Now we got a little Don Messer mixed in here, I'll admit that. We learned a few tunes from him. We didn't learn his style of playing, but we learned quite a few of his tunes. But we still played them in the old Prince Edward Island traditional music way.

Ironically, Messer's greatest impact in terms of both playing style and repertoire was in central and western Canada, where the legacy of his recordings and live media performances has established what amounts to "a national canon of repertoire and performance practice."[54] In these regions, fiddlers influenced by his rapid, straight-ahead approach have developed what can be regarded as a distinctly Canadian style of playing not directly connected to any ancestral European style.

At the Canadian Open Old-Time Fiddling Championship—founded in 1950 and held each August in Shelbourne, Ontario—Messer's style served as the standard by which old-time fiddling was defined for over forty years. In the Ottawa Valley—a hotbed of traditional fiddling that straddles the Québec-Ontario border—Messer's playing style almost completely superseded the preexisting fiddling style of that region. What's more, the styles of nearly all subsequent nationally known Canadian fiddle virtuosos outside of Cape Breton—including such popular recording artists as Ward Allen, Al Cherny, Andy DeJarlis, King Ganam, Bill Guest, Ivan Hicks, Ned Landry, Earl Mitton, and Graham Townsend—can also be traced to the Messer legacy.[55]

Because Messer's sound dominated Island radio for so long, as far as outsiders were concerned, that sound simply was Island fiddling. The notion that playing styles existed on Prince Edward Island that had little in common with Messer's was unthinkable. Meanwhile, many PE Islanders—who by the late 1940s could not help but notice that nearly everyone else's fiddle music but their own had been worthy of systematically recording and broadcasting—were left with the distinct impression that the homegrown product was of little account.

Fiddle Broadcasts and Recordings "from Away"

The same exposed position on the Atlantic Coast that made Prince Edward Island an ideal radio-transmitting site also created excellent conditions for picking up long-range radio signals. Even as Lem Jay was making his first appearance on the local airwaves, Islanders with radio sets could tune in to broadcasts featuring live or recorded fiddling emanating not only from nearby provinces but also from distant locations on the North American mainland. Ultimately, they would be exposed via media to a wide variety of alternative playing styles and a vast new repertoire.

The first off-Island fiddle-music programming to be received regularly on Prince Edward Island was broadcast by radio station CHNC of New Carlisle, Québec, on the Gaspé Peninsula and featured Québecois players. Many Islanders were quick to incorporate several tunes from this source into their repertoires, such as "The Old Man and the Old Woman," "Joys of Québec," and "St. Anne's Reel."[56]

When atmospheric conditions were favorable, Island radio sets frequently picked up fiddle-music broadcasts from the eastern United States. Broadcasts from Boston, Massachusetts, featuring Irish or southern-US fiddling, for example, were often accessible via the airwaves. Interestingly, one particularly influential music source was station WWVA of Wheeling, West Virginia (founded 1933), whose transmitter "as the crow flies" is roughly a thousand miles from Prince Edward Island. Danny MacLean (b. Garfield, Queens County), offers this account:

> I used to listen to Wheeling, West Virginia; I used to listen to that every night, and I remember I'd be out sitting in the car listening to West Virginia on the radio. I learned that tune I just played ["Mississippi Sawyer"], and I learned "Boil the Cabbage Down." And "Orange Blossom Special," that's where that came from, too.

According to John Gauthier, one part of the Island where WWVA came in loud and clear almost every night was the north shore of Queens County. Consequently, fiddlers from that part of the Island absorbed many southern US tunes into their repertoires.[57] Conversely, most Nova Scotia stations had very poor reception on the Queens County north shore. Consequently, Cape Breton fiddling was far less influential in northern Queens County than it was in many other parts of the Island (see below).

It should also be noted that CFCY, CHGS, and the other Island stations that followed in their wake often aired recorded fiddle music "from away." In the 1930s and '40s, for example, recordings of Appalachian fiddlers and other early country music artists received quite a bit of local airtime. In recent decades, recordings of Townsend, DeJarlis, Cherney, and other "pan-Canadian" fiddle virtuosos also received considerable local airplay.

Recordings and live broadcasts featuring fiddlers from neighboring Cape Breton Island first achieved a major presence on Prince Edward Island in the late 1930s and early '40s. Because Cape Breton fiddling would prove to be the most influential outside tradition to reach Prince Edward Island via the media, I discuss its history and cultural milieu in some detail.

A Brief History of Cape Breton Fiddling on Media

Although recordings of Cape Breton fiddling appeared on US labels as early as the late 1920s, the history of Cape Breton's own fiddle-recording industry really begins in 1935 with the activities of gramophone dealer Bernie MacIsaac, proprietor of the Celtic Music Store in Antigonish, Nova Scotia.[58] There was a good market for spring-powered gramophones at the time in Cape Breton and its environs, but MacIsaac figured he could improve his business if he could accommodate a large number of customer requests for recordings by Cape Breton and Antigonish-area fiddlers.[59] With this idea in mind, he "asked around to find the names of the best fiddlers in circulation; the fiddlers generally referred to as 'master fiddlers.'"[60] Ultimately, he settled on four players: three from Cape Breton (Dan J. Campbell [1895–1981; b. Glenora Falls], Angus Chisholm [1908–79; b. Margaree Forks] and Angus Allan Gillis [1897–1978; b. Upper Margaree]) and one from the Antigonish area (Hugh A. MacDonald [1889–1976; b. Lanark]).[61] Later that year, MacIsaac had all these players recorded at the studios of Compo Records in Québec, the same outfit that Don Messer was to employ a few years later.

From these first sessions, MacIsaac issued about fifteen different 78 rpm recordings on his new Celtic label and sold them out of his shop. In addition, he would periodically load up his car with recordings and peddle them to a network of dealers scattered around Cape Breton Island. These first offerings sold well enough for him to continue in the business. In his first fifteen years of operation, MacIsaac also released 78s by fiddlers Dan R. MacDonald (1911–76: b. Judique), "Little Jack" MacDonald (1887–1969; b. Creignish), Bill Lamey (1914–91; b. River Denys), Donald MacLellan (1918–2003; b. Princeville), Theresa MacLellan (b. 1925– ; b. Riverside) and Winston "Scotty" Fitzgerald (1914–87; b. White Point).[62]

In the 1950s, Celtic was joined in the Cape Breton fiddle-recording business by Rodeo Records, founded by a Scottish-born resident of Halifax, Nova Scotia, named George Taylor. Over the course of that decade, the two labels released recordings by such fiddlers as Fitzgerald, Chisholm, "Little Jack" and Dan R. MacDonald, Johnny Wilmot (1916–93; b. Centerville), Joe MacLean (1916–96; b. Lower Washabuck), Dan Joe MacInnes (1922–91; b. Sydney), Paddy "Scotty" LeBlanc (1923–74; b. East Margaree), and Elmer Briand (1922–92; b. L'Ardoise).[63]

In the 1960s and '70s, a new crop of Cape Breton media fiddlers emerged. These second-generation artists—many of whom recorded on either private labels or on such independent US labels as Rounder Records of Cambridge, Massachusetts—include John Campbell (1929–2010; b. Glenora Falls), Joe Cormier (1927– ; b. Cheticamp), Winnie Chafe (1936– ; b. Glace Bay), Jerry Holland (1955–2009; b. Brockton, Massachusetts), Sandy MacIntyre (1935– ; b. Inverness Town), Carl MacKenzie (1938– ; b. Washabuck), and Hugh "Buddy" MacMaster (1924–2014; b. Judique).[64] A third generation of Cape Breton media fiddlers reached maturity after 1990; their careers and influence are discussed in chapters 16–17.

Putting together the entire output from all company and independent labels, one observer has estimated that in the period 1935–89, roughly four thousand selections by over sixty different Cape Breton fiddlers were released.[65]

Live radio broadcasts of Cape Breton fiddling also got under way in the 1930s, with the two major stations involved being CJFX in Antigonish and CJCB in Cape Breton's largest city, Sydney. CJFX had a program called *Celtic Ceilidh*, for example, in which prominent fiddlers such as Angus Chisholm, Angus Allan Gillis, and Sandy MacLean (1893–1982; b. Strathlorne) would broadcast weekly via telephone hookup. Another popular fiddling show was *Cottar's Saturday Night*, which was broadcast on both CJCB and on the CBC-radio national network. This show featured poetry by Scottish poet Robert Burns, family chatter, and the fiddle music of Tena Campbell (1899–1949; b. Salmon River Road).[66]

Several other fiddling shows featured individual performers or ensembles. Bill Lamey, for example, had his own radio show on CJCB from 1939 to 1953 sponsored by Eastern Bakeries.[67] In the 1940s, Johnny Wilmot performed on a weekly show on CJCB called *The Irish Serenaders*.[68] Similarly, a group known as the Radio Entertainers—Winston Fitzgerald on fiddle, Estwood Davidson on guitar, and Beattie Wallace on piano—played throughout the 1950s on a weekly CJCB show sponsored by the MacDonald Tobacco Company.[69] In addition to these shows featuring live fiddling, by the early 1940s there were also several radio shows with a format devoted to playing fiddle-music recordings.

An example here is the *Clyde Nunn Show* on CJFX, which featured recordings by most of the early Celtic Records artists.[70]

Why Cape Breton?

Cape Breton Island lies only thirty-five miles east across the Gulf of St. Lawrence from the nearest point on Prince Edward Island. The two islands are quite similar in terms of land area, settlement and immigration patterns, religious and ethnic makeup, and population size. They started out with roughly the same stock of music and dance traditions. Given these parallels, just why did a major fiddle-recording and broadcast industry featuring local performers arise on Cape Breton, and why—despite a ten-year head start in broadcasting—did so little in that vein develop on Prince Edward Island? Although providing a comprehensive answer is beyond the scope of this book, my sense is that Cape Breton's musical ascendancy can be traced largely to two factors: the early formation of a cash economy and the development of pressures that drove up the general level of fiddling performance practice.

Around the turn of the twentieth century, the economies of the two islands began to move along different lines of development. With the decline of shipbuilding and shipborne commerce on Prince Edward Island, it was thrown back almost entirely on fishing and mixed farming under conditions wherein few rural families had much in the way of ready cash. Although Cape Breton had fishing ports and mixed farms aplenty, by 1900 a major coal mining and steel industry had grown up in its northeastern sector around the cities of Sydney and Glace Bay. Mining operations were also established at many other locations, notably, the towns of Mabou, Inverness, and Port Hood.[71] Because these industries offered steady wage employment, there was money in circulation on Cape Breton for the purchase of phonographs, recordings, and radio sets. Furthermore, a stronger tax base also allowed for certain infrastructural improvements to be made on Cape Breton that at the time were out of the question on Prince Edward Island. Cape Breton also benefitted simply from being in the same province as mainland Nova Scotia, which contained the port of Halifax (at least ten times the size of Charlottetown) and possessed by far the richest agricultural, natural-resource, and industrial base in the Maritimes. Because of all these factors, Cape Breton was perhaps a decade or two ahead of its sister island in acquiring such technological staples of twentieth-century life as widespread rural electrification and automobile travel.

At a time when most PEI fiddlers were isolated from each other and virtually unknown outside their immediate environs, developments on Cape Breton and among Cape Breton emigrants in Boston, Detroit-Windsor, Toronto, and other North American cities contributed to both frequent interactions among and wide exposure for better players. In 1897, the very first Mabou Parish Picnic set an important precedent by bringing fiddlers together from more than ten different Cape Breton communities.[72] Subsequently, organizers of church picnics and other local benefit events on Cape Breton would customarily send invitations far afield to prominent players.[73] This trend toward commingling was further accentuated by population movements and emigration patterns, which resulted in both the industrialized Sydney–Glace Bay region and the major emigrant population centers becoming staging grounds for contacts among fiddlers from all over Cape Breton Island.

Although dance venues on Prince Edward Island were largely village based well into the 1940s and beyond, much of the social dancing on Cape Breton moved out of the homes and into a circuit of dance halls—where providing music increasingly became the purview of touring semiprofessionals— quite early in the twentieth century. By the time of the First World War, this circuit extended from Sydney–Glace Bay across the entire length of Cape Breton's west coast, then crossed the Strait of Canso and extended roughly twenty-five miles westward to Antigonish.[74] By the 1920s, Cape Breton emigrants in such cities as Boston, Toronto, and Windsor had created their own dance venues and were routinely bringing fiddlers down from the home island to play at them.[75] Both these dance-venue circuits not only provided fiddlers with recognition and financial reward but also offered many opportunities for visiting artists to interact with local players.

As prominent Cape Breton fiddlers became increasingly aware of each other, formed social relationships, and played at the same public events, an unofficial ranking system developed among peers and public that in effect determined who got the invitations to play at the church picnics and dance halls. Consequently, when Bernie MacIsaac went looking for the "best" players to feature on his new Celtic label or when radio station organizers wanted prominent fiddlers to headline their shows, they knew exactly whom to approach.

As aspiring fiddlers strove for elite status and those who had already achieved it sought to maintain or increase their prestige, this promoted a high level of competitiveness. In such an atmosphere, an invitation to play at a dance could be seen not only as a source of income but also as an acknowledgment of status. Even when there were no financial considerations involved, fiddlers would often travel considerable distances merely in hopes of having the opportunity to outshine a rival at a dance, wedding, or musical gathering.[76]

In effect, these highly competitive conditions operated like a fully developed contest scene. The drive to excel quickly pushed up the general level of playing skill and performance practice, while the stresses inherent in continually striving for the recognition of peers and public fostered the ability to function well under pressure. Consequently, when recording and broadcasting opportunities came along, a cadre of performers was already on hand whose rigorous training allowed them to function with relative ease within the exacting standards of the new media. In addition, many fiddlers were eager to take part because appearing on a recording or broadcast was taken as a sign of superior standing.[77]

Another factor also may have contributed to an atmosphere conducive to the growth of a professional fiddling scene. Beginning in 1933, the government of Nova Scotia under the leadership of its new premier, Angus L. MacDonald (1890–1954), inaugurated a twenty-year-long campaign aimed at promoting a notion that the province—in fact a patchwork of Scottish, Irish, Acadian French, and several other ethnic groups—was the Scotland of North America. MacDonald drew on a romanticized and cherry-picked view of Scottish culture to create an image designed primarily to appeal to tourists from elsewhere in North America, Europe, and around the world. Among the outgrowths of this policy were stationing kilt-clad pipers at border-crossing points, encouraging state employees to wear kilts at public occasions, commissioning a Nova Scotia tartan, and referring officially to hilly or mountainous areas as "Highlands." Cape Breton in particular was a major beneficiary of the program, which led to the building of the Cabot Trail,[78] as well as the establishment of Cape Breton Highlands National Park and the Gaelic College in St. Ann's (the Gaelic College in turn would promote such expressions of Scottish culture as Highland Games, Highland dancing, and the aforementioned *Celtic Ceilidh* radio show). Not only was MacDonald's campaign successful in building a thriving tourist industry based on the manipulated perceptions of outsiders, but it substantially altered the local sense of identity as well; many Nova Scotians with only a smattering of Scottish heritage began to identify themselves as culturally Scottish (interestingly, MacDonald was one of them: his heritage was only about one-fourth Scottish).[79]

This province-wide emphasis on Scottish identity would have naturally played to the advantage of the fledgling Cape Breton recording and broadcast industry, which had emphasized a strong connection with Scottish culture from its inception (see below). Although there was no formal connection between the campaign and the Cape Breton fiddling scene, the notion that some form of "Scottish" musical expression was required to authenticate cultural events not only created employment opportunities for fiddlers and accompanists but also enhanced their public stature.[80] More important, now the vast majority of Nova Scotians could consider themselves part of the prime audience for Cape Breton fiddle music, and local radio stations might well have felt an obligation to both present and promote it.

The Cape Breton Influence

Most of the fiddlers who formed Cape Breton's first musical elites hailed from a relatively small number of interlocking family groups of Highland Scots ancestry based in central and southern Inverness County.[81] As one consequence, even though their ancestors had lived in the New World for over a century, many prominent Cape Breton fiddlers regarded their art as an extension of the Scottish fiddling tradition. They maintained an interest both in such Scottish-style ornamentation as snaps and cuts and in such distinctly Scottish tune genres as strathspeys and pipe marches, at a time when enthusiasm for all these phenomena on Prince Edward Island was fading. Moreover, when Cape Breton fiddlers began to focus on expanding their repertoires and increasing their technical expertise, they often sought out Scottish sources and role models. Ultimately, the Scottish identification of Cape Breton fiddling became so strong that prominent players with non-Scottish forebears, often felt compelled to draw attention away from their actual ethnic identities by adopting such nicknames as Winston "Scotty" Fitzgerald and Paddy "Scotty" Leblanc.

Any fiddler aspiring for recognition on Cape Breton was expected to perform at least some tunes that were not already associated with the approach of another player. In effect, then, it was incumbent upon each fiddler to bring new tunes into the repertoire. Some fiddlers addressed this issue by searching through the pages of old collections for tunes that had not previously been in circulation, a process that became known as "going to the books." With this aim in mind, they began to amass large assortments of these volumes—

generally such Scottish works as *The Gow Collection*, *The Gow Repository*, Fraser's *Airs and Melodies Peculiar to the Highlands*, *The Athole Collection*, *The Skye Collection*, and Skinner's *The Scottish Violinist*; other popular tune-books were O'Neill's *Dance Music of Ireland* and a New England collection known as *One Thousand Fiddle Tunes* (for more on these works, see chapter 14).[82]

Composition was, of course, another sure path to coming up with unique tunes. Although many Cape Breton fiddlers became highly active in this vein, probably the three most prominent composers prior to the 1970s were Dan R. MacDonald, Gordon MacQuarrie (1897–1965; b. Dunakin), and Dan Hughie MacEachern (1913–96; b. Queensville). Dan R. MacDonald was by far the most prolific; he is estimated to have written something in the neighborhood of two thousand tunes.[83]

Competitive pressures also affected the construction and performance of fiddle tune *groups*, or medleys. Medley playing on Cape Breton is likely to have been initially patterned on a model popularized by Scottish virtuoso James Scott Skinner. Skinner had pioneered the practice of using well-crafted medleys as a means for projecting fiddle music onto the stage, and he subsequently carried this approach into the realm of recordings.[84] His recorded selections, which averaged three or four tunes in length, followed several formats, such as reel medleys, strathspey-and-reel medleys, and *Scottish sets* (the last consisting of an air or march followed by a strathspey and reel). As Cape Breton fiddlers strove to outpace their rivals, however, the average length of such medleys grew markedly. Eventually, a typical performance of a reel or jig group might involve stringing together ten or more different tunes, while a fully developed rendition of a Scottish set could easily call for sequencing fifteen or more different tunes (a couple of airs or marches followed by a few strathspeys and ten or more reels). When fiddlers performed such tune groups at benefits, music parties, or musicians' gatherings, they would be informally rated by peers and public not only on their endurance but also on their talent for selecting tunes that both meshed well and progressed in an esthetically pleasing manner.[85] To make this process even more challenging, it was considered poor form to play any one tune more than twice through.

Because the playing of Cape Breton's elite fiddlers was so widely emulated, composition and going to the books ultimately resulted in an infusion of thousands of new tunes into the Cape Breton repertoire. Not only this, but many of the specific groups of tunes they played live and on early recordings and broadcasts also became standards.

It should also be noted in this context that since its inception the Cape Breton fiddle-recording and broadcast industry has generated a succession of superstyles. By the early 1940s, most budding Cape Breton fiddlers were actively seeking to echo the playing sounds of the first wave of recording artists, most notably, Angus Chisholm.[86] Starting in the late 1940s, the music of Winston Fitzgerald provided what might be described as a countervailing force to the media dominance of Cape Breton's first recording artists. Fitzgerald, who was of Irish and French ancestry, grew up and was first exposed to fiddle music in a small village near Cape North: far removed from much contact with Inverness County's fiddling elite. He took a while to reach playing maturity, but by the time he moved to Sydney in 1946 at the age of thirty-two he had achieved a powerful style that was as electric as it was idiosyncratic. From the moment he began to broadcast, record, and tour, Fitzgerald's sound became so influential that it served in effect as the basis for an alternative Cape Breton superstyle.[87]

Both Chisholm and Fitzgerald were frequent visitors to Prince Edward Island. Chisholm, for example, was often a guest at the home of well-known Kings County fiddler Jack Webster of Cardigan.[88] Fitzgerald toured on Prince Edward Island with some regularity during the 1950s and '60s (sometimes, as previously noted, serving as an adjudicator at local fiddle competitions), and many PEI fiddlers had the opportunity to observe his playing firsthand. According to Emmett Hughes of Dromore, Queens County, who often served as Fitzgerald's opening act on his later tours, many of these appearances would be followed by fiddlers' gatherings, where "a whole bunch would gather in and we'd play the fiddle till daylight."

In the 1970s and '80s, another superstyle grew up based on the playing of "second-generation" artists such as Buddy MacMaster, Carl MacKenzie, and Jerry Holland. Finally, in the 1990s a newer playing sound—based on the fiddling of such "third-generation" artists as Natalie MacMaster and Ashley MacIsaac—began to predominate.

"The Scottish Music Really Took over Here"

The Cape Breton fiddle-recording and broadcast scene was just hitting its stride right around the time that Don Messer was hired by CFCY. In essence, Cape Breton recordings and broadcasts filled the void left by the virtual disappearance of PEI fiddling from the media marketplace. Cape Breton fiddling was able to take on this role because it was seen by most PE Islanders as a kindred style. Here are just a few ways in which Cape Breton fiddling parallels its PEI counterpart: fiddlers hold the instrument with its belly nearly perpendicular to the collarbone, their bowing is wrist driven and composed primarily of sawstrokes, they stomp out the beat using the heel on downbeats and the toe on upbeats, they have a similar approach to using bowing accents and double-stops, the modal system is almost identical, and the most prized sound is characterized by a singing tone with plenty of "bite."

Although they felt a musical kinship with Cape Breton's media fiddlers, most PEI fiddlers saw themselves more as poor relations than as peers. To begin with, the playing on these Cape Breton broadcasts and recordings displayed a far higher level of performance practice and technical development than was prevalent at the time on Prince Edward Island. Moreover, many of the tunes played by Cape Bretoners on media were much more elaborate than those that were then circulating on Prince Edward Island. Here's how Joe MacDonald of St. Andrews, Kings County, describes the general reaction:

> When I started to play, I hadn't heard the Cape Breton fiddlers. It was the regular run of music, light tunes that we were hearing, that's what we played. But then what I call the better stuff started to filter in, and there was Angus Allan Gillis, and Angus Chisholm, and those fellows. And then of course the radio stations started to play those, and we didn't think this music could be brought out of fiddles till we heard those fellows bring it out of them. Boy, oh, boy! Then, of course, everybody [on Prince Edward Island] who could play the fiddle was dying to go to Cape Breton.

These Cape Breton fiddling broadcasts and recordings had their most powerful effect in terms of repertoire. Most PEI fiddlers were eager to learn the new tunes and were quick to incorporate new twists from these recordings into tunes they already knew. Teresa Wilson recalls,

> The Scottish music really took over here when the Antigonish [radio] station opened up, and they just played this Scottish music all the time, Cape Breton music. And this end of the Island, of course, there are a lot of Scottish people, and they just fell in love with it. And that was the first we heard of strathspeys and that kind of stuff, the first time I ever heard it. So everybody got into it, playing that kind of music.

Among the new tunes that PEI players picked up from these recordings and broadcasts were quite a few that Cape Breton's elite fiddlers had themselves only relatively recently gleaned from old tune books or composed themselves. And as each successive generation of Cape Breton recording artists redefined the standard repertoire on its home island, these same trends could also be seen taking place among PEI fiddlers.

By the 1990s, the Cape Breton influence on repertoire had become so widespread that just about every active PEI fiddler had learned at least a few tunes from Cape Breton sources. In some parts of Prince Edward Island—notably, northeastern Kings County, with its strong Scottish heritage and easy access to CJFX and CJCB broadcasts—the attraction of this new music was so profound that some younger fiddlers had ceased learning local tunes altogether. Consequently, many tunes that had flourished on Prince Edward Island prior to the media age began fading from the scene. As Johnny Joe Chaisson of Souris remarked in 1992, "The younger people, they got all this Cape Breton stuff. I never hear any of the stuff that we played. I hardly ever hear it."

Many other developments in Island fiddling likewise can be traced to the model provided by Cape Breton broadcasts and recordings. Many PEI fiddlers began to experiment again with Scottish-style ornamentation, and to a certain extent they began reexploring the strathspey genre. Some Island players adopted the Cape Breton practice of playing groups of tunes at gatherings, concerts, and dances; in some cases they adopted exactly the same tune groups that Cape Bretoners had recorded. When word got out that most Cape Breton recording and broadcast artists had expanded their repertoires by going to the books, it strengthened respect for musical literacy and encouraged many Island fiddlers to at least make the attempt to take up note-reading. Similarly, some fiddlers on Prince Edward Island were inspired by the activities of Cape Breton's prolific tunesmiths to take up tune composition themselves. Finally, many Island fiddlers started to pay increased attention to technique and performance practice. As Merlin Quinn of Cardross, Kings County, recalls, "As we got radio and we started hearing Cape Breton fiddlers, then people got more fussy about the fiddle."

Despite their high regard for the Cape Breton fiddling sound and their willingness to adopt substantial numbers of Cape Breton tunes, few Island fiddlers were motivated to alter the fundamental sound of their playing. By and large, most of them played the new tunes in their own styles and with their own assortments of twists.

The one region of Prince Edward Island where Cape Breton fiddling had its greatest stylistic impact was northeastern Kings County. This impact was amplified through the influence of a fiddler from Bear River named Joe Pete Chaisson (c. 1915–80), who was so drawn to the sound of Cape Breton playing that even as early as the 1940s he sought to make it his own. He not only convinced his brothers "Old Peter," Roddy, and Emmett to follow his example, but he also set out to bring up his three sons—"Young Peter," "Kenny Joe Pete," and Kevin—to this way of playing. As noted in chapter 9, these Bear River Chaissons ultimately created a distinctive hybrid sound that combined elements of both traditional Kings County and Cape Breton fiddling. By the 1990s, the Chaissons had successfully encouraged quite a number of other northeastern Kings players—such as Buddy and Gus Longaphie of Souris, Hughie and Dan McPhee of Bayfield, Allan MacDonald of Bangor, and Francis MacDonald of Morell—to play with more of a Cape Breton "accent."

The Legacy of Media Fiddling

Despite more than sixty years' exposure to alternative fiddling styles on radio and recordings, PEI's predominant fiddling sound was probably little different in the early 1990s from what it had been in the 1920s. No Island-based superstyle had developed, Don Messer's style had had little local effect, and—aside from northeastern Kings County—not even widespread admiration for the playing of Cape Breton's elite fiddlers was enough of an inducement to occasion the general adoption of their manner of playing. As a result, most of the many styles, substyles, and individual twists of which PEI fiddling had been composed persisted more or less intact.

Exposure to audio mass media had its principal impact in terms of repertoire. The Cape Breton media proved to be by far the most significant here, but Islanders also learned many tunes from Don Messer and from a plethora of other fiddle broadcasts and recordings (more on this in chapter 14).

Although decades of fiddle broadcasts and recordings failed to become templates *for* style on Prince Edward Island, they certainly succeeded in creating an acute awareness *of* style. Consequently, most Island fiddlers have learned to see their own tradition as existing within a constellation of different regional playing styles. Because each such style is regarded as being more or less inborn, each becomes equally valid on its own terms and within its own territory. Ultimately, there is no point in trying to sound like any particular media fiddler. For when all is said and done, one ends up just sounding like oneself.

Despite their relatively tolerant stance toward fiddling traditions of all stripes, many Island fiddlers evince an intense insecurity regarding the value of their own music. Part of this stems from the inbred sense of humility that is an important element of Island culture, but probably much of this feeling has its roots in the decades-long exclusion of Island fiddling from both airwaves and recording studios. From the late 1930s through the 1980s, there was Messer's style on one hand and that of Cape Breton's elite fiddlers on the other. Together, these two styles dominated the local media, and there were no media models to show what professional-level PEI playing might be like. At the dawn of the broadcast era in 1926, Prince Edward Island proudly sent its favorite son, Neil Cheverie, to compete for a fiddling championship in Boston against the best players of the Northeast. A half-century later, organizers of the Island's first fiddle festivals apparently felt that there was not a single Island player of sufficient stature to serve as headliner. Instead, headliners were brought in from Cape Breton, New Brunswick, and other regions, a practice that was still ongoing through the 1990s.

Interestingly, the overall relationship of Island fiddling and the media underwent a sea change beginning in the mid-1990s. As described in chapters 16 and 17, players of the younger generation have become acutely aware of performing practice, regularly record music for commercial release, and are not averse to borrowing style along with repertoire via recordings emanating from other fiddling traditions. Another noteworthy recent development among PEI fiddlers has been the rehabilitation of Don Messer's musical reputation. In 1991–92, unhappiness with Messer's approach to playing seemed almost universal. When the subject came up in 2006, however, most Island fiddlers tended to allow that perhaps many people had underestimated Messer's talents. What's more, many younger players had begun to follow in Messer's stylistic footsteps.

NOTES

1. See Hornby, "Fiddle on the Island," 91–92; and Large and Crothers, *Out of Thin Air*, 42–44, 95–96.
2. See Wiggins, *Fiddlin' Georgia Crazy*, 69; and Spielman, "Traditional North American Fiddling," 236–39, 243–44.
3. Spielman, "Traditional North American Fiddling," 236.
4. Wolfe, *Devil's Box*, xxi. Skinner's recording career is outlined on J. *Scott Skinner the Strathspey King*, Topic Records #12T280, 1975. For Irish recordings, see Maloney, "Irish Music in America," 522–29. For Québecois recordings, see Lederman, "Fiddling," 455–56.
5. Roland Jay is one of the fiddlers interviewed for our project.
6. Russell Clark's General Store was located in Mt. Stewart in northeastern Queens County.
7. Mrs. Bruce [Edith Jay] McLaren, "Lem Jay" (interview typescript), 4, Betty Rogers Large Papers, PEI Archives, Accession # 4268, Box 2.
8. Hornby, "Fiddle on the Island," 94–95.
9. Canadian federal officials initially refused to assign Charlottetown more than one radio frequency.

10. Hector MacDonald is the father of Allan MacDonald, one of the fiddlers interviewed for the project; Otis Jackson, a southern Kings County fiddler, has been mentioned several times by Archie Stewart; Robert Weeks took third prize at the Great Contest of '26.
11. *Summerside Journal-Pioneer*, Jan. 17, 1973, n.p.
12. Hornby, "Fiddle on the Island," 99–102. Kelly and McInnis was a popular Charlottetown men's clothing store.
13. Annotated photo, Betty Rogers Large Papers, PEI Archives: Accession # 4268, Box 3.
14. Hornby, "Fiddle on the Island," 101–3. Keith Rogers's daughter, Betty Rogers Large (in *Out of Thin Air*, 100) implies that there was a personality conflict between Chappelle and CFCY's new station manager Art MacDonald; at issue in part was Chappelle's level of alcohol intake.
15. Raymond Sellick, telephone interview, Aug. 10, 1999.
16. Dan MacCormack, telephone interview, Aug. 12, 1999; John Gauthier, personal interview, Nov. 16, 2006, PEIFP Interview #40.
17. Peter Doiron, telephone interview, Aug. 8, 1999; Peter Robinson, personal interview, Nov. 11, 2006, PEIFP Interview #32.
18. Paul Schurman, telephone interview, Aug. 14, 1999.
19. Unfortunately only a few of the fiddling tapes made during this period were preserved after CJRW changed hands in the mid-1990s.
20. Lowell Huestis, personal interview, Nov. 10, 2006, PEIFP Interview #30.
21. Canadians were required to take out annual licenses at the time to own and operate a radio. These figures are courtesy of historian Edward MacDonald of Charlottetown, whose cited source is the *Canada Year Book* (Dominion Bureau of Statistics).
22. O'Shea, *It Happened in Iona*, 101.
23. According to some accounts, there was actually a series of three batteries involved in powering one of these radios. Two of them were 45 volts each, were not rechargeable, and had to be replaced periodically, while the third—a 6 volt battery—frequently had to be recharged.
24. Francis MacCormack, personal interview, Oct. 15, 2006, PEIFP Interview #02.
25. John Gauthier, personal interview, Nov. 16, 2006, PEIFP Interview #40.
26. Large and Crothers, *Out of Thin Air*, 69; see pp. 35–82 for an account of the station's early days. CFCY's first transmitter had a broadcasting strength of just 50 watts.
27. Although I came across several 78 rpm disks featuring Island fiddlers that had been individually cut as souvenirs, to the best of my knowledge no recordings of Island fiddlers intended for commercial release were made prior to the modern era.
28. The Cape Breton experience is described later in this chapter. In 1923, furniture and phonograph dealer Polk Brockman of Atlanta, Georgia, pushed Okeh Records to record Fiddlin' John Carson (see Wiggins, *Fiddlin' Georgia Crazy*, 73–76). Similarly, the Irish recording industry was launched in 1916 by a New York family named Dewitt who wished to add ethnic recordings to their line of Irish retail items (Maloney, "Irish Music in America," 522).
29. For example, see Wiggins, *Fiddlin' Georgia Crazy*, 48–78; and Wolfe, *Devil's Box*, 14, 32, 81–86, and 101.
30. Hornby, "Fiddle on the Island," 94.

31. In all fairness, it should be noted that most of the tunes broadcast by the Island's early media fiddlers may already have been in general circulation.
32. Maloney, "Irish Ethnic Recordings," 92.
33. Wolfe, *Devil's Box*, 32, 83–85, and 113–14.
34. Large and Crothers, *Out of Thin Air*, 84–85.
35. *The Friendly Voice*, 1939–40 (brochure), in "Don Messer and the Islanders," Betty Rogers Large Papers, PEI Archives.
36. Large and Crothers, *Out of Thin Air*, 101.
37. Raymond Sellick, telephone interview, Aug. 10, 1999.
38. Sellick, *Canada's Don Messer*, 1–12.
39. Sellick, *Canada's Don Messer*, 13–19.
40. Sellick, *Canada's Don Messer*, 21–34.
41. Hornby, "Fiddle on the Island," 103–5.
42. Sellick, *Canada's Don Messer*, 35–56.
43. "Don Messer," Betty Rogers Large Papers, PEI Archives.
44. Sellick, *Our Musical Heritage*, 58–59.
45. Sellick, *Canada's Don Messer*, 37–38.
46. Hornby, "Fiddle on the Island," 119–20.
47. Sellick, *Canada's Don Messer*, 57–108. Sellick implies that Messer's material was considered insufficiently culturally diverse to suit what had become CBC's new management philosophy.
48. Hornby, "Fiddle on the Island," 105–6. This is a paraphrase of the liner notes for *Don Messer and the Islanders: The Good Old Days*, MCA Records Canada, # TVLP-79052, 1979.
49. Hornby, "Fiddle on the Island," 106. Wills grew up and forged his musical skills in Texas but moved his band to Tulsa, Oklahoma, in 1934.
50. Messer himself pointed to a Canadian band called George Wade and His Cornhuskers as a major influence. See Green and Miller, "Don Messer and His Islanders," 850.
51. For the Georgia Wildcats and the Dixieliners, see Wolfe, *Devil's Box*, 91 and 120, respectively; for Bob Wills, see Townsend, *San Antonio Rose*.
52. Sellick, *Canada's Don Messer*, 27.
53. "Groich" is my phonetic rendering. According to Frances MacEachern of Gaeltalk Communications in Mabou, Nova Scotia, the word involved may well be *droch*, meaning "bad."
54. Rosenberg, "Don Messer's Modern," 24.
55. For the Ottawa Valley, see Bégin, *Fiddle Music*, 6–7; for Ward Allen et al., see Lederman, "Fiddling," 456.
56. The version of "St. Anne's Reel" that spread throughout North America comes from a 1920s recording by Québecois fiddler Joseph Allard (1873–1947).
57. John Gauthier interview, Nov. 16, 2006.
58. Antigonish (pronounced with the accent on the last syllable) is a small city on the north shore of the Nova Scotia mainland, just across the Strait of Canso from Cape Breton Island.
59. McKinnon, "Fiddling to Fortune," 54–56.

60. McKinnon, "Fiddling to Fortune," 85.
61. McKinnon, "Fiddling to Fortune," 54–55. Capsule biographies for these and many other well-known Cape Breton recording artists appear in MacGillivray, *Cape Breton Fiddler.*
62. McKinnon, "Fiddling to Fortune," 53–56, 276–79.
63. McKinnon, "Fiddling to Fortune," 58–59, 279–83, 286–90.
64. McKinnon, "Fiddling to Fortune," 120–22.
65. McKinnon, "Fiddling to Fortune," 3.
66. McKinnon, "Fiddling to Fortune," 89. See also Sellick, *Our Musical Heritage*, 46; and "Tena Campbell," in MacGillivray, *Cape Breton Fiddler*, 19. The title of this show was drawn from a well-known poem by Robert Burns (1759–96).
67. McKinnon, "Fiddling to Fortune," 88. See also "Donald MacLellan," in MacGillivray, *Cape Breton Fiddler*, 144.
68. "Johnny Wilmot," in MacGillivray, *Cape Breton Fiddler*, 166.
69. McKinnon, "Fiddling to Fortune," 89.
70. "John Donald Cameron" and "Cameron Chisholm," in MacGillivray, *Cape Breton Fiddler*, 88, 96.
71. See, for example, Forbes, *Maritime Rights*, 3–6. Capsule biographies of some fiddlers who worked in the mines of Nova Scotia appear in MacGillivray, *Cape Breton Fiddler*, 8, 23, 39–40, and 56–57.
72. See, for example, "Johnny MacIsaac," in MacGillivray, *Cape Breton Fiddler*, 48. This picnic was held not long after the death of Fr. Kenneth MacDonald, the fiddle-burning priest mentioned in chapter 8.
73. McKinnon, "Fiddling to Fortune," 26.
74. Allistair MacGillivray, personal interview, Jan. 5, 1999.
75. McKinnon, "Fiddling to Fortune," 35.
76. Allistair MacGillivray interview, Jan. 5, 1999.
77. McKinnon, "Fiddling to Fortune," 85–90.
78. The Cabot Trail is a scenic highway that loops around the northern tip of Cape Breton; it is roughly 185 miles (298 km) in length.
79. McKay, "Tartanism Triumphant."
80. Graham, *Cape Breton Fiddle*, 53–54, 90.
81. Inverness County is draped along the entire northwest shore of Cape Breton Island. Progressing clockwise, Cape Breton's other administrative divisions are Victoria, Richmond, and Cape Breton Counties. A 1932 survey determined that Scots Gaelic was still spoken by over 75 percent of the population of central and southern Inverness County (reported in Kennedy, *Gaelic Nova Scotia*, 83–84).
82. McKinnon, "Fiddling to Fortune," 124–26. According to Sandy MacIntyre (personal interview, July 3, 1999), some Cape Breton fiddlers hoarded tune books to maintain the uniqueness of their repertoires.
83. A selection of Dan MacDonald's tunes was published posthumously in two volumes as *The Heather Hills Collection.*
84. See, for example, Alburger, *Scottish Fiddlers*, 181. Not only would Skinner's recordings have been readily available on Cape Breton, but he toured in North America twice:

once in 1893 and a second time in 1926 to participate in the World Champion Fiddle Contest in Lewiston, Maine.
85. McKinnon, "Fiddling to Fortune," 121–22.
86. McKinnon, "Fiddling to Fortune," 119–21.
87. McKinnon, "Fiddling to Fortune," 122.
88. Carl and Jackie Webster, personal interview, Oct. 1996.

CHAPTER FOURTEEN
The Repertoire

Dozens of descriptions and quotations in this book mention the lively, exquisitely infectious melodies that Island fiddlers play. There are also frequent references to such tune genres as jigs, reels, hornpipes, and strathspeys. This chapter looks at the structure and history of these and other tune genres and also explores the Island repertoire in detail—what tunes have been the most widely played, how tunes reached the Island, and the extent of media influence on the repertoire.[1]

Before proceeding, I will describe our method for tune collection. Fiddlers were asked at various points during their interview sessions to play selections of their own choosing. In addition, they would often spontaneously initiate pieces during the informal jam sessions that sometimes followed interviewing. All such performances were taped, and many of them were later transcribed. Nearly six hundred different tunes were identified in the course of the 1991–92 project, and approximately four hundred additional tunes were collected in 2006.[2]

Table 14.1 lists the 126 most widely played tunes of 1991–92, defined as those for which versions were collected from at least four different fiddlers

TABLE 14.1. MOST WIDELY PLAYED TUNES, 1991-92

TITLE	GENRE	KEY	ORIGIN	#	TITLE	GENRE	KEY	ORIGIN	#
1. St. Anne's Reel	Reel	D	Québec	45	22. Dismissal, The†	Reel	G	Cape Breton	13
2. Lord MacDonald's Reel	Reel	G	Scotland	36	23. Dragger's Reel, The†	Reel	G	PEI	13
3. Paddy on the Turnpike	Reel	G	Scotland	35	24. Pride of the Ball	Reel	A	Ireland	12
4. Sheehan's Reel	Reel	G	Ireland	35	25. Haste to the Wedding	Jig	D	England?	11
5. Princess Reel	Reel	G	Cdn. Mar.	30	26. Jerome's Farewell [...]	Reel	D	Ireland	11
6. Heather on the Hill†	Reel	G	Cape Breton	28	27. Mason's Apron	Reel	A	Scotland	11
7. Farmer's Reel	Reel	G	Cdn. Mar.	26	28. Angus Campbell	Reel	A	Scotland	10
8. Pigeon on the Gatepost	Reel	A	Ireland	25	29. Bonnie Lass of Fisherrow	Reel	C	Scotland	10
9. Flowers of Edinburgh	Reel	G	Scotland	24	30. Donald Cameron's Reel†	Reel	G	Cape Breton	10
10. Trip to Boston†	Reel	A	Cape Breton	24	31. High-Level Hornpipe	Reel	B♭	Scotland	9
11. Irish Washerwoman	Jig	G	Ireland	21	32. Ragtime Annie	Reel	D	US	9
12. Fisher's Hornpipe	Reel	F	Scotland	19	33. Soldier's Joy	Reel	D	Scotland	9
13. Maid Behind the Bar	Reel	D	Ireland	19	34. Southern Melody	Set	D	Cape Breton	9
14. Growling Old Man	Reel	A	Québec	17	35. Stack of Barley	Reel	G	Ireland	9
15. Homeward Bound	Reel	D	Cdn. Mar.	17	36. Stella's Trip to Kamloops†	March	A	Cape Breton	9
16. Miramichi Fire	Reel	A	Cdn. Mar.	17	37. Bird's Nest, The	Reel	A	Scotland	8
17. Mrs. McLeod of Rasay	Reel	A	Scotland	17	38. Bowing the Strings†	Reel	A	Cdn. Mar.	8
18. Ottawa Valley Reel	Reel	G	Cdn. Mar.	17	39. Carlton Co. Breakdown†	Reel	A	Cdn. Mar.	8
19. Archie Menzies	Reel	F	Scotland	16	40. Chaisson Reel	Reel	G	Cdn. Mar.	8
20. Big John MacNeil	Reel	A	Scotland	16	41. College Hornpipe	Reel	G	Scotland	8
21. Old Man & Old Woman	Reel	G	Québec	16	42. Crooked Stovepipe†	Set	G	Cdn. Mar.	8

#	Tune	Type	Key	Origin	#		#	Tune	Type	Key	Origin	#
43	Devil's Dream	Reel	A	Scotland	8		67	Black Velvet Waltz	Waltz	C	Ontario	6
44	Florence Killen Waltz†	Waltz	G	Ontario	8		68	Brae Reel, The	Reel	A	Cdn. Mar.	6
45	Jenny Dang the Weaver	Reel	D	Scotland	8		69	Dancing Fingers	Reel	D	Cape Breton	6
46	Johnny Cope Reel	Reel	A	Scotland	8		70	Dillon Brown	Reel	A	Ireland	6
47	Little Burnt Potato†	Jig	D	Cdn. Mar.	8		71	Irishman Heart to the Ladies	Jig	A	Ireland	6
48	Londonderry Hornpipe	Reel	D	Ireland	8		72	Miss Susan Cooper†	Reel	D	Shetland	6
49	Mrs. Muir MacKenzie	Reel	D	Scotland	8		73	On the Road to Skye	Reel	A	Cape Breton	6
50	Southern Waltz	Waltz	G	US	8		74	Over the Waves	Waltz	G	US	6
51	Tarbolton Lodge	Reel	E	Scotland	8		75	Pigeon on the Gate	Reel	G	Ireland	6
52	Walker Street	Reel	G	Ireland	8		76	Robert Stubbert†	Reel	D	Cape Breton	6
53	White Cockade, The	Set	G	Scotland	8		77	Silver & Gold	Set	D	US pop	6
54	Black Mill, The	Reel	A	Scotland	7		78	Trip to Windsor†	Reel	A	Cape Breton	6
55	Cock of the North	Jig	A	Scotland	7		79	Wedding Reel, Cape Br.	Reel	A	Cape Breton	6
56	Duke of Gordon's Birthday	Strath.	G	Scotland	7		80	Westphalia Waltz	Waltz	G	Europe	6
57	Jubilo	Set	D	US pop	7		81	Bonny Lea Rig	Jig	D	Scotland	5
58	Liberty	Set	D	US	7		82	Four Marys, The	Waltz	G	Scots song	5
59	Maple Sugar†	Set	D	Ontario	7		83	Girl I Left Behind Me	Set	G	Irish song	5
60	Mary Claret	Reel	B♭	Cape Breton	7		84	Glencoe March†	March	D	Cape Breton	5
61	Miss Lyall Reel	Reel	A	Scotland	7		85	High Rd. to Linton	Reel	A	Scotland	5
62	Mrs. Norman MacKeigan†	Reel	D	Cape Breton	7		86	Kenmure's Awa'	Jig	G	Scotland	5
63	North Side Tune	Set	G	Cdn. Mar.	7		87	King George IV Strathspey	Strath.	A	Scotland	5
64	Poppy Leaf Hornpipe	Reel	G	US	7		88	MacNab's Hornpipe	Reel	D	Scotland	5
65	St. Kilda Wedding	Reel	A	Scotland	7		89	Off She Goes	Jig	D	Ireland	5
66	Turkey in the Straw	Reel	G	US	7		90	Red Wing	Set	G	US pop	5

Key: # = number of fiddlers who played the tune, † = composed after circa 1925, Set = set tune, Strath = strathspey; Cdn. Mar. = Canadian Maritimes region, Messer = Don Messer, US pop = US popular song
Note: The tune with the most collected versions appears as number 1, the tune with the next-most collected versions is number 2, and so on (in the event of a tie, tunes were assigned slots alphabetically).

TABLE 14.1. MOST WIDELY PLAYED TUNES, 1991-92 (CONT'D)

TITLE	GENRE	KEY	ORIGIN	#
91. Road to the Isles	Set	D	Scots song	5
92. Sally Gardens	Reel	G	Ireland	5
93. Smash the Windows	Jig	D	Ireland	5
94. Wedding Reel, PEI	Reel	A	Cdn. Mar.	5
95. West Mabou Reel	Reel	G	Cape Breton	5
96. When You [...] Maggie	Set	G	US pop	5
97. Athole Brose	Strath.	D	Scotland	4
98. Balkan Hills	March	D	Scotland	4
99. Brenda Stubbert†	Reel	A	Cape Breton	4
100. Caber Feidh	Reel	C	Scotland	4
101. Campbell's March†	March	G	Cape Breton	4
102. Cheticamp Reel	Set	G	Cdn. Mar.	4
103. Chicken Reel	Reel	D	US	4
104. Country Waltz	Waltz	D	US	4
105. Darlin' Nelly Gray	Set	G	US pop	4
106. Devil's Delight†	Reel	A	Cape Breton	4
107. Highland Jig	Jig	G	Scotland	4
108. Island Boy	Reel	D	Cdn. Mar.	4
109. Jay's Reel	Reel	A	Cdn. Mar.	4
110. Joys of Wedlock	Jig	G	Ireland	4
111. King's Reel, The	Reel	A	Scotland	4
112. Lasses of Glenaladale	Reel	A	Cape Breton	4
113. Miss Georgina Campbell	Reel	G	Scotland	4
114. Miss Lyall Strathspey	Strath.	A	Scotland	4
115. Miss Mary S. MacLean†	Reel	D	Cape Breton	4
116. Mrs. Beattie Wallace†	Reel	D	Cape Breton	4
117. Norwegian Waltz	Waltz	G	Europe	4
118. Red Shoes, The†	Reel	A	Cape Breton	4
119. Reel à Joe Bibienne	Reel	C	Québec	4
120. Rose of Tennessee	Jig	G	US	4
121. Rothiemurchus Rant	Strath.	C	Scotland	4
122. Scourdiness†	Reel	D	Scotland	4
123. Spin 'n' Glow†	Jig	G	US	4
124. Teresa MacLellan†	Reel	G	Cape Breton	4
125. West Point Jig	Jig	G	Cdn. Mar.	4
126. Woodchopper's Breakdown	Reel	D	Messer	4

Key: # = number of fiddlers who played the tune. † = composed after circa 1925. Set = set tune. Strath. = strathspey. Cdn. Mar. = Canadian Maritimes region. Messer = Don Messer. US pop = US popular song.
Note. The tune with the most collected versions appears as number 1, the tune with the next-most collected versions is number 2, and so on (in the event of a tie, tunes were assigned slots alphabetically).

(hereafter, this is referred to as the "Top 126 List"). Titles for the less widely played tunes of 1991–92 (those collected from three fiddlers or fewer) are listed alphabetically in appendix C, table C.1; titles for all tunes first encountered in 2006 are listed alphabetically in appendix C, table C.2.[3]

At the heart of the Island repertoire in 1991–92 was a core of roughly two dozen "good old tunes" that almost every fiddler knew. All these widely known tunes were held in a position of special regard, and most fiddlers played them with a considerable amount of feeling and attention to detail. Although there are borderline cases, the titles for nearly all these core tunes appear among the first twenty-seven entries of table 14.1 (hereafter referred to as the "Top 27 List").

About half the tunes on the Top 27 List—including seven of the top ten—are played in the key of G.[4] Given prevailing playing styles, this key seems to offer Island fiddlers the most opportunity to draw power and resonance from their instruments. Among the most popular G tunes in the Top 27 List are "Lord MacDonald's Reel," "Paddy on the Turnpike," "Sheehan's Reel," "Princess Reel," "Heather on the Hill," "Farmer's Reel," and "Flowers of Edinburgh."

The two next-most-popular keys are A and D. Among popular tunes in the key of A are "Pigeon on the Gatepost" (along with its close relative "Pride of the Ball"[5]), "Mrs. McLeod of Rasay," "Big John MacNeil," "Growling Old Man," and "Miramichi Fire." Some popular tunes in the key of D are "St. Anne's Reel," "Maid Behind the Bar," "Haste to the Wedding," "Homeward Bound," and "Jerome's Farewell to Gibraltar." Other widely played keys include C, E, F, and $B_\flat$.[6]

Some tunes were more popular in certain parts of the Island than in others. For example, "Miramichi Fire" and "Growling Old Man" were most widely played in western Prince Edward Island, while "Homeward Bound" and "Jerome's Farewell to Gibraltar" were more popular in the east.

In addition to core and regionally popular tunes, most fiddlers had in their personal repertoires anywhere from a couple dozen to a few hundred additional tunes. As one might expect, the contents of individual repertoires often varied by region; fiddlers from the eastern part of the Island tended to prefer tunes of Scottish and Cape Breton origin, while fiddlers from the western part of the Island generally favored tunes from New Brunswick and the Canadian mainland.

A Capsule History of Fiddle Tunes

Although its precise time of origin is unclear, the first flowering of the style of music we now call *fiddle tunes* got under way in Scotland in the late seventeenth or early eighteenth century. The most common structures—two repeated eight-bar parts, or *turns*, or, alternatively, one repeated four-bar turn followed by a nonrepeated eight-bar turn—were dictated by the dances of the day.[7] The style of composition (that is, musical ideas) was initially adapted from preexisting Scottish musical forms, such as bagpipe music, work songs, ballads, dance songs (*puirt-a-beul*), and a legacy of older instrumental dance tunes. Later in the century, many composers of fiddle tunes began to borrow melodic and harmonic ideas consistently from baroque- and classical-era art music. By the end of the eighteenth century, the fiddle-tunes genre had become the musically dominant form of dance music throughout Britain, Ireland, and eastern North America, and composers from all these regions were actively creating new repertoire.

Since the mid-eighteenth century, an extensive written tradition for fiddle tunes has coexisted with the aural one. Systematic publication of the genre got under way with Robert Bremner's *A Collection of Scots Reels or Country Dances*, which appeared in Edinburgh as fourteen "numbers" (volumes) during the period 1751–61.[8] This was soon followed by a host of other books devoted to collected and newly composed Scottish dance tunes by such authors as Neil Stewart, Daniel Dow, Angus Cumming, and William Marshall.[9] Probably the most influential fiddle tune collections of the late eighteenth and early nineteenth centuries—often referred to nowadays as *The Gow Collection* and *The Gow Repository*—were published either directly under the imprint of well-known fiddler Niel Gow or through the firm founded by his offspring: Niel Gow and Sons of Edinburgh.[10] Some other widely circulated Scottish works published before 1860 were Captain Simon Fraser's *Airs and Melodies Peculiar to the Highlands* (1816), Joseph Lowe's *Collection of Reels and Strathspeys* (1844), and John Surenne's *The Dance Music of Scotland* (1852).[11]

The first major collection published in Ireland that featured a substantial number of fiddle tunes was O'Farrell's *Pocket Companion for the Irish or Union Pipes* (1810). Other important nineteenth-century Irish works include George Petrie's *Ancient Music of Ireland* (1851) and Patrick Weston Joyce's *Ancient Irish Music* (1873). The first large-scale North American fiddle tune compendiums were published by Elias Howe of Boston (1820–95); his works include *The Musician's Companion* (1840), *Howe's One Thousand Jigs and Reels* (c. 1867), and *Musicians' Omnibus* (7 vols., 1864–82).[12]

Several comprehensive tune collections published between 1880 and 1910 were in significant circulation on Prince Edward Island during the lifetimes of the fiddlers in our project. These include the following Scottish books: *The Athole Collection* by James Stewart-Robertson (1884), *The Skye Collection* by Keith Norman MacDonald (1887), *Kerr's Merry Melodies for the Violin* (4 vols., 1880–89), and several works by James Scott Skinner such as *The Miller O'Hirn Collection* (1881), *Harp and Claymore* (1903–4), and *The Scottish Violinist* (c. 1910). Also of local significance was a work published in Boston by a protégé of Elias Howe named William Bradbury Ryan, called *Ryan's Mammoth Collection* (1883). This book, which was devoted primarily to tunes in New England circulation (including many that were originally of Scottish and Irish origin), was later republished numerous times by the MM Cole Company of Chicago under the title *One Thousand Fiddle Tunes*. Finally, there were a few books devoted primarily to the Irish fiddling repertoire, in particular two books by Captain Francis O'Neill: *Music of Ireland* (1903) and *Dance Music of Ireland* (1907).

Fiddle Tune Genres: Reels, Hornpipes, Set Tunes, and Jigs

Fiddle tunes are divided into genres by such considerations as meter (time signature), tempo, and function. These various genres have shown great flexibility, and over the past two and a half centuries, nearly all of them have survived several major shifts in dancing styles and popular tastes. On the Island, eight such genres are represented: *reels, hornpipes, set tunes, jigs, waltzes, marches, strathspeys,* and *airs*. Table 14.2 shows the number and proportion for each genre in 1991–92, relative to both the Top 126 List and to the list of all tunes collected in those years (referred to hereafter as "the Total List"). As

TABLE 14.2. TUNE GENRES, 1991–92

GENRE	TOP 126		TOTAL LIST	
	#	%	#	%
REELS*	81	64%	312	53%
SET TUNES	14	11%	66	11%
JIGS	14	11%	88	15%
MARCHES	4	3%	18	3%
STRATHSPEYS	5	4%	51	9%
WALTZES	8	6%	38	6%
AIRS	—	—	19	3%

*Includes all hornpipes, and all marches that are played as reels on PEI.
[KEY: # = NUMBER OF TUNES COLLECTED.]

indicated in this table, reels are by far the most popular genre, with jigs and set tunes more or less tied for a distant second place. All other genres taken together make up less than 15 percent of the Top 126 List and about 20 percent of the Total List.

Islanders use four kinds of tunes for accompanying square sets: reels, hornpipes, set tunes, and jigs. All these genres tend to have two eight-bar parts (referred to on the Island respectively as the *low turn* and the *high turn*), all have two beats per measure, and all are generally played at about the same tempo—a rate roughly consistent with a metronome setting of 120 (that is, 120 beats per minute, or 2 beats per second).

Reels are generally written either in 2/2 or 2/4 time. A typical measure consists of two groups of four notes, which—depending on the time signature—can be written as either eighth or sixteenth notes (see appendix A, example 14.1). At tempo, considerable energy and skill are usually required to shape all these notes into a coherent and danceable melody. Although most reels have two repeated eight-measure parts, there is also an alternative short format consisting of one repeated four-measure low turn followed by a nonrepeated eight-measure high turn.

The term *reel* is descended from the Anglo-Saxon word *rulla*, meaning to whirl. The musical form now known as the reel originated in Scotland, probably in the last quarter of the seventeenth century or early eighteenth century. The earliest definitive record we have of the genre is the Drummond Castle Manuscript, transcribed by David Young for the Duke of Perth in 1734; the first published collection to include examples was Bremner's aforementioned 1751 work. Initially, reel tunes were employed to accompany a dance known generically as the Scotch reel. By the mid-eighteenth century, reel tunes were also being used regularly to accompany longways country-dancing (that is, *contredanse anglaise*). Later, reels were also applied to accompany cotillions, quadrilles, and other, less formal, square dances.[13] Throughout much of North America, dancing to reels eventually became so popular that many other tune genres were ultimately eclipsed.

Almost all the most widely played tunes on Prince Edward Island are reels, which some Island fiddlers refer to simply as *fast tunes*. In 1991–92, reels made up the entire top ten and forty-four of the fifty-three most popular tunes (see table 14.1). Island fiddlers seem to be at their most expressive when playing reels and to focus their greatest creative energies into ornamenting, elaborating, and otherwise making reels come alive. There are two main reasons for the predominance of reels. First, the basic mechanics of Island-style fiddling with its efficient, powerful sawstroke is particularly well-suited to the demands of reel playing.[14] Second, because the reel can be used to accompany both square sets and step dancing, it is the kind of dance tune for which there is the most consistent demand.

Hornpipes have the same structure as "long-form" reels (that is, two repeated eight-measure turns). The modern hornpipe dates from about the third quarter of the eighteenth century; it probably grew up in Britain as a slow- to medium-tempo adaptation of the reel designed to accompany step dancing.[15] The British and Irish styles of hornpipe playing stem from these fancy-stepping origins. In these traditions, hornpipes are played at a much slower tempo than are reels (that is, at about a metronome setting of 96). In addition (assuming cut time, or 2/2), the eighth notes are played with a pronounced "dotted" rhythm, which is indicated in some tune books by alternating dotted eighths and sixteenths (see appendix A, example 14.2).[16] On the Island and in most other North American fiddling traditions, however, hornpipes are almost always played at the same brisk tempo and with the same note rhythm as are reels. In order of their appearance in table 14.1, some common hornpipes played as reels on Prince Edward Island are "Fisher's Hornpipe," "Stack of Barley," "High-Level Hornpipe," and "College Hornpipe." We also encountered a few hornpipes performed in Old World style, the most common of which was "Bonaparte Crossing the Alps," a tune played for years by fiddler Lem Jay on his annual Christmas-season radio show.

The term *set tune* is a catch-all for cut-time dance tunes that are neither reels nor hornpipes. Such tunes are generally made up of a high proportion of quarter notes and are therefore much less musically dense than reels (see appendix A, example 14.3). They are relatively easy to shape into phrases and often possess a bouncy, lighthearted character, but they generally lack the rhythmic drive of reels and hornpipes. Some Island fiddlers refer to the genre as *slow tunes*—presumably because with fewer notes to play per measure, the fiddler's bow moves a bit slower than it would for reel playing. Some set tunes have sixteen bars per turn instead of eight.

Many set tunes played on Prince Edward Island are old popular-song melodies that have been adapted for use as dance tunes. Some examples in order of their appearance on table 14.1 are "Jubilo" (also known as "Kingdom Comin'"), "Red Wing," and "Darlin' Nelly Gray." Also falling within the set-tune category are *Scotch measures* such as "The White Cockade," polkas and polka-like tunes such as "Cheticamp Reel" and "Heel and Toe Polka," and tunes specifically composed to serve as set tunes such as "Crooked Stovepipe," "Maple Sugar," and "Whelan's Breakdown."[17] Set tunes derived from post–World War I popular-song melodies such as "Five Minutes More" and "Four Leaf Clover" are sometimes referred to as *fox-trots*.

The heyday of set-tune playing on Prince Edward Island was the 1950s, when the development of larger dance venues led to larger crowds, larger set sizes, and much longer dance durations. Because set tunes take much less energy to play than do jigs or reels, it was more practical under these conditions for fiddlers to use as many of them as possible (for more on Island dancing in the 1950s, see chapter 15).

Nowadays in the Anglo-Celtic tradition, the term *jig* is universally applied to all 6/8-time dance tunes. Etymologically, it probably descends from one or more among a complex of European words, such as the Italian *giga*, the Old French *gigue*, or the German *geige*, all of which mean either "bowed instrument" or "to whirl." In the seventeenth century, the term *jig* referred to any spritely dance, but by the eighteenth century the word had increasingly come to be associated with a certain class of Scottish tunes in 6/8 time with strong, lively melodies, typified by "Stool of Repentance" and "Come Under My Plaidie." Perhaps the greatest flowering of 6/8-time dance tunes in terms of both number and variety of melodies occurred in late eighteenth- and early nineteenth-century Ireland, where they were used to accompany a highly popular form of couples' step dancing.[18]

On Prince Edward Island, fiddlers recognize two categories of 6/8 tunes: Irish jigs and Scotch jigs. The category "Irish jigs" roughly coincides with what Irish fiddlers call *double jigs*; it includes tunes such as "The Irish Washerwoman" and "Larry O'Gaff," whose measures usually each contain two groups of three eighth notes (see appendix A, example 14.4). The category "Scotch jigs," in contrast, has several components. First, it includes what Irish fiddlers call *single jigs*—6/8 tunes made up primarily of quarter-eighth combinations and dotted quarter notes, such as "Pop Goes the Weasel" and "Garryowen" (see appendix A, example 14.5). Also counted as Scotch jigs are much of the aforementioned eighteenth-century Scottish 6/8 tune repertoire; *quicksteps* (6/8-time marches) converted to dance melodies, such as "Colonel Robertson"; and a curious class of 6/8 tunes with singsong melodies and sharply defined common-practice harmonies that I call *quadrille jigs*.[19] Some quadrille jigs that are widely played on Prince Edward Island are "Highland Jig," "Rose of Tennessee," and "Jackson's Jig."

During the course of the 1991–92 project, I got the impression that many Island fiddlers were a bit rusty when it came to playing jigs or were not giving tunes in 6/8 time their full attention. With square-set dancing growing increasingly rare and with no application for jigs in the step-dancing revival, local interest in this tune category as a whole was probably declining. In any event, only four of the fifty-five most widely played tunes of 1991–92 were jigs, a balance that remained substantially unchanged when results for the 2006 project were tabulated.

More Fiddle Tune Genres: Marches, Strathspeys, Waltzes, and Airs

Marches may have originally been developed for military purposes, but over the years many have been adapted for use as dance tunes. Nearly all marches played on Prince Edward Island come from the Scottish tradition. There are several kinds of Scottish marches, but certainly the most common type in the repertoire is the four-part cut-time march. Cut-time pipe marches have four repeated eight-measure parts, with a thematic sequence of ABA´B´. Generally, the last, or B´, part has a four-measure second ending that recalls the ending of part A.

The four-part pipe march developed as a by-product of the nineteenth-century Scottish piping-contest milieu, and most four-part marches played today date from the last third of the nineteenth century. At that time, such tunes were played on pipes at a brisk tempo and with relatively even eighth notes. The slower, more rhythmically complex style of march performance that one hears on pipes today, featuring dotted pairs and reversed dotted pairs (known as *Scotch snaps*) in lieu of straight eighth notes (see appendix A, example 14.6), did not predominate until approximately the time of the First World War.[20]

Most cut-time pipe marches in the Island repertoire—such as "Inverness Gathering," "MacDonald's March," and "The Drunken Piper"—are played as reels. There is no way to know for certain, however, whether Island fiddlers adapted the newer "dotted"-style marches to reel format or simply preserved the older up-tempo style of march performance.[21]

I did encounter a few four-part pipe marches played in the post–World War I style, such as "George V's Army" and "Don MacLean's Farewell to Oban." Also played in this style—and much more common in the contemporary Island repertoire—is a related subgenre known as the *fiddle march*. Fiddle marches have just two eight-measure parts, with the high turn featuring a four-measure-long second ending that reprises the ending of the low turn. Most fiddle marches now played on Prince Edward Island—such as "Glencoe March" and "Stella's Trip to Kamloops"—have been adopted relatively recently via the Cape Breton media.

Strathspeys originated in the mid- to late eighteenth century and are generally associated with the Strath Spey region (Spey River valley) of northeastern Scotland. They were originally known as *strathspey reels* (that is, reels played in the strathspey style) and, like hornpipes, are essentially slowed down, rhythmically elaborated adaptations of the reel form. Most strathspeys have two turns, each either four or eight bars in length. Four-bar turns are generally repeated, while eight-bar parts are usually played just once. On the page, the typical strathspey looks something like a hornpipe or march, with each measure made up primarily of dotted pairs and Scotch snaps (see appendix A, example 14.7). In contemporary Scotland, these note pairs are usually played pretty much as they are written (that is, with each dotted eighth note sounding three times as long as each sixteenth). In Cape Breton, Prince Edward Island, and other parts of Atlantic Canada, however, such pairs are generally played so that notes shown as dotted eighths are only twice as long as those shown as sixteenths. A Scotch snap, for example, becomes an eighth-note triplet with the second two notes tied (illustrated in appendix A, example 9.2b).

In the eighteenth century, strathspeys were often played in tandem with reels as the prime accompaniment for the then highly popular Scotch reel dance. In the most common pattern, the slower, more rhythmically complex strathspey served as a prelude to the up-tempo but rhythmically less pointed reel tune. When Scotch reel dancing began to go out of fashion on Prince Edward Island toward the end of the nineteenth century, fiddlers no longer needed to keep strathspeys in their repertoires. Consequently, most strathspeys were either converted to reels or dropped from circulation. As noted in chapter 13, strathspeys have recently come back into currency on Prince Edward Island through the influence of Cape Breton fiddling. Some strathspeys encountered with frequency on the Island in 1991–92 were "The Duke of Gordon's Birthday," "King George IV," and "Athole Brose."

Waltzes are 3/4-time tunes designed for couples' dancing. Most waltzes have two repeated sixteen-bar parts, but just about any measure format will serve. As noted in chapter 12, waltzes were practically absent from rural Prince Edward Island prior to the Second World War. Perhaps because the dance came so late to the Island, the number of true waltz tunes in circulation there is quite small, and apart from perhaps a couple of dozen examples such as "Westphalia Waltz," "Southern Waltz," and "Over the Waves," much of the waltz repertoire consists of adapted songs or airs in 3/4 or 6/8 time, such as "The Rosebud of Allenvale," "The Four Marys," and "Little Old Log Cabin in the Lane."

Fiddle airs are simply tunes intended for listening rather than dancing. The art of air playing had pretty much fallen out of favor on Prince Edward Island within the time of living memory, but it has been reviving of late through the influence of the Cape Breton media. On both Cape Breton and Prince Edward Island nowadays, one most often encounters fiddle airs in the role of opening tunes for Scottish sets (see chapter 13).

One additional point that should be stressed here is the notion of tune conversion. Good new dance melodies were often scarce in the days before radio and recordings, and there was a strong incentive to adapt available tunes to as many useful formats as possible. Consequently, folk or popular songs with either two or four beats per measure became set tunes, songs in 3/4 or 6/8 time became waltzes, marches became reels, and tunes designed to accompany outmoded dance styles were adapted for use with currently popular dances. Fr. Charles Cheverie of Charlottetown describes the process as follows:

> The fiddler would take tunes, he'd take march tunes that he heard bands playing, or take songs that they heard, put them to the fiddle, and then modify them to a beat that people could dance to. Or they'd hear a tune that was written in a book, and maybe it was a good tune but not good for dancing to. So they'd take the tune, modify it, put their beat to it, and away you go.

Fiddlers were also able to squeeze or stretch melodies to fit radically different metric formats. In western Prince County, for example, the jig "Larry O'Gaff" was converted from 6/8 to 2/2 time, resulting in a reel known variously as "Larry O'Gaff Reel" or "Island Boy." Similarly, fiddlers from all over the Island play a tune known as "The Home Waltz," an adaptation to 3/4 time of the well-known 4/4-time song "Home Sweet Home."

Origins and Stability of the Repertoire

We know that PEI's first fiddle tunes were brought along by Scottish and Irish settlers in the late eighteenth and early nineteenth centuries. We also know that in the generations since, the Island became a musical melting pot as thousands of new tunes from Britain, Ireland, and across North America appeared on the Island and entered circulation.

By examining publishing histories and cross-checking those with recorded sources and oral accounts, I was able to trace probable origins for almost all of the approximately six hundred tunes identified during the 1991–92 project (see table 14.3). This data indicates that Scotland was by far the most common tune source. A second tier of sources is formed by the Canadian Maritimes region (apart from Cape Breton), Cape Breton itself,[22] Ireland, and the United States. In addition, there are lesser contributions from Québec, central Canada (that is, Ontario and the Prairie Provinces), England, western Europe, and so on. In most cases, these proportions are roughly comparable for both the Top 126 List and the Total List.

Knowing probable origins is only part of the story, however, since in the absence of specific recollections it fails to inform us when or how the tunes in question entered the Island repertoire. Although tracing how each of the

TABLE 14.3. SOURCES OF THE ISLAND REPERTOIRE

ORIGINS	TOP 126	TOTAL
Scottish fiddle repertoire, first published prior to 1925	30%	27%
Scottish or Shetland fiddle repertoire, composed after 1925	1%	2%
Scotland, bagpipes repertoire	—	1%
Scotland, songs	2%	1%
Canadian Maritimes region, traditional (includes PEI but not Cape Breton)	11%	13%
New Brunswick and mainland Nova Scotia, composed after 1925	1%	1%
PEI, composed after 1925	1%	7%
Composed by or attributed by Island fiddlers to Don Messer or his band*	2%	3%
Cape Breton, traditional	3%	2%
Cape Breton, composed after World War I	13%	13%
Ireland, fiddle repertoire	13%	13%
Ireland, songs	1%	1%
US, fiddle repertoire	7%	7%
US, folk or popular songs	4%	5%
US, composed after 1925	1%	1%
Québec	3%	1%
"Central" Canada, traditional	2%	1%
Central Canada, composed after World War I	2%	1%
Other (England, European continent, etc.)	2%	2%

* Messer may well have been responsible for introducing many more tunes to the Island repertoire than he is given credit for here. Among the hundreds of fiddle tunes he recorded and released over the course of his career, one can find titles for at least 10 percent of the tunes in the 1991–92 repertoire. The full extent of his influence is unclear, however, because many of the tunes he recorded were already in local circulation.

many tunes on our list reached the Island lies beyond the scope of the book, some general tendencies can be pinpointed.

The process by which new tunes move into circulation among Island fiddlers is described in chapter 6. Fiddlers encounter new tunes, absorb them, and find effective ways to play them on their instruments. If new tunes are sufficiently compelling to attract the interest of other players, they begin to spread. Prior to the rise of mass media, there were essentially three ways to "encounter" new tunes: fiddlers could compose the tunes themselves, find them in published or written form, or take them directly from other musicians via aural transmission. Tunes absorbed aurally reached the Island through immigration, trade, or pursuit of work opportunities, or simply by passing among musicians along a chain of adjoining communities. As this continual stream of new tunes has entered Island circulation, a comparable number of older ones inevitably disappeared from the scene. Paul MacDonald of Charlottetown aptly describes the process.

> Tunes are like a big round table. And it's full of bottles, like bottles right to the edge. And every time you put a new bottle on, one or two drops off at the other end. And that's the way it works with tunes. Anytime you learn one, you probably forget one or two. And it probably just works like that in an unending process.

The continuous influx of new tunes was of course greatly accelerated by the introduction of mass media. Québecois tunes were absorbed directly via radio broadcasts from CHNC in New Carlisle, Québec, while Appalachian tunes came via broadcasts from station WWVA of Wheeling, West Virginia. The two media sources that were most significant in terms of introducing new repertoire were Don Messer and His Islanders (via Charlottetown station CFCY) and the Cape Breton fiddle broadcasting industry (via Nova Scotia stations CJFX in Antigonish and CJCB in Sydney).

Media influence is clearest to trace for those tunes known to have been composed after radio was first introduced to the Island in the mid-1920s. In 1991–92, such tunes amounted to roughly 20 percent of both the Top 126 List and the Total List. They break down as follows:

- New Cape Breton tunes (approximately 13 percent of both lists). Some prominent examples: "Heather on the Hill,"[23] "Trip to Windsor," and "The Glencoe March" by Dan R. MacDonald; "Sandy MacIntyre's Trip to Boston" by John Campbell; "The Dismissal" by Sandy MacLean; and "Brenda Stubbert" by Jerry Holland.

- New regional tunes (3 percent of the Top 126 List; 4 percent of the Total List). This bloc reflects the work of composers from New Brunswick and mainland Nova Scotia, such as "Little Burnt Potato" by Colin Boyd and "Carlton County Breakdown" by Earl Mitton. Also included here are tunes by Don Messer and members of the Islanders band, including "Bowing the Strings" by Ned Landry, "Blue Mountain Hornpipe" by Cec MacEachern,24 and "The Dawn Waltz" by Messer himself.
- New tunes from outside the Maritimes (approximately 4 percent of both lists). Some examples: "Maple Sugar" by Ward Allen (Ontario), "Spin 'n' Glow" by Frank Ferrell (New England), "Wissahickon Drive" by Liz Carroll (Chicago), and "Miss Susan Cooper" by Ronnie Cooper (Shetland).

Even in those cases in which tunes are known to predate the media age, their respective paths to the Island may well have involved at least some mass media input. Since the 1930s, prominent regional players—such as Don Messer, Angus Chisholm, Winston Fitzgerald, Buddy MacMaster, and Jerry Holland—have routinely mined old Scottish, Irish, and American tune books in search of fresh material to record or broadcast. They also freely borrowed from previous recordings by Scottish, Irish, Québecois, and Appalachian fiddlers. As a result, many older tunes from a variety of fiddling traditions found their way onto local and regional broadcasts or onto locally available phonograph records or tapes. In turn, such media exposure brought these tunes to the attention of Island fiddlers, who then absorbed them by ear, were motivated to look them up in tune books on their own account, and so on. Amplifying some of these trends since the late 1970s have been the activities of the Prince Edward Island Fiddlers' Society, whose leaders often selected tunes recorded by regional fiddlers to teach to the membership. Each branch of the society then further disseminated these tunes by performing them at fiddle festivals and other public events (for more on the society, see chapter 16).

Angus Chisholm and other first-generation Cape Breton recording artists, for example, introduced—or rekindled interest in—many older Scottish tunes, such as "Braes of Auchtertyre," "Rothiemurchus Rant," "Glengarry's Dirk," and "Bonnie Lass of Fisherrow." Winston "Scotty" Fitzgerald popularized many tunes of New England and general North American provenance, such as "Poppy Leaf Hornpipe," "Southern Melody," and "Southern Waltz." Similarly, Don Messer introduced tunes from a variety of North American sources, such as "Cotton-Eyed Joe," "Rippling Waters Jig," "Silver and Gold," and "Johnny Wagoner."

Taking such considerations into account, I estimate that roughly half the older Scottish tunes, a fourth of the older Irish tunes, and a substantial proportion of the older US tunes collected during the 1991–92 project originally found their way to Prince Edward Island via the broadcasts or recordings of prominent regional fiddlers.

Turning this perspective around, it also makes sense to inquire just how much of the repertoire we encountered in 1991–92 was in circulation during the era of the district dances. This issue is difficult to address with certainty, for two reasons. First, fiddlers' recollections dealing with the chronology of tune acquisition were generally not well-defined. Second, the path of modernization on Prince Edward Island was quite uneven, and the precise point that marked the end of the traditional era may have varied among districts by as much as thirty years (the process of modernization is discussed in chapter 15).

If the year 1940 is set as a point for comparison, however, I can at least suggest a plausible answer.[25] One good place to start is the *Guardian*'s coverage of the Great Fiddle Contest of 1926, which lists some of the tunes played by contestants. Among the tunes listed are "Caber Feidh," "College Hornpipe," "Deil among the Tailors," "Fisher's Hornpipe," "Flowers of May" (probably "Flowers of Edinburgh"), "Johnny Cope," "Lord McDonald's Reel," "Mrs. McLeod of Rasay," "Old Man and Old Woman," "Paddy on the Turnpike," "Pigeon on the Gatepost," "Scoldin' Wife" (probably "Growlin' Old Man and Cacklin' Old Woman"), "Queens Marriage" (an alternative name for "Pride of the Ball"), "Soldier's Joy," and "Speed the Plow."[26]

Another list in this vein comes from George Chappelle, the last Island fiddler to feature prominently on local radio before the Don Messer era. Years afterward he informally listed some of the tunes he had frequently played during his broadcasts. On this list were "Big John MacNeil," "The Drunken Piper," "Father O'Flynn," "Irish Washerwoman," "Larry' O'Gaff," "Maid Behind the Bar," "Miramichi Fire," "Money Musk," "The Ottawa [Valley] Reel," "Paddy on the Turnpike," and "St. Anne's Reel."[27]

Putting the two lists together, I can say with certainty that at least five of the top ten, fifteen of the Top 27 List (56 percent), and nineteen of the fifty-three most popular tunes (36 percent) from 1991–92 were in circulation before 1940.

In addition, many other tunes can be firmly placed in the pre-1940 repertoire by fiddlers' recollections. We were told, for example, that "The Prince

Edward Island Wedding Reel," "Christy Campbell," and "The Reel of Honor" were carried to the Island by its original Scottish settlers, and "Toganny's Tune" was attributed to eighteenth-century piper Toganny McPhee. We know that such tunes as "Jay's Reel," "Bonaparte Crossing the Alps," "Little Donald in the Pigpen," and "Arkansas Traveler" were known to Lem Jay, Hector MacDonald, and other Island fiddlers who played on local radio during the 1920s. Similarly, we were informed that "Princess Reel" and "Farmer's Reel" originated in New Brunswick and became established on the Island in the 1920s and '30s.[28]

Counted as post-1940 are tunes known to have been composed after that date; nearly all strathspeys, airs and true waltz tunes now in Island circulation; and most other tunes that were almost certainly picked up via recordings or long-range and regional broadcasts. By combining all such available information with a little bit of guesswork, I estimate that roughly three-fourths of the Top 27 List, two-thirds of the fifty-three most popular tunes, and half of the Top 126 List were in Island circulation before 1940. Given the downward trend, I would project that somewhat less than half the tunes collected in 1991–92 were in circulation on Prince Edward Island prior to 1940.

Tunes of an Island Character

What makes the Island fiddle repertoire worthy of note is not the uniqueness of its tunes but the way in which tunes from elsewhere evolve over time and develop a distinctive local flavor. As implied in chapters 6 and 9, the Island playing style serves as a lens that causes melodies to change over time in characteristic ways. Harder-to-play sequences of notes are altered to better fit fiddlers' preferred patterns of movement. Fiddlers add notes, subtract notes, or otherwise alter passages to improve their ability to mirror the characteristic rhythms of Island square and step dancing. They also continually tinker with their tunes, and what starts out as a highly personal "twist" can easily begin circulating in its own right.

There are forces at work in any aural music culture that cause tunes to decay over time, but on the Island such entropy has been kept in check by several factors. First, there is the emphasis on playing "true" versions; consequently, most fiddlers are not attracted to variants that have lost their distinctiveness. Second, most fiddlers are trained to a style of music learning in which the distinctive bits of melody that give tunes their character tend to be accurately reproduced. Finally, most common Island tunes have probably entered circulation on numerous different occasions via a variety of different routes. Although this could have become a source of confusion, in practice it has provided a means by which different versions could in effect be periodically cross-checked against each other, thereby holding decay over time to a minimum.

The Repertoire in 2006

An examination of the 2006 repertoire showed evidence of considerable flux. Many older fiddlers had been playing less regularly or had experienced declining skills because of ailments or injuries. As a result, many of them had dropped some of the more complex Scottish and Cape Breton tunes and focused instead on relatively simple standbys: mostly set tunes such as "Liberty," "Red Wing," and "Maple Sugar." The new generation of fiddlers that grew up as a result of the fiddling revival, in contrast, seemed to draw most of their new tunes from the contemporary Cape Breton and World-Celtic recording scenes. As a result, many tunes that had been popular fifteen years previously were far less frequently played or—in some cases—no longer played at all (for more on the fiddling revival, see chapters 16–17).

Because of a recent rise of interest in American bluegrass music on Prince Edward Island, both old-time and younger-generation fiddlers were becoming increasingly partial to just about any tune that remotely smacked of this genre. Consequently, tunes such as "Ragtime Annie," "Bowing the Strings," "Down Yonder," "Rubber Dolly," and "Faded Love" were achieving increased currency.

Another trend worthy of note was a marked increase both in the number of tunes being composed on Prince Edward Island and in the number of fiddlers engaged in composing them. As noted in chapter 6, only a very few fiddlers were avid composers in 1991–92, and very few locally composed tunes were circulating among other players. In 2006, in contrast, I encountered about thirty-five different composers, and quite a few of the tunes they had composed were in active circulation. Among the most active Island composers in 2006 were Edward P Arsenault, Peter Arsenault, Robert Arsenault, J.J. Chaisson, Kenny Chaisson, Kevin Chaisson, Timothy Chaisson, Roy Johnstone, Marie Arsenault Livingstone, Allan MacDonald, Ward MacDonald, Billy MacInnis Jr., Danielle Ross, Teresa MacPhee Wilson, and Richard Wood.[29]

Although there was little movement among tunes in the top ten, changes in the repertoire become increasingly striking once we move away from the very best known tunes; many tunes that were well established in 1991–92 had virtually dropped from circulation by 2006, while others barely on the radar during the earlier period had become relatively popular. Overall, less than half the tunes collected in 1991–92 were encountered again in 2006. Conversely, about 400 of the 670 different tunes recorded in 2006 (that is, roughly 60 percent of the total) had not been encountered in 1991–92.[30]

Just as significant, some of the most widely played tunes from 1991–92 showed signs of declining popularity. During the earlier project, for example, the tune considered so significant that it virtually defined Island style was "Lord MacDonald's Reel." In 2006, however, the tune was trotted out almost as an afterthought, and renditions seemed almost universally rusty and mechanical. Two other tunes that appeared to be suffering the same fate were "Princess Reel" and "Farmer's Reel."

Interestingly, fully 95 percent of the four hundred newly encountered tunes were each collected from only a single player. This points to a milieu in which musicians acquire new tunes more from outside sources than from each other. Among the most popular newly encountered tunes were "Ashokan Farewell" by Jay Unger, "Carter MacKenzie's Reel" by Kevin Chaisson, "The Mortgage Burn" by Howie MacDonald, and "PEI Ferry Crossing" by Lionel Poirier.

NOTES

1. Although the narrative is aimed primarily at the general reader, this chapter does contain some technical discussion of music, and there is frequent mention of specific tunes. Readers are highly encouraged, therefore, to consult both notation for and recorded versions of as many of the tunes mentioned here as possible. Some resources include Perlman, *Fiddle Music of* PEI (1996) plus its companion disk of field recordings, and a two-CD set of field recordings entitled *The Prince Edward Island Style of Fiddling* (Rounder). Recordings for nearly all the tunes mentioned in this chapter, along with about 150 notations from the 2006 project, have been scheduled for inclusion in a website devoted to traditional PEI fiddling. For more information, see note 4 in the introduction.
2. The actual number collected and identified during the initial project was 592, which includes about a dozen tunes first collected in 1995 during the recording project conducted by the author for Rounder Records.
3. The 1991–92 list also includes the tunes first collected by the author in 1995 during the Rounder Records project.
4. Each fiddle tune almost always has its own assigned key, based on such considerations as fingering convenience, how the melody sounds best on the instrument, and so on.
5. As noted earlier, "Pride of the Ball" also goes by several local names, including "Twin Sisters," "The Queen's Marriage," and "Roddy Joe's Reel."
6. The term *key* in this context is meant to refer to all modes with a common key center. So the "key of A," for example, refers not only to A major but also to the plethora of other A-based modes in circulation on the Island.

7. Organizing music into eight-bar phrases known as *periods* was also standard practice in the art music of that era.
8. Some tunes that were later absorbed into the fiddle tune repertoire appeared in print earlier than this, in such works as John Playford's *English Dancing Master* (1651) and his son Henry Playford's *A Collection of Original Scotch Tunes (Full of the Highland Humours) for the Violin* . . . (1700).
9. The all-too-similar titles of works by these authors are *A Collection of the Newest and Best Reels or Country Dances for the Violin* . . . (1761–64) by Stewart, *Thirty-Seven New Reels and Strathspeys for the Violin* . . . (c. 1776) by Dow, *A Collection of Strathspeys or Old Highland Reels* (1780) by Cumming, and *A Collection of Strathspey Reels* . . . (1781) by Marshall.
10. Their original titles are *A Collection of Strathspey Reels* . . . (6 vols., 1784–1822) and *A Complete Repository of Original Slow Strathspeys and Dances* . . . (vols. 1–3 published 1799–1806; vol. 4 published 1871).
11. For a detailed history of Scottish tune publishing, see Collinson, *Traditional and National Music*, 124–28, 206–27.
12. For information on Irish collections, see Breathnach, *Folk Music and Dances*, 103–16; for Howe, see Sky, "Elias Howe," 10–15.
13. See Emmerson, *Rantin' Pipe*, 55–66; and Emmerson, *Social History*, 151–53. The dances mentioned in this paragraph are discussed in chapter 12.
14. The actual process of cause and effect may have gone the other way. In other words, Island fiddling mechanics may have evolved primarily with reel-playing in mind.
15. See Emmerson, *Social History*, 205–22. Confusingly, in the sixteenth century, the name *hornpipe* was first applied to an unrelated family of British dance tunes in 3/2 time.
16. In a "dotted" rhythm, the first note of each pair appears in notation to be three times as long as the second note. In practice, generally the first note of each pair is only twice as long.
17. The Scotch measure was a dance-tune genre popular in the pre-fiddle-tune era. The polka originated in eastern Europe but was widely danced in Britain, Ireland, and North America during the second half of the nineteenth century.
18. See Emmerson, *Social History*, 193–96; Alburger, *Scottish Fiddlers*, 32; and Breathnach, *Folk Music and Dances*, 36, 58.
19. Such tunes probably grew up in association with ballroom quadrille dancing. A very large proportion of recently composed 6/8-time tunes on both Cape Breton and Prince Edward Island are modeled on the musical style of the quadrille jig.
20. Cannon, *Highland Bagpipe*, 46–47, 122–41.
21. Very likely, both forces were at work.
22. The Cape Breton contribution is treated separately from the rest of the Maritimes because of the depth and pervasiveness of its fiddle recording industry; see chapter 13.
23. "Heather on the Hill" was actually dubbed "The Heather Hill" by its composer; Islanders probably conflated its name with that of a song by Frederick Loewe from the 1950s Broadway show *Brigadoon*.
24. MacEachern was a PE Islander, but because he was a member of Don Messer and His Islanders and his tunes were disseminated by Messer, I have included his output here.

25. The year 1940 is a good dividing line because it marks both the dawn of the modernization process in some parts of rural Prince Edward Island and the point at which media influence on the Island fiddling repertoire began to be strongly felt.
26. Gleaned from the following articles in the *Charlottetown Guardian*: "Old Timers Fiddling Contest at the Strand," Mar. 30, 1926, 1ff.; "Old Timers Fiddling Contest Again Meets with Popular Favor," Mar. 31, 1926, 1ff.; "Neil Cheverie Will Represent the Island in Fiddle Contest," Apr. 1, 1926, 1ff. It is obvious from the text that reporters did not make an effort to list all tunes played.
27. "George Chappelle" (typescript), Betty Rogers Large Papers, PEI Archive, Box 4268, Box 2. The presence of "St. Anne's Reel" in this list indicates that media influence on Island repertoire was already having an effect.
28. When it was first introduced, "Princess Reel" was known as either "Charlie's Reel" or "Silver Wedding Reel." "Farmer's Reel" is usually known off-Island as "Golden Wedding Reel."
29. In 2011, fiddler Anastasia DesRoches published a collection of nearly three hundred fiddle tunes by over thirty Island composers of Acadian descent; the title is *Le vent dans les voiles* (in English, *Wind in the Sails*). See Forsyth, "De par chez nous," 234–38, 332–33.
30. This last figure somewhat exaggerates the level of change in the repertoire. Undoubtedly, some tunes that had indeed been in circulation in 1991–92 were simply never played during any of our recording sessions.

CHAPTER FIFTEEN
"It's Amazing How Quick It Did Go Down"
–Kenny Chaisson, Bear River, Kings County

Accounts differ widely as to when the decline of fiddling on Prince Edward Island actually got under way. As noted in chapter 11, during the media buildup preceding the Great Contest of 1926, the *Charlottetown Guardian* declared that fiddling had "been allowed to decline sadly from its former prominence" and that it had been "outgrown with the advent of radio and gasoline."[1] This assessment—which may have been based more on events in mainstream North America than on local conditions—turned out to be ahead of its time by a few decades. Nevertheless, many of the same social, cultural, and technological forces that brought about the demise of old-time fiddling and square dancing in mainstream North America would eventually make their way to Prince Edward Island and make themselves felt.

Comparing fiddlers' accounts makes it clear that the onset and process of decline for both fiddling and fiddle dances on the Island was not uniform. Instead, it occurred in different communities at different times, depending on a variety of local factors, such as proximity to Charlottetown, Summerside, or other sizeable towns; where and when certain technologies were first introduced; the preexisting strength of local fiddling and dance traditions; and preferences of influential individuals.

Some fiddlers trace the falling off of fiddling and community dances in their districts to the aftereffects of the Second World War. As Archie Stewart of Milltown Cross, Kings County, recalls, "There was still lots of house parties and dances in the halls, but it never was as prominent after the war as it was before the war." The dynamic stressed here is that the young men and women who went overseas returned home with marked differences in tastes and outlook.

> Most of the young people that were attending the house parties were in the services. When they came back they weren't so interested, and when I came back there was very little square dancing here. It was mostly what they call modern dancing: foxtrots and waltzes. (Neil MacCannell: b. Lorne Valley, Kings County)

> The house parties went for a little after the war, but not much. They died right down; I'm sure they did. The war changed a lot of people, eh. It changed their style of life, I think. I was different myself when I come back. (Ervan Sonier: Summerside, Prince County)

In other parts of the Island, community fiddle dances continued unabated for a decade or two longer. Jimmy O'Connor of Murray Harbour, Kings County, and Jimmy Halliday of Eldon, Queens County, for example, both estimate that the onset of decline in southeastern Prince Edward Island was in the mid-1950s. George MacPhee and his sister Teresa MacPhee Wilson of Monticello note that there was no real falling off of fiddling and fiddle dances on the Northeast Cape of Kings County until the late 1950s or early '60s. Harry Lecky of Milburn, in contrast, indicates that these activities were not on the wane in his part of western Prince County until the late 1960s.

Regardless of when fiddling first began to "go down," most fiddlers agree that by the 1970s the art was moribund throughout the Island. Most of them explain its continued falling off in more or less the same terms. In general, the decline of fiddling was traceable to changes in rural community life. These changes in turn were brought about by the introduction of twentieth-century technology on the one hand and by the implementation of government social policies on the other.

"Things Started Changing, and They Went at a Gallop"

The important technological changes that characterized twentieth-century life in much of Europe and North America—automobile travel and paved roads, mechanized agriculture, electricity, and mass communications—all came relatively late to rural Prince Edward Island. Because they were introduced at more or less the same time, their effects were all the more profound. Here is how Merlin Quinn of Cardross, Kings County, sums it up:

> I seen a lot of changes. I seen probably more changes in my lifetime than my father or grandfather, or perhaps grandfather before that. Because my father just pretty well lived and done things exactly the same as his father. The way of farming, the way of life was pretty much the same. But as I came of age, things started changing, and they went at a gallop. I wouldn't say that I'm sad about it or bitter. It's just a thing that changed. And everything *has* changed!

Horse-drawn transportation was the norm in most rural parts of the Island until well past the midpoint of the twentieth century.[2] The first paved road on the Island—connecting Charlottetown with Summerside—was built in 1935, but the majority of Island roads were not paved or plowed in winter until the late 1950s and early '60s. Automobiles first appeared in substantial numbers after the Second World War, but again it was not until the 1950s and '60s that automobile travel on the Island became commonplace.

The methods and technology of farming saw little change in most Island communities from the late nineteenth century, when horse-drawn farm machinery was introduced, until the 1950s, when tractors began to appear in serious numbers on local farms. George MacPhee (b. 1940) remembers, "When I was a little fella they used horses here—Be no tractor. Done all the work with the horses." Similarly, Reg Banks of Poplar Point, Kings County (b. 1923), notes, "I worked the horses from when I was twelve or fourteen years old right up till the '60s. I had the first tractor in the settlement, matter of fact."

The 1950s and '60s also saw the coming of rural electrification.[3] Most fiddlers have fairly clear memories of when electric power first came to their districts. Edwin Simmons of Darnley, Queens County, for example, recalls, "Back in the early '50s there was a lot of the Island that didn't have the hydro to it. My community didn't have it till '57, '58."[4] Similarly, Teresa MacPhee Wilson notes, "Electricity didn't come up on this line here until 1955. The road was paved all other places, but this was dirt road at that time. So the secondary roads didn't get the electricity until after the pavement on the roads."

Because those families who lived far off the road sometimes had to pay for their own extension lines, some Islanders went unconnected to the hydro until well into the 1960s. Louise Arsenault of Mont Carmel, Prince County, for example, tells this story:

PHOTO 15.1. *LEFT TO RIGHT*: LOUISE ARSENAULT WITH HER MOTHER, MARIE, AND SISTER, ZELMA, AT ST. TIMOTHÉE, NOVEMBER 2006 (PHOTO BY KEN PERLMAN).

We decided to plant a big cucumber garden so we could help our parents to get electricity in our house. We planted a big field of cucumbers and pumpkins, and we were going from house to house selling them. Anyways, we got enough that we put everything together, and we helped Mom and Dad to get our electricity. And my grandfather bought a television around the same time, and we got the phone around the same time. I remember that well. It would've been about 1963, the same time as I started my music.

The transition to electrified living was not without its difficulties. The electrical grid was fairly delicate at first, and nearly every time there was an electrical storm, a snowstorm, or other severe weather, something would go awry along the transmission lines and all the power in a given area would go down. According to Jackie Biggar (b. Tyne Valley, Prince County), as soon as the power in his house failed, out came the instruments, and family members would spend the rest of the evening playing music. One night as they were playing, lightning hit the transformer across the road, and some of the energy jumped to the metal strings of his father's fiddle and sister's mandolin: "They got a hell of a hoist! It was half an hour, an hour before the feeling started to come back; the whole left arm was tinglin' from the electricity."[5]

With the coming of electric power came major changes in available mass media technology. For one thing, both spring-powered gramophones and battery-powered radios were soon superseded by electric-powered phonographs and plug-in radios. In addition, because this period also coincided with the development of television as a widespread consumer product, televisions soon began to appear in rural Island homes. As Edwin Simmons recalls, the first such devices to come into an area created quite a sensation: "We used to walk I don't know how many miles across the fields to see TV one night a week. That was the big thing."

Policies put into play by both the Canadian federal government and the province would also serve as major factors. In 1951, per capita income on Prince Edward Island was still only 50 percent of the Canadian average. To ameliorate this state of affairs, in the 1950s the Canadian federal government began implementation of a program known as the National Policy, which provided generous income support programs such as Unemployment Insurance, Family Allowance, and Old Age Security; it also provided for public health care and standardized, publicly financed education.[6] In 1969, the province joined with the federal government to establish a program aimed at improving the Island economy, known as the Comprehensive Development Plan; its mandate was to address such issues as "educational reform, rural decline, tourism development, economic diversification, [and] transportation improvements."[7]

"So That Part of the Social Life Is Lost"

Each aspect of modernity undermined the tightly knit social bonds of the rural district. To begin with, the coming of paved roads and widespread automobile travel meant that leaving the immediate area—for shopping, work, or even recreation—was no longer a major undertaking. As community members ventured farther afield, each district no longer seemed the center of the universe. In the words of Jimmy Halliday, "With cars and all, people go in all directions, and it would be hard to get the community together." Similarly, Jenny O'Hanley McQuaid (b. Naufrage, Kings County) observes, "Once you got where people could own cars and travel away from their area in distances, and roads to go with it—I think the car was a major factor in changing the tenor of small areas. Everybody saw the world outside and were drawn into it."

As agriculture mechanized, farmers could get by with fewer hands. Consequently, the labor of family offspring was needed less at home, and neighbors were not called upon as often to help with such heavy tasks as seeding, plowing, and harvesting. At the same time, improved transportation allowed producers from across Canada to compete with local suppliers. Farms began to fold, and in some areas the country began to depopulate: a state of affairs that was amplified by a systematic policy aimed at reducing the number of small, "unproductive" farms put into place under the Comprehensive Development Plan.[8] Along these lines, Stewart MacIntyre (b. Fairfield, Kings County) describes the disappearance of dairying on the Northeast Cape of Kings County.

> Now there's just two dairymen in that area. That's all that's left. Most of the young people went somewhere else, you see. You might not see a cow [on the north side] from East Point to St. Peters now, or a horse for that matter. [On the south side,] there isn't a dairy farm from East Point to Souris.

Another factor that unwittingly led to a substantial decrease in the number of working farms on Prince Edward Island was the generous unemployment insurance plan put into place under the National Policy. Under this plan, any Islander who could put together approximately three months of wage employment (the exact number of weeks required has varied) was entitled to be supported for the rest of the year at about 75 percent of his or her average earning rate. Because mixed farming—which required constant hard work and was often a subsistence operation at best—did not qualify as salaried employment, this created a tremendous incentive to abandon this means of support in favor of just about any kind of job that paid a documented wage.

The National Policy also included a plan for school consolidation; all the hundreds of one-room rural schoolhouses were to be replaced by a small number of centralized schools. Consolidation was initiated on the secondary school level in 1958 and was extended to the elementary level in 1965. In 1972, as an outgrowth of the Comprehensive Development Plan, the original 217 school districts across Prince Edward Island were regrouped into 5, and all rural schools ceased operations.[9] Consolidation also contributed to the decay of district social life. As noted in chapters 1 and 2, providing for the upkeep of one-room rural schools had been a major focus for community attention and activity. When the one-room school passed from the scene, a major element that held district people together went with it.

When asked what they most miss about the old days, most Islanders lament the passing of neighborliness—the network of caring and close friendships that often forms naturally in tightly knit communities. As for the factor most responsible for its decline, these same Islanders almost always single out the introduction of television. TV provided an intoxicating alternative to the constant stream of visiting that had been an integral part of district life. And when people did come to call, the presence of television tended to significantly reduce communication between host and visitor. In the words of Joe MacDonald of St. Andrews, Kings County, "People'd rather sit home now and watch television than go to visit their neighbors, and it's just the way things transpired. So that part of the social life is lost."

"The Music Was Kind of Pushed Aside"

All these trends in district life affected the demand for fiddling. For one thing, communities no longer needed to hold so many benefit events. Farming and other forms of labor were now mechanized, so fiddle dances were not required to harness community labor. And once the rural schools were gone, the dances that had been used for generations to raise funds for their support became obsolete.

As neighborliness declined, so did the demand for house parties and other expressions of community good-fellowship. This trend was amplified by the spread of automobile travel, which made a variety of competing leisure activities—such as going on excursions, watching movies in theaters, eating in restaurants, and visiting far afield—accessible to the average Islander.

Another important consequence of the breakdown of neighborliness and the rise of automobile travel was a nearly universal change in venue for wedding celebrations. Instead of using local homes for the purpose, Islanders increasingly moved these festivities into hired halls located in towns and urban centers. At such events, music would be provided by bands that played mostly "modern" music, not by community fiddlers (more on this later).

Of all the competing leisure activities to appear in the wake of modernization, watching television was probably the most potent in terms of drawing away interest from community fiddle dances. Here's how Wilfred Gotell of Georgetown, Kings County, describes it:

> I think when television came in the houses, that's when the house parties really died down. Because before TV there was nothing else to do. But then television

came, and you weren't playing music. You don't go and meet your neighbor, or go down to where we used to have the parties. You don't seem to associate so much with your neighbors, and you miss that, too, you know. I blame it on the television, anyway. It's one of the big factors, I think.

Television also affected music making within the home. As Louise Arsenault points out, the constant stream of playing, jigging, singing, and dancing that had filled the evenings for many an Island family was suddenly faced with powerful competition.

> Once we got the television, it was a big excitement, so it seems to me like the music was kind of pushed aside a little bit there, you know. I remember that very well. I wouldn't spend so much time on my violin, and I would want to say no when my father and mother would say, "They want you to go and play." I think I would hesitate there at times because there were certain programs on the TV I wanted to watch.

With house parties and weddings no longer a major presence in district life, Islanders began to make certain changes in their homes that cemented this trend in place. For example, as Jimmy Halliday tells us, families began laying wall-to-wall carpet in the parlor, where bare wooden floors had previously provided an excellent medium for dancing.

> [*Question*: When did the dances decline?] When they started to put carpet on. People are pretty particular now, you know. You went in, let's say in the wintertime: boots, shoes, you know. But you won't get away with that now! You'll have to take your shoes off at the door most houses, and you couldn't dance anywhere.

Much more significant was a change in average kitchen size. In the old days, houses were built with kitchens large enough to accommodate the dancing of a square set. Beginning in the 1950s, as Eddy Arsenault of St. Chrysostom, Prince County, reports, most new homes were no longer built with this idea in mind.

> They used to have dances in the kitchen, because everybody had big kitchens. Now they're all small kitchens—Couldn't have a dance in a kitchen like this. But years back, the kitchen was the biggest room in the house. Now there's no more square dance. They're so scarce now, it's not even funny!

The Dance Halls

Although the onset of the modern era may have greatly reduced the number of house parties and other dances on the district level, it made possible the growth of a new venue for fiddle dances: the regional dance hall. Now that

Islanders could get around by automobile, those who still enjoyed dancing square sets could congregate in large numbers in centralized locations.

Some of these regional dances were run by charitable organizations to raise money for a cause; others were set up by independent promoters in hopes of turning a profit. They were held in community halls, in converted barns and warehouses, or in buildings specially constructed for the purpose. As noted in chapter 7, the fiddlers who provided music for these events were generally paid for their services.

Commercial dance halls featuring fiddling and square sets began to appear in Prince County as early as the mid-1930s. When Leo Farrell (b. 1916) of Central Lot 16, Prince County, was a young man, he found that he could earn more spending money by playing at dance halls than by hiring himself out for farmwork. By the late 1930s and early '40s, he was playing fairly regularly at several rural dance halls within roughly a twenty-five-mile radius of his home, in such districts as Borden, Traveler's Rest, Sherbrooke, Miscouche, Wellington, Grand River, Port Hill, and Portage. Two factors made setting up such a circuit possible: the Great Western Road—the first major road to be built in western Prince Edward Island—had just been completed, and Farrell was one of the first people in his region to own an automobile.[10]

Farrell had "retired" from dance playing and was farming full time by the mid-1940s when fiddler John Gauthier (b. Stanhope, Queens County) joined up with Tudor Baker on piano and Keith Robinson on guitar to form the Prince County Pioneers. The Pioneers—which for a while was the only touring band on the Prince County dance circuit—played at many of the same halls where Farrell had played and also played at The Diner in Summerside, at Northam Racetrack, and in Alberton. For transportation, the band chipped in and bought a 1920s-era automobile from Keith Rogers, the Charlottetown man who had founded radio station CFCY (see chapter 14). The car was so spacious that a couple of times when the Pioneers invited Don Messer's bassist Duke Nielson to join them, he was able to easily fit his "bull fiddle" in the back seat.[11]

In the late 1940s, pianist Lowell Huestis of Summerside founded the Lowell Huestis Orchestra, with a repertoire that featured big band hits, show tunes, and other popular music of that era. Before long, they were playing regularly at many of the same Prince County dance clubs that Farrell and Gauthier had frequented. As a concession to those who still preferred old-time music and dance, Huestis would often bring along a fiddler to play for a couple of square sets over the course of the evening. His favorite fiddler for the job was Russell Warren of Miminegash, Prince County, whose playing figured prominently on *West Prince Party Line*, the show Huestis would later host on CJRW radio (see chapter 14).[12]

Charlottetown had a few commercial venues in the 1940s and '50s that regularly featured square dancing. According to Billy MacInnis, Sr. (b. Charlottetown), one of the most popular was the Sportin' Club on Grafton Street—later renamed the Rollaway Club—which often featured the music of Don Messer and His Islanders. MacInnis offers this recollection.

> When I was about six or seven, there was a gangway between the Rollaway Club and the duplex building next to it, with a fire escape going up the side of the building. I used to go up that fire escape different nights when Don Messer was playing there and sit on the fire escape with the door open, lookin' in watchin' them playin'. I wasn't old enough to get in there. [Messer and his band] were popular, and back in them days they were playing almost every night of the week.[13]

Another highly popular Charlottetown dance band of that era was led by Pius Blackett, who played Hawaiian (lap) guitar and sang. Like the Huestis Orchestra, Blackett's band played contemporary pop music but had an appended fiddler who over the course of the program played for a couple of square sets. The man Blackett generally hired for that job was George Chappelle, who had been the last local fiddler to feature prominently on Island radio before the onset of the Don Messer era.[14]

By the 1950s, dance halls were also well established in rural Queens and Kings Counties. Stephen Toole of Green Road, Queens County, for example, notes that in the early 1950s he played for two years at a dance hall adjoining the nearby Bonshaw Inn and that "large crowds came, two hundred probably." Similarly, Johnny Joe Chaisson of Souris, Kings County, recalls that beginning in the mid-'50s, he played five nights a week for "near about twelve years" at Clifford Peters' Barn Dance in nearby Rollo Bay. Gary Chipman of Charlottetown describes a typical evening at a dance hall established during the early 1960s in Harrington, Queens County.

> What it was, was just a big hay barn. It had a hayloft in it and a ladder going up into the loft. So you pull in there to take the gear in. You're always about an hour before the dance—nobody around, you couldn't see anything. Then all of a sudden, the cars start pulling in. The field would be full of cars, people start climbing up the ladder and stuff. Well, the people would come in, and they'd have the canteen, and they'd all line up around the sides. There might be a couple hundred people in there if the place was big enough. We'd just start playing at 9:30, and people would be up dancing right from the start to the finish.

One of the largest dance halls in Kings County was the Beaver Club, which was run at Beaver Hall in Montague as a benefit for the local hospital. According to Howard Hancock (b. Belle River, Queens County), on some nights there could be as many as a hundred couples up on the floor.[15] The most prominent fiddler associated with this dance series was Jack Webster of nearby Cardigan. Webster was probably the most popular dance fiddler of his era throughout the eastern half of the Island, and he took on a sizable share of the available dance hall work.[16] According to Neil MacCannell (b. Lorne Valley), he "provided a good lively beat for the dancers, and we thought there was nobody like him." Reg Banks explains in part some of Webster's appeal.

> Sometimes fiddlers would go into a hall and have break after break. People would be settin' around not getting a chance to dance. But when Jack Webster went into the hall, he played right straight through the whole night. He never stopped. He'd play

PHOTO 15.2. WARD MACDONALD (FIDDLE) WITH HIS FATHER ALLAN MACDONALD, AT BANGOR, PEI, OCTOBER 2006 (PHOTO BY KEN PERLMAN).

roughly three hours with hardly ever a break. People appreciated that. He was quite a nice, pleasant man to talk to, and he was sociable. Everybody liked Jack Webster.[17]

In the mid-1960s, Hector MacDonald of Bangor, Kings County, decided he wanted to build a dance hall on his property. His son Allan MacDonald, who assisted him on the project, tells this story:

> And that spring we hauled [wood] to the mill and got it sawed, and built a big dance hall that he was wishin' he had. We thought it was pretty big, but it was only twenty-four by forty [feet]. The house [we live in] is twice as big as that now. And then we started playin' every Thursday, and it was that full, nobody had hardly any room to dance. So we [also] had to pick another night. We picked a Monday night to get clear of the other parties around the community, and we played Mondays and Thursdays and they were both pretty full.[18]

"Nobody Gets Up and Knows What to Do"

These dance halls provided a decidedly different environment from what had prevailed at the old district house parties and benefit dances. The spaces were much bigger, the crowds attending were many times as large, and—most significantly—people hailed from many different communities. The ensuing chaotic conditions had a major impact on the development of Island fiddling and dance during this period.

One major factor that complicated the fiddler's job playing at the old dance halls involved dealing with "crowd control." The tendency toward drink-induced violence that had long been associated with Island dances was often exacerbated in these new, larger halls, where aggressive impulses were no longer tempered by the need to maintain community relationships. For one thing, as Ivan Day of Kensington, Prince County, observes, the setting proved to be an ideal forum for settling grudges.

> There was always a little rivalry between different communities. There still is today; look at the hockey teams. The same thing back then, and there'd be two or three from one community, and they'd be out to get somebody from another community. And that guy would get a bunch of guys with him: "We'll settle it tomorrow night at the dance."[19]

According to John Gauthier, by the mid-1940s, coping with violent or otherwise unruly behavior at Island dance halls had become a major problem for both musicians and organizers. In fact, fights broke out so frequently at one dance hall in Traveler's Rest, Prince County, that it was nicknamed the Bucket of Blood. As Gauthier describes it, "I'm quite sure at the end of when we were playing there, that people went there for the fight and not for the dance."[20]

As discussed in chapter 12, one major source of friction at these events was competition for room on the floor while dancing Island quadrilles. To neutralize this potential flash point, the relatively space-intensive square formation was ultimately jettisoned, and all dancers present would simply form one or more large circles.

These "big-circle" quadrille sets made working a dance very tough on the fiddler. Probably the worst offender here was the swing-all-'round figure, in which each dancer swings and promenades in turn with every opposite-sex dancer. With a four-couple set, swing-all-'round made for but a few minutes' worth of playing. But in dance halls where ten, twenty, or more couples joined together to form one big set, the fiddler was looking at the fairly Herculean task of playing full tilt for up to half an hour with no break. As Leonard McDonald of Emyvale, Queens County, recalls, "If it was a big dance, it was complete murder. Because it could last forever; there could be fifty people in the set!" Similarly, Peter Doiron (b. North Rustico, Queens County) recalls, "By the time the fiddler has swung about fifteen or twenty couples, he's ready to swing out himself, eh!" Wilfred Gotell describes it as follows:

> The last figure was grand chain around and swing your partner. Perhaps you'd do it three or four times, and the set would be over. But the later years after the war was over, they'd all join in. Perhaps it was, say, twelve different sets on the floor and they'd all join in. That would make forty-eight couples, eh. And they'd all want to swing everyone in the hall when they're grand chainin'. We used to get played out; we'd just carry on so long, and then quit and that was it. There used to be an awful lot of moans and groans, but we just couldn't keep it up. But they liked to do it, and that's the way it carried on.

Another legacy from this period was a general decline in the complexity of quadrille steps and a decrease in the number of figures. Routines that did not work from circular formations were discarded, steps distinctive to particular Island communities fell by the wayside, and most maneuvers that took time to learn or required close coordination among dancers were abandoned. Similarly, the number of figures danced at regional dance halls decreased from the previously customary four to just two or three. At some halls, all figures were joined together, and the whole dance would be conducted nonstop. Eddie Martin of Eldon, Queens County, for example, offers this recollection:

> You see, when we first played, they'd dance one of those figures and stop. And we'd stop and play a different tune then. The last years they got so they kept on going,

and it got awful tiresome. Even to change to a different tune is kind of restful, you know, it's a help. But boy, they went on and on!

For Largus MacInnis of Lakeville, Kings County, these newer versions of the quadrille were merely "hogwrastles." Similarly, Leonard McDonald asserts, "Now everybody gets out and everybody does something different, and they don't go through the dance properly. It's almost obsolete because nobody gets up and knows what to do." Jimmy Banks of Poplar Point, Kings County, describes it as follows:

> I get a kick out of them now. They don't even do them. I know I often used to be playin' at dances years gone by when my family were young, and I used to say to [the dancers], "What in the heck, I'm sitting down there playin' for you and I'm playin' the same thing over and over again, 'cause you're only dancin' one part of that quadrille, and there's four more parts!" But they said, "Nobody ever learned us, so how we gonna know?" That was the answer they'd give you—Nobody instructin' them, and that's the trouble! They're just pickin' up little parts of the dance and mixin' it all up. It wasn't properly done.

The dance halls also had an unfortunate effect on Island fiddling style and repertoire. For one thing, with fiddlers' playing energies constantly overtaxed, trends were soon under way toward simplification of tune versions and toward using simpler and simpler tunes for dance accompaniment. In an effort to save wear and tear, for example, fiddlers during this era often substituted set tunes (which have fewer notes per beat) for more "notey" reels. Moreover, the search was clearly on for set tunes with fewer and fewer notes. In fact, one tune used fairly frequently to accompany the swing-all-'round figure during the 1950s and '60s was "Jingle Bells."

Dance halls packed with large, unruly crowds also created acoustical problems. In the absence of amplification, dancers often had trouble hearing the violin and sticking to the beat. Because the fiddler and his accompanists had to work hard to be heard under these conditions, there was plenty of incentive to avoid paying attention to finesse, expression, and other fine points. And although electronic pickups (amplification devices) were adopted by many fiddlers when they became available, the kind of pickups and amplification systems in general use on Prince Edward Island during that era produced a strident, unattractive fiddle tone that greatly diminished the overall appeal of the music.

By the 1960s, both fiddlers and dancers were growing increasingly disaffected with the dance hall scene. Fiddlers were unhappy with playing conditions and the degeneration of the dances, while many dancers became more and more fed up with the continual drunken disorderliness that characterized many of these events. Many dance halls were shut down because organizers despaired of ever being able to rein in attendees' behavior. Reg Banks, for example, describes the demise of one long-running commercial dance in northern Kings County.

> Down here in Little Pond they had a big dance hall and I played there every Friday night back in the '60s—Probably about 1965 they quit. A lot of people came to it, but they had a lot of trouble around the hall. As a matter of fact, lads come there pretty well ginned up—And them scraps! At the last, they had to close the hall down, and that's about the size of it.

When continued organizer disaffection and declining attendance during the 1970s forced most of the rest of the dance halls to close down, few mourned their passing.

Toward the end of the dance hall era, other trends were threatening the fiddle's dominance on Prince Edward Island as a dance-accompaniment instrument. As early as the 1940s and '50s, bands such as the Lowell Huestis Orchestra and Pius Blackett Band had pioneered the practice of appending an old-time fiddler to an ensemble that otherwise featured pop music; by the 1970s, this pattern had become the rule at nearly all Island dances and weddings. From that time through the 1990s, the typical Island dance band played a rock 'n' roll or country music repertoire and consisted of a guitar-vocalist, a keyboard player, a bassist, and perhaps a drummer. To appease the "older folks," however, most such bands would also have a fiddler on their roster. While the band performed its modern repertoire, the fiddler generally played along unobtrusively in the background. He or she would then provide the lead for a couple of square sets and perhaps a few waltzes over the course of a given program.

"The Young People's Not Interested in the Violin"

The overall decline in community music making naturally had a profound effect on Island youngsters. As house parties, benefit dances, and old-fashioned wedding celebrations became less common, young people were not sufficiently exposed to fiddling or square dancing to develop an appreciation for them. Similarly, with impromptu music making and dancing in the homes on the decline, they had less opportunity to become familiar with the old tunes or to observe playing techniques firsthand. Not surprisingly, one of the first consequences of this state of affairs was a marked decrease in the number of youngsters interested in taking up the fiddle. As Stephen Toole recounts, "I think the reason why the fiddlin' started to go back on Prince Edward Island was there wasn't too many learning. There wasn't all that many learned from the '50s [on]—Just the odd one."

Even in fiddling households, where it had been the norm for offspring to follow in a parent's musical footsteps, recruits to the instrument often failed to materialize. As Jackie Webster of Cardigan, Kings County, observes, "The young people's not interested in the violin anymore; I got four children, and they wouldn't look at the violin with me." Archie Stewart puts it this way:

> This is my father's violin. And this violin is the same age as I am. This fiddle was bought the year I was born [1917], and he passed the fiddle down to me. And this fiddle goes to my oldest daughter. [*Question*: Does she play?] No, she doesn't play. Not one of my children played. I had four girls and a boy, and not one of them plays.

Decreased exposure was only one of many factors that contributed to this falling off of interest among Island youngsters in taking up fiddle playing. Some other factors include the development of age stratification within rural communities, educational and social pressures resulting from the consolidation of schools, competition from popular music piped in via the mass media, and the development of an adolescent subculture.

In the old days, youngsters were full-fledged participants in a flourishing local social life. Young and old worked together, danced together, and conversed freely during the continual rounds of visiting. As neighborliness declined, however, all this changed. What socializing there was began to stratify by age group, and—when dancing moved out of the communities into regional dance halls—youngsters often found that they were excluded from participating. Teresa Wilson offers this account:

> Kids got separated from the parents. The adults started having bars at dances with a license to sell liquor, and children weren't allowed to go. And that is one of the big barriers that they set up between children and adults. We can blame ourselves for a lot of it. Years ago, if it was a wedding or dance, or a dance at the school or at the hall, the children went too. But then, when they had a license to sell liquor or alcohol, children weren't allowed in under drinking age, so there was sort of a barrier set up. Then the children got a different type of music goin', and they got on their own, and this separation came.

In the one-room schoolhouses, fiddle music and square dancing had often been woven into the day's schedule. In the new consolidated schools with their strictly formal attitude toward education and rigid schedules, however, there was no place for such activities. Jenny McQuaid describes the situation.

> The structure would be so different: the bells and so on. They went on buses, you had maybe a half hour of lunch—And going from class to class. There's just no time in that structured education. Whereas at noon hour in our one-room schools, well, we didn't go anywhere. We were in the same room when we ate our lunch. We tuned and sang while we ate,[21] and if you went over an hour for lunch, it didn't matter greatly. The atmosphere that consolidated schools had wouldn't lend itself to anything, only army-type regimentation—And hollerin', and lockers squealin', and doors slammin', and all this kind of thing.

There's another consideration here as well. In the one-room schoolhouses, youngsters pursued their studies in a warm, nonpressured atmosphere surrounded by siblings, relatives, and friends. Consolidated schools, in contrast, not only brought together strangers from different rural districts but also mixed rural children fresh from one-room schools with more sophisticated children from more densely populated parts of the Island. According to Jenny McQuaid, this created a situation in which spontaneous music making and dance of any kind would be subject to the not-always-kind responses of strangers.

> If you got people together who knew one another well enough, they'd dare to sit down and jig,[22] and talk and tune. You've got to know somebody fairly well before you sit down and display your talents to them. All that would be gone by the wayside once you'd get into a consolidated school, where rural kids get in with more-urbanite people. Urban kids would probably be dressed differently or better and would have talked differently, would seemingly be sitting on top of the world with their fancy books and schoolbags and all the rest. Some kids, it may make them more proud of their situation, but probably I think that [most of them] would probably recede a little bit. They would just leave all that other stuff home, and not bother.

As exposure to—and interest in—traditional music waned, television and plug-in radio served as a conduit for the importation of alternative forms of music. Because the spread of both media on Prince Edward Island coincided with the ascendancy of youth-oriented rock 'n' roll music in North American popular culture, this was bound to have a significant impact on Island youngsters. Here's how Kenny Chaisson describes it:

> The radio brought a lot of fiddle music with it, but it also brought a lot of other-type music that helps steer the people away with something new. Like, we've had the violin so long here on the Island, and this other music comes along—Something like going from the horse and the cart to the car, you know. It's just a change, and it took off. And I think the violin got left backstage.

By the 1960s, many Island youngsters had adopted contemporary commercial pop music and its associated dancing styles as their own. As far as they could see, playing and appreciating fiddle music and dancing square sets were of interest only to older generations. Before long, musically inclined youngsters were taking up guitar in lieu of fiddle, and they were playing rock 'n' roll or country music instead of jigs and reels. Dave Thomson (b. West Royalty, Queens County) notes, for example, "When I was younger, it was all Elvis Presley, you know: '56, '57. And that's what everybody done; you got a guitar and learned Elvis Presley or some of that stuff." Similarly, Gary Chipman (b. Charlottetown) observes, "After I got to be about fifteen [1959], fellows like Bill Haley and those guys came along then, and the fiddle dropped out. So I put the fiddle away for a number of years and picked up the guitar."

As Island youngsters increasingly identified with a larger world outside, they also began adopting its performance values—particularly in regard to the slick presentation styles put forward through films and television by pop artists of that era. In comparison, the plain manner and informal presentation styles of local musicians would have seemed quaint at best.

> If you had people who were performers who sang, and they had all kinds of equipment [for] their voices and the instruments and the music—The little jigging and tuning and fiddling around home sounded rather mediocre, you know. It didn't measure up to the pros, I guess. (Jenny McQuaid)
>
> Once you see TV you get all the lifestyle, and bobby-socker,[23] and all this—And here's some old feller in a beard sittin' back and playin the fiddle. Well, what are they goin' to relate to? (Edwin Simmons)

As an adolescent subculture became firmly established on the Island, any youngster who did take up the fiddle was seen as conforming to the values of the older generation. The ensuing negative social pressure was usually sufficient to make a budding fiddler give up the instrument. That this state of affairs was still going strong in the 1990s is attested to by fiddle instructor Kathryn Dau-Schmidt.[24]

> My [main] problem is about grade six with the boys and grade eight with the girls. You lose them because they have a lot of peer pressure, that it's not very cool to play fiddle. They say that there's nothing said to them but it's just something that they feel. It's just not very cool to be playing this old-fashioned music. And at Vernon River School, the girls hit grade eight and that's it, they're pretty much gone! In grade seven, you can see they're starting to waver a bit. I had one [Vernon River] girl come for instruction for a whole year in Charlottetown 'cause then her friends wouldn't know she was taking it.

Even when a youngster had an interest in pursuing traditional fiddling, a shortage of competent, systematic instruction often proved an important obstacle. In the old days, youngsters learned fiddle technique through emulation, and they learned tunes through frequent exposure. With not much fiddling going on and few opportunities to hear tunes or watch experienced musicians play, however, it would be difficult for youngsters to learn the requisite skills and repertoire without some kind of formal training.

No such training was available, however. Most old-time fiddlers were uncomfortable with the whole notion of teaching an instrument. For one thing, many felt that their inability to read music automatically disqualified them from teaching. And because they had learned instinctively and without the benefit of instruction, they had no idea how to communicate their playing skills.

Diehards

Although fiddling was rapidly losing its centrality in community life, there were still hundreds of accomplished fiddlers on the Island who enjoyed the act of playing music and sharing their art with others. Even after the process of modernization had taken hold in their respective districts, there were still a few avenues open to them that offered at least some musical satisfaction. Such activities included playing at dance halls, participating in fiddle contests or benefit concerts, and meeting regularly with accompanists or other fiddlers to "have a few tunes."

In an effort to recapture the intensity and excitement of the old community dances, several fiddlers from a given region would sometimes join together with local accompanists, step dancers, and other old-time music aficionados to create their own music-and-dance parties. Whereas the house parties of old had involved virtually the entire community, these new parties were essentially gatherings of like-minded individuals who shared a common interest. Ernie Gallant of Egmont Bay, Prince County, for example, remembers that when he was growing up in the Evangeline Coast region during the 1960s and '70s, there would be several parties per week involving the same crew of musicians and enthusiasts, who also took turns serving as hosts. The ladies would be in the kitchen all day preparing traditional Acadian fare such as *paté* and *fricot*,[25] the company would gather together, and the musicians would play all night. There would be very little square dancing at these events, but people would occasionally get up to step-dance.[26] When musician Roy Johnstone moved to Prince Edward Island from Winnipeg in 1977, he caught the tail end of this musical milieu and was deeply moved by its intensity.[27] Although this round of continual partying was gone by the mid-1980s, occasional music parties featuring the remnants of this crew were still being held in the Evangeline Coast region well into the 1990s.

Similarly, Jackie Biggar offers this description of the music parties that took place at his uncle's place near Tyne Valley during the 1960s:

> He'd have three or four parties during the summer, nine o'clock to two or three in the morning. A lot of people would go just to swing [their partners], and they'd start a square dance and you'd start swingin', and they'd just swing and swing and swing; and my God, some of them could just go like ninety mile an hour, like good at it, it just came natural to them. You had to play pretty sharp; they liked theirs stepped up pretty good, eh. It was a lot of fun. It was just the place to be; if you were a relative or a good friend you'd be there. Put the fiddle down a while, [eat] and tell jokes. And after the break was over, back at 'er again![28]

Robert Crane (b. Riverton, Kings County) reports that big music parties were still held in his area well into the 1980s. One time, "a few come in and give us the house warmin'. Eight fiddlers, about eight guitar players—Holy Jesus, fiddlin' and guitars, and dancin' in the kitchen till four o'clock in the morning!"[29] Along these lines, this writer can recall attending several music parties in northeastern Kings County during the 1991–92 project that more or less fit the above description. Some were hosted by the Chaisson family of Bear River; others were organized by friends and neighbors of George MacPhee of Monticello. Taking their example, at various times the Earthwatch research team issued invitations to local musicians and sponsored a few such events at our own headquarters.

The End of an Era

By the early 1970s, Island fiddling was clearly in trouble. There was relatively little public exposure for the art, and what exposure there was often presented it in an unattractive light. Interest in dancing square sets was also rapidly eroding, and the spread of simplified, hybrid versions of the quadrille probably did as much as anything to further this trend. Even more ominous for the future of Island fiddling was that few if any youngsters were taking up the instrument. And because there were very few practitioners under the age of thirty, it looked like only a matter of time before the art passed from the scene. Moreover, most of those youngsters who became alienated from fiddling and fiddle music during this period remained alienated, even as the revival gathered steam. At the time of the 1991–92 project, fiddlers were plentiful over the age of forty-five and under the age of fifteen, but in between—representing Islanders who reached adolescence roughly between the years 1955 and 1985—there were just a handful. From the point of view of fiddling, this group surely represents a lost generation.

There was another factor at work here as well. Fiddling had long been held responsible for much of the atmosphere of alcoholism and violence at Island dance events. By the 1970s, many Islanders—especially those who saw themselves as responsible and forward thinking— began to turn their backs on their entire musical heritage. As far as they were concerned, fiddlers were by and large just a bunch of old, not especially talented alcoholics, and fiddle dances were merely places to congregate for old-fashioned people with a taste for mayhem. For these "forward-thinking" Islanders, it was time for sensible people to say goodbye to these unsavory aspects of their past and find other ways to occupy spare time.

As this trend set in, the effect on many fiddlers was psychologically devastating. Although neighbors' unrelenting demands for music had once been irksome, their joyous reaction to fiddling—and the central role it once played in community life—had served for many fiddlers as important sources for feelings of self-worth. With such positive reinforcement gone it was easy to retreat into bitterness and isolation and to see the widespread adoption by Islanders of new leisure activities and new kinds of music as a deeply hurtful and very personal rejection.

NOTES

1. "Ye Old-Time Fiddlers Contest," *Charlottetown Guardian*, Mar. 4, 1926, 1.
2. Importing motor vehicles to Prince Edward Island was at first prohibited and later severely restricted by the provincial legislature, who feared an adverse effect on local horses. See, for example, Cousins, "Horses in the Folklore," 65–72.
3. Rural electrification on Prince Edward Island was first promoted in a 1940s political platform; the process itself took over two decades to complete. See MacDonald, *If You're Stronghearted*, 246–51.
4. At the time our project took place, the term *hydro* was used almost universally to refer to electric power of all kinds (since the early 1970s, most electrical power on Prince Edward Island has been derived from the James Bay hydroelectric project in Québec).
5. Jackie Biggar, personal interview, Nov. 23, 2006, PEIFP Interview #54.
6. Schwartz, "Economic History," 97–107.
7. MacDonald, *If You're Stronghearted*, 295.

8. MacDonald, *If You're Stronghearted*, 309. The province proposed to "buy out" small farms, pension off older farmers, and retrain younger ones.
9. Arsenault, *Island Acadians*, 243.
10. Leo Farrell, personal interview, Nov. 12, 2006, PEIFP Interview #33. The Great Western Road, which linked Summerside and Alberton, has since been incorporated into PEI Rte. 2. Farrell's father, who had a highly profitable sideline selling fox pelts, bought Leo a car when he came of age, admonishing him that if he drank to excess like many of his contemporaries and wrecked the vehicle, he would not get another one.
11. John Gauthier, personal interview, Nov. 16, 2006, PEIFP Interview #40.
12. Lowell Huestis, personal interview, Nov. 10, 2006, PEIFP Interview #30.
13. Billy MacInnis, Sr., personal interview, Nov. 26, 2006, PEIFP Interview #60. The Rollaway Club was later renamed the Silverado; the building burned down around 1990, and the club never reopened.
14. Billy MacInnis, Sr., interview, Nov. 26, 2006.
15. Howard Hancock, personal interview, Oct. 22, 2006, PEIFP Interview #10.
16. Two of Jack Webster's sons—Carl and Jackie Webster of Cardigan—were interviewed for this project in 1992 and 2006.
17. Reg Banks, personal interview, Nov. 15, 2006, PEIFP Interview #38.
18. Allan MacDonald, personal interview, Oct. 24, 2006, PEIFP Interview #14.
19. Ivan Day, in John Gauthier interview, Nov. 16, 2006.
20. John Gauthier interview, Nov. 16, 2006. Gauthier was unwilling to further identify this hall. From remarks made in passing by Ervan Sonier during his 1991 interview, however, I have been able to infer that the name of this establishment was probably the Western Star.
21. *Tuning* is Island parlance for singing fiddle tunes; see chapter 3.
22. *Jigging* is another term for singing fiddle tunes.
23. Bobby socks were ankle-length socks for females; in the early rock 'n' roll era, young female fans of pop music and associated dance styles were sometimes known as "bobby-soxers."
24. Dau-Schmidt was raised in the American Midwest and moved to Brackley, Queens County, as an adult. For decades, she was principal instructor at the Rollo Bay Fiddle Instruction Program (see chapter 16).
25. Among Island Acadians, *paté* is a meat pie; *fricot* is a stew made with meat, chicken or fish and root vegetables.
26. Ernie Gallant in Pat Doucette interview, Nov. 9, 2006, PEIFP Interview #29.
27. Roy Johnstone, personal interview, Nov. 14, 2006, PEIFP Interview #36. Johnstone would later become one of the few full-time professional fiddlers on Prince Edward Island.
28. Jackie Biggar interview, Nov. 23, 2006.
29. Robert Crane, personal interview, Nov. 29, 2006, PEIFP Interview #65.

CHAPTER SIXTEEN
"If Everybody Does a Little Bit, Great Things Can Happen"

By the mid-1970s, as Kevin Chaisson of Bear River, Kings County, puts it, "The fiddle music was pretty near done." Fiddling had been abandoned both by a younger generation who saw it as old-fashioned and by those mature Islanders who saw it as a painful reminder of an uncouth past. As for the fiddlers themselves, by and large they felt alienated both from their neighbors and from the new state of society.

If fiddling was to come back, several obstacles had to be overcome. First, the stigma attached to fiddling and related activities had to be neutralized. Second, it had to somehow be integrated into modern life. Third, conditions had to be altered so that taking up the art would once again seem an attractive alternative for youngsters. Once they were attracted to the instrument, effective methods had to be available for passing on tunes and techniques. Finally, to keep talented youngsters from abandoning the instrument at the onset of adolescence, negative peer pressure had to be blunted.

Fiddling ultimately did come back on Prince Edward Island, and at that time of this writing, the manifestations of its revitalization, or *revival*, are commonplace. Just how it returned to prominence makes for a story that is sufficiently complex to serve as the subject for an entire book in its own right. Because presenting this tale as a chronicle would result in a dizzying array of names, dates, and places, what follows instead is a thematic approach in which major leaders, strategies, and social forces are identified and their interactions analyzed.

There was no overall organization or direction to the Island's fiddling revival movement. Although in retrospect a local organization called the Prince Edward Island Fiddlers' Society may seem to have often been in the vanguard, in actual fact dozens of individuals and groups scattered around the Island with independent agendas also contributed significantly to the revitalization of fiddling.

"It Makes a Connection with Something That Has Gone"

Ironically, the very changes in Island life that threatened the survival of fiddling also put forces into motion that were ultimately to single it out for preservation. Once Islanders in general had grown used to improvements in living conditions, many of them came to realize that important aspects of the old life had disappeared and that perhaps some of these now-absent customs or activities were what had made life meaningful. This sense of lost meaning can engender a fairly intense longing for certain aspects of a former or rapidly disappearing way of life. In turn, this state of mind—which ranges from mild feelings of nostalgia to acute psychological distress—is often associated with individual or collective activities aimed at preserving or restoring these positively regarded aspects of the past.[1]

For many Islanders, fiddling came to be seen as a precious symbol of the old days. They were willing to give up their old ways of farming and transportation, their frolics and house parties, their one-room schoolhouses and community halls, and the close ties that once bound families and neighbors. But when push came to shove, they were unwilling to part completely from the musical art that graced the social life of their youth. As John Cousins of Bloomfield, Prince County, sums it up, "People love to continue to play the fiddle. It's a continuance of a tradition, and my theory about it is that this is a very therapeutic exercise. It makes a connection with something that has gone and something that was valuable in culture."

As the signs pointing to fiddling's impending demise multiplied, many fiddlers and lovers of fiddle music grew increasingly concerned. To amplify the level of their alarm, they had only to look at the fate of Island vocal music. While it had never been as central as fiddling, the singing of old Island songs was once an important aspect of rural community life. With the coming of radio, recordings, and television, however, these old songs fell into disuse within the course of a single generation. When interviewed in 1991, John Cousins summed up the situation as follows:

> The song-making traditions have died. If you ask me to go up to St. Anthony's Hall and sing, you are going to hear the old songs, and there are several people on the Island who do sing them, but they're not much in demand. At our average run-of-the-mill benefit concert, you are going to get country-and-western music.

Essentially, the old vocal tradition had died because no group came forward to act as a passionate advocate for its preservation. This made it patently clear, as noted by Libby Haywood Hubley of Kensington, Prince County, "that unless you actively pass the culture along it may not be there forever." In response, certain Islanders began thinking about taking concrete actions aimed at preserving Island fiddling. Among the various organizations and activities that grew up as a result were a fiddle association, fiddle clubs, fiddle festivals, community concerts, and fiddle instruction programs. In addition, a parallel revival involving Island step dancing both paved the way for and progressed in tandem with the fiddling revival.

Music Revival Movements

The revitalization of fiddling on Prince Edward Island can be seen as one of a long line of music revivals involving various aspects of Celtic, English, and North American traditional musics. Some such movements have already been touched on in these pages. Among them are the Irish harp and Scottish bagpipe revivals of the late eighteenth century, the Highland Games movement of the 1820s and '30s, efforts on behalf of Irish traditional music spearheaded in the 1890s by the Feis Ceoil Association and in the 1950s by Comhaltas Ceoltoiri Eireann, Henry Ford's attempts in the 1920s to resuscitate fiddling and square dancing, and the North American state and provincial fiddle association movement of the 1960s and '70s. Also of relevance here are three other movements—the development of strathspey and reel societies in Scotland and elsewhere, the Anglo-American folk song revival, and the Appalachian fiddle music revival.

The first *strathspey and reel societies*—clubs in which musicians join together to play ensemble versions of fiddle tunes from sheet music under the auspices of a conductor—developed in the 1880s as a means of remedying what was seen as a flagging interest in Scottish fiddle music. The movement got under way with the founding of the Edinburgh Highland Reel and Strathspey Society in 1881;[2] since then, such organizations have become widespread throughout the English-speaking world.

The Anglo-American folk song revival was launched by members of an educated, urban elite who undertook to preserve the music of poor, uneducated and often rural people. Enthusiasts founded folk song clubs devoted to the preservation and dissemination of this music. In the late 1920s, impulses aimed at bringing "folk music" to the world's attention led to the development of the first North American folk festivals. By the 1940s, the folk song revival in North America had become entwined with a variety of movements seeking progressive social change, and in the 1950s and '60s it generated its own pop-music scene—sometimes referred to as the "folk boom"—and its own set of pop stars.[3]

The Appalachian fiddle music revival was essentially an offshoot of the folk song revival. In the 1960s and '70s, many young men and women—most of whom likewise came from educated, urban backgrounds—sought out musical role models among the last remaining traditional fiddlers of the Appalachians. These youngsters did not merely absorb repertoire from these older players; they also closely emulated the latter's playing styles and, to a degree, their self-presentations. They then sought to promote the music by forming bands, holding regular jam sessions, and organizing concerts and festivals. From its modest beginnings, the Appalachian fiddle music revival has grown to a point at which it now involves thousands of musicians and enthusiasts scattered among several countries.

Although each music-revival movement was ultimately unique, in general these movements employed a relatively narrow range of strategies to achieve their objectives. After all, the issues with which they had to deal were often quite similar—how to keep an activity in the public eye, how to make it socially respectable and find a viable place for it within a different organization of society, how to attract a new generation of participants and find inducements to keep them active, and so on. Some common strategies that have been employed by such groups include forming advocacy organizations and social clubs, organizing ensembles, establishing competitions or other opportunities for public performance such as festivals and concerts, and developing instructional programs.

Most successful musical revivals have had at least one other characteristic in common: in fairly short order, they take on a life of their own and create dramatic changes in the revived music. There are at least three major factors driving such musical changes. First, the original social context of the music is rarely preserved during the revival process. Second, the values, attitudes, and aims of leaders are strongly reflected in a revival's outcomes. Third, the preservation of regional, local, or individual styles is generally not regarded as a significant consideration. Even in those instances where such preservation has been deemed important, certain styles—or aspects of style—are usually emphasized and others either ignored or suppressed. Taken together, all these factors produce a kind of "creative editing, a paring away of those characteristics and features deemed inappropriate and a reordering of what is left."[4]

Because the strategies employed by revival movements carry the revived art far outside its original social context, they inevitably carry change in their wake. When competitions become a major vehicle for promoting revival, for example, the criteria employed for awarding prizes tend to selectively shape musical style. Alternatively, the pressures of performance at festivals and concerts also tend to affect style. Putting music on the stage not only leads to more-polished renditions and an overall increase in tempo but also tends to bring about the dilution of dance rhythms and an emphasis on showy methods of presentation. In addition, there is always the temptation to cater to the tastes of current audiences, which can be far different from those for which the music was originally performed.

When a revival movement survives long enough, its course is also affected by the simple passage of time. Even after a decade or two, morbidity and mortality remove many of the original participants from the scene, thus clearing the way for new perspectives that are less tied to the past. What's more, the world does not stand still as a given revival progresses. As local technology, infrastructure, and attitudes change, they naturally create new sets of pressures and opportunities that affect a revival's path.

Although preservation is generally declared to be the aim of a music-revival movement, there is always the question of what exactly is being preserved. One major dichotomy can be summed up as *texts* versus *style*. Prior to the recording era, the initial focus of preservationists and collectors was on texts (lyrics and written music) because they translated easily to print. It took the onset of field recording in the 1930s and '40s before a major interest developed in preserving the actual sound of a musical genre as expressed in individual and regional playing styles.[5] Following this rubric, organizations such as strathspey and reel societies (for which both learning and performance are based on written music) can be characterized as *text centered*. Text-centered groups tend to foster an approach to fiddle music that can be described as *stylistically neutral* (that is, relatively devoid of bowing accents, ornamentation, or regional flavor). At the other end of the continuum are *style-centered* movements such as the Appalachian fiddle music revival, in which participants attempt to meticulously re-create the sound of particular artists.

Many successful revival movements create an association in the public mind between a given music or dance style and such powerful feelings as patriotism, nativism, ethnic pride, or romanticism. Thus, many Scottish and Irish revivals were set in motion by those hoping to keep aspects of local culture from being swallowed up by an imperialistic English culture. As noted in chapter 11, the North American fiddle and square dance revival of the 1920s developed in part from an impulse to insulate "native" (that is, Anglo-American) culture from "foreign" and black influences. Alternatively, romanticism is often strongly at play when revivals are initiated by cultural outsiders. For example, many activists involved in both the Anglo-American folk song and Appalachian fiddle music revivals were inspired by the notion that their adopted music was somehow "purer" than the musics to which they were born and that it somehow represented a refuge from urbanized, industrial, or bureaucratic values.[6]

Mindset of PEI's *Fiddling Revival Leaders*

The PEI fiddling revival was launched and carried out primarily by cultural insiders—Islanders who had grown up during the traditional period when house parties and community dances flourished. From these formative experiences, they absorbed certain attitudes and developed certain approaches to problem solving that strongly affected the course of this revival.

For one thing, joining together with neighbors to accomplish common goals was an important aspect of rural Island life. As described in chapters 1 and 2, districts maintained their own local schools and churches; ran benefit events such as church picnics, carnivals, and benefit dances; and organized entertainments such as St. Patrick's Day plays and Christmas concerts. Rural

Islanders also joined together in self-help groups, such as the Women's Institute, fishermen's cooperatives, and agricultural cooperatives. Once Islanders had set their minds on preserving fiddling or dancing, therefore, banding together would seem a natural thing to do.

As discussed in chapter 11, many Islanders had grown increasingly disenchanted with fiddle contests during the 1950s and '60s because of their tendency for fostering rivalries and animosities among fiddlers and their families. Unlike many other revival movements, therefore, a conscious decision was made early on to avoid holding music competitions on Prince Edward Island altogether and to focus instead on other methods of promotion, such as creating ensembles, holding festivals and concerts, and engaging in community-outreach activities such as volunteering to entertain the aged or infirm.

The early leaders of the revival were also highly aware that fiddling could not be integrated into modern Island life unless it was restored to respectability. First and foremost, fiddling had to be removed from settings where overindulgence in alcohol might come into play or where rowdy behavior might otherwise bring it into disrepute. And because attending square dances with a flask of 'shine in the back pocket or otherwise handy had become an Island custom, fiddling also had to be largely divorced from social dancing. Consequently, no consistent campaign ever materialized to promote the resurgence of dancing square sets (hereafter referred to as "old-time dancing") or to increase the number of old-time dance venues. In addition, there was little or no interest in revising or upgrading the bowdlerized versions of square sets that had spread throughout the Island since the dance hall years.

Although it was agreed that the act of fiddle playing itself had to survive, not much thought was given to what other aspects of Island fiddling might merit preservation. In particular, revival leaders never felt the need to take any special action to preserve playing styles. Because local and regional styles were traditionally considered to be inborn characteristics that appeared naturally as the player matured, there was no reason to offer this matter special attention. It was expected that once youngsters had learned to play, each would automatically adopt the style practiced in his or her community without any need for special instruction or intervention.

There were two other factors that inhibited activities aimed at stylistic preservation. First, there was the fear that singling out particular styles or players for special recognition could trigger the same kinds of rivalries and jealousies that had plagued the old contest milieu. Equally significant was the ingrained attitude—a legacy from Island fiddling's long underrepresentation on mass media—that the local product was inherently inferior to professionalized styles coming from off-Island. As Paul MacDonald of Charlottetown noted in 1992, "There is a kind of a mentality here that everything from away is better. All kids hear in the house is, 'The best player's so-and-so from away.'" Consequently, many early revival leaders were actively striving to avoid preserving the unique features of Island regional styles, in favor of promoting outside models.

Many early revival leaders were great admirers of Cape Breton fiddling and its repertoire. They were also attuned to the forces that had made the rise of the great Cape Breton players possible, such as the growth of paying venues and the development of the widespread ability to read music. Many programs and organizations that arose during the PEI revival, then, can be seen as attempts to make Prince Edward Island more like Cape Breton, in hopes that these conditions would encourage youngsters to develop the dedication and professionalism of Cape Breton's better-known performing artists. The Rollo Bay Fiddle Instruction Program, for example, was set up with the idea of imparting Cape Breton tunes in Cape Breton style. Similarly, a campaign to promote note reading was undertaken so that students would be able to emulate many Cape Breton players and "go to the books" for new repertoire.

Although as a group the leaders of the fiddling revival could by no means be described as cosmopolitan in outlook, many of them had spent sufficient time abroad to be conversant with general trends in North American and European culture. And while it is unlikely that they were aware to any great extent of other historical or contemporary music-revival movements, they were nevertheless sufficiently familiar with the manifestations of such movements—festivals, concert series, fiddle associations, music clubs, and so on—to borrow and subsequently adapt these organizational methods to their purposes.

The Prince Edward Island Fiddlers' Society

Islanders often cite the founding of the Prince Edward Island Fiddlers' Society (often referred to locally as "the PEI Fiddlers") as the step that set the fiddling revival in motion. The story is as follows. In the fall of 1975, Faber MacDonald was a young priest recently attached to St. Pius X parish in suburban Parkdale, just northeast of Charlottetown. Fr. MacDonald had grown up in a Little Pond, Kings County, fiddling family, had taken up the fiddle as a youngster, and had taught himself to read music while at seminary in Cape Breton.[7] He

PHOTO 16.1. FR. CHARLES CHEVERIE (*FOURTH FIDDLER FROM LEFT, FRONT ROW*) LEADS THE QUEENS COUNTY AND EASTERN KINGS FIDDLERS AT ROLLO BAY FESTIVAL, JULY 1992 (PHOTO BY EARTHWATCH TEAM).

was still assigned to Cape Breton in the early 1970s when local fiddlers there banded together under Fr. John Angus Rankin to form the Cape Breton Fiddlers' Association (CBFA). They had been motivated to organize in large part by the popular outcry that followed the broadcast of a television documentary called *The Vanishing Cape Breton Fiddler*. This film, written and directed by Ron MacInnes, focused on the dearth of young people taking up the instrument and predicted the eventual demise of fiddling on Cape Breton Island.[8]

Fr. MacDonald was quite impressed with two programs set in motion by the CBFA. First—in a practice almost certainly borrowed from Scotland's strathspey and reel societies—members met weekly to rehearse playing fiddle tunes on an ensemble basis.[9] These well-rehearsed performances in turn became the centerpiece for a large—and instantly successful—fiddle festival held on Cape Breton in the town of Glendale. Aside from these performances by the CBFA, the Glendale Festival very much resembled a large-scale community talent show, featuring volunteer performances by regional fiddlers and step dancers.

When Faber MacDonald arrived at Parkdale, he had a plan to organize a small fiddle ensemble. He first discussed this idea with a parishioner named Bill MacDonald (no relation; b. North Lake, Kings County). As the latter recalls, it soon became clear that the time was ripe for a much larger project.

> [Fr. MacDonald] said, "Can you find three or four more fiddlers? We should form a little group and practice, and then on occasions we can go out and play." I said to him, "That would be fine, but why couldn't we notify all the fiddlers that I know on Prince Edward Island and call a meeting and have a discussion on it?" "That would be fine," he said. "How many do you know?" So I come home here, and I made up a little list with thirty-four, thirty-five people that I knew played the violin. I sent out letters, and the date that we had the [first] meeting in the church hall there was twenty-one fiddlers there with their violins.

The new organization's membership grew rapidly. As Faber MacDonald reports, "They wanted to make sure that everybody they knew would be invited; we started with about thirty names, but [before long] they multiplied that by about three times."

The fiddlers who attended the initial meetings embraced several notions and practices that represented significant departures from Island tradition. Like their Cape Breton counterparts, they accepted the idea of playing fiddle tunes in large ensembles, despite that until then fiddling had been almost entirely a solo art. They also agreed that these ensembles would perform standard versions of tunes, which meant that fiddlers had to abandon their highly individualized twists. Because using published tune versions seemed the best way to accomplish this end, many members of the new group started learning to read music. Fiddlers also eagerly agreed to help organize and participate in fiddle festivals on the Glendale model. And as noted earlier, they agreed, with near-unanimity, to refrain from competing against each other in fiddle contests.

By the following spring, the PEI Fiddlers' Society was facing its first crisis. A substantial disagreement arose over the aims and musical focus of the new organization. As reported by Faber MacDonald, fiddlers from northeastern Kings County under the leadership of "Joe Pete" Chaisson of Bear River put forward the position that the organization should play mostly Scottish and Cape Breton music, while fiddlers from other parts of the Island felt that its focus should be more eclectic. Eventually, those who favored the more general musical focus won out. But such philosophical differences, along with logistical problems such as those caused by winter travel, soon brought about the establishment of three regional branches, each with a different character and musical focus. Eventually, most meeting, rehearsing, and performing was taking place on the branch level. In 1991–92, there were three such branches in operation: the Eastern Kings Fiddlers, with meetings in Souris; the Queens County Fiddlers, with meetings in Charlottetown; and the Prince County Fiddlers, with meetings in Summerside.[10]

The Eastern Kings branch was established under the leadership of the Chaisson family of Bear River, with Joe Pete Chaisson providing much of the inspiration and energy for the group's activities from its founding until his death in 1982. Thereafter, this role was taken up by his sons Kevin, Kenny, and "Young Peter." Kevin Chaisson recalls,

> I guess it just rubbed off on the rest of us, and I've been trying to fill his boots ever since. He just loved the music, and that's the only thing that I can see that got the thing back on track again. 'Course, we all chipped in a little bit here and there, trying to keep the thing going. Nobody has to give a great big deal, but if everybody does a little bit, great things can happen!

In 1991–92, the Eastern Kings Fiddlers was a loose association of perhaps a dozen male fiddlers and accompanists who had learned their craft during the traditional period and assimilated their repertoires primarily by ear (musicians with this life-pattern are referred to henceforth as "old-time" musicians). Among those who participated regularly at the time were the three Chaisson brothers, Gus Longaphie and his son Buddy, Allan MacDonald, Francis MacDonald, the brothers Dan and Hughie McPhee, and Charlie Sheehan. Rehearsals were informal; there was no obvious leader, repertoire was decided upon more or less on an ad hoc basis, and no one seemed overly concerned whether members played identical tune versions. Each rehearsal generally concluded with what amounted to an old-style fiddlers' gathering, where each musician took his turn at the *hot seat* next to Kevin Chaisson on piano and played a few groups of tunes.

From the beginning, the Eastern Kings branch stressed a close musical association with Cape Breton fiddling. Their repertoire consisted almost exclusively of Scottish and Cape Breton tunes, and the festival they founded in 1976—known as the Rollo Bay Scottish Fiddle Festival, or simply the Rollo Bay Festival—was almost entirely focused on Cape Breton fiddling style and repertoire. To further emphasize this connection, prominent fiddlers from Cape Breton were generally invited to serve as headliners at Rollo Bay, and each year several additional fiddlers from Cape Breton were also featured there as performers.

The Queens County Fiddlers was led throughout its early years by Fr. Faber MacDonald. MacDonald was assigned to a bishopric in Newfoundland in 1980, and after a lengthy period of transition, the job of running the branch ultimately fell to another Island clergyman, Fr. Charles Cheverie. Cheverie had grown up in relatively urban Charlottetown. Although no one in his immediate family played fiddle, he had been continually exposed to the instrument as a child. Fr. Cheverie later obtained some instruction on fiddle from family friend Joe Pete Chaisson but then abandoned the instrument during adolescence in favor of guitar. As "Father Charlie" recounts, the aftermath of Joe Pete's death was what led him back to the fiddle once again.

> I went to the funeral, and the pastor, knowing my relationship to the Chaisson family, asked me if I wanted to say the final prayers at the gravesite. After the closing prayers, "Young Peter" Chaisson come over and asked me why I wasn't playing fiddle any more. It was at that time that I was inspired to go to play the fiddle. So I've been really playing since then with some seriousness.

In 1991–92, the Queens County Fiddlers closely resembled a strathspey and reel society. Rehearsals were formal and well organized, with both repertoire and tune order selected by the leader. Most of the repertoire consisted of published versions of Scottish, Irish, and Cape Breton tunes, and there was much emphasis on playing standard tune versions.

Although the original membership of the Queens County Fiddlers consisted primarily of old-time fiddlers, not many of them remained active in the organization on a long-term basis (more on this later). By the early 1990s, most regulars at the Queens County branch could best be described as musical hobbyists in the process of developing their fiddling skills. Many of these hobbyists were older Islanders who had been attracted to fiddling during their youth but had been unwilling or unable to take it up at the time. Also included in this group were many older women, who, as noted in chapter 7, had been almost universally excluded from fiddling during the traditional period.

The Prince County Fiddlers was founded by several established musicians from western Queens and eastern Prince Counties—notably, Toussaint Arsenault, Alvin Bernard, Ivan Bowness, Ivan Day, Peter Doiron, John Gauthier, Jim MacDougall, Ed Mathews, and Ervan Sonier. From its inception through the early 1990s, the branch was directed by John Gauthier (b. Stanhope, Queens County), who, as noted earlier, had played at Island dance halls with the Prince County Pioneers in the 1940s and also had a brief stint around that time as the featured fiddler on a show broadcast by radio station CFCY. Gauthier had joined the Canadian military in 1948 and was stationed in Summerside as he was nearing retirement in the mid-1970s, just around the time that the PEI Fiddlers' Society was forming. Because he had taught himself to read music and already had some experience teaching fiddle, he figured he could be of help to the fledgling organization.[11]

Prince County Fiddlers' meetings eventually developed a two-tier format. Each session would start with Gauthier teaching a formal lesson for beginners; by the time these lessons were over, the more experienced fiddlers would have arrived and the whole company would play in ensemble. As Ivan Day recalls, each week there would generally be a new tune for the group to learn—selected either by Gauthier or by another experienced player.[12]

In the early 1990s, the Prince County Fiddlers consisted of about two dozen active members. In its makeup and method of operation, it was something of a cross between its Eastern Kings and Queens County counterparts. Membership was more or less evenly split between old-time players and newcomers; the director was more of a facilitator than a leader; rehearsals, while structured, were not hierarchical; and suggestions for improvement could come from just about anyone.

The Prince County branch played a more eclectic repertoire than did its Queens and Kings County counterparts. In addition to Scottish and Cape Breton tunes, it also performed Irish, Appalachian, New England, Québecois, and local tunes—including some composed by its own members. It was also the most adventuresome branch in terms of musical arrangements; some selections featured soloing or harmonizing, while others called for division of the group into subensembles, changes in dynamics, and a variety of other devices common to band-craft.

Taken as a whole, the activities of all three branches helped put fiddling back in the public eye. The festivals and other events they sponsored attracted thousands of people across the Island, many of whom might never have otherwise been exposed to the music. The attention they engendered not only reassured established fiddlers of the art's long-term viability but also rekindled their interest in playing. At the same time, these events impressed the general population both with fiddling's entertainment value and with its overall significance to the cultural life of the Island.

For some old-time players who were otherwise having difficulty adjusting to the modern era, the camaraderie provided by participating in the PEI Fiddlers' Society became an emotional anchor. In particular, as Faber MacDonald recalls, group activities and the resultant social ties kept many a former heavy drinker on the wagon.

> Many of these guys had been very, very turned in, to the extent that many of them are alcoholics, eh. And there was one fellow who was drinking right up to the time that he belonged to the association. But after that there was never another drink! So, it was an outlet of some kind. There was a certain sense of fulfillment or satisfaction that came as a result of belonging to a comradeship or a fellowship. And through that fellowship, giving of themselves as a group.

The activities of the PEI Fiddlers' Society also had a significant impact on Island fiddling repertoire and style. Many of the tunes introduced through the various branches began circulating via oral transmission and are now firmly established in the local canon (particularly effective in this regard were spiral-bound, photocopied tune collections distributed by the Queens County Fiddlers). Second, participation in the society brought fiddlers together from all over the Island, thereby offering them the opportunity to experience each other's repertoires, tricks of the trade, and playing sounds.

Although it effectively promoted fiddling as an activity, the PEI Fiddlers' Society never took on a preservationist role with regard to Island repertoire or playing styles. Instead of ferreting out and disseminating obscure local tunes, for example, leaders generally selected tunes to impart from among those that had been popularized on media by Don Messer or various Cape Breton fiddlers. Leaders either ignored the issue of playing style altogether or spoke out in favor of the Messer or Cape Breton models. The PEI Fiddlers' Society was also far better at outreach to the general public than it was at attracting and holding onto the old-time fiddlers it initially sought to bring together. Only a few dozen old-time players ever became regularly attending members, and by the 1990s many of them were no longer actively taking part.

This last issue proved to be a particular problem with the Queens County Fiddlers (QCF), where the influx of new and amateur players ultimately became sufficiently large to shift the focus of the organization. Almost since its inception, QCF leaders were torn between fulfilling the aspirations of established old-time players for working on interesting and challenging material, and catering to the much slower pace and simpler repertoire required by beginners and less-serious players. This conflict came to a head following the departure of Fr. Faber MacDonald from the organization. Concerned that the QCF was being turned by its transitional leadership into a social club that catered primarily to amateurs, a sizable group of well-respected old-time players left the QCF and formed their own parallel organization, which became known as the Ceilidh Fiddlers. Over the next few years, the Ceilidh Fiddlers rehearsed regularly and often performed as a unit at benefit concerts and special events. Although the group disbanded in the late 1980s, only a couple of its members ever became active again in the QCF.[13]

Other Organizations and Events

Nowhere was the grassroots nature of the Island fiddling revival more evident than in the appearance of dozens of local organizations whose activities in whole or in part were devoted to presenting or promoting fiddling and related arts. These activities can be categorized as benefits and town days, seniors' programs, fiddle clubs and amateur ensembles, old-time dances, fiddle festivals, and commercial ceilidhs.

As frolics, church or school picnics, and local benefit dances disappeared, their role in community life was filled to some degree by benefit concerts and town days. Benefit concerts raised money for local families struggling with illness or other hardship, while town days gathered funds for public causes or initiatives. Instead of offering old-time dancing as a major attraction, however, both latter-day events relied primarily on local talent shows to draw a crowd. By eliminating social dancing from the program, organizers avoided the risk of attracting the rowdy elements that been the scourge of Island dance halls.

Like the church picnics and school socials of yore, annual town days also offered a variety of nonmusical activities, such as carnival games, sales of home-prepared food, and—in some cases—the lure of agricultural or culinary themes. One such event was the Monticello Tea Party, which had been founded in the early 1980s by local residents to raise funds for converting the old district schoolhouse into a community building and museum. A few other annual town days we encountered were the Blueberry Festival in St. Peters, the Dundas Plowing Match, the Strawberry Festival in Alberton, Seniors' Day in Mill River, the Lobster Carnival in Summerside, and the Harvest Festival in Kensington.

Although benefit concerts and town days did not feature fiddling as their central focus, they nevertheless contributed significantly to its preservation. All local residents who could play an instrument, step-dance, or sing were routinely recruited to perform at these events, which served as some of the few public venues where traditional fiddling could still be heard in the years immediately following the demise of the dance halls.

A network of publicly supported senior citizens' homes (assisted living sites) and manors (nursing homes) was established on Prince Edward Island in the 1950s and '60s under the auspices of both the National Policy and the Comprehensive Development Plan. Almost from the start, individual fiddlers and their accompanists took up the practice of conducting free performances at both kinds of institutions. By the 1980s, all three branches of the Prince Edward Island Fiddlers' Society had also become heavily involved in performing on a volunteer basis at seniors' venues. These activities strongly benefitted both performer and audience. For most seniors, the sound of fiddling brought back poignant memories of youth. For active fiddlers, just being in an environment where a strong passion for their music was so much in evidence served as an important vehicle for keeping their interest in playing alive.

Opportunities to perform at benefit concerts, town days, and senior citizens venues provided many old-time players with the motivation to organize their own fiddle clubs and amateur bands. One of the largest such groups of the early 1990s was the West Prince Fiddlers of Alberton, which included Frank O'Connor, George O'Connor, Elmer Robinson, and Lee Thompson on fiddle and Dorothy Dalton Rogers on piano. Two other such groups were the Warren Leard Group of the O'Leary area, featuring Warren Leard and Harry Lecky on fiddle and Bernice Leard on piano;[14] and Reuben's Jamboree, led by Reuben Wall of Kensington and featuring, among others, fiddlers Alvin Bernard, Leo Farrell, and Lottie Lock.

The success of the Rollo Bay Festival and other fiddle festivals sponsored by the PEI Fiddlers' Society encouraged other Islanders to organize similar events. In both 1991 and 1992, for example, two major fiddle festivals were held at the local hockey rink in Abram-Village, Prince County: the Atlantic Jamboree in early August and Festival Acadien in early September.[15] Both events featured predominantly francophone headliners, and most volunteer performers were of Acadian background from either the Evangeline Coast, western Prince County, or nearby parts of New Brunswick.[16]

Although few revival leaders were keen to include old-time dancing in their events, a few local organizations bucked that trend. One such group was Abram-Village-based Club 50, which addressed the issue of crowd control by specifically excluding anyone under fifty years old from its dances.[17] Another was the Circle Club of St. Peters, Kings County, which began holding its weekly old-time dances in a decommissioned railway depot. Following in the wake of the Circle Club was the Goose River Dance, which was established

PHOTO 16.2. FINALE AT FESTIVAL ACADIEN, ABRAM-VILLAGE, SEPTEMBER 1992. THE FIDDLERS ARE EDWARD P ARSENAULT (*LEFT*) AND EDDY ARSENAULT; THE DANCER ON LEFT IS HÉLÈNE ARSENAULT BERGERON (PHOTO BY KEN PERLMAN).

in a converted blueberry warehouse about ten miles northeast of St. Peters by an informal group under the leadership of J. D. MacIntyre.

There was also a move afoot to transform community talent shows into regularly scheduled fund-raising or for-profit events. The Orwell Ceilidh— founded in the late 1970s and held in a reconstruction of the old community hall at the Orwell Corners Historic Site in southeastern Queens County—was perhaps the first venue of this type to be established. Once construction on the hall was completed, the determination was made that a social evening involving music should be held there on a regular basis. The term *ceilidh* was selected to name the event, "with the idea behind [it] being the Gaelic word traditionally used for a local informal gathering."[18] During the early 1990s, the regular house band at the Orwell Ceilidh consisted of Sterling Baker of Montague, Kings County, on fiddle and Duncan Matheson of Charlottetown on piano. Different headliners were featured each week to maintain audience interest, but most of the program generally consisted of brief, unpaid performances by local instrumentalists, step dancers, and vocalists.

Taken together, all these various activities served to both solidify and amplify the effects on Island life of the various programs that had been set in motion by the PEI Fiddlers' Society. In turn, this led to a further increase in the visibility of fiddling, a greater rapprochement between fiddling and the general public, and the continued integration of fiddling into modern Island life. In particular, the willingness of all three PEI Fiddlers' Society branches and various grassroots groups to perform tirelessly at senior citizens' homes, manors, and a variety of other charitable events contributed mightily to a positive shift in the public's attitude. Fast receding was the image of the lone drunken fiddler plying his art at violence-prone dance halls. On display instead were sober, well-dressed groups of musicians performing in good order at charitable and other respectable settings.

An Acadian Resurgence

In the heavily Acadian Evangeline Coast region of southeastern Prince County, the beginnings of the Island fiddling revival coincided with a period of cultural awakening and a growing sense of ethnic empowerment. Longstanding organized efforts aimed at asserting Acadian cultural identity and countering pressures from anglophone Canada toward assimilation had just begun to reach fruition. Among the manifestations of this resurgence were the founding of an Acadian museum, a French-language newspaper, and a bilingual secondary school known as L'École *Régionale Évangéline*. In 1963, all schools in the Evangeline were grouped under a single school board, and in 1972 this "Evangeline School Unit" was officially recognized as one of the Island's five consolidated school districts, with a special status allowing for francophone instruction.[19] In turn, presence of a French-language school district that covered the entire Evangeline created a new sense of regional identity.[20]

This budding sense of ethnic awareness may well have amplified already existing impulses in the Evangeline toward promoting and preserving fiddling and step dancing. Not only would both arts have been valued as surviving elements from an idealized past, but local variants would also be seen as distinct expressions of Acadian identity. This additional impetus for preservation may explain in part why efforts aimed at musical revival were particularly effective in and around the Evangeline region (see below). The Acadian resurgence probably also accounts for the increasing tendency since the 1990s for musicians from this region to establish artistic paths independent from trends under way elsewhere on the Island (for more on this, see chapter 17).

The Step-Dance Revival

Because there was no systematic effort to revive old-time dancing, most public exposure for fiddling during the revival was in concert settings. Because old-time fiddlers had developed their styles to play for dancing, however, they never had a reason to school themselves in the niceties of performance practice. As a result, fiddling performances in the revival's early stages generally made for poor theater. What saved the day for Island fiddling as a stage art during this period was the opportunity to accompany step dancers. This allowed fiddlers to show their art in its best light (that is, as playing for dances), while also offering audiences an exciting visual. And what provided a continuous supply of dancers in need of accompaniment was the development of a parallel revival on Prince Edward Island in the art of step dancing.

While there seems to have been some formal instruction in step dancing on Prince Edward Island as early as the 1950s and '60s, both the demand for lessons and the number of teachers began to proliferate in the mid-'70s. According to dance instructor Libby Hubley, the same nostalgia-driven impulses that fueled the fiddling revival were also at work for step dancing.

> The PEI Fiddlers' [Society] was formed at about the same time the step dancing was coming on. So they came back and rejuvenated each other to an extent. So it was all coming together. And perhaps then it was a movement in a lot of places to look back to your roots, rather than to be wiping out our past and continually trying to replace our culture: [to take] a look at the things that we have and perhaps bring them back to the fore.

By the early 1980s, the number of Island families requesting step-dancing lessons for their children had grown dramatically, and every instructor who got into the field was soon swamped with students. According to Hubley, by the early 1990s "there was more kids wanted to take it than I had time to teach them." She also estimated that at any one time during this period there were perhaps five to six hundred youngsters enrolled in step-dancing programs throughout the Island.

Step-dancing demonstrations and contests eventually became so popular that they formed an integral part of nearly every musical event and community celebration on the Island. Although the first generation of Island step-dance teachers could easily have developed the habit of sending their students on stage with predictable recorded music, to their credit they usually insisted on live fiddling. In 1991–92, Libby Hubley described how the process played out for her group, known as the Lady Slipper Dancers.

> If they call for dancers, I say, "Yes, and who will be fiddling?" Sometimes they'll say, "No one, but I can get somebody." I'd much prefer to do it to live music. And so would the kids; they love the fiddlers! That's another dimension to the dancing, is to get to know all the fiddlers.

Because live accompaniment was employed wherever possible, thousands of youngsters were exposed to fiddle music in such a way that they could not fail but appreciate its varied melodies and compelling rhythmic drive. This created a potential youthful audience for fiddle music on the Island. It also created a milieu in which many young step-dancing students were attracted to the instrument and provided with the motivation to take it up.[21]

As old-timers were quick to point out, the kind of step dancing that developed under the influence of Island step-dancing schools was fundamentally different from what had been danced during the traditional period. Because the changes in step dancing wrought by its revival presaged some of the changes that Island fiddling later experienced, it is important to at least touch on them here.

Few early teachers of Island step dancing had grown up in households where it was actually practiced. As Libby Hubley describes, most instructors had studied or taught a variety of other kinds of dance prior to taking up step dancing, and many did not have much exposure to it until they were adults.

> All those other step-dance teachers originally taught Highland dancing, tap dancing. I myself had also taken ballet and jazz. Then step [dancing] became popular, so then they taught step dancing. They brought all their training from that other dance, and that would have an effect on how they taught step, because they'd already been teaching other performance dances.

In one practice borrowed from other forms of dance pedagogy, for example, step-dancing movements were analyzed and taught as a series of routines. Although those who had learned to step dance instinctively during the traditional period had no need to think in terms of formalized steps or combinations of steps, students without such a background learned far more efficiently when a given performance was broken down into easily assimilated step sequences.

The practice of holding frequent public recitals to show student progress was another element borrowed from other forms of formal dance pedagogy.

Because Island step dancing had never before been a formal performance art, however, a version had to be devised that would work in this context. As Libby Hubley puts it, "That's a big step when you're going from the kitchen to the stage; that was the hardest thing I had to do."

One logistical issue that Hubley and her colleagues faced was how to project dancers' routines from stage to audience across the kinds of distances encountered at auditorium or festival venues. This quickly altered kitchen-era standards that called for a relatively rigid upper body and "close-to-the-floor" dancing. Since the value of many subtle movements would often be lost in environments with long, imperfect sight lines, instructors began to encourage both higher stepping and more involvement of the upper body and arms. Similar logistics—blocked sight lines and the tendency for the sound of plain leather soles beating on a stage surface to become muffled—also encouraged importing *clickers* (taps) from tap dancing into Island step dancing, which previously had been performed soft-shoe.

Within a decade, the Island step-dance revival had created a new style of step dancing that was specifically geared for stage performance. Relative to the traditional style, it was faster, louder, and replete with the kind of elaborate, virtuosic maneuvers that required no special cultural understanding to appreciate. There was also a trend toward the development of precision step-dance teams, whose performances evinced the kind of spirit that later catapulted the Irish stage production *Riverdance* to pop-cultural prominence.[22]

Many older fiddlers were not fond of the changes wrought by the step-dance revival. For one thing, they felt that the new style of dancing was too fast and too loud and that the older soft-shoe style was both more subtle and more aesthetically pleasing. They complained about the very elements of stagecraft that dance teachers had taken such pains to put in, such as the increase in upper-body movement and elevation in the plane of steps. Finally, many old-timers disliked how the dancing had been so obviously cut up into routines instead of flowing naturally from the heart. George MacPhee of Monticello, Kings County, put it this way:

> The old way of step dancing was different from the way the trained dancers do now. The trained dancers, they go in and they have certain steps they do. But the old dancers, they had a lot of style! I know I liked it better. The new ones are good dancers and all that, but I'd rather the old way of dancin'.

Fiddle Instruction

During the traditional period, learning to play the fiddle was largely an unconscious process of physical emulation and developing musical memory. As the Island modernized during the 1950s and '60s, however, this system of learning broke down. Opportunities to hear and observe fiddling in the household and community declined sharply, and even extremely observant and musical youngsters had difficulty catching on to the art. Consequently, it was recognized that formal instruction had to be made available if Island fiddling was going to survive.

It would have made a lot of sense at this stage to encourage old-time fiddlers to become involved in teaching, but this course of action was all but blocked by old attitudes. As far as the older players were concerned, if a youngster was destined to play, it would happen without any active intervention on their part. Even for those willing to take on the task, their own haphazard learning styles usually left them clueless about how to go about it. Although most old-time fiddlers were perfectly capable of teaching tunes by ear through repetition, they were generally inhibited from addressing issues of nuance and style by their inability to put their musical understanding into words.

Those old-time players who tried their hand at teaching usually did so on a volunteer basis through the auspices of Community School, an adult self-improvement program that ran after-hours in many Island school buildings during the months of February and March. Because instructors had only eight weeks per year to impart the basics to students of widely varying ages, talent levels, and speeds of assimilation, this setting usually made for a fairly limited learning environment.

Aside from Community School, most of those willing and able to take on the task of bringing the next generation along were formal violin teachers with a relatively limited understanding of local fiddling traditions. As fiddle instruction developed on Prince Edward Island, then, its focus was on rudiments of technique, on note reading, and on playing fiddle tunes by note (directly from the page) with little concern for such musical considerations as phrasing, dynamics, embellishment, rhythmic accents, and performance style. This teaching method set the pattern, and it eventually became the predominant method for teaching the instrument on the Island.

All three branches of the PEI Fiddlers' Society got involved to some degree in the process of passing on fiddle lore. As noted earlier, under John Gauthier the Prince County Fiddlers devoted the first half of each weekly meeting to instructing beginners. During its early days, the Queens County branch made time available for conducting violin lessons just prior to each weekly meeting. After these lessons were discontinued, novices were actively encouraged to use club meetings as opportunities to pick the brains of more accomplished players.

The Eastern Kings branch made the most ambitious attempt to create a systematic fiddle instruction program on the Island. As first conceived by Joe Pete Chaisson and brought to fruition by his sons, free weekly fiddle classes were set up for anyone who wanted to attend, in hopes that area youngsters would take the most advantage of the program. Funding for the enterprise would be provided by proceeds from Joe Pete's other brainchild—the Rollo Bay Festival.

The Rollo Bay Fiddle Instruction Program (hereafter referred to as the "Rollo Bay Program") started out in 1978 with about a dozen students attending a single weekly hour-long class held after-hours at the Rollo Bay Consolidated School. By the early 1990s, several hundred children and adults from the surrounding area had already participated in the program, which had expanded to three hour-long sessions per week, each attended by about thirty students.

From its inception, the primary fiddle instructor at the Rollo Bay Program was Kathryn Dau-Schmidt—a classically trained transplant from the American Midwest who had settled in Brackley, Queens County. Through a combination of advance planning and trial and error, Dau-Schmidt and the Chaisson brothers gradually created a program that seemed to work quite well for passing on the art of traditional fiddling. What evolved was a team approach in which Dau-Schmidt concentrated on basic technique and note reading, while the Chaissons made themselves available to demonstrate playing style. Kevin Chaisson describes the division of labor as follows:

> If we come across a problem with a tune—like sometimes you come across a piece of music and it don't sound right, I'll tell 'em. My brother Peter does basically the same thing. The music that they have, he'll play it for them. It's exposing the kids to how it's really played, what the music sounds like.

Because of the Rollo Bay Program and other instructional programs, scores of Islanders from all ages and walks of life were added to the list of those actively engaged in fiddling. If nothing else, this added dramatically to the number of Islanders who were sympathetic to the instrument and its music and who might eventually form an audience for both recordings and concerts featuring local fiddling.

"We Can Get to a Place Together as Long as We Play Music"

By the early 1990s, there was little doubt that fiddling's image was thoroughly rehabilitated. As far as the average Islander was concerned, the connection between fiddling and the drunken brawls of yesteryear had largely faded. In its place was a new set of associations—successful, orderly festivals; town days and ceilidhs; public-spirited charitable performances; and step-dance recitals by adolescent girls. As Jenny McQuaid (b. Naufrage, Kings County) observed in 1992, "It's more respect for fiddling, and more people are not ashamed to say they appreciate it or like it now."

One major indication of this trend was the reconciliation that developed between fiddling and organized religion. The same churches that had once been strident in their opposition to the devil's instrument completely altered their stance and began to work actively for fiddling's preservation. In fact, two of the most important leaders of and spokesmen for the fiddling revival were local clergymen—Faber MacDonald and Charles Cheverie.

Some Island churches began encouraging fiddlers to take an active role in liturgy. Harry Lecky of Milburn, Prince County, for example, reports that he has often been asked "to go around to different churches with [his] fiddle playing hymns [for] others to sing." Similarly, it became customary to invite groups of fiddlers to play en masse during funeral services. In fact, one of the first Island funerals to bring massed fiddling into the liturgy was that of Eastern Kings branch founder Joe Pete Chaisson.

Another sign of fiddling's rehabilitation was the extent to which local politicians became eager to associate themselves with the art. This led both to invitations to perform at government-sponsored events and to provincial decrees honoring fiddling organizations. In 1991, for example, the PEI Fiddlers' Society was made official ambassador to a campaign called Road to the Isles that stressed Scottish roots. Each individual member was then made an honorary ambassador and granted two items—a special vest to wear during performances and a commemorative ribbon—woven with the Island Tartan design[23]—to affix to the scroll of his or her instrument. The PEI Fiddlers' Society was also asked to perform at the opening ceremonies of the Canada Games, which were held that same year in Charlottetown.

Another important element here was the growing perception that fiddling had become an important cultural bridge among ethnic groups. Fiddlers with French surnames such as Chaisson and Cheverie, for example, had become champions of Scottish fiddling and culture. Alternatively, festivals in predominantly Acadian areas gladly welcomed participation by fiddlers with such anglophone surnames as Robinson, Jones, O'Connor, and McPhee. In 1992, Eddy Arsenault of St. Chrysostom, Prince County, summed it up as follows:

> We all play the same kind of music. I'm French, but I don't even know a French tune. And there's very little total Scotch or Irish music: they are all mixed up together, with a few French tunes, too. But we can get to a place together as long as we play music. That's just about the size of it.

Around this same period, it began to look as if Island fiddling might have a future. The Chaisson family in particular took great pains to draw attention to some of the youngsters actively studying the instrument, often by presenting youth ensembles at the Rollo Bay Festival and at other festivals and concerts around the Island. As illustrated by the following comment from Joe MacDonald of St. Andrews, Kings County, just the sight of so many youngsters effectively grasping the rudiments was regarded by many older fiddlers as a sign of great hope:

> This is what pleases me, to see those young people. And I was also to the fiddle festival at Rollo Bay, and the difference from one year to the other, now, it's just unbelievable! I know it's not going to be dropped when those young people are at it. I'd hate to see it drop. I hate to see it, because it's just too good! It pleases a lot of people.

Despite all these positive developments, there was still much cause for concern. For one thing, most active fiddlers and most of the fiddling audience were well over fifty. And while several youngsters enrolled at the Rollo Bay Program showed promise, no student there had yet emerged to join the ranks of full-fledged players. In short, despite over fifteen years of activity aimed at revival, the number of fully developed young players that had been produced to that point was precisely two—Paul MacDonald of Charlottetown and Richard Wood of nearby East Royalty.[24]

Paul MacDonald had learned his basic skills while enrolled in a provincially sponsored classical violin program called Singing Strings. He ended his classical studies at age twelve, but an encounter with the Chaisson brothers soon afterward hooked him on their style of music.

> I was at a party at my uncle's place in Bear River, and Kevin Chaisson was there, and his brothers.[25] I had already learned one medley of tunes by heart. I played it, and they all listened to me. And before the night was over, "Young Peter" Chaisson

came up to me, and he said, "Well, young fella, from now on all you're gonna be playing is Scottish fiddle music!" After that point, I kept at it!

In the years that followed, several adult Chaisson fiddlers became musical mentors to young Paul. Before long, he was performing regularly at Island festivals and concerts. In 1988, he released a cassette tape featuring his playing, which was the first commercial recording to come out of the revival.

MacDonald's activities paved the way for another youngster, named Richard Wood. Wood had started out as a step-dancing prodigy, then took up the fiddle in 1988 at age ten. Soon he was tagging along with his father, Terry, to rehearsals of the Queens County Fiddlers. By 1990, Wood was showing such great promise that his family began taking him around the Island to play at festivals, town days, and benefit concerts. They also transported him to compete in fiddle contests in New Brunswick, Nova Scotia, and Ontario, where he fared extremely well. In the summer of 1991, his playing made a major impression at the Rollo Bay Festival; his own first commercial recording, *Cutting the Bow*, was released in 1992.

The most promising fiddle student at the Rollo Bay Program in 1992 was Paul MacDonald's nine-year-old cousin Jeremy Joseph "J.J." Chaisson of Bear River, the son of Kenny Johnny Joe and Donna Chaisson.[26] To amplify hopes for J.J.'s musical future, Islanders could point to his ideal musical pedigree, which consisted of two fiddling grandfathers: Joe Pete Chaisson on the maternal side and Johnny Joe Chaisson on the paternal. Equally important, as illustrated by the following interchange between J.J.'s uncle, Kenny Joe Pete Chaisson, and distant relative Lemmy Chaisson of Rollo Bay, there was already a stream of anecdotes in circulation that portrayed a young mind "just full of music":

> **LEMMY CHAISSON:** I remember one morning in church he kept jigging [singing] these tunes. He's leaned over to Kenny, and he says, "Uncle Kenny," he says, "How does that high turn go?" And then he starts jigging!
>
> **KENNY JOE PETE CHAISSON:** This is just before Communion, too. In church! He jigged the low turn: "How's the high turn o' this tune go, Kenny?" I just looked at him, and I just about fell on the floor. I said, "Can you imagine what's going through that little mind?" He was only about six years old then, seven at the most.

This state of affairs—two fully developed young players and the promise of a third—was where matters stood in August 1992 when I conducted a joint interview with Paul MacDonald and Kevin Chaisson. When the subject inevi-

PHOTO 16.3. RICHARD WOOD AT ATLANTIC JAMBOREE, ABRAM-VILLAGE, AUGUST 1992 (PHOTO BY KEN PERLMAN).

tably turned to fiddling's survival, both were cautiously hopeful, but neither was particularly optimistic. Most worrisome to MacDonald was that the vast majority of Island youngsters seemed uninterested in traditional fiddling. To amplify his point, he compared the experience on Prince Edward Island with that of neighboring Cape Breton Island, where another fiddling revival was already producing a stream of fine young players.

> The difference over there is like if you talk to someone my age and ask 'em about fiddle music: "Gee, I like fiddle music!" Now, most times everybody has different taste, but Natalie [MacMaster] said she'd be on the [school] bus and [someone would] be saying, "Did you get the new Def Leppard tape?" and it'd be like, "Oh, yeah, really good!" And then someone would say, "Did you get that new Buddy MacMaster tape?" and "Jesus, I got that last night, and that's some good, boy!" You hear that on PEI on a bus, it'd be like *Twilight Zone* or something! I'm somewheres else, I'm not on PEI. If that could happen around here, we'd be set forever.[27]

There was certainly another factor involved here. On Cape Breton, there were many opportunities for young fiddlers to earn money and recognition playing for concerts and dances both at home and among Cape Breton émigré populations around North America. On Prince Edward Island—with contests no longer much of a factor and only a very few paying venues in operation—there was little incentive for learning to play well, apart from a sense of personal satisfaction.

The View from 1999: A *Changing of the Guard*

As things turned out, Chaisson and MacDonald had less reason for concern than they feared, and the years 1992–94 proved to be the watershed for PEI's fledgling fiddling revival. After this point, paid fiddling venues would begin to multiply, and expert young players would start appearing on the scene with almost clock-like regularity. More importantly, the activities of these new fiddlers (henceforth referred to as *new-generation fiddlers*) only served to amplify the revival's progress.

Perhaps the first sign of this sea change was the great success experienced by an event known as the Monticello Ceilidh, which had been founded in 1990 by two women with roots in northeastern Kings County—Jenny McQuaid and Teresa MacPhee Wilson (b. Monticello). McQuaid and Wilson borrowed both the term *ceilidh* and their general format from the previously mentioned event in Orwell, but they also instituted several innovations. As at Orwell, different fiddlers and singers were hired each week to serve as headliners, and much of the program was still in the form of a local talent show. Having noted the success of the nearby Circle Club Dance, however, McQuaid and Wilson decided to make old-time dancing a prominent part of the program; they also strongly encouraged local youngsters who had been studying step dancing to perform for the company. Other features that helped attract an audience included personable masters of ceremony (both McQuaid and Wilson were amateur comediennes), a 50/50 raffle, and a generous lunch.[28] In fairly short order, this formula began to attract larger and larger crowds. One measure of the event's success is the fact that the structure that housed it—a log hall built adjoining the old Monticello schoolhouse—had to be enlarged several times to accommodate a growing audience. By 1999, the log hall at Monticello was roughly four times its original size.

PHOTO 16.4. JENNY MCQUAID (*LEFT*) AND TERESA WILSON PERFORM AS THE COMIC DUO BRIDGET AND CECILY AT MONTICELLO TEA PARTY, JULY 1992 (PHOTO BY EARTHWATCH TEAM). THE ACT PARODIED ISLAND WOMEN OF THEIR GRANDPARENTS' GENERATION.

Having witnessed the success of the Monticello Ceilidh, many other Island towns and districts began to set up their own, similar events. Various solo performers and bands also borrowed the format. Because the word *ceilidh* had by this time become firmly implanted in the public mind, it soon became the generic term of choice for any Island program whose format even remotely resembled the one developed at Monticello (from now on I will refer to such events as *commercial ceilidhs*). By 1999, Islanders were talking about a "ceilidh boom," and—as Fr. Charles Cheverie reported to me—it was not uncommon on a typical summer weekend to find two full pages of classified ads in the *Guardian* announcing commercial ceilidhs taking place around the Island.[29]

To the surprise of many Islanders, a good many tourists with no particular local connection began frequenting commercial ceilidhs—a factor that grew markedly in significance after 1996 when the Confederation Bridge linking Prince Edward Island to the mainland was completed. Not only did this swell the ceilidh audience, but it also encouraged the development of entertainments aimed specifically at the tourist market.

In the Evangeline, the most significant such entertainment was a dinner theatre production called *La cuisine à Mémé* (Granny's Kitchen), which ran regularly during summer seasons near Mont Carmel at L'Étoile de Mer, a restaurant associated with a "cultural-tourism" development called Le Village de l'Acadie.[30] The production, which was founded in 1984 and ran for over twenty years, was targeted primarily at francophone tourists and featured skits based on vignettes from premodernization Acadian life interspersed with singing, fiddling, and step dancing by local artists.[31] Although *La cuisine à Mémé* resembled commercial ceilidhs in format (both were in essence glorified talent shows), it was a far more professional operation. Not only were musicians hired for an entire season and paid a salary, but the demands of working within a formal theatrical setting required them to develop a far higher level of performance practice and stagecraft than would have been necessary to function at a typical ceilidh.

By 1993–94, several students from the Rollo Bay Program had finally begun to reach musical maturity. The first to publicly emerge was Melanie Chaisson (b. 1978), daughter of Rollo Bay organizer "Young Peter" Chaisson. She began playing regularly at the Goose River Dance, and in 1995 she recorded several selections that later appeared on a CD produced by her father called *The Road to Rollo Bay*. Her playing on this recording apparently caught the imagination of several other area youngsters, who within the next couple of years had worked sufficiently hard to emerge as highly skilled players themselves. Included among this group were a few close relatives (her brother Stephen Chaisson and her cousins Kurt, Brent, and Koady Chaisson)[32] and two other youngsters who figure prominently in the next chapter (Ward MacDonald and Sheila MacKenzie).

Ward MacDonald (b. 1978) is the scion of a prominent Island fiddling family from Bangor, Kings County. His father is Allan MacDonald—an enthusiastic participant in the Eastern Kings Fiddlers. He also had two well-respected fiddling grandfathers—Hector MacDonald on the paternal side and Robert Crane (b. Riverton) on the maternal. Ward learned his first tunes from his father, put in a cameo appearance at the Rollo Bay Program, attended group classes in Montague taught by Paul MacDonald (no relation), and then continued working on his own. In the early 2000s while still a student at University of Prince Edward Island in Charlottetown, he was appointed president and music director of the Queens County Fiddlers; he has since served two terms as president of the PEI Fiddlers' Society Executive Board.

Sheila MacKenzie of Little Pond, Kings County (b. 1976), started step dancing at age five and then began studying dancing and fiddling, respectively, with Cecilia and Anne MacKinnon of Richmond, Prince County.[33] She joined the Rollo Bay Program in the late 1980s and was a student there until 1993. Following that training, she started playing for step dancers and square sets at the Monticello Ceilidh and also began playing regularly at the Goose River and Circle Club Dances. In 1997, she joined a band called Fiddlers' Sons and performed with them regularly for several years.[34] In 2006 she became the first female president of the PEI Fiddlers' Society Executive Board.

J.J. Chaisson continued to progress as originally expected, and by 1995–96 when barely into his teens he was rapidly acquiring a reputation as one of the best young fiddlers in Atlantic Canada. A couple of years later he released his first CD, entitled *In the Genes*, with a cover that featured insets with photographs of his two fiddling grandfathers. On the strength of that recording, he was booked to play at the prestigious American Festival of Fiddle Tunes in Port Townsend, Washington. He also began playing for dances and concerts throughout New England and the Maritimes.

Meanwhile, another group of young players was coming up in southeastern Prince County. Many of them had learned their skills through a new fiddle instruction program sponsored by the Prince Edward Island College of Piping, a Summerside-area music school established in 1990 by Ontario-born Scott MacAuley via a grant from the Canadian federal government. MacAuley had hired as primary fiddle instructor a New Brunswick native named Kim Vincent, a virtuoso Irish-style player then in his mid-thirties who had settled in South Granby, Queens County. Vincent's cosmopolitan background enabled him to effectively analyze and transmit skills that were specific to traditional fiddling, while being sufficiently flexible to allow students to pursue the styles of their home regions. As early as 1994, one of his students, Anastasia DesRoches (b. 1973), had made a notable local impact as a budding Prince County-style player. By the late 1990s, she was teaching individual and group fiddle lessons in her own right in her native Summerside.[35]

In another important development, by the late 1980s a few young adults from prominent Prince County fiddling families felt sufficiently encouraged by the general atmosphere of revival to take up or return to fiddling. Among this number were Albert and Peter Arsenault (sons of Eddy Arsenault of St. Chrysostom), Victor Doucette (son of Joseph Doucette of Deblois Road), and David Gaudet (nephew of Emil Gaudet of the Tignish area). Because in general their approach to fiddling closely reflected family traditions, this small coterie had the potential to serve as an important conduit for carrying distinctive local styles and variants into the new century.

New-generation fiddlers began taking over from old-time players at public events in the mid-1990s. At first, having younger fiddlers play for dances and ceilidhs was favored both as a novelty and as a sign that Island fiddling traditions might be preserved. Before long, however, organizers began to actively seek out the younger set; they were more professional in their approach to booking, more stage savvy, and appealed far more to tourists—most of whom seemed to prefer watching cute kids to wizened veterans. Increasingly since then, public fiddling (aside from playing at nursing homes) has passed to new-generation players. By 1999, it had become relatively rare to encounter old-time players performing at public venues.

One factor that led to the proliferation of young players on Prince Edward Island through the 1990s and beyond was the near-disappearance among adolescents of social stigmas attached to fiddling. Almost all of this change in attitude stemmed from the perception that fiddling proficiency could serve as a path to fame and fortune. In turn, this perception was fueled by three factors: the aforementioned predominance of young fiddlers at Island events, the development of touring opportunities for Island musicians, and the growing regional prominence of two young, high-powered fiddlers from Cape Breton—Natalie MacMaster and Ashley MacIsaac.

Prior to the modern era, the only locally based traditional-music entertainers to do any extensive touring had been Don Messer and members of his band, the Islanders. This situation changed markedly in the mid-1990s with the establishment of several annual government-sponsored regional and provincial music conventions, which offered musicians the opportunity to showcase their talents for Canadian and international presenters and agents. Most significant of these was the East Coast Music Awards (ECMAs), whose location has rotated among several major cities in Atlantic Canada. Another such event was Moncton-based Franco Fête, which catered specifically to francophone acts. Finally, PEI's own music convention—the Prince Edward Island Music Awards (PEIMAs)—was established in the late 1990s in Charlottetown.[36]

These conventions have helped several Island-based bands and solo acts achieve a national and international presence. The Chaissons proved to be one of the first beneficiaries. After a highly successful debut at the ECMAs when it was held in Charlottetown, the Chaisson Family Show—featuring Kevin, "Young Peter," and a rotating crew of offspring, nieces, and nephews—began touring in the region. In 1997, several young Chaissons—J.J., Stephen, Brent, Kurt, and Darla—formed a Celtic rock band called Celtic Tide, later renamed Kindle.[37] Kindle won best showcase at the ECMAs in 2000, was a featured main act there in 2003, and for several years toured extensively in Canada and the northeastern United States.

Another band that used the ECMAs as a springboard was Barachois (ba-ra-SHWAH), which featured fiddlers Louise Gallant Arsenault and Albert Arsenault, dancer-pianist Hélène Arsenault Bergeron, and horns player-comedian Chuck Arsenault.[38] They had come together as an ensemble while working as musicians and actors in the aforementioned dinner theater presentation, *La cuisine à Mémé*. With input from American-born manager Grady Poe, they were then transformed into a powerful stage act that blended Island fiddling and step dancing with Acadian balladry and slapstick comedy. They would go on to make three CDs—*Naturel*, *Barachois*, and *Encore*—and they toured extensively for over a decade in North America, the United Kingdom, and western Europe.[39]

Richard Wood's touring career was also successfully launched at the ECMAs. After first appearing there at the age of sixteen, he was booked to do a series of concert tours in North America, Britain, western Europe, and Japan. In the late 1990s, he toured for a year with Canadian-born country music star Shania Twain. For two years thereafter, he toured as a guest performer with the renowned Irish band the Chieftains. He has produced six CDs since his career took hold—*Come Dance with Me*, *Infectious*, *Fire Dance*, *The Celtic Touch*, *All Fired Up*, and *A Change of Reasons*.

Equally important in establishing the notion of fiddling as career path was the great success and high visibility of young Cape Bretoners MacMaster and MacIsaac. Natalie MacMaster (b. 1972) deeply impressed audiences with both her skilled playing and her electrifying stage presence. Ashley MacIsaac

(b. 1974) initially attracted attention through his vigorous approach to bowing and by mastering the ability to play fiddle and step-dance simultaneously. As he matured, he became known as much for his quirky habits of dress and self-presentation as for his music. Before long, both youngsters were being treated by the Canadian media more as pop stars than as fiddler-performers, and both ultimately began to experiment with injecting pop-music elements into their music.[40]

MacMaster and MacIsaac not only defused what remained of negative adolescent attitudes toward fiddling but also attracted many Island youngsters to the instrument and served as major influences among new-generation fiddlers in terms of repertoire, playing style, and general demeanor. Natalie MacMaster in particular became an inspiration to young girls. According to Hélène Bergeron, so great was her influence that in certain parts of Prince Edward Island, young girls began to dream of becoming fiddle players the way that young Canadian boys had long fantasized about hockey careers.[41] Above all, the examples of both young Cape Bretoners proved that world renown and considerable riches could result from the pursuit of what was once a homespun art. As Ward MacDonald puts it, "All of a sudden all the players on the Island went, 'Wow, you can make a living playing the fiddle.' That certainly changed a lot of the attitudes. It wasn't just going to be something you played in your living room or at a benefit concert."[42]

To complement the rise in the number of young fiddlers, a set of skilled young piano-accompanists was also emerging, many of whom had learned to play by actively emulating Kevin Chaisson's version of Cape Breton piano style. There was also increasing interest in playing fretted instruments, and some youngsters began experimenting with playing fiddle tunes "right out" on mandolin and guitar, a practice that was once quite rare on the Island.

By the turn of the twenty-first century, then, the generational torch had unmistakably been passed on. Most playing at Island ceilidhs and other public events was now conducted by fiddlers under the age of twenty-five. Audiences at these events had also grown younger, with many Islanders in their thirties and forties attending regularly and teenagers a not-uncommon sight. In fact, a newcomer attending commercial ceilidhs in 1999 or 2000 would have gotten a markedly different picture of the Island fiddling scene from the one we encountered in 1991–92.

In a sense, then, our story comes to a happy ending on the verge of a new century. Fiddling was rescued from the brink of extinction through the activities of literally thousands of Islanders. Even more important, a new generation of players had come to the fore, ready to take over as the older generation inexorably passed from the scene.

There were some trends, however, that struck me as problematic at the time. For one thing, the great majority of new-generation players hailed from only two parts of the Island: northeastern Kings County and the Evangeline Coast. For other Island regions, there was no mechanism in place to carry the old local styles and tunes into the future. Second, reflecting the priorities of the new Island scene, many new-generation players already seemed more concerned with developing effective stage acts than with becoming good dance players. Finally, the rapid disappearance of older generation fiddlers from the public eye meant that the next group of youngsters to come along would develop without having had much of an opportunity to hear them.

NOTES

1. See, for example, Anderson, "Voluntary Associations in History," 215–18; and Wallace, "Revitalization Movements."
2. Francis Collinson, introduction to *The Athole Collection*, vi. One of the major figures involved was James Stewart-Robertson, compiler of *The Athole Collection*.
3. Rosenberg, introduction to *Transforming Tradition*, 4–10.
4. Feintuch, "Musical Revival," 192.
5. See, for example, Rosenberg, introduction to *Transforming Tradition*, 10–17.
6. See, for example, Blaustein, "Rethinking Folk Revivalism," 270.
7. Although Mr. MacDonald was subsequently appointed bishop, because these events predate that appointment it makes sense to refer to him here simply as "Fr. MacDonald."
8. "The Vanishing Cape Breton Fiddler," in MacGillivray, *Cape Breton Fiddler*, 175–76. Although some scholars who focus on the Cape Breton fiddling milieu point out that MacInnes may have greatly overstated the case for decline (see, for example, Hennessey, "Fiddle Grooves," 44–50), the major consideration here is that at the time many Cape Bretoners did take the film's message to heart, and their activities served both as a model and as inspiration for aspects of the PEI fiddling revival.
9. Several Cape Breton fiddlers had been stationed in Scotland during World War II and were in a position to absorb various elements from contemporary Scottish culture. See, for example, "Dan R. MacDonald," in MacGillivray, *Cape Breton Fiddler*, 33.
10. A Southern Kings Fiddlers branch was initially established in Montague but soon disbanded. A second attempt to create a Southern Kings Fiddlers branch got under way in 2007; as of this writing it was still in operation.
11. John Gauthier, personal interview, Nov. 16, 2006, PEIFP Interview #40.
12. Ivan Day, in John Gauthier interview, Nov. 16, 2006, PEIFP Interview #40.

13. Margaret Ross MacKinnon, personal interview, March 11, 2008. Included among the Ceilidh Fiddlers were Bill MacDonald, Freddy McCullough, Leonard McDonald, John Dan MacPherson, Reuben Smith, Stephen Toole, and George Weatherbie. Ms. MacKinnon, who plays piano and pump organ, was their regular accompanist.
14. Cuts featuring the Leards and Lecky appear on *The Prince Edward Island Style of Fiddling: Fiddlers of Western PEI* (Rounder Records, #7014).
15. In 1971, a one-day Festival Acadien was appended to an annual agricultural fair called L'Exposition agricole. In 1974, a fiddling contest was made part of the proceedings, but in 1978 the contest was discontinued in favor of a fiddle-festival format (see Forsyth, "De par chez nous," 141–43). The timing of the switch suggests that it was made in sympathy with the anticontest stance of the Prince Edward Island Fiddlers' Society. The Atlantic Jamboree was founded by Philippe Leblanc of Mont Carmel, Prince County; a New Brunswick native, Leblanc moved to PEI in the 1980s after being hired as an art teacher by the Evangeline school district (see below).
16. Both Prince County events could also be seen as offshoots of an ongoing Acadian cultural resurgence; more on this later in the chapter.
17. The Club 50 is an offshoot of La Boueille ("The Buoy"), a social club founded in the 1970s by a local cultural organization called l'Association des Jeunes Francophones de la Région Évangéline ("Young Francophones of the Evangeline Coast"). See Forsyth, "De par chez nous," 104.
18. Margaret MacKinnon, personal communication via e-mail attachment, Dec. 1, 2007. See also the discussion of ceilidhs in chapter 2.
19. Arsenault, *Island Acadians*, 245–48, 252. One impetus for provincial action was the Official Languages Act, passed by the Canadian Parliament in 1969, that put French and English on equal footing. The school district is now known as Centre d'Education Évangéline.
20. Forsyth, "De par chez nous," 104–6. The term *Evangeline Coast* was derived from the name of the consolidated school district, which in turn was drawn from Longfellow's famous poem *Evangeline: A Tale of Acadie*.
21. Several young fiddlers who featured prominently in the PEI fiddling revival, including Anastasia DesRoches and Richard Wood, started off as step-dancing prodigies.
22. Originating in Dublin in 1994 with Michael Flatley as lead dancer and choreographer, *Riverdance* and a parallel production called *Lord of the Dance* toured worldwide; both productions were also the subject of several widely distributed videos.
23. It is customary for fiddle instructors in Scotland to present prized pupils with ribbons to tie around the scrolls or pegboxes of their fiddles. The PEI tartan was designed by Mrs. Jean Reid of Covehead, Queens County, and first adopted in 1960. The colors—selected to represent the Island milieu—consist of a main field of reddish brown and green with white and yellow accents. The impulse to commission an official Island Tartan may well have been inspired by the actions of neighboring Nova Scotia, which had acquired its own tartan design roughly a decade earlier (see chapter 13).
24. I was later made aware that at the time there had been a third such youngster—Billy MacInnis, Jr., of Village Green, Queens County—whose activities had gone largely

beneath my informants' collective radar. MacInnis went on to a professional fiddling career, and in 2006 he was touring with Stompin' Tom Connors.

25. Paul MacDonald's maternal uncle is "Kenny Johnny Joe" Chaisson, son of fiddler Johnny Joe Chaisson of Souris. Kenny Johnny Joe is married to Donna Chaisson, daughter of Joe Pete Chaisson and a sister of Kevin, "Young Peter," and "Kenny Joe Pete."
26. See previous note for Chaisson family relationships.
27. Natalie MacMaster's fiddling career is discussed later in this chapter. Her uncle Buddy MacMaster was a well-known Cape Breton fiddler of the generation born in the 1920s. Def Leppard was a popular British rock band of the 1980s; *The Twilight Zone* was an early television show that portrayed absurd or unlikely situations.
28. In a 50/50 raffle, the house retains half the intake and distributes the rest as prizes.
29. Fr. Charles Cheverie, personal interview, Aug. 12, 1999.
30. In English, the restaurant's name is "Starfish" and the development's name is "Acadian Village."
31. Forsyth, "De par chez nous," 144–47. The creator of this event was a local musician named Paul D. Gallant.
32. Kurt and Brent are sons of Kevin Chaisson; Koady is the brother of J.J. Chaisson.
33. These MacKinnons are members of a family from Cape Breton that moved to Richmond in the 1970s; soon thereafter, they began offering workshops in music and dance at different locations around the Island.
34. Sheila MacKenzie, personal interview, Oct. 29, 2006, PEIFP Interview #18. Ms. MacKinzie later married; her legal name is now Sheila MacKenzie FitzPatrick.
35. DesRosches' playing appears on *The Prince Edward Style of Fiddling: Fiddlers of Western* PEI. As mentioned in an earlier note, she recently published a collection of fiddle tunes composed by Islanders of Acadian descent.
36. To an extent the success of these artists—and also of those mentioned later in the chapter—was an outgrowth of a general music industry trend. After a Cape Breton group with traditional roots called the Rankin Family signed with EMI/Capitol Records in 1992 and experienced significant recording sales, a number of major "labels" became interested in signing and sponsoring other "Celtic"-based acts from Atlantic Canada. The various awards programs that grew up around this time seem to have been aimed at maintaining and amplifying this trend, in hopes of siphoning some music industry dollars through local players into the economies of their respective home provinces; see, for example, Hennessey, "Fiddle Grooves," 81–88.
37. Stephen is "Young Peter" Chaisson's eldest son; Darla is the daughter of "Kenny Joe Pete" Chaisson and plays piano very much like her uncle Kevin.
38. Hélène and Albert are brother and sister, the offspring of fiddler Eddy Arsenault of St. Chrysostom. Louise and Chuck are related neither to each other nor to Eddy's progeny.
39. The sound on Barachois' popular CDs was significantly shaped and polished by producer Grey Larsen. A musician and recording engineer from Bloomington, Indiana, who had been a member of popular American acoustic-music band Metamora—and

a long-time friend of manager Poe—Larsen eventually made so many trips to the Evangeline Coast that locals nicknamed him "Gris Larsenault." The band Barachois is profiled in Forsyth, "De par chez nous," 150–62.

40. For more on the careers, self-presentations, and impacts of both MacMaster and MacIsaac, see Hennessey, "Fiddle Grooves," 97–112. Natalie MacMaster's early career is also discussed in Perlman, "Cape Breton's First Family," 44–53.
41. Hélène Arsenault Bergeron, in Peter Arsenault interview, Oct. 18, 2006, PEIFP Interview #06.
42. Ward MacDonald, personal interview, Oct. 25, 2006, PEIFP Interview #13.

CHAPTER SEVENTEEN
"There's Been a Big Revival of Music on the Island"

The follow-up project of 2006 allowed me to reassess the trajectory of the PEI fiddling revival. Almost immediately upon my arrival, I realized that a second wave of modernization had taken place since the 1990s that in effect had carried the Island fully into the modern era. The building of the Confederation Bridge to the mainland was a major contributor in this regard. Not only did it make Prince Edward Island far more accessible to tourism and more attractive as a site for business and manufacturing, but it also made the major cities Moncton and Halifax far more easily accessible to Islanders. Another major contributor to modernization was the change in mass-communications technology, most notably the development of the Internet and satellite television.

As a result of such developments, Islanders as a rule seemed more tuned in to events and perspectives from the outside world. Activities in general were carried out in far stricter relationship to clocks and calendars. The local accent was losing its distinctiveness, many colorful local expressions were disappearing, and community handles had for the most part fallen into disuse.

Not only the younger generation was affected; many middle-aged and older Islanders had also undergone many of the same modifications in behavior, attitudes, and speech.

By 2006, roughly two-thirds of the fiddlers I had interviewed and recorded in 1991–92 had either passed away or stopped playing. Many of those who were still active were in a poor or reduced state of health, with their playing affected by hand injuries, arthritis, or other common afflictions of old age. Some had simply decided for reasons of their own that they did not want to play anymore. The eastern half of the Island was most severely affected; with the exception of the Northeast Kings area, there were only a very few old-time fiddlers left east of Charlottetown, and almost all that remained were over eighty. The situation in the western half of the Island was somewhat better, particularly in Prince County, where there were a few active old-time players still in their fifties and sixties.

As far as the revival was concerned, what was most apparent was the unequivocal and overwhelming success of the movement to bring back fiddling as a popular activity. This success was apparent on three levels. Hundreds of youngsters were seriously studying the fiddle in formal instruction programs, probably a similar number of adult hobbyists were actively involved in playing the instrument, and a professional elite had emerged who were in demand to play at a wide variety of publicly funded and commercial venues. Kevin Chaisson of Bear River, Kings County, offered this overall assessment:

> There's no question in my mind that there's more fiddlin' goin' on now than the last time you were here. Right across the Island: it's not just up here [Northeast Kings], and it's not just up west [the Evangeline Coast]. It's all over. It's everywheres. Music is everywheres now. There's been a big revival of music on the Island.[1]

By 2006, the Island was abuzz with the names of new-generation players—not only such holdovers from the '90s as J.J. Chaisson, Anastasia DesRoches, Ward MacDonald, Sheila MacKenzie, and Richard Wood, but also many still-younger players such as Timothy Chaisson, Nathan Condon, Aaron Crane, Elmer Deagle, Courtney Hogan, Cynthia MacLeod, and Keelan Wedge (from this point on, the original group is referred to as *first-wave fiddlers*, and the more recent lot, *second-wave fiddlers*).[2] There had also been a proliferation of fiddling CDs released by new-generation players—this on an island where prior to the 1990s there was virtually no commercial recording of fiddle music. In addition, residents of just about every part of Prince Edward Island could point to talented local youngsters whose progress portended promising fiddling careers.

Given that fiddling on Prince Edward Island was once almost exclusively a male calling, it is noteworthy that since the late 1990s a substantial majority of fiddlers at all levels—students, amateurs, and professionals—have been female. Numerous informants have offered explanations for this phenomenon. Sheila MacKenzie (b. Little Pond, Kings County), for example, posits that women make better musicians than men when given the chance, because "they naturally gravitate toward melody and timing." Hélène Bergeron (b. St. Chrysostom, Prince County) focuses on the powerful example provided by dynamic performer Natalie MacMaster. Fr. Charles Cheverie feels that the preponderance of women taking part in fiddling is in keeping with general contemporary trends in most of the arts and sciences.[3] To the above, I can add two theories of my own—that negative adolescent peer pressure had never been as effectively defused for males as for females, and that youngsters enrolled in formal step-dancing programs (the vast majority of whom have been female) are not only more likely than the general population to take up the fiddle but also more likely to progress rapidly because of their familiarity with the music and its rhythms.

Barachois and Kindle had disbanded, but fine new ensembles were forming to take their place—especially in Prince County, where the success of Barachois had opened the door for bands from Acadian communities to tour abroad. Using Franco Fête as the primary staging ground, a conduit had developed—with terminals in Moncton, the Evangeline Coast, and the Magdalene Islands[4]—whereby accomplished francophone musicians could join forces to form traditional music ensembles. In turn, a ready market for such ensembles had grown up in France, Belgium, and various francophone regions of North America. One prominent new group that had grown up to perform on this circuit was Vishten, based at the time in Mont Carmel.[5]

To match increasing demand, the number of instructors teaching private or group lessons had increased perhaps tenfold since the early 1990s. Fiddle lessons were being taught at home studios, at music stores, at community halls, and in conjunction with fiddle club meetings. At least two public schools on the Island had instituted fiddle instruction programs as part of the curriculum—one in Donagh, Queens County, and another in Ellerslie, Prince County.[6] There were also fiddle instruction courses available at dozens of Community School programs. All the private instructors I spoke with were experiencing land-office demand for their services, and some—such as Louise Gallant Arsenault in the Evangeline Coast, Robert Arsenault in the Charlottetown area, and Amy Swenson in south-central Kings County—were teaching anywhere from thirty to sixty students per week during much of the year.[7] Extrapolating from this sample, I would estimate that in the fall of 2006 there were roughly several hundred to a thousand active fiddle students on the Island, amounting to nearly 1 percent of the entire population.

The Rollo Bay Program was still in operation under the direction of the Chaisson brothers, with Kathryn Dau-Schmidt still in place as principal instructor. Given the number of competing options, however, both the program's overall attendance and its significance on the Island scene had declined markedly. The division of labor had also become more formalized, with Dau-Schmidt teaching the beginner and intermediate classes and "Young Peter" Chaisson teaching the advanced class.

The proliferation of instruction programs had created a substantial pool of Islanders with at least some fiddle training and some ability to read music. Although a few budding virtuosos aspired to becoming soloists on the commercial ceilidh circuit, most other fiddle students and amateurs had turned to ensemble playing as their main avenue for self-expression. As a result, there was an exponential increase in the number of fiddle clubs and fiddle-centered amateur bands. In addition, many Island fiddle teachers regularly rehearsed their own students for group performances, and new organizations that focused on fiddling had started up—notably, the Maritime Fiddlers (a New Brunswick–based organization devoted to the music of Don Messer and his musical heirs) and the PEI Bluegrass Society.[8]

Although fiddle tune jam sessions have been commonplace for generations in other parts of North America, they have only recently become popular on Prince Edward Island. By 2006, several regular jams devoted to tunes-playing had become established around the Island. Among them were after-hours get-togethers at the Community School in Murray Harbour, periodic gatherings of musically inclined North Side women at the home of Theresa MacPhee Wilson in Goose River, and two weekly sessions—one in Charlottetown sponsored by the PEI Bluegrass Society, and another in the Evangeline Coast, held in the basement of the Boys and Girls' Club in Wellington.[9] The Wellington Jam—led by Marie Arsenault Livingstone of Summerside—was of particular interest because it brought novices and avid amateurs into frequent contact with established fiddlers and accompanists from the Evangeline region.[10]

Another development worthy of note was a steady improvement on the Island in the general level of fretted-instrument playing, particularly guitar.

Among those aspects that had improved considerably since the 1990s were pick control, complexity of bass runs and accompaniment patterns, and the ability to play note-for-note versions of fiddle tunes up to speed.

With its job of advocacy largely completed and with so many other options available for those seeking to play in ensembles, the PEI Fiddlers' Society as a whole seemed to be in decline. The Eastern Kings branch no longer met regularly, and attendance at the two still-active branches had fallen to roughly half the levels observed in 1991–92. At the Prince County branch, neither founding director John Gauthier nor his successor, Peter Doiron, were still on the scene, and leadership of the group had passed to amateur players. Of the original founding members, only Jim MacDougall of Grand River was still a regular participant.

Fr. Charles Cheverie was still the titular head of the Queens County Fiddlers, but—well into his seventies—he was in the process of scaling down his involvement. Ward MacDonald of Bangor, Kings County, had been serving as music director of the QCF since 2003 and conducted most rehearsals and performances. Shortly after he took over, the branch decided to create its own CD. MacDonald selected the tunes, arranged them into sets, and then rehearsed the group for eight months. In May 2004, over three dozen fiddlers jammed onto the altar at Central Christian Church in Charlottetown and—with Roy Johnstone as sound engineer—recorded the entire project in twelve hours. The ensuing recording, *Forty Fiddles, Flat Out*, sold several thousand copies on the Island. The completion of this project proved to be a high-water mark, however, and thereafter attendance at branch rehearsals began to fall off.[11]

Commercial ceilidhs were still plentiful, but there were signs of trouble ahead. For one thing, as Ward MacDonald points out, there were simply too many of them in operation, resulting in both competition for audience and dilution of talent.

> You open up the paper, and there's thirty ceilidhs. For a while that's going to work, 'cause Islanders and tourists are going to want to go around and try them all. But after a few years, the ones that are good will still get the crowds, and the ones that are not, may not. The numbers of ceilidhs are starting to shrink back a bit. Maybe that's good. Maybe you're more likely to hear good music if it's not spread so thinly.[12]

Another problem arose when organizers began using the term *ceilidh* to describe nearly any kind of local entertainment. As J.J. Chaisson points out, "Everybody is using *ceilidh* as a draw, because five years ago, ceilidh was a huge thing. It's too bad, because now people are startin' to wonder, 'Is the ceilidh really a ceilidh, or is it a concert [or] a jam session?'"[13]

The audience frequenting fiddling events had also been changing. In 1991–92, much of the audience had grown up during the traditional period and thoroughly understood fiddle music. By 2006, a major proportion of this group was no longer active. Although the audiences of 2006 were just as full of gray and silver heads as their 1992 counterparts, the demographics had shifted. The new audience was largely composed of Islanders who had come of age in the 1950s and '60s, when local fiddling was in decline. Although they might have been aware of traditional fiddle music during their youth, it was not really *their* music. In fact, by 2006 many Island audiences seemed far more at home with country and western, rock 'n' roll, and other guitar-based musics than with fiddling and square dancing.

This has made for major shifts in programming and audience behavior at many commercial ceilidhs. At some events I attended, as much as three-fourths of total stage time was taken up by local country and western singers, and almost all dancing took the form of couples' dancing. During vocal performances, attendees generally waltzed to songs in 3/4 time and did the fox-trot or Lindy hop to songs in 4/4 time. And instead of forming square sets or big circles when fiddlers struck up a jig or reel, they again paired as couples and kept time to the music using fox-trot or Lindy-hop steps.

Old-time dancing had never been successfully revived and seemed well on its way to disappearing from the Island scene altogether. Although interest in dancing square sets had surged somewhat in the 1990s during the early days of commercial ceilidhs, this proved to be but a temporary interruption of a long-term decline. By 2006, most regularly scheduled square dances had been discontinued, many commercial ceilidhs had gotten away from old-time dancing, and almost all mainstream dance events—which had hitherto offered up a couple of square sets per program to appease the old folks—had dropped old-time dancing from the agenda. When attendance began to fall off at the Circle Club Dance in St. Peters, it was transformed into a commercial ceilidh.[14] The last remaining regular square dance in the Charlottetown area (featuring fiddler Elliott Wight) was discontinued in the spring of 2006.[15] Similarly, Dennis Pitre of St. Felix, Prince County, reported that in the summer of 2006 when his band asked for a show of hands on whether to continue including square sets on the program during the weekly dance at the Tignish Fire Hall, the crowd voted against it.[16] To the best of my knowledge, in the fall of 2006 there were only two remaining venues on Prince Edward Island that offered full programs of old-time dancing—the Goose River Dance and the Lorne Valley Dance—both in northern Kings County.[17]

The step-dancing revival also seemed to be in decline. In 1991–92, a substantial portion of nearly every concert, square dance, or town day had been set aside for individual and group step-dancing displays, all of which were performed to live fiddling. Although I did not attend nearly as many events in 2006 as during the 1991–92 project, my impression was that step dancing in general had fallen off markedly in participation and popularity.[18] In any event, both old-time and younger-generation players frequently voiced the complaint that the current crop of step dancers were no longer being trained to respond to fiddlers' tempos or rhythmic nuances; they either expected fiddlers to adjust to them or used recorded music. What's more, the distinctiveness of the local brand of schooled step dancing had been seriously undermined by the importation of steps, routines, and stagecraft both from Appalachian clogging and from such commercial productions of Irish step dancing as *Riverdance* and *Lord of the Dance*.

A major shift in repertoire was also apparent among both new-generation and active old-time players. As noted in chapter 14, many tunes that were widely played in 1991–92 and had been standards for generations had virtually dropped from circulation by 2006. To fill the gap, new favorites—either locally composed or adopted via the mass media—had risen to prominence.

"When All the Old-Timers Depart, Most of Their Styles Are Going with Them"

As for the old-time players themselves, for the most part they had been bypassed by the revival and did not factor significantly in the Island's new, burgeoning music scene. Continuing trends first observed in the 1990s, the accomplished new-generation fiddlers were the ones who played at the variety shows and concerts and got grants from the provincial government to make CDs. Alternatively, it was the hobbyists who generally joined the ensembles and clubs.

In 2006, the playing styles of both new-generation players and hobbyists were largely disconnected from traditional Island styles. Most hobbyists played with a stylistically neutral approach. New-generation fiddlers from northeastern Kings County (including those who came up through the Rollo Bay

Program) played an offshoot of Cape Breton style. As for second-wave fiddlers from other parts of the Island, much of what I heard can best be described as fast, clean, and rhythmically flat playing. Although this approach may be well suited to the demands of stage performance, it lacks the subtle rhythmic inflections that for generations had tied Island fiddling to the dance.

Instead of listening to or learning from older players, most younger-generation fiddlers picked up stylistic elements from each other or attempted to emulate approaches heard on popular fiddle recordings. Perhaps most influential in this regard was the recorded work of Natalie MacMaster, Ashley MacIsaac, and other young Cape Breton players. Also back in the picture were recordings by Don Messer and some of his prominent disciples, notably, Ivan Hicks and Graham Townsend. In addition, bluegrass fiddling had grown significantly in local popularity and had begun contributing to the stylistic palette.

Only in Prince County had some older styles been passed down to new-generation players. As previously noted, in the 1980s several adult scions of prominent Prince County fiddling families such as Peter Arsenault, Victor Doucette, and David Gaudet had either taken up or returned to seriously playing the instrument; by 2006 many of them had developed into strong players with styles that closely mirrored those of older generations. Moreover, the playing of some first-wave youngsters with Acadian backgrounds had also retained some regional flavor.

As PEI's old-time fiddlers disappeared from the spotlight, awareness of their fascinating playing styles and tune versions was fading rapidly from public consciousness. As Peter Arsenault notes, "I think when all the old timers depart, most of their styles are going with them, not to be duplicated. It's not that far away."[19]

These developments dramatically altered Islanders' notions regarding playing style. With so many old-time fiddlers gone from the scene, the east-west gradient of styles was no longer as evident. What most observers saw on Prince Edward Island in 2006 was just two styles: Celtic in the east and Acadian in the west. In the east, "Celtic" had replaced "Scottish" as the term of choice to describe the Cape Breton–oriented style played by most active fiddlers from northeastern Kings County. In the west, "Acadian" was the term employed for the music of francophone players from western Prince Edward Island. Many Acadians no longer recognized a stylistic kinship between the fiddling styles of eastern and western Prince Edward Island, or even among francophone and anglophone fiddlers from western Prince Edward Island. Instead, they only

PHOTO 17.1. VICTOR DOUCETTE AT HARPER ROAD NEAR TIGNISH, NOVEMBER 2006 (PHOTO BY KEN PERLMAN).

acknowledged a link between Acadian fiddlers from Prince Edward Island and francophone fiddlers from other nearby regions, notably, eastern New Brunswick and the Magdalene Islands.[20]

Also rapidly disappearing was the sense that Prince Edward Island ever had its own unique regional fiddling sound. One symptom of this state of affairs: even the term *old-time fiddling* was in the process of shifting its meaning, becoming increasingly associated with the playing of Don Messer and his heirs. To put this last development into perspective, Island fiddlers interviewed in 1991–92 had been nearly unanimous in declaring Messer's playing not stylistically akin to old-time Island fiddling.

There has been little hue and cry on the Island about the disappearance of the old Island styles. By 2006, it had been nearly a decade since most people had heard them, and frankly—without the help of recordings to keep memories refreshed—most people were not sufficiently attuned to such stylistic niceties to mourn their loss. What's more, in the natural course of events, neither youngsters nor newcomers would have even been aware that a cornucopia of playing styles had once graced the Island.

"They're Not Exposed to Them; They Don't Even Maybe Know Them"

The seeming irrelevance of older players and the disappearance of local stylistic idioms were probably inevitable given both the kinds of strategies employed by revival leaders and long-term trends in local culture and technology. In hopes of restoring respectability to the art and ensuring it a role in contemporary culture, fiddling was taken out of the kitchen and dance hall and put on the stage. And for fear of encountering the crowd-control issues that had once plagued Island dance halls, no consistent campaign was ever undertaken to revitalize old-time square dancing. Although this state of affairs did little to alter the styles of older fiddlers, the absence of opportunities to play for square sets has increasingly affected the sound of new-generation players. It is noteworthy in this regard that on neighboring Cape Breton where the old-time dance scene remained strong, younger fiddlers still play with strong dance-oriented rhythmic accents, and their playing styles in general have remained relatively close to those of older generations.

Meanwhile, strategies that in retrospect could have promoted the survival of older Island fiddling styles were eschewed—largely for fear of reactivating the rivalries and jealousies of the fiddle contest era. Fiddle clubs, organizations, and festivals never specifically promoted local styles and rarely if ever singled out older-generation players for special recognition. And after the 1970s when the PEI Fiddlers' Society declared contests off-limits to its members, no Island organization seriously considered setting up its own music competitions—even though such events have long been effectively employed by music revival movements throughout the Western world as a means for establishing stylistic standards.

Adding to the overall problem was the notion that little or nothing needed to be done via music education to pass on style. Early leaders were correct that motivated students would seek out stylistic models once they had the rudiments, but they failed to anticipate how quickly the older generation would disappear from prominence, and how instead attractive examples would arise in the media to occupy the foreground.

Because of the way that the fiddling revival progressed, contact between the musical generations declined precipitously after the mid-1990s. Youngsters from the first wave frequently shared the stage at dances and commercial ceilidhs with older players and had the opportunity to develop a sense of their repertoires, playing styles, and self-presentations. By the time the sec-

PHOTO 17.2. ANGUS MCPHEE AND CYNTHIA JAY CRANE AT CIRCLE CLUB DANCE, ST. PETERS, JULY 1991 (PHOTO BY EARTHWATCH TEAM).

ond wave came along, however, the older generation was no longer playing as much in public. Consequently, as Sheila MacKenzie points out, their music was just not sufficiently available for it to serve as a formative influence.

> I know there's a lot less interaction between some of the younger players and some of the older ones. They're not exposed to them; they don't even maybe know them. So they're maybe not getting the chance to learn from them as much. When I played, Angus McPhee would be at everything.[21] And you'd get a few stories out of him, or you'd get tunes, and even just to watch an older fiddler play.[22]

Another set of factors is involved here as well. Once fiddling had become primarily a performance medium, practitioners had to develop strategies to capture audience attention and generate excitement. As noted earlier, one of the first things brought about by these conditions was a substantial increase in average tempos. Along with the increase in speed came the notion that fiddling had to be a show and that for a given audience sometimes the show was equal to or greater in importance than the actual quality of playing. This emphasis on performance practice increased as it became clear that fiddling could serve as a path both to local renown and (in a few cases) to lucrative touring careers.

Given this state of affairs, any subtle musical insights or advice that players from the older generation might have had to offer second-wave youngsters would no longer seem particularly relevant. Sheila MacKenzie sums it up as follows:

> I think they see people like Natalie [MacMaster], or on the Island they see Cynthia MacLeod play. And they think they'd like to do that, but they don't understand everything that goes with it. Because it's very much a living tradition, and you're trying to carry something on and pass it on. And I don't think a lot of them get that and appreciate it. They don't see the value in going to see an older fiddler, because all they hear is scratchy, and they don't understand that this guy probably played four or five nights a week for thirty or forty years, and he was really good.[23]

"I Hope the Music Never Dies!"

In retrospect, the major outcomes of the PEI fiddling revival were twofold: creating a local professional fiddling scene and making the art of fiddling available as a pastime to a significant number of Islanders. Fiddling on Prince Edward Island may have changed significantly since the 1970s in terms of venue, style, and repertoire, but it might well not have survived as a widespread activity without undergoing precisely these kinds of changes.

If any old-time players felt unfairly left behind by the course of events, they did not express such thoughts to me. On the contrary, most of them seemed delighted that the activity they cherished would be carried on. As Francis MacCormack (b. St. Charles, Kings County) asserts, "Now I'm really happy with the way things are going on the Island with fiddle music. I'm surprised at all the young girls, all the young boys picking up the fiddle. It's amazing! If it keeps up we'll never have the problem [of declining interest] we had a few years ago."[24]

There was some concern expressed among both old hands and first-wave players about current trends, however. Robert Arsenault (b. Abram-Village), for example, saw the music as "better played but [not] as alive." Richard Wood warned of a loss of "soul and heart." Sheila MacKenzie feared that the music as it became disconnected from tradition was "going to get bland." J.J. Chaisson was concerned that as youngsters rely increasingly on media models, "it's gonna get harder to distinguish different styles."[25]

There was discussion in 2006 and afterward among old-time and first-wave players about acting to preserve some older Island styles, and a few concrete steps have been taken. There have been activities aimed at founding a formal fiddling school, for example, either connected with the Orwell Corner Historic Site in southeastern Queens County or at the Rollo Bay Festival grounds. Both Louise Arsenault and Ward MacDonald expressed the ambition to start up annual instructional weeks devoted to Island fiddle music and dance. MacDonald has also been looking into strategies for resuscitating old-time dancing.[26]

Precisely what path Island fiddling will take in the coming years is not at all clear. Should current trends continue, the perception that just two "traditional" styles (Celtic and Acadian) are played on Prince Edward Island will soon become the reality. The better anglophone players will be absorbed into the Cape Breton fiddling scene (this process is, in fact, already taking place), the next group of youngsters will emulate them, and eventually the playing styles of most anglophone Island fiddlers may become indistinguishable from those of their Cape Breton counterparts. Meanwhile, fiddling styles among francophone players across Atlantic Canada are in the process of merging, and the ensuing composite is likely to draw in most new-generation francophone fiddlers.[27]

Alternatively, fiddling may remain a highly popular activity on the Island, but practitioners as a whole may not follow any particular style. New influences drawn from media or new groups of immigrants will lure musicians in various directions. A decade hence, young PEI fiddlers might be little different in terms of motivation and consciousness from their counterparts in most other regions of North America. In other words, each talented player will simply find his or her own way among a host of competing musical options.

Finally, what we might be seeing on Prince Edward Island today is the gradual evolution of a new pan-Island style that draws on elements from various local, regional, and media-based styles. Something akin to this happened during the 1990s in Ontario, where what might be termed a central Canadian fiddling sound was synthesized from elements drawn from Ottawa Valley, Québecois, Cape Breton, and Don Messer styles.

Regardless of which scenario comes to pass, it is to be hoped that in the not-too-distant future an even newer generation of Island musicians might feel far enough removed from PEI's difficult, agrarian past to idealize it. Perhaps, like the young Americans of the 1960s and '70s who sparked the Appalachian fiddle music revival, these future Islanders will rediscover via the magic of field recordings their own stock of old-time fiddlers and seek to faithfully re-create their fascinating tunes, twists, and styles.[28]

I draw my narrative to a close here and will leave analysis of post-2006 musical trends on Prince Edward Island to other researchers. As the reader may already have surmised, I was drawn to the study of PEI fiddling because I saw it as pure and uncorrupted in comparison to the popular music of my own time and place. It should come as no surprise, then, when I report that I am saddened by the passing of both the old players and the old Island fiddling styles. As a musician and folk-music scholar, however, I am intrigued and excited by the prospect of the new and am filled with curiosity concerning just how Island fiddling will turn out. For after its long journey—from the crofts and clacháns of Scotland and Ireland, through pioneer days and its role as the lively focus of district life, through its resilience in the face of adverse pressures from both organized religion and the mass media, through its periods of precipitous decline and painstaking revival—we can rejoice that this lively activity will indeed survive on Prince Edward Island. I will close with this valedictory, uttered in 1992 by revival organizer Kevin Chaisson:

> Before I'm gone, I hope, by Jesus, there's an acre of 'em shoulder to shoulder! Seriously, that's how I feel about it. I hope there's all kinds of players. I hope the music never dies. It's too much fun, too much fun!

NOTES

1. Kevin Chaisson, personal interview, Nov. 30, 2006, PEIFP Interview #67.
2. Timothy Chaisson is Kevin Chaisson's youngest son, and Elmer Deagle is one of Kevin's nephews; Aaron Crane is a grandson of fiddler Roland Jay from Mt. Stewart. Both Paul MacDonald and Melanie Chaisson had left the Island in the late 1990s; at the time of this writing, neither was actively pursuing a musical career.
3. PEIFP interviews: Sheila MacKenzie (Interview #18), Oct. 29, 2006; Hélène Arsenault Bergeron (Interview #06; primary informant: Peter Arsenault), Oct. 18, 2006; Fr. Charles Cheverie (Interview #63), Nov. 28, 2006.
4. Administratively a part of the province of Québec, the francophone Magdalene Islands lie in the Gulf of St. Lawrence about seventy-five miles north of northeastern Prince Edward Island. The population of the Magdalene Islands is largely descended from

Acadian settlers who migrated there after the *grand dérangement*. See Forsyth, "De par chez nous," 285–86.

5. Vishten core personnel consists of Pastelle LeBlanc on piano accordion, Emmanuelle LeBlanc on flute and whistle (both from Mont Carmel, Prince County), and Pascal Miousse from the Magdalene Islands on fiddle. The LeBlancs are twin daughters of Philippe LeBlanc, who in the 1990s was one of the major organizers of the Atlantic Jamboree. Other musicians have sometimes joined the ensemble for extended periods; during 2006, for example, guitarist/banjoist Elmer Deagle was a regular band member. For a profile on Vishten, see Forsyth, "De par chez nous," 290–314.

6. The Donagh fiddle program was initially financed via a series of community benefit concerts and other fundraisers; in 2006 the principal instructor was Ranita Baird, daughter of fiddler Merlin Quinn of Cardross, Kings County (Amy Swenson, personal interview, Oct. 26, 2006, PEIFP Interview #15). At Ellerslie, the long-term head of the strings program was Peter Robinson, a close relative of noted West Prince fiddler Elmer Robinson and son of Keith Robinson, who played guitar on Island radio in the 1940s (Peter Robinson, personal interview, Nov. 11, 2006, PEIFP Interview #32).

7. PEIFP interviews: Louise Gallant Arsenault (Interview #55), Nov. 24, 2006; Robert Arsenault (Interview #03), Oct. 16, 2006; Amy Swenson (Interview #15), Oct. 26, 2006. Louise Arsenault and Robert Arsenault have both been mentioned many times in this volume. California-born Swenson was living in the Pacific Northwest in the late 1990s when she came across a copy of the author's tunebook, *The Fiddle Music of Prince Edward Island*, and read in the introduction about a shortage of fiddle instruction on the Island. She resolved to move to Prince Edward Island, and not long afterward she set up shop as a fiddle teacher and repairer in Caledonia, Kings County, not far from Montague.

8. In 2006, the Island branch of the Maritime Fiddlers was headed up by Mary Pineau Smith of North Rustico Harbour, Queens County; one of her duties was to organize an annual convention known as the Fiddle-Do, which that year drew about four hundred participants from across Atlantic Canada (Mary Pineau Smith, personal interview, Nov. 13, 2006, PEIFP Interview #35).

9. For Murray Harbour: Amy Swenson, personal interview, Oct. 26, 2006, PEIFP Interview #15; for Goose River: Teresa MacPhee Wilson and Friends, Nov. 14, 2006, PEIFP Interview #37; for Wellington: Marie Arsenault Livingstone, Oct. 19, 2006, in Edward P Arsenault interview, PEIFP Interview #07. In 2007, a weekly jam session focusing on fiddle tunes of all descriptions was established in Charlottetown by fiddler Roy Johnstone; at last report, it was still attracting a substantial turnout.

10. Marie Livingstone is the sister of fiddler Edward P Arsenault of Wellington; although she took up the fiddle relatively late in life, she has become a major compiler and composer of fiddle music. For more on her role and on the continued importance of the Wellington jam in the contemporary Evangeline fiddling scene, see Forsyth, "De par chez nous," 210–15.

11. According to Ward MacDonald (personal interview, Jan. 29, 2008), the QCF was then thinking of producing a second CD project.

12. Ward MacDonald, personal interview, Oct. 25, 2006, PEIFP Interview #13.
13. J.J. Chaisson, personal interview, Nov. 30, 2006, PEIFP Interview #66.
14. Anita Beaton, in St. Peters Ceilidh interview, Dec. 1, 2006, PEIFP Interview #69.
15. Judy Lowe, personal interview, Nov. 17, 2006, PEIFP Interview #41.
16. Dennis Pitre, personal interview, Nov. 9, 2006, PEIFP Interview #28.
17. While visiting the Island during the summer of 2013, I ascertained that both the Lorne Valley Dance and the Goose River Dance were still in operation.
18. This impression was corroborated by fiddler Richard Wood, personal interview, Dec. 2, 2006, PEIFP Interview #70.
19. Peter Arsenault, personal interview, Oct. 18, 2006, PEIFP Interview #06.
20. The growing separation between the francophone and anglophone music scenes on Prince Edward Island may be one consequence of the Acadian cultural resurgence discussed in chapter 16.
21. Angus McPhee of Mt. Stewart, Queens County, was one of the fiddlers interviewed for our project. He often played for the old-time dances at St. Peters and Goose River, Kings County, in the 1980s and 1990s.
22. Sheila MacKenzie, Oct. 29, 2006, PEIFP Interview #18.
23. Sheila MacKenzie interview, Oct. 29, 2006.
24. Francis MacCormack, Oct. 15, 2006, PEIFP Interview #02.
25. PEIFP interviews: Robert Arsenault (Interview #03), Oct. 16, 2006; Richard Wood (Interview #70), Dec. 2, 2006; Sheila MacKenzie (Interview #18), Oct. 29, 2006; J.J. Chaisson (Interview #66), Nov. 30, 2006.
26. MacDonald has been particularly active in this regard. In 2007, he was appointed to head up a week-long event called the Festival of Small Halls, which featured performances at dozens of different venues around the Island by fiddlers from both new and old-time generations. In 2009, he brought in dance caller Pierre Chartrand from Québec in hopes of rekindling an interest in dancing square sets. In 2010, he established the PEI Fiddle Camp, whose inaugural run had about a dozen instructors and thirty-five students.
27. With the benefit of hindsight, we can now say that this budding pan-Acadian style has been significantly shaped by the playing of two fiddlers who toured extensively with Island-based touring bands in the 1990's and early 2000's-Louise Arsenault of Barachois and Pascal Miousse of Vishten. One of the defining feature of this composite style is the increased salience of the suppressed stroke, or *shuffles* technique (chapter 9), a bowing ornament which Arsenault learned from her father and other Evangeline Coast fiddlers but then increasingly emphasized and elaborated during her Barachois years.
28. As mentioned earlier, as of this writing a home is being sought for a website devoted to field recordings of traditional PEI fiddlers. For more information, see note 4 in the introduction.

APPENDIX A: MUSICAL EXAMPLES

Chapter 2

EXAMPLE 2.1. PRINCE EDWARD ISLAND WEDDING REEL

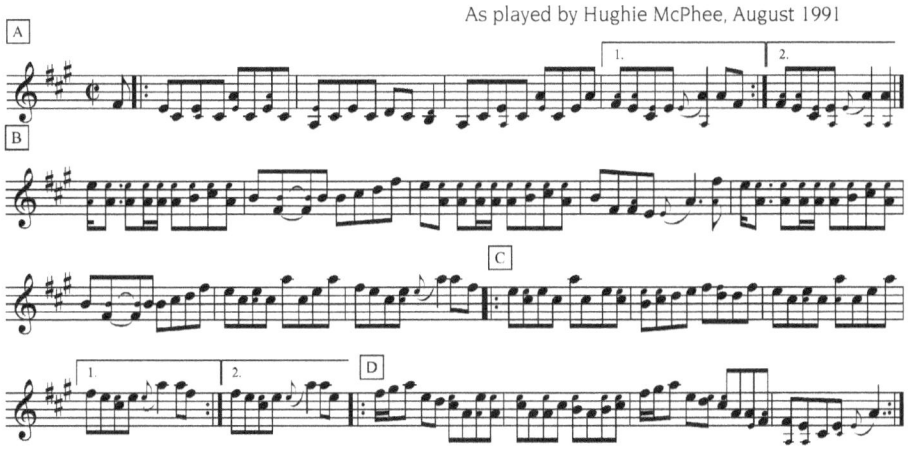

EXAMPLE 2.2. REEL OF HONOR

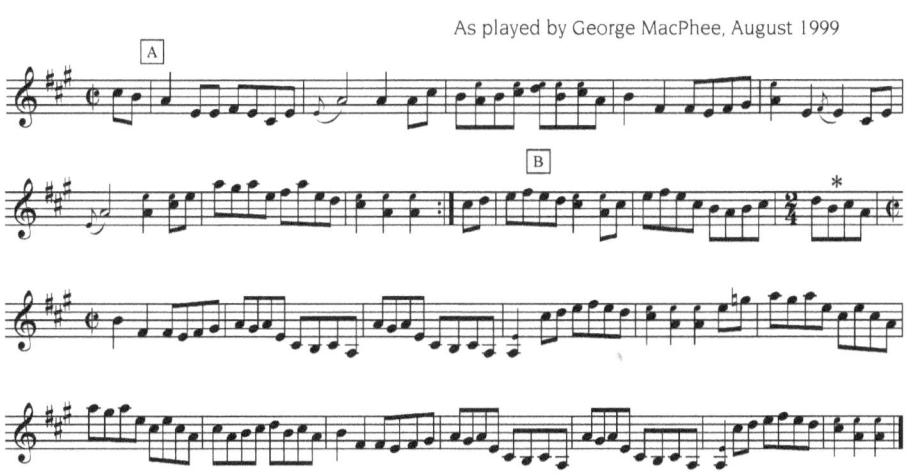

*It is unlikely that this short measure was "structural" to the Wedding Reel dance. MacPhee consistently played the tune this way during the recording session, but it may well have been a by-product of his having just dredged the tune up from memory.

Chapter 3

EXAMPLE 3.1. LOW TURN (MEASURES 1–2) OF "LORD MACDONALD'S REEL"

Chapter 6

EXAMPLE 6.1. TWISTS ON HIGH TURN CADENTIAL PHRASE (MEASURES 7–8), "LORD MACDONALD'S REEL"

"Old Peter" Chaisson, Bear River

Gus Longaphie, Souris

Wilfred Gotell, Georgetown

Dave Thomson, North River

Attwood O'Connor, Milltown Cross

Archie Stewart, Milltown Cross

Leonard McDonald, Emyvale

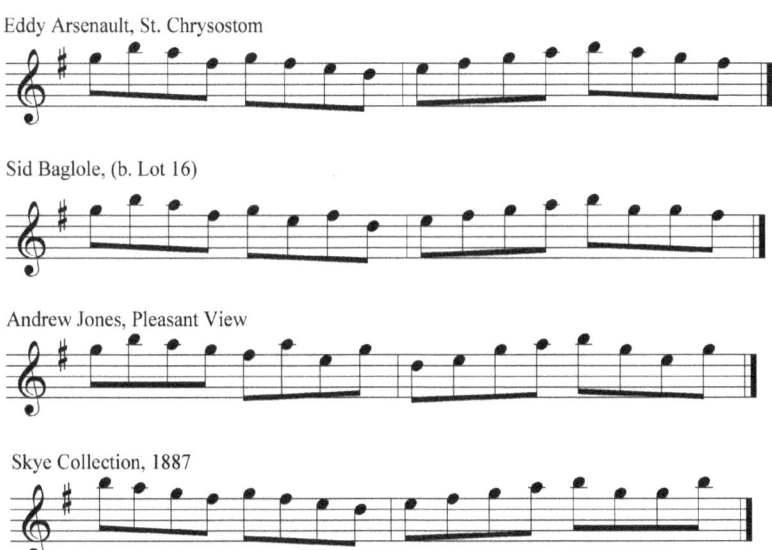

EXAMPLE 6.1a. FULL HIGH TURN, "LORD MACDONALD'S REEL"
(AS PLAYED BY ATTWOOD O'CONNOR)

EXAMPLE 6.2. TWISTS ON LOW TURN CADENTIAL PHRASE
(MEASURES 7–8), "PRINCESS REEL"

Attwood O'Connor, Milltown Cross

Sid Baglole (b. Lot 16)

Dennis Pitre, St. Felix

Archie Stewart, Milltown Cross - version 1

Archie Stewart, Milltown Cross - version 2

Edward P Arsenault, Wellington

Angus McPhee, Mount Stewart

Elliott Wight (b. Flat River)

EXAMPLE 6.2a. FULL LOW TURN, "PRINCESS REEL"
(AS PLAYED BY ELLIOTT WIGHT)

EXAMPLE 6.3. TWISTS ON HIGH TURN SECONDARY/CONNECTING PHRASE (MEASURES 3–4), "PIGEON ON THE GATEPOST"

"Old Peter" Chaisson, Bear River

Gus Longaphie, Souris

Andrew Jones, Pleasant View

George MacPhee, Monticello

Attwood O'Connor, Milltown Cross

Archie Stewart, Milltown Cross

Wilfred Gotell, Georgetown

Eddy Arsenault, St. Chrysostom

Sid Baglole (b. Lot 16)

Edward P Arsenault, Wellington

O'Neill's Music of Ireland, 1903 (Listed as Tune #1406, "Pigeon on the Gate")

**EXAMPLE 6.3a. FULL HIGH TURN, "PIGEON ON THE GATEPOST"
(AS PLAYED BY SID BAGLOLE)**

**EXAMPLE 6.4. VARIATIONS ON MAIN THEME, LOW TURN
(MEASURES 1–2), "PADDY ON THE TURNPIKE"**

Francis MacDonald, Morell Rear

George MacPhee, Monticello

Johnny Morrissey, Newtown Cross

Attwood O'Connor, Milltown Cross

Dennis Pitre, St. Felix

Archie Stewart, Milltown Cross

Dave Thomson, North River

Eddy Arsenault, St. Chrysostom

Sid Baglole, Lot 16

"Old Peter" Chaisson, Bear River

Ryan's Mammoth Collection (*1000 Fiddle Tunes*), 1883

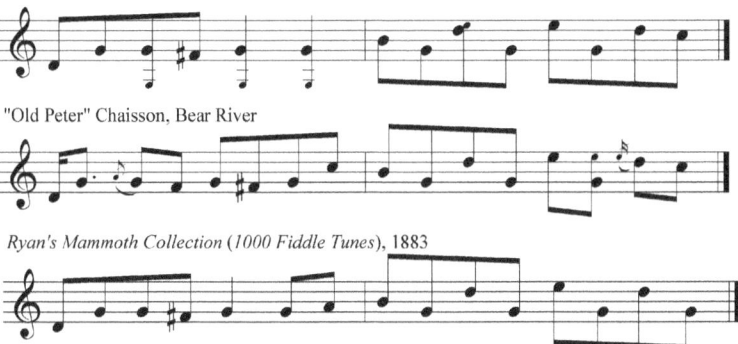

EXAMPLE 6.4a. FULL LOW TURN, "PADDY ON THE TURNPIKE"
(AS PLAYED BY GEORGE MACPHEE)

EXAMPLE 6.5. TWISTS ON HIGH TURN (MEASURES 5–8)
OF "PRINCESS REEL"

Example 6.5a. Second measure represents Arsenault's original "twist"

Example 6.5b. Second measure represents Arsenault's new "twist"

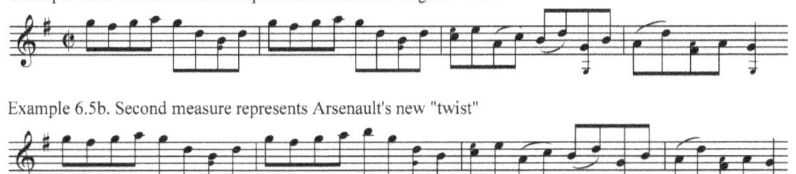

EXAMPLE 6.6. TOGANNY'S TUNE, OR FAIRY AT THE WELL

As played by Hughie McPhee, October 2006

Chapter 9

EXAMPLE 9.1. TWO-STRING FINGERING FORMS FOR G, D, AND A

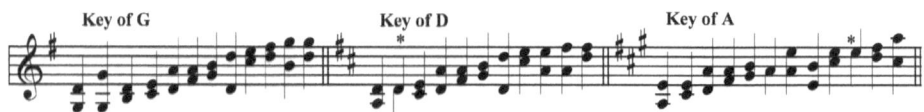

*Notes with double stems indicate "priming" (playing the same note simultaneously on adjacent strings).

EXAMPLE 9.2. BOWING ORNAMENTS

EXAMPLE 9.3. NOTING ORNAMENTS (GRACES OR GRACE NOTES)

Chapter 10

EXAMPLE 10.1. HIGH TURN, "MASON'S APRON"

Example 10.1a Mason's Apron, Standard Version: High Turn, Bars 1-4

Example 10.1b Mason's Apron, PEI Version with D#'s: High Turn, Bars 1-4

Chapter 14

**EXAMPLE 14.1. MEASURES FROM A TYPICAL REEL,
"PADDY ON THE TURNPIKE"**

As played by Victor Doucette

**EXAMPLE 14.2. MEASURES FROM A TYPICAL HORNPIPE,
"FERRY BRIDGE HORNPIPE"**

As played by "Young Peter" Chaisson

**EXAMPLE 14.3. MEASURES FROM A TYPICAL SET TUNE,
"NORTHSIDE TUNE"**

As played by Stephen Toole

**EXAMPLE 14.4. MEASURES FROM A TYPICAL "IRISH" JIG
(DOUBLE JIG), "LARRY O'GAFF"**

As played by Robert Crane

**EXAMPLE 14.5. MEASURES FROM A TYPICAL "SCOTCH" JIG,
"INVERNESS JIG"**

As played by Stephen Toole

EXAMPLE 14.6. MEASURES FROM A TYPICAL
SCOTTISH FOUR-PART PIPE MARCH, "KENNEDY STREET MARCH"

As played by Dennis Pitre

EXAMPLE 14.7. MEASURES FROM A TYPICAL STRATHSPEY,
"CAPTAIN CAMPBELL"

As played by Eddy Arsenault

APPENDIX B: LISTS OF INTERVIEW SESSIONS

Table B.1. List of Interviews, 1991–92

NAME	YEAR BORN	RESIDENCE	WHERE INTERVIEWED	PROFESSION	ACCOMPANIED BY, OR ACCOMPANIST FOR	DATE(S) INTERVIEWED
Anne-Marie Arsenault	c. 1925	Summerside	Summerside	housewife	accompanist for T. Arsenault	8/25/91
Eddy Arsenault	1921	St. Chrysostom	at residence	fisherman	Armand Arsenault, gtr	7/25/91, 8/4/92
Edward P. Arsenault	1938	Wellington	at residence	welder/mechanic	Marie Arsenault, pno	7/23/92
Jacques Arsenault	c. 1955	Mont Carmel	St. Nicholas		accompanist for Z. Poirier	8/4/92
Louise Gallant Arsenault	1956	Mont Carmel	at residence	musician	Phillipe LeBlanc, pno	7/23/92
Marie Arsenault	c. 1940	Wellington	at residence	housewife	accompanist for E. P. Arsenault	7/23/92
Robert Arsenault	1946	Meadow Bank	at residence	community development officer		7/4/92
Toussaint Arsenault	1916	Summerside	at residence	cabinet maker	Anne-Marie Arsenault, pno	8/25/91
Sidney Baglole	1912	Freetown	at residence	farmer		8/20/92
Sterling Baker	c. 1945	Montague	Monticello	merchant	Doug Matheson, pno	7/18/91
Jimmy Banks	1904	Poplar Point	at residence	farmer		7/9/91
Reg Banks	1923	Poplar Point	at residence	farmer/fisherman	Joseph Banks, gtr	7/1/92
Hélène Arsenault Bergeron	1954	Abram-Village	at residence	dancer		8/25/91
Alvin Bernard	1929	Long River	at residence	farmer, schoolbus driver	Edwin Simmons, gtr	7/21/92
Wilfred Bernard	1919	Souris Line Rd.	Monticello	farmer, mechanic	Jackie Bernard, gtr	7/23/91
Glenna Bowness	c. 1940	Kensington	Summerside			8/24/92
Donna Chaisson	c. 1955	Bear River	at residence	housewife		8/9/92

Abbreviations: C'town = Charlottetown, Nfld. = Newfoundland; gtr = guitar, pno = piano, mdl = mandolin.

NAME	YEAR BORN	RESIDENCE	WHERE INTERVIEWED	PROFESSION	ACCOMPANIED BY, OR ACCOMPANIST FOR	DATE(S) INTERVIEWED
J.J. Chaisson	1982	Bear River	at residence	student	Kevin Chaisson, pno	8/9/92
Johnny Joe Chaisson	1918	Souris	at residence	postman, trucker	Mary Chaisson, pno	7/25/92
Kenny Joe Pete Chaisson	c. 1947	Rollo Bay	at residence	factory executive	Lemmy Chaisson, gtr	8/17/91
Kenny Johnny Joe Chaisson	c. 1955	Bear River	at residence			8/9/92
Kevin Chaisson	1950	Bear River	Monticello	auto mechanic	accompanist for "Young" P. Chaisson, Paul MacDonald	7/9/91, 8/5/92
Melanie Chaisson	1978	Bear River	Monticello	student		8/25/92
"Old Peter" Chaisson	1929	Bear River	Monticello	farmer, laborer		8/2/91
Phonsey Chaisson	1929	Winnipeg	Souris	military	Mary Chaisson, pno	7/25/92
Stephen Chaisson	1977	Bear River	Monticello	student		8/25/92
"Young Peter" Chaisson	1942	Bear River	Monticello	iron worker	Kevin Chaisson, pno	7/9/91, 8/25/92
Fr. Charles Cheverie	1931	Charlottetown	Monticello	clergy		7/6/91
Gary Chipman	1944	Charlottetown	Monticello	musician		8/3/92
Joe Conway	1914	Elmira	Monticello			7/5/91
John Cousins	c. 1942	Bloomfield	at residence	teacher, folklorist		8/19/91
Katherine Dau-Schmidt	c. 1955	Brackley Beach	at residence	music teacher		9/1/92
Peter Doiron	1924	Summerside	at residence	military		7/25/91
Joseph Doucette	1910	Deblois Rd.	at residence	fisherman	Vincent Doucette, gtr	8/6/92
Vincent Doucette	1942	Tignish	St. Felix	schoolbus driver	accompanist for Dennis Pitre and Joseph Doucette	7/9/92
Connie Gallant	c. 1920	Naufrage	Monticello			7/3/91
Marlene MacKinnon Gallant	c. 1955	Tea Hill	Monticello	clerk, dancer		8/25/92
John Gauthier	1922	Belmont	Summerside	military		7/24/92
Hugh Gotell	1923	Mt. Herbert	at residence			7/24/92

Abbreviations: C'town = Charlottetown, Nfld. = Newfoundland; gtr = guitar, pno = piano, mdl = mandolin.

NAME	YEAR BORN	RESIDENCE	WHERE INTERVIEWED	PROFESSION	ACCOMPANIED BY, OR ACCOMPANIST FOR	DATE(S) INTERVIEWED
Kevin Gotell	c. 1950	Georgetown	same		accompanist for W. Gotell	8/3/92
Wilfred Gotell	1927	Georgetown	at residence	fisherman	Kevin Gotell, pno	8/3/92
Jimmy Halliday	1924	Eldon	at residence	farmer, fisherman	Eddie Martin, pno	7/20/92
James Hornby	c. 1955	Belfast	Monticello	lawyer, folklorist		7/10/91
Libby Hubley	1941	Kensington	C'town	dance teacher, provincial legislator		9/4/92
Emmett Hughes	1921	Dromore	at residence	farmer, carpenter	Gary Hughes, pno	8/8/91
Gary Hughes	c. 1950		Monticello		accompanist for A. MacDonald	7/4/91
Roland Jay	1906	Mt. Stewart	at residence	railroader	Cynthia Crane, pno	7/24/91
Andrew Jones	1918	Pleasant View	at residence	fisherman, carpenter		8/19/91
Joe Kearney	1914	Sturgeon	at residence	farmer, fisherman	Gerard Murphy, gtr	7/20/92
Bill Koughan	1926	Donagh	at residence	auto-body mechanic	Arlene Koughan Powers, pno	7/2/92
Warren Leard	1925	Coleman	Woodstock	owned flour mill	Eldon MacArthur	7/9/92
Harry Lecky	1929	Milburn	at residence	farmer	Florence Young, pno; Jerry McNally, gtr	8/24/92
Buddy Longaphie	c. 1950	Charlottetown	Monticello		Cody Myers, gtr	7/11/91
Gus Longaphie	1914	Souris	Monticello	farmer, fisherman		8/3/91
Eldon MacArthur	c. 1925	Inverness	Woodstock		accompanist for Elmer Robinson	7/9/92
Don MacCannell	c. 1947	Charlottetown	Monticello	fiddle repairer		8/5/91
Neil MacCannell	1919	Charlottetown	Monticello	salesman, fiddle repairer		8/5/91
Dot MacCauley	c. 1925		Cardigan		accompanist for C. Sigsworth, J. O'Connor	8/5/92, 8/18/92
Allan MacDonald	c. 1950	Bangor	Monticello	heavy equipment operator	Gary Hughes, pno	7/4/91
Bill MacDonald	1925	East Royalty	at residence	carpenter, composer		7/19/91

Abbreviations: C'town = Charlottetown, Nfld. = Newfoundland; gtr = guitar, pno = piano, mdl = mandolin.

NAME	YEAR BORN	RESIDENCE	WHERE INTERVIEWED	PROFESSION	ACCOMPANIED BY, OR ACCOMPANIST FOR	DATE(S) INTERVIEWED
Rev. Faber MacDonald	c. 1933	Grand Falls, Nfld.	Rollo Bay	clergy		7/20/92
Francis MacDonald	1940	Morell Rear	Monticello	farmer		7/12/91
Hilda MacPhee MacDonald	1904	Souris	Monticello	housewife		7/4/91
Joe MacDonald	1920	St. Andrews	at residence	farmer, fisherman	Heather Rose MacDonald	8/19/92
Paul MacDonald	1974	Charlottetown	Monticello	student	Kevin Chaisson, pno	8/23/91, 8/5/92
Jim MacDougall	1932	Grand River	Summerside	farmer		8/24/92
Largus MacInnis	1918	Lakeville	at residence	farmer, fisherman		7/3/92
Stewart MacIntyre	1900	Charlottetown	at residence	radio operator		8/6/92
Danny MacLean	1928	Eldon	at residence	lumberman, heavy equipment operator	Donny MacLean, gtr	8/21/92
George MacPhee	1941	Monticello	Monticello	fisherman, laborer		7/3/91, 7/7/92, 8/25/92
Ed Mathews	1919	Summerside	at residence	farmer		8/24/92
Leonard McDonald	1933	Emyvale	at residence	farmer, carpenter	Margaret Ross MacKinnon, pno; Claire McDonald, gtr	7/24/92
Angus McPhee	1929	Mt. Stewart	at residence	fisherman	Cynthia Crane, pno	7/24/91
Dan McPhee	1920	Ontario	Monticello			7/21/91
Hughie McPhee	1924	Bayfield	Monticello			7/21/91
Jenny O'Hanley McQuaid	1937	C'town (b Naufrage)	at residence	teacher		8/18/91, 8/26/92
Rita MacDonald Morrison	1919	C'town	at residence	housewife		8/20/92
Johnny Morrissey	1913	Vernon River	at residence	farmer	Margaret Ross MacKinnon, pno	8/9/92
Cody Myers	c. 1950		Monticello		accompanist for Buddy Longaphie	7/11/91
Attwood O'Connor	1923	Milltown Cross	at residence	fisherman, heavy equipment operator	Stanley Bruce, gtr; Mac MacKinnon, mdl	7/24/91, 8/22/92

Abbreviations: C'town = Charlottetown, Nfld. = Newfoundland; gtr = guitar, pno = piano, mdl = mandolin.

NAME	YEAR BORN	RESIDENCE	WHERE INTERVIEWED	PROFESSION	ACCOMPANIED BY, OR ACCOMPANIST FOR	DATE(S) INTERVIEWED
Frank O'Connor	1915	Kildare Capes	Woodstock		Eldon MacArthur	7/9/92
George O'Connor	c. 1912	Kildare Capes	Alberton			8/10/92
Jimmy O'Connor	1935	Murray Harbour	Monticello	factory worker	Dot MacCauley, gtr	8/18/92
Denny Pitre	1941	St. Felix	at residence	merchant	Vincent Doucette, gtr	7/9/92
Zélie-Anne Arsenault Poirier	1922	St. Nicholas	at residence	housewife	Jacques Arsenault, gtr	8/4/92
Merlin Quinn	1929	Cardross	at residence	farmer		8/21/92
Elmer Robinson	c. 1910	Woodstock	at residence	farmer	John Cousins, gtr; Eldon MacArthur, gtr	8/19/91, 7/9/92
Dorothy Rogers	c. 1920		Alberton		accompanist for West Prince Fiddlers	
Charlie Sheehan	1907	Bear River	Monticello	farmer, fisherman		8/8/91
Cosmas Sigsworth	1917	Cardigan	at residence	farmer, laborer	Dot MacCauley, gtr	8/5/92
Wilf Silliker	1901	Milburn	at residence	farmer	Florence Silliker Young, Gerry MacNally	8/24/92
Edwin Simmons	c. 1935	Darnley	Long River		accompanist for Alvin Bernard	7/21/92
Reuben Smith	1931	Blooming Point	Tracadie		Kay MacEachern, pno	7/29/91
Ervan Sonier	1920	Summerside	at residence	barber	Anne-Marie Arsenault, pno	8/25/91
Archie Stewart	1917	Milltown Cross	at residence	carpenter, plant foreman	Chester MacSwain, gtr	8/9/91, 7/7/92
Lee Thompson	c. 1925	Cambellton	Alberton		Dorothy Rogers, pno	
Dave Thomson	1942	North River	at residence	owns septic firm		7/3/92
Stephen Toole	1927	Green Road	at residence	experimental farmworker	Margaret MacKinnon, pno	8/20/91, 8/26/92
Carl Webster	1938	Cardigan	Monticello	farmer	Donnie MacDonald, gtr	8/19/92
Jackie Webster	1932	Cardigan	Monticello	ferry worker	Donnie MacDonald, gtr	8/19/92
Clifford Wedge (singer)	1926	Miminegash	at residence	farmer		8/10/92

Abbreviations: C'town = Charlottetown, Nfld. = Newfoundland; gtr = guitar, pno = piano, mdl = mandolin.

NAME	YEAR BORN	RESIDENCE	WHERE INTERVIEWED	PROFESSION	ACCOMPANIED BY, OR ACCOMPANIST FOR	DATE(S) INTERVIEWED
Elliot Wight	1935	North River	at residence	electrician	Judy Lowe, pno	8/8/92
Teresa MacPhee Wilson	1929	Goose River	Monticello	housewife		8/18/91, 7/8/92
Richard Wood	1978	East Royalty	at residence	student		7/19/91
Terry Wood	c. 1940	East Royalty	at residence			7/19/91

Abbreviations: C'town = Charlottetown, Nfld. = Newfoundland; gtr = guitar, pno = piano, mdl = mandolin.

Table B.2. List of Interviews, 1999

NAME	YEAR BORN	RESIDENCE	WHERE RAISED	INTERVIEW LOCATION	OCCUPATION /WHY INTERVIEWED	DATE OF INTERVIEW
Eddy Arsenault	1921	St. Chrysostom	same	same	fiddler	8/5/99
Georges Arsenault	c. 1945	Charlottetown	St. Nicholas	Charlottetown	folklorist	8/13/99
Cornelius "Lini" Bolger	1908	Summerside	Lot 11	Summerside	fiddler	8/12/99
Fr. Charles Cheverie	1931	Charlottetown	same	same	fiddler, clergyman	8/12/99
Peter Doiron	1924	Summerside	North Rustico	via telephone	fiddler	8/8/99
Lowell Huestis	1928	Summerside	Summerside	via telephone	hosted show on CJRW	8/17/99
Dan MacCormack	1923	Summerside	Broughton Island	via telephone	fiddler, played on radio	8/12/99
Cec MacEachern	1925	Charlottetown	Charlottetown	via telephone	fiddler, played with Don Messer	8/6/99
Margaret Ross MacKinnon	1941	Meadow Bank	Flat River	Eldon	accompanist	8/10/99
George MacPhee	1941	Monticello	same	same	fiddler	8/10/99
Hughie McPhee	1924	Bayfield	same	same	fiddler	8/6/99, 8/10/99
Paul Schurman	1955	Summerside	same	via telephone	family owned station CJRW	8/14/99
Raymond Sellick	1915	Brackley	same	via telephone	worked for CFCY; hosted Don Messer show	8/10/99
Archie Stewart	1917	Milltown Cross	same	same	fiddler	8/8/99

Table B.3. List of Interviews, 2006

DATE	PROJECT INTERVIEW NUMBER	INFORMANT	WHERE RAISED	INTERVIEW OR EVENT LOCATION	YEAR BORN	ACCOMPANISTS PRESENT
10/30/06	19	Joe Albert	Miminegash, PC	Summerside, PC	1927	Ivan Albert, gtr
10/18/06	05	Eddy Arsenault *	St. Chrysostom, PC	same	1921	Armand Arsenault, gtr
10/19/06	07	Edward P Arsenault *	St. Chrysostom, PC	same	1938	Marie Arsenault Livingstone, pno; Orrin Livingston, gtr
11/24/06	55	Louise Gallant Arsenault *	Mont Carmel, PC	same	1956	Zelma Gallant Arsenault, pno; Marie Gallant, pno
10/18/06	06	Peter Arsenault	St. Chrysostom, PC	Mont Carmel, PC	1959	Hélène Arsenault Bergeron, pno
10/16/06	03	Robert Arsenault *	Abram-Village, PC	Meadow Bank, QC	1946	—
11/15/06	38	Reg Banks *	Poplar Point, KC	Commercial Cross, KC	1923	Harry Buell, gtr
11/23/06	54	Jackie Biggar	Tyne Valley, PC	Summerside, PC	1953	Ken Perlman, bnj
11/30/06	66	J.J. Chaisson (interview) *	Bear River, KC	Souris, KC	1982	—
11/30/06	67b	Kevin Chaisson *	Bear River, KC	same	1950	—
11/30/06	67	"Old Peter" Chaisson *	Bear River, KC	same	1928	Kevin Chaisson, pno
11/20/06	48	Timothy Chaisson	Bear River, KC	Charlottetown, QC	1986	—
11/17/06	42	Ella Thomson Chappell	Tryon, PC	York, QC	1917	—
11/28/06	63	Fr. Charles Cheverie *	Charlottetown, QC	same	1931	Ken Perlman, bnj
11/26/06	59	Omar Cheverie	Souris, KC	Stratford, QC	1925	Randy Cheverie
11/29/06	65	Robert Crane	Riverton, KC	Pictou, Nova Scotia	1926	Ward MacDonald, pno
11/27/06	62	Kathryn Dau-Schmidt *	Colorado, USA	Rollo Bay, KC	1955	—
11/18/06	43	Harold Dockendorff	Mount Hope, KC	Brudenell, KC	1921	—

* = follow-up to 1991-91 interview; acd = accordian; bnj = banjo; gtr = guitar, mnd = mandolin, pno = piano; KC = Kings County (eastern PEI), PC = Prince County (western PEI), QC = Queens County (central PEI).

DATE	PROJECT INTERVIEW NUMBER	INFORMANT	WHERE RAISED	INTERVIEW OR EVENT LOCATION	YEAR BORN	ACCOMPANISTS PRESENT
11/9/06	29	Pat Doucette	Miminegash, PC	Summerside, PC	1936	Ernie Gallant, gtr, mnd
11/8/06	27	Victor Doucette	Deblois Rd., PC	Harper Rd., PC	1954	Cathy Doucette, bass; Vincent Doucette, gtr
11/12/06	33	Leo Farrell	Central Lot 16, PC	Same	1916	Ken Perlman, bnj
11/8/06	26	David Gaudet	Peter Rd., PC	Harper Rd., PC	1952	Cecil Arsenault, gtr; Robert Gallant, pno
11/16/06	40	John Gauthier	Stanhope, QC	same	1928	Ivan Day, gtr
10/22/06	10	Howard Hancock (with Keith Nicholson)	Belle River, QC	Flat River, QC	1932	Norman Gillis, bass; Keith Nicholson and Harold Hancock, gtr
11/23/06	53	Ralph Hardy	Alberton, PC	Burlington, QC	1927	Ken Perlman, gtr
11/10/06	30	Lowell Huestis	Summerside, PC	same	1928	n/a
11/25/06	57	Emmett Hughes *	Dromore, QC	same	1921	—
11/14/06	36	Roy Johnstone	Winnipeg, Manitoba	Argyle Shore, QC	1949	—
11/7/06	24	Harry Lecky *	Milburn, PC	Halliburton, PC	1929	Roland Cook, acd; Richard Blanchard, gtr; Shelton Hardy, gtr
11/17/06	41	Judy Lowe	Winsloe, QC	Charlottetown, QC	1944	—
10/15/06	02	Francis MacCormack	St. Charles, KC	Montague, KC	1934	George MacDonald, pno
10/24/06	14	Allan MacDonald *	Bangor, KC	same	1949	Ward MacDonald, pno
10/21/06	09	Francis MacDonald *	St. Peters Lake, KC	Morell, KC	1940	Ken Perlman, bnj
10/25/06	13	Ward MacDonald	Bangor, KC	same	1980	Alan MacDonald, gtr
11/20/06	47	Herb MacDougall	Bangor, KC	West Royalty, QC	1933	n/a
11/22/06	52	Jim MacDougall	Grand River, PC	Summerside, PC	1932	Ron Albert, gtr; Darlene Harding, pno; Peter Robinson, bass

* = follow-up to 1991-91 interview; acd = accordian; bnj = banjo; gtr = guitar, mnd = mandolin, pno = piano; KC = King County (eastern PEI), PC = Prince County (western PEI), QC = Queens County (central PEI).

DATE	PROJECT INTERVIEW NUMBER	INFORMANT	WHERE RAISED	INTERVIEW OR EVENT LOCATION	YEAR BORN	ACCOMPANISTS PRESENT
11/5/06	22	Billy MacInnis, Jr.	Village Green, QC	Charlottetown, QC	1971	Ken Perlman, bnj
11/26/06	60	Billy MacInnis, Sr.	Charlottetown	Village Green, QC	1946	—
10/29/06	18	Sheila MacKenzie	Little Pond, KC	Stratford, QC	1976	—
10/27/06	17	Clarence MacLean	Garfield, QC	Flat River, QC	1922	Rob Wilby, gtr
10/20/06	08	Hughie McPhee *	Bayfield, KC	same	1924	—
11/19/06	45	Reg Mellish	Union Road, KC, Mount Hope, KC	Montague, KC	1914	Ken Perlman, bnj
11/19/06	46	Murray Harbour Six: Cec Chapman, fiddle Amy Swenson, fiddle	n/a	Murray Harbour, KC	n/a	Kenny Chapman, mnd; Mel Geddings, gtr; Tracy MacLean Higginbotham, bass; Wayne MacLean, gtr
11/21/06	50	Bernard "Fenner" Myers	Stanhope, QC	Pleasant Grove, QC	1941	Jim Dobsen, gtr
10/22/06	10a	Keith Nicholson	Flat River, QC	same	1941	see Howard Hancock
10/15/06	01	Attwood O'Connor *	Milltown Cross, KC	same	1922	Ken Perlman, bnj
11/9/06	28	Dennis Pitre *	St. Felix, PC	same	1940	Vincent Doucette, gtr
11/6/06	23	Prince County Fiddlers	n/a	Summerside, PC	n/a	n/a
11/1/06	21	Queens County Fiddlers	n/a	Charlottetown, QC	n/a	n/a
10/24/06	12a	Merlin Quinn *	Cardross, KC	Cardigan, KC	1929	see C and J Webster
11/22/06	51	Ervin Rafferty	Rafferty Rd., PC	Foxley River, PC	1922	Ken Perlman, gtr
11/7/06	25	Fred Richard	St. Peter and St. Paul, PC	Brooklyn, PC	1936	Ken Perlman, bnj
11/11/06	32	Peter Robinson	Charlottetown	Northam, PC	1954	
11/27/06	61	Rollo Bay School Fiddle Instruction Program	n/a	Rollo Bay, KC	n/a	n/a

* = follow-up to 1991-91 interview; acd = accordian; bnj = banjo; gtr = guitar, mnd = mandolin, pno = piano; KC = Kings County (eastern PEI), PC = Prince County (western PEI), QC = Queens County (central PEI).

DATE	PROJECT INTERVIEW NUMBER	INFORMANT	WHERE RAISED	INTERVIEW OR EVENT LOCATION	YEAR BORN	ACCOMPANISTS PRESENT
10/23/06	11	Ross Family Band	Alexandra, QC	same	var.	Danielle Ross, fiddle; Jonathan Ross, pno; Stephanie Ross, gtr; Alex Ross, drums; Dorothy Arsenault Ross, manager, dancer
11/13/06	35	Mary Smith	North Rustico Harbour, QC	same	1938	Trudy Corbett, gtr; Mary Cousins, pno; Edgar Millar, fiddle; Theo Weigers, drums
11/24/06	56	Tony Smith	Tracadie Cross, QC	Rustico, QC	1939	Alfred Gallant, gtr
10/26/06	16	Malcolm "Bud" Stewart	Milltown Cross, KC	same	1936	Urban Chaisson, gtr
12/1/06	69	St. Peters Ceilidh	n/a	St. Peters, KC	n/a	n/a
10/26/06	15	Amy Swenson	Berkeley, California	Caledonia, KC	1949	—
12/1/06	68	Dave Thomson *	West Royalty, QC	Meadow Bank, QC	1942	Margaret Ross MacKinnon, pno; Alan MacRae, bass; Rupert Vessey, gtr
10/17/06	04	Cecil Trainor	Peake's Station, KC	Charlottetown, QC	1930	—
10/24/06	12	Carl and Jackie Webster *	Cardigan, KC	same	1938 1932	John Webster, gtr
10/30/06	20	Elliott Wight *	Flat River, QC	North River, QC	1935	Norman Leclair, gtr; Judy Lowe, pno
11/14/06	37	Teresa MacPhee Wilson *	Monticello, KC	Goose River, KC	1928	Tracy Warrren Burke, Marie MacIntyre, Anne McPhee, Gloria MacPhee MacInnis, Mary MacPhee Warren
12/2/06	70	Richard Wood *	East Royalty	same	1978	—

Abbreviations: * = follow-up to 1991–92 interview; acd = accordion, bnj = banjo, gtr = guitar, mnd = mandolin, pno=piano; KC = Kings County (eastern PEI), PC = Prince County (western PEI), QC = Queens County (central PEI).

APPENDIX C: LISTS OF COLLECTED TUNES

Table C.1. Additional Tunes Collected on Prince Edward Island, 1991–92†

Abercarny (Lament, Js. Moray)
Acadian Breakdown, The
Acadian Reel
Alec MacEachern's Strathspey
Allister MacGillivray's Waltz
Amazing Grace
Amazon Hornpipe
Amelia's Waltz
Andy Renwick's Ferret
Angus Chisholm's Favorite
Angus Gillis
Anna Is My Darling
Anne MacQuarrie's Reel
Annie Laurie
Ann Marie MacDonald's Jig
Archie Stewart's Reel*
Argyle Bowling Green
Arkansas Traveler
Arrochar Bridge
Athole Cummers, The
Atlantic Reel
Aunt Rose's Reel
Barry's Trip to Paris
Bashful Bachelor Hornpipe
Battle of the Boyne, The
Bear River Jig
Beautiful Lake Ainslie
Beautiful Sunday
Beautiful Swanee R. Hornpipe
Bedou's Reel
Belfast Jig
Belle Piano Reel
Belle Piano Strathspey
Benefit Waltz
Big Coffin Reel
Billy in the Lowground
Bishop MacDonald
Blackberry Blossom
Black Hoe, The
Blue Mountain Hornpipe
Blue Water Waltz
Bob Johnston
Bonaparte Crossing the Alps
Bonniest Lass in A' the World
Bonny Dundee
Bonny Kate
Bradley's Reel

Braes of Auchtertyre, The
Braes of Mar, The
Bridal Jig
Bridge of Bamore, The
Bridge of Inver, The
Bruno's Reel*
Buckley's Favorite
Burnt Leg, The
By the Fireside
Cameron Has His Wife Again
Cape Bretoner's Welcome to
  the Shetlands
Captain Campbell
Carlisle Lasses
Carl's Homecoming
Carmel Mahoney's Reel
Carnie's Canter
Cathy Hughes' Return
Cathy Hughes' Wedding
Charlie Hunter Jig
Chetticamp Jig
Chinese Breakdown
Chorus Jig
Christy Campbell
Clam Digger's Breakdown
Cobbler's Reel
Coilesfield House
Colonel Robertson
Come Under My Plaidie
Compl. to Buddy MacMaster
Confederation Reel
Constitution Breakdown
Cooley's Reel
Cornelia's Reel
Cotton Eyed Joe
Cronin's Favorite
Crossing to Ireland
Cuckoo's Nest, The
Cutting Ferns
Daisy's Jig
Darlin' Don't You Meddle Me
Dave MacNeil's Reel
Davie Taylor
Dawn Waltz, The
Delnabo
Democratic Rage Hornpipe
Denny Pitre's Reel*

Devil in the Kitchen
Don MacLean's Farewell
  to Oban
Don Messer's Breakdown
Don Side, The
Donnybrook Fair
Don't Be Teasing
Doucette's Dream*
Doucette's Reel*
Down the Tannoch Road
Down Yonder
Dr. Keith, Aberdeen
Dr. Shaw
Drunken Piper, The
Dublin Porter
Duchess' Slipper, The
Dunie Mains
Durang's Hornpipe
Duskey Meadow, The
East Newk of Fife, The
Elmer Briand's Jig
Emily's Reel
Emmett's Favorite
Ewe with the Crooked Horn
Factory Smoke Clog
Faded Love
Fairies at Monticello, The
Farewell to Sticky Buns
Farewell to Whiskey
Farmer's Jamboree
Father O'Flynn
Fay's Hornpipe
Fermoy Lasses
Ferry Bridge Hornpipe
Fisher's Wedding
Fishing with Vic
Five Mile Chase
Flags of Dublin
Flop-Eared Mule
Foncey's Tune*
Four String Polka
Fr. Francis Cameron
Freetown Reel*
Gallagher's March
Garmot Smiddy
George Mel's Dream*
George Mel's Reel*

---

† = This list represents collected tunes NOT included in table 15.1 (*the Top 126 List*).
Key: * = Titles assigned by author.

George V's Army
Georgie's Favorite Waltz
Gerard Heintzman's Piano
German Waltz
Gladstone Hornpipe, The
Glengarry's Dirk
Glennfiddich Strathspey, The
Goldenrod Jig
Golden Wedding Day
Gordon Graham's Jig
Graham's Breakdown
Greenfields of America
  (G setting)
Greenfields of America
  (D setting)
Green Meadow Reel, The
Grieg's Pipes
Haggis, The
Hamish the Carpenter
Hanged Man's Reel
Haughs of Cromdale, The
Headlands, The
Hector MacDonald's Reel*
Hector the Hero
Heel and Toe Polka
Herring Reel
Highlandman's Reel, The
Home Sweet Home
Home Waltz, The
Honeymoon, The
Honeymoon Polka
Hughie Jim Paul's Reel
Hughie Shorty's Reel
I Just Don't Want to Be Rich
Inverness Gathering
Inverness Jig
Irish-American Reel
Irish Rover
Iron Man, The
It's A Long Way to Tipperary
Jack Daniels
Jackie Chipman
Jackie Coleman's Reel
Jack Richard's Tune
Jackson's Jig
Jamie Hardie
Jerry's Beaver Hat
Jimmy's Favorite
Jingle Bells
J. MacKinnon of Smelt Brook
Jock Wilson's Ball
Joe Griffin's Tune
Joe Kearney's Reel*
Joe MacDonald's Reel
Joe MacKinnon's Reel
Joe Pete's Reel*

John Angus Beaton Strathspey
John Dan MacPherson's Jig
John J. McPhee's Reel*
John Morrison, Assynt House
Johnny Joe Chaisson's Reel*
Johnny Joe Lem's Jig*
Johnny Muise
Johnny Sullivan's Reel
Johnny Wagoner
Johnny's Jig
Johnny's Reel
Joseph and Margaret Chaisson
Joys of Mabou Mines, The
Joys of Quebec
Judique Jig
Judique Reel
Karen Chaisson's Reel
Kennedy Street March
Kevin Chaisson's Reel
Key West Hornpipe
Kiley's Reel
Killecrankie
Kimmy's Jig
Kingdom Comin'
King of the Fairies
Kitty at the Well
Koehler's Hornpipe
La Bastringue
Lad O'Beirn's Reel
Lady Anne Hope
Lady Erskine
Laird o' Drumblair, The
Land of Sweet Erin, The
La Rose
Larry O'Gaff
Lassie with the Yellow Coatie
Lass o' Gowrie
Lem Jay's Fancy*
Let's Have a Ceilidh
Levantine's Barrel
Light and Airy
Lime Hill
Little Brown Jug
Little Donald in the Pigpen
Little Old Log Cabin in
  the Lane
Lively Steps
Liverpool Hornpipe
Lochaber Gathering
Loch Leven Castle
Lord Alexander
Lord Gordon
Lord Lovat's Lament
Lord Seaforth Reel
Lovely Flora
MacDonald's March "Reel"

MacKinnon's Rant
MacSwain's Reel
Maid on the Green, The
Malcolm Finlay
Marching through Georgia
Marchioness of Huntley, The
Marchioness of Tullybardine
Margaree Reel
Margaree Valley Waltz
Margaret's Waltz
Marquis of Huntley, The
Massacre at Glen Coe, The
Mathematician, The
McDermott's Reel
McFadden's Favorite
McPhee's Rant*
Me Ain Kind Dearie
Meeting of Waters, The
Me Love's But a Lassie Yet
Merry Maiden, The
Miller o' Drone, The
Miller o' Hirn
Miller's Reel
Milltown Cross Fire, The
Minstrel's Fancy
Miss Barker's Hornpipe
Miss Drummond of Perth
Miss Gordon's Strathspey
Mississippi Sawyer
Miss Katherine Stewart
Miss MacDougall of Wallaston
Miss Maule's Strathspey
Miss Maxwell
Miss Shepherd
Misty Mountain, The
Mom's Jig
Moneymusk
Moonshine Reel, The
Mother's Reel
Mountain Road, The
Mouth of Tobique, The
Mr. Murray
Mrs. Forbes Leith
Mrs. J. Forbes
Mrs. MacCauley's Hornpipe
Mrs. MacPherson of Inveran
Mrs. Menzies of Culdares
Muckin' o' Geordie's Byre, The
Mug and Brush Reel
Munlochy Bridge
Munster Lass, The
Murray River Jig
Music Box Dancer
Mussel Breakdown
My Brother's Letter
My Cape Breton Home

† = This list represents collected tunes NOT included in table 15.1 (the Top 126 List).
Key: * = Titles assigned by author.

My Own Homestead
My Two Sons
Names Escape Me
New Brig o' Dee, The
Newcastle Hornpipe
Niel Gow's Fiddle
Niel Gow's Lament for His
    Second Wife
Nine Point Coggie
North Cape Reel*
North Shore Hornpipe
O'Brien's Reel
Old French
Old King's Reel, The
Old Peter's Reel*
Old-Timer's Reel
On a Hot Piano
On the Road to Boston
Orange and Blue Jig
Over the Briny Ocean
Pacific Slope Hornpipe
Paddy Carrey's Ship*
Paddy Cronin's Reel
Paddy in London
Parry Sound Reel
Patricia Wilmot's Reel
Patsy MacDonald's Reel
Peek-a-Boo Waltz
PEI Fiddlers' March
PEI Jamboree
Peter Baille's Wife
Petronella
Phiddlin' Phil
Picnic Reel
Ping Tune, The
Pipe Major Christie of Wick
Plaza Polka
Poplar Point Reel
Portencross Castle
President Garfield's Hornpipe
Queen Elizabeth Street March
Queen of the Priming Machine
Rakes of Mallow, The
Rally Round the Flag, Boys
Randy's Reel
Red-Haired Boy
Red River Rag
Red River Valley
Reel Made with Hilda
Reel of Honor
Reg Bank's Tune*
Regina Stubbert's Jig
Richard Brennan's Jig
Richie's Hornpipe

Rippling Waters Jig
River Bend Jig
River John Sunset Waltz
Road to Dundee, The
Road to India
Road to Skye, The
Robert Cormack, Aberdeen
Rock Valley Jig
Rollo Bay Reel*
Rosebud of Allenvale
Rose in the Garden
Rose Tree, The
Rosewood Jig
Royal Scots "March," The
Saddle the Pony
Sandy Cameron's Reel
Sandy MacIntyre's March
San Malo à Bord de Mer, À
Scotch Cove Jig
Scotch Waltz
Scotland the Brave
Sean McGuire's Reel
Seaweed Reel
Shandon Bells
Ships Are Sailing
Shores of Lough Gowna, The
Side by Side
Sidney Baglole's Reel*
Sidney Baglole's Tune*
Silvery Bell
Simply Wild Over You
Sir Archibald Dunbar
Sister Donna Kelly
Skinner's Pond Jig
Sleeping Maggie
Slocket Light
Smile Awhile
Smith's Reel
Snow Plow Reel
Souris Breakwater
Souris Reel*
Souris Waltz, The
Sow's Tail, The
Space Available
Speed the Plow
Stan's Jig
Staten Island Hornpipe
St. Francis Reel
Stirling Castle
Stone Outside Dan Murphy's
    Door
Stool of Repentance
St. Patrick's Day in Morning
Stumpie

Sugar in the Gourd
Sweetness of Mary, The
Swingin' Mémé
Tamerack 'Er Down
Tavern in the Town, The
Tea Gardens Jig
Temperance Reel
Tennessee Two-Step
Tennessee Waltz
Ten-Penny Bit
Teviot Bridge
Three O'Clock in the Morning
Till We Meet Again
Timour the Tartar
Tina's Schottische
Toganny's Tune
Tom Dey Strathspey
Tommy's Jig
Top of Cork Road
Tracy Regina's March
Tripping Up Stairs
Trips with David
Trip to Mabou Ridge
Tuggerman's Jig, The
Tullochgorum
Twin Sisters, The
Uncle Jim
Upper Denton Hornpipe, The
Up the Burn
Walkin' Uptown
Walk on Water Reel, The
Waltz You Saved for Me, The
Wandering Minstrel, The
Watermelon, The
West Point Reel
Wet Jeans
Whelan's Breakdown
When I Grow Too Old
    to Dream
Whiskey Jig
Whistlin' Jack
White River Stomp
Wight's Reel*
Wild Irish Rose, The
Wilfred's Fiddle
Wind That Shakes the Barley
Winston Scotty's Reel*
Winston's Strathspey*
Wissahickon Drive
Women of Pisquid, The
Wreck of the Old No. 9, The
Yetts of Muckart, The
Zélie-Anne's Tune

---

† = This list represents collected tunes NOT included in table 15.1 (the Top 126 List).
Key: * = Titles assigned by author.

Table C.2. Tunes Encountered for the First Time in 2006‡

Abide with Me
Acrobat's Reel
Ainsley's Reel*
Andy de Jarlis Jig
Andy's Jig
Apple Valley Breakdown
Ashland's Waltz*
Ashokan Farewell
Between Two Trees
Blackboard of My Heart
'Blige the Lady
Blue Jig*
Boghan Lochan
Boiling Cabbage Down
Bonaparte's Retreat
Bonnie Lass o' Bon Accord
Bonnie Lass of Fisherrow (B♭)
Bonnie Lass of Head Lake, The
Boo Baby's Lullaby
Bow and Arrow
Boy's Lament for His Dragon
Brenda's Reel*
Buddy's Tribute*
Buffalo Gals
Burnt Woods Breakdown*
Bury Me Beneath the Willow
Captain O'Kaine
Carmen's Tune
Carry Me Back to Old Virginny
Carter MacKenzie's Reel†
CBC's Glen and Carl
Ceilidh at 7A, The*
Celtic Touch, The†
Chocolate Pop Jig*
Christy Miller
Clamdigger's Reel*
Clamshack Reel
Comin' Round the Mountain
Commercial Cross Special*
Connaughtman's Rambles, The
Crossing, The*
Crossroads, The*
Dan Collins' Father's Jig†
Darla Chaisson's Jig
December 2nd
Delphine's Reel
Dill Pickle Rag
Dill Pickles
Dinky's Reel
Dominique
Don Messer's Centennial Waltz
Dot MacKinnon's Reel†
Douglas Jig
Duke Nielson's Jig*
Eddy and Armand*
Enduring Young Charms
Family Breakdown*
Family Ties*
Fanny Powers
Farewell to Catawba
Fiddle-Do Polka*
Fiddle Fingers
Finnegan's Landing
Fireman's Reel
Fisherman's Fiddle*
Fisherman's Reel*
Five Dionne Reel
Five-Minute Rice Reel*
Five Minutes More
Flicker's Tune, The
Fountain Filled with Blood
Francis the Miller
Frank's Jig
Fraulein
Fr. Charlie Cheverie*
Freetown Reel*
Friendly Visit Clog
Frost Is All Over, The
Funeral, The*
Galway Bay
Gascoyne, The*
Gene's Reel
George's Tune
Golden Slippers
Goodnight Irene
Grumbler, The
Half a Pound of Tea
Happy to Meet You Jig
Harmony Reel*
Harry's Reel*
Heather's Jig*
Hermine Gallant's Reel*
Home on the Range
Hull's Victory
Hummingbird Waltz
Hurricane, The
Ice on the Road
Icing on the Cake, The*
If Ever You Were Mine
Iggie and Squiggy
I'll Be All Smiles Tonight
I'll Fly Away
I'm Looking Over a Four-Leaf Clover
I'm Thinkin' of You Sweetheart
Interlake Waltz
Irish Moss Festival Reel*
Island by the Sea
Isle of My Birth†
I's the B'y
Joey Syl's Jig
John Honoree #1
John Honoree #2
Judy Cruisin'
Julie's Reel*
Kelly's Mountain
Kenny Bruce Soiree
Ken's Tune*
Lac Des Prix
Laddie with the Plaidie
Leave the Girls Alone
Le Coq et la Poule
Liam's Jig*
Life's Other Side
Lion's Den, The*
Little Dee's Reel*
Little House Clog*
Loch Earn
Logger's Breakdown
Looking in the Porch*
MacArthur Road
Maddy Brown's Jig*
March by Howard Hancock*
Mary Hughes' Jig†
Matthew's Jig*
Memories of Herbie MacLeod†
Merry Maiden Polka
Michael Rankin's Reel
Miguel's Reel*
Millburn Hornpipe†
Mockingbird, The
Mocking Bird Hill
Mom's Denial*
Montreal Breakdown
Mortgage Burn, The
My Castle's My Country House*
My Great Friend John Morris
Nancy's Waltz
Narcisse's Reel*
No Price Tag on the Doors of Nfld.
Northern Breakdown*
Ocean's Jig*
Old Brown Coat and Me
Old Dan Tucker Jig
Old Faithful
Old Red Barn, The
Ontario Swing
Operator's Reel
Orange Blossom Special
Owny's Best Jig

Paddy on the Turnpike (A setting)	Reel by Kevin Chaisson†	Tamara's Reel*
Paradise Waltz	Reel by King Gannum	Tears
Parting, The*	Reel de Forgeron	Terminal Reel*
Pathway to Light*	Reel de Placide*	Tiddle Winks*
Paul and Anne's First Waltz†	Reel des Macoques*	Topless Tavern Waltz
Paul's Jig†	Riverside Waltz	Top of Ol' Smokey
Pebble and Goose's Jig	Rollin' in My Sweet Baby's Arms	Trip to Sligo
PEI Ferry (D setting)	Rosin the Beau	Trip to Toronto
PEI Ferry Crossing (F setting)	Rubber Dolly	Tune by Kevin Chaisson†
Peter and Doreen Chaisson†	Sea People	Tune for a Paul Jones Dance
Pigeon on the Steeple*	Sheguiandah Bay	Unto the Hills
Pitchfork, The†	Sighting, The*	Vendome Clog
Planxty Brown	Simon's Great Smile	Wabash Cannonball
Point Prim Reel*	Sister Solana Beaton	Waldo Monro Shuffle*
Poor Girl Waltz	Snow Deer	Wally's Gold Cup and Saucer*
Pretty Little Cindy	Softlyand Tenderly	Waltz by Peter Arsenault*
Prince Charlie's Reel	Spinning Wheel	Warming Up the Bow*
Purple Parrot, The*	Sputnik Breakdown	Wash the Dishes*
Put Me in Your Pocket	St. Chrysostom Reel*	Wayne MacGillivery's Reel
Quadrille Waltz	Stick in Paddy's Land	Welcome Dance, The*
Railroad Tune, The	Stream of Tears*	Where the North River Flows†
It's Raining, It's Pouring*	Summerside Reel*	Where the River Shannon Flows
Reason I'm Not Pleasin'	Swamp Lake	Williey Kennedy Strathspey
Reconciliation, The	Take Me Out to the Ballgame	Wreck of the Old 97
Reel by Kenny Chaisson†		

‡ In addition to the tunes listed here, there were 170 unidentified tunes collected, consisting of 69 reels (including hornpipes and clogs), 57 jigs, 13 strathspeys, 11 waltzes, 8 set tunes, 7 marches, and 5 airs.

Key: * = Tune composed by source musician, † = tune composed since 1991–92 by another PEI musician.

APPENDIX D: PRONUNCIATION GUIDE

Place-Names

Cardross (card-ROSS)
Charlottetown (shar-la-TOWN)
Donagh (rhymes with *Jonah*)
Groshaut (gruh-HOE)
Mabou (MAH-boo)
Malpeque (mal-PEK)
Miminegash (mi-mi-ne-GASH)
Miramichi (mi-ra-mi-SHEE)
Miscouche (mis-CUSH)
Naufrage (new-FRAGE; last syllable rhymes with *beige*)
Rustico (RUSS-ti-ko)
Souris (SOO-ree)
St. Charles (Saint CHAR-less)
Tignish (tig-NISH)
Tracadie (TRA-ka-dee)

Last Names of Individuals

Albert, Joe (al-BARE)
Arsenault (AR-se-no)
Baglole (BAG-lole; last syllable rhymes with pole)
Biggar (BIG-ger)
Bearisto (BARE-is-to; last syllable rhymes with go)
Bernard, Alvin (BER-nurd)
Bernard, Wilfred (ber-NARD)
Bowness (sounds like bonus)
Chaisson (CHAY-son)
Cheverie (shev-REE)
Dau-Schmidt (Dow)
Doiron (DOR-on)
Doucette (doo-SET)
Gallant (ga-LANT; last syllable rhymes with can't)
Gaudet (Goody)
Gauthier (GO-tee-ay)
Gotell (go-TELL)
Huestis (HEW-stis; first syllable rhymes with few)
Kearney (KAR-ney)
Koughan (KEW-an (first syllable rhymes with few)
Leard (rhymes with cared)
Longaphie (LON-ga-fee; sometimes LOCK-a-bee)
MacCannell (ma-CAN-el)
MacEachern (ma-KEK-ern)
MacLean (ma-KLANE)

Pitre (Pitt)
Poirier (PWA-ree-er; sometimes Perry)
Richard, Fred (ri-SHARD)
Sonier (SONE-yay)

First Names of Individuals

Bibienne (bi-bee-EN)
Cosmas (KOZ-mus)
Ervan (er-VON)
Ervin (ER-vin)
Loughy (Locky)
Omar (rhymes with Homer)
Toussaint (TUH-sin)

APPENDIX E:
DISCOGRAPHY AND SUGGESTED LISTENING

Selected Fiddling or Fiddle-Ensemble Recordings Produced on PEI since the Onset of the Fiddling Revival*

ARTIST OR GROUP	ALBUM TITLE	YEAR	FORMAT
Arsenault Family	Party Acadien	1995	CD
Albert and Chuck Arsenault	Énergie	2009	CD
Eddy Arsenault	Piling on the Bois Sec	1993	CD
Barachois	Barachois	1996	CD
	Encore	2000	CD
	Naturel	2001	CD
Celtic Ladies	Celtic Ladies	2012	CD
Chaisson Family	The Chaisson Family	2006	CD
	Generations	2009	CD
J.J. Chaisson	In the Genes	c. 1998	CD
	Class Act	2002	CD
	The Gift	2008	CD
Melanie and Peter Chaisson	The Road to Rollo Bay	1995	CD
Nathan Condon	Playin' in the Sand	c. 2008	CD
Anastasia DesRoches	Collage	2000	CD
Melissa Gallant	Laisse-Les Aller/Let 'er Rip	1999	CD
Courtney Hogan	Swingin' on a Note	c. 2011	CD
Roy Johnstone	Rolling Waves	1991	Cassette
	Stark Ravin'	1995	CD
	Devil's Jig	1998	CD
	Summertime	2002	CD
	Longshore Drift	2008	CD
	Live at Loon	2011	CD
Kindle	Kindle	2000	CD
Fiona MacCorquodale	Eleven	c. 2012	CD
Paul MacDonald	Paul MacDonald	1988	Cassette
Ward MacDonald	Ask Her to Dance	2013	CD
Sheila MacKenzie	Sheila MacKenzie	2005	CD
Cynthia MacLeod	Head Over Heels	2002	CD
	Crackerjack	2004	CD
	Hot Off the Floor	2007	CD
	Riddle	2010	CD
	Live at the Brackley Beach Ceilidh	2012	CD

* Thanks to Judy Lowe of National Music in Charlottetown for information on recent Island recordings

Billy MacInnes	Fiddle Favorites	1984	CD
	Live at the Silverado	c. 1990	CD
	Fiddling from the Heart	c. 1997	CD
	Fiddlin' with Tradition	c. 2000	CD
	On the Bow Again	c. 2002	CD
	Fiddle Fingers	2006	CD
	The Fiddle Player from PEI	2010	CD
Queens County Fiddlers	Forty Fiddles, Flat Out	2004	CD
Matthew Reid	Born to Fiddle	2012	CD
Ross Family Band	Island Feet	2007	CD
	Prince Edward Island, I'm Coming Home	2010	CD
Various Artists	Music of / Musique de / Tignish	1999	CD
Vishten	Vishten	2004	CD
	11:11	2007	CD
	Live	2008	CD
	Mosaïk	2012	CD
Richard Wood	Cutting the Bow	1992	Cassette
	All Fired Up	1993	CD
	The Celtic Touch	1995	CD
	Fire Dance	1997	CD
	Come Dance with Me	1999	CD
	Infectious	2004	CD
	A Change of Reasons	2009	CD

More Suggested Listening

Note: Studio and live recordings of listed artists may be available on Youtube.com and other, similar Internet sites.

ANTHOLOGY FIELD RECORDINGS OF TRADITIONAL ISLAND FIDDLERS

The Fiddle Music of Prince Edward Island (CD). Mel Bay #95393CD, 1996.
The Prince Edward Island Style of Fiddling: Fiddlers of Eastern PEI (CD). Rounder #7015, 1997.
The Prince Edward Island Style of Fiddling: Fiddlers of Western PEI (CD). Rounder #7014, 1997.

DON MESSER AND HIS ISLANDERS

Don Messer. The Best of Don Messer and His Islanders, vols. 1–5 (LPs). Apex #AL-1608-1612, c. 1965.
———. Down East Dancin' with Don Messer and His Islanders, vols. 1–2 (LPs). Apex #AL-1601-2, c. 1965.

MESSER'S MUSICAL "HEIRS"

Al Cherny. Fiddle Magic (LP). RCA Camden CASX 2605, 1972.
Andy DeJarlis and His Early Settlers. Backwoods Fiddle Tunes (LP). London #EBX 4118, n.d.
King Ganam. King of the Fiddle (LP). RCA Camden #966, 1966.
Ivan Hicks. Connections. Self-published, #ME1012, 2000.
Ned Landry. Bowing the Strings (LP). RCA Camden #891, 1956. (Reissued as CD.)
Graham Townsend. The Inimitable Graham Townsend. Banff Rodeo RBS 1239, 1966. (Reissued as CD.)

IRISH AND SCOTTISH FIDDLING: A FEW EARLY RECORDINGS

Michael Coleman. *Michael Coleman—1891–1945* (2-CD set). Gael Linn / Viva Voce reissue.

Paddy Killoran and James Morrison. *From Ballymote to Brooklyn* (CD). 1997–98. (Reprinted by Coleman Irish Music Online Store.)

James Scott Skinner. *James Scott Skinner The Strathspey King* (LP). Topic #12T280, 1975. (Reissued as CD: Temple #COMD 2084, 2002.)

SOME IMPORTANT AMERICAN "ROOTS" FIDDLERS

Fiddlin' John Carson. *Complete Recorded Works*, vols. 1–7 (CDs). Doment #DOCD 8014-20, 1998.

Clark Kessinger. *Old-Time Country Music* (LP). Folkways #FA 2336, 1966. (Reissued as CD: #FW02336.)

Eck Robertson. *Old-Time Texas Fiddler* (CD). County #CO-3515-CD, 1999.

Fiddlin' Arthur Smith and His Dixieliners (LP). County #547, 1978. (Reissued as CD: County #CO-3526-CD.)

Gid Tanner and the Skillet Lickers: *Old Timey's Favorite Band* (4-CD set). Compiled by Pat Harrison, #JSP-77155-4-CD.

Various Artists. *Old-Time Fiddle Classics*. County #507, n.d.

Bob Wills and His Texas Playboys. *Legends of Country Music* (4-CD set). County CK-93858-CD.

CAPE BRETON FIDDLERS: FIRST-GENERATION RECORDING ARTISTS

Angus Chisholm. *The Early Recordings of Angus Chisholm* (LP). Shanachie 14001, 1978.

Winston "Scotty" Fitzgerald. *Winston "Scotty" Fitzgerald and His Fabulous Entertainers* (LP). Rodeo #RNT 2009, n.d.

———. *Winston Scotty Fitzgerald Classic Cuts* (CD). Cranford #FWCC-cd, n.d.

Bill Lamey. *Full Circle* (CD). An LP originally on Shanachie; now Rounder #7032.

Dan R. MacDonald. *Fiddling to Fortune* (LP). London #RLP 59, n.d.

Joe MacLean. *Old Time Fiddle Music from Cape Breton Island*. (Recorded 1977; issued as "on-demand" CD, c. 2010.)

Various Artists. *Reeling with Jigs: Canadian Fiddle Music*, vol. 1 (on-demand CD; features Dan J. Campbell, Angus Allan Gillis, Little Jack MacDonald, etc.)

CAPE BRETON FIDDLERS: SECOND-GENERATION RECORDING ARTISTS

John Campbell. *Cape Breton Violin Music* (LP). Rounder #7003, 1976. (Reissued as CD.)

Winnie Chafe. *Highland Melodies of Cape Breton* (LP). Rounder #7012, 1979.

Joseph Cormier. *Scottish Violin Music from Cape Breton Island* (LP). Rounder # 7001, 1974.

Jerry Holland. *Master Cape Breton Fiddler* (LP). Boot #7231, 1982.

Sandy MacIntyre. *Island Treasure*, vol. 1 (CD). Self-published, # SMCD9107, 1988.

———. *Cape Breton Fiddle Music: Steeped in Tradition*. Self-published, #SMCD9607, 1996.

Carl MacKenzie. *Welcome to Your Feet Again* (LP). Rounder #7005, 1977.

Buddy MacMaster. *Judique on the Floor* (LP). Sea Cape Music, n.d.

CAPE BRETON FIDDLERS: THIRD GENERATION RECORDING ARTISTS

Ashley MacIsaac. *Close to the Floor* (CD). Solar #03, 1992.

Natalie MacMaster. *Fit as a Fiddle* (CD). Rounder, 1993.

GLOSSARY

air. A fiddle tune intended for listening rather than dancing.
bee. See *frolic*.
benefit concert. A money-raising event.
"big-circle" set. A quadrille in which dancers form one or more large circles instead of multiple squares (see *square formation*).
bowing. Manipulation of the bow.
breakdown. Among older Islanders, the term is sometimes used to refer to eight-hand reels; in mainstream North American fiddling and in bluegrass music, the designation often describes a fast, showy performance piece.
camber. The concave curve of the bow stick.
ceilidh. Originally, the Gaelic term *ceilidh* (pronounced "KAY-ley") referred to a social event in which each person in turn entertains the company. In contemporary PEI, it generally refers to a fund-raising or for-profit community talent show.
chording. Accompanying the fiddle by creating a rhythmic background that incorporates an appropriate harmony for each segment of the tune.
contra dancing. A species of figure dancing in which couples face each other "longways" (in two lines).
contredanse française. See *cotillion*.
cotillion. The square-formation dance that predominated in the eighteenth century.
crooked tune. On PEI, a tune that is difficult to play. Within the Appalachian fiddle-music revival, however, the term generally refers to a tune with a variable or irregular meter.
cut. A type of bowing ornament; assuming 4/4 or 2/2 time, it consists of three rapid notes (two sixteenths and an eighth) in the space normally occupied by a quarter note.
dancing saloon. An outdoor dancing platform, often supplied with a wooden framework upon which evergreen boughs or tarpaulins can be placed to protect dancers from the elements.
dotted rhythm. A series of notes in which the first note of each pair—depending on the style of music—is either two or three times longer than the second note. In 4/4 or cut time this is written as a consistent alternation of dotted eighth notes and sixteenth notes.
double stop. A fingering pattern in which two strings are stopped, or noted simultaneously.
double-stringing. Bowing two strings at once.
doubling. Playing the melody simultaneously.
eight-hand reel. A dance performed by four couples in square formation incorporating quadrille-like routines. See also *breakdown*.
fiddle tune. A melody, generally designed for accompanying dancing and usually composed to suit the fiddle's first position range and specific tonal characteristics.

figure (of a quadrille). One of the several discrete sections of the *quadrille*, each having its own steps and music.

figure dancing. A generic term that covers all kinds of square and longways dancing.

four-hand reel. A type of Scotch reel danced by two couples (also known as a *foursome reel*).

frog. The roughly rectangular part of the bow that is held in the player's hand and which allows for adjusting the tension of the hair.

frolic. A communal work activity, often followed by a dance.

grace note(s). One or more quick notes played to decorate a melody. See also *ornamentation*.

gramophone. On PEI, the generic term for a spring-powered phonograph.

group (of tunes). Medley.

higher strings. A reference to the two highest-pitched strings of the violin (generally tuned to the A above middle C and the E above that).

high turn. The full section of a tune that is played mostly on the higher strings of the fiddle.

hornpipe. A kind of fiddle tune, generally written in 2/2 or 2/4 time. Hornpipes were originally played at moderate tempo and with a dotted rhythm, but on PEI they are usually played at "reel tempo" (quarter note = 120) to accompany square sets.

house party. The quintessential Island dance party, generally held in the kitchen or parlor of a private home.

jig. A fiddle tune in 6/8 time.

jigging. On PEI, the term describes the singing of fiddle tunes using nonsense syllables to imitate the phrasing and accents of a fiddler.

lower strings. A reference to the two lowest-pitched strings of the violin (generally tuned to the G below middle C and the D above middle C).

low turn. The full section of a tune that is played mostly on the lower strings of the fiddle.

luthier. Builder or repairer of violins or other stringed instruments.

making tunes. On PEI, this term often refers to the art of composing.

march. A tune that was originally designed to signal military maneuvers but which has been adapted by dance accompaniment; alternatively, a tune composed for fiddle in march form.

medley. Two or more tunes played in succession with no break in between, sometimes referred to as a set or *group*.

mode. A musical concept that refers not only to the ordering of notes to form a scale but also to the rules concerning how those notes are used.

noting. Forming notes on violin strings by pressing down with the fingertips.

old-time dancing. Dancing quadrilles, or square sets.

old-time fiddler. During the second half of the twentieth century, Islanders often used this term to describe a fiddler who was a good dance player and whose playing was characterized by one of the traditional Island regional styles.

open string. Sounded without being *stopped*, or pressed down to alter its pitch.

ornamentation. A way of embellishing a melody by adding such elements as grace notes, cuts, and Scotch snaps.

playing the tune right out. A term used on PEI to indicate that a nonfiddler has succeeded in playing a fiddle tune on his or her instrument note-for-note and up to speed.

prompter. Someone who calls out the routines for a quadrille or other figure-dance (also known as a "caller").

pump organ. A piano-sized reed instrument with a piano-like keyboard and treadles to pump air through the reeds.

quadrille. The predominant form of square-formation dancing on PEI (also known as *square sets*); it generally consists of four or five parts, or figures, danced in succession with pauses in between.

reel. A fast tune, generally written in 2/2 or 2/4 time. Most reels have two repeated eight-measure parts, generally with eight notes to the bar. Note: Scotch reels, four-hand reels, and eight-hand reels are types of dances.

revival. When applied to music (or more specifically, fiddling), an organized—or at least systematic—attempt to rekindle interest in a style or repertoire.

rosin. The translucent amber-colored cake derived from oil of turpentine that fiddlers rub on their bows for traction.

round dancing. A term used on PEI to refer to the waltz.

Scotch reel. An eighteenth-century Scottish dance that features fancy footwork.

Scotch snap. A rhythmic device performed by a quick pair of alternate-direction bow strokes. In 4/4 time, the rhythm is generally written as a sixteenth note followed by a dotted eighth.

set-dancing. See *quadrille*.

set of tunes. Medley.

set tune. A cut-time dance tune used to accompany set-dancing that is neither a reel nor a hornpipe. Many set tunes played on PEI are derived from popular song melodies.

slow grace. A form of ornamentation in which the player bows a note just below an important melody note and then slurs into the melody (a more technical name is *appoggiatura*).

Souris Set. The big-circle quadrille that predominates in the environs of Souris, in northeastern PEI.

square dancing. Figure dancing in which four couples stand in a square formation.

square formation. Four couples line up at right angles to form a square.

square set. See *quadrille*.

step dancing. A form of dancing in which the arms and torso remain relatively still while the legs and feet carry out intricate combinations of steps in close time to the music.

stop (a string). Pressing a string down against the fingerboard to alter its pitch. See also *double stop*.

strathspey. A moderate-tempo dance tune of Scottish origin in 4/4 time featuring elaborate rhythms.

superstyle. A stylistic template that dominates musical expression, usually deriving from a contest or recording scene.

swing (your partner). A dance routine in which couples join hands—or assume a waltz grip—and rotate quickly around a central point in time to the music.

syncopation. An unexpected accent, occurring at a position in the measure that would not ordinarily be stressed.

tea party. On PEI, a large-scale church picnic, also featuring dancing and carnival games, so named to stress its alcohol-free nature.

tempo. The speed at which a tune is played.

town day. An event to raise money for public causes or initiatives.

tune making. See *making tunes*.

tuning. Singing the melody of a fiddle tune. See also *jigging*.

turn. A term on PEI that is used to describe the sections of a fiddle tune. See also *high turn and low turn*.

twist. A personal variant of a tune or portion thereof.

waltz. A tune in 3/4 time designed for couples' dancing.

wedding reel. In Island communities with a Scottish heritage, this dance—an offshoot of the Scotch reel—was once performed by members of the wedding party to open the wedding celebrations.

BIBLIOGRAPHY

Aalen, F. H. A., Kevin Whelan, and Matthew Stout, eds. *Atlas of the Irish Rural Landscape*. Cork: Cork University Press, 1997.

Alburger, Mary Anne. *Scottish Fiddlers and Their Music*. London: Victor Gallaway, 1983.

Anderson, Robert T. "Voluntary Associations in History." *American Anthropologist* 73 (February 1971): 209–22.

Anderson, William W., and Doris M. Anderson. *Reflections on Life on a Farm at St. Peters at the Turn of the Century*. Pamphlet. N.p.: privately printed, 1979.

The Arrival of the First Scottish Catholic Emigrants in Prince Edward Island. Summerside, P.E.I.: Journal Publishing, 1922.

Arsenault, Carmella. "Acadian Celebrations of Mardi Gras." *Island Magazine* 4 (Spring/Summer 1978): 29–32.

Arsenault, Georges. *Complaintes acadiennes de l'Ile-du-Prince-Edouard*. Ottawa: Les Editions Leméac, 1980.

———. *Contes, légends et chansons de l'Ile-du-Prince-Edouard*. Moncton, N.B.: Les Editions d'Acadie, 1998.

———. *The Island Acadians*. Trans. Sally Ross. Charlottetown, P.E.I.: Ragweed Press, 1989.

———. "Le Gâteau des Rois: Twelfth Night Celebrations in Acadian Prince Edward Island." *Island Magazine* 20 (Fall/Winter 1986): 23–28.

———. "Venez Ecouter La Complainte: The Island's Acadian Balladry." *Island Magazine* 37 (Spring/Summer 1995): 3–12.

Babitz, Sol. *Differences between Eighteenth Century and Modern Violin Bowing*. Pamphlet. Los Angeles: Early Music Lab, 1970.

Baglole, Harry, ed. *Exploring Island History*. Belfast, P.E.I.: Ragweed Press, 1977.

Barz, Gregory F., and Timothy J. Cooley, eds. *Shadows in the Field: New Perspectives for Fieldwork in Ethnomusicology*. New York: Oxford University Press, 1997.

Bayard, Samuel. *Dance to the Fiddle, March to the Fife: Instrumental Folk Tunes in Pennsylvania*. State College: Pennsylvania State University Press, 1982.

———. *Hill Country Tunes: Instrumental Folk Music of Southwestern Pennsylvania*. Memoirs of the American Folklore Society, vol. 39. Philadelphia: American Folklore Society, 1944.

Beck, Boyde E. "The Fairest Land That Might Possibly Be Seen: The Image of Prince Edward Island in Some Descriptive Accounts, 1750–1860." M.A. diss., Queen's University, Kingston, Ont., 1984.

———. *PEI: An Unauthorized History*. Charlottetown, P.E.I.: Acorn Press, 1996.

Bégin, Carmelle. *Fiddle Music in the Ottawa Valley: Dawson Girdwood*. National Museum of Man Mercury Series / Canadian Centre for Folk Culture Studies Paper 52. Ottawa, 1985.

Beisswinger, Donald Andrew. "Fiddling Way Out Yonder: Community and Style in the Fiddle Music of Melvin Wine." Diss., University of Memphis, 1997.

Blaustein, Richard. "Rethinking Folk Revivalism: Grass-Roots Preservationism and Folk Romanticism." In Rosenberg, *Transforming Tradition*, 258–74.

———. "Traditional Music and Social Change." Diss., Indiana University, Bloomington, 1975.

Breathnach, Breandán. *Folk Music and Dances of Ireland*. Cork, Ireland: Mercier Press, 1971.

Brehaut, Mary, ed. *Pioneers on the Island*, part 2. Charlottetown: Historical Society of Prince Edward Island, n.d.

Bremner, Benjamin. *Island Scrap Book*. Charlottetown, P.E.I.: Irwin Printing Co., 1932.

———. *Memories of Long Ago*. Charlottetown, P.E.I.: Irwin Printing Co., 1930.

Bremner, Robert. *A Collection of Scots Reels or Country Dances . . . 14 "Numbers."* Edinburgh, 1751–61.

Bronner, Simon J. *Old-Time Music Makers of New York State*. Syracuse: Syracuse University Press, 1987.

Bunting, Edward. *General Collection of the Ancient Irish Music: Containing a Variety of Admired Airs Never Before Published, and Also the Compositions of Conolan and Carolan . . . .* Vol. 1. Dublin: W. Power, 1796; London: Preston and Son, 1796.

Butler, Gary R. "La tradition musicale des Franco-Acadiens de Terre-Neuve: Une étude descriptive." *Canadian Folk Music Journal* 23 (1995): 3–19.

Calder, Grace J. *George Petrie and the Ancient Music of Ireland*. Dublin: Dolmen Press, 1968.

Cannon, Roderick D. *The Highland Bagpipe and Its Music*. Edinburgh: John Donald Publishers, 1988.

Carmichael, Alexander. *Carmina Gadelica: Hymns and Incantations; . . . Orally Collected in the Highlands and Islands of Scotland*. Vol. 1. Edinburgh: Oliver and Boyd, 1928.

Carolan, Nicholas. *A Harvest Saved: Francis O'Neil and Irish Music in Chicago*. Cork, Ireland: Ossian Publications, 1997.

Casey, Dan. "A PEI Hallowe'en Story." *Prince Edward Island Magazine* (December 1900): 316–21.

Cash, W. T. "Taylor County History and Civil War Deserters." *Florida Historical Quarterly* 27 (July 1948): 28–58.

Cauthen, Joyce. ". . . And Bring Your Fiddle: The Fiddler in Alabama Community Life." *Alabama Heritage* 13 (Summer 1989): 2–21.

———. *With Fiddle and Well Rosined Bow: Old-Time Fiddling in Alabama*. Tuscaloosa: University of Alabama Press, 1989.

Cazden, Norman. "A Simplified Mode-Classification for Traditional American Song-Tunes." *Yearbook of the Folk Music Council* (1971).

Chiasson, Fr. Anselme. "Traditions and Oral Literature in Acadia." In Daigle, *The Acadians of the Maritimes*, 477–511.

Christeson, R. P. *The Old-Time Fiddler's Repertory*. Columbia: University of Missouri Press, 1973.

Clark, Andrew Hill. *Acadia: The Geography of Early Nova Scotia to 1760*. Madison: University of Wisconsin Press, 1968.

———. *Three Centuries and the Island*. Toronto: University of Toronto Press, 1959.

Cohen, John, and Mike Seeger, eds. *The New Lost City Ramblers Song Book*. New York: Oak Publications, 1964.

Collinson, Francis. Introduction to *The Athole Collection* by Stewart-Robinson, v–vi.

———. *The Traditional and National Music of Scotland*. Nashville, Tenn.: Vanderbilt University Press, 1966.

Combs, Josiah H. "The Highlander's Music." *Kentucky Folklore Record* 5 (October–December 1959): 108–22. Reprinted from *Vient de Paraître* (January 1926).

Conran, Michael. *The National Music of Ireland, Containing the History of the Irish Bards, the National Melodies, the Harp and Other Musical Instruments of Erin*. Collected Lectures. N.p.: J. Duffy, 1846.

Cooke, Peter. *The Fiddle Tradition of the Shetland Isles*. Cambridge: Cambridge University Press, 1986.

Cormier, Charlotte. "La Musique Traditionnelle en Acadie." *Royal Society of Canada Proceedings*, 4th series, 15 (1977): 239–59.

Cotton, W. L. *Chapters in Our Island Story*. Charlottetown, P.E.I.: Irwin Printing Co., 1927.
Cousins, John Robert. "Horses in the Folklore of Western Prince Edward Island." M.A. diss., Memorial University of Newfoundland, St. Johns, 1990.
Creighton, Helen, and Calum Macleod. *Gaelic Songs in Nova Scotia*. 1964. Reprinted, Ottawa: National Museum of Man, National Museum of Canada, 1979.
Daigle, Jean, ed. *The Acadians of the Maritimes: Thematic Studies*. Moncton, N.B.: Centre d'Études Acadiennes, 1982.
Damon, S. Foster. *The History of Square Dancing*. Barre, Mass.: Barre Gazette, 1957. Reprinted from *Proceedings of the American Antiquarian Society* 62, no. 1 (1952): 63–98.
Dart, Mary McNab. *Contra Dance Choreography: A Reflection of Social Change*. New York: Garland Publishing, 1995.
Del Ryke, Delores. "So Hell Is Full of Fiddlers—Bet It Won't Be Crowded!" *Western Folklore* 23 (July 1964): 181–86.
Devil's Box: Published Quarterly by the Tennessee Valley Old Time Fiddle Association. "The First Tennessee State Champion Fiddler." December 2, 1968: 6–7.
Dibblee, Randall, and Dorothy Dibblee. *Folksongs from P.E.I.* Summerside: PEI Centennial Commission, 1973.
Dick's Quadrille Call Book. New York: Dick and FitzGerald, 1878.
Dorson, Richard M., ed. *Folklore and Folklife*. Chicago: University of Chicago Press, 1972.
Dos Passos, John. *The Big Money*. 1930. Boston: Houghton Mifflin, 1974.
Downer, Alan S., ed. *The Memoir of John Durang, American Actor, 1785–1816*. York, Penn.: Historical Society of York County, 1966.
Dunlay, Kate, and David Greenberg. *Traditional Celtic Violin Music of Cape Breton*. Toronto: DunGreen Music, 1996.
Dunn, Charles W. *Highland Settler: A Portrait of the Scottish Gael in Nova Scotia*. 1953. Rev. ed., Toronto: University of Toronto Press, 1968.
Edwards, George Thornton. *Music and Musicians of Maine: A History of the Progress of Music . . .*, 1604–1928. Portland, Me.: Southworth Press, 1928.
Emmerson, George. *Rantin' Pipe and Tremblin' String: A History of Scottish Dance Music*. 1971. 2nd ed. London, Ont.: Galt House, 1988.
———. *A Social History of Scottish Dance*. Montreal: McGill-Queens University Press, 1972.
Feintuch, Burt. "The Conditions for Cape Breton Fiddle Music." *Ethnomusicology* 48 (Winter 2004): 73–104.
———. *In the Blood: Cape Breton Conversations on Culture*. Logan, Utah: Utah State University Press, 2010.
———. "Musical Revival as Musical Transformation." In Rosenberg, *Transforming Tradition*, 184–93.
"Fiddling to Henry Ford." *Literary Digest*. January 2, 1926, 33-38.
Fiske, Roger. *Scotland in Music*. New York: Cambridge University Press, 1983.
Fleischmann, Aloys. *Sources of Irish Traditional Music, c. 1600–1855*. 2 vols. New York: Garland Publications, 1998.
Flett, J. F., and T. M. Flett. *Traditional Dancing in Scotland*. London: Routledge and Kegan Paul, 1966.
———. *Traditional Step-Dancing in Lakeland*. London: English Folk Dance and Song Society, 1979.
Flood, Wm. H. Grattan. *A History of Irish Music*. 3rd ed. Dublin: Browne and Nolan, 1913.
Forbes, Ernst R. *The Maritime Rights Movement, 1919–1927: A Study in Canadian Regionalism*. Montreal: McGill-Queens University Press, 1979.
Ford, Ira W. *Traditional Music of America*. New York: E. P. Dutton, 1940.

Forsyth, Meghan Catherine. "De par chez nous: Fiddling Traditions and Acadian Identity on Prince Edward Island." Diss., University of Toronto, 2011.

Fraser, Capt. Simon. *Airs and Melodies Peculiar to the Highlands of Scotland and the Isles.* Edinburgh, 1816. Reprinted, Sydney, N.S.: Cranford Publications, 1982.

Fraser, Douglas. "Traditional Stepdancing in Cape Breton." In MacGillivray and MacGillivray, A *Cape Breton Ceilidh,* 24–25.

Garrison, Virginia Hope. "Traditional and Non-traditional Teaching and Learning Practices in Folk Music: An Ethnographic Field Study of Cape Breton Fiddling." Diss., University of Wisconsin–Madison, 1985.

Gellerman, Robert. *The American Reed Organ.* New York: Vestal Press, 1973.

Goertzen, Chris. "American Fiddle Tunes and the Historic-Geographic Method." *Ethnomusicology* 29 (Fall 1985): 448–73.

———. "The Transformation of American Contest Fiddling." *Journal of Musicology* 6 (1988): 107–29.

Gore, Charles. *The Scottish Fiddle Music Index: The 18th and 19th Century Printed Collections.* Musselburgh, Scotland: Amaising Publishing House, 1994.

Gow, Niel, *A Collection of Strathspey Reels* . . . Dunkeld: Niel Gow, 1784.

———. *A Second Collection* . . . Dunkeld: Niel Gow, 1788.

———. *A Third Collection* . . . Dunkeld: Niel Gow, 1792.

———. *A Fourth Collection* . . . Dunkeld: Niel Gow, 1800.

———. *A Fifth Collection* . . . Edinburgh, Niel Gow and Sons, 1809.

———. *A Sixth Collection* . . . Edinburgh, Niel Gow and Sons, 1822.

Gow, Niel, and Sons, ed. *The Beauties of Niel Gow.* 3 vols. Edinburgh, 1819. Louth, U.K.: Celtic Music, 1983.

———. Part First of the *Complete Repository of Original Slow Strathspeys and Dances.* Edinburgh: Niel Gow and Sons, 1799.

———. *A Complete Repository* . . . Part II. Edinburgh: Niel Gow and Sons, 1802.

———. *A Complete Repository* . . . Part III. Edinburgh: Niel Gow and Sons, 1806.

———. *A Complete Repository* . . . Part IV. Edinburgh: Gow and Shepherd, 1817.

Gowan, Sandra L. *Ned Landry: Master of the Fiddle.* St. Johns: New Brunswick Consortium of Professional Writers, 1996.

Graham, Glenn. *The Cape Breton Fiddle: Making and Maintaining Tradition.* Sydney, N.S.: Cape Breton University Press, 2006.

Green, Robin, and Mark Miller. "Don Messer and His Islanders." In Kallman and Potvin, *Encyclopedia of Music in Canada,* 850.

Greene, Steve. *Uncle Joe Shippee and the All New England Fiddle Contest.* Pamphlet. Orono: University of Maine, 1998.

Guilcher, Jean-Michel. *La Contredanse: Un tournat dans l'histoire francaise de la danse.* N.p.: Nouvelle Librairie de la Danse, 2003. New ed. of *La Contredanse et les renouvellements de la danse francaise,* 1969.

Harris, George W. "The Knob Dance: A Tennessee Frolic." In *Tall Tales of the Southwest: An Anthology of Southern and Southwestern Humor,* edited by Franklin Julius Meine, 55–61. New York: Alfred A. Knopf, 1930.

Harvey, D. C., ed. *Journeys to the Island of St. John, or Prince Edward Island, 1775–1832.* Toronto: MacMillan, 1955.

Hennessy, Jeffrey James. "Fiddle Grooves: Identity, Representation, and the Sound of Cape Breton Fiddle Music in Popular Culture." Diss., University of Toronto, 2008.

Herskovitz, Melville J. *Man and His Works: The Science of Cultural Anthropology.* New York: Alfred A Knopf, 1956.

Hill, S. S. *A Short Account of Prince Edward Island* . . . London: Medden and Co., 1839.
Hillgrove, Thomas. *Hillgrove's Call-Book and Dancing Master: A Complete Practical Guide to the Art of Dancing.* New York: Dick and FitzGerald, 1863.
Holmes, Skip, ed. *The Richard Wood Collection.* Vol. 1. [Charlottetown, P.E.I.]: privately printed, 1999.
Hornby, James John. "The Fiddle on the Island: The Fiddling Tradition on PEI." M.A. diss., Memorial University of Newfoundland, St. Johns, 1982.
Hornby, Jim. "The Great Fiddle Contests of 1926." *Island Magazine* 7 (Fall/Winter 1979): 25–30.
———. "Musicians of Olden Times." *Island Magazine* 10 (Fall/Winter 1981): 20–25.
———. "The Wedding Reel in Eastern Prince Edward Island." *Clansman* (August–September 1992): 14ff.
Hornby, Jim, and John Shaw. *Report on a Sound and Film Archives for PEI.* Pamphlet. Charlottetown, P.E.I.: Institute of Island Studies, 1988.
Hornby, Jim, and John Weyman. "Memories of Jack Webster." *Island Fiddler* (March 1981): 3–4.
Hornby, Susan, ed. *Belfast People.* Charlottetown, P.E.I.: Tea Hill Press, 1992.
Housewright, Wiley L. *A History of Music and Dance in Florida, 1565–1865.* Tuscaloosa: University of Alabama Press, 1991.
Howe, Elias. *Howe's Fifty Contra Dances.* No. 2. Boston: Elias Howe, [c. 1870].
———. *Howe's One Thousand Jigs and Reels.* Boston: Elias Howe, c. 1867.
———. *The Musicians Companion.* Boston: Kidder and Wright, 1840.
———. *Musicians Omnibus.* 7 vols. Boston: Elias Howe, 1864–82.
Hughes, Emmett. *A Composition of Fiddle Tunes.* Dromore, Mount Stewart, P.E.I.: privately printed, 1991.
———. *More Fiddle Tunes: Book 2.* Dromore, Mount Stewart, P.E.I.: privately printed, 2000.
Hulan, Richard. "The First Annual Country Fiddlers' Contest." *Devil's Box: Published Quarterly by the Tennessee Valley Old Time Fiddle Association* (March 15, 1969): 15–18.
Ives, Edward D. *Drive Dull Care Away: Folksongs from Prince Edward Island.* Charlottetown, P.E.I.: Institute of Island Studies, 1999.
———. *Joe Scott: The Woodsman-Songmaker.* Urbana: University of Illinois Press, 1978.
———. *Larry Gorman: The Man Who Made the Songs.* Fredericton, N.B.: Goose Lane Editions, 1993. Orig. pub., Bloomington: Indiana University Press, 1964.
———. *Lawrence Doyle: The Farmer Poet of PEI.* Orono: University of Maine Press, 1971.
———. *21 Folk Songs from Prince Edward Island.* Orono, Maine: Northeast Folklore, 1963.
———. *The World of Maritimes Folklore.* Evergreen Booklets no. 1. Halifax, N.S.: Helen Creighton Foundation, 1993.
Johnson, David. *Music and Society in Lowland Scotland in the Eighteenth Century.* London: Oxford University Press, 1972.
———. *Scottish Fiddle Music in the Eighteenth Century: A Music Collection and Historical Study.* Edinburgh: John Donald Publishers, 1984.
Johnstone, Walter. "Letters and Travels." In Harvey, *Journeys to the Island of St. John.*
Jones, James H. "Commonplace and Memorization in the Oral Tradition of the English and Scottish Popular Ballads." *Journal of American Folklore* 74 (April–June 1961): 99–112.
Kallman, Helmut, and Gilles Potvin. *Encyclopedia of Music in Canada.* 2nd ed. Toronto: University of Toronto Press, 1992.
Karpeles, Maud. *Folk Songs from Newfoundland.* Hamden, Conn.: Archon Books, 1970.
Kartchner, Kenner C. *Frontier Fiddler: The Life of a Northern Arizona Pioneer.* Edited by Larry V. Shumway. Tucson: University of Arizona Press, 1990.
Kaufman, Charles H. *Music in New Jersey, 1655–1860.* Rutherford, N.J.: Fairleigh Dickinson University Press, 1981.

Kennedy, Michael. *Gaelic Nova Scotia: An Economic, Cultural, and Social Impact Study*. Nova Scotia Museum Curatorial Report no. 97. Halifax: Nova Scotia Museum, 2002.

Kennedy, Mike. "Is Leis an Tighearna . . . : The Scottish Gaelic Settlement History of Prince Edward Island." Diss., University of Edinburgh, 1995.

[Kerr, James Spiers]. *Kerr's Collection of Merry Melodies for the Violin*. 4 vols. Glasgow: James S. Kerr, n.d. Reprint of *Kerr's Collection of Reels and Strathspeys*. Glasgow, 1870.

Laforte, Conrad. "Folk-Music, Franco-Canadian." In Kallman and Potvin, *Encyclopedia of Music in Canada*, 477–81.

LaMont, M. *Reverend Donald MacDonald: Glimpses of His Life and Times*. Charlottetown, P.E.I.: Murley and Garnum, 1902.

Large, Betty Rogers, and Tom Crothers. *Out of Thin Air* [The Story of Keith Rogers and CFCY]. Charlottetown, P.E.I.: Applecross Press, 1989.

Laufman, Dudley. "The Tradition of Fiddling and Calling in New England." *Fiddler Magazine* (Summer 1999): 31–37.

Lea, Dr. R. G. *History of the Practice of Medicine in PEI*. Charlottetown: PEI Medical Society, 1964.

Lederman, Anne. "Fiddling." In Kallman and Potvin, *Encyclopedia of Music in Canada*, 455–57.

———. "Old Indian and Métis Fiddling in Manitoba: Origins, Structure, and Question of Syncretism." *Canadian Folk Music Journal* 19 (1991): 40–60.

Lewis, J. C. "History of PEI Liquor Laws Underlines Utter Futility of Prohibition." *Wine, Beer and Spirits in Canada* (November 1957): 23–52, passim; (December 1957): 18–23.

Linn, Karen. *That Half-Barbaric Twang: The Banjo in American Popular Culture*. Urbana: University of Illinois Press, 1994.

Linton, Ralph. "Nativistic Movements." *American Anthropologist* 45 (1943): 230–40.

Lomax, Alan. "Folk Song Style: Musical Style and Social Context." *American Anthropology* 61 (December 1959): 927–53.

———. "Song Structure and Social Structure." *Ethnology* 1 (1962): 425–51.

Longstreet, A. B. [Augustus Baldwin]. *Georgia Scenes: Characters, Incidents, &c., in the First Half Century of the Republic*. 1835. New York: Sagamore Press, 1957.

Lord, Albert B. *The Singer of Tales*. Cambridge, Mass.: Harvard University Press, 1960.

Lovett, Mrs. Benjamin B., ed. *Good Morning: Music, Calls, and Directions for Old-Time Dancing as Revived by Mr. and Mrs. Henry Ford*. 3rd ed. Dearborn, Mich.: privately printed, 1941.

Lowe, Joseph. *Lowe's Collection of Reels, Strathspeys and Jigs*. 6 vols. Edinburgh, 1844.

Mac Aoidh, Caoimhín. *Between the Jigs and the Reels: The Donegal Fiddling Tradition*. Nure, Co. Leitrim: Drumlin Publications, 1994.

MacArthur, F. A. *Legends of Prince Edward Island*. 1966. 8th ed. Charlottetown, P.E.I.: H. M. Simpson, 1978.

MacDonald, Dan R. *The Heather Hill Collection*. Englishtown, N.S.: Cranford Publications. n.d.

MacDonald, Edward. *If You're Stronghearted: PEI in the Twentieth Century*. Charlottetown: PEI Museum and Heritage Foundation, 2000.

———. *New Ireland: The Irish on PEI*. Pamphlet. Charlottetown: PEI Museum and Heritage Society, 1990.

MacDonald, Keith Norman. *The Skye Collection*. 1887. Edited by Paul Cranford. London, Ont.: Scott's Highland Services, 1979.

MacDonald, Mary, and Mrs. Clinton Stewart. *Historical Sketch of Eastern Kings [County]*. Pamphlet. "Written for the Fire Dept.," 1972.

MacEachern, Dan Hugh. *MacEachern's Collection: Cape Breton Scottish Music for the Violin*. Queensville, N.S.: privately printed, 1975.

MacGillivray, Allister. *The Cape Breton Fiddler*. 1981. Marion Bridge, N.S.: Sea Cape Music, 1997.

MacGillivray, Allister, and Beverly MacGillivray. *A Cape Breton Ceilidh*. Sydney, N.S.: Sea Cape Music, 1988.

MacGregor, John. *Historical and Descriptive Sketches of the Maritime Colonies of British America*. 2 vols. London, 1828. Reprinted, New York: Johnson Reprint, 1968.

MacKinnon, Rollie, and Gordon Belsher, eds. *The Prince Edward Island Music Series*. Vol. 1. Charlottetown, P.E.I.: Garden Music Enterprises, 1991.

Mackintosh, W. A. *The Economic Background of Dominion-Provincial Relations*. Toronto: McClelland and Stewart, 1964. Reprint of "Appendix III to the Rowell-Sirois Report," Ottawa: King's Printer, 1939.

MacLeod, Ada. "The Glenaladale Pioneers." *Dalhousie Review* 11 (October 1931): 311–24.

MacPhail, Sir Andrew. *The Master's Wife*. 1939. Toronto: McClelland and Stewart, 1977.

MacQuarrie, Gordon. *The Cape Breton Collection of Scottish Melodies for the Violin*. N.p.: privately printed, 1940.

MacQueen, Malcolm A. *Hebridean Pioneers*. Winnipeg: Henderson Directories, 1957.

———. *Skye Pioneers and the Island*. Winnipeg: Stovel, 1929.

Malone, Bill C. *Country Music U.S.A.* American Folklore Society, 1968. Rev. ed., Austin: University of Texas Press, 1985.

Maloney, Mick [Michael]. "Irish Ethnic Recordings and the Irish-American Imagination." In *Ethnic Records in America: A Neglected Heritage*, 85–101. Studies in American Folklife no.1. Washington, D.C.: Library of Congress American Folklife Center, 1982.

———. "Irish Music in America: Continuity and Change." Diss., University of Pennsylvania, 1992.

Marshall, William. *Marshall's Scottish Airs, Melodies, Strathspeys, Reels, Jigs &c for the Violin*. . . . Peterborough, N.H.: Fiddlecase Books, 1978. Reprint combines four separate collections: *A Collection of Strathspey Reels with a Bass for the Violoncello or Harpsichord*, 2 vols., 1781; *Marshall's Scottish Airs, Melodies, Strathspeys, Reels, etc. for the Pianoforte, Harp, Violin, and Violoncello with Appropriate Basses*, 1822; *Volume Second of a Collection of Scottish Melodies, Reels, Strathspeys, Jigs, Slow Airs, etc., for the Piano Forte, Violin, and Violoncello*, 1845; and *Kinrara*, 1800.

McCarthy, Marie. "The Transmission of Music and the Formation of National Identity in Early Twentieth-Century Ireland." In *Irish Musical Studies: The Maynooth International Musicological Conference, 1995*, edited by Patrick F. Devine and Harry White, 146–59. Selected Proceedings, part 1. Dublin: Four Courts Press, 1996.

McCullough, Lawrence. "An Historical Sketch of Traditional Irish Music in the U.S." *Folklore Forum* 7, no. 3 (1974): 177–91.

———. "Irish Music in Chicago: An Ethnomusicological Study." Diss., University of Pittsburgh, 1978.

McKay, Dan. "Tartanism Triumphant: The Construction of Scottishness in Nova Scotia." *Acadiensis* (1992): 5–47.

McKinnon, Ian Francis. "Fiddling to Fortune: The Role of Commercial Recordings Made by Cape Breton Fiddlers in the Fiddle Music Tradition of Cape Breton Island." M.A. diss., Memorial University of Newfoundland, St. Johns, 1989.

Melin, Mats. "Local, Global, and Diasporic Interaction in the Cape Breton Dance Tradition" In *Routes and Roots: Fiddle and Dance Studies from around the North Atlantic* 4, edited by Ian Russell and Chris Goertzen, 132–44. Occasional Publications no. 8. Aberdeen: University of Aberdeen, Elphinstone Institute, 2012.

[Mellick, Harry]. *Timothy's Boyhood; or, Pioneer Country Life on PEI*. Kentville, N.S.: Kentville Publishing, 1933.

Merriam, Alan P. *The Anthropology of Music.* Chicago: Northwestern University Press, 1964.
Messer, Don. *Don Messer's Barn Dance Breakdowns.* Toronto: Gordon V. Thompson, 1954.
———. *Don Messer's Canadian Hoedowns.* Toronto: Gordon V. Thompson, 1957.
———. *Don Messer's Old Tyme Music.* Toronto: Gordon V. Thompson, 1942.
———. *Don Messer's Square Dance Tunes.* Toronto: Gordon V. Thompson, 1952.
———. *Don Messer's Way Down East Fiddlin' Tunes.* Toronto: Gordon V. Thompson, 1948.
Michaud, Neil. "Acadians and Their Music." In Daigle, *The Acadians of the Maritimes,* 617–34.
Miller, Rebecca S. "Irish Traditional and Popular Music in New York City: Identity and Social Change, 1930–1975." In *The New York Irish,* edited by Ronald H. Bayor and Timothy J. Meagher, 482–507. Baltimore, Md.: Johns Hopkins University Press, 1996.
Milnes, Gerald. *Play of a Fiddle: Traditional Music, Dance, and Folklore in West Virginia.* Lexington: University Press of Kentucky, 1999.
Mitchum, Allison. *Ivan Hicks: Fifty Years of Fabulous Fiddle Music.* Hantsport, N.S.: Lancelot Press, 1996.
Monical, William L. "Violin." In *New Harvard Dictionary of Music,* 917–22.
Moody, Ed. "The Itinerant Fiddlers of New Hampshire." *Northern Junket* (February 9, 1968): 2–13.
Moore, Marven. "The Island and the Reciprocity Treaty of 1854." In Baglole, *Exploring Island History,* 155–64.
Morgan, Edmund S. *Virginians at Home: Family Life in the Eighteenth Century.* Williamsburg, Va.: Colonial Williamsburg, 1952.
Murray, Neil J. *The Scots Fiddle: Tunes, Tales and Traditions.* Moffat, Scotland: Lochar Publishing, 1991.
Nathan, Hans. *Dan Emmett and the Rise of Negro Minstrelsy.* Norman: University of Oklahoma Press, 1962.
Nevell, Richard. *A Time to Dance: American Country Dancing from Hornpipes to Hash.* New York: St. Martin's Press, 1977.
New Harvard Dictionary of Music. Cambridge, Mass.: Belknap Press of Harvard University Press, 1986.
Nusbaum, Philip. "Bluegrass and the Folk Revival." In Rosenberg, *Transforming Tradition,* 203–19.
O Boyle, Sean. *The Irish Song Tradition.* 1976. Rev. ed., Cork, Ireland: Ossian Publications, 1989.
Ó Canainn, Tomás. *Traditional Irish Music.* London: Routledge and Kegan Paul, 1978. Rev. ed., Cork, Ireland: Ossian Publications, 1993.
O hallmhurain, Gearold. *A Pocket History of Traditional Irish Music.* Dublin: O'Brien Press, 1998.
O'Neill, Capt. Francis. *Irish Minstrels and Musicians.* 1913. Reprinted, Cork, Ireland: Mercier Press, 1987.
———. *O'Neill's Music of Ireland.* Chicago, 1903. Reprinted, Bronx, N.Y.: privately printed, 1973.
———. *O'Neills Dance Music of Ireland.* Chicago: Lyon and Healy, 1907.
One Thousand Fiddle Tunes. Chicago: M. M. Cole Publishing, 1967. Reprint of Ryan, *Ryan's Mammoth Collection.*
O'Shea, Art. *It Happened in Iona.* Charlottetown, P.E.I.: privately printed, 1990.
Perlman, Ken. "And It Was Good Pastime: Old Time Fiddling on Prince Edward Island." *Island Magazine* 35 (Spring/Summer 1994): 23–30.
———. "Cape Breton's First Family of the Fiddle: An Interview with Buddy and Natalie MacMaster." *Sing Out!* (March–April 1996): 44–53.
———. "Couldn't Have a Wedding without the Fiddler: Old Time Fiddling on Prince Edward Island." *Fiddler Magazine* (Spring 1995): 4–11.

———. "The Devil's Instrument Revisited: Prince Edward Island as a Case Study." In *Crossing Over: Fiddle and Dance Studies from Around the North Atlantic* 3, edited by Ian Russell and Anna Kearney Guigné, 228–38. Aberdeen, Scotland: Elphinstone Institute, 2010.

———. "Dwight Diller and the Music of Pocahontas County." *Sing Out!* (May–July 1997): 52–61.

———. *The Fiddle Music of Prince Edward Island: Celtic and Acadian Tunes in Living Tradition*. Pacific, Mo.: Mel Bay, 1996.

———. "A Lovely Sweet Music: Old Time Fiddling on Prince Edward Island." *Sing Out!* (November–December 1994): 32–44.

———. "Me Head Was Full of Music: Learning Fiddle Tunes on Prince Edward Island." *Old Time Herald* (Winter 1997–98): 22–27.

———. *The Prince Edward Island Style of Fiddling: Fiddlers of Eastern PEI*. Liner notes. Rounder Records #7015. 1997.

———. *The Prince Edward Island Style of Fiddling: Fiddlers of Western PEI*. Liner notes. Rounder Records #7014. 1997.

———. "Sean McGuire: Master of the Irish Violin." *Fiddler Magazine* (Spring 1998): 23–28.

———. "That Old-Time Music: Fiddlin' and Dancin' on Prince Edward Island." *The World and I* (March 1993): 240–51.

———. "Traditional Banjo Player Clyde Davenport." *Banjo Newsletter* (October 1996): 16–22.

———. "Tune-Recall among Traditional Fiddlers on Prince Edward Island." *Canadian Folk Music Bulletin* 31 (September–December 1997): 8–12.

Pichierri, Louis. *Music in New Hampshire, 1623–1800*. New York: Columbia University Press, 1960.

Plantinga, Leon. *Romantic Music*. New York: W. W. Norton, 1984.

Playford, Henry. *A Collection of Original Scotch Tunes (Full of the Highland Humours for the Violin)* . . . London: Henry Playford, 1700.

Playford, John. *The English Dancing Master*. London: Thomas Harper, 1651. Reprinted, London: Hugh Mellor, 1933. Reprinted, New York: Dance Horizons, n.d.

Posen, Sheldon. *For Singing and Dancing and All Sorts of Fun: The Story of the Ottawa Valley's Most Famous Song, "The Chapeau Boys."* Toronto: Deneau Publishers, 1988.

Pottle, Frederick A., and Charles H. Bennett, eds. *Boswell's Journal of a Tour to the Hebrides with Samuel Johnson, LL.D., 1773*. 1936. New York: McGraw-Hill, 1961.

Pratt, C. C. *A Brief History of St. Peters Bay*. N.p.: privately printed, [c. 1970].

Proctor, George A. *Old Time Fiddling in Ontario*. National Museum of Canada Bulletin 190, Contributions to Anthropology, part 2, pp. 173–91. Ottawa: Department of Northern Affairs and National Resources, 1963.

Quigley, Colin. *Music from the Heart: Compositions of a Folk Fiddler*. Athens: University of Georgia Press, 1995.

Rankin, Allan R. "Fox Farming on PEI." In Baglole, *Exploring Island History*, 166–74.

Rayburn, Alan. *Geographical Names of PEI*. Ottawa: Minister of Supply and Services, 1978.

Retí, Rudolph. *The Thematic Process in Music*. New York: Macmillan, 1951.

Rhodes, F. "Dancing in Cape Breton Island, Nova Scotia." Appendix to Flett and Flett, *Traditional Dancing in Scotland*, 267–85.

Richardson, Philip J. S. *The Social Dances of the Nineteenth Century in England*. London: Herbert Jenkins, 1960.

Ritchie, Jean. *Singing Family of the Cumberlands*. 1955. Reprinted, New York: Oak Publications, 1980.

Robinson, Geoff, and Dorothy Robinson. *Duty-Free: A Prohibition Special*. [Charlottetown, PEI]: privately printed, 1986.

Roche Collection of Traditional Irish Music, The. 1912. Reprinted, Cork, Ireland: Ossian Publications, 1982.

Rogers, Ellis A. The Quadrille: A Practical Guide to Its Origin, Development and Performance. Orpington, U.K.: C. and E. Rogers, 2003.

Rosenbaum, Art. Folk Visions and Voices. Athens: University of Georgia Press, 1983.

Rosenberg, Neil V. "Don Messer's Modern Canadian Fiddle Canon." Canadian Folk Music Journal, no. 22 (1994): 23–34.

———. "From the Sound Recordings Editor: Classification of Traditional Instrumental Music." Journal of American Folklore 108 (Spring 1995): 186–201.

———. "A Preliminary Bibliography of Canadian Old Time Instrumental Music Books." Canadian Folk Music Journal (1980): 20–22.

———. "Starvation, Serendipity and the Ambivalence of Bluegrass Revivalism." In Rosenberg, Transforming Tradition, 194–201.

———, ed. Transforming Tradition: Folk Music Revivals Examined. Urbana: University of Illinois Press, 1993.

Russell, Tony. "Additional" notes on "J. Scott Skinner, The Strathspey King." London: Topic Records #12T280, 1975.

Rutten, Gerard L. "The History of Community Bands and the Development of School Bands in Prince Edward Island." M.Ed. thesis, University of Victoria, 1997.

Ryan, Wm. Bradbury. Ryan's Mammoth Collection of More than 1050 Reels and Jigs, Hornpipes, Clogs, Walk Arounds, Slip Jigs, Essences, Strathspeys, Highland Flings and Contra Dances with Figures. Boston, 1883. Rev. ed., Pacific, Mo.: Mel Bay, 1995.

Sachs, Curt. World History of the Dance. Translated by Bessie Schönberg. New York: W. W. Norton, 1937.

Sand, George. The Master Pipers [Les Maitres Sonneurs]. Paris, 1853. Translated by Rosemary Lloyd. Oxford: Oxford University Press, 1994.

Sanders, J. Olcott. "Honor the Fiddler." In Texian Stomping Grounds, edited by J. Frank Dobie, Mody C. Boatright, and Harry H. Ransom, 78–90. Texas Folk-Lore Society Publication 17. Austin: Texas Folk-Lore Society, 1941.

Schwartz, Frank. "An Economic History of PEI." In Baglole, Exploring Island History, 93–107.

Scott, Edward. Dancing as an Art and Pastime. London: George Bell and Sons, 1892.

Sellick, Lester B. Canada's Don Messer. Kentville, N.S.: Kentville Publishing, 1969.

———. Our Musical Heritage. Hantsport, N.S.: Lancelot Press, 1984.

Semmens, Richard. "Branles, Gavottes and Contredanses in the Late Seventeenth and Early Eighteenth Centuries." Dance Research 15 (1997 [issued 1998]): 35–62.

Shapiro, Henry D. Appalachia on Our Mind: The Southern Mountains and Mountaineers in the American Consciousness. Chapel Hill: University of North Carolina Press, 1978.

Sharp, Cecil. The English Folk Song: Some Conclusions. London: Simpkin, 1907.

———. English Folk Songs from the Southern Appalachians. 1917. Edited by Maud Karpeles. Vol. 1. London: Oxford University Press, 1932, 1952.

Shaw, John. Gaelic in PEI: A Cultural Remnant. Pamphlet. Charlottetown, P.E.I.: Institute of Island Studies and Celtic Studies Committee, 1987.

Shaw, Lloyd. Cowboy Dances. Caldwell, Idaho: Caxton Printers, 1952. 1939.

Shaw, Margaret Fay. Folksongs and Folklore of South Uist. London: Oxford University Press, 1977.

Shaw, Walter. Tell Me the Tales. Charlottetown, P.E.I.: Square Deal Publications, 1975.

Shoemaker, Henry W. Mountain Minstrelsy of Pennsylvania. Philadelphia: Newman F. McGirr, 1931. 3rd. ed., titled North Pennsylvania Minstrelsy.

Shoupe, Catherine A. "Musical Families and Family Music in Scotland." *Southern Folklore* 51 (1994): 17–33.
Skinner, James Scott. *A Guide to Bowing: Strathspeys, Reels, Pastoral Melodies, Hornpipes, &c.* Bayley and Ferguson, c. 1900. Reprinted, Edinburgh: Hardie Press, 1984.
———. *The Harp and Claymore: A Volume of Music Original, Selected, and Traditional, Comprising Pastorals, Marches, Strathspeys and Reels, Laments, Song, Etc., for Voice, Violin, Bagpipe, Pianoforte, Etc.* Glasgow: Bayley and Ferguson, 1890. Reprinted, 1904.
———. *The Logie Collection of Original Music.* London: J.B. Cramer and Co., 1888.
———. *The Miller o' Hirn Collection.* Elgin: privately printed, 1881.
———. *The Scottish Violinist.* 1900. Reprinted, Glasgow: Bayley and Ferguson, n.d.
Sky, Patrick. "Elias Howe and William Bradbury Ryan." In *Ryan's Mammoth Collection*, 10–15. Pacific, Mo.: Mel Bay, 1995.
Skye Collection. See Keith Norman MacDonald.
Smith, H. M. Scott. *The Historic Churches of PEI.* Erin, Ont.: Boston Mills Press, 1986.
Spielman, Earl. "Traditional North American Fiddling." Diss., University of Wisconsin–Madison, 1975.
Spradley, James P. *The Ethnographic Interview.* New York: Holt, Rinehart and Winston, 1979.
Stewart, John. *An Account of Prince Edward Island in the Gulph of St Lawrence.* London: W. Winchester and Son, 1806. Reprinted, New York: Johnson Reprint, 1967.
Stewart-Robertson, James. *The Athole Collection of the Dance Music of Scotland.* 1884. Rev. ed., Edinburgh: Oliver and Boyd, 1961.
Strangways, A. H. Fox, with Maud Karpeles. *Cecil Sharp.* London: Oxford University Press, 1933.
Sugden, John. *Niccolo Paganini: Supreme Violinist or Devil's Fiddler.* Turnbridge Wells, England: Midas Books, 1980.
Surenne, John T. *The Dance Music of Scotland.* Edinburgh: Wood and Co., 1852.
"Suzuki and History of the Suzuki Method." *International Suzuki Journal* (Spring 1996).
Swing, Pamela Sherman. "Fiddle Teaching in Shetland Isles Schools." Diss., University of Texas at Austin, 1991.
Thomson, William. *Orpheus Caledonius.* 2 vols. London, 1725–33.
Titon, Jeff Todd. *Old Time Kentucky Fiddle Tunes.* Lexington: University Press of Kentucky, 2001.
Tolman, Beth, and Ralph Page. *The Country Dance Book.* 1937. Reprinted, Brattleboro, Vt.: Stephen Greene Press, 1976.
Townsend, Charles R. *San Antonio Rose: The Life and Music of Bob Wills.* Urbana: University of Illinois Press, 1976.
Twain, Mark. *Life on the Mississippi.* 1874. New York: Harper and Bros., 1903.
Vallely, Fintan, ed. *The Companion to Irish Traditional Music.* Cork: Cork University Press, 1999.
Voyer, Simonne. *La danse traditionnelle dans l'est du Canada.* Québec: Les Presses de L'Université Laval, 1986.
Wallace, F. C. "Revitalization Movements." *American Anthropologist* 58 (1956): 264–81.
Wallis, Mike. "The First Annual Country Fiddlers' Contest." *Devil's Box: Published Quarterly by the Tennessee Valley Old Time Fiddle Association* (March 15, 1969): 15.
Wareham, Wilfred William. "Towards an Ethnography of 'Times': Newfoundland Party Traditions, Past and Present." Diss., University of Pennsylvania, Philadelphia, 1982.
Weale, David. "No Scope for the Imagination: Another Side of Anne of Green Gables." *Island Magazine* 20 (Fall/Winter 1986): 3–8.
———. "The Time Is Come! Millenarianism in Colonial PEI." *Acadiensis: Journal of the History of the Atlantic Region* 7, no. 1 (1977): 35–48.

Webster, Gary. "Cooperatives and Credit Unions: Their Place in Island History." In Baglole, *Exploring Island History*, 175–93.

Whelan, Kevin. "Settlement and Society in Eighteenth-Century Ireland." In *The Poet's Place: Ulster Literature and Society; Essays in Honor of John Hewitt, 1907–87*, edited by Gerald Dawe and John Wilson Foster, 45–65. Belfast: Institute of Irish Studies, 1991.

Whidden, Lynn. "Métis." In Kallman and Potvin, *Encyclopedia of Music in Canada*, 851–52.

Whisnant, David E. *All That Is Native and Fine: The Politics of Culture in an American Region*. Chapel Hill: University of North Carolina Press, 1983.

Wiggins, Gene. *Fiddlin' Georgia Crazy: Fiddlin' John Carson, His Real World and the World of His Songs*. Urbana: University of Illinois Press, 1987.

Wilgus, D. K. *Anglo-American Folksong Scholarship since 1898*. New Brunswick, N.J.: Rutgers University Press, 1959.

Wilson, George. *Wilson's Modern Dances*. New York: Excelsior Publishing House, 1892.

Wolfe, Charles. *The Devil's Box: Masters of Southern Fiddling*. Nashville: Country Music Foundation Press and Vanderbilt University Press, 1997.

———. *Kentucky Country*. Lexington: University Press of Kentucky, 1982.

———. *Tennessee Strings: The Story of Country Music in Tennessee*. Knoxville: University of Tennessee Press, 1977.

Woolf, Andrew G. "The Fiddling Festival: Revivalist Old-Time Music Jam Sessions at Southern Fiddle Conventions." Diss., Tufts University, Medford, Mass., 1990.

Wynn, Afton. "Pioneer Folk Ways." In *Straight Texas*, edited by J. Frank Dobie and Mody C. Boatwright, 190–238. Publications of the Texas Folk-Lore Society no. 13. Austin: Texas Folk-Lore Society, 1937.

Yeats, Gráinne. *The Harp of Ireland: The Belfast Harpers' Festival, 1792*. Belfast, N. Ireland: Belfast Harpers' Bicentenary, 1992.

INDEX

Page numbers in **boldface** refer to illustrations.

Abram-Village (district), **2**, 26, 28, 48, 66, 79, 86, 92, 119, 140, 144–46, 184, 234, 354–55, 365, 388, 403, 409
The Acadian Reel, 116, 127n23, 413
Acadians: cultural revival, 356–57, 368, 370–71, 374n15–17, 374n19–20, 384–85, 392n20; history and immigration, 3, 5–6, 17n4, 184; language and culture, 3, 6, 19, 39–40, 44n1, 335, 338n25, 390n4; music and dance, xxvii, 18n28, 67–68, 118, 160–61; 178–82, 196n6, 217, 257, 316n29, 335, 354; post-1990s music scene, 379, 384–85, 389, 392n20, 392n27; relations with other ethnic groups, 168, 362–63. See also ensembles (professional)
accompaniment, 48, 199–211, 226, 269–70, 349; foot tapping and rhythm instruments, 24, 44n5, 48 ,72, 88, 185–86, 201–2, 211n5; local history, 199–205, 211n1; recent developments, 203, 209–11, 372, 380–81; and tonal system, 209. See also entries for individual instruments
accompanists: learning skills, 205–8, 211n8, 211n10; relations with fiddlers, 141–42, 207–9; role of, 199, 204–5
accordion, 42, 202, 391n5
agriculture (on PEI), 3, 8–10, 31–32, 56, 106, 217, 281, 319, 322–23, 345. See also frolics; community life and customs
airs (slow airs), 285, 301, 307
Airs and Melodies Peculiar to the Highlands (Fraser), 285, 300
Albert, Ivan, 409
Albert, Joe, 409
Albert, Ron, 410
Alberton, 1, **2**, 222, 258, 325, 338n10, 353–54, 407, 410
alcoholic beverages, 225; imbibing customs, 162–64, 166; Prohibition and moonshining, 9, 93, 132, 148n4, 153, 163–66, 173n32, 345. See also social role of PEI fiddlers, negative image: alcoholism
Alexander (ship), 5–6, 15
Alexandria (district), 412

All New England Fiddle Contest, 216
Allard, Joseph, 292n56
Allen, Ward, 277, 310
Almack's Assembly Room, 238, 257
American Festival of Fiddle Tunes, 369
amplification and pickups, 98, 130, 183, 330
Ancient Irish Music (Joyce), 300
Ancient Music of Ireland (Petrie), 300
Anglo-American folk-song revival. See revival movements, music
Anne of Green Gables, xi
Antigonish (Nova Scotia), 219, 279–80, 282, 287, 292n58, 309
Apex Label, 274
Appalachian and Southern US fiddling, xxviii-n3, 42, 131, 159, 172n13, 178, 182, 232n39, 233n55, 268, 273, 278; broadcast and recording industry, 195, 263–64, 268–69, 271–73, 275–76, 278, 291n28, 310; Deep South, 46n45, 101n5, 101n7, 101n12, 126n2, 127n18, 172n17, 215, 231n9, 231n11, 232n39; fiddling contests, xxvii, 195, 215–16, 229, 269; repertoire of, 278, 308–9, 351; revival of, 81n15, 126n14, 341–42, 344, 389; Texas and Southwest, xxvi, 42, 46n45, 215–16, 231n11; Upper South and West Virginia, 42, 46n45, 101n5, 101n12, 172n17, 231n10, 232n39
Appalachian clogging, 383
Argyle Shore (district), **2**, 70, 409
"Arkansas Traveler" (reel), 312, 413
Arsenault, Albert (son of Eddy), 370–71, 375n38. See also Barachois
Arsenault, Anne-Marie Gallant (wife of Toussaint) 141–42, **150**, 201, 403, 407
Arsenault, Anthony, 265
Arsenault, Armand (brother of Eddy), 403
Arsenault, Cecil, 410
Arsenault, Chuck, 371, 375n38, 421. See also Barachois
Arsenault, Eddy, 58, 79, 110, **111**, 112–13, 132, 142, 144, 160, 170, 176, 179, 181, **220**, 227, 266, 324, **355**, 363, 370, 375n38, 395, 397–99, 402, 403, 408–9, 421
Arsenault, Edward P, xxvi, 99, 114, **115**, 116, 142, 313, **355**, 391n10, 396–97, 403, 409
Arsenault, Georges (folklorist), 44n10, 408

Arsenault, Jacques (grandson of Joe "à Bibienne"), 145, 403, 407
Arsenault, Joe "à Bibienne," xxvi, 48, 66, 119, 140, 144–45, 149n22
Arsenault, Louise Gallant, 48, 63n2, 95, 113, 145–46, 193, 319, 320, 324, 371, 375n38, 379, 389, 392n27, 403, 409. *See also* Barachois
Arsenault, Marie Gallant (wife of Edward P.), 99, 116, 142, 149n18, 403
Arsenault, Medius, 265
Arsenault, Peter (son of Eddy), **28**, 313, 370, 384, 409
Arsenault, Robert, 26, 48, 79, 92, **93**, 184–85, 313, 379, 388–89, 403, 409
Arsenault, Toussaint, 141–42, 266, 350, 403
Arsenault, Zelma Gallant (sister of Louise), **320**
"Ashokan Farewell" (air), 314, 416
L' Association des Jeunes Francophones de la Région Évangéline, 374n17
"Athole Brose" (strathspey), 298, 306
The Athole Collection (Stewart-Robertson), 285, 301, 373n2
Atlanta (Georgia), 215, 263, 291n28
Atlantic Jamboree. *See* fiddle festivals
attitudes about fiddling, 65–80, 85, 175, 289; accuracy of tune versions, 76–78, 80, 99–100, 109, 124, 312; demeanor, 79–80; inborn style, 137, 176–77, 181, 224, 226, 270–71, 288–89, 345; independence of spirit, 113–14, 125, 177–78, 182, 270–71 ,277, 288–89; liveliness, 72–75, 80, 94, 147, 176, 183–85, 189, 196n4, 230, 276, 287, 312, 384; need to keep learning, 78, 139–40, 146–47; obligation to play, 70–72 , 80n1, 137–38, 153–57, 162; playing "by note," 124–25, 288; source of talent, 65–70, 80, 84, 92, 100, 113, 117, 154, 157–58, 172n4, 364, 368–69; tone quality, 74–76. *See also* social role of PEI fiddlers; new generation fiddlers; twists
aural transmission: imperfections in, 109–10; and mass media, 121, 289, 310–11; and novice fiddling, 86–88, 97, 99–100; and printed music, 118, 120–22, 124–25, 285–88, 309; processing music, 103–10, 114–15, 125, 126n2, 126n8–11; and tune diffusion, 117–22, 309; and tune titles, 122–23. *See also* twists

Baglole, Sidney, 74–75, **75**, 78, 132, 137, 180, 266, 395–99, 403
bagpipes, 15–16, 18n31, 18n36, 37, 41, 54, 59, 64n16, 116–17, 121–22, 127n34–36, 128n37, 159–60, 228, 249, 300, 341, 369; influence on fiddling, 122, 190–92, 194, 197n20, 197n24, 249, 300, 305–6, 308
Baird, Ranita, 391n6
Baker, Sterling, 85, 123, 179, 355, 403
Baker, Tudor, 325
ballet dancing, 358
Bangor (district), **2**, 74, 88, 113, 139, 208, 222, 265, 289, 327–28, 368, 381, 405, 410
banjo, xi, xii, xx , 204, 210, 265–66, 276, 391n5, 409-11
Banks, Jimmy, xxiv, 25, 29, 34, 94, 97–9, 222, 239–40, 256, 260n19, 330, 403
Banks, Joseph, 403
Banks, Reg, 74, 78, 108, 144, 319, 327, 331, 403, 409
Barachois, 44n1, 63n2, 210, 371, 379; CDs by, 371, 375n39, 421
bass, 240, 272, 274, 276, 325, 331, 410–12
Bay Fortune (district), **2**, 5
Bayard, Samuel, xx, xxviii-n3, 64n19, 126n5, 126n8–9,
Bayfield (district), **2**, 15, 116, 122, 136, 224, 260, 289, 406, 408, 411
Bear River (district), **2**, 32, 45n13, 50, 63n5, 66–67, 74, 78, 90, 94, 96, 98, 104–5, 114, 121, 123, 134–35, 161, 176, 179, 183, 192, 199, 202, 206, 221–22, 225, 255, 288–289, 336, 339, 348–9, 363–64, 378, 403–4, 409
Bearisto, Jimmy, 53, 140
Beaton, Anita, 392n14
The Beaver Club, 327–28
bees. *See* frolics
Belfast (district), **2**, 6, 15, 18n36, 49, 144, 173n39, 181, 225, 249, 405
Belfast (Ireland), 229
Belfast Harpers' Festival, 228–29, 232n51, 341
Belfast Riots, 173n39
Belgium, 379
Belle River (district), 327, 410
benefit concerts, xix, 32, 44, 121, 203, 210, 335, 341, 353–54, 364, 372, 391n6
benefit dances, xxi, 16, 35–39, 71, 97, 104, 117, 154–55, 161, 184, 199, 331, 344; church and school picnics, 16, 19, 36–37; indoor socials, 19, 36, 38; schoolhouse and community-hall dances, 16, 19, 36, 38–39, 46n31, 323, 332, 340. *See also* frolics; tea parties
Benoit, Emil, 101n5, 127n20–21
Bergeron, Hélène Arsenault, 25, 59, 72, 79, 179, 256, 355, 371–72, 375n38, 403, 409. *See also* Barachois

Bernard, Alvin, 20, 53, 67–68, 71–72, 96, 112–13, 138, 141, **198**, 350, 354, 403, 407
Bernard, Jackie, 403
Bernard, Wilfred, 403
big band music, 325
"Big John MacNeil" (reel), 296, 299, 311
Biggar, Jackie, 111–12, 220, 226, 228, 320, 336, 409
birls. See techniques of fiddling: cuts
Bisbee, Jasper "Jep," 216
Blackett, Pius, 326
Blanchard, Richard, 410
Bloomfield (district), **2**, 56, 65, 106, 136, 151, 202, 340, 404
"Blue Mountain Hornpipe," 296, 310
bluegrass music and fiddling, 172, 229, 313, 380, 384
"Boiling Cabbage Down" (set tune), 278, 416
Bolger, Cornelius "Lini," 86, 265–66, 408
Bolger, Pat, 54
"Bonaparte Crossing the Alps" (hornpipe), 265, 303, 312, 413
"Bonnie Lass of Fisherrow" (reel), 296, 310, 416
Bonnie Prince Charlie (Charles Stewart), 17n7
Bonshaw (district), **2**, 326
Bonshaw Inn, 326
Borden (district), 1, **2**, 325
Boston, Massachusetts, xxviii-n1, 137, 214, 231n15, 232n29, 232n31, 271, 273–74, 278, 282, 290, 300–1; and Maritimes emigrants, 8, 119, 211n8, 219, 230n1, 257, 260n19, 273, 282; newspapers of, 231n15, 232n31; radio broadcasts from, 219, 273, 278
La Boueille, 374n17
Bowing Down Home website, xxviii-n4, 195n2, 314n1, 392n27
"Bowing the Strings" (reel), 296, 310, 313
bowing. See also techniques of fiddling
Bowness, Glenna, 152–53, 403
Bowness, Ivan, 350
bows. See fiddles and bows
Boyd, Colin, 310
Brackley (district), **2**, 266, 338n24, 361, 404, 408
"Braes of Auchtertyre" (reel), 310, 413
branle (dance), 259n5, 259n11
breakdowns (eight-hand reels), 25, 44n6, 44n8, 235, 238, 248, 250–54, 258, 261n39
Bremner, Robert, 300, 302
"Brenda Stubbert" (reel), 298, 309
Briand, Elmer, 280
Brigadoon (play), 315n23
British Army, 121
Brockman, Polk, 291n28

Brockton (Massachusetts), 280
Brooklyn (district), 412
Bruce, Stanley, **33**, 94, 253, 406
Brudenell (district), 409
Buell, Harry, 409
Bunting, Edward, 232n51
Burke, Tracy Warren, 412
Burns, Robert, 280, 293n66

"Caber Feidh" (reel), 298, 311
Cable Head (district), **2**, 56
Cabot Trail, 283, 293n78
Cajuns, 5. See also Acadians
Caledonia (district), 122, 391n7, 412
Cambridge (Massachusetts), 280
Campbell, Dan J., 279, 423
Campbell, John, 280, 309, 423
Campbell, Steven, 121
Campbell, Tena, 280
Canada, Federal Government of, 7, 17n16–17, 44, 165, 173n32, 290n9, 321–22, 369–70, 374n19
Canada Games, 362
Canada Year Book (1927), 291n21
Canadian American Club, 230n1
Canadian Army, 93, 121–22, 136
Canadian Broadcasting Company (CBC), 266, 274–75, 280, 292n47
Canadian Centennial, 274
Canadian Maritime Provinces. See Maritimes, Canadian
Canadian Museum of History, xxiii, xxv, xxviii-n4
Canadian Open Old Time Fiddle Championship, 229, 277
Cape Breton County, 293n81
Cape Breton dancing, 252, 260n19, 261n40, 262n50
The Cape Breton Fiddler (MacGillivray), 293n71
Cape Breton Fiddlers' Association, 347
Cape Breton fiddling, 58, 176, 196n7, 277, 290, 293n71; history of, 131, 159, 172n16, 269, 281–84, 293n84; influence on PEI fiddling, 148n17, 179–80, 182–83, 192, 210, 252, 278, 286–90, 306, 308–11, 313, 315n22, 348–52, 370–72, 373n8, 384; parallels with PEI fiddling, 101n5, 101n21, 102n25, 126n2, 148n15, 281, 286–87; recording and broadcast industry, 268, 275, 278, 279–85, 289–90, 291n28; repertoire of, 196n5, 284–87, 289, 293n82–83, 299; revival of, 347, 365–66, 373n8–9, 376n40, 386; Scottish heritage, 173n37, 179, 283–84; and superstyles, 195, 271, 286. See also *names of individual fiddlers*

INDEX 443

Cape Breton Highlands National Park, 283
Cape Breton Island, xxviii-n2, **4**, 42, 159, 173n37, 260n19, 261n40, 279, 281–82, 292n58, 293n81, 346–47, 365, 375n33
Cape North (Nova Scotia), 286
"Captain Campbell" (strathspey), **402**
Cardigan (district), **2**, 54, 73, 98, 108, 126n3, 130, 140, 163, 221, 266, 286, 327, 332, 338n16, 405, 407, 411–12
Cardross (district), **2**, 8, 35, 51, 84, 176, 245, 288, 319, 391n6, 407, 411
"Carlton County Breakdown" (reel), 296, 310
Carroll, Liz, 310
Carry On Canada campaign, 39
Carson, "Fiddlin' John," 215, 263, 291n28, 423
"Carter MacKenzie's Reel," 314, 416
Carter, Jim, 59
Cartier, Jacques, 4
Cascumpec (district), 17n12
Cavendish, **2**
The Ceilidh Fiddlers, 353, 374n13
ceilidhs, 30, 31, 280, 425; in Celtic tradition, 41–42, 46n37; commercial ceilidhs, xix, xxii, 353, 362, 366–8, 370, 372, 380–82, 386; Monticello Ceilidh, **247**, 366–67, 369; Orwell Ceilidh, 355, 366
cello, 200
Celtic Ceilidh (radio show), 280, 283
Celtic Label, 279, 282
Celtic Ladies, 421
Celtic music scene, xx, 196n7, 313, 375n36
Centerville (Nova Scotia), 280
Central Christian Church, 381
CFBO (radio station), 274
CFCY (radio station), 221, 278, 350; Don Messer era, 271–75, 286, 309; founding and early days, 218, 263–67, 291n14, 291n26. *See also* Messer, Don; radio broadcasts
Chafe, Winnie, 280, 423
Chaisson family (of Bear River), 66, 179–80, 289, 336, 349, 375n25, 375n32, 375n37, 390n2, 421
Chaisson Family Show, 371
Chaisson, Brent (son of Kevin), 368, 371 375n32
Chaisson, Darla (daughter of "Kenny Joe Pete"), 371, 375n37
Chaisson, Donna (daughter of Joe Pete), 255, 364, 375n25, 403
Chaisson, Emmett (brother of Joe Pete), 288
Chaisson, J. J. (Jeremy Joseph), 67, 73, 81n3, 313, 364, 369, 371, 375n32, 378, 381, 389, 404, 409; CDs by, 369, 421

Chaisson, Joe Pete, xxvi, 50, 67, 77, 81n3, 96, 101n14, 121, 206, 222, 318, 350, 364, 375n25; advocate of Cape Breton fiddling, 179–80, 288–89; role in fiddling revival, 348–49, 361–62
Chaisson, Johnny Joe, 67, 81n3, 92, 97, 122, **130**, 132, 147, 176, 288, 326, 364, 375n25, 404
Chaisson, Kenny ("Kenny Joe Pete"), xxvi, 50, 52, 73, 77, 81n3, 114, 122, 132, 142, 161, 183, 208, 289, 313, 317, 333, 349, 364, 375n25, 375n37, 404
Chaisson, Kenny ("Kenny Johnny Joe"), 364, 375n25, 404
Chaisson, Kevin, 50, 81n3, 90, 101n14, 114, 123–24, 176, 178, **200**, 289, 313–14, 339, 375n25, 375n32, 375n37, 390n2, 404, 406, 409; accompaniment styles of, 199, 206–10, 372; role in fiddling revival, 349, 361, 363–64, 371, 378, 390
Chaisson, Koady (brother of J. J.), 368, 375n32
Chaisson, Kurt (son of Kevin), 368, 371, 375n32
Chaisson, Lemmy, 30, 47, 141–42, 161, 364, 404
Chaisson, Mary (daughter of Johnny Joe), 404
Chaisson, Melanie (daughter of "Young Peter"), 368, 390n2, 404, 421
Chaisson, Peter ("Old Peter" or "Peter Senior"), 30, 45n13, 94, 101n14, 104, 121, 134–35, 142, 192, 221–23, 288, 394, 397, 399, 404, 409
Chaisson, Peter ("Young Peter"), 32, 45n13, 81n3, 96, 123, 142, 176, **177**, 178–79, 225, **242**, 289, 368, 375n25, 375n37, 395, 401, 404, 421; role in fiddling revival, 349–50, 361, 363, 371, 380
Chaisson, Phonsey (brother of "Johnny Joe"), **130**, 404
Chaisson, Roddy (brother of Joe Pete), 288
Chaisson, Stephen (son of "Young Peter"), 368, 404
Chaisson, Timothy (son of Kevin), 313, 378, 390n2, 409
Chaisson, Urban, 412
Chaisson, William (father of Lemmy), 142
Chamberlain, Charlie, **272**, 274
Chapman, Cec, 411
Chapman, Kenny, 411
Chappell, Ella, 36, 409
Chappelle, Garfield, 266
Chappelle, George, 265–66, 271, 274, 291n14, 311, 326
Charleston (dance), 258
Charlottetown, 1, **2**, 3, 13, 54, 76, 79, 80n1, 86, 92, 106, 119–21, 129, 133, 138, 140–41, 153,

166, 178, 192, 197n19, 200, 204, 211n1, 214, 217–18, 220–22, 226–27, 231n18, 238, 249, 257, 263, 265, 266, 274, 276, 281, 290n9, 291n12, 291n21, 307, 309, 317, 319, 325–26, 334, 346, 349–50, 355, 362–63, 369, 371, 378–82, 391n9, 404–6, 408, 409–12
Chartrand, Pierre, 392n26
CHCK (radio station), 265
Cherny, Al, 277–78, 422
"Cheticamp Reel" (set tune), 298, 304
Cheticamp (Nova Scotia), 280
Cheverie, Fr. Charles, 67, 80n1, 86, 120–21, 123, 138, 142, 153, 162–63, 178–80, 204, 227, 307, 367, 379, 404, 408–9; role in fiddling revival, **347**, 350, 362, 381
Cheverie, Jim, 254, 256
Cheverie, Joseph, 231n27
Cheverie, Neil, 192, 218–19, 231n25, 290
Cheverie, Omar, 58, 87, 92, 231n25, 409
Cheverie, Randy, 409
The Chew at Campbellton Corner, 170
CHGS (radio station), 265, 278
Chicago (Illinois), 216, 264, 301, 310
The Chieftains, 371
Chipman, Gary, 79, 140, 276, 326, 334, 404
Chisholm, Angus, 58, 279–80, 286–87, 310, 423
CHNC (radio station), 278, 309
Christian Church, 153–55, 168; Catholic Church, 3, 5, 36, 40, 66, 71, 80n1, 157–60, 168, 170, 173n27, 173n38; critic of fiddling and dance, 153, 157–62, 171n3, 172n4, 172n9, 172n11–13, 172n17, 262n54, 293n72, 390; promoter of fiddling and dance, 161–62, 173n27, 362; Protestant denominations, 3, 17n2, 36–37, 71, 157–60, 168, 171n3, 231n18
"Christy Campbell" (tune), 34, 312
"Christy Miller" (tune), 34
church modes. See modes and modality
church picnics. See benefit dances; tea parties
Circle Club Dance at St. Peters. See old-time dances, contemporary
CJCB (radio station), 280, 288, 309
CJFX (radio station), 280–81, 288, 309
CJRW (radio station), 266–67, 291n19
clarinet, 240, 274, 276
Clark's General Store, 264, 268, 290n6
Clements, Vassar, 172n8
Clifford Peters' Barn Dance, 130, 326
clogging, 254, 261n49
Club 50, 354, 374n17
The Clyde Nunn Show, 281
Coast Guard (Canadian), 9, 12, 165

Cochran, "Tex," 266
"Cock of the North" (jig), 98, 102n27, 297
Coleman Corners (district), **2**, 53, 142
Coleman, Michael, 271, 423
Collection of Original Scots Tunes (Playford), 315n8
Collection of Scots Reels and Strathspeys (Lowe), 300
Collection of Scots Reels or Country Dances (Bremner), 300, 302
"College Hornpipe," 297, 303, 311
"Colonel Robertson" (jig), 304, 413
colonial era (North America), xvii, 7, 42–43, 64n19, 118, 231n10, 237–38, 253, 257
"Come Under My Plaidie" (jig), 304, 413
Comhaltas Ceoltoiri Eireann, 229, 233n52, 341
Commercial Cross (district), 409
community life and customs, 11–13, 19–20, 22–3, 35–36, 76–77, 154–57, 163–68, 321–24, 331–33; decline of community life, 321–24, 340; local words and expressions, 20, 44n1, 63n5, 63n7, 63n12, 63n14, 64n15, 127n29, 167, 173n35. See also attitudes about fiddling; social role of PEI fiddlers; decline of PEI fiddling; fiddlers's words and expressions
Community School Program, 360, 379–80
compensation for fiddling, 71, 129, 131–33, 154–55, 171n2, 222–23; payment in kind, 56, 132–33, 162–63. See also alcoholic beverages
competitiveness, dealing with, 137–40, 224, 226, 282–83; See also contests and competitions on PEI
Compo Records, 274, 279
composing, 264, 300, 304, 308–10, 312; Cape Breton composers, 232n29, 285, 287–88; Irish composers, 15, 127n21–22; on PEI, 114–15, 288, 308–9, 313, 315n19, 316n29, 351, 375n35, 383, 391n10; process of, 114–17; Scottish composers, 14, 76–77, 264, 300, 308; and the supernatural, 116–17
A Composition of Fiddle Tunes (Hughes), 114
Comprehensive Development Plan, 321–22, 354
Condon, Nathan, 378, 421
Confederation Bridge, 368, 377
Connors, "Stompin' Tom," 374n24
contests and competitions on PEI, 139–40, 146, 213–30, 230n3, 335, 374n15; Great Contest of 1926, 63n9, 148n1, 192, 213–15, 216–19, 229–30, 230n5, 263, 270, 290, 291n10, 311, 317; Island contest scene,

contests and competitions on PEI (*cont.*)
220–23; motivations of organizers, 214, 220; movement to ban, 227–30, 345, 348, 366, 374n15; negative impact of, 223–30, 269, 345
contests and competitions: other music cultures, 228–30, 231n10; Irish music and dance, 229, 232n51, 233n52, 341; North American fiddling, xxvii, 215–16, 229, 231n11, 271, 273, 344; and music revivals, 215–16, 231n9, 386; and playing styles, 229–30; Scottish music and dance, 228–29, 305; state and provincial fiddling associations, 220, 341, 364. *See also* revival movements, music
contra dances. *See* country dancing
contredanse anglaise. *See* country dancing
contredanse française. *See* cotillions
Conway, Joe, 255, 404
Cook, Roland, 410
Cooper, Ches, 266
Cooper, Ronnie, 310
cooperatives (farming and fishing), 10, 345
Corbett, Trudy, 412
Cormier, Joe, 280, 423
Cornwall (district), **2**, 36,
Corraville (district), **2**, 27, 51–52, 67, 87, 131, 142, 201, 223
cotillions, 236–37, 259n4–6, 259n10, 302. *See also* country dancing; square sets
Cottar's Saturday Night (radio show), 280, 293n66
"Cotton-Eyed Joe" (reel), 311, 413
Coughlin, Underhill, 170
country and western music, 203, 265, 341, 382
country dancing, 42, 46n40, 235–37, 259n2–4, 259n9, 302. *See also* cotillions; square sets
couples' dancing, 258. *See also* names of individual dances
courting, 51–52
Cousins, John, 56, 65, 106, 136, 151–2, 170, 202, 340–41, 404, 407
Cousins, Mary, 412
Covehead (district), 374n23
Crane, Aaron, 378, 390n2,
Crane, Cynthia Jay, **387**, 405–6
Crane, Robert, 68–9, 163, 336, 369, 401, 409
Crane, Ward, 105, 163, 182
Creignish (Nova Scotia), 279
"Crooked Stovepipe" (set tune), 297, 304
La Cuisine à Mémé (theatre production), 368, 371, 375n31
Cumming, Angus, 300
"Cutting the Bow" (recording), 364

Dallas (Texas), 215
Dalton, Art, 170
dance callers. *See* prompters
dance halls: regional, 168, 230, 246, 269, 304, 324–31, 335, 350; impact of, 329–30; venue names, 325–28. *See also* violence at dances; square sets: decline of
The Dance Music of Scotland (Surenne), 300
Dancing as an Art and Pastime (Scott), 260n26
"Darlin' Nelly Grey" (set tune), 298, 303
Darnley (district), **2**, 20, 138, 319, 407
Dau-Schmidt, Kathryn, 334, 338n24, 361, 380, 404, 409
Davenport, Clyde, 46n46
Davidson, Estwood, 280
"The Dawn Waltz," 296, 310, 413
Day, Ivan, 53, 55–56, 246, 328, 351, 410
Deagle, Elmer, 378, 390n2, 390n5
Dearborn (Michigan), 216
Deblois Road (district), **2**, 10, 26, 31, 52, 96, 201, 254, 370, 404, 410
decline of PEI fiddling, xxii, 317–37, 390; alienation of youngsters, 331–37, 339, 379, 382; changes in community life, 317–18, 321–24, 331–33, 336–37; chronology, 317–18, 336–37, 339; and fiddlers' negative image, 171, 337, 339; and mass media, 323–24, 333–34; psychological effects, 337, 339; and technological change, 317–24. *See also* dance halls
Def Leppard, 365, 375n27
"Deil Among the Tailors" (reel), 159, 311
"Deil Stick the Minister" (reel), 159
Dejarlis, Andy, 277–78, 422
Del Ryke, Dolores, 46n47
DesRoches, Anastasia, 316n29, 369, 374n21, 378, 421
Detroit (Michigan), 216, 282
"Devil and His Sister" (jig), 158
"The Devil and the Dirk" (reel), 159
"Devil in the Kitchen" (strathspey), 159, 413
"Devil in the Woodpile" (reel), 172n13
"The Devil Went Down to Georgia" (Charlie Daniels Band), 158, 172n8
The Devil's Box (Wolfe), 233n55
"Devil's Dream" (reel), 159, 297
"Devil's Hop" (tune), 159
devil's instrument. *See also* social role of PEI fiddlers, negative image
Dick's Quadrille Call Book, 260n26
Dicks, Capt. Edward, 165
"The Dismissal" (reel), 296, 309
Dixieland music, 275

446 **INDEX**

Dobson, Jim, 411
Dockendorff, Harold, 58, 71, 221, 409
Doiron, Peter, 29, 170, 227, 266, 329, 350, 381, 404, 408
"Don MacLean's Farewell to Oban" (march), 305, 413
Don Messer and His Islanders. *See* Messer, Don
Don Messer's Jubilee (TV show), 275
Don Messer's Lumberjacks, 274
Donagh (district), **2**, 104, 379, 391n6
Donegal (county of Ireland), 42, 148n12, 158
double-dancing, 253
double stops. *See also* techniques of fiddling
Doucette family (of Deblois Road), 370
Doucette, Cathy, 410
Doucette, Joseph, 10, 26, 31, 96–97, 201, 370, 404
Doucette, Pat, 75–76, 410
Doucette, Victor, 370, 384, **385**, 401, 410
Doucette, Vincent, 52, 57, 61–62, 141, 254, 404, 407, 410–11
Dow, Daniel, 300
Dowling, Al, 265–66
"Down Yonder" (set tune), 313, 413
Doyle, Arch, 170
Doyle, Babe, 274
Doyle, Jackie, 266, **272**, 274
Dromore (district), **2**, 23, 54, 87, 114, 133, 181, 209, 222, 257, 286, 405, 410
Drummond Castle Manuscript, 302
Drummond, Rev. Wm., 18n28
drums, 266, 272, 274, 276, 331, 412
"The Drunken Piper" (march), 305, 311, 413
Dublin (Ireland), 238, 374n22
"Duke of Gordon's Birthday" (strathspey), 297, 306
Dunakin (Nova Scotia), 285
Dundas (district), **2**, 353
Dunham, Allanson "Mellie," 216
Durang, John, 253, 261n48
"Durang's Hornpipe," 261n48, 413
Durant, Bill, 56

Earnscliffe (district), 22
Earthwatch, **xxi**, xxiii, xxv, xxviii-n6, 85, 336
East Coast Music Awards (ECMAs), 370–71, 375n36
East Margaree (Nova Scotia), 280
East Point, **2**, 9, 63n5, 130, 152, 221, 322
East Royalty (district), 412
Eastern Bakeries, 280
Eastern Kings Fiddlers. *See* PEI Fiddlers' Society

Eaton's of Toronto Catalog, 133, 148n7
Edinburgh Highland Reel and Strathspey Society, 342
education on PEI: consolidation of, 44, 321–23, 332–33, 356, 374n15m 374n19–20; one room schoolhouses, 12, 18n24, 36, 61, 332, 344
Egmont Bay (district), **2**, 335
eight-hand reels. *See* breakdowns
Eldon (district), **2**, 22, 125, 144, 152, 185, 251, 318, 329, 405–6, 408
elite of PEI, 216, 231n18, 270
Ellerslie (district), 218, 379, 391n6
Elmira (district), **2**, 39, 192, 218, 245, 404
EMI/Capitol Records, 375n36
Emyvale (district), **2**, 7, 24, 35, 76, 87, 142, 155, 177, 181, 253, 406
England, 236–37, 257, 261n49, 341, 344; dancing traditions of, 253–54. *See also* Great Britain
The English Dancing Master (Playford), 236, 315n8
ensembles (amateur), 378, 380, 383. *See also* revival of fiddling on PEI
ensembles (professional), dance bands, 323, 325–26, 331; orchestrated, 183, 210–11, 211n14, 269–70, 275–77; with simple backup, 133, 210; touring bands, 371–72, 375n39, 379, 391n5. *See also* names of individual bands
L' Étoile de Mer (venue), 368
Europe, xvii, 25, 108, 117, 158, 238, 257, 277, 283, 297–98, 304, 308, 315n17, 318, 346, 371
Evangeline Coast, **2**, 17n12, 48, 181, 335–36, 354, 357, 368, 373, 374n15, 374n17, 374n19–20, 375n39, 378–80, 391n10
Évangéline, Centre d'Education, 356, 374n19–20
Evangeline: A Tale of Acadie (Longfellow), 374n20
L' Exposition agricole, 374n15

"Faded Love" (tune), 313, 413
Fairfield (district) , **2**, 9, 39, 100, 136, 245, 322
"Farmer's Reel," 296, 299, 312, 314, 316n28
Farrell, Leo, 325, 338n10, 354, 410
"Father O'Flynn" (jig), 311, 413
Feis Ceoil Association, 229, 233n52, 341
female role, 63n4, 85, 101n2, 129, 142–46, 149n19, 203–205; changes in modern era, 146, 350, 379. *See also* new-generation fiddlers: development of
Ferrell, Frank, 310
"Ferry Bridge Hornpipe," **401**

INDEX 447

Festival of Small Halls, 392n26
fiddle festivals, xxii, 290, 310, 351, 353–54, 362, 364, 386; Atlantic Jamboree, **28**, **145**, **234**, 354, **365**, 374n15–16, 391n5; Festival Acadien, 354, **355**, 374n15–16; Rollo Bay Scottish Fiddle Festival, xviii-xix, **xx, 200, 347**, 349, 354, 361, 363–64, 389
fiddle instruction. See instruction in fiddling
The Fiddle Music of Prince Edward Island (Perlman), xi, xxviii-n4, 64n23, 102n29, 126n12, 127n23–24, 127n30, 127n33, 128n39, 196n14, 197n26, 232n40, 314n1, 391n7; companion CD, 422
"The Fiddle on the Island" (Hornby), xxiii, 18n35
fiddle tunes (musical genre), 103, 265; history and structure of, 107, 299–302, 315n7–12; See also tune collections ; and entries for individual tune genres
Fiddle-Do, 391n8
fiddlers' conventions, 232n39
Fiddlers' Sons, 369
fiddlers' words and expressions, 63n7, 65, 73–74, 81n15, 85, 107, 119, 126n4–5, 190–91, 196n16, 197n18, 206–8, 224, 257, 302–3
fiddlers, relations among, 27, 129, 137–41; fiddlers' gatherings, 125, 138–40, 148n15, 285–86, 335, 349. See also competitiveness; contests and competitions on PEI
fiddles and bows, 129, 133–37, 140, 219; accessories, 89, 91–92, 101n11, 136–37, 196n11, 196n16; manufacture of, 133–37, 148n14; obtaining, 88, 133, 136–37; superstitions regarding, 135, 148n9–11
fiddling families, 48–50, 370. See also entries for individual family names
fiddling in the home and community, 47–54; and holiday festivities, 39–41, 344
fiddling revival. See revival of fiddling on PEI
fiddling styles on PEI, 175–85, 390; and other Canadian styles, 175–76, 179–80, 289; and cultural experiences, 184, 196n10; general Island sound, 182–85, 191, 194, 277, 385; individual styles, 175–78, 182, 194–95, 288–89; and playing techniques, 175, 178, 181–82
fiddling styles on PEI: regional styles, 176–82, 185, 194–95, 196n3, 288–89, 369–70; central Island (Queens County), 180–82; Evangeline Coast, 181, 369–70, 373; northeast Kings County, 178–82, 185, 195, 288–89, 378, 383–84; southern Kings County, 181–82; western Prince County, 178–82, 185, 187, 195. See also Messer, Don; new generation fiddlers
50/50 Raffle, 366
"Fisher's Hornpipe," 296, 303, 311
fishing and fishermen, 4, 10, **11**, 61–62, 87, 95, 101n9, 118, 131, 156, 164, 218, 281, 345, 403–7
Fitzgerald, Winston "Scotty," 279–80, 284, 286, 310, 423; and PEI fiddle contests, 221–22, 224, 226, 286
Fitzpatrick, Sheila MacKenzie. See Sheila MacKenzie
"Five Minutes More" (set tune), 304, 416
Flat River (district), **2**, 32, 35, 72, 122, 147, 148n14, 161, 181, 267, 408, 410–12
Flatley, Michael, 374n22
"The Flowers of Edinburgh" (reel), 87, 101n6, 296, 299, 311
flute, 85, 117, 240, 391n5
"folk boom," 342
folk festivals, 342
Ford, Henry, xxvii, 215–16, 341
Fort Augustus (district), **2**, 3, 39
Forty Fiddles Flat Out (CD), 381
The Forum (venue), 221–22, 226
"Four Leaf Clover" (set tune), 304, 416
"The Four Marys" (waltz), 297, 307
fox farming, 217, 263, 338n10
Foxley River (district), **2**, 411
fox-trots (dance), 214, 235, 257–58, 304, 318, 382
France, 3–5, 58, 196n6, 211n2, 236–37, 259n6, 379
Franco Fête, 371, 375n36, 379
Fraser, Captain Simon, 300
Fraser, Iain, 197n23
Freetown (district), **2**, 75, 40
frolics (work parties), xxi, 16, 19, 31–2, 41–3, 45n14, 46n45, 71, 104, 117, 131–2, 154, 214, 273, 322–23, 340, 353. See also benefit dances

Gaelic College, 283
Gaelic language, 7, 17n11, 17n13, 18n33, 45n21, 59, 64n15, 122, 276, 292n53, 293n81, 355
Gaelic League, 229
Gaeltalk Communications, 292n53
Gallant, Alfred, 412
Gallant, Connie, 50, 404
Gallant, Ernest (Gaudet's Old Timers), 265
Gallant, Ernie (of Egmont Bay), 335, 410

Gallant, Hélaire, 265–66
Gallant, Marie, **320**
Gallant, Marlene MacKinnon, **255**, 404
Gallant, Melissa, 421
Gallant, Paul D., 375n31
Gallant, Robert, 410
Gallant, Wilfred "Moonie," 265
Ganam, King, 277, 422
Garfield (district), **2**, 11, 22, 66, 90, 119, 144, 161, 177, 188, 205–6, 278, 411
"Garryowen" (jig), 304
Gaspé Peninsula, 278
Gaudet, David, 96, 370, 384, 410
Gaudet, Emil, 370
Gaudet, Ernest "Lippy," 265
Gaudet, Joseph "Joe Bun," 265
Gaudet's Old Timers, 265
Gauthier, John, 69, 268, 278, 328–29, 338n20, 404, 410; performing and broadcasting, 266, 325; and Prince County Fiddlers, 350–51, 360–61, 381
Geddings, Mel, 411
General Collection of the Ancient Irish Music (Bunting), 232n51
George Chappelle and the Merry Islanders, 265–66, 270, 274
"George Mel's Dream" (air), 127n24
"George V's Army" (march), 305, 414
George Wade and the Cornhuskers, 292n50
Georgetown (district), **2**, 30, 38, 54, 66, 85, 114, 119, 133, 207, 211n9, 222, 256, 323, 405
Getson, Howie, 266
Gillis, Angus Allan, 279–80, 287, 423
Gillis, Norman, 410
Glace Bay (Nova Scotia), 280–82
Glenaladale pioneers, 5, 15, 249
"Glencoe March," 297, 306, 309
Glendale Fiddle Festival, 347
"Glengarry's Dirk" (strathspey), 310, 414
Glenora Falls (Nova Scotia), 279
Goose Bay Airforce Base, 58
Goose River (district), **2**, 62, 242, 248, 380, 392n21, 408, 412
Goose River Dance. *See* old-time dances, contemporary
Gorman, Larry, 11
Gotell, Hugh, 114, 123, 404
Gotell, John Charles, 75
Gotell, Kevin, 207–8, 405
Gotell, Wilfred, 30, 38, 54, 66, 74, 75, 85, 94, 133, 222–23, 256, 323, 329, 394–95, 397, 405
The Gow Collection, 285, 300, 315n10

The Gow Repository, 127n18, 285, 300, 315n10
Gow, Niel, 300
Grand Falls (Newfoundland), 44n2, 406
Grand Ole Opry, 264
Grand River (district), **2**, 52, 90, 98, 105, 406, 410
Grand River (dance). *See also* square sets: in big-circle format
Great Britain, 164, 173n38, 237, 264, 371, 375n27; colonial period, 4–7, 17n2, 17n4, 17n7, 17n11, 17n17, 18n28, 18n33, 173; dancing in, 235–38, 249, 257, 260n13, 260n21, 262n52, 315n17; fiddling and music traditions of, xxviii, 16, 138, 158–59, 101n21, 121, 127n36, 178; and tune genres, 300, 303, 307, 315n15. *See also* England; Scotland
Great Depression, 9, 89, 217, 229, 265
Great Western Road, 325, 338n10
"The Green Fields of America" (reel), 119, 127n32, 414
Green Road (district), **2**, 40, 69, 91, 113, 181, 326, 407
Griffin, Joe, 185
Groom, Percy, 265
groups of tunes (medleys), 139, 148n17, 211n12, 252, 285, 288
"Growling Old Man" (reel), 296, 299
Guardian (Charlottetown), 129, 148n1, 214, 216–19, 230n3, 311, 316n26, 317, 368
Guest, Bill, 277
guitar, 85, 190, 211n6, 334, 350, 372, 380–82, 403–407, 409–412; as accompaniment instrument, xvii, 24, 29–30, 35, 38, 48–49, 51–52, 57–58, 61, 98, 133, 138, 141–44, 146, 149n19, 201–206, 210, 269, 336; in professional ensembles, 133, 266, 274, 276, 280, 325–26, 331, 391n5
Gulf of St. Lawrence, **2**, 3, **4**, 179, 281, 390n4

Haley, Bill, 334
Halifax (Nova Scotia), 58, 211n8, 266, 275, 279, 281, 377
Halliburton (district), 410
Halliday, Jimmy, 22–24, 125, 152, 185, 251, 318, 321, 324, 405
Hancock, Harold, 327, 410–11
Harding, Darlene, 411
Hardy, Ralph, 258, 410
Hardy, Shelton, 410
harmonica, 72, 50, 91, 204, 265
Harp and Claymore (Skinner), 301
Harper Road (district), 385, 410
harpsichord, 200

Harrington (district), 326
Hart, Joseph, 260n16
Harvey Station (New Brunswick), 273
Harvey, William "Will," 69, 81n6, 218, 220–21, 231n25
"Haste to the Wedding" (jig), 296, 299
The Heather Hills Collection (MacDonald), 293n83
"Heather on the Hill" (reel), 296, 299, 309, 315n23
Heatherdale (district), **2**, 253
Hebrides, 15, 34
"Heel and Toe Polka" (set tune), 304, 414
"Hell Among the Yearlings" (reel), 172n13
"Hell Broke Loose in Georgia" (reel), 172n13
Hickey's Twist Tobacco, 17n14
Hicks, Ivan, 228, 277, 384, 422
Higgenbotham, Tracy MacLean, 411
"High Level Hornpipe," 224, 232n40, 296, 303
Highland bagpipes. *See* bagpipes
Highland dancing, 18n36, 121, 252, 261n46, 262n50, 283, 358
Highland games, 18n36, 121, 228, 283, 341
"Highland Jig" (tune), 298, 304
Highlanders, Scottish. *See* Scotland: history and immigration from
Highlands (Nova Scotia), 122, 283
hillbilly music era, 215–16, 273
Hillgrove's Call Book, 240, 260n17
Hogan, Courtney, 378, 421
Holland, Jerry, 280, 286, 309–10, 423
Holman's Department Store, 265
"Home Sweet Home" (set tune), 307, 414
"The Home Waltz," 307, 414
"Homeward Bound" (reel), 296, 299
Hornby, James "Jim," xxiii, 225, 230n3, 231n27, 405
hornpipe dancing, 253
hornpipes (tune genre), 14, 25, 78, 103, 214, 253–54, 261n48, 295, 301–303, 306, 401; history and structure of, 301–3, 315n15–16; titles of, 224, 261n48, 296–97, 303, 310–11, 315n15, 413–17
house parties (dances), 20–31, 44n1, 50, 60–61, 71, 74, 97, 104, 131, 154–55, 166, 183, 199, 257, 268, 273; decline of, 317–318, 323–24, 331, 340; high spirits at, 25–26; procedures and logistics, 21–24, 29–31 *See also* ceilidhs; parallels with other fiddling cultures; square sets; step-dancing
Howe, Elias, 300–1
Howe's One Thousand Jigs and Reels, 300

Hubley, Libby Haywood, 254, 341, 357–59, 405
Huestis, Harold, 265
Huestis, Lowell, 266–67, 325–26, 331, 408, 410
Hughes, Emmett, 23, 25, 33, 39, 54, 87, 114, 127n19, 133, 181, 209, 222, 225–26, 257, 286, 405, 410
Hughes, Gary, 405
Hunter River (district), **2**

Immigration. *See* Ireland; Scotland
In the Genes (CD), 369
instruction in fiddling: formal, 146, 335, 339, 341, 360, 369–70, 373, 378–80, 391n6–7; Rollo Bay Instructional Program, 338n24, 346, 361, 363–64, 368–69, 380, 383, 411. *See also* learning to play fiddle
Intercolonial Club of Boston, 214, 216, 219, 230n1, 232n29
Inverness (district), 405
Inverness County (Nova Scotia), 284, 286, 293n81
"The Inverness Gathering" (march), 305, 414
"Inverness Jig," **401**
Inverness Town (Nova Scotia), 280–81
Iona (district), 9, 22, 267
Ireland
—dance traditions of: 15, 181–82, 237, 253, 261n45, 303–4, 315n17, 359, 383
—fiddling and musical heritage of: xxvi, 14–16, 18n31, 41–42, 44n10, 59, 64n15, 64n17, 64n20, 67, 81n2, 101n5, 101n21, 109, 117, 126n2, 126n5, 127n21–22, 127n27, 128n42, 138, 148n12, 158–59, 173n27, 178, 180–82, 196n9, 265, 273, 359; broadcasts and recordings of Irish fiddling: 195, 264, 268, 270–71, 278, 290n4, 291n28, 310–11; contemporary players: 369, 371; revivals of music and dance: 228–29, 232n51, 233n52, 341, 344
—fiddling repertoire of: 15, 18n29, 64n18, 100, 109, 126n12–13, 127n32, 273, 275, 285, 296–98, 300–1, 303–4, 307–8, 310–11, 315n12, 350–51, 363. *See also* tune collections
—immigration from: xvii, xxvi, 3, 6, 14, 118, 158, 184, 283, 286, 390
—language and cultural heritage: 6, 17n11, 29, 46n37, 59, 217; religion of. *See* Christian church
Irish descent, Islanders of, 54, 67, 173n39, 168, 180–81, 196n9, 217
Irish Jig (dance), 253

The Irish Serenaders, 280
"The Irish Washerwoman" (jig), 296, 304, 311
"Island Boy" (reel), 298, 307
Isle of Coll, 15
Isle of Mull, 15
Ives, Sandy, 44n10, 46n30

Jabbour, Alan, xi, xx, xxviii-n3, **186**
Jackson, Otis, 105, 119, 127n32, 182, 265, 291n10
"Jackson's Jig," 304, 414
Jacobite Rebellion, 5, 17n7
jam sessions, 380, 391n9–10
jaw harp, 265
Jay, Lem, 263–65, 268, 270, 277, 303
Jay, Roland, 95, 264, 290n5, 390n2, 405
"Jay's Reel," 265, 298, 312
Jenkins, Lot, 131
"Jerome's Farewell to Gibraltar" (reel), 296, 299
jigging, 58–63, 64n15, 64n17, 64n23, 84, 97, 123, 146, 208, 269, 324, 333–34, 338n21–22, 364; as children's play, 61–63; as communication method, 59, 64n17, 123; as dance accompaniment, 59–62, 64n20, 72, 202, 245; and tune transmission, 64n16, 84, 86–88, 90, 95, 99–100, 101n7, 104, 117–19, 245, 273; vocables for, 58–60, 62. See also aural transmission; puirt-a-beul
jigs (dance genre), 253, 261n46
jigs (tune genre), xix, 14–15, 24–25, 78, 64n15, 78, 87, 103, 158, 192, 214, 222, 241, 258, 260n13, 285, 295, 307, 334, 382, 401; history and structure of, 301–2, 304–5; kinds of, 304, 315n19, 401; titles of, 102n27, 126n12, 296–98, 304, 310–11, 413-17
"Jingle Bells" (set tune), 330, 414
"Johnny Cope" (reel), 297, 311
"Johnny Wagoner" (reel), 311, 414
Johnson, Andrew, 96
Johnstone, Roy, 313, 335, 338n27, 381, 391n9, 410, 421
Jones, Andrew, 27, 89, 156, **174**, 180, 189, 196n8, 222–23, 266, 395, 397, 405
Joyce, Patrick Weston, 300
"Joys of Québec" (set tune), 278, 414
"Jubilo" (set tune), 297, 303
Judique (Nova Scotia), 279–80

KDKA (radio station), 263
Kearney, Joe, 85, 147, 181–82, 405
Kearney, William, 147
Keefe, Peter, 170

Kelly and McInnis Program (radio show), 265, 291n12
"Kennedy Street March," **402**
Kennedy, "Big Joe," 163
Kensington, 1, **2**, 53, 140, 152, 254, 328, 341, 353–54, 403, 405
Kerr's Merry Melodies for the Violin, 301
Kessinger, Clark, 271, 423
Kildare Capes (district), **2**, 23, 38, 91, 98, 166, 407
Killoran, Paddy, 271, 423
Kindle (band), 371, 379, 421
"King George IV" (strathspey), 297, 306
Kings County, xxx, 1, 2, 3, 5, 13, 37–39, 49, 63n5, 69, 74, 116, 119, 127n32, 132, 152, 159–61, 178–82, 192, 195, 196n5, 217–19, 222, 225, 238, 242, 245–46, 260n19, 265, 286, 288–89, 291n10, 318, 322, 326–27, 331, 336, 348, 351, 378, 366, 378, 380, 383–84. *See also* fiddling styles of PEI; *and entries for individual towns and districts*
Kings County Fiddlers. *See* PEI Fiddlers' Society
Koughan, Bill, 104, 405

Lachine (Québec), 274
Lady Slipper Dancers, 358
Lakeville (district), **2**, 7, 27, 50–51, 241, 243, 245, 268, 330, 406
Lamey, Bill, 279–80, 423
Lanark (Nova Scotia), 279
The Lancers (Lancer's Quadrille), 238–39, 241–42, 244, 260n16, 260n25. *See also* square sets
Landry, Ned, 274–75, 277, 310, 422
L'Ardoise (Nova Scotia), 280
Large, Betty Rogers, 271, 291n14
Larry O'Gaff (jig), 304, 307, **401**, 414
Larsen, Grey, 375n39
Leard, Bernice, 142, 354, 374n14
Leard, Warren, 53, 142, 354, 374n14, 405
learning to play fiddle: assistance from adults, 94–97, 99–100, 104, 211n7; basic skills, 80, 92–98, 102n22 (*see also* techniques of fiddling); fiddle toys and surrogates, 63, 84–86, 101n5; first tunes, 83, 86–88, 95–97, 99–100, 102n22 (*see also* aural transmission); getting started, 62–63, 83–92; no formal instruction, 92–94, 100, 335. *See also* attitudes about fiddling; fiddle instruction (formal)
Leblanc, Bill, 266, 274
LeBlanc, Emmanuelle, 391n5

LeBlanc, Paddy "Scotty," 280, 284
LeBlanc, Pastelle, 391n5
LeBlanc, Philippe, 374n15, 391n5, 403
Lecky, Harry, 318, 354, 362, 374n14, 405, 410
Leclair, Norman, 412
Leeco, Harper, 120
Lepage, Richard, 148n14
Lewiston (Maine), 216, 219, 231n15, 293n84
Life on the Mississippi (Twain), 64n22
Lindy hop (dance), 258, 382
"Little Burnt Potato" (jig), 297, 310
"Little Donald in the Pigpen" (reel), 312, 414
"Little Old Log Cabin in the Lane" (waltz), 307, 414
Little Pond (district), **2**, 20, 71, 155, 227, 331, 346, 369, 379, 411
Livingstone, Marie Arsenault, 313, 380, 391n9–10, 409
Livingstone, Orrin, 409
Lock, Lottie, 354
Loewe, Frederick, 315n23
Lomax, Alan, xx, xxviii-n3, 196n10
Lomax, John, xx, xxviii-n3
London, 228, 236, 238
Long River (district), **2**, 20, 53, 67, 96, 112, 138, 174, 198, 403, 407
Longaphie, Buddy, 113, 180, 289, 349, 405–6
Longaphie, Gus, 23, 66, 78, 105, 131, 146, **187**, 289, 349, 394, 397, 405
Longfellow, Henry Wadsworth, 374n20
longways dancing. *See* country dancing
"Lord MacDonald's Reel," 64n23, 109, 222, 256, 296, 299, 314, **394–95**
Lord of the Dance (stage production), 374n22, 383
Lorne Valley (district), **2**, 22, 133, 219, 318, 327, 383, 392n17
Lorne Valley Dance. *See* old-time dances, contemporary
Lot 11 (district), **2**, 7, 86, 266, 408
Lot 16 (district), **2**, 7, 74, 132, 266, 325, 410
lot system, 5–7, 17n16, 168, 173n39
Louisiana, 5
Louisville (Kentucky), 216
Lowe, Joseph, 300
Lowe, Judy, 141, 231n25, 408, 410, 412
Lowell Huestis Orchestra, 325–26
Lower Washabuck (Nova Scotia), 280
Lowlands, Scottish. *See* Scotland
lumber woods, 10–11, 29; music making in, 57, 90, 119–20. *See also* aural transmission

M. M. Cole Company, 301
Mabou Parish Picnic, 282, 293n72
Mabou (Nova Scotia), 159, 281–82, 292n53
MacAdam, J. D., 50, 74–75
MacArthur, Eldon, **220**, 405, 407
MacAuley, Dot, 405, 407
MacAuley, Scott, 127n35, 369
MacCannell, Don, 405
MacCannell, Neil, 22, 133–35, 219, 318, 327, 405
MacCauley, Loman, 266
MacCormack family (of Cardigan), 266
MacCormack, Dan, 266, 408
MacCormack, Francis, 86, 93, 267, 388, 410
MacCormack, Mary, 266
MacCormack, Therese, 266
MacDonald clan, 5
MacDonald Tobacco Company, 280
MacDonald, Allan, 113, 139, 208, **255**, 289, 291n10, 313, **327**, 328, 349, 368, 405, 410
MacDonald, "Big Alec," 170
MacDonald, Angus L. (Premier of Nova Scotia), 283
MacDonald, "Billy Lauchy," 56, 63n11
MacDonald, Dan (Intercolonial Club champion), 219
MacDonald, Dan R. (Cape Breton composer), 279–80, 285, 309, 373, 423
MacDonald, Donnie (accompanist), 407
MacDonald, Edward (historian), 291n21
MacDonald, Bishop Faber, 20, 44n2, 71, 155–57, 373n7, 406; role in fiddling revival, 227, 346–48, 350–52, 362
MacDonald, Francis, 15, **82**, 84, 191, 289, 349, 398, 406, 410
MacDonald, George (accompanist), 410
MacDonald, Heather Rose (daughter of Joe), 406
MacDonald, Hector, 74, 222, 265, 291n10, 312, 328, 369
MacDonald, Hilda MacPhee, 56, 68, 81n4, 95, 134–35, 144, 406
MacDonald, Howie (Cape Breton fiddler), 314
MacDonald, Hugh A. (fiddler from Lanark, NS), 279
MacDonald, "Little Jack " (Cape Breton fiddler), 279–80, 423
MacDonald, Joe, 13, 36–37, 47, 54, 66–67, 71, 77, 86, 124, 132, 135, 138, **165**, 168, 199, 205, 287, 323, 363, 406
MacDonald, John (Laird of Glenaladale), 5–6

MacDonald, Keith Norman, 301
MacDonald, Fr. Kenneth, 159, 293n72
MacDonald, L. A. "Art," 271–72, 291n14
MacDonald, Paul, 76, 106, 192, 197n19, **200**, 309, 346, 363–65, 369, 375n25, 390n2, 404, 406, 421
MacDonald, Ward, 313, **327**, 368–69, 372, 378, 381, 389, 391n11, 392n26, 409–10, 421
MacDonald, William "Bill," 27, 30, 114–15, 120, 164, 205, 254, 348, 374n13, 405
"MacDonald's March," 305, 414
MacDougall, Herb, 88, 91, 101n10, 410
MacDougall, Jim, 52, 90, 98, 105, 350, 381, 406, 410
MacEachern, "Big Dan," 219, 232n29
MacEachern, Cec, 274–75, 310, 315n24, 408
MacEachern, Dan Hughie, 232n29, 285
MacEachern, Frances, 292n53
MacEachern, Kay, 407
MacEachern's Collection, vol. 2, 232n29
MacGregor, John, 16, 31, 249
MacInnes, Dan Joe, 280
MacInnes, Gloria MacPhee, 45n11, 412
MacInnes, Ron, 347, 373n8
MacInnis, Billy, Jr., 313, 374n24, 411, 422
MacInnis, Billy, Sr., 326, 411
MacInnis, Largus, 7, 27, 50, **51**, 56, 241, 243, 245, 251, 268, 330, 406
MacIntyre, J. D., 248, 355
MacIntyre, James, 136
MacIntyre, Marie, 96, 412
MacIntyre, Sandy, 280, 293n82, 309, 423
MacIntyre, Stewart, 9–12, 39, 100, 136, 245, 251, 322, 406
MacIsaac, Angus, 222
MacIsaac, Ashley, 222, 286, 370–71, 384, 376n40, 423
MacIsaac, Bernie, 279, 282
MacKay, Lorne, 69, 221
MacKenzie, Capt. Alec, 136
MacKenzie, Carl, 280, 286, 423
MacKenzie, Sheila, 368–69, 378–79, 387–89, 411, 421
MacKinnon, Anne, 369
MacKinnon, Cecilia, 369
MacKinnon, Janie, 60
MacKinnon, Mac, 406
MacKinnon, Margaret Ross, 32, **33**, 122, 161, 374n13, 406–8, 412
MacKinnon, "Big Peter," 256
MacLean, Angus Leslie, 49, 73–74, 144, 147, 161

MacLean, Clarence, 90, 101n15, 188, 411
MacLean, Danny, 11, 22, 49, 57, 78, 90, 119, 125, 147, 177, 181, 183, 205, 278, 406
MacLean, Donny, 406
MacLean, Elsie, 144
MacLean family (of Garfield), 66, 144, 149n21
MacLean, Joe, 280, 423
MacLean, Lauchy, 161
MacLean, Sandy, 280, 309
MacLellan, Donald, 279
MacLellan, Theresa, 279
MacLeod, "Alec Thrasher," 200
MacLeod, Cynthia, 378, 388, 421
MacMaster, Hugh "Buddy," 280, 286, 310, 365, 375n27, 423
MacMaster, Natalie, 286, 365, 370–72, 375n27, 376n40, 379, 384, 388, 423
MacPhail, Sir Andrew, 54
MacPhee clan, 15
MacPhee, George, xxiii, xxvi, 32, 34, 45n11, 45n19, 59, 61, 73–75, 84, 87, 94–96, 107, 116, 138, 147, 226, **255**, 318–19, 336, 359, 393, 397–99, 406, 408
MacPhee, Mel, xxv, 32, 45n19, 116, 147
MacPhee, Roddy Joe, 45n11, 123, 314
MacPhee, Ronnie Archie, 120
MacPherson, John Dan, 122, 374n13
MacQuarrie, Gordon, 285
MacQuorquodale, Fiona, 421
MacRae, Alan, 412
Macrae, Harold, 274
Macrae, Warren, **272,** 274
MacSwain, Chester, **21**, 61, 120, 141, 407
"MacSwain's Reel," 120, 127n33, 414
Magdelene Islands, 379, 385, 390n4
Mahann, Angus, 69
"Maid Behind the Bar" (reel), 296, 299, 311
Maine, **4**, 10, 119, 136, 216, 219, 231n15, 293n84
mandolin, 85, 133, 143–44, 204, 210, 321, 372, 406
"Maple Sugar" (set tune), 297, 304, 310, 313
maps of PEI, 2, 4
marches (tune genre), 103, 191–92, 240, 284–85, 301, 401; history and structure, 305–6, 315n21; titles of, 265, 296–98, 305–6, 309, 401, 413–17
Margaree Forks (Nova Scotia), 279
Maritime Fiddlers, 380, 391n8
Maritimes Fiddling Contest, 222
Maritimes, Canadian, 3, 8, 15, 17n17, 137, 178, 271, 274, 281, 293n71, 369; music and dance

Maritimes, Canadian (*cont.*)
  from, 58, 162, 222, 253, 296–98, 308, 310, 315n22, 371, 375n36, 380, 391n8. *See also* New Brunswick; Nova Scotia
Marshall, William, 300
Martin, Eddie, 329, 405
"Mason's Apron" (reel), 209, 296, **400**
mass media: and fiddling, 171, 195, 263–90, 309–11, 316n25, 316n27, 319, 390; and pop culture, 333–34, 341; recent developments in, 290, 377; technology, xxviii–n5, 267–68, 281, 291n23, 321. *See also* radio broadcasts; sound recordings and phonographs; television
Matheson, Duncan, 355, 403
Mathews, Ed, 350, 406
McCarran, Phonsey, 169
McCullough, Fred, 207, 211n9, 374n13
McDonald, Claire Arsenault, 142, **156**, 406
McDonald, Rev. Donald, 160, 173n21
McDonald, Leonard, 24, 28, 30, 35, 39, 76, 87, 142, 146, 155, **156**, 163, 177, 181, 191, 253, 329–30, 374n13, 406
McDonaldites, 160
McLaren, Edith Jay, 264–65
McMichen, Clayton, 215, 233n55, 271; and McMichen's Georgia Wildcats, 276
McNally, Jerry, 405
McPhee, Angus, 154, **387**, 392n21, 406
McPhee, Anne, 412
McPhee, Dan, 15, 122, 255, 260n19, 289, 406
McPhee, Hughie, 15, 116–17, 120, 136, 224, 232n41, 260n19, 349, 393, 399, 406, 408, 411
McPhee, John Joe, 120
McPhee, Toganny, 15, 116–17, 312, 399
McQuaid, Jenny O'Hanley, 12–13, 50, 60–61, 68, 118, 241, 321–22, 333–34, 362, 366, **367**, 406
Meadowbank (district), 93, 403
medleys. *See* groups of tunes
Mellish, Reg, 411
The Merry Makers, 265–66
Messer, Don: Don Messer and His Islanders, 148n3, 210, 271, **272**, 274–77, 315n24, 326, 370, 422; formative years, 42, 273–74; influence of, 180, 266, 274, 276–77, 289–90, 380, 385, 389; media and performing career, 264, 266–67, 271–75, 292n47–48, 311, 326; playing style and musical style, 180, 182–83, 269, 275–77, 286, 289, 292n50; repertoire of, 275–77, 308–11, 352, 384
Messer, Emma, 273
Messer, Jim, 273

Metamora, 375n39
Mi'kmaqs, 3, 4, 16n1, 63n9, 135, 218
Millar, Edgar, 412
Millburn: Kings County district, 87; Prince County district, 106
The Miller O'Hirn Collection (Skinner), 301
Milltown Cross (district), v, **2**, 10, 20–21, 33, 47, 49, 60, 66, 72, 83, 97, 104, 131, 134, 144, 155, 168, 177, 179, 200, 222, 242, 253, 272, 318, 406–408, 411–12
Miminegash (district), **2**, 29, 62, 75, 266, 407, 409–10
Miousse, Pascal, 391n5, 392n27
"The Miramichi Fire" (reel), 296, 299, 311
Miramichi Valley, 11
Miscouche, 1, **2**, 325, 419
"Miss Susan Cooper" (reel), 297, 310
"Mississippi Sawyer" (reel), 278
Mitton, Earl, 222, 277, 310
modernization on PEI: digital age, 377–78; post World War II, xx, 217, 311, 317–24, 336–37. *See also* community life and customs; decline of PEI fiddling
modes and modality, musical, 108, 126n7, 148n17, 184, 193–94, 197n23–26, 208, 211n11–12, 287, 314n6
Monaghan (county of Ireland), 6
Moncton (New Brunswick), 371, 377, 379
"Money Musk" (reel), 311
Mont Carmel (district), **2**, 48, 95, 113, 193, 319, 368, 374n15, 379, 391n5, 403, 409
Montague, 1, **2**, 74, 85, 119, 123, 148n8, 179, 181, 222, 244, 327, 355, 369, 373n10, 391n7, 403, 410–11
Monticello (district), xxi, xxiii–xxiv, xxvi, xxx, **2**, 3, 15, 32, 36, 39, 45n11, 48, 55, 59, 61–62, 66, 73, 82, 84, 107, 116, 120, 138, 143, 177, 187, 203, 221, 226, 244, 247, 255, 267, 318, 336, 353, 359, 366, 367, 369, 403–8, 412
Monticello Ceilidh. *See* ceilidhs
Monticello Tea Party. *See* town days
Montréal, Québec, 118, 253
morbidity and mortality, 147, 313, 378
More Fiddle Tunes: Book 2 (Hughes), 127n19
Morell, **2**, 15, 84, 191, 289, 406, 410
Morrison, James, 271, 423
Morrison, Rita MacDonald, 40, 71, 143, 146, 206, 406
Morrissey, Johnny, 22, 84, 86, 105, 132, 144, 181, 398, 406
"The Mortgage Burn" (reel), 314, 416

Mount Herbert (district), 404
Mount Hope (district), **2**, 71, 221, 409, 411
Mount Pleasant (district), 35
Mount Stewart, **2**, 13, 36, 154, 263, 268, 290n6, 390n2, 392n21, 405–406
Mounties (Royal Canadian Mounted Police), 163–64
mouth music. *See* jigging
"Mrs. McLeod of Rasay" (reel), 296, 299, 311
Murphy, Billy, 182
Murphy, Frank, 56
Murphy, Gerard, 405
Murray Harbour (district), **2**, 55, 86, 133, 224, 380, 407, 411
Murray River (district), **2**
music-and-dance parties, 335–36
The Musicians' Companion (Howe), 300
The Musicians' Omnibus (Howe), 300
Myers, Bernard "Fenner," 411
Myers, Cody, 180, 405–6

"Names Escape Me" (reel), 122, 128n39
Napoleonic Wars, 238
Nashville (Tennessee), 216, 264
The National Barn Dance (radio show), 264
National Old-Time Fiddlers Contest, 229
National Policy, 321–22, 354
Naufrage (district), **2**, 12, 50, 68, 118, 241, 321, 362, 404, 406
negative image (of fiddlers). *See* social role of PEI fiddlers
Nelly J. Banks (ship), 165
New Brunswick, xxii, 2–3, **4**, 10–11, 17n4, 90, 144, 196n6, 252, 369, 371, 374n15, 377, 379; fiddling and dance of, 42, 57, 118–19, 176, 179, 196n6, 222, 252, 266, 273, 290, 354, 364, 380, 385; fiddling repertoire of, 102n29, 275, 299, 308, 310, 312
New Carlisle (Québec), 278, 309
New England, 8, 42, 237, 240; fiddling and fiddle music from, 64n19, 216, 275, 285, 301, 310, 351, 369. *See also* Boston (Massachusetts); Maine
new generation fiddlers: changes in attitudes and demeanor, 80, 290, 372–73, 387–88; changes in playing style, 195n1, 383–89, 392n27; changes in repertoire, 312–13, 383–84; development of, 363–73, 374n24, 378–80; emergence of professional players, 378, 380, 383; first vs. second wave, 378, 386–89; recordings by, 364, 369, 378, 383, 421–22. *See also* female role; *and entries under individual names*
New Haven (district), **2**, 180
New London (district), **2**
"The New Rigg'd Ship" (jig), 126n12
New York City, 119, 261n48, 264, 274, 291
New York (state), 42, 45n24
New Zealand (district), 255
Newfoundland, xxvi, **4**, 44n2, 58, 119, 127n31, 164, 350, 406; music of, xxvi, 42, 64n19, 69, 81n2, 81n11, 81n17, 101n5, 119, 127n20–21, 158
Newtown Cross (district), **2**, 22, 58, 84, 105, 132
Nicholson, Keith, 410
Niel Gow & Sons of Edinburgh, 300
Nielson, "Duke," **272**, 274, 325
Norboro (district), **2**, 53, 56, 246
North Lake (district), **2**, 27, 114, 130, 164, 205, 254, 348
North River (district), **2**, 169, 407–8, 412
North Rustico (district) **2**, 29, 170, 227, 266, 329, 408
North Rustico Harbour (district) 391, 412
Northam Racetrack, 325
"Northside Tune" (set tune), **401**
Norway (Maine), 216
noting. *See* techniques of fiddling
Nova Scotia Highlanders (pipe band), 122
Nova Scotia: mainland, 176, 252, 364; province of, xxii, 2–3, 4, 10, 17n4, 57, 118–20, 122, 176, 196n6, 203, 219, 274, 278, 279, 281, 292n53, 292n58, 293n71, 308–10, 364, 374, 409; tartanist campaign, 283–84, 374n23. *See also* Cape Breton

O'Connor family (of Milltown Cross), 144
O'Connor, Arnold, 49
O'Connor, Attwood, 10, **33**, 34, 47, 49, 52, 57, 60, 66, 83, 94, 96, 104, 131, 147, 168–69, 177, 181–82, 189–90, 253, 394–98, 406, 411
O'Connor, Elsie, 49
O'Connor, Frank, 23–24, 38, 91, 354, 407
O'Connor, George, 98, 166–67, 354, 407
O'Connor, Jimmy, 55, 86, 178, 224, 318, 405, 407
O'Connor, Melville, 49
O'Connor, Phillip, 49, 144
Official Languages Act, 374n19
"The Old Man and the Old Woman" (reel), 278, 296, 311
old-time dances: contemporary, 43, 383; Circle Club Dance of St. Peters, xix, 354–55, 366,

old time dances (cont.)
382, **387**, 392n21; Goose River Dance, **242**, 354–55, 368–69, 383, 392n17, 392n21; Lorne Valley Dance, 382, 392n17

O'Leary, 1, **2**, 354

Olson, Ted, xiii

One Thousand Fiddle Tunes. See *Ryan's Mammoth Collection*

O'Neill, Capt. Francis, 301

O'Neill's Dance Music of Ireland, 285, 301

O'Neill's Music of Ireland, 64, 109, 301, 397

Ontario, 8, 127n35, 229, 277, 297, 308, 310, 364, 369, 389, 406

oral transmission. See aural transmission

"Orange Blossom Special" (tune), 278

Orwell (district), **2**, 54, 123, 355, 366, 389

Orwell Bay, 6, 22

Orwell Ceilidh. See ceilidhs

Orwell Corners Historic Site, 355, 389

Osborne, Marg, 274

O'Shea, Art, 9, 267

Ottawa Valley fiddling, 277, 389

"The Ottawa Valley Reel," 296, 311

Outports Show (CFCY), 265

"Over the Waves" (waltz), 297, 307

"Paddy Carrey's Fortune" (jig), 126n12

"Paddy Carrey's Ship" (jig), 126n12, 415

"Paddy on the Turnpike" (reel), 109, 296, 299, 311, **398–99, 401**

Paganini, Niccolò, 158

Panmure Island, **2**, 162

parallels with other fiddling cultures, xxvi, xxviii-n8, 41–43, 64n19. See also entries under individual fiddling cultures

Parkdale (district), 346, 348

Paul Jones (dancing game), 258

Peakes (district), **2**, 412

PEI, administrative organization of, 1, 17n24, 173n29

PEI Bluegrass Society, 380

PEI College of Piping, 121, 127n35, 369

"PEI Ferry Crossing" (reel), 314, 417

PEI Fiddle Camp, 392n26

PEI Fiddlers' Society, xix-xx, xxii, 113, 310, 340, 354, 360, 362, 369, 381; anti-contest stance, 227–28, 230, 345, 348, 386; founding and early struggles, 340, 346–49; and fiddling revival, 351–54, 356 (see also revival of fiddling on PEI); musical influence, 310, 348–52, 386. See also fiddle festivals; instruction in fiddling (formal)

PEI Fiddlers' Society, branches of: Eastern Kings County, **347**, 349, 351, 361, 381; Prince County, 349, 350–51, 360–61, 381, 411; Queens County, **347**, 349–53, 361, 369, 381, 391n11, 411, 422; Southern Kings County, 373n10

PEI Fiddling and Step Dancing Competition, 228

PEI fiddling, decline of. See decline of PEI fiddling

PEI fiddling, revival of. See revival of fiddling on PEI

PEI Highlanders (pipe band), 121

PEI, history of, 1, 4–8, 17n4, 17n7, 17n11–12, 17n16–17; introduction of fiddling and fiddle music, 14–16, 18n28, 18n31, 18n33, 18n36. See also Acadians; Great Britain; Ireland; Scotland

PEI Liquor Commission, 166

PEI, maps of, **2, 4**

PEI Route 2, 338n10

PEI Tourist and Publicity Association, 214, 230n1

PEI statistics (climate, topography, geography, population), 1–4

PEI Music Awards (PEIMAs), 370–71, 375n36

PEI, Provincial Government of, 44, 164, 166, 321, 337n1, 338n8, 383

PEI Tartan, 362, 374n23

"The PEI Wedding Reel," 34, 312, 393

Pennsylvania, fiddling in, 64n19, 126n8–9

pentatonic scales. See modes and modality

performance practice (professional), 131, 171, 268–72, 282–83, 287–88, 290, 334

Perlman, Ken, **xxi**, xxviii-n4, **21**, **255**, 409–11

Peter Road (Prince County district), 96, 410

Peters Road (Kings County district), 61, 265

Peters, Clifford, 130, 326

Petrie, George, 300

phonographs. See sound recordings and phonographs

piano, 52, 85, 193–94, 197n25, 272, 273, 276, 325; as accompaniment instrument, 24, 27, 138, 141–44, 146, 185, 199–210, 211n1, 264–66, 280, 349, 354–55, 372, 374n13, 375n37, 403–412; playing the tune right out, 85, 207–8. See also pump organ

"The Picnic at Groshaut" (song), 37, 46n30

Pictou (Nova Scotia), 409

"Pigeon on the Gatepost" (reel), 109, 296, 299, 311, **397–98**

Pitre, Dennis, 23, 26, 61–62, 78, 87, **88**, 94–95, 101n9, 111, 141, 147, 382, 396, 398, 402, 404, 407, 411

Pittsburgh (Pennsylvania), 263
Pius Blackett Band, 326, 331
Playford, Henry, 236
Playford, John, 236, 315n8
Pleasant Grove (district), 411
Pleasant View, **2**, 89, 156, 174, 180, 222, 266, 405
Pocket Companion for the Irish or Union Pipes (O'Farrell), 300
Poe, Grady, 371
Poirier, Lionel, 314
Poirier, Zélie-Anne Arsenault, 48–49, 63n1, 86, 119, **145**, 407
polkas (tune genre), 214, 303–4, 315n17; titles of, 303–4, 413, 413–16
"Pop Goes the Weasel" (jig), 304
Poplar Point (district), xxiv, **2**, 25, 74, 94, 108, 144, 222, 239, 319, 330, 403, 409
"Poppy Leaf Hornpipe," 297, 310
popular music, 258, 265, 325–26, 342, 372
Port Hill (district), 325
Port Hood (Nova Scotia), 281
Port Townsend (Washington), 369
Portage (district), **2**, 325
Powers, Arlene Koughan, 405
Presley, Elvis, 204, 334
"Pride of the Ball" (reel), 123, 296, 299, 311, 314n5
Prince County, 1, **2**, 3, 5, 7, 11, **12**, 38, 53, 61, 118–19, 141, 160, 166, 170, 178–81, 187, 192–93, 195, 217, 246, 265, 266–67, 276, 307, 318, 325, 350, 354, 356, 369–70, 374n16, 378–79, 384. *See also* fiddling styles of PEI; and entries for names of individual towns and districts
Prince County Fiddlers. *See* PEI Fiddlers' Society, branches of
Prince County Pioneers, 325, 350
The Prince Edward Island Style of Fiddling (CD), xii, 314n1, 374n14
Prince Edward Theatre, 218, 263
"The Princess Reel," 100, 102n29, 109, 112, 117, 296, 299, 312, 314, 316n28, **395–96, 399**
Princeville (Nova Scotia), 279
print tradition of fiddle tunes. *See* tune collections
professional fiddling scene on PEI, 148n3, 370–73, 378–80, 383–84, 386–88
professional music circuits, 210, 370–71, 379
Prohibition. *See* alcoholic beverages
prompters, 240, 245, 247–48
Proveau, Gill, 254
Proveau, Jack, 57, 117
Providence (Rhode Island), 216

Pugliese, Patri, 260n21, 260n26
puirt-a-beul, 59–60, 300. *See also* jigging
pump organ, 24, 48, 50, 90–91, 100, 120–21, 149n19, 200–4, 206, 211n2, 374n13

quadrille. *See* square sets
Quadrille and Flux. *See* square sets: in big-circle format
Québec, **4**, 10, 58, 149, 173n27, 196n6, 252–53, 262n54, 279, 337n4, 390, 392n26; city of, 253; dancing styles of, 252–53; fiddling and fiddle music from, 64n19, 119–20, 126n13, 149n22, 176, 182, 189, 264, 274–75, 277, 290n4, 292n56, 296, 308–10, 351, 389; radio broadcasts and recordings from, 182, 189, 264, 275, 278, 290n4, 292n56, 309–10
Queens County, 1, **2**, 3, 5–6, 69, 159–61, 180–81, 217, 241, 246, 249, 278, 326, 350–51, 355, 389. *See also* fiddling styles of PEI
Queens County Fiddlers. *See* PEI Fiddlers' Society; *and entries for names of individual towns and districts*
Queensville (Nova Scotia), 285
quicksteps, 304
Quinn, Merlin, 8, 13, 35–36, 51–3, 84, 92, 96, 176–77, 245–46, 251, 257, 288, 319, 391n6, 407, 411

radio broadcasts, 180; history of, xxviii-n5, 100, 215, 217–18, 223, 263–64, 290n9; influence of, xxii, 182–83, 203, 210, 267–71, 273–74, 277–78, 286–90, 292n31, 346; PEI fiddling on radio, 263–73; technological constraints, 267–68, 291n21, 291n23; and tune transmission, 104 ,123, 189, 270, 278, 303, 309–11. *See also* Appalachian and Southern US fiddling; Boston; Cape Breton Fiddling; CFCY; Messer, Don; Québec
The Radio Entertainers, 280
Rafferty Road (district), **2**, 34, 411
Rafferty, Ervin, 34–35, 45n23, 61, 411
"Ragtime Annie" (reel), 296, 313
Rankin Family (band), 375n36
Rankin, Eachan and Con Duiligh, 15–16, 18n33, 18n36
Rankin, Fr. John Angus, 347
Rankin, Neil, 15
Reavy, Ed, 127n21–22
Red Cross (Canadian), 9
"Red Wing" (set tune), 98, 102n27, 297, 303, 313
"Red-Haired Boy" (reel), 59, 64n18

"Reel à Joe Bibienne," 119, 127n30, 298
"Reel of Honor," 34, 312, 393
reels (tune genre), xviii, xix, xix, 14–15, 24–25, 34, 40, 42, 59, 78, 87, 103, 179, 185, 192, 208–9, 214, 222, 241, 256, 260n13, 295, 305, 382; history and structure, 301–3; illustrations of, **393–401**; titles of, 34, 59, 64n18, 87, 108–9, 100, 101n6, 102n29, 109, 112, 116–17, 119–20, 122–23, 127n23, 127n30, 127n32–33, 128n39, 189, 196n14, 209, 221–22, 225, 256, 258, 265, 278, 285, 292n56, 296–99, 309–13, 330, 334, 413–17
reels (dance genre). See Scotch reels; breakdowns
regional styles of PEI fiddling. See fiddling styles on PEI
Reid, Jean, 374n23
repertoire, PEI fiddling: changes over time, 311–13, 316n25, 316n30, 383, 390; lists of collected tunes, 296–98, 413–17; popular tunes, tune genres, and keys, 295–99, 301–2, 314n4, 314n6; and printed music, 120–21, 288, 300–301, 348, 350; regional differences, 178, 299; sources of, 118–21, 180, 287–89, 299, 307–12; tune conversion, 301, 303–7. See also aural transmission; tune collections
Reuben's Jamboree, 354
Revenuers, Canadian. See alcoholic beverages
revival movements, music, xxvii, 341–44; Anglo-American folk song revival, 341–42; in Ireland, 228–29, 233n52, 344; in Scotland, 228–29, 341–42, 344; strategies and dynamics, 342–44, 346, 348. See also Appalachian fiddling; Cape Breton Fiddling; contests and competitions; step dancing; strathspey and reel societies
revival of fiddling on PEI, xxii; aims and strategies, 340, 344–46, 386–87; charitable outreach, 75, 353–54, 356, 362 (see also benefit concerts; town days); creating a career path, 370–72, 388; fiddling societies and clubs, 113, 340–41, 346–54, 378–80, 383, 386 (see also PEI Fiddlers' Society; ensembles [amateur]); history of, 346–57, 360–66, 373n8, 377–78, 390; rehabilitation of image, 339, 351, 356, 362–63, 370–72, 386; motivating youngsters, 339, 358, 361, 363–66; new role for fiddling, 339–41, 351, 356, 362–63, 378, 388; and "old-time" dancing, 345, 353–55, 382–83, 386–88; and "old-time" fiddlers, 351–53, 383–84, 386–88;

future preservation efforts, 389, 392n26; and step-dancing revival, 357–59; stylistic consequences, 383–88. See also Acadians: cultural and music revival; ceilidhs; fiddle festivals; fiddle instruction (formal); new generation fiddlers
Richard, Fred, 53, 91, 411
Richmond (district), **2**, 369, 375n33
Richmond County (Nova Scotia), 293n81
Ricketts' Circus of Philadelphia, 253, 261n48
"Rickett's Hornpipe," 261n48
Ricketts, Samuel, 253
Riot Act, 170
"Rippling Waters Jig," 311, 415
River Denys (Nova Scotia), 279
Riverdance (stage production), 359, 374n22, 383
Riverside (Nova Scotia), 279
Riverton (district), **2**, 68, 163, 221, 336, 369, 409
The Road to Rollo Bay (CD), 368
Road to the Isles Campaign, 362
Robertson Library, xxviii-n4
Robertson, Eck, 215, 264, 423
Robinson, Elmer, 35, 45n23, 69, 166–67, 180, 196n14, **220**, 221, 228, 231n25, 267, 354, 391n6, 405, 407
Robinson, Keith, 266, 325, 391n6
Robinson, Peter, 232n49, 291n17, 391n6, 410, 411
Rock Barra (district), 15, 116, 152
rock 'n' roll music, 204, 331, 333–34, 338n23, 382
Rodeo Records, 279–80
Rogers, Dorothy Dalton, 166, 354, 407
Rogers, Keith, 263, 271, 291n14, 325
Rollaway Club, 326
Rollo Bay (district), **2**, 30, 47, 141, 161, 326, 404, 406, 409, 412
Rollo Bay Fiddle Instruction Program. See fiddle instruction (formal)
Rollo Bay Scottish Fiddle Festival. See fiddle festivals
"Rose of Tennessee" (jig), 298, 304
"Rosebud of Allenvale" (waltz), 307, 415
Rosengarten, Michael D., 149n23
Ross Family Band, 412, 421
Ross, Alex, 412
Ross, Danielle, 313, 412
Ross, Dorothy Arsenault, 412
Ross, Jonathan, 412
Ross, Stephanie, 412
"Rothiemurchus Rant" (strathspey), 298, 310
Rotterdam (Netherlands), 136

round dancing. See waltzes (dance genre)
Rounder Records, 280, 314n1–3, 374n14
"Rubber Dolly" (tune), 313, 417
rum-running. See alcoholic beverages
Rustico, 1, 5, 17n12, 69, 170, 265
Ryan, William Bradbury, 301
Ryan's Mammoth Collection, 109, 128n40, 285, 301, 399

Salmon River Road (Nova Scotia), 280
San Antonio (Texas), 216
"Sandy MacIntyre's Trip to Boston" (reel), 296, 309
Sapphere, Noel ("Blind Newell"), 54, 218
saxophone, 272, 274
schoolhouse dances. See benefit dances
schottisches, 214
Schurman, Paul, 408
scordatura. See techniques of fiddling: alternative tunings
Scotch Gathering, 18n36, 121
Scotch Guards, 127n36
Scotch measures, 303, 315n17
Scotch reels (dance genre), 14–15, 25, 34, 37, 42, 44n6, 235, 238–39, 258, 261n29, 261n36, 302, 306; connection with step-dancing, 249–54; history of and structure, 248–53; legacy of, 252–54; wedding reel, 34, 45n21, 252
Scotch snaps. See techniques of fiddling
Scotland, 58, 197n23, 273;
—dancing heritage of, 14–16, 34, 45n21, 235–36, 238–39, 248–54, 257–58, 261n29, 261n36, 261n49, 307 (*see also* breakdowns; country dancing; Scotch reels; square sets)
—fiddle recordings from, 231n15, 264, 285, 290n4
—fiddling and musical heritage of, xxvii, xix, xxvi, xxviii-n2, 14–16, 41–42, 44n10, 59, 67–68, 76–77, 81n2, 81n11, 81n16, 114, 117, 121, 127n18, 127n34, 127n36, 129, 158–59, 192, 196n12, 196n16, 197n20, 201, 216–17, 252, 285–88, 363, 373n9, 374n23 (*see also* bagpipes; ceilidhs)
—fiddling repertoire of, 15, 18n29, 100, 101n6, 102n27, 122, 126n12–13, 127n34, 159, 172n13, 178, 180, 191, 196n3, 275, 284–85, 288, 296–308, 310–13, 315n8, 315n11, 315n17, 348–51, 363 (*see also* composing; tune collections)
—history and immigration from, 3, 5–7, 14–16, 17n2, 17n7, 18n31, 18n33, 118, 160, 173n39, 184, 235, 273, 390

—language and cultural heritage of, xxviii-n7, 6–7, 17n11, 18n36, 29, 34–35, 45n11, 45n15, 46n37, 64n15, 76–77, 184, 280, 283–84, 287–88, 293n81 (*see also* Gaelic language; Christian church)
—revivals in music and dance, 228, 341–42, 344, 347
Scottish descent, Islanders of, 168, 173n37, 173n39, 178, 257, 362
Scottish ornaments. See techniques of fiddling
Scottish sets, 285, 307. See also groups of tunes
The Scottish Violinist (Skinner), 285, 301, 423
Scully, Peter, 135
Sears, Roebuck and Company Catalog, 148n7, 264
Selkirk (district), **2**, 56, 81n4, 95, 134, 140
Selkirk, Fifth Earl of (Thomas Douglas), 6
Sellick, Raymond, 266, 272, 408
senior citizens' homes and manors, 74–75, 353–54
set tunes, 24–25, 103, 307, 313, 330, **401**; origins and structure, 301–2, 303–4, 315n17; titles of, 98, 102n27, 278, 297–98, 303–4, 313, 413–17
Sharp, Cecil, xx, xxviii-n3
Sheehan, Charlie, 78, 98, 105, 135, 202–3, 349, 407
Sheehan, James, 135
"Sheehan's Reel," 296, 299
Sherbrooke (district), 325
Shetland Isles, 81n11, 126n2, 127n18, 297, 308, 310
shivarees. See weddings
Sigsworth, Cosmas, 12, 27, 30, 51–52, 60, 67, 73, 87, 99, 131, 142, 201, 223, 407
Sigsworth, Rita Flynn, 51–52, 142
Silliker, Wilf, 407
"Silver and Gold" (set tune), 297, 311
Silverado Club, 338n13
Simmons, Edwin, 20, 72, 138, 141, **198**, 319, 321, 334, 403, 407
Simmons, Rae, **272**, 274,
Singing Strings, 363
The Skillet Lickers, 210, 215, 274, 423
Skinner, James Scott, 216, 231n15, 264, 285, 290n4, 293n84, 301; his tune collections, 285, 301
Sky, Pat, 315n12
The Skye Collection, 109, 285, 301, 395
Skye, Isle of, 6
Sligo (county of Ireland), 271

slow airs. *See* airs

Smith, "Fiddlin' Arthur," 233n55, 271, 276, 423; and the Dixieliners, 276

Smith, Larry, 226

Smith, Mary Pineau, 391n8

Smith, Reuben, 89, 124–25, 374n13, 407

Smith, Tony, 92, 221, 226, 258, 412

social role of PEI fiddlers, 20–21, 72, 79–80; community entertainers, 47–48, 52, 84, 100n1, 154; community obligations, 20, 43, 70–72, 130–33, 137, 153–57, 162, 337; providing music for dancing, 23–24, 54–57, 98, 130–31, 138, 147, 230. *See also* female role

social role of PEI fiddlers, negative image: alcoholism, 151–53, 157, 162–66, 168, 171, 171n1, 337, 352; devil's instrument, 157–62, 171n3, 172n4, 172n11–13, 172n17; fomenters of violence, 131, 153, 166–71, 171n1, 246, 328–31, 337; laziness, 80, 90, 125, 131, 151–57, 171, 171n1; morally suspect activity, 153, 228. *See also* attitudes about fiddling; Christian Church

socials. *See* benefit dances

"Soldier's Joy" (reel), 296, 311

songs of PEI. *See* vocal tradition on PEI

Sonier, Ervan, 24, 28, 57, 62–63, 85, 87, 132, 141, **150**, 152, 224, 266, 318, 338n20, 350, 407

sound recordings and phonographs: gramophones, 87, 104, 264, 268–69, 279, 321; history of, 215, 264, 291n27–28, 321, 344; influence of, 123, 128n41, 203, 268, 277, 286–90, 309–11, 310. *See also* new generation fiddlers

Souris, xix, xxiii, 1, **2**, 9, 15, 23, 37, 58, 66–67, 87, 92, 105, 113, 119, 122, 130, 131, 161, 176, 179, 196n3, 217, 222, 224–25, 231n27, 250, 261n38, 271, 288–89, 322, 326, 349, 375n25, 403–406, 409

Souris Line Road (district), 403

Souris set, xix, 246–48. *See also* square sets

South Granby (district), 369

Southern Kings Fiddlers. *See* PEI Fiddlers' Society

"Southern Melody" (set tune), 296, 310

Southern Summits (CD), xii

Southern United States, fiddling from. *See* Appalachian and Southern US fiddling

"Southern Waltz," 297, 307, 310

"Speed the Plow" (reel), 311, 415

"Spin 'n' Glow" (jig), 298, 310

Sportin' Club, 326

"The Spree at Montague," 74, 81n13, 148n8

square dancing, xxi, 33, 40, 58, 61, 73, 85, 160–61, 215–16, 236, 244, 260n24, 302, 317–18, 324, 326, 331–32, 335–36, 341, 344–45, 382–83, 386. *See also* cotillions; square sets

square sets, xix, 44n7, 235–49, 336; at benefit dances, 35–39; in big-circle format; 235, 246–48, 258, 261n26, 329–30; decline of, 246–48, 329–331, 336, 382–83 (*see also* revival of fiddling on PEI: and "old-time" dancing); history of, 25, 235–42, 250, 258, 259n10–12, 260n13–16, 260n19, 260n24; in the home, 48–49; at house parties, 21–22, 24–27, 30–31, 40, 42–43, 257; learning to dance; 61, 240, 244–45; musical accompaniment for, 25, 60–61, 237–38, 240–41, 302–3, 315n19, 325–26, 331; revival of on PEI, 43, 345, 354–55, 366, 369 (*see also* old-time dances, contemporary); structure and steps, 24–25, 27, 235–44, 250, 261n28, 262n50; varieties of, 238, 241–44, 260n25; at weddings, etc., 32–35. *See also* cotillions; country dancing; Lancers; Souris set; stepdancing

St. Andrews (district), **2**, 36, 40, 47, 54, 66, 71, 86, 124, 132, 135, 165, 199, 206, 218, 287, 323, 363, 406

"St. Anne's Reel," 189, 196n14, 221, 278, 292n56, 296, 299, 311, 316n27

St. Anthony's Hall, 341

St. Charles (district), **2**, 37, 86, 256, 267, 388, 410

St. Chrysostom (district), **2**, 25, 58–59, 72, 79, 110, 142, 160, 176, 179, 196n3, 227, 256, 266, 324, 363, 370, 375n38, 379, 403, 408–9

St. Felix (district), **2**, 23, 61, 78, 87, 111, 382, 404, 407, 411

St. John (New Brunswick), 211n8, 274

St. Margarets (district), **2**, 130

St. Nicholas (district), **2**, 403, 407, 408

St. Peter and St. Paul (district), 53, 91, 411

St. Peters (district), xix, **2**, 39, 130, 322, 353–54, 355, 382, 412

St. Peters Bay, 37

St. Peters Dance. *See* old-time dances

St. Peters Lake, 410

St. Philippe (district), 72

St. Pierre and Miquelon, **4**, 164, 166

St. Pius X parish, 346

St. Teresa's (district), 163

"Stack of Barley" (hornpipe), 296, 303
Stanhope (district), **2**, 69, 266, 268, 325, 350, 410–11
state and provincial fiddle associations. *See* contests and competitions
"Stella's Trip to Kamloops" (march), 296, 306
step dancing, xvii-xix, 32, 43–44, 54, 59, 235, 335, 353, 371; competitions in, 214, 218, 232n29, 357; evolution of, 249–54; in home and community, 48–49, 61–62; at house parties and dances, 25, 34, 27–29, 40, 251, 257; launching pad for fiddlers, 358, 374n21, 379; learning how, 254–55, 357–58; musical accompaniment for, 28–29, 189, 254–56, 301, 303; procedures and aesthetics, 254–56, 257–58, 359; revival in, 258, 341, 357–59, 362, 366, 369, 383, 392n18; during square sets, 25, 251–52
Stephens, "Uncle Bunt," 216
Stewart, Archie, **V**, 20, **21**, 23–26, 29, 31–2, 38, 60–61, 72, 77, 97, 104–7, 113, 119–20, 134, 139–41, 155, 160, 163, 166–69, 179, 181–83, 191, 200, 208, 222, 241, 244, 251, 272, 277, 291n10, 318, 332, 394–98, 407–8
Stewart, Malcolm "Bud," 412
Stewart, Neil, 300
Stewart-Robertson, James, 301, 373n2
Stokes, Lowe, 215, 233n55, 271
"Stool of Repentance" (jig), 304, 415
Stradivarius, 86, 101n3
Strait of Canso, 292n58
Strand Theatre, 214, 217, 263
Stratford, 409
Strathlorne (Nova Scotia), 280
strathspey and reel societies, 341–42, 344, 347, 350
strathspeys (tune genre), xxvii, 14, 103, 192, 249, 252, 284–85, 287–88, 290n4, 295, 300–301, 312, 315n9–10, **401**; history and structure, 306; titles of, 297–98, 306, 310, 413–17
Sturgeon (district), **2**, 85, 147, 405
styles of fiddling. *See* fiddling styles
Subury (Massachusetts), 216
Sullivan, Lizzie, 61
Summerside, 1, **2**, 24, 57, 74, 118–19, 121, 132, 137, 141–2, 148n5, 150, 152, 176, 196n3, 200–201, 211n1, 212, 222, 224–26, 231n18, 265–66, 317–19, 325, 329, 338n10, 349, 351, 353, 369–70, 380, 403–404, 406–411
superstyles, development of, 195, 229–30, 271, 286, 289

Surenne, John, 300
Swenson, Amy, 380, 391n6–7, 411–12
swing music, 229, 275
Sydney (Nova Scotia), 280–82, 286, 309

Tanner, Gid, 215, 423
tap dancing, 358–59
tartanist campaign. *See* Nova Scotia
Taylor, George, 279–80
tea parties, xxviii-n1, 16, 37, 39, 214. *See also* benefit dances
Teahill (district), 404
techniques of fiddling, 175, 185–93; alternative tunings, 190–91, 196n16; bowing , 92, 94–96, 178, 181, 183–84, 187–93, 229, 233n52, 287, 303, 315n14; cuts (birls), 183, 192 ,195, 197n19–20, 284; double-stringing/double-stops, 111, 184, 190–91, 195, 287; foot-tapping styles, 184–86, 194, 287; grace notes, 111, 178, 183–84, 191–93, 195, 197n22, 287–88; holding fiddle and bow, 184, 186–88, 195, 196n12, 196n15, 287; noting, 94, 96–97, 101n22, 188, 196n13, 232n41; Scotch snaps, 192, 284, 305–6; suppressed stroke ("shuffles"), 178, 192–93, 195, 392n27
technology. *See* transportation and technology
television broadcasts, 266, 275, 321, 323–24
Tennessee Mixer (dance), 261n28
Thibodeau, Willie, 75–76
Thompson, Lee, 354, 407
Thompson, Uncle Jimmy, 233n55
Thomson, Dave, 97, 140, 169, 189, 334, 394, 398, 407, 412
Tignish, 1, **2**, 10, 17n12, 53, 57, 61, 75, 176, 179, 196n3, 217, 222, 370, 382, 404, 422
Tignish Fire Hall, 382
"Togannys Tune," 116, 312, **399**, 415
tonal system, 184, 193–94, 197n24, 209
Toole, Stephen, 40, 69, **70**, 73, 76–78, 91, 113, 181, 241, 326, 332, 374n13, 401, 407
Toombs, Lawrence, 266
Toronto, Ontario, 46n26, 119, 133, 137, 282
tourism on PEI, 214, 321, 368, 381
town days, xvii, xix, xxii, xxiv, 44, 121, 228, 353–54, 362, 364, 383; Monticello Tea Party, xvii, **255**, 353, 367; names of events, 353
Townsend, Graham, 228, 277–78, 384, 422
Tracadie (district), **2**, 92, 221, 226, 258, 407, 412
Tracadie Bay, 5, 15, 44
Trainor, Cecil, 412

transportation and technology (on PEI), 321; automobile travel and paved roads, xx, 13, 181, 246, 267, 281, 318–19, 321–23, 325, 337n2, 338n10; electric power, xx, xxviii-n5, 45n11, 48, 90, 98, 130, 217, 267–68, 281, 319–21, 330, 337n3–4; ferry service, 17n16, 217, 314; horse-drawn, 8–10, 12–14, 22–24, 32, 35, 55–56, 89, 95, 98, 106, 108, 121, 137, 152, 156, 184, 245, 319, 333, 337n2; mechanization of farming, 319, 322–23; railroad, xix, 10, 14, 17n16, 54, 57, 217, 354. *See also* decline of PEI fiddling; mass media; modernization on PEI; radio broadcasts; sound recordings and phonographs; television

Traveler's Rest (district), 325, 328
treepling, Scottish, 254, 261n49
"Trip to Windsor" (reel), 297, 309
Trois Rivieres, Québec, 253
trumpet, 274
Tryon (district), **2**, 409
tune collections, 300–301; and aural transmission, 120–22; from bagpipes, 121–22; Irish, 275, 285, 300–1, 310, 315n12; North American, 275, 285, 300–1, 310; Scottish, 109, 127n18, 275, 284–85, 300–1, 310, 315n9–11. *See also* repertoire, PEI fiddling; *and entries for individual titles*
tuning. *See* jigging
turluter. See jigging
Twain, Shania, 371
Tweedside (New Brunswick), 42, 273–74
The Twilight Zone, 365
"Twin Sisters" (reel), 123, 314n5, 415
the twist (dance), 258
twists (personal tune variations), 27, 78, 103, 107–14, 124–25, 138–39, 181–82, 194, 270–71, 287–89, 312, 348, 390, **394–99**. *See also* aural transmission
two-step (dance), 258
Tyne Valley (district), **2**, 111, 220, 228, 320, 336, 409
Tyne Valley Oyster Festival, 228

ukulele, 86
Unger, Jay, 314
Union Road (district), **2**, 411
United Church of Canada, 3, 71
United States, 46n47, 126n5, 148n7, 164, 215, 232n39, 237, 261n28, 274, 275, 278, 308, 311, 371

University of Prince Edward Island, xxviii-n4, 369
Upper Margaree (Nova Scotia), 279

The Vanishing Cape Breton Fiddler (film), 347, 373n8
V-E day, 58
Les vent dans les voiles (Desroches), 316n29
Vernon River (district), **2**, 121, 334, 406
Vernon River School, 334
Vessey, Rupert, 412
Victoria (district), **2**
Victoria County (Nova Scotia), 293n81
Vienna (Austria), 257
Village de L'Acadie, 368
Village Green (district), **2**, 374n24, 411
Vincent, Kim, 369
viola da gamba, 201
violence at contests, 227
violence at dances, 37, 166–71, 246, 269, 328–31, 337. *See also* dance halls; social role of fiddlers
Virginia Reel (Sir Roger de Coverley) 237
Vishten, 210, 379, 390n5, 422
vocal tradition on PEI, 29, 37, 44n10, 46n30, 74, 270, 341

Wall, Reuben, 354
Wallace, Beattie, 280
waltzes (tune genre), 78, 103, 222, 224, 301, 305–7, 312; titles of, 297–98, 307, 310, 413–17
waltzes (dance genre), 173n27, 235, 257–58, 262n52, 318, 331, 382
War of 1812, 237
Warner, Frank, xx, xxviii-n3
Warren, Mary MacPhee, 412
Warren, Russell, 266, 326
Washabuck (Nova Scotia), 280
waulking (milling) of cloth, 31, 42, 45n15
Weatherbie, George, 92, 222, 374n13
Weatherbie, William "Bill," 92, 121
Webster, Carl, 54, **55**, 132, 338n16, 407, 411–12
Webster, Jack, 54, 55, 73, 98, 108, 126n3, 130, 132, 140, 221, 286, 327–28, 338n16
Webster, Jackie, **55**, 98, 130, 332, 338n16, 407, 411–12
Webster, John, 412
wedding reel. *See* Scotch reels
weddings, 19, 32–35, 43, 71, 76, 117, 131, 154, 166, 169, 184, 199–200, 214, 323–24, 331–32; shivarees, 35; wedding showers, 19, 35, 43, 154. *See also* square sets; step dancing

Wedge, Clifford, 29, 62, 407
Wedge, Keelan, 378
Weeks, Robert, 218, 231n25, 232n29, 265, 291n10
Weigers, Theo, 412
Wellington (district), **2**, 99, 114–15, 142, 325, 380
Wellington Jam, 380, 391n10
West Indies, 17n17, 158, 164
West Lake Ainslie (Nova Scotia), 159
West Prince Fiddlers, 354
The West Prince Party Line (radio show), 266–67, 326
West Royalty (district), 97, 140, 169, 189, 334, 410, 412
The Western Star (venue), 338n20
western swing music, 203, 229, 276, 292n49–51
"Westphalia Waltz," 297, 307
Wheeling, West Virginia, 278, 309
"Whelan's Breakdown" (set tune), 304, 415
"The White Cockade" (set tune), 297, 303
White Point (Nova Scotia), 279
Wight, Elliott, 35, 72, 76, 141, 147, 181, 267, 382, 396, 408, 412
Wilby, Rob, 411
Wills, Bob, 275, 292n49; and the Texas Playboys, 210, 276, 423
Wilmot, Johnny, 280
Wilson, Teresa MacPhee, 3, 36, 39, 40–41, 48, 51, 59–62, 66, 68, 84, 89, 96, 99–100, 117, 120, 143–44, 146–47, 203–4, 207, 221, 244, 257, 267, 276, 287, 313, 318–19, 332, 366, **367**, 380, 408, 412
Windsor, Ontario, 282
Winnipeg, Manitoba, 335, 404, 410
Winsloe (district), **2**, 218
"Wissahickon Drive" (reel), 310, 415
WLS (radio station), 264
WNAC (radio station), 219
Wolfe, Charles, xiii, 233n55
Women's Institute, 36, 46n26, 345
Wood Islands (district), **2**
Wood, Richard, 313, 363–64, **365**, 371, 374n21, 378, 389, 392n18, 408, 412; CDs by, 371, 422
Wood, Terry, 408
Woodstock (district), **2**, 69, 166, 196n14, 220, 267, 405, 407
World Champion Old-Time Fiddlers' Contest, 216, 219, 231n15, 294n84
World War I, 42, 44n6, 238, 258, 282, 304–5, 308
World War II, 8–9, 19, 24, 32, 34–5, 39, 58, 122, 136, 141, 373n9; as precursor to modernization, xxvii, 16, 139, 148n2, 168, 203, 246, 257, 306, 318–19
WSB (radio station), 263
WSM (radio station), 264
WWVA (radio station), 278, 309

York (district), 36, 409
Young, David, 302
Young, Florence, 405

www.ingramcontent.com/pod-product-compliance
Lightning Source LLC
Chambersburg PA
CBHW020348080526
44584CB00014B/931